THE OXFORD HANDBOOK OF
AMERICAN BUDDHISM

THE OXFORD HANDBOOK OF AMERICAN BUDDHISM

Edited by
ANN GLEIG
and
SCOTT A. MITCHELL

Oxford University Press is a department of the University of Oxford. It furthers
the University's objective of excellence in research, scholarship, and education
by publishing worldwide. Oxford is a registered trade mark of Oxford University
Press in the UK and certain other countries.

Published in the United States of America by Oxford University Press
198 Madison Avenue, New York, NY 10016, United States of America.

© Oxford University Press 2024

All rights reserved. No part of this publication may be reproduced, stored in
a retrieval system, or transmitted, in any form or by any means, without the
prior permission in writing of Oxford University Press, or as expressly permitted
by law, by license, or under terms agreed with the appropriate reproduction
rights organization. Inquiries concerning reproduction outside the scope of the
above should be sent to the Rights Department, Oxford University Press, at the
address above.

You must not circulate this work in any other form
and you must impose this same condition on any acquirer.

Library of Congress Cataloging-in-Publication Data
Names: Gleig, Ann, editor. | Mitchell, Scott A., 1973– editor.
Title: The Oxford handbook of American Buddhism / Ann Gleig
and Scott A. Mitchell.
Description: 1. | New York : Oxford University Press, 2024. |
Series: Oxford handbooks series | Includes bibliographical references and index.
Identifiers: LCCN 2024004660 (print) | LCCN 2024004661 (ebook) |
ISBN 9780197539033 (hardback) | ISBN 9780197539057 (epub) |
ISBN 9780197539064
Subjects: LCSH: Buddhism—United States.
Classification: LCC BQ732 .O985 2024 (print) | LCC BQ732 (ebook) |
DDC 294.30973—dc23/eng/20240209
LC record available at https://lccn.loc.gov/2024004660
LC ebook record available at https://lccn.loc.gov/2024004661

DOI: 10.1093/oxfordhb/9780197539033.001.0001

Printed by Sheridan Books, Inc., United States of America

Contents

List of Contributors   ix

    Introduction   1
    Ann Gleig and Scott A. Mitchell

PART I   FOUNDATIONS

1. American Buddhism, Modernity, and Globalization   17
   Christopher Emory-Moore

2. The History of Buddhism in the United States   36
   Thomas Calobrisi

3. Identities I: Race and Whiteness in American Buddhism   54
   Ann Gleig

4. Identities II: Gender and Sexuality in American Buddhism   74
   Amy Paris Langenberg

5. American Buddhist Studies and Scholar-Practitioners   92
   Scott A. Mitchell

PART II   TRADITIONS

6. Chinese Buddhism in America   115
   Rongdao Lai

7. Pure Land Buddhism in America   129
   Jesse J. Lee

8. Zen Buddhism in America   144
   Ben Van Overmeire

9. Korean Buddhism in America 161
   CLAUDIA SCHIPPERT

10. Theravāda Buddhism in America 177
    ERIK BRAUN

11. Nichiren Buddhism in America 196
    RALPH H. CRAIG III

12. Vietnamese Buddhism in America 211
    TODD LEROY PERREIRA

13. Tibetan Buddhism in America 230
    HOLLY GAYLEY AND JOSHUA BRALLIER

14. American Buddhism and Judaism 249
    JAY MICHAELSON

PART III PRACTICES

15. Buddhist Monasticism in North America 271
    LUKE CLOSSEY AND KAREN FERGUSON

16. Food in American Buddhism 288
    MELISSA ANNE-MARIE CURLEY

17. Mindfulness and Meditation in the United States 303
    NALIKA GAJAWEERA

18. American Buddhism and Healthcare 322
    C. PIERCE SALGUERO

19. Ritual, Rituals, and Ritualizing in American Buddhism 339
    RICHARD K. PAYNE

20. Engaged Buddhism in the United States 359
    FUNIE HSU/CHHI

PART IV FRAMES

21. American Buddhism and Secularism 377
    KIN CHEUNG

22. American Buddhism and Psychotherapy IRA HELDERMAN	395
23. American Buddhism and Technology GREGORY PRICE GRIEVE AND DANIEL VEIDLINGER	414
24. American Buddhist Education and Pedagogy JUDITH SIMMER-BROWN	428
25. American Buddhist Chaplaincy Supervision JITSUJO T. GAUTHIER	446
26. Buddhist Material Culture in the United States PETER ROMASKIEWICZ	462
27. American Buddhism and Visual Culture WINSTON C. KYAN	483
28. Buddhism and American Literature KIMBERLY BEEK	499
Index	517

Contributors

Kimberly Beek is a Ronin Institute Research Scholar who focuses on the emergence of popular fiction with a Buddhist worldview. She is interested in story and discourse that reveal the processes of religious acculturation and demythologization. She created the *Buddhist Fiction Blog* in 2011 and, along with contributing editors, regularly posts novel and short story announcements and reviews.

Joshua Brallier is a doctoral candidate in Buddhist Studies at Northwestern University with interests in gender and sexuality in Buddhist tantra, Buddhist narrative literature, and the critical study of men and masculinities. His dissertation research focuses on the life, writings, and reception history of Do Khyentsé Yeshé Dorjé, the deer-hunting, alcohol-drinking, gun-wielding tantric master from the Golok region of eastern Tibet. Joshua has published "The Mighty Siddha and the Arrogant King" in *Longing to Awaken* (University of Virginia Press, 2024), "The Siddha Who Tamed Tibet" in *Buddhist Masculinities* (Columbia University Press, 2023), "The Fists of My Perfect Teacher" in *NEXT* (2019), and "We Need to Think About the Dalai Lama's Actions Very Carefully" in *Tricycle: The Buddhist Review* (2023). Prior to his doctoral studies, Joshua earned an MA in Buddhist Studies from the University of Colorado Boulder, an MDiv in Indo-Tibetan Buddhism from Naropa University, and a BA in Religious Studies and English Literature from Georgetown University.

Erik Braun is an Associate Professor in the Department of Religious Studies at the University of Virginia. He is the author of *The Birth of Insight: Meditation, Modern Buddhism, and the Burmese Monk Ledi Sayadaw* (University of Chicago Press, 2013), a co-winner in 2014 of the Toshihide Numata book prize in Buddhism. Besides writing various articles, he also co-edited with David McMahan the volume *Meditation, Buddhism, and Science*. He focuses on Burmese Buddhism in the nineteenth and early twentieth centuries, as well as matters related to Pali literature and to globalizing forms of meditative practice.

Thomas Calobrisi received his PhD in Religious Studies from the Graduate Theological Union in 2021. His research focuses on the recontextualization of Buddhist ideas, practices, and artifacts in contemporary American culture. His publications include "Early Modern European Encounters with Buddhism" (Oxford Reference Encyclopedia, 2022), "Presenting the Dharma Essence in an American Vocabulary: Apologetic Strategies in the Writings of Jon Kabat-Zinn" (*Pacific World: Journal of the Institute of Buddhist Studies*, 2021), and "The Quantum Leap from Karma to Dharma:

Moral Narrative in the Writings of Jon Kabat-Zinn" (*Journal of Dharma Studies*, 2018). He co-edited a 2021 special issue in the *Journal of Dharma Studies* with Devin Zuckerman entitled "Buddhism and the History of Science." He is currently a research fellow at the Institute of Buddhist Studies.

Kin Cheung is Associate Professor of East and South Asian Religions and Chair of the Philosophy Department and Global Religions Department at Moravian University. He researches how contemporary agents use Buddhist doctrine and ritual practices in Chinese and American contexts as well as transnational networks. He has published on Buddhists engaging with healing, meditation, ethical dilemmas, economics, capitalism, and secularism. He is co-editor of *Buddhism and Healing in the Modern World* (University of Hawai'i Press, 2023). His work also appears in *The Journal of the American Academy of Religion*; *Religion, State and Society*; *The Journal of Buddhist Ethics*; *Miracles: An Exercise in Comparative Philosophy of Religion*; *Teaching about Asia in a Time of Pandemic*; *Buddhism and Medicine: An Anthology of Modern and Contemporary Sources*; *Studies in Chinese Religions*; and *Handbook of Ethical Foundations of Mindfulness*.

Luke Clossey is Associate Professor at Simon Fraser University, where he teaches and researches world history and the history of religion. With Karen Ferguson he is investigating the history of Theravāda monasticism in North America; their "Birken Buddhist Forest Monastery: Asian Migration, the Creative Class, and Cultural Transformation in the New Pacific British Columbia" appeared in *BC Studies* 208 (2020–2021). His new book, *Jesus and the Making of the Modern Mind*, is forthcoming with Open Book Publishers.

Ralph H. Craig III is Assistant Professor in the Department of Religion at Whitman College. He received his BA in Theological Studies at Loyola Marymount University and his PhD in Religious Studies at Stanford University. He is the author of *Dancing in My Dreams: A Spiritual Biography of Tina Turner* (Eerdmans Publishing, 2023), which explores the place of religion in the life and career of Tina Turner and examines her development as a Black Buddhist teacher.

Melissa Anne-Marie Curley works on modern Buddhism and Japanese philosophy. She is interested particularly in how twentieth-century intellectuals, artists, and social reformers borrow elements from the popular Buddhist imagination in articulating what the future of Japan (and the world) should look like. Her first book, *Pure Land/Real World: Modern Buddhism, Japanese Leftists, and the Utopian Imagination*, examines leftist interpretations of Buddhist images of paradise and exile in the context of the Fifteen Years' War (1931–1945). She is currently collaborating on a translation of Japanese philosopher Keta Masako's *Philosophy of Religious Experience: An Elucidation of the Pure Land Buddhist World* and beginning work on a new study of Buddhism and the culture of self-help in East Asia and North America.

Christopher Emory-Moore is an independent scholar of North American religious diversity based in qathet, British Columbia. Recent publications include "Invisible

Presence and Inferred Absence: Theologies of Nothingness and Emptiness in Hasidic Judaism and Geluk Buddhism" in *Canadian Readings of Jewish History: From Knowledge to Interpretive Transmission* (2023) and "Branding a New Buddhist Movement: The New Kadampa Tradition's Self-identification as 'Modern Buddhism'" (*Journal of Global Buddhism*, 2020).

Karen Ferguson is a Professor of Urban Studies and History at Simon Fraser University in Vancouver, British Columbia. She is the author most recently of "A Monastery for Laypeople: Birken Forest Monastery and the Monasticization of Convert Theravada in Cascadia," *Journal of Global Buddhism* 23, no. 2 (2022): 203–218, and, with Luke Clossey, "Birken Buddhist Forest Monastery: Asian Migration, the Creative Class, and Cultural Transformation in the New Pacific British Columbia," *BC Studies* 208 (2021): 17–44.

Nalika Gajaweera is a cultural anthropologist with specializations in the intersections of Buddhism, race, ethno-nationalism, and gender. She has studied these issues most in-depth in the context of Sri Lanka and the United States. Her current book project focuses on documenting the struggles, experiences, and practices of ethnic and racial minority leadership within North American meditation-based insight institutions, and their efforts to confront issues of race, racism, and whiteness within these institutions.

Jitsujo T. Gauthier is an Associate Professor and Co-chair of Buddhist Chaplaincy at the University of the West. Her practice and pedagogy invite more tenderness and breath into meditation and the classroom. She teaches Buddhist Homiletics, Spiritual Care and Counseling, Spiritual Leadership, and Engaged Zen Buddhism. Her research focuses on the practical application of Buddhism within the fields of contemplative education, ministry, and peacemaking work. Her dissertation, "An On-the-Job Mindfulness Intervention for Pediatric ICU Nurses," was published in the *Journal of Pediatric Nursing* (2015). Other publications include "Hope in the Midst of Suffering" in the *Journal of Pastoral Theology* (2016); "Formation and Supervision in Buddhist Chaplaincy" in *Reflective Practice: Formation and Supervision in Ministry* (2017); and "Buddhist Chaplaincy in the U.S." in *The Oxford Handbook of Buddhist Practice* (2023).

Holly Gayley is a scholar and translator of contemporary Buddhist literature in Tibet and Associate Professor in the Department of Religious Studies at the University of Colorado, Boulder. Her research areas include gender and sexuality in Buddhist tantra, ethical reform in contemporary Tibet, Tibetan and Himalayan women writers today, and theorizing translation, both literary and cultural, in the transmission of Buddhist teachings to North America. She is author of *Love Letters from Golok: A Tantric Couple in Modern Tibet* (2016); translator of *Inseparable across Lifetimes: The Lives and Love Letters of Namtrul Rinpoche and Khandro Tāre Lhamo* (2019); editor of *Voices from Larung Gar: Shaping Tibetan Buddhism for the Twenty-First Century* (2021); and co-editor of *Living Treasure: Buddhist and Tibetan Studies in Honor of Janet Gyatso* (2023). Her articles on Nyingma communities in eastern Tibet have appeared in the *History of Religions, Journal of Buddhist Ethics, Contemporary Buddhism, Journal of Religious Ethics, Religions*, and *Himalaya Journal*. She has recently co-authored two articles with

Somtso Bhum about Buddhist themes in contemporary Tibetan women's writings: "Parody and Pathos: Sexual Transgression by 'Fake' Lamas in Tibetan Short Stories" (*Revue d'Etudes Tibétaines*, April 2022) and "Capturing the Quotidian in the Everyday Renunciation of Buddhist Nuns in Tibet" (*Journal of Tibetan Literature*, July 2023).

Ann Gleig is Associate Professor of Religion and Cultural Studies at the University of Central Florida. She is author of *American Dharma: Buddhism beyond Modernity* (Yale University Press, 2019). She is currently working on a co-written book with Amy Langenberg on sexual abuse in American Buddhism (under contract with Yale University Press). She serves as an editor at the *Journal of Global Buddhism*.

Gregory Price Grieve is a Professor of Religious Studies at the University of North Carolina, Greensboro, specializing in religious studies and popular culture. His research focuses on the intersection of Buddhism and digital religions, focusing on ethics and cultural values. He has authored multiple books and articles in the field.

Ira Helderman is Visiting Assistant Professor in the Department of Religious Studies and Adjunct Assistant Professor of Religion, Psychology, and Culture in the Divinity School at Vanderbilt University. His research examines how psychotherapists' definitions of what is and is not religious shape their understandings of caregiving, health, and illness. He has published in peer-reviewed journals such as *The Journal of the American Academy of Religion* and book collections like *Mysticism and Depth Psychology*. His monograph *Prescribing the Dharma: Psychotherapists, Buddhist Traditions, and Defining Religion* (University of North Carolina Press, 2019) is the first comprehensive examination of the surprisingly diverse ways that psychotherapists have approached Buddhist traditions.

Funie Hsu/Chhi (she/they) is a transdisciplinary scholar whose work melds American Studies, Asian American Studies, Education, Buddhist Studies, Critical Animal Studies, and other fields. Hsu/Chhi is currently Associate Professor of American Studies at San José State University and was a former University of California President's Postdoctoral Fellow at the University of California, Davis. She received a PhD in Education with a Designated Emphasis in Women, Gender, and Sexuality (UC Berkeley). Prior to her academic career, she was an elementary school teacher in Los Angeles Unified. She is completing her first book, *Instructions for (Erasing) Empire: English, Domestication, and the US Colonization of the Philippines* (under contract, University of Washington) and is currently working on a second book project that examines the popular secularization of mindfulness in the context of American public schools. It pays particular attention to Asian American racialization, Asian American Buddhist alterity, and structures of global capitalism. This work is sponsored in part by a Spencer Foundation grant. Her recent publications include "A Theory of Reciting as Asian American Buddhist Practice: The Young Buddhist Editorial as a Discursive Site of Recitation" in the *Journal of Global Buddhism*. Other scholarship and essays have appeared in *American Quarterly, Educational Studies, CATESOL, L2 Journal, The Immanent Frame, Lion's Roar*,

Buddhadharma, *The Progressive*, and elsewhere. Hsu/Chhi is a co-organizer of May We Gather, a national Buddhist memorial ceremony for Asian American ancestors.

Winston C. Kyan is an Associate Professor in the Art/Art History Department at the University of Utah. He is currently engaged in researching and publishing on traditional Buddhist art of Asia, Buddhist visual culture of the Asian diaspora, and Buddhism-inspired contemporary Asian art.

Rongdao Lai is Assistant Professor of Chinese Religions (Buddhism) at McGill University. Her areas of specialization are modern Chinese Buddhism, Buddhism and the state, Buddhist education, transnational religious networks, and religion and social activism in Asia.

Amy Paris Langenberg is Professor of Religious Studies at Eckerd College. Her work focuses on gender and sexuality in Indian Buddhism, female Buddhist monasticisms, contemporary Buddhist feminisms, and, more recently, sexual abuse within American convert Buddhism. She is the author of *Birth in Buddhism: The Suffering Fetus and Female Freedom* (Routledge, 2017). She is currently working on a co-written book with Ann Gleig on sexual abuse in American Buddhism (under contract with Yale University Press).

Jesse J. Lee is a doctoral candidate at Florida State University, studying American Religious History. His research areas include Asian American history, Buddhism in North America, race, law, and citizenship. His dissertation focuses on Japanese American Pure Land Buddhists in the early twentieth century, particularly the legal incorporation of Buddhist congregations, religious conceptions of land, and the consequences of linguistic translation.

Jay Michaelson is an affiliated Assistant Professor at Chicago Theological Seminary, as well as a well-known journalist and meditation teacher. He holds a PhD in Jewish Thought from Hebrew University, a JD from Yale Law School, and nondenominational rabbinic ordination. His most recent book, *The Heresy of Jacob Frank: From Jewish Antinomianism to Esoteric Myth*, won the 2022 National Jewish Book Award for scholarship. Dr. Michaelson is authorized to teach in a Sri Lankan Theravādan Buddhist lineage, was a member of the Barre Center for Buddhist Studies Board of Directors for six years, and was an editor and podcast host at the Ten Percent Happier meditation start-up for four years. Other books include *Evolving Dharma: Meditation, Buddhism, and the Next Generation of Enlightenment* and *The Gate of Tears: Sadness and the Spiritual Path*.

Scott A. Mitchell is the Yoshitaka Tamai Chair of Jōdo Shinshū Buddhist Studies at the Institute of Buddhist Studies in Berkeley. He is the author of *The Making of American Buddhism* (Oxford University Press, 2023) and *Buddhism in America: Global Religion, Local Contexts* (Bloomsbury, 2016), as well as co-editor with Natalie Fisk Quli of *Buddhism beyond Borders* (State University of New York Press, 2015) and *Methods in Buddhist Studies: Essays in Honor of Richard K. Payne* (Bloomsbury, 2019).

Richard K. Payne is Professor Emeritus at the Institute of Buddhist Studies, Berkeley. His main research focus is tantric Buddhist ritual. His recent publications include: *Language in the Buddhist Tantra of Japan: Indic Roots of Mantra* (Bloomsbury Academic, 2018), the edited volume *Secularizing Buddhism: New Perspectives on a Dynamic Tradition* (Shambhala, 2021), and the co-edited volume with Fabio Rambelli (University of California, Santa Barbara) *Buddhism under Capitalism* (Bloomsbury, 2022). He is Founding Editor-in-Chief of the Oxford Bibliographies/Buddhism, co-editor together with Georgios A. Halkias (University of Hong Kong) of *The Oxford Encyclopedia of Buddhism* (online and forthcoming in print, 2024), and co-editor with Glen A. Hayes (Emeritus, Bloomfield College) of *The Oxford Handbook of Tantric Studies*.

Todd LeRoy Perreira is a Lecturer in Comparative Religious Studies at San José State University where he teaches courses in contemporary Buddhism and world religions. He specializes in the history of Asian religions in the United States and has published a number of articles on the Thai aspects of Southeast Asian Buddhism in North America as well as a genealogical history on the use of the term Theravāda in modern discourse. His current research focuses on a cultural history of Buddha images in American life.

Peter Romaskiewicz earned his doctorate in Religious Studies from the University of California, Santa Barbara. His dissertation explores the use of smell and scented materials in medieval Chinese religions and the impact of trade in supra-regional aromatics on religious practice. His dissertation includes a translation of the earliest extant Chinese perfuming catalogue, the *Materia Aromatica* (*Xiang pu*), compiled by the Song official Hong Chu (1066–c. 1127). His research interests include Buddhist olfactory culture and material culture in medieval China as well as the historical reception of Buddhist imagery in the West.

C. Pierce Salguero is a transdisciplinary scholar of health humanities who is fascinated by historical and contemporary intersections between Buddhism, medicine, and cross-cultural exchange. He has a PhD in History of Medicine from the Johns Hopkins School of Medicine (2010), and teaches Asian history, medicine, and religion at Penn State University's Abington College. He is the Editor-in-Chief of the journal *Asian Medicine* and has published widely on the topic of Buddhism and Asian medicine, including most recently *A Global History of Buddhism and Medicine* (Columbia University Press, 2022).

Claudia Schippert was Associate Professor of Humanities and Cultural Studies at the University of Central Florida until 2023. They are now serving as Executive Director of the American Academy of Religion. Schippert's research interests are queer theory and religion in America, contemporary Buddhism, and digital Humanities.

Judith Simmer-Brown is Distinguished Professor of Contemplative and Religious Studies at Naropa University in Boulder, Colorado, where she was a founding faculty member. As Buddhist practitioner since the early 1970s, she served as an *acharya* (senior teacher) for Shambhala International from 2000 to 2022, where she continues to lead beginning meditation and advanced Vajrayāna programs. Active in North American

Buddhism, she has been planner and leader for a number of conference gatherings of western Buddhist teachers and leaders over the past thirty years. She is also a thought leader in Buddhist chaplaincy education in the United States. Her books are *Dakini's Warm Breath: The Feminine Principle in Tibetan Buddhism* (Shambhala, 2001) and *Meditation and the Classroom: Contemplative Pedagogy for Religious Studies* (State University of New York Press, 2011). She and her husband, Richard, have two adult children and four grandchildren.

Ben Van Overmeire is Assistant Professor of Religious Studies at Duke Kunshan University. A comparatist, he examines how pre-modern Zen Buddhist genres and ideas are understood today, particularly in popular literature. He has just finished a book manuscript on American Zen autobiography, describing how and why such narratives incorporate koan, Zen riddles revolving around seemingly unsolvable questions such as "What is the sound of one hand clapping?" Recent publications have appeared in *Religions* and *Contemporary Buddhism*.

Daniel Veidlinger is Chair of the Department of Comparative Religion and Humanities at California State University, Chico, where he focuses on Asian religions. He has written extensively about Buddhism and technology and co-edited *Buddhism, the Internet and Digital Media: The Pixel in the Lotus* (Routledge, 2015) which was one of the first volumes on this topic. He is also the Editor of *Digital Humanities and Buddhism: An Introduction* (De Gruyter, 2019) and the author of *From Indra's Net to Internet: Communication, Technology and the Evolution of Buddhist Ideas* (University of Hawai'i Press, 2018) which traces the history of Buddhism's association with media technologies from the earliest times until the present.

INTRODUCTION

ANN GLEIG AND SCOTT A. MITCHELL

IN 2020, in the midst of the global COVID pandemic and international Black Lives Matter protests against systemic racism sparked by the murder of African American George Floyd, a new Buddhist website and virtual community launched: The Young Buddhist Editorial (YBE).[1] A YouTube video on the site features five young Japanese American Jōdo Shinshū Buddhists who explain that they had decided to create a virtual space to connect and support their community as they are no longer able to attend their local temples due to the pandemic. The vision and values of YBE—articulated through the categories of Dharma, Culture, Interdependence, Sangha, and Social Justice—center Jōdo Shinshū as one of the 84,000 paths to end suffering taught by the Buddha; emphasize the importance of Buddhism as a religious, cultural, and community practice for Asian Americans; and express their commitment to overcoming the structural suffering of white supremacy, patriarchy, capitalism, and imperialism.

Reflecting the YBE's subtitle "Connecting our Community through Stories and Art," other notable features on the site include the MakerSpace, with various creative expressions such as music, spoken word, poetry, illustrations, photography, and videography. One offering is "Humans of Buddhism," a photo series that attempts to disrupt what it sees as the Buddhist stereotype in a Christian-majority country—"a shaven head monk in robes"—through portraits of young Buddhists in jeans and sweatshirts, on escalators and in gardens.[2] YBE also runs a book club with a thematic focus on Asian American histories and experiences, and hosts "Face to Face," a conversation series featuring topics such as Ecodharma and Collective Karma, which apply traditional Buddhist doctrines to contemporary social concerns.

Aesthetically stylish and easy to navigate with accompanying Instagram, Facebook, Twitter, and YouTube accounts, YBE's website embraces technological innovations to express and expand American Buddhist identity, practice, and community. It also

---

[1] The Young Buddhist Editorial, https://www.youngbuddhisteditorial.com.
[2] Humans of Buddhism, https://www.youngbuddhisteditorial.com/humans-of-buddhism.

forefronts and honors Asian American Buddhist history and tradition by articulating its mission as follows: "to preserve the stories of those who came before" and to create dialogue between older and younger generations of Buddhists. The undoing of binary categories such as traditional/modern, religious/political, ritual/meditation, immigrant/convert, and Asian/Western Buddhism that have often operated in the construction of American Buddhism is notable on YBE.

It is fitting to open *The Oxford Handbook of American Buddhism* with a snapshot of an American Buddhist project which connects contemporary Asian American experiences with Asian American history. American Buddhism begins with the establishment of Buddhist communities by Chinese and Japanese immigrants in the nineteenth century. The first Buddhist temple in the United States was built in San Francisco in 1853 by the Sze Yap Company, a Chinese American fraternal society. By the 1880s, Japanese immigrants in Hawai'i had begun establishing temples; and in 1899, the Buddhist Churches of America (BCA) was founded in San Francisco.[3] Thus, the ancestors whom the YBE honors in its project are the same Jōdo Shinshū Buddhists who established the oldest continually operating Buddhist community in North America. In his pointedly titled *The Making of American Buddhism*, Scott Mitchell (2023) shows the foundational role that Japanese American Jōdo Shinshū Buddhists played in the 1950s in constructing "American Buddhism" as a uniquely modern form of Buddhism. While their contributions were obscured by the Beat generation and counterculture writers such as D. T. Suzuki, Alan Watts, and Jack Kerouac who are commonly heralded as popularizing Buddhism in the United States, Mitchell shows it was actually the labor, organizing, and hospitality of Jōdo Shinshū Buddhists that made this possible.[4]

Young Buddhist Editorial serves as an instructive site to reflect on the development and central features of Buddhism in the United States as well as several of the themes explored in the following chapters. One of these is *a (re)centering of Asian American Buddhist history and experience*. Despite making up nearly two-thirds of American Buddhists, Asian American Buddhists have been routinely marginalized in both mainstream and academic narratives of Buddhism in the United States, which have tended to privilege majority-white convert communities and their offshoots such as the "secular" mindfulness movement. Take, for instance, the claim made in the 1990s by Helen Tworkov, the founding editor of the popular Buddhist magazine *Tricycle: The Buddhist Review*, that Asian Americans had not figured prominently in the creation of American Buddhism.[5] Or, the reproduction of the figure of the white female meditator on successive covers of popular magazines such as *TIME* as the face of Buddhist-derived meditation.[6] Asian American Buddhist practitioners and scholar-practitioners have

---

[3] Originally named the Buddhist Mission of North America, the organization was officially renamed the Buddhist Churches of America during the illegal incarceration of Japanese and Japanese Americans during World War II.

[4] Scott A. Mitchell, *The Making of American Buddhism* (New York: Oxford University Press, 2023).

[5] Helen Tworkov, "Many Is More," *Tricycle: The Buddhist Review*, Winter 1991, 4.

[6] Joanna Piacenza, "TIME's Beautiful, Blonde, White 'Mindfulness Revolution,'" *Huffpost*, January 29, 2014, https://www.huffpost.com/entry/time-mindfulness-revolution_b_4687696.

highlighted the white supremacy undergirding the centering of white convert Buddhists and have countered the erasure of Asian Americans through recovering their central role in transmitting, preserving, and transforming Buddhism in the United States.[7]

The recentering of Asian Buddhists *forefronts Buddhist diversity.* American Buddhist scholar Jane Iwamura notes the omnipresence of the mystical Buddhist monk in American popular culture, an orientalist stereotype which has been supplemented by the white, blonde female mindfulness meditator.[8] Asian and Asian American monks and white meditators, however, represent only a slice of the tremendous diversity of Buddhism in North America. This diversity is expressed institutionally and demographically, across and within Buddhist lineages. Institutionally, nearly every form of Buddhism present in Asia has some presence in North America, from a large cross section of Zen lineages, to Chinese communities from both mainland China to the broader Chinese diaspora, Buddhists from Thailand, Sri Lanka, and elsewhere in Southeast Asia, to say nothing of the variety of "convert" communities, hybrid communities, or "secular" Buddhist networks. Demographically, majority white meditation-based convert communities have witnessed major shifts in racial demographics and the establishment of diversity, inclusion, and equity initiatives through racial justice efforts and initiatives that are impacting Buddhist teaching and practice formats.[9]

Inextricable from the centering of Asian American Buddhism and a celebration of racial and cultural diversity within and across Buddhist lineages is *an emphasis on the historical and social context* of American Buddhism. The relationship between Asian American Buddhism and the social conditions of white supremacy, patriarchy, and capitalism were signified in a memorial ceremony for Asian American victims of a mass shooting in Atlanta, Georgia. The ceremony, named "May We Gather: A National Buddhist Memorial Ceremony for Asian-American Ancestors," occurred on May 4, 2021, at the Higashi Honganji Buddhist Temple in Los Angeles. In attendance were forty-nine Buddhist leaders from various Chinese, Japanese, Khmer, Korean, Sri Lankan, Taiwanese, Tibetan, Thai, and Vietnamese Buddhist lineages. Duncan Ryûken Williams, Funie Hsu, and Chenxing Han, the organizers of the ceremony, placed these murders in a long history of anti-Asian and anti-Buddhist violence.[10] In her ethnographic study of American meditation-based convert lineages, Ann Gleig identifies a similar feature in what she calls the "contextual turn," namely an increasing awareness among convert practitioners of how Buddhist practice is shaped by the specific social and cultural contexts in which it unfolds, particularly in relationship to issues of power

---

[7] See, for instance, Duncan Williams, *American Sutra: A Story of Faith and Freedom* (Cambridge, MA: Harvard University Press), 2019. Chenxing Han, *Be the Refuge: Raising the Voices of Asian American Buddhists* (Berkeley, CA: North Atlantic Books, 2021), 189.

[8] Jane Iwamura, *Virtual Orientalism: Asian Religions and American Popular Culture* (Oxford: Oxford University Press, 2010).

[9] For an overview of some of these initiatives, see Ann Gleig, *American Dharma: Buddhism beyond Modernity* (New Haven, CT: Yale University Press, 2019), 139–175.

[10] May We Gather, https://www.maywegather.org/.

and privilege.[11] The close intersections between religious, social, and political contexts is expressed on a doctrinal level through concepts such as collective karma, collective liberation, radical dharma, queer dharma, and Ecodharma, which articulate, extend, and revision foundational Buddhist concepts through a social justice lens.

Our opening snapshot of the YBE points to the impact of *generational shifts* across and within both heritage and convert-based communities of Buddhist practice in the United States. While indebted to and drawing inspiration from earlier generations, younger generations of American Buddhists forefront shifting social contexts and new political and environmental realities. Moreover, many "convert-based" communities are now several decades old, with multiple generations practicing the dharma in North America.[12]

Whereas the *utilization of modern technology* is often associated with younger generations, American Buddhists have long been on the vanguard of new trends and have used contemporary *art and literature* to (re)produce and promote Buddhist identity, practice, and community. From Buddhist periodicals in the 1950s to the establishment of virtual communities under COVID, from the hip-hop of the Wu Tang Clan to Zen priest and author Ruth Ozeki's award-winning *The Book of Form and Emptiness* (2022), North American Buddhists have long demonstrated creativity and innovation in the multiple configurations and representations of their traditions. Such technological and artistic pursuits have had an impact on American culture writ large, beyond the confines of Buddhist communities. Buddhist-derived practices such as mindfulness meditation have been deployed in healthcare and educational settings, the military, and the business sector, and as a result have become, according to some, a multimillion-dollar industry.[13] Silicon Valley and Wall Street cultures have extracted Buddhist practices and principles for entrepreneurial motivation and capital gains. Basketball coach Phil Jackson credits Zen Buddhism for his coaching philosophies and sporting success, and Michael Jordan includes a mindfulness coach as an essential part of his training regime. Reworkings of Buddhist concepts such as *karma* are belted out by pop star Taylor Swift, and Buddhist statues have become a mainstream of home and garden décor.[14] Aiming to capture these hybrid identities and the traces of Buddhist influence, scholars have suggested terms such as "nightstand Buddhists" and "Buddhish."[15] Thus, despite

---

[11] Gleig, *American Dharma*.

[12] For a consideration of the impacts of Generation X and millennials in meditation-based convert lineages, see Gleig, *American Dharma*.

[13] Jeff Wilson, *Mindful America: The Mutual Transformation of Buddhist Meditation and American Culture* (New York: Oxford University Press, 2014).

[14] Justin Curto, "Grading Taylor Swift's 'Karma' with a Buddhist-Studies Professor," *Vulture Magazine*, October 27, 2022, https://www.vulture.com/2022/10/taylor-swift-karma-explained-professor.html; Jiemin Bao and William M. Willis, "The Cultural Appropriation of Buddhism in Advertisements," *Journal of Global Buddhism* 23(1) (2022): 46–62.

[15] Thomas A. Tweed, "Night-Stand Buddhists and Other Creatures: Sympathizers, Adherents, and the Study of Religion," in *American Buddhism: Methods and Findings in Recent Scholarship*, ed. Duncan Ryûken Williams and Christopher S. Queen, Curzon Critical Studies in Buddhism (Richmond, Surrey: Curzon, 1999), 71–90; C. Pierce Salguero, *Buddhish: A Guide to the 20 Most Important Buddhist Ideas for the Curious and Skeptical* (Boston, MA: Beacon Press), 2022.

self-identifying Buddhists making up a mere one percent of the population, it is fair to say that Buddhism has had a substantial influence on American culture.

"American Buddhism": Which America? Whose America?

Buddhism was brought to the United States in the mid-nineteenth century by Chinese and Japanese immigrants. As noted, despite bringing Buddhism to the United States and preserving the tradition under intense conditions of xenophobic violence and discrimination, Asian Americans have been routinely erased from mainstream narratives of American Buddhism. To understand this erasure, we need to understand the racist history of personhood and citizenship in the United States wherein there has long been an implicit assumption that to be "American" is to be a "white Christian."[16] The project of making America a white Christian nation was founded on the genocide of Native Americans. Since their arrival in the fifteenth century, European colonizers have stolen and forcibly removed indigenous peoples from their land and Christian missionaries have waged war against indigenous worldviews, religions, and cultures through institutionalizing forced Christian conversions and assimilation. The equation of American personhood with white Christianity is expressed in the 1892 speech of Captain Richard H. Pratts, wherein he declared, "Kill the Indian in him, save the man." Pratt was speaking in support of the Christian Indian boarding school system, which aimed to "civilize" and "Americanize" Native American children.[17] Despite being the first peoples of North America, it was not until 1924 that the US Congress granted US citizenship to Native Americans.

Forcibly brought to the Americas through the transatlantic slave trade, African Americans were also excluded from American personhood and citizenship. The chattel slavery industry defined Black people and their children as the legal property of white slave owners. The 1790 Naturalization Act conflated whiteness and Americanness by granting citizenship only to white males over the age of 21. It was only in 1868, three years after the abolishment of slavery, that the ratification of the Fourteenth Amendment granted, at least in principle, legal citizenship to African Americans. Despite this constitutional protection, discrimination, inequality, and violence toward Black Americans

---

[16] Katheryn Gin Lum, *Heathen: Religion and Race in American History* (Cambridge, MA: Harvard University Press, 2022).

[17] For a full copy of the speech and further details, see Carlisle Indian School Digital Resource Center, https://carlisleindian.dickinson.edu/. Murder of "the Indian" was not confined to their familial and cultural erasure. It is estimated that over 500 Indian children died in boarding schools. See Bryan Newland, "Federal Indian Boarding School Initiative Investigating Report," May 2022, Bureau of Indian Affairs, 9. https://www.bia.gov/sites/default/files/dup/inline-files/bsi_investigative_report_may_2022_508.pdf.

was legalized for more than century by the pejoratively named Jim Crow laws passed in nearly every state of the Union.[18]

This was the deeply racist and racialized context that Asian Buddhists found themselves situated in when arriving as immigrants in the mid-nineteenth century. As both non-white and non-Christian, they faced double stigmatization as racial and religious others. Asian immigrant Buddhists were dubbed "heathens" and their temples and centers were vandalized and destroyed. Successive discriminatory laws resulted in the prohibition of immigration from Asia, beginning with the Chinese Exclusion Act of 1882 and culminating in the Asian Exclusion Act of 1924. In 1922, the US Supreme Court ruled against the application for citizenship from Takao Ozawa, a Japanese immigrant in Hawai'i, concluding that Japanese could not be considered white. Asian American Buddhists' vulnerability and perpetual status as suspicious "Others" was demonstrated in the forced relocation of Japanese Americans to internment camps after the bombing of Pearl Harbor. As Williams shows, Buddhist practice was a deep source of comfort and resilience for those incarcerated who preserved their religion in the face of intense violence and discrimination.[19]

Thus, the making of "American Buddhism" has happened at the intersection of Buddhist and Anglo-American cultural frameworks. Even as American Buddhists have critiqued and discarded a normative white Christianity, the American context brings a set of implicit assumptions, values, and norms rooted in whiteness, Protestantism, individualism, secularism, psychotherapy, and liberal feminism, all of which have shaped the emergence of American Buddhism. Recognizing the diversity of America's cultural influences beyond white Protestant individualism, however, brings many more conversation partners to the table. African American Buddhist scholar Rima Vesely-Flad, for instance, shows how Black American Buddhists are encountering Buddhism through the lens of the Black Radical tradition expressed through figures such as James Baldwin and Audre Lourde.[20] Driven by indigenous Buddhist practitioners and scholars, an emerging dialogue between Buddhism and indigenous, decolonial worldviews is also underway.[21] These conversations are supported by the recovery of neglected Buddhist histories. In short, the past and present of Buddhism in the United States looks quite different when narrated from the perspective of racialized minorities rather than white converts.

---

[18] They would not be overturned until the 1960s Civil Rights movement, although numerous studies demonstrate the continuing impacts of structural racism on the health and well-being of African Americans. See, for instance, Michelle Alexander, *The New Jim Crow: Mass Incarceration in the Age of Colorblindness* (New York: The New Press, 2010).

[19] Williams, *American Sutra*.

[20] Rima Vesely-Flad, *Black Buddhists and the Black Radical Tradition: The Practice of Stillness in the Movement for Liberation* (New York: New York University Press, 2022).

[21] Raymond Lam, "Restoration and Justice: An Interview with Dr. Natalie Avalos on Indigenous Spiritualities and Buddhist Allies," *Buddhistdoor Global*, December 2021, https://www.buddhistdoor. net/features/restoration-and-justice-an-interview-with-dr-natalie-avalos-on-indigenous-spirituality-and-buddhist-allies/. Spirit Rock Meditation Center has begun to host retreats exploring the relationship between indigenous spirituality and Buddhism.

Many scholars, practitioners, and scholar-practitioners have questioned the utility of the label *American Buddhism*, rooted as it is in mainstream narratives of whiteness while referring to a tradition with ongoing transnational and global connections. Acknowledging these limitations, in this volume we use the term *American Buddhism* "under erasure," encouraging ongoing critique and interrogation—asking, whose America? Which Buddhism? And whose and which Buddhism is overlooked when we invoke the term? Whereas we suggest a disruption, complication, and enlargement of the term, practically speaking, we must name our subject *something*; and to the extent that our subject is Buddhisms/Buddhists in North America, we have chosen *American Buddhism*, recognizing that this term necessarily includes everything Buddhist in the United States (and North America more broadly). A first step in this project is to (re)center Asian American Buddhists, recovering neglected histories and marginalized communities while critiquing the essentialized binaries that have operated within the study and practice of American Buddhism.[22]

One example of such a reconfiguration is provided by Kevin Chen in an article written for the YBE. In the provocatively titled "Also American Buddhist," he offers a nuanced reflection on his own Buddhist identity, particularly his relationship to the term *American Buddhism*. Shen grew up in the Tzu Chi Buddhist community, a modern Taiwanese Humanistic Buddhist community, which has a strong focus on humanitarian work. However, he shares that before reading Chenxing Han's *Be the Refuge: Raising the Voices of Asian American Buddhists*, and learning about the history of Buddhism in America, "it had never even occurred to me to identify my parents' volunteer work with Tzu-Chi as a facet of the multicultural phenomenon of American Buddhism writ large."[23] The reason for this is because for Shen, as for many members of the YBE, the synonymous terms of *American Buddhism* and *Western Buddhism* functioned largely "as a boogeyman, a catch all to describe problems we saw in Buddhism around us."

For Shen and his young Buddhist sangha, American Buddhism signified the reproduction of whiteness, the decontextualization and commodification of their tradition and heritage. Yet, Shen reflected further, "was this usage not itself alienating and reinforcing barriers between ourselves and our home in the West?" He suggests rather than simply reversing the binaries that have constituted white Buddhism by separating between pure/real Asian-heritage Buddhism and impure/inauthentic American white Buddhism, a better way forward is to embrace "the messy reality of Buddhism as practiced." This involves *both* a reclaiming of Asian American Buddhist communities and history *and* an inclusion of other forms of American Buddhism—an affirmation to self and other Buddhists that they are "also American Buddhists." Offering the signifier as a way to express multiplicity, for Shen, "Also American Buddhist" expresses a "larger,

---

[22] Leading the way in such a reconfiguration is the conversation series "Re-Orienting the Study of Buddhism in the West," produced by the Institute for the Study of Humanistic Buddhism in the West. See https://www.ishb-uwest.org/copy-of-ishb-scholarly-working-group.

[23] Kevin Chen, "Also American Buddhist," *The Young Buddhist Editorial*, https://www.youngbuddhisteditorial.com/articles/also-american-buddhist.

more inclusive vision" of what American Buddhism is, one which "creates space for diversity without being monolithic."[24]

Heritage Buddhism, digital Buddhism, Taiwanese Humanistic Buddhism, Buddhism as labor and service, Pure Land Buddhism, white Buddhism, Buddhism as community, Buddhism through creativity and art, Buddhist practice as ritual, reading, and mindfulness, collective karma, Ecodharma, American sutras, Buddhism in the twenty-first century, temple Buddhism, Buddhism as resistance and refuge against racism, socially situated Buddhism, therapeutic Buddhism, hybrid Buddhism, Buddhism as fuel for and retreat from capitalism, Black, Brown and white Buddhists, multigenerational, first-generation, and convert Buddhists, gendered Buddhists, survivors of abuse in Buddhism—inspired by Shen's powerful first-person reflection, and the multiplicity expressed by and through the YBE, it is the "Also American Buddhist" that the *Oxford Handbook of American Buddhism* particularly seeks to reflect and retrieve.

Mapping the Terrain of American Buddhism: Volume Overview

The Oxford Handbook of American Buddhism guides the reader through the rich terrain of American Buddhism, illuminating the diversity of practice communities and wide varieties of Buddhist identities, considering the multiple configurations that have resulted from the cross-fertilization of Buddhism and American cultural conditions and discourses, and extending the broader theoretical and methodological parameters that have shaped the study of American Buddhism. We have organized the *Handbook* into four parts: (I) Foundations, (II) Traditions, (III) Practices, and (IV) Frames. These parts build on, but go beyond previous scholarship by updating foundational topics such as traditions and practices, as well as including new areas of focus such as the recovery of neglected histories and marginalized identities and analyzing the intersections of Buddhist practice and scholarship.

Part I: Foundations sets out the broader historical and theoretical contexts and concerns of the field of American Buddhism studies while situating North American Buddhist traditions within the wider global context of Buddhist modernism. In Chapter 1, "American Buddhism, Modernity, and Globalization," Christopher Emory-Moore begins the reorientation of the study of American Buddhism by disrupting the Eurocentric assumption that modernization is a uniquely Western phenomenon. He situates American Buddhism in broader transnational patterns, showing that American Buddhism is just one local expression of global "multiple modernities." Thomas Calobrisi's "The History of Buddhism in the United States," Chapter 2, celebrates the diversity of American Buddhism, both in terms of its multiple lived practice communities

---

[24] Ibid.

and the various hydridic formations—identities, practices, and cultural products—resulting from its encounter with ever-shifting cultural conditions.

If Buddhism as an object of practice or scholarship is always mediated through the bodies of practitioners and scholars, what vectors of embodied identity have particularly shaped American Buddhism? In Chapter 3, "Identities I: Race and Whiteness," Ann Gleig traces the central role that race and whiteness have played in the formation and practice of American Buddhism. She documents the multiple ways that Asian American heritage Buddhists and convert Buddhists of Color have disrupted whiteness, and calls on white scholars of American Buddhism to also resist the disciplinary reproduction of whiteness in Buddhist Studies. Amy Langenberg models such resistance in Chapter 4, "Identities: II: Gender and Sexuality," through advancing an intersectional approach to gender and sexuality that undoes the common narrative that white liberal feminism is the sole creator of a gender egalitarian Buddhism. Langenberg discusses the multiple Buddhisms emerging from the lived experiences of Asian American and Asian immigrant lay and ordained women, Black women, trans and queer Buddhists, and sexual abuse survivors. The move away from a supposedly "universal" abstract subject to socially situated Buddhist practitioners is applied to the field of Buddhist studies by Scott Mitchell. In Chapter 5, "American Buddhist Studies and Scholar-Practitioners," Mitchell troubles the normative ideal of objectivist scholarship through an exploration of the symbiotic relationship between Buddhist scholarly and practice communities, systems, and institutions.

Having considered the broader historical context and theoretical concerns of American Buddhism, *Part II: Traditions* focuses on specific Buddhist communities and lineages. While Buddhism is a minority religion in the Americas, it is nevertheless profoundly diverse, with roots in virtually all parts of Asia. *Traditions* aims to give a sense of this vibrant multiplicity by including lineages that have received little previous scholarly attention and centering marginalized voices. The reader will note that we have included in this section both specific lineages (e.g., "Zen") as well as country-specific traditions (e.g., "Vietnam"). This is necessary for a number of reasons. On the one hand, as is the norm in the case of Japan, sectarianism is a defining feature of some Buddhist schools, and owing to the length of their presence in North America, they have had unique experiences in need of focused attention. On the other hand, some forms of Buddhism are directly related to specific Asian cultural spheres and the transnational historical events that similarly define these traditions, as is the case with refugee communities from South and Southeast Asia. Finally, as is clear in this part, the level of overlap and connections between different traditions, lineages, communities, and histories serves to highlight the often-arbitrary character of academic categorization schemes.

Chief among these schemes is the well-known "two Buddhisms" typology which has come under necessary and sustained interrogation for producing a racialized hierarchy between "immigrant/heritage" and "(white) convert" Buddhists. Two chapters suggest that it can be applied descriptively without reproducing racism.[25] In Chapter 10,

---

[25] See Wakoh Shannon Hickey, "Two Buddhisms, Three Buddhisms, and Racism," *Journal of Global Buddhism* 11 (2010): 1–25.

"Theravāda Buddhism in America," Erik Braun makes a case that the "two Buddhism" model still retains some heuristic utility, if it is used to differentiate between two interrelated Theravāda Buddhist cultures—one oriented to meditation, the other to cosmology—rather than two racialized Buddhist communities. Moreover, in Chapter 9, "Korean Buddhism in America," Claudia Schippert documents the simultaneous existence of two forms of Korean Buddhism in the United States: those practiced by Koreans or Korean Americans and those practiced by communities of non-Korean, largely white practitioners. Far from exalting white converts, Schippert is sensitive to the "double minority" status of American Korean Buddhists, calling for more scholarly attention to their complex negotiations of ethnic identity and religious heritage.

Buddhism as a living religion was first brought to North America by Chinese immigrants in the nineteenth century, the subject of Chapter 6, "Chinese Buddhism in America," by Rongdao Lai. The Chinese diaspora has further diversified these communities, which include various forms of Humanistic Buddhism from Taiwan as well as communities with ties to the Chinese mainland. Through a focus on a Chinese nun Man Chu (1930–2014), who has been neglected in existing scholarship, Lai nuances both the history and category of American Buddhism. Japanese Buddhism has a similarly long pedigree, as discussed in Chapter 7, "Pure Land Buddhism in America," by Jesse Lee. Whereas this chapter focuses primarily on Japanese forms of Pure Land Buddhism, Lee rightly critiques the simplistic equation of Pure Land Buddhism with a specific Japanese sectarian identity and rightly calls for more research on Pure Land influences across the (Mahāyāna) Buddhist world.

Zen Buddhism has similarly had a long and broad impact on American culture, which is demonstrated via a focus on literary production in Chapter 8, "Zen Buddhism in America," by Ben Van Overmeire. Continuing the theme of highlighting marginalized voices within in Buddhist communities, this chapter helpfully includes the work of African American Zen teachers such as Zenju Earthlyn Manuel, as well as the "usual suspects" of D. T. Suzuki and Philip Kapleau. Moreover, the Tibetan diaspora has increasingly impacted American culture more broadly, primarily via the visibility of the Dalai Lama. In Chapter 13, "Tibetan Buddhism in America," Holly Gayley and Joshua Brallier center the perspectives of Tibetan agents for enacting the transmission of Tibetan Buddhism to new cultural contexts.

In Chapter 12, "Vietnamese Buddhism in America," Todd Perreira rightly notes that the Vietnamese Buddhist community may represent one of the largest ethnic groups in all of Buddhist America; however, with some notable exceptions, there remains a dearth of scholarship on the tradition.[26] His contribution is a welcome intervention. A similarly understudied lineage is Nichiren Buddhism. Filling a lacuna in scholarship, Ralph H. Craig III in Chapter 11, "Nichiren Buddhism in America," introduces the four main Nichiren Buddhist sects that came to the United States in the late nineteenth and

---

[26] See Allison Truitt, *Pure Land in the Making: Vietnamese Buddhism in the US Gulf South* (Seattle: University of Washington Press, 2021).

twentieth centuries—Nichirenshū, Nipponzan Myōhōji, Nichiren Shōshū, and Sōka Gakkai/SGI-USA—with particular focus on SGI-USA.

A number of scholars have articulated the hybrid figure of the "JewBu" as a distinct type of American Buddhist identity.[27] Do these JewBus also make up a distinct tradition? In the final chapter of this part, "American Buddhism and Judaism" (Chapter 14), Jay Michaelson analyzes five modes of interaction between Buddhism and Judaism, ranging from "converts" who fully embrace a Buddhist identity to "responders" who reject Buddhism but create forms of Jewish practice heavily indebted to Buddhist techniques.

Michaelson's chapter raises questions about the porousness and creativity of Buddhist identities and serves as a useful transition to *Part III: Practices*. The chapters here explore the various ways in which Buddhist individuals and communities have adapted their practices to the cultural conditions of North America, while illuminating the broader historic and social forces undergirding such adaptations. In Chapter 15, "Buddhist Monasticism in North America," for instance, Luke Clossey and Karen Ferguson show how the roles of resident monks and nuns in community temples from multiple Buddhist lineages, situated across North and Central America, have been largely determined by the cultural and social needs of ethnic/heritage communities, such as the facilitation of communication between immigrants and their American-born children. In Chapter 16, "Food in American Buddhism," Melissa Anne-Marie Curley explores what American Buddhist food practices, such as alms giving, home cooking, and virtuous eating, tell us about Buddhist identities and community-making across heritage and convert communities.

In Chapter 17, "Mindfulness and Meditation in the United States," Nalika Gajaweera attends to undoubtedly the most popularized of Buddhist practices in the US: mindfulness meditation. Disrupting the utopic promise of the "mindfulness revolution," she unpacks mindfulness's entanglements with colonialism, whiteness, and neoliberalism. Further decentering comes from C. Pierce Salguero, who notes that the popularity of mindfulness has overshadowed the wide array of Buddhist practices for health and well-being. In Chapter 18, "American Buddhism and Medicine," Salguero considers the wide spectrum of Buddhist healing practices currently being used by diverse American Buddhist populations.

Richard Payne takes a more theoretical approach toward dismantling the conflation of Buddhist practice with meditation in Chapter 19, "Ritual, Rituals, and Ritualizing in American Buddhism." He interrogates an enduring legacy of Protestant Buddhism: the binary discourse that distinguishes meditation from ritual and valorizes the former as positive and the latter as negative. *Part III: Practices* ends with the disruption of another enduring legacy in American Buddhism: the disavowal of Asian American Buddhists. In Chapter 20, "Engaged Buddhism in the United States," Funie Hsu/Chhi points out that

---

[27] See Emily Sigalow, *American JewBu: Jews, Buddhists, and Religious Change* (Princeton, NJ: Princeton University Press, 2019).

scholars and practitioners of engaged Buddhism have failed to examine the racialized "American-ness" of engaged Buddhism, which continues to operate through the exclusion and neglect of Asian American Buddhists.

Payne and Hsu/Chhi's respective illuminations of enduring harmful legacies shaping American Buddhism prepare the reader for the final stretch of the journey. *Part IV: Frames* explores the main interpretive frameworks, popular mediums, and dialogue partners that Buddhism has encountered and through which Buddhism has been expressed in its American context. As Kin Cheung shows in Chapter 21, "American Buddhism and Secularism," these frameworks can reflect and reproduce ethnocentric assumptions. He analyzes the ways in which the hierarchical and racialized binaries of the "secular/religious," "universal/cultural," and "rational/superstitious" operate in the beliefs and practices of self-identified secular Buddhist networks and communities.

The next four chapters consider the mutual impacts and transformations produced by the meeting of Buddhism and American cultural discourses, practices, and products. In Chapter 22, "American Buddhism and Psychotherapy," Ira Helderman charts the multiple encounters between American convert Buddhist communities and psychotherapy, paying particular attention to the different ways that Buddhists articulate the relationship between the two. And Gregory Grieve and Daniel Veidlinger trace the innovative ways that American Buddhists have utilized technologies ranging from radios to phone apps to develop and promote Buddhist practices in Chapter 23, "American Buddhism and Technology." How do practitioners bring a Buddhist approach to trainings and institutions rooted in non-Buddhist histories, assumptions, and values? In Chapter 24, "American Buddhist Education and Pedagogy," Judith Simmer-Brown analyzes the diversity of American Buddhist educational offerings, ranging from children's temple school programs to accredited universities. Buddhist chaplaincy has emerged as a significant area of education and training within Buddhist higher educational programs; through a focus on "American Buddhist Chaplaincy Supervision," Jitsujo T. Gauthier in Chapter 25 examines the ways in which Buddhists have adapted and reformulated chaplaincy supervision from a Christian context to a Buddhist one.

The final three chapters explore both how Buddhism has functioned as a source of artistic inspiration and how Buddhist art has become a form of Buddhist practice, as well as tackling critical issues such as orientalism. In Chapter 26, "Buddhist Material Culture in the United States," Peter Romaskiewicz focuses on the ways in which Buddhist artifacts such as Buddhist icons have played a key role in diasporic and heritage Buddhist identity, practice, and community formation. Art historian Winston Kyan explores the diversity of American Buddhism through the lens of visual culture with particular attention to race, class, and gender in Chapter 27, "American Buddhism and Visual Culture." Similarly, in Chapter 28, "Buddhism and American Literature," Kimberly Beek discusses the broad range of Buddhist literary offerings, which she concludes now deserve their own specific genre of "Buddhist American literature." Beek's observation seems a fitting one to conclude on: the multiple deep encounters between Buddhism and America have birthed not just an *American Buddhism* but a *Buddhist America*.

Conclusion

Contributions from Michaelson, Hsu/Chhi, and others defy the four sections the editors have chosen for this volume. Are these chapters discussing theoretical or methodological questions about the study of religion in North America? Practices of specific communities or individuals? New Buddhist lineages or traditions? Or all of the above? Such contributions point to the growing diversity of the (sub)field and its relationship to other disciplines. Indeed, the study of Buddhism in North America necessarily contributes to larger academic conversations around, among others, racial formation, religion and material culture, and multiple religious belonging.

As a subfield of Buddhist studies, American Buddhism studies has been in conversation with and contributed to the larger field's development over the past several decades. Whereas many of the field's foundational scholars were classically trained buddhologists, the study of American Buddhism has benefited greatly from increasingly diverse methodologies and approaches. Our contributors include scholars trained primarily in anthropology, Asian American studies, art history, sociology, and urban planning. The questions, theoretical frames, and insights of this scholarship have, in turn, influenced Buddhist studies, which has become increasingly self-reflective and open to self-critique.

We anticipate these trends to continue. Indeed, whereas we have attempted to produce a comprehensive volume on the rich diversity and histories of Buddhism in North America, there is much more that can be said. There remain communities largely understudied or merely hinted at in these chapters. There remain questions and topics deserving of future scholarship approached beyond the confines of received academic tropes. It is said that there are 84,000 gates to awakening—surely there remain a similar number of academic projects waiting to be written.

PART I
FOUNDATIONS

CHAPTER 1

AMERICAN BUDDHISM, MODERNITY, AND GLOBALIZATION

CHRISTOPHER EMORY-MOORE

Introduction

EARLY in the telling of Siddhartha Gautama's youth in the 2010 PBS documentary *The Buddha*, His Holiness the Dalai Lama identifies in the Buddha a quality of self-reliance that might equally please Benjamin Franklin and Ralph Waldo Emerson: "Everybody, every human being wants happiness. And Buddha, he acts like teacher: 'You are your own master. Future, everything depends on your own shoulder.' Buddha's responsibility is just to show the path; that's all." Soon thereafter, the film's narrator, actor Richard Gere, tells us how "Siddhartha had put his faith in two gurus. They hadn't helped him.... Now, he knew what he must do: to find the answer to his questions, he would look within, and trust himself."

Later in the film, poet Jane Hirshfield describes the immanence of the Buddha's transcendence: "Nirvana is this moment seen directly.... There's nowhere to go. There's nothing else to be. There's no destination. It's not something to aim for in the afterlife. It's simply the quality of this moment." Since "at any moment what the Buddha found, we can find," Hirshfield insists that the Buddha's Noble Eightfold Path is a mere collection of suggestions—"a set of possible recipes that you can try on your own life and you can see which one makes the best soup."

Directed by American television biographer David Grubin, this humanistic, pragmatic, romantic account of the historical Buddha reflects a different genre of "awakened one" than the one typically conceptualized by Buddhists in Asia a century and a half ago—for example, within the classical Theravāda *Buddha-vandana* ritual of venerating the deified Buddha through prostrations, chanting, and offerings, or the *bhakti*-inspired Vajrayana practices of venerating the living *bla-ma lha* (guru-deity) through service and devotion. Here, rather, we are assured that the Buddha was no deity, miracle-worker, or guru, but an ordinary human with an extraordinary interest in examining and explaining the highs and lows of human experience. This is an unmistakably American Buddha, but it can also be described as a modernist Buddha—reflecting a broader, longer lineage of Buddhism's "modern" reformation at the hands of European, Asian, and American Buddhists and sympathizers.

This chapter provides a sketch of some of the key characters and characteristics constituting this diverse lineage of global, modern Buddhism in which Grubin's PBS Buddha is a rather late participant. In particular, this chapter makes two broad claims about two interpenetrating processes of social change which have fundamentally shaped Buddhism in North America:[1] globalization and modernization—the geographical and ideological adaptation of traditional Buddhist social forms to a post-feudal, "modern" historical period defined by liberal humanism, industrial capitalism, and the democratic nation-state.

1. *Buddhism's modernization has been Western.* Buddhism's modernization has developed largely in response to the colonial globalization of European Protestant modernity.
2. *Buddhism's modernization has been global.* Buddhism's modernization has been variably led and effected by non-European Buddhists in a variety of local Asian contexts.

The first point highlights the fact that Buddhist modernity has been significantly shaped by the ideological commitments of the Protestant Reformation and Enlightenment—particularly by liberalism (the ideal of individual freedom rooted in a conception of personhood which posits an inviolable, private self whose will must be liberated) and progressivism (the ideal of human progress through scientific, technological, economic, and social advancement). The second point highlights the diversity of Buddhist modernity, or modernities, which, as the product of "different communities, nations, and religious groups selectively adopt[ing] and adapt[ing] elements of Western modernity, combining them in unique ways with local concepts" (McMahan 2015, 182), extend well beyond the typically drawn features of Western modernity.

Significantly, this combination of tangibly Christian and non-Christian cultural elements is an apt description of the United States itself, and thus of the cultural environments in which contemporary American Buddhist communities continue to variably respond to modernity's nebulous, ineluctable legacy.

---

[1] In this chapter, I use the designation "North America" to refer primarily to the United States and Canada.

BUDDHIST MODERNISM

The noun "modernity" generally refers either to a post-traditional historical period typically starting with the Reformation, or to a set of cultural convictions (e.g., egalitarianism) and conditions (e.g., diversity) emerging from the European social transformations of that period's early stages. The adjective "modern" is commonly used to connote a particular sense of historical novelty: "[M]ore than merely referencing a particular epoch, modernity in important ways references modern people's sense of leaving a particular past and entering into a new time" (Mitchell 2016, 233). While such an embrace of modern cultural development has motivated liberal Protestants since the mid-nineteenth century (Hutchison 1992), the Roman Catholic Church's mid-twentieth-century program of official *aggiornamento* (Casanova 1994), or "bringing up to date," captures the common referent of the cognate noun "modernization."

At the turn of the twenty-first century, scholar-practitioner B. Alan Wallace observed the proliferation of a number of seemingly novel patterns in Western Buddhist formations that scholars before and after him have referred to as "Protestant"[2] or "modernist:"[3]

> It appears that a kind of Buddhist protestant reformation is in the making. The role of monks, nuns, priests, and professional contemplatives is on the decline; there is an erosion of the very distinction between laity and clerics; and the importance of the laity, including women, is on the rise. These changes are induced by individualism and nonconformism, democracy and egalitarianism, humanistic psychotherapy, feminism, modern science, and of course Christianity and Judaism. (2002, 46)

Wallace is confident that Buddhism's traditional (i.e., historically characteristic) elite and popular patterns of religious action and identity (e.g., guru/disciple; renouncer/householder) are being transformed under the influence of an individualistic conception of self-reliant personhood with roots in the dominant religion of this continent's European settlers: Protestant Christianity.

Coined by scholars to describe the product of Buddhism's so-called protestant reformation, "Buddhist modernism" is a form of Buddhism which has been in the making since the late-nineteenth-century clash of European colonial powers and Buddhist cultures across Asia. In his foundational study of the phenomenon, David McMahan describes it as a "modern hybrid tradition" (2008, 5) which reinterpreted traditional Asian Buddhist ideas and practices along the lines of Western modernity's defining

---

[2] See Abeysekara 2019 for an exhaustive critical review of scholarship since 1991 aiming to problematize Gananath Obeyesekere's (1970) inaugural account of "Protestant Buddhism" in late-nineteenth-century Ceylon.

[3] Ann Gleig (2019, 21–34) provides a genealogy of the term "Buddhist modernism" in Western scholarship.

discourses, as theorized by Charles Taylor (1989): Christianity, scientific rationalism, and romantic expressivism.

McMahan argues that Buddhist modernism has not only tracked Western Christianity, science, and Romanticism, but also carved out a place for itself in the tensions between the three. Specifically, modernists have aligned Buddhism with scientific rationalism to make a case that it is a "rational religion" over against Christianity, while drawing on the language of Romanticism and psychology with their emphases on interior depths, to counter the materialistic implications of science (2008, 23). The strategic alignment of Buddhism with Christianity, scientific rationalism, and Romantic expressivism has, according to McMahan (2008, 42), been effected by such modernizing cultural processes as detraditionalization, demythologization, and psychologization.

Detraditionalization

Commonly referred to as the "axial age," the sixth century BCE saw a wave of world renunciation sweep through Asia and the Near East, internalizing public community cults into religions of personal salvation (e.g., Platonism, Jainism, Buddhism, Zoroastrianism). Two millennia later, suggests Jose Casanova, the Protestant Reformation's analogous inward turn toward otherworldly individualism pioneered a process of differentiation that forced religion to withdraw from universal monism embodied in a state church to competing private denominations within a newly created and institutionalized private sphere (1994, 49–51).

Emerging from the "subjective turn" of post-Reformation Christian inwardness, "which liberated the modern individual from the external, ritual, and sacramental control of the church" (Casanova 1994, 51), McMahan defines detraditionalization as the shift of orientation from external to internal authority and the associated reorientation from institutional to privatized religion. The popular reallocation of religious authority from clerical decree to lay personal experience has been one of Protestant Christianity's most important global religious influences (Gombrich and Obeyesekere 1988, 216).

The internalization, or privatization, of religious authority and experience which marks both Protestant Christianity and "Protestant Buddhism" often also entails, according to McMahan, a shift from transcendence to immanence, from negative to positive evaluations of human nature, and from a concern with the future to living life fully in the present (2008, 43). In modern Buddhist formations, detraditionalizing trends can lead to the secularization of elements of Buddhism (e.g., meditation) under the influence of such beliefs in immanentism and progressivism emphasizing human-divine continuity over discontinuity (e.g., Grubin's PBS Buddha).

Another component of religious detraditionalization commonly concomitant with such humanistic convictions is the process of democratization (understood broadly as the action of making religious authority widely accessible), which, in the case of Buddhism, often entails both laicization and feminization—that is, increased potentials for both non-monastic and female authority over Buddhist practice.

Demythologization and Psychologization

Arguably rivaling the modernizing power of Protestant-inspired individualism, the discourse of natural science[4] has such immense cultural authority in contemporary North American society that alignment with it is one of the surest means for a new religious movement, domestic or immigrant, to cultivate respectability and minimize cultural discontinuity. This particular strategy of identity construction and audience attraction has therefore been a common one for North American Buddhist figures and groups, as it has for religious movements more broadly.[5]

Buddhism's demythologization refers to the extraction, or reconstruction, of meanings viable in post-Enlightenment modernity from teachings embedded in ancient Asian worldviews (McMahan 2008, 46). The secularized version of Buddhism presented in the Stephen Batchelor's best-selling 1997 book *Buddhism Without Beliefs*, or the Romanticist reformulation of the Buddhist doctrine of interdependence (*pratitya-samutpada*) from a description of unsatisfactory samsaric phenomena to a "world-affirming ecological worldview" (McMahan 2008, 24) are exemplary. The demythologization of Buddhist concepts often entails the psychologization of traditionally ontological realities. Examples are Chögyam Trungpa's reformulation of samsara's six realms from literal places of rebirth to symbols of psychological states (McMahan 2008, 45–46) and Carl Jung's internalization of Tibetan Buddhism's pantheon of Buddhas, gods, and spirits that the modern West's Christian monotheism and scientific rationalism "could not abide" (McMahon 2008, 54).

Besides the extraction of practices (e.g., meditation) and meanings (e.g., samsara) from broader ritual and doctrinal frameworks prevalent in Asian Buddhist history, another popular strategy for aligning Buddhism with Western science has been the selective appropriation of doctrine—laying emphasis, for example, on scriptures like the *Kalama Sutta* from the Pali *Anguttara Nikaya* in which the Buddha appears to endorse an agnostic discipline of self-reliant empiricism.

Like the American editor Paul Carus's influential 1894 book, *The Gospel of Buddha*, which espoused a Protestantized version of Buddhism as a religion of scientific rationalism, demythologized and psychologized transformations of Buddhism have often been more creative than expository. For Martin Verhoeven, Carus's work offers a cautionary case of American Buddhist modernism's ethnocentric biases: "The continuing effort to link science and Buddhism may conceal a similar cultural hubris, as it embraces those elements of Buddhism that seem consonant with the modern Western way of life and give short shrift to the rest" (1998, 227).

---

[4] These two foremost discourses of modernity—Protestant Christianity and scientific rationalism—share sociohistorical roots in early modern Western Europe, specifically the Protestant Reformation and "scientific revolution."

[5] For further reading on Buddhism and science, see Lopez 2008, 2012; Braun and McMahan 2017; Payne 2020.

Meditation

If Buddhist modernism had an emblem, it would be the cross-legged figure of a meditator—a self-disciplined individual absorbed in contemplative examination of their own consciousness and cosmos. The privileging of meditation is a dominant characteristic of monastic-led North American Buddhist sects such as the Tibetan-inspired Foundation for the Preservation of the Mahayana Tradition, as well as laicized, de-Buddhified lineages of practice such as Insight and mindfulness which have adapted meditation from "an arduous, lifelong training attempted in a renunciatory, monastic context" to a purportedly easy and instant cure-all for daily lay life (Wilson 2014, 52–53).

As such, popular, lay emphasis on the traditionally elite ritual practice of meditation is at the foreground of Donald Lopez's portrait of "Modern Buddhism":

> The strong emphasis on meditation as the central form of Buddhist practice marked one of the most extreme departures of modern Buddhism from previous forms. The practice of meditation had been throughout history the domain of monks, and even here meditation was merely one of many vocations within the monastic institution. . . . In modern Buddhism, however, meditation is a practice recommended for all, with the goal of enlightenment moved from the distant future to the immediate present. (2002, xxxviii)

And according to McMahan, "The vast majority of Asian Buddhists have practiced the dharma through ethics, ritual, and service to the sangha" (2008, 183). This historical pattern of popular Buddhist action contrasts sharply with a paradoxical pattern of adaptation in modernist Buddhist formations in which, "while meditation is often considered the heart of Buddhism, it is also deemed the element most detachable from the tradition itself" (185).

McMahan begins his discussion of Buddhism's modernist alignment with Western Romanticism (embodied by the American Transcendentalists, Theosophists, and Beat poets) with a quote from the American mindfulness pioneer most responsible for Buddhism's modern medicalization, the American doctor Jon Kabat-Zinn: "Buddhism is fundamentally about being in touch with your deepest nature and letting it flow out of you unimpeded" (2008, 119). Kabat-Zinn's Mindfulness-Based Stress Reduction Program is "perhaps the most successful" (2008, 56) of a variety of new experimental psychotherapies functioning to detraditionalize Buddhism via psychologization, "allowing meditation to operate in non-Buddhist therapeutic settings, often for non-Buddhist goals and without requiring commitment to explicitly Buddhist values" (2008, 57). For McMahan, this idea is rooted in an extension to all of Buddhism of D. T. Suzuki's Romanticist interpretation of "Zen" as a universal mystical experience.[6]

---

[6] See Sharf 1995b for an overview of the role of Suzuki's writings in the popular proliferation both in the West and in Japan of a modernist "rhetoric of meditative experience."

While the foregoing snapshot appears to support a reading of Buddhist modernism as a syncretic blend of traditional Asian Buddhist and Western non-Buddhist elements, the historical making of Buddhist modernism has been far more complex than a simple narrative of "East meets West." As McMahan points out, Buddhist modernism emerged both as a form of resistance to Western colonial forces and an appropriation of Western philosophical, religious, and social forms. In other words, modern Buddhism has always been global Buddhism.

Buddhism's Modernization in Global, Historical Perspective

European scholarly interest in "Buddhism" emerged in the mid-nineteenth century when philologists like Max Muller and Thomas Rhys-Davids began viewing it as something other than pagan heathenism (Lopez 1995), indeed as a second qualitatively non-national, universalistic *world* religion in addition to Christianity (Masuzawa 2005). Scholars like Muller and Rhys-Davids set out to reconstruct the Buddhist tradition in their own Protestant intellectualist mold from Pali and Sanskrit texts collected by British colonial officials in India. This idealized and ahistorical tradition of high textuality formed the basis of Western Orientalists' construction of "classical" Buddhism, which they contrasted with the various degraded forms of local, vernacular Asian Buddhisms. Nineteenth-century translations by the Pali Text Society were then appropriated by Asian Buddhist reformers like Anagarika Dharmapala and Soyen Shaku, and by Western sympathizers like the founders of the Theosophical Society, Helena Blavatsky and Henry Olcott, nourishing both Asian anti-colonial universalisms and popular Western Orientalisms which variably aimed "to assert Buddhism as a fully modern religion that was relevant to the contemporary world, and equal (or superior) to Christianity in its compatibility with science" (Harding, Hori, and Soucy 2020b, 1–2).

For the reason that "Theravada and Zen established many of the enduring motifs of Buddhist modernism from the early period" (McMahan 2008, 23), the following brief historical tour of modernization movements in global Buddhism begins with these regional Asian traditions.

South Asia: Theravāda

When Sri Lanka's Theravāda Buddhism began to modernize under erudite reformers in the late nineteenth century, the country had been colonized and missionized by European powers for 400 years, first by the Portuguese, then by the Dutch, and finally by the British since 1796. When Hikkaduve Sumangala became a monk at the age of thirteen in 1840, "Christian churches, schools, and printing presses attacked Buddhist texts and practices," and "Buddhist responses to Christianity were on the rise" across the island (Blackburn 2010, x). A major player in such Lankan responses, Sumangala "interacted with leading scholars from Europe and Asia as well as with the colonial governor and other high-ranking colonial officials on the island," and was seen by the British as "an archbishop of Canterbury-like figure, whom they considered a spokesman for Buddhist opinion on the island" (2010, xi).

The generation of Lankan monks with whom Sumangala ordained and trained "became a powerful force of opposition" (2010, x) to British Christian missionizing. Mohottivatte Gunananda, for example, with whom Sumangala collaborated closely (2010, 37), "founded the Society for the Propagation of Buddhism in imitation of the Society for the Propagation of the Gospel, and on a press originally imported by the Church Missionary Society began to print replies to Christian propaganda" (Gombrich and Obeyesekere 1988, 203). Gunananda spoke powerfully in defense of Buddhism at the famous Buddhist-Christian "Panadura debate" in 1873, an event which Lopez suggests "marked the beginning of modern Buddhism" (2002, ix).

The anti-colonial rationalization of Buddhism fashioned by Sumangala, Gunananda, and their monastic peers led to what has been called "Protestant Buddhism" (Obeyeskere 1970) for its laicizing reform, key elements of which were an increase in the participation of women and disdain for the intercession of gods and demons (Kemper 2005, 24).[7] This Protestant-inflected style of Sinhala Buddhism was subsequently internationalized by the likes of European-educated Anagarika Dharmapala, who was heavily influenced by the Euro-American new religious movement, Theosophy, particularly its co-founder Henry Steel Olcott. As versed in Orientalist occultism as Protestant rationalism, Dharmapala was well situated to carve out a place for Theravāda Buddhism between Christianity, scientific rationalism, and romantic expressivism.

Kemper describes Dharmapala as an "antimissionary missionary" who resisted Christianity's hegemony by appropriating the values and social forms of Victorian England to both return Buddhism to its historical place in his homeland and to spread it beyond. He accomplished the latter task quite effectively during his visit to Chicago's World Parliament of Religions in 1893, where, as the first Theravāda missionary in America, Dharmapala delivered a speech titled "The World's Debt to Buddha" in which he presented the law of karma as a theory of evolution and Buddhism as a strictly empirical science which "earnestly enjoins that nothing whatever be accepted on faith" (quoted in Deming 2015, 91).

Elsewhere around the same time, the Theravāda monk Ledi Sayadaw was busy laicizing and popularizing Buddhist study and meditation in an effort to defend the Buddhist doctrine (śāsana) against the British. As in Sri Lanka, Burmese Buddhism's forced disestablishment under British rule caused the laity to fill the patronage vacuum, which also had the effect of laicizing typically monastic practices

---

[7] See Blackburn 2010 for further information on strategic Sri Lankan Buddhist resistance to Western colonial forces.

like meditation. Braun (2013) traces a genealogy of Theravāda vipassanā meditation's globalizing detraditionalization from the initial anti-colonial reforms of Ledi Sayadaw to the measured modernisms of U Ba Khin and S. N. Goenka, to the enthusiastic modernism of the American founders of the Insight Meditation Society, to the secularized mindfulness training developed by Jon Kabat-Zinn.

East Asia: Mahayana

Even in Japan, which was never directly colonized by European powers, Victorian-era Protestant Christianity was seen as a model for the role of religion in modern society (Snodgrass 2003). Such privatized, rationalist, and activist religion seemed to facilitate Britain's colonial might, which loomed on Japan's doorstep following Britain's Opium Wars with China from 1839 to 1860. Buddhism's South Asian Protestantization was used by Japanese reformers like the Rinzai Zen monk Soyen Shaku as a guide for the rationalization of Japanese Buddhism and the formation of *shin bukkyo* ("new Buddhism"). Shaku played a major role in the proliferation of Zen Buddhism in the West, following his delegation to Chicago in 1893 (where he was the first Zen missionary to America) and subsequent authorship of the first book in English on Zen in 1906, *Sermons of a Buddhist Abbot*, in which he too claimed that "Buddha's teachings are in exact agreement with the doctrines of modern science" (1993, 122).

Perhaps the most influential figure in the development of Buddhist modernism (McMahan 2008, 122), Shaku's student and translator, D. T. Suzuki, studied with Paul Carus in La Salle, Illinois, from 1897 to 1909, learning the rhetorical means to appropriate and combine the ideals of Western rationalism and Romanticism in his own introduction of a modernist version of Zen to millions of Americans in the 1950s. In *Essays in Zen Buddhism*, for example, Suzuki pitched Zen Buddhism as a form of "radical empiricism" (1949, 140) and a pure pre-theoretical experience at once transcultural and yet only fully available to the Japanese.

Western imperialism was also a catalyst for the modernization of Chinese Buddhism. In the decades following Britain's defeat of Qing China in the Opium Wars, Han (Mahayana) Buddhism came to be viewed as a reason for the country's defeat and ensuing European economic exploitation: "Humanistic or *renjian* Buddhism constitutes one Buddhist answer to the crisis of Han Buddhism perceived by many Chinese at the turn of the 19th century. . . . [Han] was criticized as superstitious, world denying, and a hindrance to the modernization and strengthening of Chinese society" (Reinke 2018, 3).

The monk Taixu was a particularly influential Han Buddhist reformer, most known for his skillful integration of this-worldly liberal Protestant ideals of social activism, science, and inter-religious dialogue (Pittman 2001), for example in his 1926 essay "On the Establishment of the Pure Land in the Human Realm." Confounding a tidy conception of Buddhist modernism as a product *solely* of detraditionalization, demythologization, and psychologization, however, Taixu, not unlike Hikkaduve Sumangala before him, went about crafting such "modernist" reforms in concert with an energetic "traditionalist" effort to revive a devotional cult of Buddha Maitreya (Ritzinger 2017).

Perhaps the most globalized Chinese form of "humanistic" or "socially engaged" Buddhism (*renjian fojiao*) in the lineage of Taixu is Taiwan's Foguang Shan ("Buddha's Light Mountain"), which has hundreds of thousands of lay devotees and 1,300 monastics across five continents (Chandler 2005, 2004), the largest Buddhist monastery in the Western world, California's Hsi Lai Temple, and accredited universities in Taiwan and the United States. Victor Hori identified Foguang Shan and the global Nichiren lay revival movement, Soka Gakkai ("Value Creation Society"), as clear refutations of the idea that Buddhist modernism is a uniquely Western phenomena: "Modern Asian Buddhist organizations like Foguang Shan and Soka Gakkai of Japan are not quaint Buddhisms lifted from the rice paddies of the East to serve the Asians who've come to the West. They are large, sophisticated organizations comfortably taking the globe as home base" (Hori 2010, 33).

Today in Taiwan, six of the largest Buddhist groups claiming to be socially engaged (*renjian fojiao*) comprise 20 percent of the country's adult population, and share a conviction "that the Pure Land will not be in some faraway paradise but on this earth and in this world" framing a mission of "preparing the world—i.e. society—for its realization" (Schak and Hsiao 2005, 1–2).

Central Asia: Vajrayana

Due in part to Tibet's comparatively curtailed interaction with European colonizers, although Tibetan Buddhism may be the most global form of Buddhism, it has not gone through as thorough a modernizing process as other forms of Asian Buddhism (Harding, Hori, and Soucy 2014, 17).[8] McMahan points out, for example, that "some strains of Tibetan Buddhism have not been as quick to embrace the world-affirming, egalitarian, and democratic reinterpretations of the path as have other forms of Buddhism catering to western converts" (2008, 247).

The ambiguous state of Tibetan Buddhism's modernization is affirmed by "the Shugden affair" (Lopez 1998)—an ongoing internal Tibetan dispute between pluralistic modernists, led by the Dalai Lama, and sectarian Geluk-pa traditionalists like Kelsang Gyatso, founder of the New Kadampa Tradition, both of whom see the Tibetan "protector" deity Dorje Shugden as a living supernatural agent: evil spirit versus Buddha (McMahan 2008, 55).

In addition to internal sectarian divisions, specific tenets of Tibetan doctrine and practice seem particularly resistant to modernist detraditionalization. According to Martin Mills, for example, the principles of individualism and egalitarianism are at

---

[8] This is besides the fact that Western perceptions of Tibetan Buddhism have often yielded orientalist images of a quintessentially pre-modern religion: ritualistic, magic-obsessed, and hierarchical (Lopez 1995, 1998).

sharp odds with the "inherently unequal social" framework of Buddhist tantra rooted in the guru/disciple hierarchy (2003, 141–142). Nyingma lama Penor Rinpoche supports such a portrait of inherent hierarchy in his conservative dismissal of Buddhism's democratization: "There is no benefit to following the democratic spiritual path.... They are just wasting time.... [There must be] transmissions and blessings from a lama, the master... [who is from] a very pure lineage" (McMahan 2008, 247).

Despite the fact that Tibetan Buddhism has been modernizing for roughly half as long as Buddhist traditions such as Theravāda and Zen that encountered Western colonial powers over a century ago, McMahan suggests that the diasporic "privatization, deinstitutionalization, and detraditionalization" of Tibetan Buddhist meditation is well under way:

> Chögyam Trungpa's Shambhala training, for example, offers methods of mind training stripped of traditional rituals and requiring minimal doctrinal commitment. The Dalai Lama also encourages non-Buddhists to practice meditation, offering it as a Buddhist contribution to a turbulent world, one that cultivates peace of mind, compassion, and ethical responsibility in anyone, regardless of religious commitments. (2008, 187)

Although Buddhist modernism did not exist in Tibet, Lopez identifies the Dalai Lama as Buddhist modernism's "leading proponent" (1998, 185) since the 1959 Tibetan diaspora. In addition to his modernist emphasis on non-sectarian ecumenicism and his embrace of popular Western culture, he has taken an active interest in modern physics and psychology, hosting "Mind Science" conferences in Dharamsala and the United States. Jeannine Chandler suggests that the leading factor behind Tibetan Buddhism's entry into "the American consciousness by way of the media and popular culture" was "the growing reputation and international image of the Dalai Lama" (2009, 76), whose self-help books had become popular literature by the mid-1990s.

Religious detraditionalization is also well under way within post-Mao Chinese Tibet, where, since the 1980s, the imperatives of cultural preservation and innovation have fueled a revival of Tibetan Buddhist monasticism shaped by monks and nuns "vigorously promot[ing] education and ethics in terms compatible with an unfolding neoliberal modernity" (Gayley 2021, xii) which is at once ideological and economic (Caple 2019).

Modern Buddhism: Global Buddhism

Buddhism has been adapting to American culture since the establishment of the first Chinese and Japanese temples in Hawai'i and on the West Coast in the late nineteenth century, and in greater numbers since the 1960s with increases in both Asian immigration and non-Asian American interest in Buddhism. But the arrival of particular

Asian Buddhist formations on Canadian and American shores has rarely precipitated or coincided with their modernization. Scholars of Buddhism in the West are becoming increasingly aware that Buddhist modernism is not simply a product of the modernized West receiving and revitalizing Buddhism from pre-modern Asia.

Thirty years after its initial formulation by Charles Prebish (1979), Hori (2010) argued that the "two Buddhisms" typology of Asian-ethnic/Western-convert commonly adopted in early studies of North American Buddhism[9] imported ethnocentric value judgments that denigrate the Asian "ethnic" other by contrasting her inherited, unthinking Buddhism with the Euro-Canadian "convert" seen to have freely chosen her Buddhism. Instead, Hori called for scholars to recognize that Canadian Buddhism is as ethnic (i.e., culturally particular) as any Asian Buddhism.

As early as 1998, Kenneth Tanaka pointed to the Buddhist Churches of America (BCA) as illustrative of the ethnic/convert dichotomy's tendency to obscure ethnic heterogeneity and overlap between the two categories. Martin Baumann (2002) pointed out that the categories of immigrant and convert become increasingly meaningless when applied to consecutive generations whose members no longer fit into one or the other. American Scholars Wakoh Shannon Hickey (2010) and Joseph Cheah (2011) have since demonstrated that the two Buddhisms typology contains not only racist nuances supporting a white supremacist representation of American Buddhism, but the historically inaccurate assumption that Buddhism began modernizing in the West. Harding, Hori, and Soucy (2014, 2020) have built on such critiques to identify a tired theoretical paradigm contained in the implicit conflation of three sets of binaries: Asian-ethnic/Western-convert, traditional/modern, and inauthentic/authentic.[10]

Wherever the progressivist ideals of the European Enlightenment had an impact, "tropes of modernism were taken up, interpreted, and adapted to local circumstances, and then exported in . . . 'glocalization' processes" (Harding, Hori, and Soucy 2020b, 2). Buddhism's "modern" evolution has always also been a global geographical one. As such, Harding, Hori, and Soucy (2014, 2020a) argue for increased and continued awareness of the simultaneously global and local, or *glocal* (Robertson 1995), nature of contemporary North American Buddhist phenomena. Following Roland Robertson, Peter Beyer outlines the global-local interplay of glocalization in general:

> There is (1) the spread of various particular social forms across the globe, which constitutes their universalization. . . . These universalized forms . . . (2) become particularized to various other local situations. . . . Such transformation, in turn, can become the particular subject of (3) another universalization, which in turn becomes reparticularized in other contexts and other times. And so on. The global expresses itself only as local, and the local expresses itself in global terms. (2006, 24)

---

[9] See Numrich 1996; Fields 1998; Queen and Ryuken Williams 1999; Coleman 2001; and Cadge 2005.

[10] Natalie Quli critiques a converse orientalist tendency among Buddhist studies scholars who "have become preoccupied with protecting authentic, 'traditional' Asian Buddhism from the contamination of Western-influenced 'Buddhist modernism'" (2009, 5).

By this account, David Grubin's PBS Buddha could indeed be interpreted as a local American particularization—that is, an *Americanization*—of a universalized social form, in this case the life story of the Buddha. Alexander Soucy points out, however, that Buddhist adaptations in Canada (or by extension the United States) are not the result of Buddhism's transformation to become suitable for Canadians, but local manifestations of greater trends in global Buddhism (2014, 50). This is a subtle but important distinction. In the case of Grubin's PBS Buddha, it calls us to identify this particular self-reliant, rationalist, romantic meditator as not simply an Americanized Buddha, *nor* a primitivist Indian Buddha, but a modernist one—an icon cast in the Protestant-inflected mold of global Buddhist modernity by predominantly, but not exclusively, Asian Buddhist reformers such as Anagarika Dharmapala since well before the Buddha was a popular American icon. In other words, a similarly "Protestantized" Buddha pre-dates its popular portrayal in the United States—a local manifestation of a trend in greater global Buddhism.

Patterns of religious adaptation previously identified as American can thus be revisited with a global, or glocal, perspective. The patterns of democratization, pragmatism, and engagement which Christopher Queen saw emerging among the three to four million American Buddhists in 1999 (three-quarters of whom were of Asian heritage), for example, should be understood not as emerging characteristics of a "new," uniquely modern "American Buddhism," but as local American manifestations of greater global Buddhist trends—that is, as recognizable patterns of global Buddhism's American localization.

These patterns of adaptation reflect reformist tendencies in the North American localization of a variety of global Buddhist formations. But where there is reformist modernism, there are often also strong undercurrents of reactionary neo-traditionalism (Emory-Moore 2020a), and nearly everything in between—a continually evolving plethora of Buddhist lifeways that consistently reflect and persistently resist the categorizations of modern and traditional, global and local.

POSTCOLONIAL BUDDHIST POSTMODERNITY

Discussing "retraditionalization" as one of a variety of trends in "the postmodern condition of Buddhism," McMahan reminds us that, "[i]n fact, we see across the globe a number of movements attempting to reappropriate tradition, to cast off some of the staples of Buddhist modernism, and to reassert more conventional views of the dharma. Such 'returns' are themselves products of modernity" (2008, 246).

Wendy Cadge (2005), for example, described teachers at the Cambridge Insight Meditation Centre who, after years of decontextualized vipassanā meditation practice, have for entirely pragmatic reasons begun (re)introducing what she refers to as other supporting branches of the Theravāda Buddhist tree—rituals, ceremonies, precept gatherings—recognizing that the health of a tree's heartwood relies on its bark.

Meanwhile, viewing "their tradition's strict adherence to the vinaya [as] the only path forward for Theravada in the West" (Clossey and Ferguson 2020, 37), non-Asian pioneer monks of the global Thai Forest Tradition (the roots of which go back to a nineteenth-century Thai monastic reform movement) harken back to an ultra-conservative form of early Theravāda Buddhist monastic practice in the forests of central British Columbia (Birken Forest Monastery) and southern California (Metta Forest Monastery).

Although scholars have linked the development of "various hybrid combinations of the traditional and modern" (Gleig 2019, 5) with Buddhist *post*modernity, the historical diversity of Buddhism's global modernization has seen reformers who have often been as concerned with preservation as innovation. Ledi Sayadaw's efforts to promote the combination of meditation and doctrinal study (Braun 2013, 5) as a means of protecting Buddhism under British colonialism in Burma is exemplary.[11] Soorakkulame Pemaratana's (2020) recently recovered archival evidence of the conservative ritual reforms of Buddhist activists in colonial Ceylon represents a comparable contemporaneous case of "traditionalist" Theravāda Buddhist modernism. Echoing Blackburn's caution against overstating the Protestant nature of Sri-Lankan Buddhist modernism (2010, xiii), Pemaratana observes that the scholarly account of the novelty of such modern-traditional hybridities has been selective and elite, often "emphasiz[ing] only reforms that were rationalist or styled after Christian forms of religious practice" (2010, 33).

Ann Gleig's research confirms that "American meditation-based convert Buddhism" increasingly reflects characteristics identified by Mitchell (2016) as key features of postmodernity: "(1) its critical skepticism toward modern narratives of scientific rationalism, universal truth, and human progress; and (2) its embrace of diversity in contrast to the modern tendency toward the erasure of difference" (Gleig 2019, 290). Casanova's claim that "modern privatized religiosity . . . is the true harbinger of the postmodern condition" (1994, 230) suggests that both these developments—the relativization of meta-narratives and celebration of minority perspectives—may be best understood as extensions of religious detraditionalization.

Gleig derives her conclusion that "new [American Buddhist] developments . . . cannot be fully explained within the parameters of Buddhist modernism" (2019, 281) from ethnographic studies of critical turns in the mindfulness movement, psychotherapy in Zen sex scandals, and reorientations of vipassanā practice. Gleig argues that these cases respectively challenge "three key components of Buddhist modernism—the scientific-rational lineage, the Romantic lineage, and the privileging of meditative experience" (2019, 12). The gap between lived American Buddhism and received theory on Buddhist modernism leads her to ask, "How, then, are we to name such emerging trends?" (2019, 281). After reviewing the utility of several existing categories, Gleig proposes a "three-forked 'post-' analysis"—postmodern, postcolonial, and postsecular—as a method

---

[11] Analogously, "conservation through adaptation" is how one scholar (Kay 2004, 100) has characterized what I have referred to as the "hybrid fundamentalism" (Emory-Moore 2020a, 25) of the New Kadampa Tradition.

to "identify the specific currents of modernity that are undergoing transformation in American Buddhism" (2019, 298).

Following Mitchell and other scholars of postmodern religion, Gleig's portrait of American Buddhist postmodernity extends the above portrait of selective de-/retraditionalization by highlighting a pattern of diverging reactionary trends leaning toward the respectively conservative and secularizing extremes of fundamentalism and deinstitutionalized spiritualities (2019, 10): "These two seemingly contradictory trends—innovation and preservation, radicalism and recovery—are indicative of postmodernity in which a revalorization of tradition appears alongside an acceleration of secularization" (2019, 5).

Buddhism has always been characterized by an ongoing tension between attempts to preserve tradition and adapt to changing social conditions. A common emic analogy for the interplay between tradition and adaptation in Buddhist history refers to the preservation of Dharma tea by reconstructing its cultural cup: "The globalization of Buddhism involves a trend toward isolating the active ingredient of enlightenment; what is the essential Dharma distinct from cultural accretions?" (Sumegi 2014, 229). A guiding question for the study of Buddhist adaptation, modern-colonial or postmodern-postcolonial, is therefore: What does the Buddhist community at hand perceive to be the essential Dharma distinct from cultural accretions? Whatever this is will likely not be made available for detraditionalization and may become the basis of retraditionalization when seen to be threatened.

Conclusion

To delineate the contours of Buddhist modernity and globalization is to delineate theories of interpretation, or hermeneutics (Mitchell 2016, 238)—theories grounded in conceptual and linguistic categories which simultaneously communicate and constitute the "modern" and the "global" in implicit or explicit contrast with their opposites, the "traditional" and the "local." In an important respect, then, to populate these categories by describing the real sociohistorical properties and processes to which they refer is to talk about talking.

In the words of Quli and Mitchell, "the category of 'modernity' represents a type of discourse (a *narrative*) that is deeply colored by the cultural patterns and subjectivities of the storyteller. This is as true about scholars using the term as it is about the people scholars seek to describe and understand" (2015, 212). The New Kadampa Tradition's successful internet promotion of conservative Geluk teachings under the banner of "Modern Buddhism" (Emory-Moore 2020a), for example, makes it plain that "narratives of modernity have been appropriated by [Buddhist] individuals, groups, and institutions in a variety of creative ways and integrated into the already-existing cultures underlying them, producing unique forms with their own logics and histories" (Quli and Mitchell 2015, 203). Just like "modern," the "traditional" narrative is also rhetorically deployed by Buddhist communities in strategies of audience attraction and identity formation.

Beside the fact that the terms are so often deployed to evaluate positions and identities, "the application of the labels 'modern' and 'traditional' to specific Buddhist traditions is uneven and culturally arbitrary" (Mitchell 2016, 237). For these reasons and others, including its tacit rhetoric of "radical rupture," Quli and Mitchell suggest abandoning "modernism" as an analytical tool for the study of Buddhism in the United States (2015, 213).[12] Harding, Hori, and Soucy (2014) make a similar suggestion with regard to Buddhism in Canada, arguing for the replacement of modern/traditional with global/local.

If we choose to employ modernity and globalization as hermeneutic techniques for making sense of Buddhist history and cultural geography, as this chapter has done, let us do so with self-conscious attentiveness to the double-edged utility of theoretical categories which always simultaneously reveal and obscure (Wilson 2012, 232). Rather than locating semantic value in an individual term, for example by identifying "modernity" with "an absolute set of characteristics applied evenly across Buddhist traditions" (Mitchell 2016, 238) or "Buddhist globalism" as "a type of Buddhism with a set of characteristics" (Soucy 2014, 38), let us enshrine the spectral dis/continuities between binary categories in our maps and street views of American Buddhist phenomena: global and local, modern and traditional, and perhaps finally, appearance (*samvrti-satya*) and emptiness (*paramartha-satya*).

References

Abeysekara, Ananda. 2019. "Protestant Buddhism and 'Influence.'" *Qui Parle* 28, no. 1: 1–75.
Baumann, Martin. 2002. "Protective Amulets and Awareness Techniques, or How to Make Sense of Buddhism in the West." In *Westward Dharma: Buddhism Beyond Asia*, edited by Charles S. Prebish and Martin Baumann, 51–65. Berkeley: University of California Press.
Beyer, Peter. 2006. *Religions in Global Society*. London: Routledge.
Blackburn, Anne M. 2010. *Locations of Buddhism: Colonialism and Modernity in Sri Lanka*. Chicago: University of Chicago Press.
Braun, Erik. 2013. *The Birth of Insight: Meditation, Modern Buddhism, and the Burmese Monk Ledi Sayadaw*. Chicago: University of Chicago Press.
Braun, Erik, and David L. McMahan, eds. 2017. *Meditation, Buddhism, and Science*. New York: Oxford University Press.
Cadge, Wendy. 2005. *Heartwood: The First Generation of Theravada Buddhism in America*. Chicago: University of Chicago Press.
Caple, Jane E. 2019. *Morality and Monastic Revival in Post-Mao Tibet*. Honolulu: University of Hawai'i Press.

---

[12] Elsewhere (Emory-Moore 2020b), I attempt to take up Quli and Mitchell's call by employing the less colored term "adaptationism" (Hutchison 1992, 6) subdivided into the categories of "enthusiastic" and "measured" to chart patterns of detraditionalization in Tibetan-inspired, English-language children's meditation manuals.

Casanova, José. 1994. *Public Religions in the Modern World*. Chicago: University of Chicago Press.

Chandler, Jeannine. 2009. *Hunting the Guru: Lineage, Culture and Conflict in the Development of Tibetan Buddhism in America*. PhD dissertation, University at Albany, State University of New York.

Chandler, Stuart. 2005. "Spreading Buddha's Light: The Internationalization of Foguang Shan." In *Buddhist Missionaries in the Era of Globalization*, edited by Linda Learman, 162–184. Honolulu: University of Hawai'i Press.

Chandler, Stuart. 2004. *Establishing a Pure Land on Earth: The Foguang Buddhist Perspective on Modernization and Globalization*. Honolulu: University of Hawai'i Press.

Cheah, Joseph. 2011. *Race and Religion in American Buddhism*. New York: Oxford University Press.

Clossey, Luke, and Karen Ferguson. 2020. "Birken Buddhist Forest Monastery: Asian Migration, the Creative Class, and Cultural Transformation in the New Pacific British Columbia." *BC Studies* 208: 17–44.

Coleman, James William. 2001. *The New Buddhism: The Western Transformation of an Ancient Tradition*. Oxford: Oxford University Press.

Deming, Willoughby. 2015. *Understanding the Religions of the World: An Introduction*. Chichester: John Wiley & Sons.

Emory-Moore, Christopher. 2020a. "Branding a New Buddhist Movement: The New Kadampa Tradition's Self-identification as 'Modern Buddhism.'" *Journal of Global Buddhism* 21: 11–28.

Emory-Moore, Christopher. 2020b. "Present Peace, Future Freedom: Children's Meditation Instruction in Two Diasporic Tibetan Buddhist Lineages." *Religious Studies and Theology* 39, no. 1: 57–74.

Fields, Rick. 1998. "Divided Dharma: White Buddhists, Ethnic Buddhists and Racism." In *The Faces of Buddhism in America*, edited by Charles S. Prebish and Kenneth Tanaka, 196–206. Berkeley: University of California Press.

Gayley, Holly, ed. 2021. *Voices from Larung Gar: Shaping Tibetan Buddhism for the Twenty-First Century*. Boulder, CO: Snow Lion Publications.

Gleig, Ann. 2019. *American Dharma: Buddhism beyond Modernity*. New Haven, CT: Yale University Press.

Gombrich, Richard, and Gananath Obeyesekere. 1988. *Buddhism Transformed: Religious Change in Sri Lanka*. Princeton, NJ: Princeton University Press.

Harding, John S., Victor Sōgen Hori, and Alexander Soucy. 2014. "Introduction." In *Flowers on the Rock: Global and Local Buddhisms in Canada*, edited by John S. Harding, Victor Sōgen Hori, and Alexander Soucy, 3–24. Montreal: McGill-Queen's University Press.

Harding, John S., Victor Sōgen Hori, and Alexander Soucy, eds. 2020a. *Buddhism in the Global Eye: Beyond East and West*. London: Bloomsbury.

Harding, John S., Victor Sōgen Hori, and Alexander Soucy. 2020b. "Introduction: Alternate Buddhist Modernities." *Journal of Global Buddhism* 21: 1–10.

Hori, Victor Sōgen. 2010. "How Do We Study Buddhism in Canada?" In *Wild Geese: Buddhism in Canada*, edited by John S. Harding, Victor Sōgen Hori, and Alexander Soucy, 12–38. Montreal: McGill-Queen's University Press.

Hickey, Wakoh Shannon. 2010. "Two Buddhisms, Three Buddhisms, and Racism." *Journal of Global Buddhism* 11: 1–25.

Hutchison, William R. 1992. *The Modernist Impulse in American Protestantism*. Durham, NC: Duke University Press.

Kay, David N. 2004. *Tibetan and Zen Buddhism in Britain: Transplantation, Development and Adaptation.* London: Routledge Curzon.

Kemper, Steven. 2005. "Dharmapala's *Dharmaduta* and the Buddhist Ethnoscape." In *Buddhist Missionaries in the Era of Globalization*, edited by Linda Learman, 22–50. Honolulu: University of Hawai'i Press.

Lopez, Donald S., Jr. 1995. *Curators of the Buddha: The Study of Buddhism Under Colonialism.* Chicago: University of Chicago Press.

Lopez, Donald S., Jr. 1998. *Prisoners of Shangri-La: Tibetan Buddhism in the West.* Chicago: University of Chicago Press.

Lopez, Donald S., Jr. 2002. *A Modern Buddhist Bible: Essential Readings from East and West.* Boston: Beacon Books.

Lopez, Donald S., Jr. 2008. *Buddhism and Science: A Guide for the Perplexed.* Chicago: University of Chicago Press, 2008.

Lopez, Donald S., Jr. 2012. *The Scientific Buddha: His Short and Happy Life.* New Haven: Yale University Press.

Masuzawa, Tomoko. 2005. *The Invention of World Religions, Or, How European Universalism Was Preserved in the Language of Pluralism.* Chicago: University of Chicago Press.

McMahan, David L. 2008. *The Making of Buddhist Modernism.* New York: Oxford University Press.

McMahan, David L. 2015. "Buddhism and Multiple Modernities." In *Buddhism beyond Borders: New Perspectives on Buddhism in the United States*, edited by Scott A. Mitchell and Natalie E. F. Quli, 181–195. New York: State University of New York Press.

Mills, Martin A. 2003. *Identity, Ritual and State in Tibetan Buddhism: The Foundations of Authority in Gelukpa Monasticism.* London: Routledge Curzon.

Mitchell, Scott A. 2016. *Buddhism in America: Global Religion, Local Contexts.* London: Bloomsbury.

Numrich, Paul David. 1996. *Old Wisdom in the New World: Americanization in Two Immigrant Theravada Buddhist Temples.* Knoxville: University of Tennessee Press.

Obeyesekere, Gananath. 1970. "Religious Symbolism and Political Change in Ceylon." *Modern Ceylon Studies* 1, no. 1: 43–63.

Payne, Richard K. 2020. "Buddhism and the Sciences: Historical Background, Contemporary Developments." *Journal of Dharma Studies* 3, no. 2: 219–243.

Pemaratana, Soorakkulame. 2020. "Reviving the Buddha: The Use of the Devotional Ritual of Buddha-Vandanā in the Modernization of Buddhism in Colonial Sri Lanka." *Journal of Global Buddhism* 21: 29–50.

Pittman, Don A. 2001. *Toward a Modern Chinese Buddhism: Taixu's Reforms.* Honolulu: University of Hawai'i Press.

Prebish, Charles S. 1979. *American Buddhism.* North Scituate, MA: Duxbury Press.

Queen, Christopher. 1999. "Introduction." In *American Buddhism: Methods and Findings in Recent Scholarship*, edited by Duncan Ryuken Williams and Christopher S. Queen, xiv–xxxvii. Surrey: Curzon Press.

Quli, Natalie. 2009. "Western Self, Asian Other: Modernity, Authenticity, and Nostalgia for 'Tradition' in Buddhist Studies." *Journal of Buddhist Ethics* 16: 1–38.

Quli, Natalie E. F., and Scott A. Mitchell. 2015. "Buddhist Modernism as Narrative: A Comparative Study of Jodo Shinshu and Zen." In *Buddhism Beyond Borders: New Perspectives on Buddhism in the United States*, edited by Natalie E. F. Quli and Scott A. Mitchell, 197–215. Albany: State University of New York Press.

Reinke, Jens. 2018. "Sacred Secularities: Ritual and Social Engagement in a Global Buddhist China." *Religions* 9, no. 11: 338.
Robertson, Roland. 1995. "Glocalization: Time-Space and Homogeneity-Heterogeneity." In *Global Modernities*, edited by M. Featherstone, S. Lash, and R. Robertson, 25–44. London: Sage Publications.
Ritzinger, Justin. 2017. *Anarchy in the Pure Land: Reinventing the Cult of Maitreya in Modern Chinese Buddhism*. New York: Oxford University Press.
Ryuken Williams, Duncan, and Christopher S. Queen, eds. 1999. *American Buddhism: Methods and Findings in Recent Scholarship*. Surrey: Curzon Press.
Schak, David, and Hsin-Huang Michael Hsiao. 2005. "Taiwan's Socially Engaged Buddhist Groups." *China Perspectives* 59: 1–18.
Shaku, Soyen. 1993. *Zen for Americans: Including the Sutra of Forty-two Chapters*. New York: Barnes & Noble Books.
Sharf, Robert H. 1995b. "Buddhist Modernism and the Rhetoric of Meditative Experience." *Numen* 42: 228–283.
Snodgrass, Judith. 2003. *Presenting Japanese Buddhism to the West: Orientalism, Occidentalism, and the Columbian Exposition*. Chapel Hill: University of North Carolina Press.
Soucy, Alexander. 2014. "Buddhist Globalism and the Search for Canadian Buddhism." In *Flowers on the Rock: Global and Local Buddhisms in Canada*, edited by John S. Harding, Victor Sōgen Hori, and Alexander Soucy, 25–54. Montreal: McGill-Queen's University Press.
Sumegi, Angela. 2014. "Reflections on a Canadian Buddhist Death Ritual." In *Flowers on the Rock: Global and Local Buddhisms in Canada*, edited by John S. Harding, Victor Sōgen Hori, and Alexander Soucy, 225–244. Montreal: McGill-Queen's University Press.
Suzuki, Daisetz Teitaro. 1949. *Essays in Zen Buddhism*. New York: Grove Press.
Tanaka, Kenneth K. 1998. "Epilogue: The Colors and Contours of American Buddhism." In *The Faces of Buddhism in America*, edited by Charles S. Prebish and Kenneth K. Tanaka, 287–298. Berkeley: University of California Press.
Taylor, Charles. 1989. *Sources of the Self: The Making of the Modern Identity*. Cambridge: Cambridge University Press.
Verhoeven, Martin J. 1998. "Americanizing the Buddha: Paul Carus and the Transformation of Asian Thought." In *The Faces of Buddhism in America*, edited by Charles S. Prebish and Kenneth K. Tanaka, 207–227. Berkeley: University of California Press.
Wallace, B. Alan. 2002. "The Spectrum of Buddhist Practice in the West." In *Westward Dharma: Buddhism Beyond Asia*, edited by Charles S. Prebish and Martin Baumann, 34–50. Berkeley: University of California Press.
Wilson, Jeff. 2012. *Dixie Dharma: Inside a Buddhist Temple in the American South*. Chapel Hill: University of North Carolina Press.
Wilson, Jeff. 2014. *Mindful America: The Mutual Transformation of Buddhist Meditation and American Culture*. New York: Oxford University Press.

CHAPTER 2

THE HISTORY OF BUDDHISM IN THE UNITED STATES

THOMAS CALOBRISI

Introduction

THE history of Buddhism in United States is deceptively simple. The relatively brief presence of Buddhism in America, no more than a century and a half, belies the complexity of its transmission, dissemination, and growth. Few places in the world hold such a diversity of Buddhist traditions and lineages, new and old alike, operating together. As such, narrating this history in a way that captures its nuances and intricacies is tricky. In what follows, I present *a* (not *the*) brief history of Buddhism in America. I make the case that the Transcendentalists of the mid-nineteenth century set a pattern of free adaptation that is, consciously or otherwise, repeated across the next century and a half. Following Thomas Tweed, I describe this pattern of adaptation as "collaging," as it takes up circulating bits and pieces of Buddhism and presses them into new forms that meet new needs and exert cultural influence on Buddhists and non-Buddhists alike.

My historical narrative begins in the mid-nineteenth century, with the Transcendentalists and the arrival of Chinese Buddhists on the West Coast. In the next section, on the late nineteenth and early twentieth centuries, I focus on the "Buddhist sympathizers" of the Victorian period and the establishment of Shin Buddhism in Hawaii and the United States. The interwar period follows this, looking at the resilience of Japanese Buddhists during and after their internment. The penultimate section looks at the "Zen boom" of the postwar period, and the final one observes the introduction of *vipassanā*, the rise of mindfulness, and the advent of the internet during the late twentieth and early twenty-first centuries. I conclude with reflections on the "postmodern" turn in American Buddhism, considering its prospects and limitations.

The Twin Arrival of Buddhism

Thomas Tweed's chronicling of American Buddhism begins in the late nineteenth century, with what he refers to as the first wave of "Buddhification"; and yet, the history of Buddhism in the United States arguably begins several decades earlier. The turn of the nineteenth century saw the birth of the modern disciplines of Indology and Sinology. These fields were bolstered by the creation of learned societies across Europe and the United States. Such organizations gathered scholars for regular meetings and disseminated the research of their members to the broader public through journals and lectures. Figures involved with these societies produced studies, translations, and even provided manuscripts from Chinese, Mongolian, Tibetan, Burmese, Sanskrit, and Pāli Buddhist sources (Lopez 2013, 174–187). These scholars helped establish that the variety of traditions witnessed across Asia by Europeans were the same religion, now called "Buddhism," and that Buddhism originated in ancient India and spread into East, Southeast, and Central Asia. That said, perhaps no one did more to shape the Euro-American understanding of Buddhism than the French philologist Eugène Burnouf (1801–1852).

Relying primarily on the Sanskrit manuscripts dispatched from Nepal by Brian Houghton Hodgson to the Société Asiatique in the late 1830s, Burnouf produced in 1844 a pioneering study entitled *Introduction to the History of Indian Buddhism*. What Burnouf would do in his *Introduction* would prove monumental not only for the academic study of Buddhism but for its public reception as well. As Donald S. Lopez, Jr., states, "Burnouf described the Buddha and Buddhism for the first time in ways that would become so ingrained and natural that their origins in an 1844 French tome would eventually be forgotten," which include "that Buddhism is an Indian religion, that the Buddha is a historical figure, and perhaps of particular consequence, that the Buddha was a human teacher of a religion, or perhaps a philosophy, that preaches ethics and morality without recourse to dogma, ritual, or metaphysics" (Lopez 2013, 210–211).

Prior to the debut of the *Introduction*, Burnouf published two excerpts from his manuscript and his translation of the *Lotus Sutra* as standalone essays in the April and May 1843 issues of *Revue indépendante*. These essays caught the attention of a group of spiritual seekers in Cambridge, Massachusetts. This group, Hedge's Club or "Transcendental Club," had begun in 1836 among liberal Unitarians. The Club included Frederic Henry Hedge (the Club's namesake), as well as Ralph Waldo Emerson, Henry David Thoreau, Margret Fuller, and Elizabeth Palmer Peabody. They composed the core of American Transcendentalism, a loose-knit, break-away movement from Unitarianism. Transcendentalism taken together was characterized by an emphasis on the intrinsic goodness of humanity, on the power of the mind to shape and reshape one's reality, and on both nature and nonbiblical literature as sources of divine inspiration; their optimism and relative openness were in reciprocal relationship with their progressive sensibilities. While the Transcendentalists had initially published their views in several

New England journals, their material became increasingly unwelcome in the late 1830s, with the *Christian Examiner* and the *North American Review* eventually refusing to publish them altogether (Belasco 2010, 374).

In 1840, the *Dial*, a quarterly journal, was established; it was initially edited by Margaret Fuller and George Ripley. When Fuller stepped down from her position in 1842, Emerson took her place and established a new column within the *Dial* entitled "Ethnical Scriptures" (Belasco 2010, 379–380). In his preface to the series, Emerson claims the intention of it is to present "selections from the oldest ethical and religious writings of men," with the Hebrew and Greek scriptures excluded (Emerson 1842, 82). Each nation has its own "bible" in which can be found "grand expressions of moral sentiment in different ages and races, the rules of the guidance of life, the bursts of piety and of abandonment to the Invisible and Eternal" (Emerson 1842, 82). Sarina Isenberg and Arthur Versluis have pointed out that Emerson and Thoreau were drawn to certain translations not for their faithfulness to their original texts, but for their fit with Transcendentalist sentiments (Isenberg 2013, 22–26; Versluis 1993, 191). We see this selective approach to the entry entitled "The Preaching of Buddha," included in the January 1844 issue of the *Dial*.

The excerpted passages present the Buddha in a fashion all too familiar today: as a young prince who renounced his home and family, taught a path of moral cultivation and philosophical insight, and rejected the dogmas of his day, particularly that of caste. The portion drawn from the *Lotus Sutra* contains two parables, that of the blind man and that of the many plants, the latter of which explains that the Buddha's teaching, though singular (that is, the bodhisattva path to Buddhahood), speaks to beings regardless of their specific capabilities and dispositions, just as a great rain falls equally on the plants of the forest regardless of their size and shape.

Lopez has commented that the *Dial* entry presents a "quite misleading pastiche" (2016, 166); in his view, the piece conflates the young prince with the cosmic Buddha of the *Lotus Sutra* whose bodhisattva path supersedes the prince's path of solitary liberation. True as that may be, Lopez misses what is remarkable about the piece. In it, we find a Buddha who embodies Transcendentalist values; he is a spiritual seeker who renounces his worldly status, confronts the corrupt institutions of his time, and teaches a path of spiritual advancement accessible to all equally.

Isenberg points out that Emerson was indifferent to debates among translators about the arcane details of method; rather, what was important to him was the meaning that could be glossed from any translation (2013, 25). Similarly, Thoreau did not consider himself an academic translator but was focused on, as Isenberg states, "a general feeling that the texts evoke, rather than an accurate portrayal" (Isenberg 2013, 25). This is to say, if we evaluate "The Preaching of Buddha" by contemporary academic standards, then we are using the wrong yardstick. Isenberg notes that these translations do not simply "carry over"—as the etymology implies—texts and peoples, but that translators create something new in their efforts (2013, 24–25). Here, I want to return to Tweed's concept of "Buddhification" I mentioned above.

Buddhification is a process which "allowed some decontextualized Buddhist beliefs, practices, and artifacts to circulate widely, especially among Americans who did not identify with that tradition" (Tweed 2013, 194). When these beliefs, practices, and artifacts were freed from their traditional contexts, they took on a certain malleability (Tweed 2013, 213). These circulating bits and pieces of Buddhism were found objects that non-Buddhist Americans picked up and collaged into new forms, ones that "exerted wide cultural influence and met multiple needs" (Tweed 2013, 213). "The Preaching of Buddha" can be considered the first case of Buddhification, as it presents not only a case of circulating bits and pieces of Buddhist artifacts being collaged into new forms that meet new needs, but also one that, considering the reach of the *Dial* in its heyday, likely exerted wide influence in American culture (Belasco 2010, 381; Isenberg 2013, 32).

The 1840s in America saw Buddhism introduced not once but *twice*; there was the *Dial* entry, as well as the arrival of Buddhists from China in 1849, who traveled across the Pacific to the United States to work in the newly established gold mines. They would build thriving diaspora communities and establish places of worship over the ensuing decades. By the turn of the twentieth century, there were hundreds of "joss houses"— small shrines or temple buildings which draw their namesake from a corruption of the Portuguese word *deos*—dotting the West Coast (Stewart 1998, 16). These "joss houses" were not Buddhist per se but included Taoist and Chinese folk deities alongside Buddhist ones (Stewart 1998). As Rick Fields claims, the Chinese were likely the first to bring images of the Buddhas and bodhisattvas to America, enshrining them in these new temples (Fields [1981] 2022, 86). The temples were not only sites of worship but places of refuge for their patrons. Considering the etymology of the term, we can understand the temples as yet another translation of Buddhism, one that included artifacts and practices as well as beliefs.

Unfortunately, Chinese American communities were met with fear and hostility, as they were perceived not simply as a threat to the livelihoods of their white counterparts, but as perpetual foreigners who brought disease and immorality. Fear of the "yellow peril" culminated in the Chinese Exclusion Act of 1882, which banned the immigration of Chinese workers. Though it was initially made to last only ten years, the legislation was active until its replacement by the Magnuson Act of 1943. The use of Chinese laborers as strikebreakers in the 1870s drew the ire of labor organizations and led to their support for the Chinese Exclusion Act—the Industrial Workers of the World were the exception, opposing the law since the organization's inception in 1905 (Choi 1999, 8). This discrimination precipitated a decline in the Chinese American population, dropping from nearly 100,000 in 1880 to around 61,000 in the 1920s (Chandler 1998, 16–17). Lack of interest from successive generations of Chinese Americans lowered the patronage of the temples, leading to their closure in the 1930s and 1940s (Chandler 1998). That said, some of these temples, such as Tin Hou and Kong Chow Temples in San Francisco's Chinatown, are still in operation to this day.

The First Wave of Buddhification, 1853–1918

The opening of trade relations between the United States and Japan in the late nineteenth century marks for Tweed the first wave of Buddhification. The "arrival of the black ships" (*kurofune raikō*), the first US naval ships in Edo Bay in 1853, is an infamous event in Japanese history. The Perry expedition to Japan was an attempt by the United States to break by threat of force the centuries-old Japanese policy of national seclusion. Once the Americans had made headway, other imperial nations followed suit. The appeasement of foreign forces by the Tokugawa shogunate led to a loss of confidence among its people, who turned toward the Imperial court for leadership. This came to a head with the restoration of the Imperial court as the government of Japan in 1868 in what is known as the Meiji Restoration.

The Meiji era (1868–1912) overall had a profound impact on every aspect of the daily life in Japan, as it sought to rapidly modernize the nation; it allowed not only the influx of goods, ideas, and practices from Europe and America, but also the efflux of Japanese people westward to Hawaii and the Americas. This itself had ramifications for Buddhist institutions in Japan. The Meiji government loosened its ties with Buddhist institutions, going so far as to remove policies that banned Buddhist monastics from consuming meat and taking spouses (Jaffe 2001). The period saw an intensification of anti-Buddhist sentiments, as Buddhism was deemed a foreign doctrine out of step with Japanese sensibilities; amid the introduction of Western scientific knowledge, it was castigated as superstitious and backward (Ketelaar 1990, 43–87; Snodgrass 2003, 16–44). During the 1870s, temples were destroyed, lands seized, and priests defrocked (Josephson 2012, 186–191). Buddhist institutions were on the backfoot and sought ways to bring themselves in line not only with modern science and philosophy but with the interests of the Meiji government.

Buddhist priests in the Jōdo Shinshū (hereafter Shin) and Zen sects were at the forefront of the effort to modernize Buddhism. Figures such as the Shin Buddhist priests Inoue Enryo and Shimaji Mokurai and the Zen priest Shaku Sōen (1860–1919) devoted themselves to studying Buddhism in order to portray it as consonant with the findings of modern science, secular government, Japanese nationalism, and the latest trends in Western philosophy (Snodgrass 2003, 115–154; McMahan 2008, 63–69; Josephson 2006). Sōen and his students Daisetsu Teitarō Suzuki (1870–1966) and Nyogen Senzaki (1876–1958) traveled to the United States on several occasions to lecture and teach; it is hard to understate their influence here. Just as these figures sought to give Buddhism a new face for the modern world, many Japanese men and women were migrating to new lands, bringing Buddhist beliefs and practices with them.

Japanese immigration to Hawaii had begun in the 1860s, and it picks up in the Americas in the mid-1880s (Mitchell 2016, 52). From 1890 to 1910 the number of Japanese immigrants and natural-born citizens in the United States increased dramatically, from

2,039 in 1890 to 127,000 in 1908 (Kashima 2011, 30). The numbers for Japanese laborers followed similar patterns in Hawaii. There, they worked primarily on sugar plantations and would begin to establish Buddhist organizations in the 1890s. The regions from which the Japanese laborers emigrated were predominantly Shin, and hence they brought that tradition with them (Mitchell 2016, 52).

In Hawaii, the Shin Buddhist priest Soryu Kugai (or Kagahi) arrived in 1889 and established the first official Buddhist temple in Hilo eight years later (Mitchell 2016). In 1898, the first Shin Buddhist priests, Eryu Honda and Ejun Miyamoto, arrived in the United States for a tour of the West Coast. In 1900, they established the Young Men's Buddhist Association (YMBA) and were officially recognized as an overseas mission of the Nishi Hongwanji (Mitchell 2016, 52). The YMBA was later reorganized as the Buddhist Church of San Francisco and the Buddhist Mission of North America (BMNA). The BMNA would be renamed as the Buddhist Churches of America (BCA) following World War II and is the longest continually running Buddhist institution in North America (Mitchell 2016). Other Japanese Buddhist sects, such as Sōtō Zen and Shingon, also established temples and overseas missions in Hawaii and the United States in 1910s and 1920s (Mitchell 2016, 53).

These institutions, particularly the BMNA/BCA, are often misconstrued as homogeneously Japanese American. Even in their earliest iterations, however, they were outward-facing and sought to attract non-Japanese Americans to their communities (Mitchell 2016, 55). In Hawaii, Yemyo Imamura, who led Hawaii's Shin Buddhist mission from 1900 until his passing in 1932, made inroads with the broader public. As Scott Mitchell explains, "Imamura was interested in propagating a pan-sectarian version of Shin Buddhism throughout Hawai'i, one that was rooted in their particular denomination but that was of appeal beyond the confines of one sect" (2016, 55). Ernest and Dorothy Hunt, two early converts to Shin Buddhism, were instrumental in reaching out to Anglo Americans. The Hunts in Hawaii, as well as Julius Goldwater in Los Angeles and Gladys Sunya Pratt in Tacoma, were given ordination as ministers, helping to produce English-language materials and develop new ritual forms (Ama 2011, 70–80; Ama 2015; Mitchell 2016, 55–56). Like Imamura, they promoted a "trans-sectarian Buddhism" focused on the ethical teachings of Śākyamuni rather than the salvific power of Amitābha (Ama 2011, 72, 94).

Though Buddhist organizations like the BMNA and the Shin Buddhist mission in Hawaii did successfully interest white Americans, this did not exempt them from discrimination and alienation. Japanese Americans were excluded from the process of naturalization and were prohibited from owning land and property (Mitchell 2016, 54). Japanese American Buddhists were viewed as anti-American and anti-Christian. Shin temples offered Japanese American Buddhists some respite from the prejudice they faced. This prejudice, however, Mitchell notes, "had the effect of pressuring the community to acculturate or bend its customs toward American norms, effecting changes in both language and religious customs" (2016, 54). Much of the material produced by these white American ministers at this time—including hymnals, books, and journals—drew not only from Shin sources but also from Pāli Theravāda ones as well (Mitchell

2016, 56). Their interest in these sources is downstream from shifts in the academic study of Buddhism in Europe and the appropriation of this scholarship by other white Americans and Europeans.

Late-nineteenth- and early-twentieth-century figures such as Max Müller, Hermann Oldenberg, Émile Senart, and Caroline and Thomas Rhys Davids did much to expand Western knowledge of Buddhism through studies and translations. Figures in this generation turned their attention toward Pāli literature preserved by the Theravāda traditions of Southeast Asia, which they took to be more ancient than Burnouf's Sanskrit texts and hence more authoritative. Importantly, this new scholarship not only sought to highlight Śākyamuni Buddha as a human figure, but also explicitly racialized him as "Aryan" (Trautmann 1997). The emphasis they placed on identifying the Buddha as an "Aryan" was part of an overtly white-supremacist project meant to inoculate the Buddha against his image as "Asian." This dovetailed with a growing interest in Buddhism, particularly with more wealthy, educated white Americans, and served to provide legitimacy to claims made among them about "authentic" Buddhism (Snodgrass 2009; Quli 2018; Anningson 2021). This growth in public interest was spurred by the founding of the Theosophical Society in 1875 by Helena Petrovna Blavatsky, William Quan Judge, and Henry Steel Olcott and the 1879 publication of *The Light of Asia*—a poetic English-adaptation of the *Lalitavistara*—by Sir Edwin Arnold.

Theosophy was a collage of the kind Tweed describes; a new "confluence" drawn not only from different Buddhist traditions but also from a variety of religious movements. At the center of Theosophy was the notion that there is a single truth expressed differently by diverse religions and that this truth was revealed to Blavatsky by Tibetan yogis or "Mahatmas," whom she channeled spiritually. Arnold's *The Light of Asia* was widely popular, selling as many copies as such well-known titles from the period as Mark Twain's *Huckleberry Finn* and Frances Hodgson Burnett's *Little Lord Fauntleroy* (Tweed 2000, 29). Between this new scholarship, the popularization of Buddhism through literature, and new religious movements, the final decades of the nineteenth century only saw the interest in Buddhism among Americans increase.

In his history of the period, Tweed categorizes Americans interested in Buddhism or "Buddhist sympathizers" into three ideal-types: esoterics, rationalists, and romantics. The esoteric Buddhists Tweed identifies were nearly, to a person, Theosophists, and, as the name implies, had an intense interest the occult. For the esoterics, their interest in Buddhism was an extension of their involvement with Theosophy as well as other occult movements such as spiritualism, mesmerism, and Swedenborgianism. Rationalist types inflected Buddhism with an American rational religiosity which emphasized the rational-discursive over the experiential, took the individual as a primary source of authority, and fiercely advocated for religious and political tolerance (Tweed 2000, 61). Tweed identifies Paul Carus, a German-born theologian-turned-philosopher based in the Chicago area, as exemplary of the rationalist approach (2000, 64). Whereas rationalists stressed the discursive, and the esoterics the experiential, romantic or "exotic-culture" Buddhists focused on the aesthetic. For romantics, Tweed explains, "the attraction of Buddhism was part of an immersion in, and attachment to, a Buddhist culture as a whole—its art, architecture, music, drama, customs, language, and literature as well as its religion" (Tweed 2000, 69). Further, in contrast to their counterparts, romantic Buddhists, given their interest in the exotic features of Buddhist cultures, were more interested in Tibetan and Japanese Buddhism than in Ceylonese Buddhism.

Tweed stresses that his three ideal-types are not perfectly embodied by any historical individual but are composite categories that express general tendencies among larger groups. Indeed, there was as much convergence as polemics between them. Romantics and esoterics respectively showed rationalist tendencies, and rationalists also displayed esoteric and romantic tendencies. Moreover, all these figures were linked by a network of print publications, including Carus's *Monist* and *Open Court* as well as the *Buddhist Ray*, the *Light of Dharma*, and other materials put out by the BMNA (Tweed 2012).

In their own way, members of each type inherited different tendencies within the earlier Transcendentalist movement: their romantic penchant for the exotic, their search for occult meaning, their fierce rationalism. Further still, just as the Transcendentalists had fashioned together circulating Buddhist ideas and practices into new forms that met their needs and exerted influence, these Buddhist sympathizers, now with far more information and access, reworked them into new forms amid the challenges of the late nineteenth century. They presented Buddhism as rational and ethical, as spiritual but not dogmatic, as progressive, and as compatible with the latest findings of modern science.

A highpoint of the first wave of Buddhification was the 1893 Parliament of World's Religions. While the Parliament, held in Chicago, was billed as an inclusive and tolerant event, the language used by its promoters betrayed a white, Christian supremacism (Ketelaar 1990, 136–173; Snodgrass 2003, 65–84). The Parliament was a veritable who's who of turn-of-the-century American religion; it included Anagārika Dharmapāla from Ceylon and Sōen from Japan, but also Swami Vivekananda, a pivotal figure in the introduction of Hinduism to the United States, and a slate of other Japanese delegates representing various "Northern" Buddhist traditions.

From their appearances at the Parliament, Sōen and Dharmapāla would be invited back to the United States for lecture tours, serving to further popularize Buddhism among the American public. Suzuki and Senzaki, as well as Sokei-an Sasaki—all students of Sōen—would do much to introduce Zen Buddhism. Albeit, in the case of Suzuki, it was done in a rather idiosyncratic manner (Sharf 1995). By the end of World War I, most of the Buddhist sympathizers of the late nineteenth century had passed away. That said, the cultural forms they had collaged together between the 1870s and 1910s would remain influential for future generations of American Buddhists—as we observed with the Hunts, Pratt, and Goldwater. And though interest in Buddhism among white Americans took a dive in the interwar years, Japanese Americans would serve to keep their traditions alive despite the harrowing circumstances they would face as a community when war broke out across the world yet again in the late 1930s.

The Interwar Years and the Second Wave of Buddhification, 1919–1973

Turn-of-the-century policies such as the Chinese Exclusion Act and the Alien Land laws were still in effect during the interwar period—the former until 1943 and the latter until 1952. Thus, the forms of institutionalized discrimination established previously did not cease to impact the lives of Asian Americans at this time. Indeed, Japanese communities in Hawaii came under increasing surveillance as American military intelligence officials believed, wrongly, that diaspora communities would function to subvert American interests from within. Duncan Ryūken Williams has shown that, contrary to these suspicions, the evidence gathered from their surveillance over several decades indicated that Japanese Americans were neither disloyal to the United States nor willing to act subversively against it (Williams 2019, 27–38). Despite the evidence, when Pearl Harbor Naval Base in Hawaii was attacked by Japanese forces on December 8, 1941, the effort to round up and interrogate community leaders, particularly Buddhist clergy, was undertaken swiftly (Williams 2019, 39–67). Executive Order 9066, signed by President Franklin Delano Roosevelt on February 16, 1942, authorized the military to engage in any means necessary to secure the country against subversion. Williams notes that the Order does not mention Japanese Americans explicitly; nonetheless, it provided the legal authorization for their forced internment (2019, 68).

The internment of Japanese Americans ran from February 1942 to March 1946. Initially, Buddhist internees were denied the ability to congregate, conduct services, or possess any unapproved Japanese-language materials by the overseeing authorities; however, internees pressed the issue, citing their First Amendment rights, and gained permission to create places of worship and hold services by the spring of 1943 (Williams 2019, 118). Williams observes that interned Japanese Americans were able to "reinvent" American Buddhism during this time. First, they began to sponsor social events such as dances and pageants, tournaments for baseball and ping-pong, and oratory contests (2019, 122–126). Second was the "Anglicization" of Shin Buddhist services, which included the singing of Buddhist hymns to Western tunes, as well as adoption of Christian terminology (2019, 127–130). Third was the move to create Buddhist rituals that would have a trans-sectarian appeal (2019, 130–134). Fourth was their outreach to and cooperation with Christians, which involved the celebration of Christmas and Thanksgiving, as well as the establishment of ecumenical monuments such as the Manzanar Ireitō (2019, 135–141). Fifth, which was specific to the Nishi Hongwanji Shin Buddhists, was the creation of a democratically organized, English-language Buddhist organization; this organization is the BCA mentioned above, which was founded in Ogden, Utah, in 1944 (2019, 146–148).

Upon the release of the Japanese Americans from internment in March 1946, the new challenge was adjusting into a society that had viewed them dangerously anti-American for several years. Many returned to find their homes, businesses, and places of worship occupied by others, who often refused to leave. Despite these adversities, the developments of the internment period would serve Japanese Americans well for decades to come and allow them to play a vital role in in the second wave of Buddhification in the postwar period (Mitchell 2023).

In 1946, Kanmo Imamura, son of Yemyo mentioned above, was assigned as the minister for the Berkeley Buddhist Temple. He and his wife Jane, a trained musician, were deeply dedicated to educating young people. Shortly following their arrival, the Imamuras began running a study group aimed at English-language Buddhist education. While the study group began as a small affair, it would attract wider attention from the Berkeley community, including Gary Snyder—now a well-known poet and author. Snyder was so impressed with the study group that he invited three friends of his—Jack Kerouac, Alan Ginsberg, and Philip Whalen—to sit in.

Snyder, Kerouac, Ginsberg, and Whalen would become key figures in the literary "Beat" movement of the 1950s. "Much of early Beat writing," Mitchell explains, "can be seen as a rejection of or even escape from postwar American culture and an attempt at embracing alternative sources of creative and spiritual inspiration" (2016, 60). Mitchell further points out that the nonconformism of the Beats can be seen as "a continuation of late-Victorian-era thinking, especially as exemplified by the Transcendentalists who rejected the normative religious thinking of their day" (2016, 60). The Beats' engagement with Buddhism was more cultural and aesthetic than discursive. Another Beat-adjacent figure present at the Berkeley study group meetings was Alan Watts, who had studied Zen in the late 1930s under the guidance of Sasaki and would himself become an important popularizer of Zen and Asian religion generally.

The Beats and Watts contributed to a revival of print culture among Japanese American Buddhists; just as the BMNA had disseminated the *Light of Dharma* generations before, now BCA members were establishing new publications such as the *Berkeley Bussei*, *Tri-Ratna: Buddha*, and the *American Buddhist* (Mitchell 2016, 60; Mitchell 2023). However, the perspectives offered by the Beats and other white contributors were often at odds with their Japanese American counterparts (Masatsugu 2008; Mitchell 2023). What was at stake in the pages of these publications was not simply what place Buddhism was to have in American life or how to practice Buddhism authentically, but *who* could answer those questions and *by what means*. The Beats saw Buddhism as a kind of antidote to the malaise of mid-century American life. Yet, the desire to construe Buddhism in this way did not sit well with Japanese Americans, whose memories of internment were all too fresh (Mitchell 2016, 63). By the end of the 1950s, the connection between the Beats and the Berkeley study group had dissolved. The study group would continue—even being organized into the Institute of Buddhist Studies and incorporated as a graduate school in 1969—as would the Beats; however, their attention turned more so to Zen Buddhism.

Concurrent with the Beats and the Berkeley group was the return of Suzuki, and his idiosyncratic brand of Zen, to the United States. "For Suzuki," Mitchell states, "Zen is universal in that it apprehends transcendent truths that are gleaned through an experiential path that is necessarily ahistorical and acultural," and yet it is also "uniquely and quintessentially Japanese" (2016, 46). While "*Suzuki Zen*," as Tweed calls it, was largely the product of Suzuki's oeuvre, others such as Watts, Nancy Wilson Ross, and Eugen Herrigel also contributed to the image of Zen as "a tradition that centered experience, eschewed constraints, encouraged spontaneity, shaped culture, and inspired art" (Tweed 2013, 203). Tweed goes on to say, "Zen emerged as a tradition that seemed to be applicable to all aspects of everyday life" (2013, 203). The writings of Suzuki, Watts, Ross, and Herrigel inspired an entire genre of literature in the late 1950s and early 1960s that sought to do that, with titles in the style of "*Zen and the Art of X*" or "*Zen and Y*" (2013, 203). *Suzuki Zen* also had an impact on the fine arts. John Cage, Robert Rauschenberg, and Nam June Paik, for example, were influenced in their works by the presentation of Zen as embodying spontaneity, absurdism, and irreverence toward received or traditional forms and concepts (2013, 203–211).

To make the confluence of flows even more complex, Zen Buddhism was also being popularized at this time by other, more traditional figures. Taizan Maezumi and Shunryu Suzuki, two priests in the Sōtō Zen tradition, had come to the United States to serve in Japanese American temples. Each would branch out beyond these communities to offer Zen training to white sympathizers. In doing so, Suzuki and Maezumi established two important American Zen traditions—those of the San Francisco Zen Center and the White Plum Asanga, respectively. Students of Maezumi and Suzuki alike would go on to open major Zen Buddhist temples, training centers, and organizations across the United States. Philip Kapleau, who underwent Zen training in Japan, established the Rochester Zen Center in New York; his 1965 book *Three Pillars of Zen* continues to be a popular English-language introduction to the tradition. While it was founded in 1930 by Sokei-an Sasaki, the First Zen Institute, under the direction of his late wife Ruth Fuller Sasaki and Mary Farkas, would continue its operations, hosting teachers such as Jōshū Sasaki, a Rinzai Zen priest who opened several Zen centers and training monasteries, and funding Snyder's travels to Japan in the 1950s and 1960s. Eidō Shimano, another Rinzai Zen priest, founded two meditation centers in New York during the late 1960s and mid-1970s. Sasaki, Shimano, and Maezumi, it should be noted, faced allegations of sexual misconduct by their followers. In each case, several students came forward with stories of unwanted advances from and inappropriate relations with their teachers. Scandals around sexual misconduct would be sadly common among budding Buddhist communities in the United States (Mitchell 2016, 82–83; Gleig 2019, 84–110).

The mid- to late 1960s marked several important developments for the history of Buddhism in the United States: the Immigration and Nationality Act of 1965, better known as the Hart-Cellar Act; the escalation of American involvement with the Vietnam War; and the counterculture movements. All of these developments tied into the Cold War; indeed, so much of the development of Buddhism in America from this time onward happened under the shadow of the Cold War. The Hart-Cellar Act opened new opportunities for people from South, Southeast, and East Asia to come to the United States by dropping restrictions on immigration from places other than Northern Europe (Mitchell 2016, 67–69). Amid the counterculture, Buddhism was taken up by another generation of Americans eager to reject mainstream culture and the Vietnam War effort.

Thousands of immigrants from nearly every part of Buddhist Asia would begin entering the United States and establishing places of worship. Since the 1970s and 1980s, Taiwan-based transnational groups such as Fo Guang Shan, founded by Hsing Yun, and Dharma Drum Mountain, founded by Sheng Yen, have made significant inroads in the United States. Such organizations, Mitchell states, "while established initially to meet the needs of Chinese American populations, have grown in size, serve ethnically diverse populations, engage in explicit charitable and engaged practices, have established links to the broader culture though publication and educational projects" (2016, 73). From the late 1960s onward, the diversity of Buddhist traditions in the United States would only increase, offering sympathetic Americans a staggering variety of environments and communities for practice (Mitchell 2016, 84–85).

The transnational flow of Buddhist ideas, practices, and artifacts was not unidirectional, however. Americans, such as Jack Kornfield, Joseph Goldstein, and Sharon Salzberg, traveled to Asia in search of new spiritual practices. While abroad they would encounter revivalist and modernizing Buddhist movements, including the Thai Forest movement represented by the charismatic Ajahn Chah and the Burmese *vipassanā* ("insight") movement represented by Satya Narayana Goenka and Mahāsī Sayādaw (Mitchell 2016, 78–79, 98–99). Kornfield, Goldstein, and Salzberg alike were deeply interested in the practice of *vipassanā* meditation and sought to adapt this practice to the concerns and needs of American lay life; their introduction of lay-oriented *vipassanā* meditation would be transformational for American Buddhism.

The Third Wave of Buddhification, 1974–2014

Tweed only identifies two periods of Buddhification, namely, the turn of the twentieth century and the post-war decades; however, the period from 1974 to 2014 saw Buddhification intensify. From the introduction of *vipassanā*, beginning in 1974, meditation would become the *sine qua non* of Buddhism in the American social imagination. When the growing *vipassanā* movement was encountered by Americans in the 1970s, particularly at retreats led by Goenka, the practice was presented as the authentic quintessence of the Buddha's teaching. Moreover, Goenka thought of *vipassanā* practice as universal, secular, and even scientific; anyone from any walk of life could do it because it was not "religion" in Goenka's view (Mitchell 2016, 98–99). Kornfield, Salzberg, and Goldstein, while well-aware of the Theravāda roots of *vipassanā* practice, were strongly influenced by Goenka's distinctive approach in their own transmission of this practice to Americans.

Another key figure in all of this is Chögyam Trungpa. Trungpa had fled Tibet in 1959, coming to the United Kingdom in the early 1960s to study at Oxford University. After he was injured in a car accident, Trungpa relinquished his monastic vows and took up life as a lay teacher; he established meditation centers, and his charismatic yet unconventional approach to instructing Westerners garnered him great attention (Mitchell 2016, 149). In 1973 and 1974, Trungpa established an organization he called Vajradhatu (now Shambhala International) and the Naropa Institute (now Naropa University) in Boulder, Colorado. He invited not only Beat poets like Ginsberg and Zen-inspired artists like Cage to teach at Naropa, but also the freshly returned *vipassanā* instructors Kornfield and Goldstein. In 1975, these two, along with Salzberg and Jaqueline Mandell, purchased a large mansion in Barre, Massachusetts, and converted it into a *vipassanā* retreat center, the Insight Meditation Society (IMS).

As Wendy Cadge explains, teachers at IMS "concerned themselves . . . with what it meant to take the Buddhist tradition, steeped in the imagery and metaphor of Asia, to try to find its unchanging essence, and then to express that essence in the imagery of a new time and place" (2005, 30). The effort to express this "unchanging essence" most often meant translating it into the terms of Western psychotherapy; this is most evident in the West Coast variety of *vipassanā* (Fronsdal 1998; Gleig 2019, 114–120). While *vipassanā* meditation has become quite popular in the United States, the movement exists alongside Theravāda institutions organized by diaspora communities (Mitchell 2016, 99–105). This is to say, it exists among diverse expressions of the Theravāda tradition which serve semi-overlapping, multiethnic and multiracial communities.

As the founders of the *vipassanā* movement were getting started on the East Coast and Trungpa was established in Colorado, yet another key figure would appear on the scene: the Vietnamese monk Thich Nhat Hanh. Thich had ties to the United States going back to the 1960s; however, he only made inroads with the American public with his 1975 publication *The Miracle of Mindfulness*. Like the Zen literature of the 1960s, Thich's book showed how mindful awareness could be applied in ordinary settings. Thich was formative not only for the popularization of meditation in the United States, but also for the international phenomenon of "engaged Buddhism" (Mitchell 2016, 213–218); he was an outspoken proponent of peace during the Vietnam War and used his notoriety as a Buddhist leader to advocate for interfaith cooperation, environmentalism, and vegetarianism. For these reasons, Thich played a significant role in shaping American Buddhism as it is lived and practiced today across the diversity of traditions.

Before turning to the emergence of mindfulness meditation in the late 1970s and early 1980s, it should be noted that "Buddhist studies" as an academic field was coming into its own at this time. In the 1960s, "religious studies," that is, the non-confessional, humanistic, and social-scientific study of religion, was taking shape. Nathan McGovern notes that religious studies served a specific ideological purpose in the milieu of the Cold War, namely, to construe religion as a *sui generis* category irreducible to material conditions (2017, 710). In this way, religious studies was one more weapon in the American arsenal against the "godless" communism of the Soviet Union. Buddhist studies departments, groups, and programs began to crop up in the United States around the same time and drew influence not only from religious studies but from area studies as well.

The introduction of "Buddhist studies," alongside the growing popularity of Zen, *vipassanā*, and Tibetan varieties of Buddhist practice, set the stage for the emergence of mindfulness meditation from the research and writing of Jon Kabat-Zinn (b. 1944). Trained as a molecular biologist, Kabat-Zinn encountered Buddhism in the 1960s as a student at the Massachusetts Institute of Technology. In the 1970s, he would attend retreats at the IMS and practiced regularly at the Cambridge Zen Center established by the Korean Sŏn teacher Seung Sahn (Kabat-Zinn 2011, 286). Similar to the pioneers of the *vipassanā* movement, Kabat-Zinn wanted to present Buddhist practices without reference to the "metaphor and imagery of Asia," to use Cadge's words. This led him to establish the Stress Reduction Clinic at the University of Massachusetts Medical School, where he had been made a professor in 1976.

What came out of Kabat-Zinn's Stress Reduction Clinic was a program he referred to as "Mindfulness-Based Stress Reduction" (MBSR). Designed for those suffering from chronic pain, MBSR was modeled on a ten-day *vipassanā* retreat spread over ten weeks and drew on themes from Tibetan and Indian Buddhist traditions for concepts as well as Zen and *vipassanā* practices (Wilson 2014, 94). Kabat-Zinn's MBSR is a collage par excellence, as perhaps no other assemblage of Buddhist ideas and practices into a new form has been so adaptable and thus capable of exerting incredible cultural influence. Access to clinical spaces allowed Kabat-Zinn to collect data on the efficacy of MBSR, from which he would produce studies touting its medical benefits. The "medicalization" of mindfulness through Kabat-Zinn's MBSR and his studies of its effects opened the possible avenues for influence exponentially (Wilson 2014, 95–97).

The popularity of MBSR would grow steadily through the 1980s and into the late 1990s. According to Wilson, the first decade of the twenty-first century was a "crossover decade" for mindfulness meditation, as it had become "a basic part of the spiritual vocabulary of North America" entirely apart from Buddhism: "authorized by science, endorsed by Oprah, marketed by Buddhists, appropriated by self-help gurus, it appeared in such a tidal wave of publications and applications that it seemed that everyone was doing mindfulness, in every conceivable situation, without any need to announce one's commitment to Buddhism to do so" (Wilson 2014, 40). Among the factors contributing to the successful mainstreaming of mindfulness, Wilson identifies "the explosion of books with 'mindfulness' in the title," as an important one (2014, 40). Like the Zen literature before it, mindfulness literature applied its namesake concept to all facets of life: work and career advancement, eating and weight loss, rehabilitation, relationships and sex, parenting, education, sports, and so on.

The further mindfulness was applied, however, the further it got from its grounding in Buddhist thought—particularly the ethical framework that was a key feature of *vipassanā* retreats. The growing gap between the Buddhist practice and its mainstream adaptation began to be troubling to many in the mid-2010s, spurring what Ann Gleig has referred to as the "Buddhist backlash" to mainstream mindfulness (Gleig 2019, 56). Alongside the concern for ethics, Buddhist critics of mainstream mindfulness claimed that its construal as "bare attention" has a tenuous canonical basis and that the focus on scientific justification constitutes a form of neo-colonialism (Gleig 2019, 57–62). Gleig observes that while some came to the defense of mainstream mindfulness, many took these criticisms to heart. Teachers of mindfulness have sought to introduce contextual, ethical, and social-justice dimensions to their programs, challenging the individualist and universalist paradigms through which mindfulness was initially mainstreamed (2019, 72–82).

I would be remiss if I did not mention the importance of the internet in the more recent history of American Buddhism. Media technologies, print media in particular, have always been central to Buddhism in America. And while print publications like *Tricycle* and *Lion's Roar* have simply transitioned into online formats, the internet has also allowed for new forums and communities to emerge, unencumbered by the confines of physical location. Crucially, the internet has been a site of contention and critique, particularly across generational gaps.

Both Mitchell and Gleig point to how blogs and podcasts, such as *Buddhist Geeks* podcast created in 2007 and *Angry Asian Buddhist* blog created in 2008, have critiqued what they call "consensus Buddhism" and "white Buddhism" of the baby boomers (Mitchell 2016, 167–170; Gleig 2019, 259–262). They each note how forums such as *Speculative Non-Buddhism* and publications by its participants have sought to bring contemporary critical theory to bear on mainstream American Buddhism (Mitchell 2016, 169; Gleig 2019, 263–365). Recent research by Gleig and Brenna Artinger has shown that online dissent among Buddhists is not solely progressive in character. Rather, these progressive developments themselves have become the subject of conservative backlash, giving voice to white supremacist, far-right appropriations of Buddhism and critiques of both consensus Buddhism and the progressive developments by far-right figures (Gleig and Artinger 2021). What the cacophony of online voices at the end of the 2010s reveals is that American Buddhism is undergoing a moment of reflection and reform, one which will I touch on the concluding section of this narrative.

Future History?

The history of Buddhism in America coincides quite neatly with the phenomenon known as "Buddhist modernism." According to David McMahan, Buddhist modernism has three broad characteristics: detraditionalization, demythologization, and psychologization (McMahan 2008, 42). Though the diversity of American Buddhisms betrays any blanket statement to such an effect, it is easy to see how American Buddhists have broken with tradition, reconsidered the "imagery and metaphor of Asia," and sought to press Buddhist thought and practice to fit the psychologically coded concerns of lay life. However, both Mitchell and Gleig have described recent developments in American Buddhism as "postmodern" in character (Mitchell 2016, 155–171; Gleig 2019, 4). By "postmodern" here they mean that hallmarks of Buddhist modernism—an individualistic orientation, a focus on meditation, the discarding of ritual practices, a stress on rationality, nonliteral interpretation, and the psychologization of cosmology—have come into question. Younger, more diverse Buddhist communities are looking to reform the way they have received the tradition, often with an eye to how their places of worship can be more inclusive across lines of race, class, and gender.

Throughout this chapter, I have come back to Tweed's metaphor of collage. Americans, whether they were born into a Buddhist household or not, have found bits and pieces of Buddhism circulating through flows of media and have collaged them together into new cultural forms. In breaking with the modernism of their forebearers, postmodern Buddhists are repeating the same patterns that have persisted throughout the past century and a half. Of course, this is not to downplay the novelty of their formulations, but simply to put them in a broader scope.

What will have to be seen is how successful these postmodern iterations of American Buddhism will be in the coming decades. To turn once again to Tweed, with regard to the Zen literature of the 1960s, he pointed out that what captivated readers was the adaptability of Buddhist practices. Certainly, the adaptability of secular mindfulness can be credited for its success. Though it is not clear that adaptability is the *only* barometer by which success can be measured, postmodern developments in American Buddhism certainly must meet new needs in a way that is meaningful to Americans broadly. This, I think, will be a serious challenge, for in a moment of skyrocketing inequality, declining life expectancy, and increasing disaffection with organized religions, what do these postmodern iterations of American Buddhism have to offer? The promise of these tendencies may come in the emphasis on community and shared practice, as the isolation and alienation experienced by so many amid the COVID-19 pandemic has Americans searching for ways to reunite with others and create meaningful connections.

REFERENCES

Ama, Michihiro. 2011. *Immigrants to the Pure Land: The Modernization, Acculturation, and Globalization of Shin Buddhism, 1898–1941.* Honolulu: University of Hawai'i Press.

Ama, Michihiro. 2015. "'The First White Buddhist Priestess': A Case Study of Sunya Gladys Pratt at the Tacoma Buddhist Temple." In *Buddhism beyond Borders: New Perspectives on Buddhism in the United States*, edited by Scott A. Mitchell and Natalie E. F. Quli, 59–74. Albany: State University of New York Press.

Anningson, Ryan. 2021. *Theories of the Self, Race, and Essentialization in Buddhism: The United States and the Asian "Other," 1899–1957.* New York: Routledge.

Belasco, Susan. 2010. "The *Dial*." In *The Oxford Handbook of Transcendentalism*, edited by Harbert Petrulionis, Laura Dassow Walls, and Joel Myerson, 373–383. New York: Oxford University Press.

Chandler, Stuart. 1998. "Chinese Buddhism in America: Identity and Practice." In *The Faces of Buddhism in America*, edited by Charles S. Prebish and Kenneth K. Tanaka, 13–30. Berkeley and Los Angeles: University of California Press.

Choi, Jennifer Jung-Hee. 1999. "The Rhetoric of Inclusion: The I.W.W. and Asian Workers." *Ex Post Facto* VIII: 1–8.

Emerson, Ralph Waldo. 1842. "Veeshnoo Sarma." *Dial: A Magazine for Literature, Philosophy, and Religion* 3, no. 1 (July): 82.

Fields, Rick. [1981] 2022. *How the Swans Came to the Lake: A Narrative History of Buddhism in America*. Boulder, CO: Shambhala.

Gleig, Ann. 2019. *American Dharma: Buddhism beyond Modernity*. New Haven, CT: Yale University Press.

Gleig, Ann, and Brenna Artinger. 2021. "The #BuddhistCultureWars: BuddhaBros, Alt-Right Dharma, and Snowflake Sanghas." *Journal of Global Buddhism* 22: 19–48.

Isenberg, Sarina. 2013. "Translating World Religions: Ralph Waldo Emerson's and Henry David Thoreau's 'Ethnical Scriptures' Column in *The Dial*." *Comparative American Studies* 11, no. 1 (March): 13–36.

Jaffe, Richard M. 2001. *Neither Monk Nor Layman: Clerical Marriage in Modern Japanese Buddhism*. Princeton, NJ: Princeton University Press.

Josephson, Jason Ānanda. 2006. "When Buddhism Became a 'Religion': Religion and Superstition in the Writings of Inoue Enryō." *Japanese Journal of Religious Studies* 33, no. 1: 143–168.

Kabat-Zinn, Jon. 2011. "Some Reflections on MBSR, Skillful Means, and the Trouble with Maps." *Contemporary Buddhism* 12, no. 1 (May): 281–306.

Kashima, Tetsuden, and Commission on Wartime Relocation and Internment of Civilians. 2011. *Personal Justice Denied*. Seattle: University of Washington Press.

Ketelaar, James Edward. 1990. *Of Heretics and Martyrs in Meiji Japan: Buddhism and Its Persecution*. Princeton, NJ: Princeton University Press.

Lopez, Donald S., Jr. 2013. *From Stone to Flesh: A Short History of the Buddha*. Chicago: University of Chicago Press.

Lopez, Donald S., Jr. 2016. *The Lotus Sutra: A Biography*. Princeton, NJ: Princeton University Press.

Masatsugu, Michael K. 2008. "'Beyond This World of Transiency and Impermanence': Japanese Americans, Dharma Bums, and the Making of American Buddhism during the Early Cold War Years." *Pacific Historical Review* 77, no. 3: 423–451.

McGovern, Nathan. 2017. "The Contemporary Study of Buddhism." In *The Oxford Handbook of Contemporary Buddhism*, edited by Michael Jerryson, 701–714. New York: Oxford University Press.

McMahan, David L. 2008. *The Making of Buddhist Modernism*. New York: Oxford University Press.

Mitchell, Scott A. 2016. *Buddhism in America: Global Religion, Local Contexts*. New York: Bloomsbury Academic.

Mitchell, Scott A. 2023. *The Making of American Buddhism*. New York: Oxford University Press.

Palmer Peabody, Elizabeth [Anonymous]. 1844. "The Preaching of Buddha." *Dial: A Magazine for Literature, Philosophy, and Religion* 4, no. 3 (January): 391–402.

Quli, Natalie Fisk. 2018. "On Authenticity: Scholarship, the Insight Movement, and White Authority." In *Methods in Buddhist Studies: Essays in Honor of Richard K. Payne*, edited by Scott A. Mitchell and Natalie Fisk Quli, 154–172. New York: Bloomsbury Academic.

Seager, Richard Hughes. 2012. *Buddhism in America*. Revised and expanded edition. New York: Columbia University Press.

Sharf, Robert H. "The Zen of Japanese Nationalism." In *Curators of the Buddha: The Study of Buddhism under Colonialism*, edited by Donald S. Lopez, Jr., 107–160. Chicago: University of Chicago Press, 1995.

Snodgrass, Judith. 2003. *Presenting Japanese Buddhism to the West: Orientalism, Occidentalism, and the Columbian Exchange*. Chapel Hill: University of North Carolina Press.

Snodgrass, Judith. 2009. "Discourse, Authority, Demand: The Politics of Early English Publications on Buddhism." In *TransBuddhism: Transmission, Translation, Transformation*, edited by Nalini Bhushan, Jay L. Garfield, and Abraham Zablocki, 21–41. Amherst: University of Massachusetts Press.

Trautmann, Thomas R. 1997. *Aryans and British India*. Berkeley and Los Angeles: University of California Press.

Tweed, Thomas A. 2000. *The American Encounter with Buddhism, 1844–1912: Victorian Culture and the Limits of Dissent*. 2nd edition. Chapel Hill: University of North Carolina Press.

Tweed, Thomas A. 2012. "Tracing Modernity's Flows: Buddhist Currents in the Pacific World." *The Eastern Buddhist* 43, no. 1–2: 35–56.

Tweed, Thomas A. 2013. "Buddhism, Art, and Transcultural Collage: Toward a Cultural History of Buddhism in the United States, 1945–2000." In *Gods in America: Religious Pluralism in the United States*, edited by Charles L. Cohen and Ronald L. Numbers, 193–227. New York: Oxford University Press.

Versluis, Arthur. 1993. *American Transcendentalism and Asian Religions*. New York: Oxford University Press.

Williams, Duncan Ryūken. 2019. *American Sutra: A Story of Faith and Freedom during the Second World War*. Cambridge, MA: Harvard University Press.

Wilson, Jeff. 2014. *Mindful America: The Mutual Transformation of Buddhist Meditation and American Culture*. New York: Oxford University Press.

CHAPTER 3

IDENTITIES I

Race and Whiteness in American Buddhism

ANN GLEIG

On May 4, 2021, a group of Asian American Buddhists gathered at the Higashi Honganji Buddhist Temple in Los Angeles for a memorial service called "May We Gather: A National Buddhist Memorial Ceremony for Asian-American Ancestors." The service took place forty-nine days after the murder of eight people, including six Asian American women, across three beauty spas in Atlanta. It was attended by forty-nine Buddhist leaders from various Chinese, Japanese, Khmer, Korean, Sri Lankan, Taiwanese, Tibetan, Thai, and Vietnamese Buddhist lineages. As the description of the event noted: "We will chant sutras, recite the name of our ancestors, heal in ceremony and share Dharma perspectives from leading American Buddhists to repair an important aspect of our nation's racial karma."[1]

"May We Gather" was organized by three Asian American Buddhists: scholar-practitioners Funie Hsu, Duncan Ryuken Williams, and Chenxing Han. In her reflection, Hsu shared the xenophobia and systematic violence faced by Asian American Buddhists and emphasized that healing only occurred through community. Williams referenced the abolitionist Frederick Douglass's speech on America as a "composite nation" in which he linked the emancipation struggles of Black Americans with the struggles of Chinese immigrants, and connected the Atlanta murder of Korean American Buddhist Yong Ae Yue with the murder of African American George Floyd. Han offered light and incense to seven memorial tablets, one for each of the six women murdered and one for all those victims of racial violence, recognizing how suffering has connected people across difference ethnic and spiritual communities.

"May We Gather" was marked by a number of characteristics—the centering of Asian American Buddhist communities, cultures, and histories, the articulation of a Buddhist hermeneutics of structural racism, an intersectional approach to social violence,

---

[1] May We Gather, https://www.maywegather.org/.

the expression of solidarity with other marginalized Buddhists of Color, and the role of Buddhist scholar-practitioners in shaping conversations on racism in American Buddhism. Taking a historical and ethnographic "thick descriptive" approach, which both describes actions and illuminates the interpretive context in which they occur, this chapter will survey some of the ways these patterns can also be seen across the broad landscape of American Buddhism. It will begin by showing how whiteness shaped the construction of Buddhist modernism in Asia and the very formation of the category of American Buddhism. Next, it will identify the ways in which Asian American Buddhists, particular Japanese Americans, have been subject to and have resisted whiteness, before moving to consider how Buddhists of Color have disrupted whiteness in meditation-based convert lineages. Finally, it will reflect on emerging directions in Buddhist racial justice work, such as the negotiation of differences between marginalized communities and the role of scholars of Buddhism.

Colonialism, Whiteness, and Buddhist Modernism

The modernization of Buddhism that began in Asia in the late nineteenth and early twentieth centuries under the conditions of colonialism provides the historic context for the multiple ways by which Buddhism in the United States has been highly racialized, being both shaped by and reproducing whiteness.[2] Buddhist reforms occurring during this time demonstrated both resistance and assimilation to colonialism and white supremacy.[3] Picking up the assimilative thread, scholars have focused on the role that white supremacy and racial hierarchies played in the construction of Asian Buddhism and its amplification in a North American context marked by whiteness and structural racism. At the forefront of these is Joseph Cheah's work, which has illuminated a legacy of white supremacy and racial hierarchy from the Western orientalists' racialized rearticulation of Asian Buddhism in the late and middle Victorian era to the present-day exclusion of lived communities of Asian American heritage Buddhists.[4]

Orientalists were writing at a time in which Enlightenment, social Darwinism, and eugenic conceptions of race were prevalent in Europe and North America. Orientalists'

---

[2] See Christopher Emory Moore, Chapter 1 in this volume, for a thorough examination of Buddhist modernism.

[3] Erik Braun, *The Birth of Insight* (Chicago: University of Chicago Press, 2013); Richard Jaffe, *Seeking Shakyamuni: South Asia in the Formation of Modern Japanese Buddhism* (Chicago: University of Chicago Press, 2019).

[4] Joseph Cheah, *Race and Religion in American Buddhism: White Supremacy and Immigrant Adaptation* (Oxford: Oxford University Press, 2011). Joseph Cheah, "Buddhism, Race, and Ethnicity," in *Oxford Handbook of Contemporary Buddhism*, ed. Michael Jerryson (Oxford and New York: Oxford University Press, 2016), 650–661.

rearticulations of Asian Buddhism were intricately linked to and reflected these racist discourses and colonial projects. One dominant theme here was the construction of a "real" or "pure" textual Buddhist that needed to be rescued from a "cultural" or "degenerate" Buddhism. Scholars such as Eugene Burnouf, Brian Houghton Hodgson, and T. W. Rhys Davids dismissed the ritual merit-making and devotional aspects of Buddhism as "superstitious cultural accretions" that had distorted the real Buddhism of the Pali Canon. In their ethnocentric arrogance they declared that Asian Buddhists were ignorant of "true" Buddhism, which only the objective scholarship employed by white philologists could recover. Asian monastic elites were also complicit in granting authority to such perspectives. Theosophist Henry Steel Olcott's "Protestant Buddhism," which shaped Theravada Buddhist through a white Protestant lens, was legitimated through the traditional authority of the Singhalese sangha.[5]

Another dominant thread in the construction of Buddhist modernism was the fashioning of the Buddha as Aryan. In response to colonial claims that Asian people were biologically inferior to Europeans and that Buddhism was a less evolved form of religion than Christianity, Asian Buddhist modernists and Western sympathizers subversively employed "race sciences" to fashion the Buddha as a racially superior Aryan and Buddhism as a superior scientific religion.[6]

While the modernist construction of real Buddhism as textual Buddhism, the model of the Buddha as an Aryan, and the scientific presentation of Buddhism were fashioned by and have served both Asian and Western Buddhist ends, the underlying racialized characteristics of these formations have been amplified in a North American cultural context marked by ongoing legacies of whiteness and racial discrimination and violence.[7] While it is beyond the parameters of this chapter to fully describe the racialized context of the United States, the field of critical whiteness studies offers broad insights into how whiteness functions. Key analytic insights of this field include the recognition that (i) white supremacy has functioned both explicitly as actions of overt violence and discrimination and as a subtler expression of structural dominance; (ii) white identity is constructed as normative and universal; (iii) white dominance is naturalized and presented as ahistoric; (iv) individualism is central to whiteness; and (v) whiteness is a source of ongoing harm to People of Color.[8] All of these characteristics are evident in the history of Buddhism in North America.

Joseph Cheah's distinction between cultural and racial rearticulation offers one explanatory framework for how whiteness has shaped Buddhism in the United States. Cheah adopts this distinction from Michael Omi and Howard Winant and extends

---

[5] For a helpful summary of scholarship on the orientalist history of Buddhist studies, see Adeana McNicholl, "Buddhism and Race in the United States," *Religion Compass* 15, no. 8 (2021): 1–13.

[6] Ryan Anningson, "Once the Buddha Was an Aryan: Race Sciences and the Domestication of Buddhism in North," *Journal of Religion & Culture* 27, no. 1 (2017): 51–57.

[7] For the ways in which whiteness has operated within secular Buddhism and the mindfulness movement, see Nalika Gajaweera, Chapter 17, and Kin Cheung, Chapter 21, in this volume.

[8] For more details, see Joy Brennan and Ann Gleig, "Whiteness Is a Sankhara: Racial Justice as Buddhist Practice," *Yin-Cheng Journal of Contemporary Buddhism* 1, no. 1 (2023): 30–57.

their work to define cultural rearticulation as "a way of representing religious tradition from another's culture into ideas and practices that are familiar and meaningful to people of one's own culture." Such a process is inevitable when religions travel across cultural contexts, and examples from Buddhist history include the sinicization of Buddhism in China. By contrast, racial rearticulation is "the acquisition of the beliefs and practices of another's religious tradition and infusing them with new meanings derived from one's own culture in ways that preserve the prevailing system of racial hegemony."[9]

In many ways, the history of Buddhism in the United States is the story of the enforcement, subversion, and overcoming of the racial rearticulation of whiteness. Put simply by Adeana McNicholl: race is not incidental to, but constitutive of American Buddhism.[10] One expression of racial rearticulation, for example, has been the "two Buddhisms typology," which distinguishes between Asian American immigrant/heritage and white convert American Buddhist communities.[11] Originally a descriptive distinction, a racial hierarchy was soon established whereby white American convert Buddhists were positioned as practicing "real" Buddhism and Asian American heritage communities were positioned as practicing "cultural" Buddhism. Wakoh Shannon Hickey identifies three specific ways in which whiteness came to function in the two Buddhisms typology: (i) the presumed authority of white convert Buddhists to define what counts as real "American Buddhism"; (ii) the assumption that "white Buddhism" is authentically American and Asian Buddhism is a foreign tradition located in America; and (iii) the fact that white American Buddhists have received a disproportionate amount of attention from both academic and popular quarters.[12]

Hickey's critique demonstrates that it is essential to adopt the categories of American heritage and convert Buddhism cautiously, in careful and qualified ways, in order not to reproduce the white supremacy that has operated within them.[13] Nonetheless, focusing on these different, but often overlapping, lineages does enable one to see the multiple overt and covert ways that whiteness has *both* operated *and* been resisted and overcome within them. Given my own research specialty, my focus here will be meditation-based convert lineages, which have historically been populated by majority white demographic, rather than convert lineages such as Soka Gakkai that have drawn a much more multi-racial audience.[14]

---

[9] Cheah, *Race and Religion in American Buddhism*, 60.

[10] McNicholl, "Buddhism and Race in the United States," 1.

[11] Charles S. Prebish, "Two Buddhisms Reconsidered," *Buddhist Studies Review* 10 (1993): 187–206.

[12] Wakoh Shannon Hickey, "Two Buddhisms, Three Buddhisms, and Racism," in *Buddhism Beyond Borders: New Perspectives on Buddhism in the United States*, ed. Scott A. Mitchell and Natalie E. F. Quli (Albany: State University of New York Press, 2015), 44–46.

[13] For a summary of critiques of American Buddhist typologies see McNicholl, "Buddhism and Race in the United States," 4.

[14] For more information on Soka Gakkai, see Ralph Craig III, Chapter 11, in this volume.

Asian American Buddhists: Violence and Exclusions

Buddhism was brought to the United States by Chinese and Japanese immigrants who came to work as laborers. The first Buddhist temple in the United States was built in San Francisco in 1853 by the Sze Yap Company, a Chinese American fraternal society. The first Buddhist organization was the Buddhist Churches of America (BCA), which traces its roots to the Japanese Shin Buddhist Rev. Soryu Kagai, who came from Kyoto to minister to the growing Japanese Buddhist community in Hawaii in 1889. From the onset, Chinese and Japanese Buddhist communities faced considerable social, religious, and legal forms of racist discrimination and violence. Anti-Asian sentiments led to religious sites and community centers, including Buddhist spaces, being vandalized and burned down, with Buddhists dubbed as "heathens" and "pagans" and depicted with racist stereotypes. Asian immigrants were often the victims of physical violence, such as the Los Angeles massacre of Chinese immigrants in 1871 which resulted in the death of seventeen Chinese men and boys. In 1882 Congress passed the Chinese Exclusion Act, which prohibited Chinese laborers from immigrating to the United States. This was followed by the Asiatic Barred Zone Act of 1919, which primarily targeted Asian immigrants. In 1922, the Supreme Court ruled against the application for citizenship from Takao Ozawa, a Japanese immigrant in Hawaii, concluding that the Japanese could not be considered white. By 1924, immigration from Asia effectively stopped and would not resume fully until the lifting of the Asian Exclusion Act in 1965.[15]

Ongoing racism and discrimination against Japanese Americans reached an apex after the Japanese Empire attacked Pearl Harbor on December 7, 1941. In response, President Roosevelt issued Executive Order 9066, which resulted in the forced removal of the entire Japanese American population from the West Coast into concentration camps for most of the war. Over 125,000 Japanese men, women, and children were detained in inhumane conditions. As Duncan Ryuken Williams notes, while all Japanese Americans were subject to displacement and detention, Buddhist priests were particularly targeted as Buddhism was positioned as inherently incompatible with American values. Under conditions of intense loss and hardship, Japanese American Buddhists preserved their Buddhist practice, drawing strength, resilience, and comfort from it.[16] Pre- and post-internment Japanese Buddhist communities assimilated in various ways as strategies of survival. For instance, in 1944 the Buddhist Mission of North America changed its name to the Buddhist Churches of America. The COVID-19 pandemic has reignited the long

---

[15] Joseph Cheah, "US Buddhist Traditions," in *Oxford Handbook of Contemporary Buddhism*, ed. Michael Jerryson (Oxford and New York: Oxford University Press, 2016), 316–331. See Funie Hsu, Chapter 20 on Engaged Buddhism in this volume, for more details and theoretical sophistication.

[16] Duncan Williams, *American Sutra: A Story of Faith and Freedom* (Cambridge, MA: Harvard University Press, 2019), 258.

history of racist rhetorical and physical violence against Asian Americans, including the vandalization of Asian Buddhist temples.[17]

"WE'VE BEEN HERE ALL ALONG": RECOVERING ASIAN AMERICAN VOICES

Another major expression of racial discrimination against Asian American Buddhists has been the exclusion and marginalization of Asian American heritage communities from mainstream narratives of Buddhism in America. Despite making up nearly two-thirds of Buddhists in the United States, Asian Americans are routinely excluded in discussions and representations of American Buddhism. One example of the white dominance of American Buddhism is seen in the slippage between "white" and "American." Take, for example, former *Tricycle* editor Helen Tworkov's reflection on the development of American Buddhism in which she claimed that Asian Americans had "not figured prominently in the development of something called American Buddhism." Third-generation Jōdo Shinshū priest, Rev. Ryo Imamura, whose grandfather and father were bishops of the Honpa Hongwanji Mission of Hawaii, wrote an immediate rebuttal of Tworkov's claim in a letter to *Tricycle*. He pointed out that it was Asian Americans who had brought, implanted, and preserved Buddhism in America for 100 years under intense racial hostilities and bigotry, as well as welcoming white Americans into their Buddhist temples and helping them start their own communities.[18]

A number of practitioners and scholar-practitioners have followed Rev. Imamura's disruption of the false and racist equation of "American Buddhism" with "white Buddhism" by recovering the foundational role and impact that Asian American heritage communities have had on the development of Buddhism in the United States. One example is Aaron J. Lee, who began a blog titled "Angry Asian Buddhism" under the pseudonym of Arun in 2019. The Angry Asian Buddhist was groundbreaking in highlighting the multiple erasures of Asian American Buddhism in mainstream American Buddhism.[19] Another is Funie Hsu's 2016 *Buddhadharma* article, "We've Been Here All Along," which shows how Jōdo Shinshū had been marginalized and calls on white American Buddhist converts to confront their racism as an integral part of their Buddhist practice.[20] "Engaged Jodo Shinshu Buddhism," an anonymous social media project, shares the pivotal contributions that North American Jōdo Shinshū

---

[17] Chenxing Han, "Stay Safe... Both from the Virus and the Racism," *Tricycle: The Buddhist Review*, April 9, 2020. https://tricycle.org/article/coronavirus-racism/.

[18] For a critical analysis of this exchange, see Natalie Quli, "Western Self, Asian Other: Modernity, Authenticity and Nostalgia for 'Tradition' in Buddhist Studies," *Journal of Buddhist Ethics* 6 (2009): 1–38.

[19] An archive of Angry Asian Buddhism is available at http://www.angryasianbuddhist.com/.

[20] It is important to note that Hsu's article received a high volume of complaints, including personal attacks.

communities have made to social justice activism, thereby undermining narratives of engaged Buddhism as an essentially white modernist convert project.[21]

Scott Mitchell shows that recovering the contributions of Japanese American Buddhists not only brings more diversity and inclusion to the narrative of American Buddhism, but also rewrites the very history of American Buddhism. He demonstrates how Nisei (second-generation Japanese Americans) saw themselves as uniquely placed to bridge Japanese and American culture through Buddhism itself. These Buddhists, who have been typically relegated to the "cultural" Buddhism category, played a fundamental role in birthing a distinctly modern American form of Buddhism, a role that has been inaccurately attributed to white converts from the Beat and counterculture movement.[22]

INTERSECTIONALITY AND GENERATIONAL PATTERNS

"May We Gather" recognized that the six Asian American women murdered in Atlanta were the victims of both racism and misogyny. Paying attention to the intersections of race and gender, Buddhist scholar Sharon Suh seeks to render visible those Asian American Buddhists who are doubly marginalized by virtue of their race and gender identity. In an ethnography of a group of first-generation Korean American Buddhists in Los Angeles, Suh illuminates distinct gender differences in how these Korean Americans practices Buddhism, with females drawing on the psychological healing resources of the tradition and males favoring an intellectual approach. Through focusing on the lived experience of Korean American Buddhist women, Suh shows how Buddhism functions as a source of self-empowerment that offers emotional resilience and relief in the daily lives of her racialized and gendered subjects. In this sense, Suh's research populations disrupt both the privileging of white convert Buddhists and the male renunciate body that marks elite canonical Buddhism and has been reproduced in Western orientalist scholarship, which has historically prioritized Buddhist text and philosophy over lived experience.[23]

Chenxing Han extends the intersectional thread to consider issues of race, gender, and sexuality in her ethnography of young Asian American Buddhists. Situating herself

---

[21] See, for example, @engagedpureland on Mastodon, Facebook, or Instagram. See also Funie Hsu, Chapter 20 in this volume, and Alexander O. Hsu, "Coming to Terms with Engaged Buddhism: Periodizing, Provincializing, and Politicizing the Concept," *Journal of Global Buddhism* 23, no. 1 (2022): 17–31.

[22] Scott Mitchell, *The Making of American Buddhism* (Oxford and New York: Oxford University Press, 2023).

[23] Sharon Suh, *Being Buddhist in a Christian World: Gender and Community in a Korean American Temple* (Seattle and London: University of Washington Press, 2004).

as a "first-generation" Buddhist who feels neither completely at home in the white space of American convert Buddhism nor within Asian American heritage communities, Han makes visible the thriving networks of young Asian American Buddhists, ranging from multi-generational Jōdo Shinshū Buddhists to new converts. Across their differences, she finds that these young adults all share a commitment to an "intersectional Buddhism," one that is "keenly attuned to issues of race, gender, sexuality." As Han explains, for young Asian American Buddhists "the many manifestations of culture—race, ethnicity, gender, sexuality, and so on—are not a grime to be wiped off or a dross to be transcended, but phenomena that we must thoroughly explore and fully engage with if we are to realize a truly inclusive American Buddhism."[24]

An intersectional Buddhism is also advanced by the Young Buddhist Editorial (YBE), an Asian American Buddhist organization formed to honor and preserve their community heritage and to share their own particular life experiences as young Buddhists in a racially hostile culture. As co-founder Devon Matsumoto shares, "I joined YBE because I feel that the strength of community is how we fight white supremacy and that an Asian American Buddhist community is uniquely positioned to help in this fight." Based primarily in the Japanese American Jōdo Shinshū community but with membership open to all, YBE has a strong intersectional social justice commitment and has produced a series of webinars to explore how topics such as queerness, abolition, colonization, and environmentalism relate to Buddhism. For social committee member Juliet Bost, the aim is to work "towards the radical dismantlement of systems of racist, patriarchal, cisheterosexist, and colonial oppression, and ultimately build new, supportive and liberatory ways of being."[25] These young intersectional Asian American Buddhists have formed community around the inspiration of "Be the Refuge," which is the title of Han's book and was originally the title of a blog post by the Angry Asian Buddhist. For Han, the words function on multiple ways—as a teaching, an invitation, a practice—and point to community as an antidote to whiteness.[26]

"White Buddhism": Meditation-Based Convert Lineages

American meditation-based convert Buddhist communities began to grow in the 1960s and 1970s. Cutting across the different denominational forms of Insight, Zen,

---

[24] Chenxing Han, *Be the Refuge: Raising the Voices of Asian American Buddhists* (Berkeley, CA: North Atlantic Books, 2021), 189.
[25] "About Us" The Young Buddhist Editorial, https://www.youngbuddhisteditorial.com/about.
[26] Chenxing Han, "Young. Asian. American. Buddhist: What These Words Cannot Say," *Tricycle: The Buddhist Review*, March 9, 2021. https://tricycle.org/article/be-the-refuge-chenxing-han/.

and Tibetan Buddhism, these communities were characterized by a strong focus on individual meditation practice and Buddhist philosophy. They de-emphasized cosmological, devotional, and ritual elements and were psychologically oriented. Participants were overwhelmingly white, middle to upper-middle class, tended to be politically liberal, and prioritized individual development over community-building. Within these communities, there had been a call for democratization, seen in both a move toward gender equality, with an increasing number of women in positions of authority, and the blurring of authority between monastic and lay populations.[27]

The normative whiteness of these meditation-based convert lineages has been documented across scholarly and practitioner contexts. In the early 1990s, Rick Fields identified how racism showed up among white Buddhists. Starting with a description of overt racism in the United States, Fields added that "[a] deeper and perhaps equally powerful aspect of racism, however, is the power to define, always the paramount power in a racist society." This power of naming was evident in white Buddhists who declared their meditation-focused approach as "real" Buddhism and dismissed the devotional Buddhism of Pure Land as "cultural baggage" which Chinese and Japanese immigrants had brought to the United States over a hundred years before their convert communities had begun. In claiming to pioneer "American Buddhism," such white practitioners were unconsciously equating "American" with "white" and reproducing legacies of white supremacy and structural racism.[28]

Twenty-five years after Field's identification of "white Buddhism," psychologists Craig Hase, James Meadows, and Stephanie Budge adopted sociologist Elijah Anderson's concept of the "white space" to better understand how white experience and values become established as the norm in meditation-based convert sanghas. Anderson's concept refers to how a range of spaces—including neighborhoods, leisure space, schools, workplaces, and churches—construct and reinforce a "taken for granted reality" in which white people and white norms dominate and Black people are "typically absent, not expected, or marginalized when present." Hase, Meadows, and Budge identified a number of ways in which People of Color (POC) experience, negotiate, and disrupt Buddhist meditation-based convert sanghas as white spaces.[29]

---

[27] Charles S. Prebish, *Luminous Passage* (Berkeley and Los Angeles: University of California Press, 1999); James William Coleman, *The New Buddhism: The Western Transformation of an Ancient Tradition* (New York: Oxford University Press, 2001); Wendy Cadge, *Heartwood: The First Generation of Theravada Buddhism in America* (Chicago: University of Chicago Press, 2005).

[28] Rick Fields, "Confessions of a White Buddhist: Dharma, Diversity and Race," *Tricycle: The Buddhist Review*, Fall 1994, https://tricycle.org/magazine/confessions-white-buddhist/.

[29] Craig Nicholas Hase, James C. Meadows, and Stephanie L. Budge. "Inclusion and Exclusion in the White Space: An Investigation of the Experiences of People of Color in a Primarily White American Meditation Community," *Journal of Global Buddhism* 19 (August 2019): 1–18.

Disrupting "White Buddhism": Diversity, Equity, and Inclusion Initiatives

Practitioners of Color and their white allies have been tackling racism and white supremacy within meditation-based lineages since the 1990s. In June 2000, a small group distributed a booklet titled *Making the Invisible Visible: Healing Racism in Our Buddhist Communities* to the Buddhist teachers in the West conference at Spirit Rock Meditation Center in June 2000. This compilation declared that for many years, Euro-American middle-class sanghas had been resistant to the efforts of POC to raise awareness of the reproduction of oppressive racial and socioeconomic structures within them. Interweaving personal experiences of racism with Buddhist teachings and critical race theory, this landmark collection offered a number of resources to combat racism, ranging from institutional diversity trainings to addressing racism in Dharma talks. *Making the Invisible Visible* is one of a number of attempts and initiatives by Buddhists of Color over the last two and a half decades to overcome whiteness in American Buddhism.[30]

One major area has been to raise awareness through forums and literature. Examples here include the 2004 *Dharma, Color, and Culture: New Voices in Western Buddhism*, edited by Hilda Gutiérrez Baldoquín, a lineage holder in the Soto Zen tradition, which was the first collection to bring together the voices of Western Buddhist practitioners of color, and *Buddhadharma*'s 2016 summer issue on "Free the Dharma: Race, Power, and White Privilege in American Buddhism."[31] A second area is the emergence of POC-specific retreats and sitting groups. Spirit Rock has held POC retreats almost annually since 1999. First-person narratives and scholarship on POC affinity spaces has shown that they function as invaluable places of refuge for Buddhists of Color. In her rich ethnographic study of POC Insight meditators, for example, Nalika Gajaweera found that these groups were "safe spaces" in which meditators could process painful embodied emotions around racialized trauma, develop radical resilience, and build community.[32]

A third area is the emergence of POC teachers who are actively promoting Buddhist racial justice initiatives, including developing Buddhist hermetical frameworks. Such teachers cut across Boomer and Generation X generations and represent a variety of

---

[30] *Making the Invisible Visible: Healing Racism in Our Buddhist Communities*, https://www.dharma.org/wp-content/uploads/2017/02/Making-the-Invisible-Visible.pdf.

[31] Hilda Gutiérrez Baldoquín, *Dharma, Color, and Culture: New Voices in* Western Buddhism (Berekely, CA: Parallax Press, 2004); "Free the Dharma: Race, Power, and White Privilege in American Buddhism," *Buddhadharma: The Practitioner's Quarterly* (Spring 2016).

[32] Nalika Gajaweera, "Sitting in the Fire Together: People of Color Cultivating Radical Resistance in North American Insight Meditation," *Journal of Global Buddhism* 22, no. 1 (2021): 121–139.

Buddhist lineages.[33] Closely related is the development of communities with specific attention to issues of multiculturalism and racism: at the forefront of these is the East Bay Meditation Center in Oakland, California.[34] Similarly, there is the impact of nonsectarian Buddhist organizations that have taken up racial justice work as a major concern. The Buddhist Peace Fellowship (BPF) has a long history in developing and promoting racial justice initiatives within American convert lineages, and Dharma Relief, a new organization founded in 2020, has turned its focus to "Healing Race Relations."[35] The impact of these teachers, communities, and organizations can be seen in the embrace of racial justice in trans-sectarian gatherings such as the 2021 International Dharma Teachers Gathering, which ran under the theme of "Facing Truth: Waking Up to Love, Justice and Equity."[36]

A fourth area is the adoption of diversity, inclusion, and equity plans and staff as well as teacher diversity and anti-racist trainings by Buddhist centers such as Insight Meditation Society and the San Francisco Zen Center. A fifth area is recent initiatives that focused on the Insight leadership and teacher training demographics. In 2016, Larry Yang estimated that there were only ten teachers who identified as POC among the 350 trained Insight teachers. As a result, both Insight Meditation Society (IMS) and Spirit Rock Meditation Center ran teacher training programs designed to increase POC representation: 90% of Spirit Rock's program trainees and 75% of IMS's trainees identified as POC. Together, they have resulted in a 330% increase of teachers of color in the Insight community.[37]

A sixth area is the development of Buddhist teachings and practices to combat racism. These trainings are rooted in multiple Buddhist hermeneutics of racial justice, which interpret Buddhist doctrine through the lived experiences of marginalized practitioners of color. While differing across lineages, these emergent "buddhologies" commonly advance a collective articulation of foundational Buddhist teachings such as dukkha, karma, and liberation. One example from the Insight tradition is Larry Yang's "multicultural hermeneutics of Buddha, Dharma and Sangha," in which he suggests that specific cultural experiences and values should be integrated into Buddhist practice. Another is Zen teacher Zenju Earthlyn Manuel's Buddhist hermeneutics in which the "embodied differences" of race, gender, and sexuality are placed at the very core of awakening in a soteriological model that seeks to integrate social identities and spiritual liberation.[38]

---

[33] See, for example, Larry Ward, *America's Racial Karma* (Berkeley, CA: Parallax Press, 2020); and Larry Yang, *Awakening Together: The Spiritual Practice of Inclusivity and Community* (Somerville, MA: Wisdom Publications, 2017).

[34] See Ann Gleig, "Dharma Diversity and Deep Inclusivity at the East Bay Meditation Center: From Buddhist Modernism to Buddhist Postmodernism?," *Contemporary Buddhism* 15, no. 2 (2014): 312–331.

[35] "Healing Racial Trauma," *Dharma Relief*, https://dharmarelief.org/healing-racial-trauma/.

[36] International Western Dharma Teacher Gathering, https://www.dharmateachergathering.org/

[37] Gina Sharpe and Larry Yang, "Training the Buddhist Leaders of Tomorrow," *Lion's Roar: Buddhist Wisdom for Our Time*, August 21, 2018. https://www.lionsroar.com/training-the-buddhist-leaders-of-tomorrow/.

[38] See Ann Gleig, "Undoing Whiteness in American Buddhist Modernism," in *Buddhism and Whiteness*, ed. George Yancy and Emily McRae (London: Lexington Books, 2019), 21–42.

Analyzing the characteristics of racial justice work across meditation-based convert lineages, Gleig argues that they are marked by three turns—critical, contextual, and collective—and indicate a shift from colonial/modernist formations of Buddhism to Buddhisms forged in a postmodern/postcolonial context.[39]

BLACK LIVES MATTER AND BLACK BUDDHISM

Within the wider POC American Buddhist community, there has emerged a distinct Black Buddhist community. Black American teachers and practitioners have been exploring the specific relationship between Buddhism and Black histories and experiences through literature, retreats, and other program offerings. Groundbreaking figures include Jan Willis, whose 2001 memoir *Dreaming Me* charted her path from a Baptist upbringing through the 1960s civils rights movement and into Tibetan Buddhist practice and scholarship, and intersectional feminist bell hooks, who was a student of Thich Nat Hanh and delivered early critiques of the whiteness of American Buddhism.[40] Inspired by the Black Lives Matter movement, Rev. angel Kyodo williams, Lama Rod Owens, and Jasmine Syedullah's *Radical Dharma: Talking Race, Love, and Liberation* explores how Buddhist practice can disrupt white supremacy and envisions a collective liberation that combines social and spiritual freedom.[41] Another is the anthology *Black and Buddhist: What Buddhism Can Teach Us about Race, Resilience, Transformation and Freedom*, in which a number of prominent teachers share how their lived experiences as Black Americans shape their understanding of Buddhism and how Buddhism provides them with ways of navigating racial trauma.[42]

In August 2002, Spirit Rock hosted the first ever African American Dharma Retreat and Conference. More recently there have been two cross-lineage events for Black Buddhist teachers. The first was called "The Gathering," held in 2018 at Union Theological Seminary in New York City.[43] The second was called "The Gathering II: Buddhist Sangha of Black African Descent" and took place at Spirit Rock in October 2019. Insight teacher Konda Mason, who was one of the co-organizers of The Gathering

---

[39] Gleig, *American Dharma: Buddhism beyond Modernity* (New Haven, CT: Yale University Press, 2019), 249–304.

[40] bell hooks, "Waking Up to Racism," *Tricycle: The Buddhist Review* 4, no. 1 (Fall 1994). https://tricycle.org/magazine/waking-racism/.

[41] Rev. angel Kyodo williams, Lama Rod Owens, and Jasmine Syedullah, *Radical Dharma: Talking Race, Love, and Liberation* (Berkeley, CA: North Atlantic Books, 2016).

[42] Pamela Ayo Yetunde and Cheryl A. Giles, eds., *Black and Buddhist: What Buddhism Can Teach Us about Race, Resilience, Transformation and Freedom* (Boulder, CO: Shambhala, 2021).

[43] "Power and Heart: Black and Buddhist in America," *Lion's Roar: Buddhist Wisdom for Our Time*, January 30, 2019. https://www.lionsroar.com/power-heart-black-and-buddhist-in-america/.

II, identified its two key components as a celebration of community, and an exploration of how to make the Dharma relevant for Black communities given their particular social histories.[44] One such Black Buddhist pedagogy is Deep Time Liberation, a retreat program developed by Insight teachers Noliwe Alexander Way and Devin Berry. It explores the impact of ancestral legacy and intergenerational trauma on Black Americans and draws on multiple healing practices set within the wider context of mindfulness practice.[45]

The Black Lives Matter movement has also had a significant impact on American Buddhism. On May 14, 2015, a delegation of 125 Buddhists from sixty-three different organizations gathered for the first "White House-U.S. Buddhist Leadership Conference." Here they presented two letters: one on climate change and one titled "Buddhist Statement on Racial Justice." The inspiration for this letter was attributed to the courage of the people of Ferguson and the Black Lives Matter movement and seamlessly interweaved the language of Buddhism—suffering, interdependence, non-harm, and compassion—with racial justice.[46] After the police murder of African American George Floyd, Buddhist organizations across lineages such as the BCA, the Soto Zen Buddhist Association, and Soka Gakkai International-US released public statements vowing to transform "deep-rooted" structural racism.[47]

While racial justice has recently come to the forefront of meditation-based convert lineages, it has been centered more in other convert lineages. In her playfully titled "Why Are There So Many Black Buddhists?," Jade Sassar reflects on her positive experience as a Black woman in the multiracial Nichiren Buddhist organization Soka Gakkai International (SGI).[48] She emphasizes that SGI's commitment to social transformation resonates with Black Americans, and she connects the (purported) struggles of SGI's Japanese teachers against Japanese imperialism with the struggle against structural racism.[49] Black Buddhism is also providing new spaces for community building across convert lineages. Myokei Caine Barret, for instance, the first African Japanese American Bishop of the Nichiren Order of North America, was one of the co-organizers

---

[44] "Black Buddhist Konda Mason and The Gathering II," *Lion's Roar: Buddhist Wisdom for Our Time*, November, 2019. https://www.lionsroar.com/podcast/7-konda-mason-black-buddhist/.

[45] Rima Vesely-Flad, "Free at Last," *Lion's Roar: Buddhist Wisdom for Our Time*, September 3, 2019. https://www.lionsroar.com/free-at-last/.

[46] Jack Kornfield, "Statement on Racism from Buddhist Teachers and Leaders in the United States," May 14, 2015, https://jackkornfield.com/statement-on-racism-from-buddhist-teachers-leaders-in-the-united-states/.

[47] Ann Gleig, "Buddhist and Racial Justice: A History," *Tricycle: The Buddhist Review*, July 24, 2020. https://tricycle.org/article/buddhists-racial-justice/.

[48] Jade Sassar, "Why Are There So Many Black Buddhists?," *Tricycle: The Buddhist Review*, October 16, 2018, https://tricycle.org/article/black-buddhists/.

[49] Scholars have actually contested Soka Gakkai's own narrative that they resisted Japanese imperialism. See, for example, Brian Victoria, Sōka Gakkai Founder, Makiguchi Tsunesaburō, "A Man of Peace?," *The Asia-Pacific Journal*, 12, no. 37: 3. https://apjjf.org/2014/12/37/Brian-Victoria/4181/article.html.

of The Gathering and has been an active participant in cross-lineage American Buddhist events.

Scholars have provided rich ethnographies, theoretical framings, and historic context for Black American Buddhism. Drawing on interviews with over seventy Black Buddhists, Rima Vesely-Flad offers a layered portrait of how Black American Buddhists draw from Buddhist doctrine and practice to heal racialized trauma, build community, and forge new soteriological visions of collective liberation.[50] She shows how they read Buddhism through the Black radical tradition, connecting the wisdom of the Dharma with the writings of Audre Lourde and James Baldwin. Adeana McNicholl analyzes and historically situates contemporary Black Buddhist writings, arguing that they function to empower Black Americans within the white space of American convert Buddhism by romantically constructing Asia as "Other" to the hegemonic West, thereby simultaneously extending and disrupting white orientalist discourse.[51] Similar to Mitchell's work, McNicholl demonstrates that the history of American Buddhism and Buddhist modernism itself looks quite different when centered around racial minorities rather than white converts.[52]

WHITE BUDDHIST RESISTANCE AND RECEPTIVITY

The increasing emergence of racial justice initiatives within meditation-based American Buddhism has been met with both resistance and receptivity by white practitioners. While typically populated by a liberal demographic, many white Buddhists have opposed diversity, equity, and inclusion (DEI) initiatives, claiming they are either irrelevant or even in opposition to Buddhist practice. Buddhists of Color advocating for racial justice have been accused of a range of offenses from "being too angry" to causing disharmony and division in the sangha. White Buddhists have also dubbed POC affinity groups as spaces of "segregation" and reverse racism. Teachers have reported that white practitioners have complained or walked out of classes when they have discussed racism in their Dharma talks.[53]

Ann Gleig and Brenna Artinger have traced the white reactionary backlash to Buddhist DEI work through an examination of online activity and rhetoric. They chart the emergence of a broad spectrum of self-identified "anti-woke" white Buddhists who have targeted racial justice work, organizing them into three distinct but overlapping

---

[50] Rima Vesely-Flad, *Black Buddhists and the Black Radical Tradition: The Practice of Stillness in the Movement for Liberation* (New York: New York University Press, 2022).

[51] Adeana McNicholl, "Being Buddha, Staying Woke: Racial Formation in Black Buddhist Writings," *Journal of the American Academy of Religion* 86, no. 4 (2018): 883–911.

[52] McNicholl, "Buddhism and Race in the United States," 9–10.

[53] Gleig, *American Dharma*, 154–156.

categories: reactionary centrists, the Buddhist Right, and alt-Right Buddhists. Gleig and Artinger argue that common to all three groups is the attempt to delegitimate Buddhist ant-racist work as political and not Buddhist, and to naturalize their own political positionalities as Buddhist but not political. They interpret reactionary right-wing Buddhists through the model of postmodern conservatism, which is marked by a nostalgia for racial and gender hierarchies.[54] McNicholl fleshes out how religion, race, and gender intersect in the alt-Right Buddhists through their anti-Semitism and idealization of white masculinity and patriarchy.[55]

Other white Buddhists have responded more enthusiastically to calls for racial justice in American Buddhism. Following the lead of Buddhists of Color, these white allies frame becoming aware of whiteness, or "white awareness practice," as both a community-making necessity and a Buddhist soteriological practice.[56] One main area has been the production of "white awareness literature." A number of prominent white Buddhist teachers and leaders have published articles in mainstream Buddhist magazines calling on fellow white practitioners to confront white supremacy as an integral part of their Buddhist practice. One example is Insight teacher Tara Brach's 2016 article, "Facing My White Privilege," which calls on white practitioners to recognize their "collective conditioning" as white people in white awareness groups for their own liberation as well as to build inclusive sanghas.[57] Another area is the emergence of white awareness groups, affinity groups for white Buddhists to explore their conditioning as white people through a Buddhist lens. "White Awake" at New York Insight, led by Elaine Retholtz and Gary Singer, for instance, presents itself as a "course for white practitioners to create a space to examine our privilege, blind spots and racial conditioning in the context of Dharma teachings and practice."[58]

Emerging Directions: Differences between "People of Color"

The umbrella terms "POC" or "BIPOC" (Black, Indigenous, People of Color) have functioned as a pragmatic way for Buddhists of Color to build solidarity and resist white

---

[54] Ann Gleig and Brenna Grace Artinger, "#Buddhist Culture Wars: BuddhaBros, Alt-Right Dharma, and Snowflake Sanghas," *Journal of Global Buddhism* 22, no. 1 (2021): 19–48. Ann Gleig, "Reactionary Right-Wing Buddhists Have Joined the Fight against Critical Race Theory," *Religion Dispatches* (March 23, 2022). https://religiondispatches.org/reactionary-white-buddhists-have-joined-the-fight-against-critical-race-theory/.

[55] McNicholl, "Buddhism and Race in the United States," 5.

[56] Brennan and Gleig, "Whiteness Is a Sankhara: Racial Justice as Buddhist Practice."

[57] Tara Brach, "Facing My White Privilege," *Lion's Roar: Wisdom for Our Time*, December 26 2016. https://www.lionsroar.com/facing-my-white-privilege/.

[58] For an examination of White Awake at NYC Insight, see Brennan and Gleig, "Whiteness Is a Sankhara: Racial Justice as Buddhist Practice."

supremacy in American Buddhism. As noted by a number of commentators, the celebration of community is a key characteristic of racial justice work in American Buddhism. As well as strengthening relationships in the present, Buddhist scholar-practitioners such as Duncan Williams and Rima Vesely-Flad have emphasized historical solidarities between Asian Americans and Black Americans.[59] It is important, however, to acknowledge differences, including tensions, as well as commonalties between distinct ethnic and racial minority Buddhist groups. One response to these differences, for example, is the emergence of specific racial affinity groups and retreats. In 2020, Spirit Rock hosted a retreat for Asian Americans. In reflecting on the need for an Asian American retreat, co-teacher Louije Kim noted that it was important to avoid conflating the experiences of People of Color. As she explained, within Buddhist conversations "diversity is always in response to being in a white dominant space, or in a space that's influenced by white supremacy. The result is often an unfortunate flattening of the experiences of people of color as singular and undifferentiated."[60]

Within the category of Asian American Buddhism itself, there is tremendous diversity. While this chapter has focused on the experiences of Japanese American Buddhists, attention to how Korean, Vietnamese, and Tibetan Buddhists, and South and Southeast Asian Theravāda Buddhist communities navigate their religious and racialized identities in local, national, and global contexts brings more nuance to discussions of American Buddhism and race.[61] Studies of Asian American Buddhist communities reveal differences in how individuals articulate their racial identities in relationship to religious, social, and political structures, as well as intra-Asian Buddhist ethnic tensions.[62] Sri Lankan American anthropologist Nalika Gajaweera offers a first-person reflection on her experiences as a racialized Buddhist across two very different cultural contexts. As a second-generation Asian American Buddhist in the white space of American convert Buddhism, her embrace of "cultural" Buddhism serves to disrupt the racialized hierarchy between so-claimed "real" and "cultural" Buddhism. As a Sinhalese Buddhist in a Sri Lankan context, however, she seeks to distance herself from the violence of Buddhist ethnocentric nationalism.[63]

The Buddhist Peace Fellowship (BPF) is one site in which relationships between Asian American and Black American Buddhists have been honestly and painfully confronted. On the one side, this has involved tackling legacies of anti-Blackness in Asian American communities and the ways in which the "model minority myth" has been weaponized against Black Americans. On the other, it has involved tackling the

---

[59] Vesely-Flad, *Black Buddhists and the Radical Tradition*, 51–62.

[60] Louije Kim, quoted in Atia Sattar, "A Sangha for Asian American Buddhists in the West," *Tricycle: The Buddhist Review*, June 9, 2022, https://tricycle.org/article/asian-buddhists-sangha/.

[61] See the respective chapters on these traditions in this volume.

[62] See, for example, Allison J. Truiett, *Pure Land in the Making: Vietnamese Buddhism in the US Gulf South* (Seattle: University of Washington Press, 2021). Jiemin, Bao, *Creating a Buddhist Community: A Thai Temple in Silicon Valley* (Philadelphia: Temple University Press, 2015).

[63] Nalika Gajaweera, "Reclaiming Our So-Called "Cultural Baggage," *Lions Roar: Buddhist Wisdom for Our Time* (Winter 2021). https://www.lionsroar.com/reclaiming-our-so-called-cultural-baggage/.

ways in which POC convert Buddhists have also participated in orientalism and the marginalization of Asian American Buddhists. Funie Hsu, a former board member of BPF, was a driving force in educating the community about the histories and exclusions of Asian American heritage communities. Despite efforts to heal past harms, however, ongoing frustrations resulted in her and other board members' resignations and BPF entering a period of retreat. Sarwang Parikh, the interim director, shared that the organization was committed to bridging the divide between Western convert and heritage Buddhist sanghas.[64]

Just as American Buddhists on the ground are thinking across Asian American and Black American communities, scholars working across Asian studies, Asian American studies, and Black studies are generating new directions in research on American Buddhism.[65] Similarly, Indigenous studies research on settler colonialism and decolonization and conversations between Indigenous and Buddhist scholars and activists are an emerging area in both practice and academic communities.[66] One area that remains underdeveloped, however, is research into how class differences, both in terms of economic and cultural capital, impact racial identity and racial justice work in American Buddhism. For instance, the "white space" of American meditation-based convert Buddhism is a classed as well as racialized space, which some Buddhists of Color have been able to navigate through their class privilege.[67] Is DEI work in American Buddhist communities characterized by assimilative approaches, which seek to increase diverse representation within preexisting structures, or radical transformative approaches, which seek to create new structures?[68] How might Black Marxist concepts of racial capitalism and elite capture extend understandings?[69] Could class consciousness forge new solidarities across racialized American Buddhists as well as disrupt the commodification of Buddhism, which is also marked by whiteness? Such questions point to how research on how class, as well as gender and sexuality, intersects with race would enrich understandings of race and whiteness in American Buddhism.

---

[64] Buddhist Peace Fellowship, "BPF Spring Update: New Growth." email announcement March 1, 2022.

[65] See, for instance, Adeana McNicholl's "The Black Buddhism Plan: Buddhism, Race, and Empire in the Early Twentieth Century," *Religion and American Culture* 31, no. 3 (2021): 332–378.

[66] Raymond Lam, "Restoration and Justice: An Interview with Dr. Natalie Avalos on Indigenous Spiritualities and Buddhist Allies," *Buddhistdoor Global*, December 2021, https://www.buddhistdoor.net/features/restoration-and-justice-an-interview-with-dr-natalie-avalos-on-indigenous-spirituality-and-buddhist-allies/.

[67] Ann Gleig, "Beyond the Upper Middle Way," *Lion's Roar: Buddhist Wisdom for Our Times*, September 13, 2019. https://www.lionsroar.com/beyond-the-upper-middle-way/.

[68] Ann Gleig, "Enacting Social Change Through Meditation," in *The Oxford Handbook of Meditation*, ed. Miguel Farias, David Brazier and Mansur Lalljee (Oxford and New York: Oxford University Press), 771–791.

[69] Olufemi Taiwo, *Elite Capture: How the Powerful Took over Identity Politics (and Everything Else)* (Chicago: Haymarket Books, 2022).

Conclusion: The Role of Scholars

The colonial and orientalist history of Buddhist studies has been well documented. Scholars such as Joseph Cheah and Natalie Quli have shown that orientalist constructions of what does and does not count as real Buddhism have resulted in the exclusion of Asian American Buddhists.[70] When white Buddhists claim that Buddhist anti-racism work is illegitimate as there is no textual precedence for it, they are also reflecting and reproducing this history. As Gleig and Artinger show, alt-right Buddhists explicitly draw on Buddhist studies scholarship to support their white supremacist and misogynist interpretations of the tradition. Some scholars—many, but not all of whom are also Buddhist practitioners—are intentionally aiming to disrupt the legacies of white supremacy in Buddhist studies through anti-racist-informed research.[71] One avenue through which this is occurring is increasing representation of Asian American Buddhist heritage communities that have been neglected in the field.[72] This scholarship does not merely add more diversity to preexisting structures, but rewrites histories of American Buddhism and reorients the academic subfield field of American Buddhist studies.[73] Another is the production of scholarship that legitimates racial justice work as Buddhist through providing historical and/or textual precedence, or framing it through a lived religious approach.[74] A third avenue is through scholars engaging in public scholarship that brings academic knowledge and authority into Buddhist communities. Notably much of this research is coming from scholars located outside of Buddhist studies in fields such as Asian American studies and anthropology, or scholars working across these fields.

Common to these approaches is a self and disciplinary reflexivity in which the whiteness of Buddhist studies and American Buddhist studies is critiqued.[75] As with Buddhist racial justice work, such scholarship has received pushback from other scholars who view it as an overreach of identity politics and activism in the field.[76] In researching

---

[70] Natalie Quli, "On Authenticity: Scholarship, the Insight Movement, and White Authority," in *Methods in Buddhist Studies: Essays in Honor of Richard K. Payne*, ed. Scott A. Mitchell and Natalie Fisk Quli (London: Bloomsbury Press, 2019), 154–172.

[71] Ryan Anningson, *Theories of the Self, Race, and Essentialization in Buddhism* (Routledge, 2021); Gleig and Artinger, "#Buddhist Culture Wars."

[72] For example, Williams, *American Sutra*, and Mitchell, *The Making of American Buddhism*.

[73] See Funie Hsu, Chapter 20 on Engaged Buddhism in this volume, for an example of such a reorientation. See also McNicholl, "The Black Buddhism Plan."

[74] George Yancy and Emily McRae, eds., *Buddhism and Whiteness* (London: Lexington Books, 2019); Joy Brennan, "Deconstructing Whiteness," *Buddhadharma: The Practitioner's Quarterly* (Summer 2021): 28–43.

[75] See, for example, Sharon Suh, "We interrupt your regularly scheduled programming to bring you this very important public service announcement . . ." : aka Buddhism as Usual in the Academy," in *Buddhism and Whiteness*, ed. George Yancy and Emily McRae (London: Lexington Books, 2019), 1–20.

[76] Jorn Borup, "Who Owns Religion? Intersectionality, Identity Politics, and Cultural Appropriation in Postglobal Buddhism," *Numen* 67 (2020): 226–255.

race and whiteness in American Buddhism, scholars should therefore be cognizant of their own positionality, the ways in which the field has participated in the construction of racialized forms of Buddhism, and the impact of scholarship on the ground in American Buddhist communities. In short, a disruption of the whiteness of American Buddhism necessitates an interdisciplinary disruption, reinvigoration, and reorientation of the field of Buddhist studies itself.

References

Anningson, Ryan. *Theories of the Self, Race, and Essentialization in Buddhism.* Abingdon, Oxfordshire, UK: Routledge, 2021.

Anningson, Ryan. "Once the Buddha Was an Aryan: Race Sciences and the Domestication of Buddhism in North." *Journal of Religion & Culture* 27, no. 1 (2017): 51–57.

Bao, Jiemin. *Creating a Buddhist Community: A Thai Temple in Silicon Valley.* Philadelphia: Temple University Press, 2015.

Borup, Jorn. "Who Owns Religion? Intersectionality, Identity Politics, and Cultural Appropriation in Postglobal Buddhism." *Numen* 67 (2020): 226–255.

Brennan, Joy. "Deconstructing Whiteness." *Buddhadharma: The Practitioner's Quarterly* (Summer 2021): 28–43.

Brennan, Joy, and Ann Gleig, "Whiteness Is a Sankhara: Racial Justice as Buddhist Practice." *Yin-Cheng Journal of Contemporary Buddhism* 1, no. 1 (2023): 30–57.

Cheah, Joseph. *Race and Religion in American Buddhism: White Supremacy and Immigrant Adaptation.* Oxford: Oxford University Press, 2011.

Cheah, Joseph. "US Buddhist Traditions." In *Oxford Handbook of Contemporary Buddhism*, edited by Michael Jerryson, 316–331. Oxford and New York: Oxford University Press, 2016.

Cheah, Joseph. "Buddhism, Race, and Ethnicity." In *Oxford Handbook of Contemporary Buddhism*, edited by Michael Jerryson, 650–661. Oxford and New York: Oxford University Press, 2016.

Fields, Rick. "Confessions of a White Buddhist: Dharma, Diversity and Race," *Tricycle: The Buddhist Review*, Fall 1994, https://tricycle.org/magazine/confessions-white-buddhist/.

Gajaweera, Nalika. "Reclaiming Our So-Called 'Cultural Baggage.'" *Lions Roar: Buddhist Wisdom For Our Time* (Winter 2021). https://www.lionsroar.com/reclaiming-our-so-called-cultural-baggage/.

Gajaweera, Nalika. "Sitting in the Fire Together: People of Color Cultivating Radical Resistance in North American Insight Meditation." *Journal of Global Buddhism* 22, no. 1 (2021): 121–139.

Gleig, Ann. *American Dharma: Buddhism beyond Modernity.* New Haven, CT: Yale University Press, 2019.

Gleig, Ann. "Enacting Social Change through Meditation." In *The Oxford Handbook of Meditation*, edited by Miguel Farias, David Brazier, and Mansur Lalljee, 771–791. Oxford and New York: Oxford University Press, 2021.

Gleig, Ann. "Engaged Buddhism." In *Oxford Research Encyclopedia of Religion*. Oxford and New York: Oxford University Press.

Gleig, Ann. "Undoing Whiteness in American Buddhist Modernism." In *Buddhism and Whiteness*, edited by George Yancy and Emily McRae, 21–42. London: Lexington Books, 2019.

Gleig, Ann. "Buddhist and Racial Justice: A History." *Tricycle: The Buddhist Review*, July 24, 2020. https://tricycle.org/article/buddhists-racial-justice/.

Gleig, Ann, and Brenna Grace Artinger. "#Buddhist Culture Wars: BuddhaBros, Alt-Right Dharma, and Snowflake Sanghas." *Journal of Global Buddhism* 22, no. 1 (2021): 19–48.

Han, Chenxing. *Be the Refuge: Raising the Voices of Asian American Buddhists.* Berkeley, CA: North Atlantic Books, 2021.

Hase, Craig Nicholas, James C. Meadows, and Stephanie L. Budge. "Inclusion and Exclusion in the White Space: An Investigation of the Experiences of People of Color in a Primarily White American Meditation Community." *Journal of Global Buddhism* 19 (August 2019): 1–18.

Hickey, Wakoh Shannon. "Two Buddhisms, Three Buddhisms, and Racism." In *Buddhism beyond Borders: New Perspectives on Buddhism in the United States*, edited by Scott A. Mitchell and Natalie E. F. Quli, 44–46. Albany: State University of New York Press, 2015.

McNicholl, Adeana, "The Black Buddhism Plan: Buddhism, Race, and Empire in the Early Twentieth Century," *Religion and American Culture* 31, no. 3 (2021): 332–378.

McNicholl, Adeana. "Buddhism and Race in the United States." *Religion Compass* 15, no. 8 (2021): 1–13.

McNicholl, Adeana. "Being Buddha, Staying Woke: Racial Formation in Black Buddhist Writings." *Journal of the American Academy of Religion* 86, no. 4 (2018): 883–911.

Mitchell, Scott. *The Making of American Buddhism.* Oxford and New York: Oxford University Press, 2023.

Quli, Natalie. "Western Self, Asian Other: Modernity, Authenticity and Nostalgia for "Tradition" in Buddhist Studies." *Journal of Buddhist Ethics* 16 (2009): 1–38.

Quli, Natalie. "On Authenticity: Scholarship, the Insight Movement, and White Authority." In *Methods in Buddhist Studies: Essays in Honor of Richard K. Payne*, edited by Scott A Mitchell and Natalie Fisk Quli, 154–172. London: Bloomsbury Press, 2019.

Suh, Sharon. "We interrupt your regularly scheduled programming to bring you this very important public service announcement . . .": aka Buddhism as Usual in the Academy." In *Buddhism and Whiteness*, edited by George Yancy and Emily McRae, 1–20. London: Lexington Books, 2019.

Taiwo, Olufemi. *Elite Capture: How the Powerful Took over Identity Politics (and Everything Else).* Chicago: Haymarket Books, 2022.

Truiett, Allison. J. *Pure Land in the Making: Vietnamese Buddhism in the US Gulf South.* Seattle: University of Washington Press, 2021.

Vesely-Flad, Rima. *Black Buddhists and the Black Radical Tradition: The Practice of Stillness in the Movement for Liberation*. New York: New York University Press, 2022.

Yancy, George, and Emily McRae, eds. *Buddhism and Whiteness*. London: Lexington Books, 2019.

Williams, Duncan. *American Sutra: A Story of Faith and Freedom.* Cambridge, MA: Harvard University Press, 2019.

Willis, Jan. *Dreaming Me: Black, Baptist, Buddhist: One Woman's Spiritual Journey*. Somerville, MA: Wisdom Publications, 2001.

CHAPTER 4

IDENTITIES II
Gender and Sexuality in American Buddhism

AMY PARIS LANGENBERG

On May 4, 2021, "May We Gather," a "national Buddhist memorial service for Asian American ancestors"[1] was held in Los Angeles at a temple that had recently been vandalized as part of a spike in anti-Asian violence related to the perceived Chinese origins of COVID-19. "May We Gather" brought together Buddhist nuns, monks, and priests from many Asian American Buddhist communities with the purpose of gathering the Asian American Buddhist sangha and mending bodies, minds, and communities harmed by racialized violence. "May We Gather" marked the 49th day after eight people, including six women of Asian or Asian American descent, were gunned down in Atlanta in a mass shooting. One of the six murdered women was a Buddhist Korean American mother of two, Yong Ae Yu. Ae Yu was represented by ancestor tablets and memorialized during the event, along with five other Asians or Asian Americans killed in acts of racialized violence during almost 150 years of Asian American history.

In her greeting, one of the principal organizers of "May We Gather," Funie Hsu, a Buddhist practitioner and scholar of American studies, promised the assembled Buddhist community, and the large virtual audience watching the livestream, that together they would "chant sacred texts, transfer merit to Asian American Buddhist ancestors, and pray for the protection of all beings."[2] While all three of these actions—chanting, making and transferring merit, and praying for protection—along with the event's focus on community harmony and respect for ancestors—are central to many Asian Buddhist communities, they are not universally taken to be central to all forms of American Buddhism. According to some scholarship on American Buddhism, predominately white and affluent "convert Buddhists" prefer, rather, to place meditation

---

[1] https://www.maywegather.org/49-days. Last accessed December 28, 2022.
[2] https://www.maywegather.org/. Last accessed December 28, 2022.

and individual spiritual development at the center of their Buddhist practice, a tendency that is said to differentiate "ethnic" or "heritage" Buddhism from so-called convert Buddhism. More recently, an ethnographic study of young Asian American Buddhists by Chenxing Han, another of the event's organizers, has troubled this "two Buddhisms" framework, demonstrating its flattening effect. Based on sixty-nine interviews with young adult Asian American Buddhists, Han's book, *Be the Refuge: Raising the Voices of Asian American Buddhists*, maps often ignored generational differences *within* Asian American Buddhist families, as well as religious differences between and within Asian American communities. As an example, Han surfaces the voices of young Asian Americans who, contrary to expectations, "convert" to Buddhism, in part because they are interested in meditation and doctrine.[3]

As noted by Buddhist studies scholar Adeana McNicholl, dominant (white) power structures, however provincial or ethnocentric, influence what can be known, including the knowledge produced by academic fields like Buddhist studies. In McNicholl's words, "If we are to provincialize hegemonic religious and racial categories, we must prioritize scholarship that centers the religio-racial subjectivities of Asian American and other racialized Buddhists."[4] Taking its cue from the historic "May We Gather" event, and Han's groundbreaking study, this cross-sectional overview of gender and sexuality in contemporary American Buddhism centers those that have been less visible—some would say structurally erased—in much Buddhist studies scholarship. Informed also by the intersectional and postcolonial feminisms of thinkers like Sara Ahmed, Saba Mahmood, and Chandra Talpade Mohanty, the analysis starts from the premise that gender and sexual orientation in American Buddhism is inextricable from other strong vectors of identity, especially race and ethnicity. Stepping around the narrative that white converts and their liberal feminisms have created an egalitarian Buddhism in America,[5] this chapter offers instead a different story by exploring the Buddhisms of Asian and Asian American lay women, ordained women of Asian heritage, celibate women, Black teachers, trans and queer individuals, and sexual abuse survivors—often overlapping categories—at the seams of sex and gender.[6] It concludes that, while they may be demographic minorities, and minoritized in white American Buddhist communities, the Buddhism of the multiply sexed and gendered individuals and communities profiled here should not be relegated to the margins; rather, the rich multidimensionality of contemporary American Buddhism is in large part their creation.

---

[3] Han 2021. See also McNicholl 2021, 4.

[4] McNicholl 2021, 2.

[5] For example, Seager 1999, 185–200; Boucher 1988; "Women in American Buddhism."

[6] While this overview essay "centers" non-dominant genders and sexualities in an effort to "provincialize" Buddhist forms of white masculinity, the latter are implicit in the analysis as a contrast class, a source of bias, and sometimes a source of violence. For scholarship on white masculinity in American Buddhism, see Gleig and Artinger 2021 and McNicholl 2021.

Asian and Asian American Lay Women

The "two Buddhisms" framework has manifested in descriptions of American Buddhism in many forms and permutations, some of them scholarly,[7] some popular.[8] In a seminal 2010 essay, Wakoh Shannon Hickey made a cogent critique of this typology in its various forms, illuminating the effects of racism it produces.[9] As Hickey points out, the "two Buddhisms" typology lends itself to imagining a hierarchy of Buddhisms that is racialized in the American context. This is a hierarchy that upholds meditation and doctrinal study as central to the Buddhist path to enlightenment and dismisses "cultural" practices such as chanting, making offerings, Buddhist arts, prostration, dance or other movement traditions, festivals, and communal meals as non-essential "cultural baggage." Since these common activities are also associated with lay women's practice at "heritage" temples, and are contrasted with the doctrinal concerns and meditation practices of male monastic elites, this imagined hierarchy is also implicitly gendered. But, as the work of scholars such as Sharon Suh, Tamara Ho, Patricia Usuki, and Karma Lekshe Tsomo demonstrates, summarizing the Buddhist practices of Asian American Buddhist lay women as transactional or "cultural"—in other words, feeding monks, cooking for the community, and making merit—is highly misleading.

Suh and Ho, whose research focuses on a Los Angeles Korean Buddhist temple and the Burmese community in Southern California, respectively, both note that the Buddhist immigrant women they interviewed spoke of community networking, service, and ethical behavior when asked about their Buddhist commitments. Both scholars also emphasize the role that Buddhism plays in helping first-generation immigrant women nurture a resilient self and critical mind while negotiating the disorienting, and sometimes violent, experiences of dislocation and immigration. Buddhism as a practice of chanting, meditating, listening, and worshipping "provides," in Tamara Ho's words, "an organizational framework through which [immigrant] women can reflect on institutions of power, critique master narratives of Western supremacy and patriarchy, and practice a contingent, open-ended relationality."[10] Sharon Suh's ethnographic work with lay women members of Sa Chal Temple also makes plain their keen interest in self-cultivation, not only transactional merit making or socializing. She writes:

> The main goals of [women's] religious practice were self-transformation and the development of individual agency that they interpreted through the Buddhist doctrines of karma, the universal Buddhist Nature, and the potential enlightenment

---

[7] For an overview of variations on the "two Buddhisms" framework, see Hickey 2010. See also McNicholl 2021.

[8] Mitchell 2016, 63; Hickey 2010, 8–9; Han 2021, 21–24.

[9] Hickey 2010.

[10] Ho 2020, 184.

in all beings. Women often claimed that finding and knowing one's mind was the essential aspect of the Buddha's teachings—not teaching children about religion or praying for one's husband's business as many men seemed to believe.[11]

In reflecting on her interviews with Jōdo Shinshū women (most of whom were second-, third-, or fourth-generation Japanese Americans), Patricia Usuki, an ordained minister in the Buddhist Church of America (BCA), also stresses their critical engagement with doctrine, as well as a widespread sentiment among emergent female leaders within Jōdo Shinshū that "the main focus of the BCA should be religion," not social networking for the Japanese American community.[12] Karma Lekshe Tsomo makes a similar point in her recent study of Jōdo Shinshū *fujinkai* (Buddhist women's organizations) in Hawai'i, quoting the ex-president of the Buddhist Women's Association Toko Umehara's assertion that these are "religiously oriented, rather than primarily social organizations."[13] In looking at the interview-based ethnographic research of these scholars, what surfaces is a picture of Asian American women nurturing supportive networks with co-nationals, celebrating festivals, or making merit, *but also* exploring Buddhist ideas and practices for reasons of ethical self-cultivation and critical reflection on self, power, and community. In other words, they engage thoughtfully with Buddhism in ways that are not dissimilar to the ways that white converts are said to engage it.

The emphasis in white convert communities (and also in Buddhist studies scholarship) on meditation and doctrine derives in part from the priorities of elite Asian monasticism. For instance, in his study of Thai Buddhist immigrant women, Todd LeRoy Perreira quotes two Theravāda monk-scholars, one Thai and one American, who make a distinction between lay women's Buddhism and the "actual practice of Buddhism."[14] The privileging of monastic over lay practice also means that, despite their demographic and institutional significance in American Buddhism, fewer scholars have studied the Buddhism of Asian and Asian American lay women, especially if they have not gained prominence as leaders. We hope that this is changing.

Ordained Asian American Women

Cristina Moon, a resident priest at Daihonzan Chozen-ji Rinzai Zen temple in Honolulu, Hawai'i, is one emergent female Asian American Buddhist leader who *has* attracted notice in the Buddhist media and beyond. Moon was one of six Buddhist teachers (three of whom were Asian or Asian American women)[15] invited to speak on the six Buddhist

---

[11] Suh 2004, 21.
[12] Usuki 2007, 78.
[13] Tsomo 2022, 36.
[14] Perreira 2020, 172.
[15] The other two were Myokei Caine-Barrett and Sister Kinh Nghiem.

*pāramitā*s (perfections) at the "May We Gather" memorial. Moon spoke on *vīrya*, which she glossed as "spiritual strength," and upheld as foundational for the practice of compassion or "suffering with" the oppressed, violated, and marginalized. In particular, Moon held up the resilience of the six women killed in the Atlanta shootings as a key instance of *vīrya*. In Moon's words, the "strength they had to make America their home, working multiple jobs and navigating a new world for the sake of their families was tremendous."[16] As she recited the women's names, Tan Xiaojie, Feng Daoyou, Hyun Jung Grant, Park Soon Chung, Kim Suncha, and Yue Yong Ae, Moon's voice broke with emotion.

Moon, who is Korean American, has been a particularly sharp critic of the erasure of Buddhism's Asian traditional roots in predominantly white convert communities. In a 2020 *Tricycle* article, she comments on the "cosplay" of white Buddhists' fetishization of Asian teachers, as well as their superficial imitation of Asian cultural behaviors, even while they denigrate other Asian Buddhist traditions as "cultural baggage"[17] and marginalize Asian and Asian American people within their sanghas.[18] Moon extols Chozan-ji as one of the few American Zen temples that was not only founded by, but is still run by Asian Americans. At Chozan-ji, students learn what Moon calls "reorienting practices," which are integral to Asian Buddhisms but not always prioritized in white sanghas. These include giving to Buddhist institutions without expecting to receive something, offering to help with whatever needs to be done, and humbly learning from those with more experience.

Moon emphasizes the importance of the Buddhist lifeways passed down in Asian cultural settings from teachers to students over many centuries. Although on occasion she has mentioned patriarchy as a source of suffering and oppression, her focus on resisting anti-Asian hate, marginalization, and erasure has so far taken precedence over noting dynamics of inequity or abuse related to gender and sexuality within Buddhism. This alignment is likely motivated at least in part by a resistance to what Funie Hsu has described as "the paternalistic idea that Buddhism needs saving from its 'traditional' Asian heritage" common among white convert Buddhists.[19] Moon also emphasizes that studying the Dharma at Chozen-ji need not be gendered:

> Asian culture—as well as Western culture—is pretty patriarchal.... The challenge to any of us who are training seriously in Buddhism though is to not let our minds get stuck on that.... You can't let that dictate how you train or your engagement with the Dharma.... Those are the limitations of human beings as imperfect creatures but the Dharma transcends that.[20]

---

[16] https://www.cristinamoon.com/speaking/may-we-gather-pan-asian-pan-buddhist-memorial-service. Last accessed December 29, 2022.
[17] See Gajaweera 2021 for a reframing of this term in the context of diasporic Asian Buddhism.
[18] See Hsu 2017.
[19] Hsu 2021.
[20] Interview, October 25, 2021.

Patricia Kanaya Usuki, another American Buddhist woman leader of Asian heritage, emphasizes different dimensions of the Asian American Buddhist experience. For instance, she has written at length about challenges to female leadership and agency in traditionally male-dominated, culturally Japanese Jōdo Shinshū communities in America. Her 2007 book, *Currents of Change*, is a systematic study of women's experiences within this oldest of American Buddhist communities. Originally written as an M.A. thesis for the Berkeley-based Institute of Buddhist Studies, her book surfaces the voices of Jōdo Shinshū women and tracks generational shifts within the community. In particular, Usuki notes the subtle ways in which the women she surveyed reconcile gender hierarchical patterns of authority in American Jōdo Shinshū temples with the inherent gender egalitarianism of the Jōdo Shinshū founder Shinran Shonin's teachings. In her study, she also surveys the attitudes of young people in BCA temples, reporting that many of them drift away after leaving their parents' home. One reason for this, Usuki speculates, could be "unresolved gender issues."[21] At the same time, Usuki notes the ordination of women as BCA ministers, increasing numbers of women occupying seats on temple boards or other leadership positions, and the changing focus of the Buddhist women's groups (*fujinkai*) from kitchen work and event organizing to promotion of the Dharma and other sorts of education.[22]

Usuki's experience within her own Buddhist organization differs significantly from Moon's, leading her to take a different approach to the Asian cultural dimensions of Jōdo Shinshū temples. BCA temples historically have emphasized Japanese language and culture and have acted as important social gathering places for Japanese Americans. Now officially retired, Usuki served sixteen years as the head minister of the San Fernando Valley Hongwanji Buddhist Temple. Usuki, who did not grow up in the BCA, describes beginning her tenure at San Fernando, which was losing membership at that time, with the intention of keeping her focus on the Dharma. "If you want to have your Japanese cultural events, that's fine, that's great, but for me those are secondary," she told her new sangha. "The one thing that ties us all together should be the Dharma."[23] The main vehicle of Dharma training at San Fernando is the Sunday service, rather than meditation or other practices like the martial arts taught at Chozan-ji. By her own description, Usuki's approach to teaching Buddhism on Sundays, or at funerals and other events where she is called to speak, is pedagogical. She never uses "lingo" or references concepts without explaining them in layman's terms to her listeners. This feels to her more appropriate and necessary in an American environment that is not what she refers to as "culturally Buddhist." Although Usuki thinks it's possible that the changes she brought led to some traditionalists leaving the temple, the San Fernando sangha did, in fact, experience net growth during her tenure. According to Usuki, most of these new members were "non-traditional," meaning, not Japanese and/or not from a Jōdo Shinshū background.

---

[21] Usuki 2007, 76. See also Tsomo 2022, 50.
[22] Interview, September 24, 2021. See also Tsomo 2022, 49.
[23] Interview, September 24, 2021.

Still, Usuki is quick to say, "I don't care about numbers. All I cared about was to keep the Dharma going in that area (of Southern California)."[24]

CELIBACY AS GENDER RADICAL

Moon and Usuki are both ordained non-celibates in Mahāyāna lineages. Tathālokā Therī, on the other hand, upholds Theravāda female Buddhist celibate traditions in North America. Although celibate monasticism is a cherished ideal in many Asian Buddhist contexts, it has much less cultural visibility in the North American context. In this way, Tathālokā Therī has lived a gender-radical American Buddhist life. A Washington, D.C., native born to ethnically non-Asian parents, Tathālokā Therī began her Buddhist studies in 1988 at age nineteen in Europe, eventually ordaining in 1995 as a novice-level monastic with the *bhikkhunī* elder Myeong Seong Sunim in South Korea. After returning to the United States, Tathālokā Therī received her *bhikkhunī* (full ordination) vows from a Sri Lankan *bhikkhu* (male monastic) at the International Meditation Center in Los Angeles in 1997. As she later came to appreciate, in entering the ranks of fully ordained monastic women holding full vows (*bhikkhunī*), Tathālokā Therī took her place in an international movement of Buddhist monastic women, one described by scholar Susanne Mrozik as a "robed revolution."[25] This movement was striving to restore the highest monastic ordination status to women in lineages where it had long been lost, or to establish it where it had never existed. Since that time, Tathālokā Therī has been pivotal in supporting the global *bhikkhunī* revival.

Tathālokā Therī has worked toward the goal of nurturing female forms of Buddhist monasticism in North America and internationally on multiple fronts. The first non–Sri Lankan woman to be appointed as a *bhikkhunī* preceptor in her lineage, Tathālokā Therī has facilitated sixty-seven ordinations since 2009 for women at all stages, including *anagārikā*s, novice *sāmaṇerī*s, and fully ordained *bhikkhunī*s, some of European, Hispanic, and Native American heritage from the United States, Canada, Europe, New Zealand, and Australia, and some of South and Southeast Asian heritage from Sri Lanka, Malaysia, Singapore, and Thailand. She is also the senior monastic advisor for the Alliance for Bhikkhunis, a pioneer lay organization that financially supports Theravāda *bhikkhunī*s worldwide.[26] Money is a perennial problem for female monastics in South and Southeast Asia, Himalayan areas, and in the West, as systems of lay and government support either simply don't exist, or neglect women. At home in Northern California, Tathālokā Therī has founded her own community, called Dhammadarini ("female upholders of the dharma") with the help of lay supporters.[27] Dhammadharini

---

[24] Interview, September 21, 2021.
[25] Mrozik 2009.
[26] https://www.bhikkhuni.net/. Last accessed April 15, 2022.
[27] https://www.dhammadharini.net/. Last accessed April 15, 2022.

is located in Penngrove, Sonoma County, and supports a small community of monastics at various stages in the monastic path.

Tathālokā Therī is notable for her active scholarship into the history of *bhikkhunī*s and their textual traditions.[28] Scholarly work is an essential element of her larger goal to support female monastics practicing in Theravāda lineages. Surfacing the voices and experiences of historical Buddhist women provides important inspiration and modeling for contemporary monastic women marginalized in androcentric institutions, or as a result of living in cultural contexts like North America where the celibate path of Buddhist discipline is not well understood. Similarly, direct access to canonical and commentarial texts on monastic discipline, which are internally diverse and historically layered, provides vital spiritual support for women walking that ancient path while living day-to-day in contemporary America or other new cultural contexts.

Tathālokā Therī says she has, from the beginning, been conscious of and intentional around issues of diversity and inclusivity at Dhammadharini, but she is also aware of dynamics of whiteness there. "People see a place where there are white people becoming monastics and white *women* becoming monastics, and as soon as people see two white monastics together, or three, then there are others—white women—who think that this is the place to go," Tathālokā admits, referencing the community's optics on social media.[29] The work of diversity continues within the Dhammadharini Sangha and the Dhammadharini Support Foundation, both of which support ordained women of Asian, Hispanic, African, and Native American heritage and are holding conversations about whiteness internally in order to more skillfully welcome and include non-white postulants and retreatants. According to Tathālokā Therī, several years of conversations have also been held at leadership and monastic community levels with regard to gender diversity. A remarkable feature of the current Dhammadharini community is its inclusion of both male-identified and gender-diverse monastics and visitors, and its recent achievement in supporting a nonbinary individual's entry into the ordained sangha.

BLACK BUDDHIST TEACHERS

As Han's 2021 book, *Be the Refuge*, illustrates so compellingly, binaries like the "two Buddhisms" framework inscribe hierarchies of gender and race that can be harmful to Buddhist communities. As her work also demonstrates, they fail to accurately represent all possibilities and realities of the American Buddhist landscape by automatically occluding whatever doesn't fit into one domain or the other. Recent scholarship on Black Buddhist teachers also disrupts the two Buddhisms framework by lifting up Buddhisms practiced by Black Americans, which both overlap with and diverge from the categories

---

[28] https://independent.academia.edu/TathaalokaBhikkhuni. Last accessed April 17, 2022.
[29] Interview, November 4, 2021.

of "convert" and "heritage" Buddhism. Black Buddhist teachers emphasize the importance of ancestors, place of origin, and lineage and also make use of Buddhist doctrines, practices, and institutions to work with the trauma of marginalization, uprooting, and racial violence, as do many immigrant Buddhist communities.[30] Like many white convert Buddhists, Black Buddhists sometimes participate in an orientalist vision of Asian Buddhism as a civilizational alternative to Euro-American Christian society, though the social ills they identify are racial oppression and racialized trauma rather than neurosis, depression, or alienation.[31]

According to Black studies scholar and Buddhist practitioner Rima Vesely-Flad, Black Buddhist teachers are innovative and distinctive in drawing on the Black radical tradition to, in Vesely-Flad's words, elevate "the body as a site for liberation, that allows for the presence, joy, and innate sensuality named by Lorde and Baldwin."[32] Many prominent Black Buddhist teachers are women, and a strikingly large number identify as nonbinary, bisexual, and/or queer. In elevating the body, Black Buddhist teachers elevate gender and sexuality, as well as race, as legitimate domains of Buddhist practice. As the Soto Zen priest Zenju Earthlyn Manuel, who is Black and identifies as queer, notes in her moving treatise on awakening through race, gender, and sexuality, titled *The Way of Tenderness*, "When I set out on the path of Dharma, the question of what this life was dealt squarely with my immediate physical reality, meaning, in my case, my race, sexuality, and gender."[33]

Raised in Los Angeles, Zenju Earthlyn Manuel practiced in the Soka Gakkai (Nichiren Buddhist) tradition for fifteen years before joining the San Francisco Zen Center (SFZC) community in 2001. There she started again as a beginner, becoming a student of Blanche Hartman, who was known for her advocacy for women in the SFZC community. In 2018, two years after Hartman's death, Manuel was ordained as a Soto Zen priest by Victoria Austin. She is now head of Still Breathing Zen Sangha, a refuge for Zen Practitioners of Black African descent. Holding a PhD, Manuel is a prolific writer who has published in multiple Buddhist publications and has contributed to many anthologies and collaborative projects. She has also authored five books, including *The Shamanic Bones of Zen: Revealing the Ancestral Spirit and Mystical Heart of a Sacred Tradition*, which explores the relationship of indigenous practices to Buddhism. The ideas expressed in Manuel's writings are rooted in her Zen training, but also engage multiple other traditions, including the Christianity of her childhood, Native American traditions, and African Indigenous traditions.

Like many of her Black Buddhist peer teachers, Manuel regards ceremonies that connect to the land and rituals to honor ancestors as central to community wellness and individual spiritual progress. She describes, for instance, how early in her Zen practice the task of sweeping the temple, cleaning the toilets, and doing laundry, all of which are

---

[30] Vesely-Flad 2022.
[31] McNicholl 2018, 2021.
[32] Vesely-Flad 2022, 224.
[33] Manuel 2015, 79.

supposed to create humility in the practitioner, triggered instead harmful feelings related to racial identity. She writes, "Because so many of the work leaders were white, in the beginning I could only see the work as what my ancestors did as slaves, sharecroppers, wet-nurses, and maids. The memory of my black ancestors and slavery was visceral."[34] By receiving inspiration from her ancestors, Manuel transformed this experience of inappropriate humility into a reconnection with ancestral memory.[35] Manuel also broadens Zen Buddhist rituals for honoring lineages by including traditions for honoring female teachers and sustainers as well as practitioners' own family lineages, along with the lands and ecologies that supported them. By the same token, Manuel characterizes the Buddha as an important "shamanic ancestor" of modern practitioners, one to whom Buddhist practitioners must "make offerings . . . across all genders and in all places and times."[36]

Manuel's articulation of suffering and liberation directly engages, rather than seeking to transcend, her embodied experiences of race, sexuality, and gender, which she has referred to as "fiery gateways" to the spiritual realizations she longs for.[37] In *The Way of Tenderness*, she writes, "The body I inhabit has experienced nearly every category of hatred that exists within this society, directed toward the various unacceptable differences that characterize its appearance."[38] White, cis, and straight practitioners may fear discussing race, gender, and sexuality, claiming that doing so creates division in the sangha, or that such topics are not "spiritual."[39] Manuel teaches directly against such views, stating that "these things are exactly spiritual and we must start with the fire."[40] Racialized and embodied experiences of gender and sexuality, in fact, constitute the Buddhist path she walks, rather than being experiences to be transcended.

In 2020, for the first time, Spirit Rock Meditation Center's prestigious four-year advanced teacher-training course graduated a cohort comprised entirely of individuals from non-dominant cultures. Ninety percent of this historic cohort identified as PoC, and 55 percent identified as LGBTQIA+.[41] Among these was Gen-X meditation instructor, writer, and organizational consultant Kate Johnson. A Chicago native, Johnson began her meditation practice while working as a dancer in New York City and earning an MFA in performance studies at New York University. A mixed-race Black woman who identifies as queer, Johnson has described her experiences in Buddhist meditation centers as both racially harmful and lifesaving. As Johnson's practice deepened, she entered a one-year teacher-training program with Ethan Nichtern and

[34] Manuel 2021b.
[35] Ibid.
[36] Manuel 2021a.
[37] https://www.resources.soundstrue.com/transcript/through-the-fire-to-liberated-tenderness/. Last accessed December 28, 2022.
[38] Manuel 2015, 11.
[39] See, for instance, Gleig and Artinger 2021.
[40] https://www.resources.soundstrue.com/transcript/through-the-fire-to-liberated-tenderness/. Last accessed June 25, 2022.
[41] Miller 2020.

the Interdependence Project in 2011. She also studied in the Insight tradition with PoC teachers Gina Sharpe, Spring Washam, and DaRa Williams, to name a few, before entering the advanced course at Spirit Rock. In addition to her somatic-based work with individual clients and organizations, Johnson now works with well-known mindfulness teachers Tara Brach and Jack Kornfield as a meditation and DEIA (diversity, equity, inclusion, and accessibility) consultant. In 2021, Johnson published *Radical Friendship: Seven Ways to Love Yourself and Find Your People in an Unjust World*, which she intends as "a guide to reopening spaces for collective friendship."[42]

Johnson's elaboration of the Buddhist teaching on spiritual friendship (*kalyāṇa mittatā*) is aimed at bringing about liberatory relationships, what she refers to as "radical friendships," at the personal, community, and societal levels. The idea for her book grew from a short talk that she presented at the Buddhist Geeks conference in 2013, titled "Waking Up to Power and Privilege in Our Communities." Johnson used the image of a gated community—the sort of place a Black teenager might get shot just for wearing a hoodie and looking out of place to a security guard—to describe the racial homogeneity and willful "color-blindness" of many Buddhist spiritual communities. Relying on the softening effect of first-person plural pronouns as she delivered her message to a mostly white audience, she called upon Buddhists ("us") to use the power of mindful reflection to address their own ("our own") implicit bias, and to do the work of inclusivity in their ("our") Buddhist communities. She also named the emotional and spiritual labor performed by Black practitioners such as herself when they show up in those white Buddhist spaces as the only person of color. Laughing about the time a white practitioner at a retreat asked her, "Why don't Black people like the Dharma?" she quipped: "We love the Buddha. We're down with the Dharma. . . . Don't talk to us about the Sangha."[43]

Radical Friendship started with the core idea that "as practitioners of Buddhist meditation, our training could uniquely position us to uproot racial bias and other forms of delusion—if we were willing to apply our practice to those particular forms of suffering."[44] Borrowing from insights from transformative justice thinkers such as adrienne marie brown, Johnson grounds her discussion in the notion that racial and other forms of structural violence occur at all levels of relationship—institutions, communities, families, friendships, or romantic relationships—and must be healed at all levels as well. In her book, Johnson traverses these levels, from the culture of white supremacy to bad roommate vibes, moving up and down registers to offer a comprehensive relational Buddhist practice for a more just world.

For Johnson, dancer and yogi, "Mindfulness isn't a thought. It's a full-bodied sensory experience."[45] Like Manuel and many other Black Buddhist teachers, Johnson describes experiences of marginalization as a person inhabiting a queer Black body, and locates

---

[42] Johnson 2021, 1.
[43] https://www.youtube.com/watch?v=ZM9I9gj77Nk. Last accessed August 3, 2022.
[44] Johnson 2021, 6.
[45] Ibid., 164.

liberation in that same body. For instance, in her reflections on the Buddhist friendship practice of "not abandoning," Johnson advises loyalty and gratitude toward the body, even though, or especially because, it is a storehouse of trauma and something often objectified, sexualized, and pathologized. Johnson does not, in fact, refer to specific bodies in this section, but writes, neutrally, that "[o]ur bodies receive our attention as love, and under the soft glow of loving awareness, knots start to unwind and deep holdings start to release."[46] Still, the framing of her book in terms of transformative justice, as well as Johnson's centering of her own experiences as a mixed-race Black queer woman, suggests to the reader that her teaching on loyalty to the body as a Buddhist practice is particularly important for Black bodies, queer bodies, and female-identified bodies.

LGBTQI+ Buddhist Teachers and Practitioners

In the American context, Buddhist communities have been tolerant of LGBTQI+ individuals, but not necessarily welcoming. Larry Yang, a prominent queer meditation teacher of Color in the Insight tradition, recounts an early experience of attending a ten-day residential retreat focused on the practice of *mettā* (often translated as "loving kindness"). Rather than feeling lovingly held by the retreat experience, Yang felt instead "awkward, lonely, and even unsafe," affirming his view that despite their aspirations to universal love, spiritual communities were "typically unable, unwilling, or unskilled at directing love toward those aspects of life important to *me*, someone outside the dominant hetero-normative American culture."[47] Building on pioneering efforts to create community spaces for LGBTQI+ identified Buddhist practitioners by Arinna Weisman and Eric Kolvig, Yang was instrumental in founding the East Bay Meditation Center (EBMC), alongside J. D. Doyle, in 2007. EBMC was, from the beginning, organized around the primary aim of incorporating cultural diversity into Dharma practice and supporting underrepresented communities. Among its practice groups, which include a people of color sangha and groups for teens and people with disabilities, is the Alphabet Sangha, whose membership is limited to LGTBQIA+ individuals.[48]

Caitriona Reed, trained in both the Zen and Insight traditions, and co-founder of the Manzanita Village Retreat Center in Southern California, is said to be the first American Buddhist teacher to come out as transgender.[49] In 1998, Reed published an

---

[46] Johnson 2021, 166.
[47] Yang 2017, 83.
[48] See Gleig 2012.
[49] For a more recent and different trans perspective on Buddhist practice in America, see Buckner 2020.

essay titled "Coming Out Whole" in *Inquiring Mind* (a long-standing Buddhist magazine that is no longer in print) in which she described her coming out journey, the role that Buddhism played in that journey, and the ways that living into her transgender identity released a "softness" in her body and a "sweetness and energy in her life." Not passing as a woman (at that time) and six-foot-two-inches tall, she also articulated the wish to visibly and physically "challenge the rigidity of gender stereotypes" that are so dangerous to live outside of and that result in so much violence to gender nonconforming people.[50]

Tricycle magazine republished Reed's essay in honor of Pride month in 2019. Also in 2019, *Tricycle* published a new interview with Reed entitled "A Transgender Buddhist Trailblazer 20+ Years Later." Noting her earlier emphasis on the nonbinary, fluid nature of her gender experience, the interviewer questioned Reed about how core Buddhist teachings on nondual awareness informed her transgender identity. Reed responded, "Non-dualism lays the ground for questioning any binary system—in our context, normative heterocentric notions regarding sexual orientation and gender. Non-dual implies no binary. No doubt there's an ethical component too: refraining from judging others based on an unexamined, inherently binary, notions about people, situations, and events." She then connected the anxiety of her own "big scary decision" to the more ordinary unease of even cisgendered heterosexual individuals "looking for a greater ability to relax in the ambiguity they feel in their own identity."[51] Such people may not be transgender, gay, or overtly genderqueer, she notes, but they share an aspect of queerness. Thus, offering herself as an embodied teaching on nonduality and impermanence in place of a fixed notion of the self, Reed generously seeks to expand, sweeten, and soften fixed identity categories for everyone.

Reed's generous interpretation of queerness to include some straight cisgendered people does not dilute her understanding of the importance of LGBTQI + exclusive spaces in sanghas. The Alphabet Sangha members interviewed by Ann Gleig for her ethnographic study of EBMC stressed their invisibility and alienation in predominantly straight Buddhist spaces. One explained to Gleig, "If queer identity isn't addressed explicitly it can prevent queers practicing as they often feel isolated in straight spiritual communities."[52] Responding to this felt isolation, Kevin Manders expresses his wish to connect trans, genderqueer, and nonbinary Buddhists to one another through the publication in 2019 of a collection of essays by trans Buddhists that he co-edited with Elizabeth Marston. "This book has helped with healing my heart," he writes, "and I hope it does the same for yours."[53]

---

[50] Reed 2019.
[51] Reed and Newton 2019.
[52] Gleig 2012, 207. See also Hu 2017.
[53] Manders 2019, 2.

Buddhist Survivors of Sexual Abuse and Their Advocates

Buddhist survivors of sexual abuse, many of whom are white cisgender females, also experience the effects of marginalization in American sanghas.[54] They feel unsafe, unseen, and silenced in their communities, and their experiences are routinely denied or rationalized through the pernicious use of Buddhist teachings. As a result, they often choose to leave their communities in hopes of finding another that feels safer, and sometimes they abandon the Buddhist path altogether. Their stories are also not well represented in Buddhist studies scholarship, a reflection of their systemic erasure. Like ordained Buddhist women, immigrant lay women, Black Buddhist teachers, and queer Buddhist teachers, however, abuse survivors and their advocates are shaping American Buddhism by interpreting Buddhist doctrines and restructuring Buddhist communities in alignment with their own experiences. Some of them are speaking out against abusive teachers and complicit sanghas on social media and in the popular press, others are creating new ethics and grievance policies for existing communities, and still others are creating trauma-informed Buddhist spaces that attend carefully to configurations of power and sexual ethics.

Revelations of sexually abusive teachers have rocked American Buddhist sanghas since the 1980s, but only a small number of prominent Buddhist teachers, some themselves survivors, have responded to these revelations. One such leader is Willa Blythe Baker, a qualified teacher in the Kagyu lineage of Tibetan Buddhism, who has spoken powerfully and publicly about her own experiences of sexual abuse. Baker was involved in a long-term secret sexual relationship with her Tibetan teacher, Lama Norlha Rinpoche, who initiated the liaison just a few days after he ordained her as a celibate Buddhist nun. Years after Baker ended her relationship with Norlha and left his community at Kagyu Thubten Choling monastery (KTC), she learned of several other women who had also been involved in secret sexual relationships with him. Wishing to prevent further harm and break the secrecy that had up to this point protected Norlha from accountability, Baker began to take steps to bring the situation to the attention of the KTC community. This included the initiation of a formal public disclosure process at KTC in 2017 during which Baker and one other woman read impact statements aloud and a taped apology from Norlha was screened.[55] Since that time, Baker has

---

[54] In the case of Triratna, a community started in the 1960s by Dennis Lingwood, a British man, known by his Buddhist name, Sangharakshita, the survivors are male. More recently, allegations against the Karmapa have come from three Asian women.

[55] Deveaux 2017. A civil law case was filed in New York State in November 2023 on behalf of three women alleging that Norlha inflicted psychological coercion, physical violence, and sexual abuse, including rape.

published a number of detailed articles in Buddhist publications narrating her own confusion, emotional harm, and journey toward healing, and offering specific advice for survivors and their allies.[56] She has also been active in supporting other survivors of Buddhist sexual abuse, working at times with Zen teachers Jan Chozen Bays and Grace Schireson, and a lawyer with expertise in corporate sexual harassment law, Carol Merchasin.

Baker, who completed two three-year retreats and earned a PhD from Harvard Divinity School, is the founding teacher of the Natural Dharma Fellowship (NDF), based in Boston, Massachusetts, and the co–spiritual director of the affiliated Wonderwell Retreat Center alongside Liz Monson. Baker and Monson take as their mission "bringing the practices of Tibetan Buddhism into the contemporary world in accessible, relevant, and creative ways."[57] In characterizing NDF's approach and relationship to Tibetan Buddhist lineage teachings, Baker uses the term "mindful pruning." The socioreligious structures of Tibetan Buddhism are, Baker explains, "caught up in institutionalized patriarchy." While professing a deep love and respect for the tradition in which she was trained, Baker believes that "we really do need to think deeply about how we are going to undermine patriarchy in our own traditions and replace it with egalitarian dharma. This involves a lot of micro-choices."[58] As an example, the NDF sangha does not recite the long lineage prayers customary in Tibetan Buddhist sanghas. While the community does practice with lineage prayers, these are selected or re-translated to reflect a more equal gender balance.

Baker's approach to leading the NDF community, as well as her commitment to accessible and relevant Dharma teachings, has been shaped by her formative but abusive relationship with Lama Norlha. In an impactful 2018 *Lion's Roar* article, Baker reflects on this journey and its radical effects on her own understanding of Buddhist teachings. She writes:

> I wondered whether disillusionment is not in fact the plague of the spiritual path but rather its catalyst. Don't get me wrong—I would not wish this experience on anyone or any community. But perhaps true refuge can't be found without a falling away of our false sense of security. It may be that the deepest teachings are not the ones transmitted in the dharma hall but rather the life experiences that challenge everything we believed to be true.[59]

In the same essay, Baker tackles the controversial issue of *samaya*, often understood in Western Vajrayāna Buddhism to denote a relationship in which the student accepts her teacher's actions and requests as enlightened teachings, no matter what they might be.

---

[56] Baker 2017, 2018, 2019.
[57] https://naturaldharma.org/natural-dharma-fellowship/. Last accessed August 20, 2022.
[58] Interview, May 25, 2022.
[59] Baker 2018.

Baker challenges what she feels is a misinterpretation, stressing transparency and mutual accountability over obedience. Similarly, Baker critiques the hierarchical pyramid-like structures usual in Vajrayāna communities, with teachers occupying the throne at the front of the Dharma hall and a place of unquestioned authority at the head of communities. By contrast, the authority structure and community processes of NDF are designed to be a consensus-based system of checks and balances, where nobody makes decisions alone, and teachers, community, and board members must answer to one another. This nonhierarchical "community of circles" or mandala approach[60] reflects Baker's commitment to a horizontal "spiritual friendship" (rather than guru-based) teaching model in the wake of abuse. Notably, Baker, Monson, and other members of NDF modeled their governing structure on the Unitarian Universalist Church and a Boston-based nonprofit organization called Haley House, not on any American Buddhist communities.[61]

Conclusion

Attempting to describe gender and sexuality in American Buddhism without an intersectional lens that also analyzes other dimensions of identity and experience inevitably leads to distortions. Accounts of gender and sexuality that repeat the dominant narrative about a more gender-egalitarian convert Buddhism in America have disproportionately elevated the stories of the white cisgender middle-class women, while obscuring other perspectives, and even, in the case of sexual abuse, certain aspects of the white cisgender experience. This chapter intentionally gives space to female-identified, trans, and queer Buddhists doing innovative work and shaping the landscape of American Buddhism in ways simultaneously informed by gender identity and/or sexual orientation *and* other strong aspects of identity and social position, especially race and ethnicity but also celibacy and survivorhood.[62] Acceptance and equal access have not, necessarily, been a hallmark of their lives as American Buddhists, contrary to dominant narratives. Their innovative interpretations of Buddhist teachings and lifeways are shaped, however, by their complex identities and experiences of disruption and violence, as are the Buddhist communities they found, lead, and join. In fact, Asian and Asian American lay women, women and queer Buddhists of color, monastic and other ordained women, trans individuals, and survivors of sexual abuse cannot really be said to be at the margins anymore; rather, the rich multidimensionality of contemporary American Buddhism is now in large part their creation.

---

[60] Baker 2022.
[61] Interview, May 25, 2022.
[62] A deeper reckoning with class as a factor in Buddhist identities and experiences is a desideratum.

References

Baker, Willa Blythe. 2017. "Advice for Women in a Secret Sexual Relationship with Their Buddhist Teacher." *Lion's Roar*. https://www.lionsroar.com/advice-for-women-in-a-secret-sexual-relationship-with-their-buddhist-teacher/.

Baker, Willa Blythe. 2018. "Breaking the Silence on Sexual Misconduct." *Lion's Roar*. https://www.lionsroar.com/breaking-the-silence-on-sexual-misconduct/.

Baker, Willa Blythe. 2019. "How You Can Support a Victim of Clergy Sexual Misconduct." *Lion's Roar*. https://www.lionsroar.com/support-victim-sexual-misconduct/.

Baker, Willa Blythe. 2022. "Building Blocks of Belonging." *Lion's Roar*. https://www.lionsroar.com/building-blocks-of-belonging/.

Boucher, Sandy. 1988. *Turning the Wheel: American Women Creating the New Buddhism*. Boston: Beacon Press.

Buckner, Ray. 2020. "Zen in Distress: Theorizing Gender Dysphoria and Traumatic Remembrance with Soto Zen Meditation." *Religions* 11: 582.

Deveaux, Tynette. 2017. "Kagyu Thubten Choling Addresses Sangha about Lama Norlha's Sexual Misconduct with Students." *Lion's Roar*. https://www.lionsroar.com/kagyu-thubten-choling-addresses-sangha-about-lama-norlha-rinpoches-sexual-misconduct-with-students/.

Gajaweera, Nalika. 2021. "Reclaiming Our So-called 'Cultural Baggage.'" *Lion's Roar*. https://www.lionsroar.com/reclaiming-our-so-called-cultural-baggage/.

Gleig, Ann. 2012. "Queering Buddhism or Buddhist De-Queering?" *Theology & Sexuality* 18, no. 3: 198–214.

Gleig, Ann. 2013. "From Buddhist Hippies to Buddhist Geeks: The Emergence of Buddhist Postmodernism?" *Journal of Global Buddhism* 15: 15–33.

Gleig, Ann, and Brenna Artinger. 2021. "#BuddhistCultureWars: BuddhaBros, Alt-Right Dharma, and Snowflake Sanghas." *Journal of Global Buddhism* 22, no. 1: 19–48.

Han, Chenxing. 2021. *Be the Refuge: Raising the Voices of Asian American Buddhists*. Berkeley, CA: North Atlantic Books.

Hickey, Wakoh Shannon. 2010. "Two Buddhisms, Three Buddhisms, and Racism." *Journal of Global Buddhism* 25: 1–25.

Ho, Tamara C. 2020. "Women of the Temple: Burmese Immigrants, Gender, and Buddhism in a U.S. Frame." In *Emerging Voices: Experiences of Underrepresented Asian Americans*, edited by Huping Ling, 183–198. New Brunswick, NJ: Rutgers University Press.

Hsu, Funie. 2017. "We've Been Here All Along." *Lion's Roar*. https://www.lionsroar.com/weve-been-here-all-along/

Hsu, Funie. 2021. "Those Poor Women." *Lion's Roar*. https://www.lionsroar.com/those-poor-women/.

Hu, Hsiao-lan. 2017. "Buddhism and Sexual Orientation." In *The Oxford Handbook of Contemporary Buddhism*, edited by Michael Jerryson, 662–677. New York: Oxford University Press.

Johnson, Kate. 2021. *Radical Friendship: Seven Ways to Love Yourself and Find Your People in an Unjust World*. Boulder, CA: Shambhala Publications.

Manders, Kevin. 2019. "Introduction." In *Transcending: Trans Buddhist Voices*, edited by Kevin Manders and Elizabeth Marston, 1–2. Berkeley, CA: North Atlantic Books.

Manuel, Zenju Earthlyn. 2015. *The Way of Tenderness: Awakening through Race, Sexuality, and Gender*. Somerville, MA: Wisdom Publications.

Manuel, Zenju Earthlyn. 2021a. "Making Offerings to Our Ancestors." *Lion's Roar*. https://www.lionsroar.com/making-offerings-to-our-ancestors/.

Manuel, Zenju Earthlyn. 2021b. "Sweeping my Heart." *Lion's Roar*. https://www.lionsroar.com/sweeping-my-heart/.

McNicholl, Adeana. 2018. "Being Buddha, Staying Woke: Racial Formation in Black Buddhist Writing." *Journal of the American Academy of Religion* 86, no. 4: 883–911.

McNicholl, Adeana. 2021. "Buddhism and Race in the United States." *Religion Compass* 15, no. 8: 1–13.

Miller, Andrea. 2020. "Historic Class of Diverse Dharma Teachers Graduates." *Lion's Roar*. https://www.lionsroar.com/historic-class-of-diverse-dharma-teachers-graduates/.

Mitchell, Scott A. 2016. *Buddhism in America*. London: Bloomsbury Academic.

Moon, Cristina. 2020. "From 'Just Culture' to a Just Culture." *Tricycle: A Buddhist Review*. https://tricycle.org/trikedaily/asian-american-erasure-buddhism/.

Mrozik, Susanne. 2009. "A Robed Revolution: The Contemporary Buddhist Nun's (Bhikṣuṇī) Movement," *Religion Compass* 3, no. 3: 360–378.

Perreira, Todd Leroy. 2008. "The Gender of Practice: Some Findings among Thai Buddhist Women in Northern California." In *Emerging Voices: Experiences of Underrepresented Asian Americans*, edited by Huping Ling, 160–182. New Brunswick, NJ: Rutgers University Press.

Reed, Caitriona. 2019. "Coming Out Whole." *Tricycle: the Buddhist Review*. https://tricycle.org/trikedaily/transgender-buddhist/.

Reed, Caitriona, with Jennifer DeMaio Newton. 2019. "A Transgender Buddhist Trailblazer 20+ Years Later." *Tricycle: A Buddhist Review*. https://tricycle.org/trikedaily/caitriona-reed/.

Seager, Richard Hughes. 1999. *Buddhism in America*. New York: Columbia University Press.

Suh, Sharon A. 2004. *Being Buddhist in a Christian World: Gender in a Korean American Temple*. Seattle: University of Washington Press.

Tsomo, Karma Lekshe. 2022. "Japanese Buddhist Women in Hawai'i: Waves of Change." *Pacific World* 4, no. 3: 25–51.

Usuki, Patricia Kanaya. 2007. *Currents of Change: American Buddhist Women Speak Out on Jodo Shinshu*. Berkeley, CA: Institute of Buddhist Studies.

"Women in American Buddhism." The Pluralism Project. Harvard University. https://pluralism.org/women-in-american-buddhism. Last accessed December 28, 2022.

Vesely-Flad, Rima. 2022. *Black Buddhists and the Black Radical Tradition: The Practice of Stillness in the Movement for Liberation*. New York: New York University Press.

Yang, Larry. 2017. *Awakening Together: The Spiritual Practice of Inclusivity and Community* Someville, MA: Wisdom Publications.

CHAPTER 5

AMERICAN BUDDHIST STUDIES AND SCHOLAR-PRACTITIONERS

SCOTT A. MITCHELL

Introduction

In the early 1950s, a visiting scholar of Tibetan Buddhism from Japan, Tokan Tada, was in the San Francisco Bay Area. He regularly gave lectures at Stanford University as well as the American Academy of Asian Studies, founded in 1951. Tada was also friends with the resident minister of the Berkeley Buddhist Temple and his wife, Kanmo and Jane Imamura. During this period, they had developed a robust educational program at their temple, one that attracted many notable figures in the Beat and West Coast countercultural movements. These programs also attracted young Buddhist studies scholars such as Alex Wayman. Tada spent the bulk of 1953 at the Berkeley Temple working with the Imamuras and other young students in the community translating the *Śrīmālādevī Siṃhanāda Sūtra* and the *Vimalakīrti Nirdeśa Sūtra*. Neither of these translations was published in its entirety, though Wayman, who undoubtedly met his wife Hideko at the temple, would later go on to a rather successful career as a Buddhist scholar and would publish his own translation of the *Śrīmālādevī* in the 1970s.[1]

This brief anecdote is used to illustrate how Buddhist studies scholars, from both Asia and North America, and American Buddhist practitioners have often and in a quite literal sense been in the same room, how their histories have overlapped and intersected. This should not be surprising. As detailed in several chapters of this volume, Buddhists have been living and practicing in North America since the mid-nineteenth century.

---

[1] Scott A. Mitchell, *The Making of American Buddhism* (New York: Oxford University Press, 2023), 153–156.

Whereas Buddhist studies got its start in the nineteenth century, its North American iteration more fully developed during the immediate decades after World War II. The histories of American Buddhism and Buddhist studies are coterminous.

This chapter thus has two aims. First, I trace out the history of academic Buddhist studies generally and the subfield of American Buddhism studies[2] specifically, and I pay particular attention to the intersections between communities of Buddhist scholars and communities of Buddhist practice. Second, and more importantly, I focus on the implications of these intersections. To the extent that Buddhist studies as a field has retained some of its colonialist and orientalist assumptions about religions, cultures, and their study, scholars continue to privilege an objectivist scholarship that assumes a sharp distinction between "insiders" and "outsiders" to the tradition. However, to the extent that Buddhist studies scholars and Buddhist practitioners are often interconnected and intertwined via specific contexts, institutions, and networks, is this distinction even possible? What might a collapsing of the insider/outsider dichotomy mean for the ideal of objective scholarship? And what new research vistas are opened by refocusing our gaze from the individual of the "scholar-practitioner" to the interconnected communities that most scholars inhabit?

Buddhist Studies as a Field

Buddhist studies began as an orientalist project. I make this claim to foreground the primary aims of early scholarship on Buddhism, both colonial and philological. Whereas colonialism implies the displacement and genocide of Indigenous peoples, colonization also includes the active *control* of colonized persons. For example, in the case of British colonial rule over South Asia, the colonial project included the process of collecting knowledge of local culture, customs, and systems of government, which were then deployed in the service of colonial management. By exploiting knowledge of caste-based Indian politics, British colonial civil servants elevated local and Indigenous bureaucrats and magistrates in service of the Crown and at the expense of the Indian people. It is thus within the context of knowledge gathering for the purposes of colonial control that the project of orientalist scholarship emerged.

To be an "orientalist" in the "long nineteenth century" meant to be a specialist in the cultures, peoples, flora, and fauna of the "Orient"—essentially everything east of the

---

[2] As will be discussed later in this chapter, there is no clearly defined "subfield" of American Buddhist studies. There are specific programs and publications—such as the Buddhism in the West Unit at the American Academy of Religion or the journals *Global Buddhism* and *Contemporary Buddhism*—which prioritize scholarship in non-Asian locales. But the very title of these projects speaks to the porous and fuzzy boundaries of "the West." This chapter, located within a volume on "American Buddhism," is concerned with scholarship on Buddhism in the United States or North America more broadly.

Mediterranean. Orientalist scholars in South and East Asia came into contact with a wide array of cultic and religious practices from Benares to Kyoto which, at first glance, seemed wildly dissimilar. Over time, however, it became clear that these practices all had a common origin in the Indian sage Siddhartha Gautama, the Buddha. Thus, vast resources were expended to study the histories and texts associated with the Buddha and the religion that was founded in his name. At the same time, orientalist projects were also linked to the burgeoning field of philology. The similarities between such disparate languages as Sanskrit and Latin suggested to European philologists a common origin, one that could be variously understood as either a uniting feature of a "brotherhood of man" or as proof of one culture's inherent superiority over others—a project directly linked to the racial politics of Aryanism, as discussed elsewhere in this volume. It was within this complex of colonial control and European chauvinism that the academic study of Buddhism began.

Stanley Abe's contribution to the seminal 1995 volume *Curators of the Buddha* well describes the colonialist construction of knowledge on Buddhism in his summary of Rudyard Kipling's novel *Kim*. The novel's opening scene depicts a meeting at the Lahore Museum between a British curator and art historian and a Tibetan lama on pilgrimage to Buddhist sacred sites. The curator (who claims "I am here to gather knowledge") leads the lama on a tour of the museum and explains the artifacts and artworks collected therein by reference to French and English scholarly books. To the lama's amazement, the curator even has photographs of his own monastery, evidence of the reach of colonial control and surveillance. However, during the tour the curator is pleased to discover that the lama is not an ignorant mendicant but a scholar in his own right. "This is an important distinction in the West," writes Abe, "where scholarship, grounded in notions of scientific objectivity that require critical distance, is juxtaposed to subjective expressions such as religious faith."[3] Abe's reading of *Kim* thus illustrates the processes of colonial knowledge collection:

> In the idealized world of the [museum], Buddhist images are by definition alien and different, yet under certain circumstances, that is, through appropriate interpretative and disciplinary techniques, they are totally knowable. The Curator, in possession of the material remains of Buddhist art, the stacks of European books, and the training of an art historian, directs the process through which the incommensurable, Buddhist art, is transformed and rendered recuperable to the West as a version of the known. Such an appropriation is only possible, however, through the meticulous control and, when necessary, exclusion of the native presence, their history and their voice, from the discourse of art history. In one respect, this procedure must delete certain traces of otherness in order to possess Buddhist art as the other. In another respect, the difference that necessarily marks Buddhist art as alien must be maintained even as art history seeks to incorporate Buddhist art into Western knowledge. This is

---

[3] Stanley K. Abe, "Inside the Wonder House: Buddhist Art and the West," in *Curators of the Buddha: The Study of Buddhism under Colonialism*, ed. Donald S. Lopez (Chicago: University of Chicago Press, 1995), 66.

the operation of colonial discourse as an apparatus of power "that turns on the recognition and disavowal of racial/cultural/historical differences."[4]

It has become passé among scholars to make the claim that "Buddhism" is a Western invention to the extent that Buddhism-as-religion emerged within the contexts of colonialism. This claim, however, obscures how colonialism was the context for not only the invention of "Buddhism" but also the invention of "Buddhist studies"; and it further obscures the role played by Buddhists in the construction of both Buddhism and Buddhist studies. In short, local and Indigenous Buddhists cooperated with colonial civil servants in the construction of what we now take for granted as Buddhism. As but one example, Brian Houghton Hodgson is well known for his role in sending Sanskrit texts to Eugène Burnouf. But Hodgson's ability to send these texts to Paris was entirely contingent on his relationship with a local *pandit*, Amritananda. Amritananda's motivations were a complicated mix of both the political and the religious, whatever those terms may mean. Leaving that issue aside (as we can never know exactly what motivated the *pandit* to collaborate with the civil servant), it is simply a matter of fact that local Buddhists were always engaged in the process of defining Buddhism during the colonial period. Other examples, such as the Sri Lankan monk Hikkaduve Sumangala and of course Anagarika Dhamarapala, attest to Asian Buddhists' engagement with and reaction to the forces of colonialism which sought to define Buddhism as a modern religion.[5] Simply put, to claim that Asian Buddhists were the passive victims of a Western project that sought to define their religion for them, that they were not active participants in this project, is to replicate the orientalist move of simultaneously disavowing and representing the "other" and does nothing to advance our understanding of the field's history.

Moreover, this early period of (Western) Buddhist studies was not free from polemical accounts of the tradition. In addition to Burnouf's early translation of Buddhist texts, another important moment in the history of Buddhist studies was the establishment of the Pali Text Society by the Rhys Davidses (as discussed by Emory-Moore and Calobrisi, Chapters 1 and 2 in this volume). The Society's foundation and ongoing influence illuminate several important aspects of modern academic Buddhist studies and its methodological assumptions. First, being primarily concerned with the translation of the Pali canon, we see the field's focus on the *text*. The textual turn, of course, is a hallmark of a Protestant-influenced Buddhist modernism whereby the text becomes more authoritative than either ecclesiastic authorities or the living tradition.[6] Second, as the *Pali* Text Society, we see the elevation of the Pali canon as more authoritative than other Buddhist textual traditions and the concomitant focus on the "founder" over and

---

[4] Ibid., 69.

[5] As but one example, see Anne M. Blackburn, *Locations of Buddhism: Colonialism and Modernity in Sri Lanka* (Chicago: University of Chicago Press, 2010).

[6] Broadly speaking, this process is described as detraditionalization by McMahan. See David L. McMahan, *The Making of Buddhist Modernism* (New York: Oxford University Press, 2008).

against the living tradition. This focus on the Pali canon as representative of an "original" Buddhism rests on the uncritically accepted belief that all Pali texts are necessarily older than other Indic sources, conveniently aligns with modern Theravāda apologetics, and is, at the end of the day, an example of the appeal to tradition logical fallacy. Finally, as will be discussed later in this chapter, whereas Thomas Rhys Davids and the Pali Text Society are often centered in histories of academic Buddhist studies, we should be mindful of the polemical nature of his writings; that is, whereas contemporary Buddhist studies scholars may want to claim a critical distance from the tradition, some of our founding figures did not live up to this ideal.

These colonial-era projects shaped many of the theoretical and methodological assumptions of early Buddhist studies; however, the actual *field* of Buddhist studies as we know it is really a twentieth-century—and more specifically a post–World War II—project. At the turn of the twentieth century, the fields of theology and religious studies were growing more and more distinct. Whereas theology at the time was almost by definition a normative Christian project, religious studies was concerned more with the study of non-Christian religions, on the one hand, and the "hermeneutics of suspicion," on the other. Following from nineteenth-century critiques of religion by Freud, Marx, and Nietzsche, among others, religious faith was seen as something of a character flaw, and religious cultures, histories, and practices as something which could, and *should*, be studied at a distance.[7] Or, as we saw earlier in Abe's read of *Kim*, it was assumed that scholarship ought to be grounded in scientific objectivity. In the later part of the twentieth century, however, and especially in the ecumenical wake of Vatican II, the field of religious studies grew increasingly diverse both in terms of its methods and the religious traditions under study. Nevertheless, it has more or less maintained its distance from theology by drawing a distinction between descriptive and normative studies. In short, whereas theology is something done by committed religious persons from within the tradition, religious studies is presumed to be done from outside the tradition, at a distance.

By the mid-twentieth century, at the conclusion of World War II and the end of direct European colonial control over much of "the Orient," Cold War politics replaced and replicated the colonial project of managing and controlling the non-Western world. That is, in the power vacuum of a postcolonial Asia and in the West's fight against global communism, how might the emergent superpower of the United States control and manage the "other" as a bulwark against Soviet-style socialism? It was in this context that the area studies took hold in North American universities. Via either direct government funding or via clandestine means (e.g., the Asia Foundation[8]), area studies

---

[7] Ann Gleig, "Researching New Religious Movements from the Inside Out and the Outside In," *Nova Religio: The Journal of Alternative and Emergent Religions* 16, no. 1 (2012): 88–103.

[8] See Laura Harrington, "The Greatest Movie Never Made: The Life of the Buddha as Cold War Politics," *Religion and American Culture* 30, no. 3 (2020): 397–425; and Justin Ritzinger, "Tinker, Tailor, Scholar, Spy: Holmes Welch, Buddhism, and the Cold War," *Journal of Global Buddhism* 22, no. 2 (2021): 421–441.

was extremely well funded in the postwar years, allowing a generation of scholars to focus their attention on learning the languages, cultures, and religions of discrete areas of Asia. This influx of cash and (re)turn to the Orient had enormous benefits for a generation of Buddhist studies scholars who were able to do necessary language training and secure employment. It is worth noting that in addition to replicating the colonialist project of gathering knowledge on the "other" for the benefit of the "West," this era of scholarship was also directed on Buddhist cultures, histories, locales, and persons that were necessarily outside of the United States. As we will see in a moment, this had a direct impact on the development American Buddhism studies.

This era of Buddhist studies was, in a sense, without a home. As Jose Cabezón and others have noted, during the 1950s and 1960s, most buddhologists were trained in area studies departments; most scholarship was being published in country-specific journals; and many scholars presented their work at the Association for Asian Studies.[9] Over the course of the 1960s and 1970s, however, the situation changed dramatically. Religious studies as a field had continued to develop, diversify, and establish itself within higher educational institutions, leading to the situation where most of the scholars who received their PhDs in the 1960s did not stay in area studies but instead found appointments in religious studies departments. To date, Cabezón notes, only two of the more than two dozen programs in North American universities that offer advanced degrees in Buddhist studies are in departments associated with area studies—the rest are all in religious studies departments.[10] More importantly, the 1970s saw the founding of the International Association of Buddhist Studies and its related journal, which represents "a decision on the part of buddhologists to fashion an identity, an institutional home, separate from Asian Studies."[11] Additionally, by the late 1970s and into the 1980s, scholars began gravitating toward the American Academy of Religion (AAR) which, since the 1960s, had become increasingly diverse and open to the academic study of non-Christian religions. By 1980, George Bond, Colleen Cox, Leslie Kawamura, and Charles Prebish had firmly established the Buddhist Studies Unit at the annual AAR meeting, and to this day the Unit remains one of the primary academic homes for Buddhist studies scholars in the Anglophone world.

Whereas Cabezón well details the rise and diversification of Buddhist studies within the AAR and its associated journal, he also makes the following, somewhat offhand, observation:

> In the early 2000s several of us who were keen on adding Buddhist Theology to the portfolio of our scholarly activities had proposed paper panels to the Buddhism [Unit] but met resistance. (For a variety of reasons that lie beyond the scope of

---

[9] José I. Cabezón, "2020 AAR Presidential Address: The Study of Buddhism and the AAR," *Journal of the American Academy of Religion* 89, no. 3 (2021): 793–818.

[10] Cabezón, "2020 AAR Presidential Address," 794 n.4.

[11] Ibid., 802.

this address, Buddhist Studies has never been hospitable to normative, theological work.)[12]

Whereas over the past two decades the field of Buddhist studies has diversified methodologically, and whereas since 2019 the AAR's Buddhism Unit has held several important and self-reflective panels on the field that push at its boundaries, Cabezón's observation here that the field has generally been inhospitable to normative studies is well taken. Indeed, whereas the field of Buddhist studies has increasingly welcomed studies on Buddhism and Buddhists outside Asia and has embraced methods and theoretical perspectives beyond philology, at the end of the twentieth century the colonial-era assumption that the proper focus of Buddhist studies is Asia and the text remained largely unchallenged; and perhaps the first buddhologist to challenge this assumption was Charles Prebish.

In the 1970s, curious to learn more about the growing number of Buddhist communities in North America, Prebish set out to research the phenomenon. He was almost immediately met with resistance on the assumption that there was no Buddhism in America. Nevertheless, he persisted, and his 1979 volume, *American Buddhism*, was one of the first sustained studies of Buddhism outside Asia.[13] Despite this landmark study, very little scholarship was directed toward American Buddhism over the subsequent two decades. By the turn of the twenty-first century, however, the situation changed dramatically. The past twenty years have seen a marked increase in the number of monographs, edited volumes, special editions, and entire journals dedicated to the study of Buddhisms outside Asia. In 2008, the Buddhism in the West Unit was begun at the AAR, in large part due to the efforts of Jeff Wilson. And major conferences such as those held at the Institute of Buddhist Studies in Berkeley in 2010 signaled the growth and professionalization of the subfield.

In his contribution to the 2008 volume *North American Buddhists in Social Context*, Paul David Numrich argues that establishing a field of study requires specialization, organization, and publication. In the case of American Buddhism studies, the (sub)field meets the second two criteria, as evidenced by the wealth of scholarly publications, dissertations, journals, and monographs, and professional organizations such as the Buddhism in the West Unit and conferences dedicated to the subject. Numrich defines "specialization" as "scholarly training, theoretical assumptions, technical terminology, and research questions and methods" which more or less define the parameters of study within the field.[14] Specialization in the (sub)field of American Buddhism studies can be seen in the repeated focus and ongoing research on such topics as acculturation and

---

[12] Ibid., 813.

[13] See Charles S. Prebish, *American Buddhism* (North Scituate, MA: Duxbury Press, 1979); and Charles S. Prebish, *Luminous Passage: The Practice and Study of Buddhism in America* (Berkeley: University of California Press, 1999).

[14] Paul David Numrich, "North American Buddhists: A Field of Study?," in *North American Buddhists in Social Context*, ed. Paul David Numrich (Boston: Brill, 2008), 1.

cultural adaptation; globalization, localization, and transnational studies; and the ever-present "two Buddhisms" debate, which remains something of a thorn in the field's side.[15] However, here we turn our attention to a different research question central to the field of American Buddhism studies, one that was first articulated by Prebish—namely, the role of the scholar-practitioner. It is worth recalling here that American Buddhism studies emerged within the larger field of Buddhist studies at a particular moment in history wherein scholars were more or less focused exclusively on Asia and the text; that the field had inherited specific methodological assumptions from its colonialist and orientalist legacy; and that there was an overall assumption in the field of religious studies that scholarship ought to be conducted at a distance, by outsiders to the religious traditions under study. Prebish's early work on scholar-practitioners, however, demonstrated that there was an ever-increasing number of North American Buddhist studies scholars who also identified as Buddhists (publicly or privately). The existence of "scholar-practitioners" thus raises important questions regarding the ideal of "scientific objectivity" the field was purportedly founded upon, an issue to which we now turn.

Scholar-Practitioners and the "Silent Sangha"

In his contribution to Williams and Quuen's *American Buddhism: Methods and Findings in Recent Scholarship* (1999), Prebish makes the claim that half of all Buddhist scholars are also Buddhist practitioners, but half of these "scholar-practitioners" are afraid to self-identify as such. This hesitancy to be "openly Buddhist" is, according to Prebish, a reflection of the assumption that good scholarship is necessarily done at an arm's length from the tradition, reflecting the hermeneutics of suspicion embedded within religious studies, as noted earlier. Prebish quotes Cabezón here, who states plainly: "Critical distance from the object of intellectual analysis is necessary. Buddhists, by virtue of their religious commitment, lack such critical distance from Buddhism."[16] Prebish's work, however, complicates this assumption. After all, several foundational figures in Buddhist studies were also practicing Buddhists. Anecdotally, Prebish describes a visit to the University of Wisconsin by Edward Conze, "the world's foremost scholar of that complicated form of Mahāyāna literature known as *prajñāpāramitā*," during which he admitted to a student that he practiced Buddhist meditation.[17] In his surveys of

---

[15] Mitchell, *The Making of American Buddhism*, 160.
[16] Charles S. Prebish, "The Academic Study of Buddhism in America: A Silent Sangha," in *American Buddhism: Methods and Findings in Recent Scholarship*, ed. Dunan Ryûken Williams and Christopher S. Queen (New York: Curzon, 1999), 190.
[17] Ibid., 183.

academic Buddhist studies at the close of the twentieth century, Prebish does not necessarily name who self-identifies as a Buddhist or not, but his list of Buddhist studies faculty at major institutions across North America certainly includes many figures who are also well-known as self-identified and practicing Buddhists.[18]

Many of the scholars whom Prebish identifies as "scholar-practitioners" are, like Prebish himself, converts to the tradition. However, I believe it is important to note that the postwar generation of North American Buddhist studies scholars includes some foundational figures who were born and raised in the tradition, a tradition which itself was established in North America in the late nineteenth century. As but one example, we may look to Masatoshi Nagatomi. Prebish describes Nagatomi as one of the "leading professors" of a postwar Buddhist studies boom due to his appointment to a position at Harvard University. This appointment led to Harvard becoming one of the most important Buddhist studies programs in North America. Nagatomi was born into a Jōdo Shinshū Buddhist family, one that was illegally incarcerated during World War II due to anti-Japanese hysteria in the first half of the century. Nagatomi's father held Buddhist services as Manzanar, as documented by Williams in his *American Sutra*.[19] Furthermore, another "leading professor" of the era, Richard Robinson, who was instrumental in establishing the highly respected Buddhist studies program at the University of Wisconsin, had his first encounter with Buddhism via another Jōdo Shinshū priest in Alberta, Canada, Yutetsu Kawamura; Kawamura's son, Leslie, as we saw earlier, was one of the founders of the Buddhism Unit at the AAR.[20] These connections between North American academic Buddhist studies and preexisting North American Buddhist communities complicate the assumption that critical distance is a necessary component of good scholarship. There appears to be little "distance" between communities of scholarship and practice. Moreover, to the extent that persons such as Nagatomi and Kawamura were raised within a Buddhist community with its own tradition of scholarship, one wonders whether the dual-identity of "scholar-practitioner" would have had the same problematic valences it did for later converts. Leaving aside such speculations, the point here is to simply note that there are different ways an individual may relate to the tradition and to draw our attention to the already existing scholar-practitioners in the field who have made sizable contributions.

Following on the work of Prebish, Mikael Aktor takes up the question of religious self-identification in his article "Asymmetrical Religious Commitments? Religious Practice, Identity, and Self-Presentation among Western Scholars of Hinduism and Buddhism." Aktor's approach is comparative—what is the relationship between scholarly study and personal practice in Buddhist studies as compared to Hindu studies? Aktor begins with the anecdotal reflection that it appears scholar-practitioners are more welcome in Buddhist studies and attempts to quantify this observation via public statements and

---

[18] Ibid., 204–205.
[19] Duncan Ryûken Williams, *American Sutra: A Story of Faith and Freedom in the Second World War* (Cambridge, MA: Harvard University Press, 2019).
[20] Mitchell, *The Making of American Buddhism*, 170.

surveys conducted on scholarly list-servs. In short, the situation is complicated. As we have seen, in the early decades of the twenty-first century, Buddhist studies has grown more welcome to a diversification of perspectives, methodologies, and field sites. As such, the "Buddhist Theology" project Cabezón mentioned eventually did find a home at the AAR in the form of the Buddhist Critical-Constructive Reflection Unit, which sets itself apart from other Buddhism-related units by being self-consciously normative. According to Aktor, the same is not true in Hindu studies. "Books by Western scholars of Hinduism of the sort that I am specialized in, i.e., in classical Brahminical textual tradition, generally tend to be written by authors who seem distanced from these traditions: 'objective' academics who study 'another culture.'"[21] Part of the reason for this asymmetry, Aktor suggests, has to do with the lingering association between the practice of Hinduism and ethno-nationalist Indian identity. Leaving that aside, however, Aktor's work strongly suggests that in the two decades since Prebish did his initial surveys, not only has Buddhist studies grown more accepting of "normative" scholarship, but the number of self-identified and "out" scholar-practitioners may be considerably higher.

Oddly, Aktor's approach is to focus on what he terms "Western scholars," and it is clear that by "Western" he means "white." He notes that whereas "Western academic departments of Hindu and Buddhist scholarship include immigrants, or descendants of immigrants, from countries with Hindu and Buddhist cultures," for the purposes of his study he does not include them.[22] The reason for this exclusion is so that he can compare the experiences of "ethnically Western" (read "white") scholars across academic disciplines, presumably because they share the same cultural and racial background (and perhaps are more likely to be converts to the religious traditions). This is a perfectly reasonable approach to his study, even if one may quibble about terminology.[23] Nevertheless, it is still an odd choice, as it raises an obvious question: at what point do the "descendants of immigrants" become included in the category of "Western"? As mentioned, some of the foundational figures of Buddhist studies in North America (e.g., Nagatomi and Kawamura) were the "descendants of immigrants," born and raised in the United States and Canada, not Japan. Thus, one cannot help but feel that this exclusion from the category of "Western" replicates the perpetual foreigner stereotype and essentializes Asian American identity based on ancestry, rather than their experiences as persons raised in a Western cultural context.[24] Put another way, if we take for granted the "Western-ness" of scholars born and raised in the (American) Buddhist tradition,

---

[21] Mikael Aktor, "Asymmetrical Religious Commitments? Religious Practice, Identity, and Self-Presentation among Western Scholars of Hinduism and Buddhism," *Numen* 62, no. 2–3 (2015): 266.

[22] Aktor, "Asymmetrical Religious Commitments?," 267.

[23] It seems clear from context that "ethnically Western" is to be read as "white" in the sense of whiteness as ideology and not necessarily personal identity; cf. Mitchell, *The Making of American Buddhism*, 22–23.

[24] See Chenxing Han, *Be the Refuge: Raising the Voices of Asian American Buddhists* (Berkeley, CA: North Atlantic Books, 2021), 114.

does this change some of the assumptions or questions which undergird the research projects of Aktor and Prebish?

A further limitation of the "scholar-practitioner" line of research is a focus on the individual, a point to which we will return shortly. Before we do, however, it is worth noting how these questions remain at issue a quarter century after Prebish's original work on the subject. As but one example, consider Jørn Borup's "Who Owns Religion? Intersectionality, Identity Politics, and Cultural Appropriation in Postglobal Buddhism." This comprehensive but ultimately meandering essay wends its way through various contentious topics, such as cultural appropriation, the rising popularity of secular mindfulness practices, the "two Buddhisms" typology, and "identity politics," a term Borup never defines but which nevertheless is apparently a problem for both Buddhist scholars and Buddhist practitioners. The through-line of the essay is its titular question—"Who owns religion?"—and Borup's concern is that identity politics merely reinscribes essentialist notions of religion and a dangerous subjectivity and reification of individual experience, both at the expense of "typical non-confessional 'European-style' scholarship" wherein one needs some type of distance from one's subject.[25] What seems at stake for Borup here is the extent to which postmodern—"including feminist, post-Orientalist, intersectionalist"[26]—scholarship is used not as a corrective to an earlier generation of scholarship, but as a cudgel in the form of an (again not defined) "identity politics" whose aim is to merely "de-white-wash" the study and practice of religion, at best; at worst, to paraphrase his sources, a type of "white male bashing" which seeks to purge both Buddhism and Buddhist studies from "white contamination."[27] Of course, this concern about the displacement of the white male perspective, in either scholarly or practice communities, is unfounded. Rather than relying on the anxious and anecdotal accounts of individual scholars, one need only collect quantifiable data on the number of white persons who occupy positions of leadership in Buddhist and scholarly communities, serve on the editorial boards of academic journals, and hold tenure-track positions at prestigious universities. One would think that such data would allay the emotional fears of scholars purportedly committed to the scientific and objective study of religion. To be clear, critiquing someone based solely on their "identity" (as a white man or otherwise) is not fair, is at best lazy scholarship, and does little to advance the field of Buddhist studies or the humanities more generally. At the same time, it is also demonstrably false that white men are suffering institutionally to the extent that they remain published and employed.[28]

---

[25] Jørn Borup, "Who Owns Religion? Intersectionality, Identity Politics, and Cultural Appropriation in Postglobal Buddhism," *Numen* 67, no. 2–3 (April 20, 2020): 246.

[26] Ibid., 248.

[27] Ibid., 244.

[28] Kecia Ali, et al. "Living It Out: Manthologies," *Journal of Feminist Studies in Religion* 36, no. 1 (2020): 145–158.

Beyond the Individual: Structures and Institutions

Before continuing, it is worth clarifying what I mean by "the individual," as apparently this term has caused some confusion.[29] In the following, I am neither ascribing value to individualism nor making metaphysical or ontological claims about what constitutes the individual. I use the term in its simplest and most colloquial sense—an individual person, as opposed to a collective or community of persons. My argument here is that scholarship on the "scholar-practitioner" takes as the level of analysis the individual person. This type of research is, in the end, concerned with the question of personal or individual (self-)identity. Whether or not that identity is "individualistic," is embedded within the ideologies of Western modernity, or is a byproduct of Buddhist modernism is beside the point. The point is to note the level of analysis (an individual person). My question is simply, what if our level of analysis was not on an individual person but the institutional, communal, and networked contexts within which individuals are located? Rather than asking "who is (or who identifies as) a Buddhist?," I am asking where does the *work* or labor of Buddhist studies happen? How is this work impacted by the various contexts within which we do it? And, finally, do these contexts shape what we know (or think we know) about Buddhism and Buddhists? In other words, when we focus our analysis not on the anecdotal experiences of individual persons but, instead, on the systems and institutions within which they do their scholarly work, what is revealed?

Aktor hints at larger institutional contexts and networks when he discusses the Numata Foundation or Bukkyō Dendō Kyōkai (BDK). One of the BDK's "main projects is to 'promote and introduce Buddhism to the world,' partly through supporting academic Buddhist Studies at top-ranking universities. Many of the most eminent international scholars of Buddhism have been funded by this organization."[30] Elsewhere, I have discussed the relationship between the BDK and academic Buddhist studies largely through the lens of economics and a critique of late-stage global capitalism.[31] My aim

---

[29] Donna Brown (Donna Lynn Brown, "Is Buddhism Individualistic? The Trouble with a Term," *Journal of Buddhist Ethics* 28 (2021): 55–99) has expressed confusion over the term "individualism" in her exhaustive literature review of scholarship on Buddhism, Buddhist modernity, and Western Buddhism. Despite being in many ways an important intervention on the dangers of polemics and stereotypes being uncritically promulgated in scholarship, Brown nevertheless misrepresents several of her sources, mine included, claiming that I present "Euro-American Buddhists as individualistic and Asian-Americans as not" (83) in my 2016 *Buddhism in America*. The careful reader will note that on the pages she cites for this claim nowhere do I make the argument that different racial groups are more or less individualistic and, in fact, am merely summarizing other scholars' work; therefore, in that book, I am neither presenting my own argument nor making any claims about the individualistic tendencies of any particular group.

[30] Aktor, "Asymmetrical Religious Commitments?," 276.

[31] Scott A. Mitchell, "Drawing Blood: At the Intersection of Knowledge Economies and Buddhist Economies," in *Buddhism under Capitalism*, ed. Richard K. Payne and Fabio Rambelli (London: Bloomsbury Academic, 2022), 169–183.

there was to draw our attention to the structures and contexts which shape scholarly work and the often unacknowledged impulses or motivations that lie behind them, in this case the logics of neoliberalism. Leaving aside this economic critique, here I would merely draw our attention to interconnections between scholarly communities and communities of practice, and the BDK/Numata Foundation is a primary example of how these communities intersect. Bukkyō Dendō Kyōkai translates to "Society for the Promotion of Buddhism" (not Buddhist studies). And whereas scholars may be well familiar with their funding of academic programs, professorial chairs, research and travel grants, book awards, and academic journals, the BDK is also responsible for placing tens of thousands of copies of the book *Teachings of the Buddha* in hotel nightstands alongside Gideon's Bible.[32] Again, as I have stated elsewhere, "I am in no way suggesting that financial support of Buddhist studies [by BDK or other foundations] represents something untoward or compromises the integrity of the scholars and institutions that benefit from them."[33] I am merely drawing our attention to a *relationship* between communities of scholarship and practice. A structural or systemic relationship is neither inherently positive nor negative, and in this case its benefits go both ways. Intuitively scholars understand the profound benefit of funding for their research, publications, and students. Conversely, the products of our labors bring Buddhism (and the Dharma) to the attention of a larger public. Thus, funding from Buddhists has benefits for scholars; and Buddhist studies scholarship has benefits (dare we say *karmic benefits*) for the Dharma.

The relationship between academic Buddhist studies and communities of Buddhist practice goes beyond funding. At the level of the individual, as we have seen before, figures such as Nagatomi and Kawamura were raised within Buddhist communities. These communities are also sites of interaction between scholars and practitioners. Indeed, as discussed in multiple chapters in this volume, Buddhists have been living and practicing Buddhism in North American since the mid-nineteenth century. It would be odd to think that somehow this activity did not, in some way, intersect with academic Buddhist studies communities and networks.

For example, in the 1950s the Jōdo Shinshū–affiliated Berkeley Buddhist Temple established a study center and a series of educational programs. One impulse for these programs was the education and training of future priests for the North American Jōdo Shinshū Buddhist community. However, far from being solely the project of a sectarian organization, and far from being the provenance of an isolated ethnic community, the project attracted the attention of white converts, intellectuals, artists, and scholars. This included many well-known mid-century artists and poets, such as printmaker Will Peterson and countercultural poet and environmentalist Gary Snyder. It also included buddhologists and academics such as Glen Grosjean, Frederic Spiegelberg, and Alex Wayman, all of whom studied or led classes at the Berkeley Temple's educational center. Wayman at the time was a graduate student at the University of California,

---

[32] Like a great many things, COVID brought an end to the hotel industry's practice of leaving books in nightstands.
[33] Mitchell, "Drawing Blood," 175.

Berkeley, studying Tibetan. And as we saw in the opening vignette for this chapter, a visiting Japanese scholar of Tibetan Buddhism, Tokan Tada, was also in attendance. Thus, working together in the same room on a translation of the *Śrīmālādevī Siṃhanāda Sūtra* and the *Vimalakīrti Nirdeśa Sūtra* were both "Western scholars" and scholars from Japan, as well as Japanese American Buddhists. From our vantage point here in the present, it would be nearly impossible to make definitive claims about the personal identities of all the individuals in that room and whether or not they each identified as Buddhist (or not), let alone what that identity may have meant for them. However, we cannot deny the fact that they were all in the same room together, regardless of their individual identities. Once this translation project was complete, they each went their separate ways, and in Wayman's case, his journey led him to becoming one of the most important figures in academic Buddhist studies in the late twentieth century.[34] Thus, when we shift our level of analysis away from the individual and to the larger contexts and networks within which scholarly work takes place, what is revealed are connections between and intersecting the supposedly separate worlds of Buddhist practice and academia. Academia, it seems, is rarely "at an arm's length" from the subjects of its studies.

In making this claim, I am following on the work of Pema McLaughlin and their article "Imagining Buddhist Modernism: the Shared Religious Categories of Scholars and American Buddhists." McLaughlin attempts to complicate the relationship between scholars and those that they study, noting that ordinarily objectivist approaches foreground the differences between them. American Buddhist studies is an ideal location to complicate this approach due to the overlap between (particularly convert) American Buddhists and Buddhist studies scholars. "It is a demographic fact that religious scholars and American converts to Buddhism are culturally and often geographically close," they note.[35] Convert Buddhists are more often found in urban settings and/or in close proximity to universities and colleges. (And though McLaughlin does not mention it, so-called immigrant communities are also statistically more likely to be in close proximity to urban centers.) American Buddhist converts and scholars are also culturally close, more likely to come from middle- or upper-class white backgrounds. Institutionally, as we have seen in this chapter, the development of American Buddhist communities and academic communities overlaps as well. Drawing on Prebish's work, McLaughlin notes that "Buddhist Studies as a discipline is a product of the same cultural factors that prompted the formation of many convert communities: the counterculture movements of the 1960s, an explosion of interest in Asian cultures and religions, 'and the growing dissatisfaction with (and perhaps rejection of) traditional religion.'"[36] As a result of this common origin, (convert) Buddhists and scholars have co-created a "normative modernity," a rhetoric wherein it is assumed that as Buddhism moves to the West, it necessary

---

[34] Mitchell, *The Making of American Buddhism*.
[35] Pema McLaughlin, "Imagining Buddhist Modernism: The Shared Religious Categories of Scholars and American Buddhists," *Religion* 50, no. 4 (2019): 531.
[36] McLaughlin, "Imagining Buddhist Modernism," 532; cf. Prebish, "The Academic Study of Buddhism in America: A Silent Sangha," 187.

becomes modern. This rhetoric rests on and reinforces a series of assumptions: the equation of the West with modernity and the subsequent dismissal of Asian Buddhism as "traditional"; the scholarly project of authenticating "true" Buddhism as located in the text and in the past and therefore the dismissal of convert Buddhists in America as "not really Buddhist"; the reinforcement of the "two Buddhisms" trope which marginalizes both Asian American Buddhists and other Buddhists of color; and, finally, the creation of a shared textual space wherein both (convert) Buddhists and Buddhist scholars use the "native term" religion to make prescriptive and normative claims about Buddhism.[37] Not only do Buddhists and scholars deploy the same rhetorics about religion and occupy the same textual space, as we have seen here, at times they occupy the same literal or physical spaces as well. This may take the form of individuals who identify as "scholar-practitioners" and thus move in and between academic and religious spaces; it may take the form of philanthropic funding from Buddhist organizations toward academic or presumably "secular" projects; it may take the form of close collaboration in the form of the translation or preservation of texts or cultures (see Gayley and Brallier, Chapter 13 in this volume). Regardless of what form it takes, Buddhists and scholars are in relationship, institutionally and structurally.

In conducting a self-reflective study on the origins of American Buddhism studies and/or American Buddhism itself, when one takes as the level of analysis communities, networks, or institutions rather than individuals, what is often revealed are the interconnections between communities and the shared cultural assumptions between them. One line of research here could be a greater focus on the issue of class. To the extent that, as McLaughlin has shown, convert American Buddhists and Buddhist scholars generally come from the same socioeconomic and racial backgrounds, it is reasonable to assume that they will share particular cultural values, interests, and perspectives. As Caroline Starkey has argued, scholars of Buddhism in the West would be well served by a greater attention to the issues of class, within the communities we study as well in our own communities.[38] How have the values and cultural assumptions implicit with middle-class and elite academic and university communities influenced, implicitly or explicitly, the ways in which we have approached our studies?

Scholarly Objectives and Objective Scholarship

In his 2007 essay, "The Disciplines of Buddhist Studies: Notes on Religious Commitment as Boundary-Marker," Oliver Freiberger focuses squarely on the

---

[37] McLaughlin, "Imagining Buddhist Modernism," 545.
[38] Caroline Starkey, "Don't Ignore Class: Material Relationships, Economic Conditions, and Buddhism in the West," *Annual Meeting of the American Academy of Religion* (Denver, CO, 2022).

insider-outsider dichotomy in the study of Buddhism. He begins by reflecting on the nature of academic disciplines and fields of study and suggests that Buddhist studies is a field, not a discipline, precisely because it lacks sustained "boundary-work"—that is, Buddhist studies is interdisciplinary by its nature. Nevertheless, the bulk of the essay is concerned with how the issue of religious commitment is itself a boundary-maker in the field. Freiberger brings us back to Thomas Rhys Davids and presents a lengthy and "meaty" quote whereby the Pali scholar dismisses in harsh terms "Northern Buddhism" (e.g., Mahāyāna and tantric Buddhism) as "immoral" and "absurd" derivations from the founder's true intent. Rather than dismissing this perspective as merely "orientalist," however, Freiberger argues that Rhys Davids's condemnation of non-Pali Buddhism was *Buddhist* in orientation, that he was writing what amounted to an apologetic in defense of Pali-based Buddhism—that he was, in short, an "insider" to the tradition, not an outsider. "Note," writes Freiberger, "that I do not take 'outsider perspective' to imply objectivity; the term merely denotes the methodological decision not to describe religious phenomena from within the tradition one studies. For the sake of argument, I ignore for the moment other biases and agendas that may come into play."[39]

It goes without saying that I am in agreement with Freiberger here, that Rhys Davids was writing as an insider to the tradition, an apologist for a particular sectarian and historically situated version of Buddhism. As discussed here, Rhys Davids is one of a long line of scholars who have shaped not only the academic study, but the practice of Buddhism in North America. Moreover, I am in agreement with Freiberger that the dichotomy between insiders and outsiders has been one of the central points of contention within the field of Buddhist studies. However, he also sets up a dichotomy between Buddhist studies and Buddhist theology and suggests that the latter is necessarily defined by scholars who have religious commitments to Buddhism, thus implying that Buddhist studies scholars do not. Leaving aside for the moment whether or not this is an accurate depiction of the two fields (or even whether or not it is possible to so cleanly cleave the two), let us linger for a moment on the role of the scholar.

Whether a scholar considers themself an insider or outside, what is their role? Are they to be a dispassionate and objective reporter on sociocultural phenomena? Or are they to be advocates for the tradition? This question was taken up by a trio of essays in a special section of the *Journal of Global Buddhism*. In his contribution, John Makransky argues in favor of the Buddhist critical-constructive (i.e., Buddhist theological) approach as being informed by the rigorous standards of traditional Buddhist studies but offering something of value to both Buddhists and the broader contemporary world.[40] In contrast, Ian Reader argues strongly against advocacy in scholarship, claiming that

---

[39] Oliver Freiberger, "The Disciplines of Buddhist Studies: Notes on Religious Commitment as Boundary-Marker," *Journal of the International Association of Buddhist Studies* 30, no. 1–2 (2007): 306.

[40] John Makransky, "The Emergence of Buddhist Critical-Constructive Reflection in the Academy as a Resource for Buddhist Communities and for the Contemporary World," *Journal of Global Buddhism* 9 (2008): 113–153.

objectivity is what defines the modern approach to the study of religion and gives the field its integrity. Confessional scholarship, for Reader, is dangerous, and he uses the case of new religious movements (NRM) studies as an example. Reader claims that some scholars of NRMs feel compelled to advocate on behalf of their research subjects due to the fact that there is a strong anti-cult bias in the modern world following in the wake of such well-publicized disasters as Jonestown, Waco, and Aum Shinrikyo. A truly objectivist scholarship is presumably better positioned to critique religion and new religious movements.[41]

Duncan Ryûken Williams takes the "middle path" between these positions in his essay "At Ease in Between: The Middle Position of a Scholar-Practitioner." Williams rightly argues that one can both encourage students to sympathetically understand the Buddhist tradition and simultaneously develop critical distance based on the tradition's long history. By "sympathetically understand" the tradition, Williams means engendering in students an appreciation for how Buddhists see the world, either through primary texts, art, or ethnographic sources. But seeing the world through another's eyes does not necessarily mean one must subscribe to the same worldview. Invoking his graduate school mentor, Masatoshi Nagatomi, Williams describes the importance of critical distance on the tradition by reminding us that "Buddhism is not monolithic." Helping students understand how the Buddhist tradition is historically situated and mutable over time "affords us the ability to recognize how different Buddhists . . . approach, discuss, and practice towards the alleviation of suffering."[42]

Williams's focus on *teaching* is, I believe, crucial. It is a reminder that scholarship does not exist in a vacuum. That is, whether one is an advocate of the tradition (like Makransky) or against advocacy (like Reader), these positions do not exist as disembodied platonic ideals, but rather in specific institutional contexts. As scholars, the fruits of our labors are manifest in university classrooms, academic monographs, and peer-reviewed journals. A scholar teaching Buddhism to undergraduates at a public university in, say, Florida, is going to be constrained by legal systems completely beyond her control and, even if she wanted to advocate for the tradition, may be legally prohibited from doing so. This same scholar may be invited to speak to a local Buddhist sangha wherein she will not only be free to advocate for the tradition but expected to do so. Thus, rather than trapping this one person in the amber of *either* advocate *or* scholar, we can intuitively understand how context gives shape and meaning to their work, how they can present and represent Buddhism according to the structures of different times, places, and communities.

The notion that one can stand apart from the tradition is, arguably, part of Buddhist studies' colonialist legacy. As Natalie Quli has expertly argued, Buddhist studies has inherited imperialist nostalgia in the formulation of the "Western Self/Asian Other"

---

[41] Ian Reader, "Buddhism and the Perils of Advocacy," *Journal of Global Buddhism* 9 (2008): 83–112.
[42] Duncan Ryûken Williams, "At Ease in Between: The Middle Position of a Scholar-Practitioner," *Journal of Global Buddhism* 9 (2008): 155–163.

dichotomy.⁴³ If we uncritically accept that the proper subject of Buddhist studies is limited to "those people, over there" (or, more accurately, "these texts composed in the past"), then keeping the tradition at arm's length is a matter of course for, from this perspective, Buddhism is not a living thing practiced by living persons in the real world but something confined to the past. Buddhism, of course, is a living tradition, practiced by living persons, many of whom are also paid to do academic and scholarly work for some of the most prestigious universities in the modern world. And to that extent, the field of Buddhist studies and communities of Buddhist practice are in relationship. Perhaps the projects of "outing" scholar-practitioners (as per Prebish), or asking whether or not scholars are more comfortable being practitioners in Buddhist studies than in other disciplines (as per Aktor), or whether or not being an advocate is a good thing or a bad thing (as per Reader), are not the most interesting lines of research to be pursued. Perhaps tracing out the systems and relationships between persons and institutions will reveal more about our interconnections, will reveal that in some way we are all already "inside" the tradition.

To be clear, I am not using the term "interconnection" here in its Buddhist (modernist) sense, though that is a happy coincidence. If we have learned nothing since 2020, I assume we have learned that the world is, indeed, interconnected. Our interconnection makes possible a global pandemic. Our climate crisis will affect everyone, eventually. To borrow from Melissa Anne-Marie Curley, Buddhist studies scholars should dispense with the field's educational status quo and instead begin teaching its students about "medicine and healing, small-scale and collective food production, alternative economies and strategies of mutual aid."⁴⁴ Indeed, when the tragic consequences of climate collapse come, fretting about identity politics (as per Borup) will hardly be a useful pastime in the face of more immediate survival projects. Discourses that seek to divide and ignore our relationships will no doubt be weaponized precisely to enable some to survive over and against others. So, regardless of whether or not you, as an individual, are concerned about our collective liberation as sentient beings or our collective survival as a species, a focus on individuality must come second to an understanding of our relationality. How are we connected to one another? How are these connections sustaining or destructive? What institutions, systems, and communities support our collective well-being, and which hinder, suppress, or oppress? Future research on both American Buddhism and Buddhist studies as a field will necessarily need to address these questions and adapt themselves to new realities. Our scholarship (and our practice) ought to be oriented toward collective (political, social, cultural, religious) liberation rather than discourses of mutual distrust which will surely only hasten our mutual destruction.

---

⁴³ Natalie E. Quli, "Western Self, Asian Other: Modernity, Authenticity, and Nostalgia for 'Tradition' in Buddhist Studies," *Journal of Buddhist Ethics* 16 (2009): 1–38.

⁴⁴ Melissa Anne-Marie Curley, "Let Buddhist Studies Die," Collective Buddhist Studies Manifesto, December 31, 2021, http://buddhiststudiesmanifesto.net/let-buddhist-studies-die/.

References

Abe, Stanley K. "Inside the Wonder House: Buddhist Art and the West." In *Curators of the Buddha: The Study of Buddhism Under Colonialism*, edited by Donald S. Lopez, 63–106. Chicago: University of Chicago Press, 1995.

Aktor, Mikael. "Asymmetrical Religious Commitments? Religious Practice, Identity, and Self-Presentation among Western Scholars of Hinduism and Buddhism." *Numen* 62, no. 2–3 (2015): 265–300.

Blackburn, Anne M. *Locations of Buddhism: Colonialism and Modernity in Sri Lanka*. Chicago: University of Chicago Press, 2010.

Borup, Jørn. "Who Owns Religion? Intersectionality, Identity Politics, and Cultural Appropriation in Postglobal Buddhism." *Numen* 67, no. 2–3 (April 20, 2020): 226–255.

Brown, Donna Lynn. "Is Buddhism Individualistic? The Trouble with a Term." *Journal of Buddhist Ethics* 28 (2021): 55–99.

Cabezón, José I. "2020 AAR Presidential Address: The Study of Buddhism and the AAR." *Journal of the American Academy of Religion* 89, no. 3 (2021): 793–818.

Curley, Melissa Anne-Marie. "Let Buddhist Studies Die." Collective Buddhist Studies Manifesto, December 31, 2021. http://buddhiststudiesmanifesto.net/let-buddhist-studies-die/.

Freiberger, Oliver. "The Disciplines of Buddhist Studies: Notes on Religious Commitment as Boundary-Marker." *Journal of the International Association of Buddhist Studies* 30, no. 1–2 (2007): 299–318.

Gleig, Ann. "Researching New Religious Movements from the Inside Out and the Outside In." *Nova Religio: The Journal of Alternative and Emergent Religions* 16, no. 1 (2012): 88–103.

Han, Chenxing. *Be the Refuge: Raising the Voices of Asian American Buddhists*. Berkeley, CA: North Atlantic Books, 2021.

Harrington, Laura. "The Greatest Movie Never Made: The Life of the Buddha as Cold War Politics." *Religion and American Culture* 30, no. 3 (2020): 397–425.

Makransky, John. "The Emergence of Buddhist Critical-Constructive Reflection in the Academy as a Resource for Buddhist Communities and for the Contemporary World." *Journal of Global Buddhism* 9 (2008): 113–153.

McLaughlin, Pema. "Imagining Buddhist Modernism: The Shared Religious Categories of Scholars and American Buddhists." *Religion* 50, no. 4 (2019): 529–549.

McMahan, David L. *The Making of Buddhist Modernism*. New York: Oxford University Press, 2008.

Mitchell, Scott A. *Buddhism in America: Global Religion, Local Contexts*. London: Bloomsbury Academic, 2016.

Mitchell, Scott A. "Drawing Blood: At the Intersection of Knowledge Economies and Buddhist Economies." In *Buddhism under Capitalism*, edited by Richard K. Payne and Fabio Rambelli, 169–183. London: Bloomsbury Academic, 2022.

Mitchell, Scott A. *The Making of American Buddhism*. New York: Oxford University Press, 2023.

Prebish, Charles S. "The Academic Study of Buddhism in America: A Silent Sangha." In *American Buddhism: Methods and Findings in Recent Scholarship*, edited by Dunan Ryûken Williams and Christopher S. Queen, 183–214. New York: Curzon, 1999.

Prebish, Charles S. *American Buddhism*. North Scituate, MA: Duxbury Press, 1979.

Prebish, Charles S. *Luminous Passage: The Practice and Study of Buddhism in America*. Berkeley: University of California Press, 1999.

Quli, Natalie E. "Western Self, Asian Other: Modernity, Authenticity, and Nostalgia for 'Tradition' in Buddhist Studies." *Journal of Buddhist Ethics* 16 (2009): 1–38.

Reader, Ian. "Buddhism and the Perils of Advocacy." *Journal of Global Buddhism* 9 (2008): 83–112.

Ritzinger, Justin. "Tinker, Tailor, Scholar, Spy: Holmes Welch, Buddhism, and the Cold War." *Journal of Global Buddhism* 22, no. 2 (2021): 421–441.

Williams, Duncan Ryûken. *American Sutra: A Story of Faith and Freedom in the Second World War*. Cambridge, MA: Harvard University Press, 2019.

Williams, Duncan Ryûken. "At Ease in Between: The Middle Position of a Scholar-Practitioner." *Journal of Global Buddhism* 9 (2008): 155–163.

PART II
TRADITIONS

CHAPTER 6

CHINESE BUDDHISM IN AMERICA

RONGDAO LAI

THE story about the transmission and development of Chinese Buddhism in the United States is one of exclusion. On the one hand, as the result of a series of restrictive immigration laws starting with the Chinese Exclusion Act in 1882, Chinese Buddhist clergy arrived relatively late in the United States compared to their Japanese counterparts. On the other hand, scholarly narratives and typologies for what constitute "American Buddhism" often mean that American Chinese Buddhists, who make up a significant percentage of Buddhists in the country, are systematically overlooked. The implicit biases and problems with taxonomies such as "ethnic" and "convert" Buddhism are beyond the scope of the present chapter—they have also been critically addressed by scholars in recent years.[1] Further adding to this marginality is the category "Chinese Buddhism" itself. According to scholars of American Buddhism, the religion practiced by early Chinese migrants in the mid-nineteenth century was "a mixture of Confucian ancestor veneration, popular Taoism, and Pure Land Buddhism" that cannot be properly classified as Buddhism.[2] Even with the arrival of monastics who founded Buddhist temples since the 1960s, their practice is "highly eclectic and often includes various

---

[1] Joseph Cheah, *Race and Religion in American Buddhism: White Supremacy and Immigrant Adaptation* (New York: Oxford University Press, 2011); Chenxing Han, *Be the Refuge: Raising the Voices of Asian American Buddhists* (Berkeley, CA: North Atlantic Books, 2021); Wakoh Shannon Hickey, "Two Buddhisms, Three Buddhisms, and Racism," *Journal of Global Buddhism* 11 (2010): 1–25; Scott Mitchell, *Buddhism in America: Global Religion, Local Contexts* (New York: Bloomsbury, 2016), 207–209; Natalie Quli, "Western Self, Asian Other: Modernity, Authenticity, and Nostalgia for 'Tradition' in Buddhist Studies," *Journal of Buddhist Ethics* 16 (2009): 1–38. For earlier typologies on Buddhism in America, see Jan Nattier, "Who Is a Buddhist? Charting the Landscape of Buddhist America," in *The Faces of Buddhism in America*, ed. Charles S. Prebish and Kenneth K. Tanaka (Berkeley: University of California Press, 1998), 183–195; Paul David Numrich, *Old Wisdom in the New World: Americanization in Two Immigrant Theravada Buddhist Temples* (Knoxville: University of Tennessee Press, 1996); Charles S. Prebish, *American Buddhism* (North Scituate, MA: Duxbury Press, 1979).

[2] Richard Hughes Seager, *Buddhism in America* (New York: Columbia University Press, 2012), 181.

aspects of all five traditional Chinese schools."³ One could argue that this is representative of the orientalist biases, Protestant presuppositions, and influence of modern Japanese Buddhist studies scholarship—which insist on the institutional boundaries between the different religious traditions as well as the various schools within Buddhism. In fact, the syncretism of the three institutional traditions of Buddhism, Confucianism, and Daoism has been a prominent feature of Chinese religiosity since at least the late imperial era.⁴ Furthermore, even within institutional Chinese Buddhism, it is common for learned monastics to study the doctrines of the various schools and to view the practice of Chan and Pure Land as complementary rather than mutually exclusive, although Chan has remained a dominant institution.

The Chinese were the first Asian migrants to the United States. The first ship carrying Chinese gold miners arrived in 1849, only a year after the discovery of gold in Northern California. Their numbers grew steadily in the next three decades. In 1860, 10 percent of all Californians were Chinese, at around 60,000. By the 1880s, there were slightly over 100,000 Chinese living in the United States, mostly along the West Coast.⁵ When they were forced to leave the mining fields due to anti-Chinese sentiment among white Americans, they moved east to work in the construction of the transcontinental railway. Over time, they settled in major urban areas such as Los Angeles and San Francisco. These first migrants were almost exclusively male and originated from Guangdong. Due to racism and exclusion, they were forced to live in ethnic enclaves that would become Chinatowns.

To serve the religious needs of the growing community, places of worship started to appear. Similar to other Chinese diasporic communities, shrines were built by kinship organizations (*huiguan* 會館)—based on shared identity such as family names, native places, and dialects—and fraternal organizations (*tang* 堂).⁶ These "joss houses," as they are often called in literature and media reporting on Chinese religion, housed Buddhist, Daoist, and other popular deities such as Guanyin, Mazu, and Guangong. The first Chinese shrines in San Francisco were the Tin How Temple and Kong Chow Temple, both constructed in the early 1850s. By the turn of the century, there were hundreds of such shrines up and down the US West Coast. However, with the passage of the Chinese Exclusion Act in 1882, which virtually barred all Chinese immigration, the number

---

³ Charles S. Prebish, *Luminous Passage: The Practice and Study of Buddhism in America* (Berkeley: University of California Press, 1999), 27.

⁴ On the issue of syncretism in Chinese religion, see Timothy Brook, "Rethinking Syncretism: The Unity of the Three Teachings and Their Joint Worship in Late-Imperial China," *Journal of Chinese Religions* 21, no. 1 (1993): 13–44.

⁵ Stuart Chandler, "Chinese Buddhism in America: Identity and Practice," in *The Faces of Buddhism in America*, ed. Charles S. Prebish and Kenneth K. Tanaka (Berkeley: University of California Press, 1998), 16; Rick Fields, *How the Swans Came to the Lake: A Narrative History of Buddhism in America* (Boston: Shambhala Publications, 1992), 72–73.

⁶ Philip A. Kuhn, *Chinese among Others: Emigration in Modern Times* (Lanham, MD: Rowman & Littlefield, 2008), 44–45. For the organizational structure of *huiguan* in the US, see Him Mark Lai, *Becoming Chinese American: A History of Communities and Institutions* (Walnut Creek, CA: AltaMira Press, 2004), part II.

of Chinese started to decline, and these temples were abandoned over time.[7] None of temples in the San Francisco Chinatown survived the 1906 earthquake and fire.

Although the Chinese Exclusion Act was repealed by the Congress in 1943, a strict quota privileging migrants from Northern and Western Europe remained in place until the passage of the Immigration and Nationality Act in 1965. This new era of ethnic Chinese mobility, driven also by geopolitics and socioeconomic changes in Asia, saw the arrival of migrants from Hong Kong, Taiwan, and Southeast Asia, later followed by those from the Chinese mainland after the Reform and Opening Up in 1978. Compared to the nineteenth century, these Chinese were more diverse in terms of educational level and socioeconomic status. There were students, entrepreneurs, and refugees, among others. The Buddhists among them formed lay groups and temples. Monks and nuns were soon invited to lead these communities.

The 1980s saw a proliferation of Chinese Buddhist temples in the United States. Among them, reformist groups from Taiwan, identified as the heirs of Humanistic Buddhism promoted by the twentieth-century monk Taixu 太虛 (1890–1947), have been the primary focus in scholarship on global Chinese Buddhism.[8] These reformist groups, including Fo Guang Shan, Dharma Drum, and Tzu Chi, were founded by charismatic teachers in postwar Taiwan. Their coherent, carefully curated identities and personnel are centrally managed by the respective headquarters in Taiwan. Yet, this is a relatively new development, whereas little is known about the vast array of other Buddhist actors and networks that followed different paradigms in forming transnational connections.[9]

The present chapter is an attempt to document the activities of Chinese monastics outside the reformist groups from Taiwan. In doing so, I follow Thomas Tweed's axioms for a translocative analysis in the study of global Buddhism: follow the flows; notice all the figures crossing; attend to all the senses; consider varying scales; and notice how flows start, stop, and shift.[10] Although smaller in both number and scale, these Buddhist

---

[7] Chandler, "Chinese Buddhism in America," 17.

[8] Stuart Chandler, *Establishing a Pure Land on Earth: The Foguang Buddhist Perspective on Modernization and Globalization* (Honolulu: University of Hawai'i Press, 2004); C. Julia Huang, *Charisma and Compassion: Cheng Yen and the Buddhist Tzu Chi Movement* (Cambridge, MA: Harvard University Press, 2009); Jens Reinke, *Mapping Modern Mahayana Chinese Buddhism and Migration in the Age of Global Modernity* (Berlin: De Gruyter, 2021). On the reformist monk Taixu, see Don Pittman, *Toward a Modern Chinese Buddhism: Taixu's Reforms* (Honolulu: University of Hawai'i Press, 2001); Justin Ritzinger, *Anarchy in the Pure Land: Reinventing the Cult of Maitreya in Modern Chinese Buddhism* (New York: Oxford University Press, 2017).

[9] Rongdao Lai, "Tiantai Transnationalism: Mobility, Identity, and Lineage Networks in Modern Chinese Buddhism," in *Transnational Religious Spaces*, ed. Philip Clart and Adam Jones (De Gruyter, 2020), 210–224; Lina Verchery, "Impersonal Intimacy: Relational Ethics and Self-Cultivation in a Transnational Chinese Buddhist Monastic Network," PhD dissertation, Harvard University, 2021; Yoshiko Ashiwa and David Wank, "The Globalization of Chinese Buddhism: Clergy and Devotee Networks in the Twentieth Century," *International Journal of Asian Studies* 2, no. 2 (2005): 217–237.

[10] Thomas A. Tweed, "Theory and Method in the Study of Buddhism: Toward 'Translocative Analysis,'" in *Buddhism beyond Borders: New Perspectives on Buddhism in the United States*, ed. Scott A. Mitchell and Natalie E. F. Quli (Albany: State University of New York Press, 2015), 3–19.

teachers were nonetheless instrumental in paving the ground for the vibrant growth of Chinese Buddhism in the United States since the 1980s. This is a study of the life and career of one nun, Man Chu (,[11] the founding abbess of the Western American Buddhist Association, also known as the Perfect Enlightenment Temple (Yuanjue si 圓覺寺) in Los Angeles. This chapter is divided into three sections. It begins with a biographical sketch of Man Chu, which is followed by an overview of her voluminous published works. It closes with a discussion of the role of border-crossing experience in her identity as a global Chinese Buddhist.

An Extraordinary Life

During a conversation with me in the early 2000s, Man Chu brought up the title for an article she penned on the one-year anniversary of the passing of her teacher, the scholar-monk Minzhi 敏智 (1909–1996). The piece was titled "An Extraordinary Memoir" (*Bu pingfan de huiyi* 不平凡的回憶).[12] I asked whether it was her teacher's life or hers that was extraordinary. Without answering, she turned around and went into her study. Moments later, she reappeared with a book in her hand. It was the autobiography of the famed scholar-monk Yinshun 印順 (1906–2005) titled *An Ordinary Life* (*Pingfan de yisheng* 平凡的一生).[13] She then said, "Modesty is only a virtue for monks. Nuns don't have that luxury." I took it that she meant it was *her* experience that was extraordinary!

Man Chu's extraordinary life story began in Zhanjiang, Guangdong province, in Southeastern China. She was born into the Zhan 詹 family in 1930. She suffered prolonged illnesses since birth. Worrying that she might not survive, her family sent her to a local nunnery called Fushoushan Temple (Fushoushan si 福壽山寺) when she was eighteen months old.[14] The abbess Yuanshen 遠慎 (n.d.) made sure that Man Chu attended school. She was ordained when she was sixteen. At this time, the monk Hairen 海仁 (1886–1978) had returned to Guangdong from Hong Kong after it fell to the Japanese during the Second World War. Hairen frequently lectured in temples in the Zhanjiang area. The newly ordained Man Chu was among the audience. Hairen was reportedly impressed with the young nun's intelligence. When he returned to Hong

---

[11] Throughout this chapter, I follow the romanization of her name as Man Chu, which is the Cantonese pronunciation that Man Chu herself used. In the reference list, however, her name is romanized according to *Hanyu pinyin* as Wenzhu.

[12] Wenzhu, *Juehai Diandi* 覺海點滴 [Droplets in the Sea of Awakening] (Los Angeles: Western American Buddhist Association, 2013), 4:1222–1240.

[13] Yinshun 印順, *Pingfan de yisheng* 平凡的一生 [An Ordinary Life] (Taipei: Zhengwen chubanshe, 1994).

[14] It should be noted that Man Chu's family did not abandon her. It was customary in some regions of China to send sickly children to temples hoping that they would be protected by the Buddha and other deities. In most cases, the families continued to provide for their children. Man Chu remained close to her birth family.

Kong in 1947, he brought Man Chu with him. This marks the beginning of nearly seven decades of her living, practicing, and teaching Chinese Buddhism in the transnational context. For six years, in Hairen's humble hermitage on Lantau Island, Man Chu studied the *Śūraṃgama Sūtra*, *Lotus Sūtra*, and other Tiantai texts.[15] This training in monastic scholasticism had a significant impact in shaping her identity as a teacher and writer.

In 1952, she was in the inaugural class at the Zhengxin Buddhist Academy (Zhengxin foxueyuan 正心佛學院) founded by Mingchang 明常 (1898–1977). It was the first and only school for nuns in Hong Kong. Minzhi served as the principal instructor, teaching a class of eight nuns the Chinese classics and composition, in addition to Yogācāra philosophy—his specialization. Due to financial hardship, the school closed three years later, after graduating its first class. Discouraged by the lack of educational opportunities for nuns within Buddhism, Man Chu turned to secular education. In 1955, she won a scholarship to attend the United College, which would later form the Chinese University of Hong Kong together with two other colleges. When she graduated with a bachelor's degree in Social Education in 1958, she became one of the first Chinese nuns to have received a university degree. In the same year, she left to attend the graduate school at Taisho University in Japan.

Upon returning from Japan in 1961, she started to play an active role in social and religious arenas. She held regular public lectures at the Hong Kong City Hall, founded a Buddhist youth association that offered classes and activities,[16] became the principal for a government-subsidized secular school, and served as a board member for the Hong Kong Buddhist Association. Within a few years, she emerged as a prominent figure in the Hong Kong Buddhist community.

Man Chu visited the United States and Canada in the summer of 1972 on the invitation of several lay followers. At the end of her tour, she realized that there were Chinese Buddhist temples in major cities such as San Francisco, New York, and Toronto, but not Los Angeles. She decided to stay to establish the first Chinese Buddhist temple there. A year later, the Western American Buddhist Association was incorporated. At first, the temple was housed in a residential building in Chinatown. As the congregation grew, a church across the street from the original location was acquired in 1976. For the next forty years, Man Chu and the Perfect Enlightenment Temple served the Chinese community in Los Angeles and beyond through its charity, Dharma classes, and ritual activities. When tens of thousands of refugees were relocated to Camp Pandleton in San Diego following the Fall of Saigon in 1975, Man Chu and temple volunteers made weekly visits to the camp, distributed basic necessities, and led chanting sessions for the

---

[15] Xianggang Fajiao lianhehui, "Wenzhu Fashi," *Xianggang Fojiao* 香港佛教 [Hong Kong Buddhism], July 2016, 38; Lingbo Yu, *Minguo gaoseng zhuan sanbian* 民國高僧傳三編 [Biographies of Eminent Monks of the Republican Period, Part III] (Taipei: Huiming wenhua, 2001), 227; Lingbo Yu, *Zhongguo Fojiao Haiwai Hongfa Renwu Zhi* 中國佛教海外弘法人物誌 [Records of Overseas Propagators of Chinese Buddhism] (Taipei: Huiju chubanshe, 1997), 420.

[16] Man Chu's Hong Kong Buddhist Youth Association was one of several youth associations founded in the 1960s. See *Jiazhou Deng, Xianggang Fojiao Shi* 香港佛教史 [A History of Buddhism in Hong Kong] (Hong Kong: Zhonghua shuju, 2015), 161–164.

refugees. The temple also sponsored over 300 refugees and helped them settle into a new life in Southern California.

In 1983, Man Chu returned to her home temple in Zhanjiang for the first time since her departure as a teenager. Most of the buildings in the temple had been occupied by local residents during the Cultural Revolution. While some nuns remained, the main hall was severely dilapidated. She helped negotiate with the authorities to reclaim the temple as a religious site. She also funded the reconstruction project, which was completed in 1990.[17] Today, the Fushoushan Temple remains one of the major nunneries in the Zhanjiang area. When her teacher Minzhi passed away in New York in 1996, Man Chu was named one of the executors in his will. Under her leadership, the Minzhi Memorial Educational Foundation donated to Buddhist academies in China, offered annual scholarships for students pursuing Buddhist Studies in higher education, and built schools in impoverished areas in China.

Man Chu's career as a Buddhist teacher has spanned both sides of the Pacific Ocean. When she was not teaching in California, she was often found on lecture tours in Hong Kong, Guangdong, and Southeast Asia. Her published works were also widely circulated in the Chinese Buddhist world, both in physical form and on the internet. It is hard to estimate the total circulation of her works as they have been printed and reprinted by various groups as Dharma books for free distribution. In the early 2000s, she started to systematically make her work available on the internet.[18] This eventually led to her decision to curate her own complete work, published in fifteen volumes and consisting of over 2.5 million characters. A short analysis of her work will be provided in the next section. Although widely respected in the transnational Chinese Buddhist world, Man Chu remains unknown beyond the Chinese community in the United States. Her followers in the United States are exclusively ethnic Chinese, with the majority being Cantonese speakers. All of her lectures were given in Cantonese. Following Verchery's point about communities that are "locally isolated but globally connected," I argue that this contradiction is the basis of Man Chu's identity as a global Chinese Buddhist based in America—to be further addressed in the last section of this chapter.[19]

---

[17] Overseas Chinese were instrumental to the reconstruction of temples and revival of religious life in post-Mao China. See Kenneth Dean and Zhenman Zheng, *Ritual Alliances of the Putian Plain*, Volume 1: *Historical Introduction to the Return of the Gods* (Leiden: Brill, 2010), 229–254; Khun Eng Kuah, *Rebuilding the Ancestral Village: Singaporeans in China* (Hong Kong: Hong Kong University Press, 2011). On the revival of monastic Buddhism, see Brian Nichols, "Tourist Temples and Places of Practice: Charting Multiple Paths in the Revival of Monasteries," in *Buddhism after Mao: Negotiations, Continuities, and Reinventions*, ed. Zhe Ji, Gareth Fisher, and André Laliberté (Honolulu: University of Hawai'i Press, 2019), 97–119.

[18] Wenzhu, "Wenzhu Fashi Zuopin Ji 文珠法師作品集 [Collection of Venerable Wenzhu's Work]," accessed June 3, 2023, http://wabala.org/tc/wenzhu_work.php.

[19] Lina Verchery, "An Alternative to the 'Westernization' Paradigm and Buddhist Global Imaginaries," in *Buddhism in the Global Eye: Beyond East and West*, ed. John S. Harding, Victor Sōgen Hori, and Alexander Soucy (New York: Bloomsbury, 2020), 161.

Droplets in the Sea of Awakening

Man Chu's reputation as a talented writer began during her university days, when she regularly wrote for newspapers and other Buddhist publications. In 1957, she joined her fellow United College students on a tour of Taiwan. The group was sponsored by the ruling Guomindang in part of a larger campaign to mobilize overseas Chinese. Upon returning to Hong Kong, she started a column for the Buddhist magazine *Humanity* (*Rensheng* 人生) in which she recorded her visits to different attractions, meetings with lay and monastic Buddhists, her impression of the vitality of Buddhism on the island, as well as her longing for a "free China." The series was reportedly so popular among the readership that the magazine decided to publish it as a stand-alone volume the next year. The famed female writer and literature professor Xie Bingying 謝冰瑩 (1906–2000) contributed the preface for the book.[20]

In her seventies, Man Chu began to compile and revise her written works. Titled *Droplets in the Sea of Awakening* (*Juehai diandi* 覺海點滴), her complete work was published between 2005 and 2013. It consists of five parts: a major commentary on the *Śūraṅgama Sūtra* (*Lengyan jing* 楞嚴經), lecture notes and commentaries on various sūtras, public lectures on Buddhism, essays and miscellany, and a commentary on the *Lotus Sūtra*. A quick glance of its table of contents reveals the breadth of her interest and the depth of her expertise. Her public lectures cover topics from Buddhism and science to cultivating harmonious family relationships. Her commentaries include seminal texts in Chinese Buddhism—from the *Lotus* to the *Diamond* and Pure Land sūtras. The compilation was mostly a lone endeavor. In her late sixties, she learned to write using a computer with a digital writing pad.

Of her voluminous works, the most influential is undoubtedly the commentary on the *Śūraṅgama Sūtra*, which she began studying during her time with Hairen as a teenage nun in Hong Kong. Before his death, Hairen handed Man Chu notes from his lectures that some of his students had copied down. He urged Man Chu to carry on his lifelong efforts in promoting the scripture and its teaching. Based on Hairen's notes, Man Chu composed her own commentary. It follows the traditional Chinese Buddhist exegetical practice of sectional analysis (*kepan* 科判) as both an organizational and interpretive strategy. The sūtra is divided into chapters and sections in a line-by-line exegesis that explicates the structural relationship between the different sections.[21] It is a highly sophisticated work that heavily cross-references other sūtras and commentaries. While clearly expounding a doctrinal position, it also systematically integrates other teachings in Chinese Buddhism. The commentary is written in vernacular Chinese, making it

---

[20] Wenzhu, *Baodao Lüxing Ji* 寶島旅行記 [Taiwan Travelogue] (Beitou, Taiwan: Rensheng zazhi, 1958); Wenzhu, *Droplets* 4:3, 1352–1494.

[21] Alexander Mayer, "Commentarial Literature," in *Encyclopedia of Buddhism*, ed. Robert E. Buswell, Jr. (New York: Macmillan, 2004), 168.

more accessible to modern readers than earlier commentaries composed in classical Chinese.[22]

The *Śūraṅgama* is one of the most important scriptures in later Chinese Buddhism. To this day, the standard morning liturgy in Chinese monasteries still begins with the *Śūraṅgama Dhāraṇī*. It has informed the Chinese Buddhist worldview and practices such as meditation, body burning, and vegetarianism. Despite its claim as the translation of a scripture of Indic origin, the consensus among modern scholars is that it is an apocryphal scripture composed in China in the eighth century.[23] Unlike some of her peers, Man Chu did not engage with modern debates in defending the authenticity of the scripture. Instead, she emphasized the beauty and sophistication of its language, its profound teachings, its magical power in revealing and overcoming heterodoxies, and the importance to uphold the scripture, especially in the end of the Dharma age (*mofa* 末法):

> [The sutra] does not only epitomize scientific analysis, ethics, and human relations, it also explains the reality of the universe and human life based on philosophical principles. It reveals the origins of the world, sentient beings, and karma. It shows the way to return to the truth and attain awakening. It is not only the essence of all of the Buddha's teachings, but also the gate to all bodhisattva practices... and subsequently Buddhahood.[24]

Teaching a dense text like the *Śūraṅgama* requires considerable commitment from both the teacher and students. Man Chu had lectured on the sūtra many times in the United States and Hong Kong. Her advanced classes on the *Śūraṅgama* usually lasted one to two years. From time to time, she expressed concerns about the listeners' lack of preparedness and perseverance to follow her lectures. This anxiety about the potential discontinuity of a scripture that was regarded as the perfect embodiment of the threefold training of morality, concentration, and wisdom compelled her unremitting efforts in teaching, preserving, and circulating the *Śūraṅgama*. The last revised edition of her commentary was printed the year before her death. The *Śūraṅgama*, therefore, bookended her career as a Dharma teacher. It can be argued that she responded to modern scholarship on the authenticity of the sūtra by ensuring that it continued to be taught and studied.

Her other commentaries follow similar exegetical style. If her scholasticism represents certain cultural and religious conservatism, the other half of her collected work suggests that she is at the same time a complex maker of Buddhist modernism.[25]

---

[22] Wenzhu, "Da Foding Shoulengyan Jing Jingji 大佛頂首楞嚴經講記 [A Commentary of the Śūraṅgama Sūtra]," in *Droplets* 1:1–3.

[23] James A. Benn, "Another Look at the Pseudo-Śūraṃgama Sūtra," *Harvard Journal of Asiatic Studies* 68 (June 2008): 57–89.

[24] Wenzhu, "Lengyan Jing Qichu Powang Shifan Xianjian 楞嚴經七處破妄十番顯見 [The Seven Negations of False View and Ten Metaphors for Seeing the Nature of Reality]," *Droplets* 4:2, 717–718.

[25] David L. McMahan, *The Making of Buddhist Modernism* (Oxford: Oxford University Press, 2008), 6–9, 18–21.

Like her co-religionists pressed to respond to the discourse of modernity, Man Chu was keenly aware of the cultural authority of science. Rather than simply arguing for the compatibility between Buddhism and science or positioning Buddhism in a competition for truth claims with science, she participated in what Erik Hammerstrom terms the "discursive field of the philosophies of life" by reflecting on human origins, the ontological and epistemological status of the human being, and an ethics that was linked to self-cultivation.[26] She critiqued the limits of scientific knowing and posited that Buddhist empiricism represented a more superior form of knowing, free from delusion, that would lead to the ending of suffering. She was concerned with the ethical implications of science. In her lectures aimed primarily at laypeople, she asserted that Buddhism provided the foundation for an ethical life in a modern and global world. In addition to her critique of materialism, she also spoke of the devastation of wars and the danger posed by destructive weapons. Driven by compassion, she claimed, Buddhism would inspire new discoveries in science and also serve as its guiding principle with the ultimate aims of improving human life and alleviating suffering.[27]

Man Chu embodied what I call a modern student-monk identity. The early twentieth century saw the emergence of a group of young monastics who thought of themselves as members of a unique community distinct from the rest of the Chinese *saṃgha*. Having attended new-style Buddhist academies, they paid close attention to sociopolitical issues, were critical of the traditional Buddhist establishment, and passionately participated in the textual community made up of the numerous Buddhist newspapers and periodicals. This collective identity therefore became a discursive tool for student-monks to redefine Buddhism in new social orders.[28] Over the course of the twentieth century, the locale for the production of this identity expanded into a transnational one as a result of migration or displacement.

Man Chu's ideas about the place of Buddhism in the modern world were informed by the above-mentioned textual community. They were also its driving force. She wrote and lectured extensively on how to live a Buddhist way of life by engaging with issues such as family relationships, youth engagement, human psychology, and war and peace. Like her fellow student-monks, she was optimistic about the role of Buddhism in modern societies, if Buddhist practices and soteriology were redefined to focus on actions taken by ordinary individuals in everyday life. Her career exemplifies the hybridity of modern Buddhism by challenging the dualistic tropes of tradition-modernity and Asian-Western. While accepting the discourse of modernity into the categories of Buddhism, she did not hesitate to criticize its weaknesses. Furthermore, she insisted on the particularities of her tradition in

---

[26] Erik J. Hammerstrom, *The Science of Chinese Buddhism: Early Twentieth-Century Engagements* (New York: Columbia University Press, 2016), 10.

[27] Wenzhu, "Zongjiao Fojiao Yu Kexue 宗教佛教與科學 [Religion, Buddhism, and Science]," in *Droplets* 3:3, 417–424.

[28] Rongdao Lai, "The Wuchang Ideal: Buddhist Education and Identity Production in Republican China," *Studies in Chinese Religions* 3, no. 1 (2017): 63.

interpreting scriptural sources to define what it meant to be a good Buddhist citizen in a global world.

Mobility and Identity

Border crossing underlines Man Chu's career. She had lived all of her adult life outside of China—first in the British colony of Hong Kong and later in the United States. Her identity as a Buddhist teacher, therefore, was formed at the intersection of modern Chinese Buddhist institutions, diasporic ethnic consciousness, and transnational spatial imagination. Yet, the fluidity of categories such as "Chinese," "American," and "Buddhist" necessitates attention to the particular processes in which the dynamic flow and exchange of religio-cultural capital and identity take place.

First, by "Chinese," I refer to "an association with and a cultural and linguistic literacy in a social space that is comprised of links to certain geographic localities" (be it mainland China, Hong Kong, or Taiwan), rather than any modern nation-state.[29] While links to China through cultural symbols and social practices define the identity and experience of the Chinese diaspora, it is also important to note its internal differences. The transnational circulation of Man Chu's teaching is ethno-culturally specific and takes place exclusively in Chinese. Yet, her lectures in Cantonese added another layer of linguistic-cultural specificity. Native Cantonese speakers inevitably find a stronger bond with Man Chu, compared to Dharma teachers who preach in Mandarin. At the same time, her written works are widely read beyond the Cantonese-speaking world. Therefore, this layered Chineseness is fluid. One's experience of Chinese Buddhism is conditioned by how one encounters her—whether through attending her lectures in person, watching them on the internet with subtitles, or reading her various works in both physical and digital formats.

Her stature as a Chinese Buddhist teacher is at least partially grounded in her distance from the People's Republic of China. The country witnessed devastation to its religious life and institutions during various political campaigns such as the Cultural Revolution. As part of a generation of Chinese monastics who fled communist China, Man Chu saw herself as a custodian of orthodox Chinese Buddhism. She is also perceived as such by those in the diasporic community. Her authority and authenticity, therefore, depend on her uprootedness.[30] The revitalization of Buddhism in contemporary China owes much to the Chinese diaspora. When Chinese Buddhism was recovering from the destruction of the Cultural Revolution, it was overseas monastics such as Man Chu who provided financial support and religious expertise. However, one has to avoid viewing these movements as unidirectional. Driven primarily by politics, these nodes of authority and legitimacy are constantly shifting. The history, institution, and practices of

---

[29] Reinke, *Mapping Modern Mahayana*, 10.
[30] Verchery, "An Alternative to the 'Westernization' Paradigm and Buddhist Global Imaginaires," 159.

modern Chinese Buddhism should be understood as a connected history of Buddhism in China and the diaspora. Jack Chia, in his study of Chinese Buddhism in maritime Southeast Asia, proposes the notion of "South China Sea Buddhism," which challenges assumptions about center and the periphery.[31] In fact, the diaspora *can be* a center for Buddhism where new institutions, expressions, and practices emerge. The circulation of resources and ideas between China and its diaspora, therefore, is part of the connected history of Chinese Buddhist modernism. Building on Chia's work, one might reasonably raise the possibility of conceptually framing this history as part of "Pacific World Buddhism."

Second, the case study of Man Chu offers (yet another) opportunity to reflect on ongoing debates about American Buddhism. Recognizing the racial stereotypes that often underscore the dichotomy between Buddhism in America (usually associated with Asian American Buddhists) and American Buddhism (of white converts), I appreciate Scott Mitchell's adoption of the more neutral term "US Buddhism" to refer to the variety of forms and expressions of Buddhism in the United States.[32] Yet, I choose to describe Man Chu and her community in Los Angeles as a form of American Buddhism. This is solely due to the issue of self-described identity and representation. Most of the members of Man Chu's temple I met referred to themselves as Americans (*Meiguoren* 美國人) *and* Chinese (*Zhonggouren* 中國人 or *huaren* 華人), whether they were recent immigrants or American-born Chinese. Therefore, I refer to their Buddhism as American Buddhism, regardless of the citizenship status of its adherents. Although often excluded by observers as "too Asian to be American," these American Chinese Buddhists are embedded in a global, cultural Buddhist China, and they are also active makers of a unique form of American Buddhism. Just as their Chineseness is layered, the hybridity of Americanness should be recognized in theorizing American Buddhism.[33]

Similarly, Man Chu is often introduced in Asia as Master Man Chu of America (*Meiguo de Wenzhu fashi* 美國的文珠法師). However, unlike her contemporaries such as Xingyun 星雲 (1927–2023) and Hsuan Hua 宣化 (1918-1995), the mission to transmit Buddhism to the West is not featured prominently in her biographical accounts. In additional to the scale of her activities, gender might also play a role in such depictions. Xingyun, the founder of the global Foguangshan order, has made a vow to bring Buddhism to all five continents of the world. Hsuan Hua, who founded the Dharma Realm Buddhist Association in Northern California, is touted as the "first American Patriarch of orthodox Buddhism."[34] Compared to the global presence and branch temples of these organizations, Man Chu's Perfect Enlightenment Temple is modest in scale—it never expanded beyond its Los Angeles Chinatown location, and she was usually aided by no more than one or two nuns at the temple. This diffused, fluid, and

---

[31] Jack Meng-Tat Chia, *Monks in Motion: Buddhism and Modernity across the South China Sea* (New York: Oxford University Press, 2020), 85.
[32] Mitchell, *Buddhism in America*, 8.
[33] Quli, "Western Self, Asian Other," 16–20.
[34] Verchery, "An Alternative to the 'Westernization' Paradigm and Buddhist Global Imaginaires," 161.

decentralized institutional model in modern Chinese Buddhism represents the majority. Most Chinese Buddhist temples in the United States were founded by individual teachers who are loosely connected to various regional, tonsure, and Dharma transmission networks—a model that has yet to be carefully theorized. Therefore, the study of the mobility and adaptability of these individual Buddhist teachers will shed light on a significant aspect of American Buddhism.

Lastly, it might be a cliché to say that Buddhism is not a static, homogenous entity. There is indeed no shortage of scholarly work drawing attention to the varieties and forms of Buddhism across different cultures and localities. Nonetheless, transnational Buddhists in the diaspora are not merely passive transmitters of Buddhism, but agents of knowledge production. Although often framed as authentic and orthodox Buddhism, these teachers selectively reconfigure Buddhist doctrines through their (re)interpretation of classical, scriptural sources. In the case of Man Chu, she accepted the discourse of modernity in making a case for the relevance of Buddhism in the modern world, while simultaneously defending ethno-culturally specific forms of Buddhism as not only authentic, but a superior way of knowing the nature of reality. If we take diasporic consciousness as cultural perceptions and historical memories, border crossings for these Buddhists shape the continuous production of identity and orthodoxy. Put another way, what it means to be Chinese, American, and Buddhist is informed as much by their border-crossing experiences as their places of origin. To return to Tweed's axioms, following the flows and paying attention to lesser-known figures and their activities at varying scales allow us to observe the hybridity, flexibility, and mobility of border crossings and identity production in global Buddhism.

Conclusion

As a nun from a small temple in Southern China who lived through one of the most tumultuous times in modern Chinese history, Man Chu's journey in becoming one of its most-learned Buddhist teachers is, to use her word, extraordinary. Her border crossings also epitomize the struggles and hopes of Chinese monastics of her generation. By situating her in the narrative of migration, race, and belonging in the United States, I show that the transmission of Buddhism is a significant aspect of transnational Chinese diasporic connectivity. As part of *The Oxford Handbook of American Buddhism*, this chapter is neither an overview of the history of Chinese Buddhism in the United States, nor is it an introduction to the largest Chinese Buddhist groups in the country. By focusing on an almost unknown nun, at least in Western academia, it identifies the social and historical processes in which ethnic and religious identities were (re)formulated through border-crossing. Ultimately, I hope this offers both a catalyst for the many books and dissertations that can be written, and an opportunity to test, challenge, revise, and complicate current discourse on what it means to be global, Chinese, American, and Buddhist in the twenty-first century.

REFERENCES

Ashiwa, Yoshiko, and David Wank. "The Globalization of Chinese Buddhism: Clergy and Devotee Networks in the Twentieth Century." *International Journal of Asian Studies* 2, no. 2 (2005): 217–237.

Benn, James A. "Another Look at the Pseudo-Śūraṃgama Sūtra." *Harvard Journal of Asiatic Studies* 68 (June 2008): 57–89.

Brook, Timothy. "Rethinking Syncretism: The Unity of the Three Teachings and Their Joint Worship in Late-Imperial China." *Journal of Chinese Religions* 21, no. 1 (January 1993): 13–44.

Chandler, Stuart. "Chinese Buddhism in America: Identity and Practice." In *The Faces of Buddhism in America*, edited by Charles S. Prebish and Kenneth K. Tanaka, 13–30. Berkeley: University of California Press, 1998.

Chandler, Stuart. *Establishing a Pure Land on Earth: The Foguang Buddhist Perspective on Modernization and Globalization*. Honolulu: University of Hawai'i Press, 2004.

Cheah, Joseph. *Race and Religion in American Buddhism: White Supremacy and Immigrant Adaptation*. New York: Oxford University Press, 2011.

Chia, Jack Meng-Tat. *Monks in Motion: Buddhism and Modernity across the South China Sea*. New York: Oxford University Press, 2020.

Dean, Kenneth, and Zhenman Zheng. *Ritual Alliances of the Putian Plain*, Volume 1: *Historical Introduction to the Return of the Gods*. Leiden: Brill, 2010.

Deng, Jiazhou. *Xianggang Fojiao Shi* 香港佛教史 [A History of Buddhism in Hong Kong]. Hong Kong: Zhonghua shuju, 2015.

Fields, Rick. *How the Swans Came to the Lake: A Narrative History of Buddhism in America*. 3rd ed., rev. and updated. Boston: Shambhala Publications, 1992.

Hammerstrom, Erik J. *The Science of Chinese Buddhism: Early Twentieth-Century Engagements*. New York: Columbia University Press, 2016.

Han, Chenxing. *Be the Refuge: Raising the Voices of Asian American Buddhists*. Berkeley, CA: North Atlantic Books, 2021.

Huang, C. Julia. *Charisma and Compassion: Cheng Yen and the Buddhist Tzu Chi Movement*. Cambridge, MA: Harvard University Press, 2009.

Kuah, Khun Eng. *Rebuilding the Ancestral Village: Singaporeans in China*. Hong Kong: Hong Kong University Press, 2011.

Kuhn, Philip A. *Chinese among Others: Emigration in Modern Times*. Lanham, MD: Rowman & Littlefield, 2008.

Lai, Him Mark. *Becoming Chinese American: A History of Communities and Institutions*. Walnut Creek, CA: AltaMira Press, 2004.

Lai, Rongdao. "The Wuchang Ideal: Buddhist Education and Identity Production in Republican China." *Studies in Chinese Religions* 3, no. 1 (2017): 55–70.

Lai, Rongdao. "Tiantai Transnationalism: Mobility, Identity, and Lineage Networks in Modern Chinese Buddhism." In *Transnational Religious Spaces*, edited by Philip Clart and Adam Jones, 210–224. De Gruyter, 2020.

Mayer, Alexander. "Commentarial Literature." In *Encyclopedia of Buddhism*, edited by Robert E. Buswell, Jr., 166–169. New York: Macmillan, 2004.

McMahan, David L. *The Making of Buddhist Modernism*. Oxford: Oxford University Press, 2008.

Mitchell, Scott. *Buddhism in America: Global Religion, Local Contexts*. New York: Bloomsbury, 2016.

Nichols, Brian. "Tourist Temples and Places of Practice: Charting Multiple Paths in the Revival of Monasteries." In *Buddhism after Mao: Negotiations, Continuities, and Reinventions*, edited by Zhe Ji, Gareth Fisher, and André Laliberté, 97–119. Honolulu: University of Hawai'i Press, 2019.

Numrich, Paul David. *Old Wisdom in the New World: Americanization in Two Immigrant Theravada Buddhist Temples*. Knoxville: University of Tennessee Press, 1996.

Pittman, Don. *Toward a Modern Chinese Buddhism: Taixu's Reforms*. Honolulu: University of Hawai'i Press, 2001.

Quli, Natalie. "Western Self, Asian Other: Modernity, Authenticity, and Nostalgia for 'Tradition' in Buddhist Studies." *Journal of Buddhist Ethics* 16 (2009): 1–38.

Reinke, Jens. *Mapping Modern Mahayana Chinese Buddhism and Migration in the Age of Global Modernity*. Berlin: De Gruyter, 2021.

Ritzinger, Justin. *Anarchy in the Pure Land: Reinventing the Cult of Maitreya in Modern Chinese Buddhism*. New York: Oxford University Press, 2017.

Tweed, Thomas A. "Theory and Method in the Study of Buddhism: Toward 'Translocative Analysis.'" In *Buddhism beyond Borders: New Perspectives on Buddhism in the United States*, edited by Scott A. Mitchell and Natalie E. F. Quli, 3–19. Albany: State University of New York Press, 2015.

Verchery, Lina. "An Alternative to the 'Westernization' Paradigm and Buddhist Global Imaginaires." In *Buddhism in the Global Eye: Beyond East and West*, edited by John S. Harding, Victor Sōgen Hori, and Alexander Soucy, 150–162. New York: Bloomsbury, 2020.

Verchery, Lina. "Impersonal Intimacy: Relational Ethics and Self-Cultivation in a Transnational Chinese Buddhist Monastic Network." PhD dissertation, Harvard University, 2021.

Wenzhu. *Baodao Lüxing Ji* 寶島旅行記 [Taiwan Travelogue]. Beitou, Taiwan: Rensheng zazhi, 1958.

Wenzhu. "Da Foding Shoulengyan Jing Jingji 大佛頂首楞嚴經講記 [A Commentary of the Śūraṅgama Sūtra]." In *Juehai Diandi* 覺海點滴 [Droplets in the Sea of Awakening], Vol. 1:1–3. Los Angeles: Western American Buddhist Association, 2013.

Wenzhu. *Juehai Diandi* 覺海點滴 [Droplets in the Sea of Awakening]. Los Angeles: Western American Buddhist Association, 2013.

Wenzhu. "Lengyan Jing Qichu Powang Shifan Xianjian 楞嚴經七處破妄十番顯見 [The Seven Negations of False View and Ten Metaphors for Seeing the Nature of Reality]." In *Juehai Diandi* 覺海點滴 [Droplets in the Sea of Awakening], 4:2:717–782. Los Angeles: Western American Buddhist Association, 2013.

Wenzhu. "Wenzhu Fashi Zuopin Ji 文珠法師作品集 [Collection of Venerable Wenzhu's Work]." 2016. Accessed June 3, 2023. http://wabala.org/tc/wenzhu_work.php.

Wenzhu. "Zongjiao Fojiao Yu Kexue 宗教佛教與科學 [Religion, Buddhism, and Science]." In *Juehai Diandi* 覺海點滴 [Droplets in the Sea of Awakening], 409–424. Los Angeles: Western American Buddhist Association, 2013.

Xianggang Fajiao lianhehui. "Wenzhu Fashi." *Xianggang Fojiao* 香港佛教 [Hong Kong Buddhism], July 5, 2016.

Yu, Lingbo. *Minguo gaoseng zhuan sanbian* 民國高僧傳三編 [Biographies of Eminent Monks of the Republican Period, Part III]. Taipei: Huiming wenhua, 2001.

Yu, Lingbo. *Zhongguo Fojiao Haiwai Hongfa Renwu Zhi* 中國佛教海外弘法人物誌 [Records of Overseas Propagators of Chinese Buddhism]. Taipei: Huiju chubanshe, 1997.

CHAPTER 7

PURE LAND BUDDHISM IN AMERICA

JESSE J. LEE

Introduction

PERHAPS the most significant challenge of any history is the problem of definition. Conventionally, Pure Land Buddhism has largely been defined by three key elements: devotion to Amitābha Buddha, hope for rebirth in Amitābha's buddha-realm (Sukhāvatī), and ritual practice of buddha-name recitation (*nembutsu/nianfo*), especially as an expression of faith in the other-power (*tariki*) of Amitābha. However, more recent scholarship has recognized that such elements are generally associated with Japanese expressions and perceptions of Pure Land Buddhism. Indeed, much modern research on the history of Pure Land Buddhism rests upon the foundation of Japanese Buddhist sectarian scholarship, especially from the imperial period, which sought to assert the religious legitimacy and (arguably) supremacy of their traditions. Consequently, these Japanese scholars emphasized the importance of Japanese Pure Land Buddhist ideologies, practices, textual sources, and genealogies. Subsequently, many Western scholars in the latter half of the twentieth century reified the implicit association of Pure Land Buddhism with specific Japanese definitions and categories, including in histories of Buddhist transmissions from Japan to the West. As such, it necessarily precludes the inclusion of other potential Pure Land traditions and practices, such as devotion to buddhas other than Amitābha and hope for rebirth in their buddha-realms. Therefore, recent scholarship has attempted to expand the boundaries of what constitutes Pure Land Buddhism in order to more comprehensively understand the networks of Pure Land traditions, expressions, and histories (Yu 2014).

Perhaps the most common narrative of Pure Land Buddhism in North America begins with the arrival of two Jōdo Shinshū priests arriving in California on September 1, 1899.

While undoubtedly a significant moment for the history of the Buddhist Churches of America (BCA), the largest and oldest Pure Land organization in North America, emphasis on this particular origin point carries with it some implicit preconceptions of the definition and scope of Pure Land Buddhism in America. First, it privileges an institutional history of Pure Land Buddhism, whereby those associated with an official organization are granted greater significance since they are historically more recognizable and traceable. Second and subsequently, a focus on the institutional history of Pure Land in America is predominantly a history of Japanese Pure Land Buddhism. As such, other expressions and evidences of Pure Land practice or ideology are often overlooked, especially if they do not fit neatly into a distinct denominational definition or institution. Third, the Nishi Honganji branch of Jōdo Shinshū Buddhism is often at the center of common Pure Land Buddhist histories in America, minimizing the influence and presence of other Japanese Pure Land Buddhist sects and non-Japanese Buddhist movements. In this way, many introductory histories of Pure Land Buddhism in America only cursorily address Higashi Honganji Jōdo Shinshū, Jōdoshū, various Asian Buddhist movements, and American intellectual and popular engagements with Pure Land Buddhism. While the BCA remains an essential element in the story of Pure Land Buddhism in North America, the present chapter hopes to explore this history in a more expansive way that better represents its great historical diversity and dynamism.

This project of definitional expansion, however, is complicated when studying and telling the history of Pure Land Buddhism in North America. To begin with, most of the established research on Pure Land Buddhism in North America focuses on Japanese Pure Land Buddhism. This is not only due to the influence of Japanese sectarian scholarship, but also due to the fact that the most recognizable Pure Land institutions and movements in North America have been associated with Japanese immigrants and missionaries. Indeed, Japanese Buddhism has largely dominated the discourse of Buddhism in America, both popularly and academically, especially before 1965. Moreover, as already mentioned, most historical sources concerning Buddhism in North America before 1965 are either Japanese Buddhist sources or white American intellectual and convert encounters with various types of Buddhism. As such, the history of Pure Land Buddhism in North America necessarily centers the stories, texts, and practices of Japanese Buddhists and Japanese Buddhism. At times, Pure Land Buddhism is even eclipsed by and amalgamated into the broader category of "Japanese Buddhism" or "Mahayana Buddhism," which presents its own set of methodological issues. Nevertheless, it is important to acknowledge the ways in which older paradigms of thought and categorization are perpetuated, while simultaneously gesturing toward necessary future areas of research. While the history told here will include a significant focus on Japanese Buddhism, there is much work to be done to deepen, broaden, and nuance the story of Pure Land Buddhism in America.

THE FIRST INTRODUCTIONS

The first adherents of Pure Land practice and/or ideology in the United States were likely Chinese immigrants in the nineteenth century. As Chinese immigrants came to the United States to labor in mining, agriculture, or construction, they brought with them their religious beliefs and practices. The dynamics of lay Chinese religiosity did not require strict adherence to any single religion, denomination, or school of thought. As such, even though Chinese immigrants established many temples, derogatorily labeled "joss houses" by white American observers, they often included a variety of religious artifacts from Daoist, Confucian, Buddhist, and other indigenous Chinese religious cosmologies. Such religious syncretism and fluidity among Chinese laborers suggest that Pure Land practices and ideologies would likely have been present in some fashion. Since at least the writings and interpretations of Tan-Luan (476–542), devotion to Amitābha Buddha and the practice of buddha-name recitation were a form of general salvation accessible to all people, not just monastics. Later developments of Pure Land ideology became associated with death and dying rituals, particularly communal buddha-name recitation as a practice to ensure rebirth in the Pure Land. As Kathryn Gin Lum has noted, death and funeral rites were a significant element of Chinese American religious experience (Gin Lum 2019). As such, it is likely that such ideologies and practices were tied to some form of Pure Land Buddhism, though not exclusively. Additionally, since Chinese Pure Land monks also traveled to the United States and performed religious rituals for the immigrant communities, it is likely that many of these funerals had significant Pure Land elements (Shen 2017). However, the extent to which such Pure Land practices were evident among Chinese American immigrant communities remains an area for further research.

While the everyday religiosity of Chinese American immigrants in the nineteenth century is methodologically difficult due to the scarcity of historical sources, especially from an emic perspective, the joss houses that remain can provide some insight into the religious dynamics of early Chinese American communities. Indeed, the prominence of the color gold and lavish ornamentation inside these houses of worship may have been intentional artistic representations of the heavenly Western Paradise, Amitābha's Pure Land, thereby elevating the senses and consciousness of worshippers away from the mundane to the divine (Gordon 2022). Moreover, some of these joss houses have rooms specifically dedicated to Buddhist meditation and practice, such as the "Moon Temple" at the Oroville Chinese Temple, which houses three buddha statues. Many of these early temples had statues dedicated to a variety of Daoist, Confucian, and Buddhist deities, especially Guanyin, the Chinese manifestation of Avalokiteśvara. However, while Buddhist architecture and iconography are present in these places, the specific dynamics of such Buddhism remain understudied. Further research into the art and architecture of these religious artifacts may provide a glimpse into the varieties of

Buddhism represented in early Chinese American communities. For instance, Guanyin is also known as Amitābha's attendant in his Pure Land, aiding individuals in their rebirth there. Moreover, devotion to the Medicine Buddha (Bhaiṣajyaguru), who is also associated with Amitābha, was commonly incorporated into traditional Chinese medicinal principles and practice. Thus, it is likely that early Chinese immigrant communities venerated the Medicine Buddha, especially through buddha-name recitation and belief in his buddha-realm (Vaiḍūryanirbhāsa), alongside other Chinese deities, such as Hua Tuo, the Daoist deity of medicine. In these ways, further investigation into the art and architecture in joss houses can provide additional insight into how Pure Land ideologies and practices were embraced by early Chinese American immigrants.

Early American Intellectual Encounters

While Chinese immigrants were certainly the first to introduce Pure Land ideologies and practices to North America, white Americans rarely recognized the specific Buddhist elements in such religious communities. Often, white American observers would categorize all Chinese religiosity as heathenism and superstition, without attendance to particular dynamics within and between such communities. The first American encounters with Buddhism *qua* Buddhism were through orientalist translations of religious texts and encountering Buddhist missionaries and representatives (Tweed 1992). Notably, the three main Pure Land Buddhist texts (the Visualization Sutra, the Larger Sukhāvatī Sutra, and the Shorter Sukhāvatī Sutra) were first translated into English in 1894 by F. Max Müller and Takakusu Junjirō. Orientalist translations of Asian religious texts were deeply influential in Western engagement with and appropriation of such traditions, especially in literature and religion. While the influence of specific books from Müller's *Sacred Books of the East* series on American Romanticism, Transcendentalism, and Theosophy (among others) has been explored in existing scholarship, the particular reach and influence of these Pure Land texts remain understudied. However, it is notable that Paul Carus, the famous author and editor, published *The Gospel of Buddha* in the same year as Müller and Takakusu's translations. This book took existing translations of Buddhist texts and deeply edited them to resemble Christian New Testament parables and teachings. Notably, Carus's book included one chapter entitled "Amitabha, the Unbounded Light," which gives a presentation of Pure Land Buddhist ideology from the identity of Amitābha, to the qualities of his Pure Land, to the practice of buddha-name recitation. In this way, American audiences were certainly engaging Pure Land ideologies and texts, albeit in their own distinctive ways.

One year prior to the publication of these texts, the World Parliament of Religions was meeting in Chicago, offering another opportunity for Americans to engage with Buddhist leaders and teachers. In the years leading up to the World Parliament, Japanese

Buddhists, both lay and clerical, were intentionally making international contacts and traveling to foreign countries in order to raise Japanese cultural prestige on a global scale. While some were skeptical of the normative Christian nature of the World Parliament, especially since the organizers were all Christian theologians, six delegates of Japanese Buddhism decided to attend (Zheng 2019). Four of the delegates were monks representing different traditions: Shaku Sōen (Zen), Ashitsu Jitsuzen (Tendai), Toki Hōryū (Shingon), and Yatsubuchi Banryū (Nishi Honganji Jōdo Shinshū). In addition to Yatsubuchi's presence at the World Parliament, the Japanese delegates brought with them some pamphlets on Japanese Buddhism to distribute. Notably, two such pamphlets were *Skeleton of a Philosophy of Religion* by Kiyozawa Manshi, a notable Higashi Honganji Shin Buddhist reformer, and *A Brief Account of Shin-Shiu* by Akamatsu Renjō, a notable Nishi Honganji Shin Buddhist reformer (Hardings 2008). Despite this representation of Pure Land Buddhism at the World Parliament of Religions, the delegates had a common objective: to assert the legitimacy of Japanese Mahāyāna Buddhism over and against Theravāda Buddhists for Western audiences. As such, Pure Land ideology was eclipsed and integrated into a broader presentation of Japanese Buddhism. Nevertheless, the World Parliament of Religions marks an important American encounter with Japanese Buddhism, including its Pure Land aspects.

EARLY JAPANESE PURE LAND IN AMERICA

Prior to the World Parliament of Religions and intellectual engagements with Pure Land ideology and texts, Japanese immigrants were already bringing with them their religious identities and traditions. As larger waves of Japanese immigration came to Hawaii and the continental United States, often to work as agricultural laborers, there grew a greater need for spiritual and religious leadership among immigrant communities. Like the Chinese Pure Land Buddhist monks discussed above, several Shin Buddhist priests traveled with Japanese immigrants to serve such communities. Perhaps the most notable of these was Sōryū Kagahi of the Nishi Honganji sect. After arriving in Honolulu, Hawaii, he established the first Shin Buddhist temple on the Big Island in 1889. Importantly, Kagahi was communicating his efforts with the religious leadership of his denomination, located in Kyoto. Recognizing the need for Shin priests to minister to the Japanese Hawaiian communities, he requested additional missionaries and resources. His requests went largely unfulfilled until 1897, when Nishi Honganji leaders properly assessed the situation in Hawaii and sent several groups of missionaries to the islands, as well as recognizing independent Shin priests already ministering to the immigrant communities (Ama 2011). In the meantime, other sects of Japanese Pure Land Buddhism sent their own missionaries to establish their own sectarian religious communities. For example, the first Jōdoshū temple in Hawaii was established in Honolulu in 1894, and the first Higashi Honganji temple was established on Kauai in 1899. While there was some sectarian competition and tension at times, most Japanese

Pure Land lay Buddhists coexisted fluidly. Religious institutions, along with educational institutions, were often locations for immigrant cultural solidarity and solace, which often meant that the finer details of Pure Land sectarian difference mattered less to lay populations than their communal experience as foreign laborers.

Like the situation in Hawaii, Japanese immigrant populations on the American mainland required clerical leadership and aid. In 1897, a Shin Buddhist layperson from San Francisco, named Nisaburō Hirano, petitioned the Nishi Honganji headquarters for priests and missionaries. The next year, on July 6, 1898, two Shin Buddhist priests, Eryū Honda and Ejun Miyamoto, arrived in San Francisco. Later that year, they would meet with local Japanese immigrants and establish a Young Men's Buddhist Association (YMBA) and the first Buddhist church in the United States, which would become the headquarters for the Buddhist Mission of North America (BMNA). Over the next few years, the BMNA would further establish additional para-organizational associations and services, such as the YMBA Newsletter (*Bukkyo Seinenkai Kaiho*, 1900), the Buddhist Women's Association (*Fujinkai* 1900), and Japanese-language schools, among others. Additionally, the number of temples or churches, as the organization began to call them in 1905, increased steadily at a rate of at least one church per year from 1898 until 1946. In spite of this incredible growth in population size and social reach, the BMNA often encountered considerable difficulties, which most scholars recognize as the underlying motivation for the transformation of their organizational structures and functions. Indeed, the virulent anti-Japanese sentiment experienced by Japanese Buddhist immigrants fostered a greater need for ethnic and communal solidarity, which in turn accelerated the establishment and growth of Buddhist churches (Kashima 1977).

FURTHER DEVELOPMENTS OF JAPANESE PURE LAND

While the presence of anti-Japanese sentiment in the United States was seemingly pervasive throughout the first half of the twentieth century, there were several significant moments that especially mobilized militant attitudes (and occasionally attacks) against Japanese immigrants. First, the Russo-Japanese War precipitated strong anti-Japanese sentiment among the general American public, which found expression not only in physical attacks on Japanese persons and property, but also in the formation of the Japanese and Korean Exclusion League in 1905, which was later renamed as the Asiatic Exclusion League in 1907. Consequently, these racial antagonisms may have been the catalyst for the encouraged name changes to Anglicized Buddhist *churches*. In 1905, the fourth director of the BMNA, Reverend Koyu Uchida, changed the previous title of the Hongwanji Branch Office, the BMNA headquarters in San Francisco, to the Buddhist Church of San Francisco, and he encouraged other BMNA communities (*bukkyokai*, literally Buddhist association) to also call themselves Buddhist churches. Moreover, with the passing of the California Alien Land Laws of 1913 and 1920 and the Oriental Exclusion Act of 1924, the BMNA intensified efforts to organize and mobilize Buddhist communities and associations to meet the needs of the Japanese American community and adapt to their American context.

One significant way that the BMNA did this was through legal negotiations with the state. While the first Buddhist church to file articles of incorporation was the Fresno Buddhist Church in 1901, most churches began incorporating after 1913, thereby legalizing their designation as religious organizations, or "churches," with the state of California. Notably, both the San Francisco Buddhist Church and the Buddhist Church of Stockton were officially incorporated in 1913, the same year as the first California Alien Land Law. Moreover, the BMNA officially adopted an organizational constitution to coordinate their various churches in 1924, the same year as the Oriental Exclusion Act.

Another significant way that the BMNA sought to adapt to their American context was to assert their American identity. Indeed, the establishment of the first Boy Scout troop associated with a Buddhist church was in Fresno, California, in 1920. Furthermore, one of the most notable and noticeable transformations within the BCA throughout its history is the way in which Jōdo Shinshū Buddhism was linguistically translated from Japanese to English. The purpose of the linguistic developments in the BMNA was primarily to translate the religious nature and standard of their communities to their American context, both to the state and wider American audiences. This translation project developed gradually. For example, some of the earliest Buddhist missionaries from Japan often referred to themselves as reverends, ministers, or priests; Buddhist communities were first called churches in 1905; and the leader of the BMNA was changed from director (*kantoku*) to bishop (*socho*, which might be better translated as "president") in 1918. However, it was not until the 1920s that the BMNA started translating their religious positions, structures, and beliefs into English on a wider scale. For example, *gatha* was translated as "hymn," *dana* as "gift," *sangha* as "brotherhood of Buddhists," and *shinjin* as "faith." The BMNA would continue this project of anglicization and Americanization as they continued to face xenophobic hostility, both culturally and legally.

However, the transformations of Japanese Pure Land Buddhism in America were not unilaterally reactive to anti-Asian sentiment and Christian-centric legal and cultural values. Not only did Pure Land missionaries seek to minister to Japanese immigrant communities, but they also intentionally sought to share and spread their religion among white Americans. In response to the reports made by the two Shin Buddhists priests in San Francisco in 1898, the headquarters of the Nishi Honganji in Kyoto sent two Buddhist missionaries to California. Shuye Sonoda and Kakuryo Nishijima arrived in San Francisco on September 1, 1899, an event publicized by an article in the *San Francisco Chronicler*. Not only did these two missionaries help build up the North American Buddhist Mission for Japanese immigrant communities, but they actively sought to make Pure Land Buddhism available and accessible to the American public. As such, they quickly began holding English-language services and messages in November 1899 and initiated an English-language Buddhist periodical, *The Light of Dharma*, in April 1901.

Notably, Sonoda was a founding chairman (alongside six white American directors) of a nondenominational American Buddhist organization, the Dharma Sangha of Buddha, established in 1900. The purpose of this organization, according to its foundational documents, was to propagate and teach the doctrines of Buddha Shakyamuni "embraced in the generic term, Buddhism." In this way, Japanese Pure Land Buddhist leaders cooperated with American Buddhists to encourage greater public awareness of their religion, regardless of denominational or doctrinal distinction. Such pansectarian Buddhist associations and collaborations were common practices for Japanese Buddhists, both in Japan and abroad. As already discussed, Japanese Buddhist attendees of the World Parliament of Religion collaborated together to represent Japanese Mahāyāna Buddhism, largely guided by the *Bukkyō Kakushū Kyōkai* (Buddhist Transdenominational Committee), established in 1890. Especially since Western audiences were most familiar with orientalist translations and descriptions of Buddhism that emphasized the Indian origins of the tradition, many Japanese Buddhists developed a broader presentation of their religion that included Theravāda and Pali texts and terms, as well as a greater emphasis on the historical Buddha. Indeed, the first bishop of the Honpa Honganji Mission of Hawaii, Emyō Imamura, often engaged with white American Buddhist sympathizers and converts in this way. Not only did he ordain and employ several white converts, but he also embraced those interested in the broader and more generalized tenets of Buddhism, including Theosophists. He even invited Henry Steele Olcott, one of the founders of the Theosophical Society, to lecture on Buddhism when he visited Hawaii in 1901 (Ama 2019).

In their mission to spread greater awareness of Buddhism in their American context, Japanese Pure Land Buddhists necessarily responded to popular American perceptions and expectations of the Buddhist tradition, sometimes without denominational distinction. Consequently, some Japanese Pure Land Buddhists de-emphasized the unique elements of their denomination to reach greater audiences, sometimes incorporating non–Pure Land Buddhist practices and ideologies into their services. Indeed, even some of the first white initiates and priests of the BMNA during the 1920s and 1930s had various perspectives of Buddhism, at times diminishing the significance of Shinran's doctrines for more Theravāda understandings of karma, nirvana, and enlightenment. Especially since white converts were active participants in the proliferation of Buddhism to wider American audiences, playing important roles in the English propagation programs in Hawaii and on the mainland, such Western perspectives of Buddhism certainly influenced the ways Japanese American Buddhists understood their organizational mission and identity (Mitchell 2016).

Japanese Pure Land Buddhism necessarily adapted to the many dynamics of the American political, religious, and cultural context. Japanese religious institutions became sites of cultural and linguistic solidarity for immigrant communities, especially in response to widespread anti-Asian sentiment. In order to make the peaceable religious nature of their organization visible to the American state and public, the BMNA undertook a series of strategic transformations and translations. Furthermore, outreach to and engagement with Americans interested in Buddhism required further adaptations in their religious collaborations and presentation, especially considering the wide variety of perspectives and expectations such Americans had of Buddhism. In this way, while Japanese Pure Land institutions were still deeply connected to religious leadership in Japan, these Japanese American Buddhist churches were developing a unique American expression of Pure Land Buddhism in response to the multifarious American context (Mitchell 2023).

Japanese Pure Land in Internment and Afterward

Despite such strategies of assimilation and adaptation, the height of anti-Japanese sentiment erupted after the attack on Pearl Harbor on December 7, 1941. Shortly thereafter, President Franklin Delano Roosevelt signed into action Executive Order 9066 on February 19, 1942, which called for the forced internment of all persons of Japanese descent, regardless of citizenship status, in designated strategic military zones. After the attack on Pearl Harbor, the BMNA released public statements condemning the Pearl Harbor attack and reasserting their loyalty to the United States. Moreover, Buddhist churches organized other patriotic campaigns, including donating money to the war effort (contributing to the Red Cross or through buying defense bonds) and giving public patriotic sermons and lectures, which would continue into internment. Despite persistent insistence of their loyalty to the United States and public actions to demonstrate such loyalty, most BMNA church communities, which were located on the West Coast, were interned. The ministers and leaders associated with the BMNA headquarters in San Francisco were all interned at the camp in Topaz, Utah, where they met with other BMNA leaders from other camps in a series of meetings between February and July 1944 to completely restructure their organization, rewrite their constitution, and officially file their Articles of Incorporation as the Buddhist Churches of America.

All such legal assimilation and linguistic translation that developed in the early twentieth century took on greater significance and consequence with the advent of World War II and Japanese internment, indisputably the most remarkable period and transition in Japanese American history. Duncan Williams argues that the wartime experience of internment, military endeavors, and relocation shaped and eventually defined Japanese American Buddhism as distinctly American and Buddhist. While the Christian American ethos was consistently put into conflict with the presence and identities of Japanese American Buddhists, especially through the popular and structural prejudices set against them, most Japanese American Buddhists attempted to assert the compatibility of Buddhism with American identity. As such, they articulated and asserted their right to freedom of religion in the camps and the military in order to make room for themselves in the American religious landscape. Moreover, Japanese American Buddhists who participated in the draft or in the military in general, either through intelligence, administration, or as translators, in the Pacific theater or as combat personnel in Europe, were seen as asserting Japanese American loyalty (and Buddhist compatibility) with American identity and goals. In this way, Japanese Americans contended that it was their specific Buddhist Dharmic duty to participate in the war effort with the express purpose of fomenting greater acceptance of Buddhism, which would aid Americans in practicing one of their greatest defining values: religious liberty (Williams 2019).

While the 1944 reincorporation as the Buddhist Churches of America instigated many changes, two of the most significant were transitioning all organizational authority to the Nisei (the American-born second generation) and severing organizational ties with the Jōdo Shinshū headquarters in Kyoto. In regard to the first, the necessity for all organizational leaders and legal incorporators to be Nisei established American citizenship as a requirement for institutional authority. While the older generations still held considerable spiritual and religious authority, the ownership and function of the new BCA belonged to the younger generations (Masatsugu 2023). Moreover, while Shin Buddhist priests were formerly required to go to Japan for their religious education and ordination, such organizational ties to Japan became unpopular and impractical during and after internment. Consequently, while English religious education programs were initiated in both the United States and Japan in the 1930s, the Buddhist Study Center was established in 1949 in Berkeley, California. This would become the official center for ministerial training for all North American Shin Buddhist priests, officially incorporating with the State of California in 1969 as a religious seminary and graduate school (now called the Institute of Buddhist Studies). In this way, religious education and organizational leadership became aligned with American citizenship, legal incorporation, and the English language. Especially in regard to the English language, all services were required to be in English during the internment camps, and this practice largely continued after resettlement. Not only was this an outward expression of American cultural loyalty, but this was also a practical implementation for Nisei leaders and American-educated priests.

As Japanese Americans were slowly released from internment, there loomed a great uncertainty about the future. While there were some people of goodwill protecting the assets of interned Japanese Americans, such as Shin convert priest, Julius Goldwater, in Los Angeles, many Japanese Americans who returned to the West Coast found their homes, businesses, and educational and religious institutions either destroyed, occupied, and/or seized by the government. Since many Japanese American properties were lost on the West Coast, resettlement drove a large population of Japanese Americans eastward into the Midwest and the East Coast. While eastward expansion was happening before internment, most Japanese Pure Land churches were established in places where Japanese immigrants already resided. As such, because most Japanese immigrant populations lived on the West Coast, this was where the majority of Buddhist churches were. Unlike Zen Buddhist traditions, which in many cases specifically catered to and sought out white American converts, Jōdo Shinshū largely remained an immigrant religious tradition and moved to meet the needs of Japanese immigrant communities. With the movement of many Japanese Americans eastward, the BCA became a truly national organization.

Much like before internment, religious institutions became sites of cultural solidarity and aid, helping Japanese American Buddhists slowly rebuild their lives and communities. Even after the war ended, prevalent anti-Japanese sentiment persisted, making such religious and cultural institutions foundational to Japanese American community life. As such, the BCA continued to strategically transform their organization to assert its authentic American identity. For example, the BCA began using the pipe organ in their services in the late 1940s, installing an organ in the San Francisco Buddhist Church in 1947. Moreover, the BCA published its first hymnal, entitled "Service Book and Hymnal: A Manual of Religious Observances and Hymns for the Use of the Buddhist Churches of America," in 1953. Many of these hymns were English translations of Buddhist texts and chants from a variety of Buddhist traditions from Japan, China, and India, set to Western musical arrangements. Since American definitions of religion are often informed by Christian traditions, especially Protestantism, such developments continued to assert Japanese American Buddhist religiosity and its right to belong in the American religious and cultural landscape, especially in response to persistent anti-Asian prejudice. The BCA also continued to engage with other forms of Buddhism and popular American perceptions of Buddhism. Notably, Zen/Beat Buddhist converts were often included and accommodated in BCA study groups, conferences, and publications during the Cold War era (Masatsugu 2008). Moreover, the BCA was formative in the establishment of the Buddhist Council of America in 1952, which was a pan-Buddhist organization that sought to encourage interdenominational Buddhist cooperation, greater interfaith dialogue, and greater public awareness and acceptance of Buddhism in America.

While the BCA remains an important religious and cultural institution in the twenty-first century, like many other institutional religious organizations in America, membership numbers have dramatically declined since the 1970s. While it was estimated that the BCA was made up of about 50,000 families in 1960, that number had fallen to about 18,000 families by 1995 (Aquino 1996). The most recent estimate according to the BCA website is around 12,000 members across over sixty churches, with declining membership exacerbated by the COVID pandemic. There is no clear consensus on why membership numbers have dropped so dramatically over the past several decades, but some attribute it to the greater assimilation and acceptance of Japanese Americans to broader American culture and society. Others have argued that the BCA itself has become too Americanized, overly resembling Protestant Christianity, thereby becoming another ritualized institutional religion of which many younger generations are disinterested and critical. Indeed, many Buddhist churches that were largely composed of Japanese Americans a few decades ago are experiencing shifting racial dynamics, becoming more multiethnic and sometimes even minority Japanese American communities as Buddhist churches continue to attract diverse converts but struggle with youth retention (Spencer 2014).

Regardless of the reasons for their membership decline, the BCA remains a strong and important institution, deeply embedded into the fabric of American society. For example, the BCA is associated with many other American religious organizations, participating in their regular meetings, such as the World Parliament of Religions, the National Buddhist Prison Sangha Gathering, and the American Buddhist Congress, among others. Moreover, the BCA has regularly participated in social protest movements since the 1960s, from the 1963 "March on Washington" to the 2018 "Thousand Ministers March for Justice" in Washington, D.C. Notably, the BCA issued a public statement condemning the Trump administration's 2017 travel ban against seven Muslim-majority countries and suspending the settlement of Syrian refugees, arguing that the executive order spurns the basic values of both American liberty and Buddhist compassion. In this way, and many others, the BCA continues to be an active and integral participant in American society and culture.

New Pure Lands in America

The end of World War II brought dramatic changes to the American landscape, which necessarily altered the communities and movements of Pure Land Buddhism in America. Especially, postbellum legal changes to immigration restrictions significantly changed the future developments of Pure Land Buddhism in America, especially the Magnuson Act of 1943, the McCarran-Walter Act of 1952, and the Hart-Cellar Act of 1965. The Magnuson Act allowed a small number of Chinese immigrants to the United States for the first time since the Chinese Exclusion Act of 1882. The McCarran-Walter Act not only increased the number of Asians allowed to immigrate into the country, but also granted Asian immigrants the right to naturalize as American citizens. Lastly, the Hart-Cellar Act abolished the national quota system, greatly increasing the numbers of immigrants from Asia, among other regions of the world formerly discriminated against in previous immigration laws. Such legislation not only brought in more diverse representations of Buddhism to the United States, but also revitalized many Chinese American religious communities, bolstering membership through immigration and strengthening transnational support networks. Notably, in the wake of these changes in immigration legislation, new and different forms of Chinese Buddhism found their way to the United States. Especially due to the economic and political turmoil caused by the Chinese Civil War, many found it necessary to evade the influence and political endeavors of the Chinese Communist Party. Consequently, many Chinese Buddhists left their homes to build diasporic religious communities throughout the world, though most prominently in Hong Kong and Taiwan. Due to updated American immigration legislation, the United States was another such location for religious diasporic growth.

For instance, the Venerable Master Hsuan Hua (1918–1995) was a notable Chan Buddhist monk who fled China in 1949, traveling throughout Asia and founding his Buddhist Lecture Hall in Hong Kong in 1956. Some of his disciples immigrated to the United States and, at the direction of Hsuan Hua, established the Sino-American Buddhist Association in San Francisco in 1958, later renamed the Dharma Realm Buddhist Association. He would later join his students in the United States in 1963. He then traveled and taught widely throughout the United States, eventually establishing the City of Ten Thousand Buddhas in 1976, the first Chan Buddhist monastery in the United States and one of the largest in the Western Hemisphere. While Hsuan Hua is formally the Dharma heir to the Weiyang (Guiyang) lineage of Chan Buddhism, his work and teachings were intentionally pan-Buddhist, building bridges between and syncretizing beliefs and practices of various Buddhist schools, especially Pure Land and Tientai. Indeed, Hsuan Hua encouraged his students to practice devotion to Amitābha Buddha through buddha-name recitation, especially as a form of meditative contemplation. Many other notable Chinese and Taiwanese Buddhist teachers and reformers engaged with Pure Land Buddhist teachings and practices, finding expression in American diasporic communities. For example, many Chinese Buddhists associated with the development of modernist and humanistic Buddhism have advocated for Pure Land practices, especially endorsing the concept of creating a Pure Land in the human realm. This concept, primarily developed by Taixu (1890–1947), has been passed on and propagated through many international Buddhist movements, like Hsing Yun's Fo Guang Shan and Sheng Yen's Dharma Drum Mountain, both of which have established communities in the United States. Notably, such organizations not only advocate for newer interpretations of the Pure Land to encourage social engagement, they also often incorporate buddha-name recitation into their regular ritual observation, as well as in their funeral rites. In this way, transnational Chinese Humanistic Buddhist organizations feature both traditional and modernist interpretations and practices of Pure Land traditions (Reinke 2021).

With the advent of greater immigration and globalization in the latter half of the twentieth century, the United States has seen a rise in greater diversity of Buddhist traditions, as well as general American knowledge and awareness thereof. Indeed, some Buddhist figures, such as Thich Nhat Hahn (1926–2022) and the 14th Dalai Lama (1935–), have been elevated to celebrity status in many Western countries, thereby popularizing various Buddhist ideologies and practice throughout American culture and society. While neither *Thiền* nor Tibetan Buddhism are usually categorized as Pure Land traditions, both historically have included the practice of buddha-name recitation and the recognition of various Pure Lands, especially *Tusita*, the Pure Land of the Maitreya. Indeed, some Tibetan Buddhist teachers, especially those who proselytize Western audiences, emphasize the significance of various Pure Land practices and devotion. For example, Lama Zopa Rinpoche (1946–), who established the Foundation for the Preservation of the Mahayana Tradition in Portland, Oregon, in 1975, has often expressed to his students the importance of several buddhas and their Pure Lands, such as Avalokiteśvara, Vajrayogini, and Amitābha. Furthermore, Thich Nhat Hanh has also engaged with Pure Land ideology in a few of his books, including a commentary on the Amitābha Sutra. In these ways, the greater encounters with various forms of Buddhism, through both immigration and popular Buddhist figures, have developed Pure Land Buddhist organizations, perceptions, and practices in new and different ways. While many diverse forms of Buddhism now proliferate through American religious and popular culture, the ways in which and the extent to which such movements can rightly be considered an expression of Pure Land Buddhism remain a continuing question of categorization and definition.

Conclusion

While the history of Pure Land Buddhism in America is usually unilaterally associated with the BCA, the category of Pure Land Buddhism can be expanded to include many other instances of Pure Land ideology, devotion, and practice. Many immigrants from Asia brought with them their religious traditions, which necessarily changed due to the dynamics of the American legal and cultural context. Whether it was legal discrimination, especially through internment and restrictions on immigration or citizenship, or cultural prejudice, many Pure Land communities strategically assimilated to American definitions and performances of proper religion. Moreover, such Buddhist communities inevitably encountered Americans interested in Asian religions, bringing with them preconceived expectations and perceptions of Buddhism, largely informed by orientalist literature and/or popular representations thereof. Consequently, many Buddhist communities and organizations advantageously embraced more generalized understandings of Buddhism, diminishing sectarian doctrinal differences to appeal to the wider American society. Such transformations were also consistent with global developments of various Buddhist traditions to meet changing national and transnational political, social, and religious challenges in the twentieth century. In these ways, various Pure Land Buddhist movements and organizations developed in interesting and dynamic ways, intentionally or unintentionally acquiring an American character.

More than demonstrating the various influences the American context had on the development of various Pure Land Buddhist movements in America, this history demonstrates that the very category and definition of Pure Land Buddhism need greater theoretical exploration. If scholars rely on conventional definitions of Pure Land Buddhism, focus will continue to remain on the Japanese American experience. Without discounting the significance of Japanese American Buddhism, there remain many other instances of Pure Land ideology and practice that are only discussed in other contexts, such as Chinese American religiosity, orientalist scholarship, and Buddhism in popular culture. Recognizing the specific ways that Pure Land texts, traditions, ideologies, and practices are addressed, represented, and engaged in these and various other movements will hopefully provide greater insights into the unique dynamics of not only Pure Land Buddhism, but also of American religious history. As such, there are many fertile areas of American Buddhist history that require greater research and analysis, identifying the many nuances of Buddhist communities and their encounters with their American context.

References

Ama, Michihiro. 2011. *Immigrants to the Pure Land: The Modernization, Acculturation, and Globalization of Shin Buddhism, 1898–1941*. Honolulu: University of Hawai'i Press.

Ama, Michihiro. 2019. "The Imamura Families and the Making of American Buddhism." In *Oxford Research Encyclopedia, Religion*. Oxford: Oxford University Press, online publication. https://doi.org/10.1093/acrefore/9780199340378.013.600.

Aquino, Jorge. January 26, 1996. "Buddhism in America: Buddhist Churches of America Roiled by Change, Dissension." *Religion News Service* (San Francisco). https://religionnews.com/1996/01/26/top-story-buddhism-in-america-buddhist-churches-of-america-roiled-by-change/.

Gin Lum, Kathryn. 2019. "Religion on the Road: How Chinese Migrants Adapted Popular Religion to an American Context." In *The Chinese and the Iron Road: Building the Transcontinental Railroad*, edited by Gordon H. Chang and Shelley Fisher Fishkin, 159–178. Stanford, CA: Stanford University Press.

Gordon, Robert. 2022. *Buddhist Architecture in America: Building for Enlightenment*. London: Routledge.

Harding, John S. 2008. *Mahayana Phoenix: Japan's Buddhists at the 1893 World's Parliament of Religions*. New York: Peter Lang.

Kashima, Tetsuden. 1977. *Buddhism in America: The Social Organization of an Ethnic Religious Institution*. Westport, CT: Greenwood Press.

Masatsugu, Michael K. 2008. "'Beyond This World of Transiency and Impermanence': Japanese Americans, Dharma Bums, and the Making of American Buddhism during the Early Cold War Years." *Pacific Historical Review* 77, no. 3 (August): 423–451.

Masatsugu, Michael K. 2023. *Reorienting the Pure Land: Nisei Buddhism in the Transwar Years, 1943-1965*. Honolulu: University of Hawai'i Press.

Mitchell, Scott A. 2016. *Buddhism in America: Global Religion, Local Contexts*. New York: Bloomsbury Academic.

Mitchell, Scott A. 2023. *The Making of American Buddhism*. New York: Oxford University Press.

Reinke, Jens. 2021. *Mapping Modern Mahayana: Chinese Buddhism and Migration in the Age of Global Modernity*. Berlin: Walter de Gruyter GmbH.

Shen, Meilee. 2017. "Chinese Buddhism in the United States." *Prajñā Vihāra* 18, no. 1 (Jan–Jun): 73–97.

Spencer, Anne C. 2014. "Diversification in the Buddhist Churches of America: Demographic Trends and Their Implications for the Future Study of U.S. Buddhist Groups." *Journal of Global Buddhism* 15: 35–61.

Tweed, Thomas A. 1992. *The American Encounter with Buddhism, 1844–1912: Victorian Culture and the Limits of Dissent*. Chapel Hill: University of North Carolina Press.

Williams, Duncan Ryuken. 2019. *American Sutra: A Story of Faith and Freedom in the Second World War*. Cambridge, MA: Harvard University Press.

Yu, Jimmy. 2014. "Pure Land Devotion in East Asia." In *The Wiley Blackwell Companion to East and Inner Asian Buddhism*, edited by Mario Poceski, 201–220. Malden, MA: John Wiley & Sons.

Zheng, Aihua. 2019. "Buddhist Networks: The Japanese Preparation for the World's Parliament of Religions, 1892–1893." *Japanese Journal of Religious Studies* 46, no. 2: 247–275.

CHAPTER 8

ZEN BUDDHISM IN AMERICA

BEN VAN OVERMEIRE

Introduction

CHENXIN Han's recent book of interviews with Asian American Buddhists contains one striking comment by Nora, a Shin Buddhist priest. When asked whether she associates Zen with Japanese Americans, she vehemently responds: "I don't! . . . I don't think of Japanese Americans, I think of Caucasians."[1] Nora's comment reflects both the general perception of Zen among Americans and the main focus of scholarship on Zen in America: white communities affiliated with Japanese teachers who practice meditation at the expense of other ritual practices. The lines that have dominated research on this specific subgroup are as follows. First, driven by the question of authenticity, in turn generated by Zen's status as a "new religion" on American soil, scholars have investigated how similar American Zen is to its direct predecessor and most significant cultural influence, Japanese Zen. This has involved a quest for the origins of Zen in America. Often, these origins privilege the Chicago World Parliament of Religions of 1893 and the Japanese scholar-practitioner Daisetz Teitaro Suzuki. Second, due to the association between Zen and aesthetics, scholars have explored how Zen has affected American literature, particularly the writing of convert authors associated with the so-called Beat Generation. Third, in the wake of the sex scandals that have ravaged Zen communities across the United States since the 1980s, scholars have started paying attention to the institutional history of Zen and the question of what Zen ethics in America should be. Finally, over the past two decades scholars have increasingly started using the categories of gender and race to scrutinize American Zen. This has resulted in increasing (though still comparatively minimal) attention to heritage communities whose practice of

---

[1] Chenxing Han, *Be the Refuge: Raising the Voices of Asian American Buddhists* (Berkeley CA: North Atlantic Books, 2021).

Zen can be significantly different from those of the white communities that are often presented as the face of Zen in America.

Apart from the dearth of scholarship on heritage communities, there are other dimensions of Zen in America that have remained relatively unexamined. Scholars are just beginning to consider, for example, those Zen Buddhists who do not directly affiliate with a temple or center but have built their religious practice through reading and their community on the internet.[2] Some scholars have begun to look at what rituals other than meditation characterize Zen religious life in America.[3] The focus on how Japanese Zen was adapted to America has left out how American Zen has in turn shaped Zen in other places. This focus has also led to a significant neglect of American Chinese, Korean, and Vietnamese Zen lineage communities, both convert and cradle, even when these are associated with celebrity masters such as Thich Nhat Hanh and Seung Sahn.

This chapter is structured to trace the different lines in scholarship outlined above. First, it looks at Zen in Asia and the impact of the Chicago World Parliament. Then, it examines the ideas and influence of D. T. Suzuki, probably the most important figure for American convert Zen. As it shows, one important effect of Suzuki's work was the association of Zen with aesthetics in literature, music, and performance. Then, it discusses two prominent Zen teachers who taught convert American Buddhists to meditate. Finally, the impact of the Zen sex scandals and the relatively new angles of gender and race are brought to the foreground.

THE ORIGINS OF ZEN IN ASIA

Zen originated as a Chinese school of Buddhism that called itself "Chan" ("Zen" is the Japanese pronunciation of this character, which in turn was a transliteration of the Sanskrit term *dhyāna*, meaning meditation). Emerging in China as early as the sixth century CE, Zen Buddhists gradually distinguished their school from other schools by stressing a "special transmission outside the scriptures." As time went by, Zen Buddhists started claiming that their masters had received a special instruction from the Buddha,

---

[2] Thomas A. Tweed, "Night-Stand Buddhists and Other Creatures: Sympathizers, Adherents, and the Study of Religion," in *American Buddhism: Methods and Findings in Recent Scholarship*, ed. Duncan Ryūken Williams and Christopher S. Queen (Routledge, 1999), 71–90; Helen J. Baroni, *Love, Rōshi: Robert Baker Aitken and His Distant Correspondents* (Albany: State University of New York Press, 2012). From Tweed, I adopt the distinction between "cradle" and "convert" Buddhists.

[3] Jeff Wilson, *Mourning the Unborn Dead: A Buddhist Ritual Comes to America* (New York: Oxford University Press, 2009), https://doi.org/10.1093/acprof:oso/9780195371932.003.0001. Senryo Asai and Duncan Ryūken Williams, "Japanese American Zen Temples: Cultural Identity and Economics," in *American Buddhism Methods and Findings in Recent Scholarship*, ed. Duncan Ryūken Williams and Christopher S. Queen (Richmond, Surrey: Curzon, 1999), 20–35. For ritual in American Buddhism, also see Chapter 19 in this volume.

a teaching beyond words. This instruction was far superior to textual understandings of enlightenment and, they said, had been transmitted across the ages through an enduring lineage of masters.

In a well-noted irony though, Zen Buddhists produced the largest amount of Buddhist literature in China.[4] One scholarly interpretation of this paradox has been to see the Zen school as a "community of memory" which "denotes socially interdependent groups that share certain practices and are bound together by their communal remembrance of the past, which provides them with a sense of collective identity and a common heritage."[5] In other words, a narrative of the past that is articulated in sacred literature reinforces a certain idea of group identity, however much that identity might change over time.

Due to China's massive cultural prestige in medieval Asia, the Zen school's ideas and practices found their way into other states, such as Vietnam, Korea, and Japan. By the Song Dynasty, the school had ideologically split into two different factions, one named the Linji (Japanese: Rinzai) lineage after the famous Zen master Linji Yixuan, the other named Caodong (Japanese: Soto) after the masters Dongshan Liangjie and Caoshan Benji. The split partly concerned the usage of koan, seemingly nonsensical exchanges between Zen students and their teachers, who as living Buddhas represent a spontaneous freedom unburdened by worries or rules. With the Song master Dahui Zonggao, the Linji lineage had adopted the usage of such texts in formal Zen study: gaining insight into a koan was considered as gaining insight in enlightened behavior and enlightenment itself. The Caodong lineage refused such tools and maintained that enlightenment was achieved through "silent illumination."[6]

In Japan, the famous Zen masters Eihen Dogen (Soto) and Hakuin Ekaku (Rinzai) solidified these doctrinal differences, with Dogen rejecting the specific type of koan meditation Dahui had designed and Hakuin revitalizing the koan curriculum. There was also a class difference, with Rinzai appealing more to the higher educated classes and Soto priests going out to educate people in the countryside.[7] This might explain why Rinzai Zen apologists such as D. T. Suzuki associated certain elite practices such as the tea ceremony and flower arrangement with Zen. It also explains how Rinzai Zen became associated with samurai training, an association that would deeply influence how Zen continues to be perceived in the United States.

---

[4] John R. McRae, *Seeing through Zen: Encounter, Transformation, and Genealogy in Chinese Chan Buddhism* (Berkeley: University of California Press, 2003), 3.

[5] Mario Poceski, *The Records of Mazu and the Making of Classical Chan Literature* (New York: Oxford University Press, 2015), 25.

[6] Morten Schlütter, *How Zen Became Zen: The Dispute over Enlightenment and the Formation of Chan Buddhism in Song-Dynasty China*, Studies in East Asian Buddhism 22 (Honolulu: University of Hawai'i Press, 2008).

[7] Martin Colcutt, *Five Mountains: The Rinzai Zen Monastic Institution in Medieval Japan* (Cambridge, MA: Harvard University Press, 1981); William Bodiford, *Sōtō Zen in Medieval Japan* (Honolulu: University of Hawai'i Press, 1993).

Zen Modernism and the Parliament of World Religions

With the turmoil of Japanese modernization, Japanese Zen Buddhists found themselves under immense pressure to meet the needs of the state.[8] One solution to this problem was to essentialize Zen as the essence of Japanese culture, a bastion against the changes that capitalism and modernity brought to the country. Zen was presented as a religion on par with or even superior to Christianity, compatible with the findings of modern science. To accomplish this successfully, though, the orientalist preference of Western scholars for the earliest Buddhist texts, and their idea that South Asian Theravāda most closely corresponded to these texts, had to be countered by the assertion that Japanese Zen was the most developed and supreme form of Buddhism altogether.[9] This idea of Zen was proposed at the 1893 Chicago World Parliament of Religions by the Meiji-trained Rinzai Zen master Shaku Soen.[10] In his speech to the audience, Soen took care not to refer to any specific religious practices that take place in Zen temples. Rather, he referred to Zen as a universal "idea."[11]

Soen would exert the most influence on American Zen through his students Nyogen Senzaki and Daisetz Teitaro ("D. T.") Suzuki. Neglected by Western scholars, Senzaki lived a life of poverty. After Soen abandoned him in San Francisco, he survived by working odd jobs while establishing a "floating zendo" where he provided instructions on sitting meditation to anyone who wanted it. After the attack on Pearl Harbor, he was imprisoned, along with so many other Japanese Americans. His writings were conserved by his students.[12]

---

[8] Harry D. Harootunian, *Overcome by Modernity: History, Culture, and Community in Interwar Japan* (Princeton, NJ: Princeton University Press, 2000).

[9] Richard King, *Orientalism and Religion: Post-Colonial Theory, India and "the Mystic East"* (London and New York: Routledge, 1999), 143–160; Judith M. Snodgrass, "Publishing Eastern Buddhism: D. T. Suzuki's Journey to the West," in *Casting Faiths: Imperialism and the Transformation of Religion in East and Southeast Asia*, ed. Thomas David DuBois (Basingstoke, UK: Palgrave Macmillan, 2009), 46–72.

[10] On Soen, see especially Michel Mohr, "The Use of Traps and Snares: Shaku Soen Revisited," in *Zen Masters*, ed. Steven Heine and Dale S. Wright (New York: Oxford University Press, 2010), 183–216.

[11] Larry A. Fader, "Zen in the West: Historical and Philosophical Implications of the Chicago World's Parliament of Religions," *Eastern Buddhist* 15, no. 1 (1981): 122–145; Richard Hughes Seager, *The World's Parliament of Religions: The East/West Encounter, Chicago, 1893* (Bloomington: Indiana University Press, 1992); Judith M. Snodgrass, *Presenting Japanese Buddhism to the West: Orientalism, Occidentalism, and the Columbian Exposition* (Chapel Hill: University of North Carolina Press, 2003); Snodgrass, "Japan's Contribution to Modern Global Buddhism: The World's Parliament of Religions Revisited," *The Eastern Buddhist*, new series 43, no. 1 (2012): 81–102.

[12] Duncan Ryūken Williams, *American Sutra: A Story of Faith and Freedom in the Second World War* (Cambridge, MA: Harvard University Press, 2019), 5–9; Rudiger V. Busto, "Disorienting Subjects: Reclaiming Pacific Islander/Asian American Religions," in *Revealing the Sacred in Asian and Pacific America*, ed. Jane Naomi Iwamura and Paul Spickard (London: Routledge, 2003), 15–21.

D. T. Suzuki had a very different career. He was much better funded than Senzaki, eventually becoming a professor at Otani University in Japan and giving guest lectures at Columbia University. In the wake of the Parliament he came to the United States and helped the American author and publisher Paul Carus with various translation tasks. In helping Carus with his projects, which included a translation of the Daoist classic *Daode jing* and the compilation of a *Life of the Buddha* modeled on the Christian gospels, Suzuki picked up a variety of skills and intellectual influences that would help make his version of Zen uniquely appealing to American tastes. Particularly important is the influence of the ideas of the American philosopher William James, who in his *The Varieties of Mystical Experience* had proposed that the foundation of religion is mystical experience, and that ritual and institutions are all byproducts, or even aberrations, of what originally is something deeply individual and personal.[13]

Broadly speaking, Suzuki's presentation of Zen, which has been studied extensively, is as follows: following James, he cast Zen as primarily experiential. He recast Zen notions that have been translated as "enlightenment" (such as *kensho* and *satori*) as terms denoting religious experience, which is arguably very different from how such notions were understood in premodern Zen.[14] Suzuki also connected Zen with various elements of Japanese culture, such as the tea ceremony, the rock garden, and the haiku poetic form.[15] There is a clear tension in his work between Zen as the province of Japanese culture, inaccessible to non-Japanese, and a Zen that points to a universally available enlightenment experience.[16] This stress on Japanese-ness has led some scholars to connect Suzuki with Japanese wartime imperialism, but the nature of his politics remains the subject of intense debate.[17]

Stylistically, D. T. Suzuki's books rely heavily on koan, which should be no source of wonder given his Rinzai background. Like Soen, Suzuki did not tell his readers how to sit in meditation. It is for this reason that many, including the American Zen master Philip Kapleau, have called his Zen "intellectual." The work of Alan Watts has also been

---

[13] Robert H. Sharf, "The Zen of Japanese Nationalism," *History of Religions* 33, no. 1 (August 1993): 1–43; Sharf, "Buddhist Modernism and the Rhetoric of Meditative Experience," *Numen* 42, no. 3 (October 1995): 228–283; Snodgrass, "Publishing Eastern Buddhism: D. T. Suzuki's Journey to the West."

[14] Sharf, "Buddhist Modernism and the Rhetoric of Meditative Experience."

[15] Daisetz Teitaro Suzuki, *Zen and Japanese Culture*, ed. Richard M. Jaffe, Bollingen Series 64. (Princeton, NJ: Princeton University Press, 2010); Shōji Yamada, *Shots in the Dark: Japan, Zen, and the West*, Buddhism and Modernity 9 (Chicago: University of Chicago Press, 2009).

[16] Bernard Faure, *Chan Insights and Oversights: An Epistemological Critique of the Chan Tradition* (Princeton, NJ: Princeton University Press, 1993); Sharf, "The Zen of Japanese Nationalism"; Sharf, "Buddhist Modernism and the Rhetoric of Meditative Experience"; David L. McMahan, *The Making of Buddhist Modernism* (Oxford and New York: Oxford University Press, 2008), 117–148.

[17] Brian Daizen Victoria, *Zen at War*, 2nd ed. (Lanham, MD: Rowman & Littlefield, 2006); Kemmyō Taira Satō and Thomas Kirchner, "DT Suzuki and the Question of War," *The Eastern Buddhist* 39, no. 1 (2008): 61–120; Victoria, "The 'Negative Side' of DT Suzuki's Relationship to War," *The Eastern Buddhist* 41, no. 2 (2010): 97–138; Satō and Kirchner, "Brian Victoria and the Question of Scholarship," *The Eastern Buddhist* 41, no. 2 (2010): 139–166; Suzuki, *Zen and Japanese Culture*; Suzuki, *Selected Works of D. T. Suzuki: Zen*, ed. Richard M. Jaffe, Vol. 1, (Oakland: University of California Press, 2015); Grace, "The Political Context of D. T. Suzuki's Early Life," *The Eastern Buddhist* 47, no. 2 (2016): 83–100.

described in this manner. Deeply influenced by Suzuki, Watts's *The Way of Zen* takes, as its title implies, a philosophical direction, relying on an understanding of Daoism (The Chinese term *dao* can be translated as "the Way") to explain what Zen is and what it is not.[18] Though Watts later wanted to correct loose interpretations of Zen that his own work had generated, his books open up an interpretation of Zen where anything goes, an interpretation that would be the hallmark of the Beat generation's engagement, literary and otherwise, with the school.[19]

ZEN AS A VISUAL AND LITERARY AESTHETIC

The work of Suzuki and Watts made it possible for American artists to see Zen as an aesthetic aimed at inducing and expressing enlightenment. This interpretation is very clear in Jack Kerouac's *The Dharma Bums*, one of the most famous Beat novels engaging Zen in America.[20] *The Dharma Bums* revels in many of the classical Zen koan that had been introduced by D. T. Suzuki (whom Kerouac had met in New York) and uses them as material to envision a different type of America, where a "rucksack revolution" would upend the military-industrial complex and return to an earlier, more bucolic time envisioned through the happy saints of Zen koan. Suzuki's influence on *The Dharma Bums* is also apparent in the main character's ardent chase for enlightenment, a theme Kerouac would continue to develop in his later work. Like most of Kerouac's other novels, *The Dharma Bums* speaks without censorship, a technique Natalie Goldberg would later connect with Zen Buddhist practice in her influential writing manual, *Writing down the Bones: Unleashing the Writer Within* (1986).[21] For Goldberg, who studied with the Japanese master Dainin Katagiri, writing is encountering the mind, and in principle not different from meditation.[22]

As the association between Zen and aesthetics was explored by many artists and writers, it itself became a significant subject of scholarly inquiry, particularly as it appears in the work of Kerouac, Gary Snyder, Philip Whalen, Jane Hirshfield, and Charles Johnson. Such scholarship has often attempted to see how these authors represent Zen ideas and refer to Zen genres.[23] Detective novels and science fiction movies

---

[18] Alan Watts, *The Way of Zen* (New York: The New American Library of World Literature, 1959).
[19] Alan Watts, "Beat Zen, Square Zen, and Zen," *Chicago Review* 12, no. 2 (1958): 3–11.
[20] Jack Kerouac, *The Dharma Bums* (New York: Penguin Books, 2000). For more on the Beats, see Chapter 28 in this volume.
[21] Kerouac, "Belief and Technique for Modern Prose," David L. McMahan, *The Making of Buddhist Modernism* (Oxford and New York: Oxford University Press, 2008), 226–227.
[22] Natalie Goldberg, *Writing down the Bones: Freeing the Writer Within*, 1st ed. (Boston: Shambhala, 1986).
[23] Miriam Levering, "Jack Kerouac in Berkeley: Reading the Dharma Bums as the Work of a Buddhist Writer," *Pacific World*, Third Series, 6 (2004): 7–26; Paul F. Rouzer, *On Cold Mountain: A Buddhist Reading of the Hanshan Poems* (Seattle: University of Washington Press, 2015); John Whalen-Bridge and Gary Storhoff, *The Emergence of Buddhist American Literature* (Albany: State University of New York

have also employed Zen tropes and ideas for various purposes.[24] Outside of literature and film, the music of John Cage and the performances of the avant-garde performance group Fluxus have also merited scholarly attention.[25] An important analysis of the relationship between Zen and aesthetics has been Gregory Levine's *Long Strange Journey*.[26] The process of Zen becoming a vague placeholder for any type of East Asian aesthetics or spirituality went hand in hand with orientalist portrayals of its key figures in film, photography, and in various other media.[27] Less attention has been paid to how Zen is portrayed in numerous documentaries, with some notable exceptions, for example

Press, 2009); Whalen-Bridge and Storhoff, *Writing as Enlightenment: Buddhist American Literature into the Twenty-First Century* (Albany: State University of New York Press, 2011); Anthony Hunt, *Genesis, Structure, and Meaning in Gary Snyder's Mountains and Rivers without End*, Western Literature Series (Reno: University of Nevada Press, 2004); Yoshinobu Hakutani, *Jack Kerouac and the Traditions of Classic and Modern Haiku* (Lanham, MD: Lexington Books, 2019). Timothy Gray, *Gary Snyder and the Pacific Rim: Creating Countercultural Community*, Contemporary North American Poetry Series (Iowa City: University of Iowa); David Schneider, *Crowded by Beauty: The Life and Zen of Poet Philip Whalen* (Oakland: University of California Press, 2015); Patricia Sieber, "Acts of Translation: Jane Hirshfield, Chinese Poetics and the Practice of Zen," *Contemporary Buddhism* 1, no. 2 (2000): 119–139; Deirdre C. Byrne and Garth Mason, "Two Gates into Jane Hirshfield's Poetry," *Contemporary Buddhism* 21, no. 1–2 (2020): 328–350; Ling Chung, "Modernist Elements in Jane Hirshfield's Voice and Zen Meditation," *Connotations* 21, no. 1 (January 1, 2011): 101–125; Richard Collins, "Honoring the Form: Zen Moves in Charles Johnson's Oxherding Tale," *Religion and the Arts (Chestnut Hill, Mass.)* 14, no. 1–2 (2010): 59–76; Kyle Garton-Gundling, *Enlightened Individualism: Buddhism and Hinduism in American Literature from the Beats to the Present* (Columbus: Ohio State University Press, 2019). Also see Chapter 27 in this volume.

[24] Sheng-mei Ma, "Zen Keytsch: Mystery Handymen with Dragon Tattoos," in *Detecting Detection: International Perspectives on the Uses of a Plot*, ed. Peter Baker and Deborah Shaller (New York: Continuum, 2012), 115–138; Christian Feichtinger, "Space Buddhism: The Adoption of Buddhist Motifs in Star Wars," *Contemporary Buddhism* 15, no. 1 (January 2, 2014): 28–43; Ben Van Overmeire, "Hard-Boiled Zen: Janwillem Van De Wetering's The Japanese Corpse as Buddhist Literature," *Contemporary Buddhism* 19, no. 2 (July 3, 2018): 382–397, https://doi.org/10.1080/14639947.2018.1480890; Seton, "Killing the Buddha: Ritualized Violence in Fight Club through the Lens of Rinzai Zen Buddhist Practice," *Religions (Basel, Switzerland)* 9, no. 7 (2018): 206; Jason Andrew Bartashius, "White Samurai in a Fascistic House of Mirrors: Fight Club, Zen and the Art of (Re)constructing Ethno-Nationalism," *Culture and Religion* 20, no. 4 (2019): 351–370.

[25] Rob Haskins, "Aspects of Zen Buddhism as an Analytical Context for John Cage's Chance Music," *Contemporary Music Review* 33, no. 5–6 (November 2, 2014): 616–629; Kay Larson, *Where the Heart Beats: John Cage, Zen Buddhism, and the Inner Life of Artists* (New York: Penguin, 2012); David Nicholls, *John Cage* (Urbana: University of Illinois Press, 2007); Ken Friedman, *The Fluxus Reader* (New York: Academy Editions, 1999), @friedman_fluxus_1999; Natasha Lushetich, *Fluxus: The Practice of Non-Duality* (Amsterdam: Editions Rodopi, 2014); Owen F. Smith, *Fluxus: The History of an Attitude* (San Diego: San Diego State University Press, 1998).

[26] Gregory P. A. Levine, *Long Strange Journey: On Modern Zen, Zen Art, and Other Predicaments* (Honolulu: University of Hawai'i Press, 2017).

[27] Jane Naomi Iwamura, *Virtual Orientalism: Asian Religions and American Popular Culture* (New York: Oxford University Press, 2011); Elisabetta Porcu, "Staging Zen Buddhism: Image Creation in Contemporary Films," *Contemporary Buddhism* 15, no. 1 (January 2, 2014): 81–96; Sharon A. Suh, *Silver Screen Buddha: Buddhism in Asian and Western Film* (London: Bloomsbury Academic, 2015); Scott A. Mitchell, "The Tranquil Meditator: Representing Buddhism and Buddhists in US Popular Media," *Religion Compass* 8, no. 3 (2014): 81–89.

Andreas Becker's study of a movie made about the famous San Francisco Zen Center cook Edward Brown.[28]

MEDITATION AS THE ESSENCE OF ZEN: PHILIP KAPLEAU AND SHUNRYU SUZUKI

Suzuki and Watts did not explain how to sit in meditation. Meditation also did not play an important role in the Zen temples attended by first- and second-generation Japanese immigrants, which instead focused on funerary services and on hosting Japanese cultural events (much like temples in Japan itself).[29] It would be a series of eccentric teachers who would teach convert Americans how to meditate, and who would elevate meditation above any other practice.

Two representative examples of such teachers are the American Zen teacher Philip Kapleau and the Japanese Zen master Shunryu Suzuki. Kapleau went to Japan in 1953 and after four years of practice attained *kensho* (one of the two terms frequently used for Zen enlightenment). His Zen handbook *Three Pillars of Zen* (1965) was remarkable because it provided a combination of practical instructions with autobiographical accounts of individuals (like Kapleau himself) who had attained *kensho*.[30] This combination made the book a huge success, and its stress on enlightenment as an attainable goal for committed laypeople deeply influenced the expectations Americans had of Zen practice.[31]

Perhaps the most influential Japanese teacher in the United States was Shunryu Suzuki. By the time he set off for the United States, he had completed the necessary step of a training at the rigorous Soto monastery Dogen had founded at Eiheiji. Unlike some other Japanese teachers (such as Kapleau's teacher Yasutani Hakuun), Suzuki did not come to America to convert Americans to Buddhism, but to serve the needs of the Japanese community in San Francisco. It was only gradually after his arrival in 1959 that his primary occupation became teaching convert Buddhists. Under his leadership and that of his Dharma heir, Richard Baker, San Francisco Zen Center grew into a large and complex organization. Suzuki had many lineage teachers, though he initially only transmitted the Dharma to Richard Baker. Due to its venerable history and institutional presence, San Francisco Zen Center and the communities affiliated with it have

---

[28] Andreas Becker, "'When You Wash the Rice, Wash the Rice': About the Cinematic Representation of Cooking and Zen in Doris Dörrie's How to Cook Your Life (2007)," *Contemporary Buddhism* 15, no. 1 (2014): 97–108.

[29] Asai and Williams, "Japanese American Zen Temples."

[30] Philip Kapleau, *The Three Pillars of Zen: Teaching, Practice, and Enlightenment*, 35th ed. (New York: Anchor, 2000).

[31] Kenneth Kraft, *Zen Teaching, Zen Practice: Philip Kapleau and the Three Pillars of Zen* (Trumbull, CT: Weatherhill, 2000).

been a particular focus of scholarship.³² An edited collection of dharma talks by Suzuki, published as *Zen Mind, Beginner's Mind*, would be immensely influential.³³ Unlike D. T. Suzuki's work, *Zen Mind, Beginner's Mind* aimed to talk about what it is to sit in meditation without chasing after enlightenment. The stress of all these teachers on meditation would be decisive for American Zen modernism, further reinforcing the idea that this practice was the essence of Zen.³⁴

Zen Sexual Misconduct, Gender, and Racial Identity

From the 1980s onward, it became public knowledge that many of the most influential teachers of American Zen convert lineages, including Richard Baker, Eido Shimano, Taezan Maezumi, Joshu Sasaki, and Dainin Katagiri, had maintained sexual relationships with their students or had even sexually assaulted them.³⁵ The sex scandals spurred a deep rethinking of the ethical responsibilities of teacher and student in American Buddhism, and what could be done to prevent such abuses in the future.³⁶ Instead of trusting one single individual with total authority, organizations like the San Francisco Zen Center have since reformed toward a more democratic way of governance. Practitioners have adopted a variety of perspectives to interpret the actions of their teachers, ranging from the "logic of transcendence," the idea that these actions were enlightened ways of instruction incomprehensible to unenlightened individuals, to "projection theory," a Zen modernist idea derived from psychoanalysis, where teachers can "become an idealized daddy figure" who "encourages women to compete for their attention and affection."³⁷ As the latter term implies, one influential perspective has been

---

³² Peter Brown, "Enjoying the Saints in Late Antiquity," *Early Medieval Europe* 9 (2000): 1–24; Michael Downing, *Shoes Outside the Door: Desire, Devotion, and Excess at San Francisco Zen Center* (Washington, DC: Counterpoint, 2001); Stephanie Kaza, "Finding Safe Harbor: Buddhist Sexual Ethics in America," *Buddhist-Christian Studies* 24, no. 1 (2004): 23–35; Jason C. Bivins, "'Beautiful Women Dig Graves': Richard Baker-Roshi, Imported Buddhism, and the Transmission of Ethics at the San Francisco Zen Center," *Religion and American Culture: A Journal of Interpretation* 17, no. 1 (2007): 57–93; Baroni, *Love, Rōshi*.

³³ Shunryu Suzuki, *Zen Mind, Beginner's Mind* (Boston: Weatherhill, 1973).

³⁴ David McMahan and Erik Braun, *Meditation, Buddhism, and Science* (Oxford: Oxford University Press, 2017). See Chapter 17 on mindfulness and meditation in this volume.

³⁵ Downing, *Shoes Outside the Door*.

³⁶ Kaza, "Finding Safe Harbor: Buddhist Sexual Ethics in America"; Wakoh Shannon Hickey, "Regarding Elephants in the Room: What Buddhists Could Learn from Christians about Preventing Teacher Misconduct," *Buddhist-Christian Studies* 41, no. 41 (2021): 95–125, https://doi.org/10.1353/bcs.2021.0013.

³⁷ Grace Schireson, *Naked in the Zendo: Stories of Uptight Zen, Wild-Ass Zen, and Enlightenment Wherever You Are* (Boulder, CO: Shambhala, 2019), 114. For the "the logic of transcendence," see Bernard Faure, *The Red Thread: Buddhist Approaches to Sexuality* (Princeton, NJ: Princeton University Press,

psychoanalysis. The German psychoanalyst Carl Jung had early in the twentieth century connected Zen with psychoanalysis, and this approach was solidified by the publication of the edited volume *Zen Buddhism and Psychoanalysis* in 1960.[38]

The investigation of the sex scandals has gone hand in hand with feminist investigations and critiques of the androcentric attitude that dominated both Zen's history in general and the Beat version of Zen in particular.[39] *The Dharma Bums*, for example, portrays women as either sexual objects or motherly caretakers, never as serious practitioners of Buddhism. Together with the scholar Miriam Levering, the practitioner Grace Schireson has drawn attention to remarkable female masters and students in Zen's history.[40] This historical recovery combines with an attention to women's experiences with Zen in America.[41] Sometimes, both historical recovery and contemporary experience mapping are combined.[42] Such feminist projects are often articulated by scholar-practitioners like Schireson, who in her other publications has examined how American convert Zen can be a hostile space for bodies that are not male or able.[43] Like Schireson, black convert Buddhists Zenju Earthlyn Manuel and angel Kyodo williams center their own experiences of marginalization in their work, mixing Zen teaching, autobiography, biography and poetry.[44]

Accounts like those of Schireson, Manuel, and williams parallel scholars' questioning of the construct of an "American Zen" that privileges white male converts.

1998), 98–99. For more on projection theory, see Ann Gleig, *American Dharma: Buddhism beyond Modernity* (New Haven, CT: Yale University Press, 2019), 84–110.

[38] Daisetz Teitaro Suzuki, Erich Fromm, and Richard J. DeMartino, *Zen Buddhism and Psychoanalysis* (New York: Harper, 1960); Anne Harrington, "Zen, Suzuki, and the Art of Psychotherapy," in *Science and Religion, East and West*, ed. Yiftach Fehige (London: Routledge, 2016), 48–69; See also Chapter 22 on Buddhism and psychotherapy in this volume.

[39] See also Chapter 4 on gender and sexuality in this volume.

[40] Grace Schireson, *Zen Women: Beyond Tea Ladies, Iron Maidens, and Macho Masters* (Somerville, MA: Wisdom Publications, 2009).

[41] Susanne Mrozik and Peter N. Gregory, *Women Practicing Buddhism: American Experiences* (Somerville, MA: Wisdom Publications, 2008).

[42] Zenshin Florence Caplow and Reigetsu Susan Moon, eds., *The Hidden Lamp: Stories from Twenty-Five Centuries of Awakened Women* (Somerville, MA: Wisdom Publications, 2013); Ben Van Overmeire, "'Mountains, Rivers, and the Whole Earth': Koan Interpretations of Female Zen Practitioners," *Religions* 9, no. 4 (April 2018): 125, https://doi.org/10.3390/rel9040125.

[43] Schireson, *Naked in the Zendo*.

[44] Zenju Earthlyn Manuel, *The Way of Tenderness: Awakening through Race, Sexuality, and Gender* (Somerville, MA: Wisdom Publications, 2015); Manuel, *Sanctuary: A Meditation on Home, Homelessness, and Belonging* (Somerville, MA: Wisdom Publications, 2018); angel Kyodo williams, *Being Black: Zen and the Art of Living with Fearlessness and Grace* (Harmondsworth, UK: Penguin, 2002); Ann Gleig, "Undoing Whiteness in American Buddhist Modernism: Critical, Collective, and Contextual Turns," in *Buddhism and Whiteness: Critical Reflections*, ed. Emily McRae and George Yancy (Lanham, MD: Lexington Books, 2019); Gleig, "Buddhists and Racial Justice: A History," *Tricycle: The Buddhist Review* (July 24, 2020), https://tricycle.org/trikedaily/buddhists-racial-justice/; Adeana McNicholl, "Being Buddha, Staying Woke: Racial Formation in Black Buddhist Writing," *Journal of the American Academy of Religion* 86, no. 4 (July 13, 2018), 883–911, https://doi.org/10.1093/jaarel/lfy019; see also Chapter 3 on race and whiteness in this volume.

Scholars such as Iwamura and Wakoh Shannon Hickey have shown that the heritage of colonialism, orientalism, and racism continues to affect Zen and its representation today.[45] Parallel to Manuel and williams's observations that Zen Centers have very few members of Color, there has been a remarkable absence of heritage communities in discussions of Zen. As a corrective, Duncan Williams has shown how many distinctive features of American Zen (such as its ecumenical approach to practice), were formed it the Second World War internment camps. In doing so, Williams tells the story of what Zen meant to those who had nearly everything taken away from them, and how in some cases the solidarity among the interned fostered a cross-sectarian and inter-religious solidarity.[46]

Discussions of convert or heritage communities not affiliated with Japanese teachers have tended to be even rarer than discussions of Japanese American communities. Thus, whereas there are some discussions of famous teachers like Thich Nhat Hanh (Vietnam), Seung Sahn (Korea), and Shengyen (Taiwan), the communities associated with these teachers have remained relatively invisible in scholarship.[47] Instead, scholarship on Thich Nhat Hanh has focused on his ethical stance, his connection to mindfulness meditation, and his relation to Christianity.[48]

Conclusion

During the pandemic, I found myself in Numazu, Japan, the home of my in-laws. Exploring local temples, I discovered to my delight that one nearby temple, Daichu-ji, had been founded by Zen poet Muso Soseki. During my conversation with the abbot of this temple, he told me that the temple had been visited by Gary Snyder in 2012, who came to pay his honors to Muso. The celebration had been elaborately photographed, and I was regaled with plenty of pictures of a smiling Snyder amid a host of Japanese

---

[45] Iwamura, *Virtual Orientalism*; Wakoh Shannon Hickey, "Two Buddhisms, Three Buddhisms, and Racism," *Global Buddhism* 11 (2010), http://dx.doi.org/10.5281/zenodo.1306702.

[46] Williams, *American Sutra: A Story of Faith and Freedom in the Second World War*.

[47] Sor-Ching Low, "Seung Sahn: The Makeover of a Modern Zen Patriarch," in *Zen Masters*, ed. Steven T. Heine and Dale S. Wright (New York: Oxford University Press, 2010), 267–285Stuart Chandler, "Chinese Buddhism in America: Identity and Practice," in *The Faces of Buddhism in America*, ed. Charles S. Prebish and Kenneth K. Tanaka (Oakland: University of California Press, 1998), 30. I also refer the reader to Chapter 6 on Chinese Buddhism in America in this volume.

[48] Jeffrey Daniel Carlson, "Pretending to Be Buddhist and Christian: Thich Nhat Hanh and the Two Truths of Religious Identity," *Buddhist-Christian Studies* 20, no. 1 (2000): 115–125; Nathan Eric Dickman, "Linguistically Mediated Liberation: Freedom and Limits of Understanding in Thich Nhat Hanh and Hans-Georg Gadamer," ed. Scott D. Churchill, *The Humanistic Psychologist* 44, no. 3 (2016): 256–279; Sallie B. King, "Transformative Nonviolence: The Social Ethics of George Fox and Thich Nhat Hanh," *Buddhist-Christian Studies* 18, no. Journal Article (1998): 3–36; Mathias Schneider, "Mindfulness, Buddha-Nature, and the Holy Spirit: On Thich Nhat Hanh's Interpretation of Christianity," *Buddhist-Christian Studies* 41, no. 1 (2021): 279–293.

monks. I also was given an edited volume with writings on and by Soseki.[49] This volume opens with a dedicatory poem by Snyder, titled "For Daichu-ji and its people throughout the years." This vignette to me captures a final promising direction of research: the influence that Zen in America has had on the development of Zen in other countries, including those countries such as Japan with a strong historical Zen Buddhist tradition.[50] In many ways, American Zen has become the Zen that is known around the world.

References

Asai, Senryo, and Duncan Ryūken Williams. "Japanese American Zen Temples: Cultural Identity and Economics." In *American Buddhism: Methods and Findings in Recent Scholarship*, edited by Duncan Ryūken Williams and Christopher S. Queen, 20–35. London: Routledge, 1999.

Baroni, Helen J. *Love, Rōshi: Robert Baker Aitken and His Distant Correspondents*. Albany: State University of New York Press, 2012. http://ebookcentral.proquest.com/lib/duke/detail.action?docID=3408645.

Bartashius, Jason Andrew. "White Samurai in a Fascistic House of Mirrors: Fight Club, Zen and the Art of (Re)constructing Ethno-Nationalism." *Culture and Religion* 20, no. 4 (2019): 351–370. https://doi.org/10.1080/14755610.2020.1842475.

Becker, Andreas. "'When You Wash the Rice, Wash the Rice.' About the Cinematic Representation of Cooking and Zen in Doris Dörrie's How to Cook Your Life (2007)." *Contemporary Buddhism* 15, no. 1 (2014): 97–108. https://doi.org/10.1080/14639947.2014.890345.

Bivins, Jason C. "'Beautiful Women Dig Graves': Richard Baker-Roshi, Imported Buddhism, and the Transmission of Ethics at the San Francisco Zen Center." *Religion and American Culture: A Journal of Interpretation* 17, no. 1 (2007): 57–93. https://doi.org/10.1525/rac.2007.17.1.57.

Bocking, Brian. "Mysticism: No Experience Necessary?" *Diskus* 7 (2006): 1–13.

Bodiford, William. *Sōtō Zen in Medieval Japan*. Honolulu: University of Hawai'i Press, 1993.

Breen, John, and Shōji Yamada. *Suzuki Daisetsu: Zen Wo Koete [Daisetz Suzuki: Beyond Zen]*. Kyoto: Shinbunkaku, 2021.

Brown, James. "The Zen of Anarchy: Japanese Exceptionalism and the Anarchist Roots of the San Francisco Poetry Renaissance." *Religion and American Culture* 19, no. 2 (2009): 207–242. https://doi.org/10.1525/rac.2009.19.2.207.

Brown, Peter. "Enjoying the Saints in Late Antiquity." *Early Medieval Europe* 9 (2000): 1–24.

---

[49] Isao Kumakura and Gensho Takenuki, eds., *Zen Master Musō Soseki: Life and Legacy* (Tokyo: Shunjuisha, 2012).

[50] Judith M. Snodgrass, "'Budda No Fukuin': The Deployment of Paul Carus's 'Gospel of Buddha' in Meiji Japan," *Japanese Journal of Religious Studies* 25, no. 3–4 (Autumn 1998): 319–344; Joshua A. Irizarry, "Putting a Price on Zen: The Business of Redefining Religion for Global Consumption," *Journal of Global Buddhism* 16 (2015): 51–69; Joseph Laycock, "Zen Meets New Thought: The Erhard Seminars Training and Changing Ideas about Zen," *Contemporary Buddhism* 15, no. 2 (2014): 332–355, https://doi.org/10.1080/14639947.2014.932490. I also refer the reader to Chapter 1 on Buddhist modernity and globalization in this volume.

Busto, Rudiger V. "Disorienting Subjects: Reclaiming Pacific Islander/Asian American Religions." In *Revealing the Sacred in Asian and Pacific America*, edited by Jane Naomi Iwamura and Paul Spickard, 9–28. London: Routledge, 2003.

Byrne, Deirdre C., and Garth Mason. "Two Gates into Jane Hirshfield's Poetry." *Contemporary Buddhism* 21, no. 1–2 (2020): 328–350. https://doi.org/10.1080/14639947.2021.1977013.

Caplow, Zenshin Florence, and Reigetsu Susan Moon, eds. *The Hidden Lamp: Stories from Twenty-Five Centuries of Awakened Women*. Somerville, MA: Wisdom Publications, 2013.

Carlson, Jeffrey Daniel. "Pretending to Be Buddhist and Christian: Thich Nhat Hanh and the Two Truths of Religious Identity." *Buddhist-Christian Studies* 20, no. 1 (2000): 115–125. https://doi.org/10.1353/bcs.2000.0003.

Chandler, Stuart. "Chinese Buddhism in America: Identity and Practice." In *The Faces of Buddhism in America*, edited by Charles S. Prebish and Kenneth K. Tanaka, 13–30. Oakland: University of California Press, 1998.

Chung, Ling. "Modernist Elements in Jane Hirshfield's Voice and Zen Meditation." *Connotations* 21, no. 1 (January 1, 2011): 101–125. http://go.gale.com/ps/i.do?p=LitRC&sw=w&issn=09395482&v=2.1&it=r&id=GALE%7CA287183061&sid=googleScholar&linkaccess=abs.

Colcutt, Martin. *Five Mountains: The Rinzai Zen Monastic Institution in Medieval Japan*. Cambridge, MA: Harvard University Press, 1981.

Collins, Richard. "Honoring the Form: Zen Moves in Charles Johnson's Oxherding Tale." *Religion and the Arts (Chestnut Hill, Mass.)* 14, no. 1–2 (2010): 59–76. https://doi.org/10.1163/107992610X12592913031829.

Dickman, Nathan Eric. "Linguistically Mediated Liberation: Freedom and Limits of Understanding in Thich Nhat Hanh and Hans-Georg Gadamer." Edited by Scott D. Churchill. *The Humanistic Psychologist* 44, no. 3 (2016): 256–279. https://doi.org/10.1037/hum0000023.

Downing, Michael. *Shoes Outside the Door: Desire, Devotion, and Excess at San Francisco Zen Center*. Washington, DC: Counterpoint, 2001.

Elkins, Andrew. *Another Place: An Ecocritical Study of Selected Western American Poets*. Fort Worth: Texas Christian University Press, 2002.

Fader, Larry A. "Zen in the West: Historical and Philosophical Implications of the Chicago World's Parliament of Religions." *Eastern Buddhist* 15, no. 1 (1981): 122–145.

Faure, Bernard. *Chan Insights and Oversights: An Epistemological Critique of the Chan Tradition*. Princeton, NJ: Princeton University Press, 1993.

Faure, Bernard. *The Red Thread: Buddhist Approaches to Sexuality*. Princeton, NJ: Princeton University Press, 1998.

Feichtinger, Christian. "Space Buddhism: The Adoption of Buddhist Motifs in Star Wars." *Contemporary Buddhism* 15, no. 1 (January 2, 2014): 28–43. https://doi.org/10.1080/14639947.2014.890348.

Fields, Rick. *How the Swans Came to the Lake: A Narrative History of Buddhism in America*. Boston: Shambhala, 1992.

Foulk, T. Griffith. "'Authentic': Rehabilitating Two Chan Buddhist Masters Neglected in Zen Studies." *Harvard Journal of Asiatic Studies* 77, no. 2 (2017): 465–486. https://doi.org/10.1353/jas.2017.0034.

Friedman, Ken. *The Fluxus Reader*. New York: Academy Editions, 1999.

Garton-Gundling, Kyle. *Enlightened Individualism: Buddhism and Hinduism in American Literature from the Beats to the Present*. Literature, Religion, and Postsecular Studies. Columbus: Ohio State University Press, 2019.

Gleig, Ann. *American Dharma: Buddhism beyond Modernity*. New Haven, CT: Yale University Press, 2019.

Gleig, Ann. "Buddhists and Racial Justice: A History." *Tricycle: The Buddhist Review*, July 24, 2020. https://tricycle.org/trikedaily/buddhists-racial-justice/.

Gleig, Ann. "Undoing Whiteness in American Buddhist Modernism: Critical, Collective, and Contextual Turns." In *Buddhism and Whiteness: Critical Reflections*, edited by Emily McRae and George Yancy, 21–42. Philosophy of Race. Lanham, MD: Lexington Books, 2019.

Goldberg, Natalie. *Writing down the Bones: Freeing the Writer Within*. 1st ed. Boston: Shambhala, 1986.

Grace, Stefan. "The Political Context of D. T. Suzuki's Early Life." *The Eastern Buddhist* 47, no. 2 (2016): 83–100.

Gray, Timothy. *Gary Snyder and the Pacific Rim: Creating Countercultural Community*. Contemporary North American Poetry Series. Iowa City: University of Iowa Press, 2006.

Han, Chenxing. *Be the Refuge: Raising the Voices of Asian American Buddhists*. Berkeley, CA: North Atlantic Books, 2021.

Hakutani, Yoshinobu. *Jack Kerouac and the Traditions of Classic and Modern Haiku*. Lanham, MD: Lexington Books, 2019.

Harootunian, Harry D. *Overcome by Modernity: History, Culture, and Community in Interwar Japan*. Princeton, NJ: Princeton University Press, 2000.

Harrington, Anne. "Zen, Suzuki, and the Art of Psychotherapy." In *Science and Religion, East and West*, edited by Yiftach Fehige, 48–69. London: Routledge, 2016.

Haskins, Rob. "Aspects of Zen Buddhism as an Analytical Context for John Cage's Chance Music." *Contemporary Music Review* 33, no. 5–6 (November 2, 2014): 616–629. https://doi.org/10.1080/07494467.2014.998426.

Hickey, Wakoh Shannon. "Regarding Elephants in the Room: What Buddhists Could Learn from Christians about Preventing Teacher Misconduct." *Buddhist-Christian Studies* 41 (2021): 95–125. https://doi.org/10.1353/bcs.2021.0013.

Hunt, Anthony. *Genesis, Structure, and Meaning in Gary Snyder's Mountains and Rivers Without End*. Western Literature Series. Reno: University of Nevada Press, 2004.

Irizarry, Joshua A. "Putting a Price on Zen: The Business of Redefining Religion for Global Consumption." *Journal of Global Buddhism* 16 (2015): 51–69. https://go.exlibris.link/C5X8jgWK.

Iwamura, Jane Naomi. *Virtual Orientalism: Asian Religions and American Popular Culture*. New York: Oxford University Press, 2011.

Kapleau, Philip. *The Three Pillars of Zen: Teaching, Practice, and Enlightenment*. 35th edition. New York: Anchor, 2000.

Kaza, Stephanie. "Finding Safe Harbor: Buddhist Sexual Ethics in America." *Buddhist-Christian Studies* 24, no. 1 (2004): 23–35. https://doi.org/10.1353/bcs.2005.0023.

Kaza, Stephanie. "Western Buddhist Motivations for Vegetarianism." *Worldviews: Environment, Culture, Religion* 9, no. 3 (2005): 385–411. https://doi.org/10.1163/156853505774841650.

Kerouac, Jack. "Belief and Technique for Modern Prose." *The Evergreen Review* 2, no. 8 (1959). https://jacket2.org/commentary/jack-kerouac-belief-technique-modern-prose.

Kerouac, Jack. *The Dharma Bums*. Penguin Classics. New York: Penguin Books, 2000.

King, Richard. *Orientalism and Religion: Post-Colonial Theory, India and "the Mystic East."* London and New York: Routledge, 1999.

King, Sallie B. "Transformative Nonviolence: The Social Ethics of George Fox and Thich Nhat Hanh." *Buddhist-Christian Studies* 18 (1998): 3–36. https://doi.org/10.2307/1390434.

Kraft, Kenneth, ed. *Zen Teaching, Zen Practice: Philip Kapleau and the Three Pillars of Zen*. Trumbull, CT: Weatherhill, 2000.

Kumakura, Isao, and Gensho Takenuki, eds. *Zen Master Musō Soseki: Life and Legacy*. Tokyo: Shunjuisha, 2012.

Larson, Kay. *Where the Heart Beats: John Cage, Zen Buddhism, and the Inner Life of Artists*. New York: Penguin, 2012.

Laycock, Joseph. "Zen Meets New Thought: The Erhard Seminars Training and Changing Ideas about Zen," *Contemporary Buddhism* 15, no. 2 (2014): 332–355. https://doi.org/10.1080/14639947.2014.932490.

Levering, Miriam. "Jack Kerouac in Berkeley: Reading *The Dharma Bums* as the Work of a Buddhist Writer." *Pacific World*, third series, 6 (2004): 7–26.

Levine, Gregory P. A. *Long Strange Journey: On Modern Zen, Zen Art, and Other Predicaments*. Honolulu: University of Hawai'i Press, 2017.

Low, Sor-Ching. "Seung Sahn: The Makeover of a Modern Zen Patriarch." In *Zen Masters*, edited by Steven T Heine and Dale S. Wright, 267–285. New York: Oxford University Press, 2010.

Lushetich, Natasha. *Fluxus: The Practice of Non-Duality*. Amsterdam: Editions Rodopi, 2014. http://site.ebrary.com/lib/ucsd/docDetail.action?docID=10907837.

Ma, Sheng-mei. "Zen Keytsch: Mystery Handymen with Dragon Tattoos." In *Detecting Detection: International Perspectives on the Uses of a Plot*, edited by Peter Baker and Deborah Shaller, 115–138. New York: Continuum, 2012.

Manuel, Zenju Earthlyn. *Sanctuary: A Meditation on Home, Homelessness, and Belonging*. Somerville, MA: Wisdom Publications, 2018.

Manuel, Zenju Earthlyn. *The Way of Tenderness: Awakening through Race, Sexuality, and Gender*. Somerville, MA: Wisdom Publications, 2015.

Masatsugu, Michael K. "'Beyond This World of Transiency and Impermanence': Japanese Americans, Dharma Bums, and the Making of American Buddhism during the Early Cold War Years." *Pacific Historical Review* 77, no. 3 (August 2008): 423–451. https://doi.org/http://dx.doi.org/10.1525/phr.2008.77.3.423.

McMahan, David, and Erik Braun. *Meditation, Buddhism, and Science*. Oxford and New York: Oxford University Press, 2017.

McMahan, David L. *The Making of Buddhist Modernism*. Oxford and New York: Oxford University Press, 2008.

McNicholl, Adeana. "Being Buddha, Staying Woke: Racial Formation in Black Buddhist Writing." *Journal of the American Academy of Religion* 86, no. 4 (July 13, 2018): 883–911. https://doi.org/10.1093/jaarel/lfy019.

McRae, Emily, and George Yancy, eds. *Buddhism and Whiteness: Critical Reflections*. Philosophy of Race. Lanham, MD: Lexington Books, 2019.

McRae, John R. *Seeing through Zen: Encounter, Transformation, and Genealogy in Chinese Chan Buddhism*. Berkeley: University of California Press, 2003.

Mitchell, Scott A. *Buddhism in America: Global Religion, Local Contexts*. London: Bloomsbury Academic, 2016.

Mitchell, Scott A. "The Tranquil Meditator: Representing Buddhism and Buddhists in US Popular Media." *Religion Compass* 8, no. 3 (2014): 81–89. https://doi.org/10.1111/rec3.12104.

Mohr, Michel. "The Use of Traps and Snares: Shaku Soen Revisited." In *Zen Masters*, edited by Steven Heine and Dale S. Wright, 183–216. New York: Oxford University Press, 2010.

Nicholls, David. *John Cage*. American Composers. Urbana: University of Illinois Press, 2007.

Poceski, Mario. *The Records of Mazu and the Making of Classical Chan Literature*. New York: Oxford University Press, 2015.

Porcu, Elisabetta. "Staging Zen Buddhism: Image Creation in Contemporary Films." *Contemporary Buddhism* 15, no. 1 (January 2, 2014): 81–96. https://doi.org/10.1080/14639947.2014.890354.

Rouzer, Paul F. *On Cold Mountain: A Buddhist Reading of the Hanshan Poems*. Seattle: University of Washington Press, 2015.

Satō, Kemmyō Taira, and Thomas Kirchner. "Brian Victoria and the Question of Scholarship." *The Eastern Buddhist* 41, no. 2 (2010): 139–166.

Satō, Kemmyō Taira, and Thomas Kirchner. "DT Suzuki and the Question of War." *The Eastern Buddhist* 39, no. 1 (2008): 61–120.

Schireson, Grace. *Naked in the Zendo: Stories of Uptight Zen, Wild-Ass Zen, and Enlightenment Wherever You Are*. Boulder, CO: Shambhala, 2019.

Schireson, Grace. *Zen Women: Beyond Tea Ladies, Iron Maidens, and Macho Masters*. Somerville, MA: Wisdom Publications, 2009.

Schlütter, Morten. *How Zen Became Zen: The Dispute over Enlightenment and the Formation of Chan Buddhism in Song-Dynasty China*. Studies in East Asian Buddhism 22. Honolulu: University of Hawai'i Press, 2008.

Schneider, David. *Crowded by Beauty: The Life and Zen of Poet Philip Whalen*. Oakland: University of California Press, 2015.

Schneider, Mathias. "Mindfulness, Buddha-Nature, and the Holy Spirit: On Thich Nhat Hanh's Interpretation of Christianity." *Buddhist-Christian Studies* 41, no. 1 (2021): 279–293. https://doi.org/10.1353/bcs.2021.0026.

Seager, Richard Hughes. *The World's Parliament of Religions: The East/West Encounter, Chicago, 1893*. Bloomington: Indiana University Press, 1992.

Seton, Gregory. "Killing the Buddha: Ritualized Violence in Fight Club through the Lens of Rinzai Zen Buddhist Practice." *Religions (Basel, Switzerland)* 9, no. 7 (2018): 206. https://doi.org/10.3390/rel9070206.

Sharf, Robert H. "Buddhist Modernism and the Rhetoric of Meditative Experience." *Numen* 42, no. 3 (October 1995): 228–283. http://www.jstor.org/stable/3270219.

Sharf, Robert H. "The Zen of Japanese Nationalism." *History of Religions* 33, no. 1 (August 1993): 1–43. http://www.jstor.org/stable/1062782.

Sieber, Patricia. "Acts of Translation: Jane Hirshfield, Chinese Poetics and the Practice of Zen." *Contemporary Buddhism* 1, no. 2 (2000): 119–139. https://doi.org/10.1080/14639940008573728.

Smith, Owen F. *Fluxus: The History of an Attitude*. San Diego: San Diego State University Press, 1998.

Snodgrass, Judith M. *Presenting Japanese Buddhism to the West: Orientalism, Occidentalism, and the Columbian Exposition*. Chapel Hill: University of North Carolina Press, 2003.

Snodgrass, Judith M. "'Budda No Fukuin': The Deployment of Paul Carus's 'Gospel of Buddha' in Meiji Japan." *Japanese Journal of Religious Studies* 25, no. 3–4 (Autumn 1998): 319–344.

Snodgrass, Judith M. "Japan's Contribution to Modern Global Buddhism: The World's Parliament of Religions Revisited." *The Eastern Buddhist* New Series 43, no. 1 (2012): 81–102.

Snodgrass, Judith M. "Publishing Eastern Buddhism: D. T. Suzuki's Journey to the West." In *Casting Faiths: Imperialism and the Transformation of Religion in East and Southeast Asia*, edited by Thomas David DuBois, 46–72. Basingstoke, UK: Palgrave Macmillan, 2009.

Snyder, Gary. *The Practice of the Wild: Essays*. San Francisco: North Point Press, 1990.

Suh, Sharon A. *Silver Screen Buddha: Buddhism in Asian and Western Film.* London: Bloomsbury Academic, 2015.

Suzuki, Daisetz Teitaro. *Selected Works of D. T. Suzuki: Zen.* Edited by Richard M. Jaffe. Vol. 1. Oakland: University of California Press, 2015.

Suzuki, Daisetz Teitaro. *Zen and Japanese Culture.* Edited by Richard M. Jaffe. Bollingen Series 64. Princeton, NJ: Princeton University Press, 2010.

Suzuki, Daisetz Teitaro, Erich Fromm, and Richard J DeMartino. *Zen Buddhism and Psychoanalysis.* New York: Harper, 1960.

Suzuki, Shunryu. *Zen Mind, Beginner's Mind.* New edition. Boston: Weatherhill, 1973.

Tweed, Thomas A. "Night-Stand Buddhists and Other Creatures: Sympathizers, Adherents, and the Study of Religion." In American Buddhism: Methods and Findings in Recent Scholarship, edited by Duncan Ryūken Williams and Christopher S. Queen, 71–90. London: Routledge, 1999.

Van Overmeire, Ben. "Inventing the Zen Buddhist Samurai: Yoshikawa Eiji's Musashi and Japanese Modernity." *The Journal of Popular Culture* 49, no. 5 (2016): 1125–1145.

Van Overmeire, Ben. "'Mountains, Rivers, and the Whole Earth': Koan Interpretations of Female Zen Practitioners." *Religions* 9, no. 4 (April 2018): 125. https://doi.org/10.3390/rel 9040125.

Van Overmeire, Ben. "Hard-Boiled Zen: Janwillem Van De Wetering's The Japanese Corpse as Buddhist Literature," *Contemporary Buddhism* 19, no. 2 (July 3, 2018): 382–397, https://doi.org/10.1080/14639947.2018.1480890.

Victoria, Brian Daizen. *Zen at War.* 2nd edition. Lanham, MD: Rowman & Littlefield, 2006.

Victoria, Brian Daizen. "The 'Negative Side' of DT Suzuki's Relationship to War." *The Eastern Buddhist* 41, no. 2 (2010): 97–138.

Watts, Alan. *The Way of Zen.* New York: New American Library of World Literature, 1959.

Watts, Alan W. "Beat Zen, Square Zen, and Zen." *Chicago Review* 12, no. 2 (1958): 3–11.

Whalen-Bridge, John, and Gary Storhoff. *The Emergence of Buddhist American Literature.* Albany: State University of New York Press, 2009.

Whalen-Bridge, John, and Gary Storhoff. *Writing as Enlightenment: Buddhist American Literature into the Twenty-First Century.* Albany: State University of New York Press, 2011.

Williams, Duncan Ryūken. *American Sutra: A Story of Faith and Freedom in the Second World War.* Cambridge, MA: Harvard University Press, 2019. http://www.hup.harvard.edu/catalog.php?isbn=9780674986534&content=reviews.

williams, angel Kyodo. *Being Black: Zen and the Art of Living with Fearlessness and Grace.* Harmondsworth, UK: Penguin, 2002.

Wilson, Jeff. *Mindful America: The Mutual Transformation of Buddhist Meditation and American Culture.* New York: Oxford University Press, 2014.

Wilson, Jeff. *Mourning the Unborn Dead: A Buddhist Ritual Comes to America.* New York: Oxford University Press, 2009. https://doi.org/10.1093/acprof:oso/9780195371932.003.0001.

Yamada, Shoji. *Shots in the Dark: Japan, Zen, and the West.* Buddhism and Modernity 9. Chicago: University of Chicago Press, 2009.

CHAPTER 9

KOREAN BUDDHISM IN AMERICA

CLAUDIA SCHIPPERT

Introduction

On a Sunday morning, during the circle talk that concludes a multi-day Zen retreat, twenty participants reflect on their experience during the just concluded *yongmaeng jeongjin* (an intensive meditation retreat).[1] They sit on padded mats and cushions on the floor of the main meditation room at Dae Won Sa, a Korean Buddhist temple associated with the Jogye Order of Korean Buddhism.[2] The temple is located in a rural/suburban stretch between Fort Lauderdale and Miami. The Zen students gathered look fairly representative of the surrounding area: all are non-Korean, primarily Caucasian and some Hispanic, and they range in age from their early twenties to late sixties. While they are all lay practitioners (rather than monks or nuns), the Zen students have spent the previous two and a half days following a (slightly modified) Korean monastic retreat schedule: getting up at 4 a.m. for 4:30 a.m. bowing practice, where they completed 108 full prostrations in vigorous unison and silence. Following daily ceremonial chanting in Korean, they spent each day until 9:30 p.m. alternating sitting and walking meditation with the rare interruption of "work period," which refers to an hour of collective cleaning the temple or preparing food for the three daily meals cooked by retreat

---

[1] While originally referring to the one week of intensive practice with little to no sleep during the traditional twice annual three-month-long meditation retreats in Korean monasteries, the Zen group in this opening vignette uses the term to describe any multi-day intensive meditation retreat.

[2] All names identifying persons or temples in this chapter are pseudonyms. In rendering Korean terms in English, I mostly follow the "Revised Romanization of Korean." The older McCune-Reischauer system is maintained in quotations or for names/terms that continue to rely on it. While *Seon* is the Korean term for (the Japanese-derived) "Zen," in the American context, "Zen" is used also in many Korean-lineage contexts, e.g., the "Zen School" mentioned in this opening vignette.

participants in the temple kitchen. Meals have been eaten in "traditional" Korean temple style: Practitioners unstack their four nested bowls in unison, following the sound cues provided by the wooden clapper (*jukbi*). They eat their rice, soup, and side dishes/salad in silence, rinsing their bowls with roasted barley tea before restacking the bowls and waiting for another auditory cue to remove and clean the communal pots in the large temple kitchen, and then everyone returns to the main "Dharma Room" for more sitting meditation.

The only exception to the unlikely group of retreatants gathered at this Korean Buddhist Temple is the one Korean monk who currently lives at Dae Won Sa. Much to the appreciation of the American Zen students, Bon Jin Sunim has joined the group periodically during their weekend meditation retreat and also for the congratulatory circle talk at the end of the retreat. While Sunim (the Korean honorific term for a monk or nun) is the only Korean monastic present, many of the Zen students in attendance wear the gray short (bowing) robes, or even the longer formal monastic robes with wide sleeves (*jangsam*) and the brown *gasa* (an intricately sewn bib-like garment worn around the neck, similar to the Japanese *rakusu*). While wearing *jangsam* and *gasa* is associated with monastics in the Korean Jogye tradition, in this Zen group the robe and *gasa* are also worn by Zen students who have taken lay precepts or have become Dharma teachers. Zen Master Mu Sahn (a white Jewish man from New York who has visited the Florida Zen group for the occasion of the retreat) gives the final short talk during the sharing circle, and then participants hurry to clear the space by picking up cushions and sweeping any remaining dust from the Dharma room.

Preparations immediately commence for the Korean service that will start at 10:30 a.m. Several Korean men and women rush into the room to arrange the many mats into the appropriate order in preparation for the Sunday service. Many other Korean women have already gathered in the kitchen or in the large yard outside the suburban house to chop mushrooms or seaweed on folding tables and to cook soup on makeshift stoves, in addition to ongoing activities in the temple kitchen inside, where a group is preparing an elaborate vegetarian lunch of rice, noodles, soup, and multiple side dishes for the large group of people who will gather after the service. They will sit on the floor surrounding low tables placed in the main hall, or on the several dozen chairs around folding tables in the temple's dining room, as well as on the back patio surrounded by mango trees and rows of palmetto palms indigenous to Florida.

Inside the kitchen, some women chop kimchi into bitesize chunks, while others create various additional dishes or check on the multiple rice cookers. Throughout the bustling activities, everyone can listen to the service, which is broadcast directly into the kitchen and other areas of the house through loudspeakers. While those in the kitchen or in outside spaces primarily hear chanting of sutras by the resident monk, accompanied by the sound of a large bell, the activities inside the main worship hall include some Korean men and women participating in vigorous bowing practice during the sutra chanting; others sit and chant along, yet others quietly say mantras as they face the three large golden statues that dominate the wide altar: Shakyamuni Buddha, flanked by Kwan

Seum Bosal and Ji Jang Bosal. The resident monk continues to chant various sutras while hitting the impressive large Korean temple bell or a wooden *moktak* (fish-belly shaped wooden instrument mainly used to keep rhythm), which resonates powerfully in the room with a low ceiling.

With the exception of some visitors from the prior Zen center retreat, almost all participants in the service are Koreans. While on this Sunday morning friendly words are exchanged and invitations to join the lunch are taken up, such overlap between the two groups is very unusual. Indeed, in most other locations where we might observe "Korean Buddhism in North America," we might not find any such overlap, as these two types of groups likely occupy entirely different meeting spaces.

The opening vignette resembles what Kim has described in a case study "of a Korean ethnic Buddhist temple in metropolitan Boston" (2008, 163) and also what Sharon Suh's *Being Buddhist in a Christian World* (2004) explores in Los Angeles. At Dae Won Sa in Florida, the Korean community supports the temple as a place for occasional ceremonies and regular Sunday worship, but also as an important place for communal gathering, networking, and shared meals. Indeed, on this Sunday morning, there are likely more people involved in the preparation of the elaborate lunchtime meal than are present inside the main room where Sunim is chanting and where he subsequently delivers a brief sermon in Korean.

The non-Korean Zen group (which is part of the Kwan Um School) functions independently and parallel to the Korean temple. Although the local teacher of the Zen group has periodically also served on the board of the temple and maintains friendly collegiality with the resident monks, there is no real overlap of the two groups' planned activities or members. While the Zen Center expresses gratitude for being able to use a beautiful and "authentic" space such as Dae Won Sa, it is unclear whether members of the Korean temple consider the Zen group a comparable institution.[3]

The coexistence and lack of overlap among these two groups that practice forms of Korean Buddhism in Florida, like similar communities in other cities, here serves as introduction to the two main groups that constitute "Korean Buddhism in North America."

This chapter first describes the difference between the two groups. Then, Korean heritage communities are contextualized historically and by describing form and function of one temple. The next section introduces as "translation into English" the major North American convert communities founded by Korean teachers. In the final section, three relevant themes central to academic explorations of Korean Buddhism in America are briefly suggested: the legacy of Jinul's inclusive style in the formation and transmission of Korean Buddhism; the double minority status of Korean Buddhists in North America; and the complex legacy of resistance to Japanese colonial rule in changing geopolitical and transnational contexts.

---

[3] Similar to Kim 2008, 174.

Caveat and Sources

The chapter draws on currently available documents and scholarly resources published in English, on archival records of Zen Master Seung Sahn—also largely limited to those available in English—and on the author's participant observation and interviews in contexts described in the chapter. While there is much more to be written about Korean-speaking Buddhists and their practice in North America, that work will need to be addressed by an author more proficient in the Korean language. Given the overall great dearth of scholarship about Korean Buddhism in North America, this chapter is intended as a first, though certainly partial and incomplete, step in attempting to fill that gap.

Two Groups of "Korean Buddhism in North America"

As explored here, "Korean Buddhism in North America" includes two distinct (and thus far almost mutually exclusive) sets of communities.

First, "Korean Buddhism" names the style of Buddhism that developed in Korea, starting with the introduction of Buddhism from China in the fourth century CE, and that in the twentieth century was brought to North America in the context of immigration. This Korean Buddhism is practiced almost exclusively by Korean heritage communities. The vast majority of formally organized congregations belong to the Korean Jogye (Chogye) Order of Buddhism, with communities relying on Korean monastic teachers who come to live in North America for a period of time. A smaller number of Korean Buddhist communities belong to other Korean orders, or they may be practitioners of popular Korean Buddhism-based religious movements such as Won Buddhism (see Choi 2015; Ching 1997; Kim 2001).[4]

Second, the other groups associated with Korean Buddhism in North America are founded by or follow the teachings of Korean Buddhist teachers; practitioners in these groups are predominantly non-Korean and English-speaking. The largest such group is the Kwan Um School of Zen, founded by Korean Zen Master Seung Sahn. Samu Sunim called the groups I identify as "English-speaking" in terms of the "nonethnic Korean Sŏn Buddhist movement in the West" (2001, 230). His terminology points to the close connection of language and ethnic heritage/cultural traditions.

---

[4] Other orders of Korean Buddhism in North America include Taego, Chontae and Jingak. Won is a modern reform movement within Buddhism, established in Korea in 1916 by Pak Chungbin, later known as Sot'aesan (1891–1943). Roughly twenty-five Won Buddhist centers exist in larger cities in North America, and practitioners assert the importance of adapting Buddhist practice to changing social circumstances.

It should be noted that a conceptual division into "two Buddhisms" has been criticized (see, e.g., Hickey 2015; Han 2021; Numrich 2006). The typology homogenizes all immigrant communities and does not allow for the necessary attention to local phenomena and contexts. "Asian versus convert" unhelpfully mixes categories of origin and ethnic identity with religious practice status, and such a distinction does not adequately account for, among other aspects, differences among multiple generations of heritage practitioners, as well as complex dynamics in communities founded within the American contexts, not to mention regional differences. The distinction can also reinscribe orientalist notions or can import white supremacist expressions or racial hierarchies of convert (largely white) and heritage (largely non-white immigrant) groups.

In this chapter, I do not seek to reinscribe a hard distinction between "heritage" and "convert" communities. Nonetheless, I suggest that in the case of Korean Buddhism in North America, a (related but not identical) distinction based on the primary language used within the community appears operative. We can observe (exclusively/primarily) Korean-speaking communities on the one hand, and communities that practice some form of Korean-lineage Buddhism but are (exclusively/primarily) English-speaking on the other hand. To be sure, some Korean temples offer English-language services or meditation classes, but their institutional context is firmly rooted in Korean language and culture and often an ongoing connection to South Korean institutions such as the Jogye Order.[5]

Focusing on primary language familiarity and linguistic usage as a distinguishing factor might also help account for the fact that, as Kim claims, second- and third-generation Koreans may well be sufficiently unfamiliar or uncomfortable with the dominant Korean language and culture operating in the Korean temples that they might opt to re-discover or connect to the non-Korean convert forms of "Korean Buddhism" such as those in the Zen Centers of the Kwan Um School (2008, 182).

A particularly unique resource is the 2012 online publication by *The Korean Buddhist News USA*: "The Sangha Book of Korean Buddhism." Its editor Jong Kweon Yi introduces the publication as follows (emphasis added):

> This is a book of Sangha specifically dedicated to the Korean Buddhist community in North America. **This is the first serious effort to bring together all groups representative of Korean Buddhism run by Koreans and Americans here.** Since Korean Buddhism became established in North America, it has served Korean immigrant communities as [a] spiritual and cultural shelter. Eminent teachers and masters from Korea have also transmitted Dharma to Western students. They opened a number of Buddhist centers across the country and they have been run by their

---

[5] Many in contemporary Korean heritage communities are functionally bilingual—which cannot be said of the second category. Perhaps the second group should be called "only English speaking" to reflect the limitation or loss of Korean language and cultural context in the convert communities—where members may have memorized some Korean chants, but mostly function exclusively in English for instruction.

Western students. These centers are very important in the Korean community. We have compiled a list of these English speaking centers for this directory, too. This is the first resources [*sic*] to include **these two streams of Korean Buddhism in North America.**

Yi further defines how he views these "two streams" of Korean Buddhism in North America:

> **In the book, we defined and declared the boundary of what we call "our community."** . . . One of the notable things about the Sangha book was that it included the English-speaking Korean Buddhist groups in America as an independent category. Although there are many English-speaking practitioners in the New World, many of them remain unknown to Koreans. **We believe that Korean Buddhism is not about language, but about lineage.** In this regard, it is natural that they should be considered as part of the Korean Buddhist community. Once we believe, we just do it. (2012, n.p.)

Yi here seeks to validate to the heritage community the English-speaking Buddhist groups that are founded by Korean teachers. Even while Yi acknowledges the simultaneous existence of "two streams," he asserts that a shared lineage of Korean teachers serves as an important factor in identifying certain North American English-speaking Buddhist groups as part of "Korean Buddhism." (It should be noted that Yi and his organization acknowledge their debt to Seung Sahn.)

Korean Buddhists in North America

Korean immigration to the United States began in 1903 with workers recruited for pineapple and sugar plantations in Hawaii. After establishing communities in Hawaii and then Southern California, immigration from Korea slowed after the 1924 Oriental Exclusion Act and became largely limited to individual students or politicians. While after 1945 some immigration began again, the most significant increase occurred after the Immigration Act of 1965 removed the severe restrictions on Asian immigrants. More than 30,000 Koreans immigrated to the United States each year from 1976 to 1990, when the pace of immigration began to slow. The total number of immigrants from Korea to the United States by 2010 exceeded one million. While the earlier waves of immigrants were primarily laborers, war victims, or political refugees, the Korean immigrants after 1965 were primarily white-collar workers in Korea. Today, "more than 95% of Korean Americans consist of post-1965 immigrants and their children" (Min 2011, 196).

A noticeable shift in religious affiliation from pre- to post-immigration has been observed among Koreans in North America. Among the Korean or Korean American population, only a small minority practice Buddhism (numbers reported range from

1.5 percent to 15 percent Buddhists vs. 40 percent to 80 percent Christians). This pattern of majority Christian adherence (versus minority status for Korean Buddhists) is replicated across all regions in North America. The pace of Korean immigration has significantly slowed since the 1990s, but the predominantly Christian identification of Korean Americans continues to be valid, rendering Korean Buddhists a double minority.

One indicator of Korean Buddhist communities in North America are existing temples that fulfill the function of providing religious instruction and care for the local community.[6] Estimates of the number of exiting temples throughout North America vary. Suh (2004) identified "eighty-nine temples serving the Korean American community in the larger United States." Yi (2012) lists 93 proper temples, but lists addresses for almost 200 individual groups, centers, or temples in the United States and Canada. The Jogye Order website currently (2022) lists 82 distinct Temples in North America.[7]

A Korean Buddhist Temple

Returning to the opening vignette, Dae Won Sa's interior, especially the main Dharma hall, is easily identified as a Korean Buddhist worship space. The spacious room has a wooden floor, carefully cleaned and ready for the many rectangular mats and cushions that are usually stacked in a corner until they are used during services or other activities. With the exception of a small standup piano in one corner and the large ornate Korean brass bell hanging from a sturdy wooden frame, there are few additional decorations on the walls. However, hundreds of colorful paper lotus lanterns hang neatly arranged from the low ceiling, each with the name of the person or family who made a donation attached on a small piece of paper; when lit with the small electric lights strung throughout the bright pink and yellow paper lanterns, the room becomes bright and colorful. Also immediately recognizable to Korean Buddhists are the multiple altars and statues in the front of the room. As one would find in other Korean Buddhist temples, one side altar (or platform) is dedicated to ancestor commemoration/the spirits of the deceased (*hadan*) and the other to the Dharma protectors (*sinjungdan*), while the expansive main altar at the center (*sangdan*) supports various candles, incense holders, and the three large golden statues of (the Korean versions of) Sakyamuni Buddha, JiJang Bosal (*Kstigarbha*) and Kwan Seum Bosal (*Avalokiteśvara*).

While the interior is unmistakably a Korean-style Buddhist temple space, the outside resembles the neighborhood's ranch houses with large yards. Unlike the Hindu Shiva Vishnu Temple down the road, which sports exterior decorations more clearly

---

[6] But also note Cheah 2011 for the importance of religiosity not located within temples.
[7] Whether examined regionally or nationally, Korean Jogye is the predominant institutional representation: "The largest and most mainstream order, encompassing approximately 60 percent of the over 20 Buddhist orders in Korea" (Kim 2008, 164).

indicative of "authentic" Indian temple architecture, the Korean temple easily blends into the South Florida horse country neighborhood, with only the occasional festivities like Buddha's birthday or particularly well attended Sunday services bringing a great number of Korean community members and thus potential attention from neighbors to the temple.

While in some metropolitan areas with a high concentration of Koreans and Korean Americans (such as Los Angeles, Seattle, Chicago, Detroit, New York, or Honolulu) we find temple buildings with exteriors in "traditional" Korean style, the majority of Korean Buddhist temples in North America are housed in buildings that have been bought or rented and repurposed by the Korean community to support the (monastic-led) Buddhist community. Former churches, garages, barns, residential homes, or storefronts are marked as temples by ornate calligraphy or practical printed signs affixed to posts or front doors. On occasion a statue or a small multi-tiered structure resembling a peace pagoda is visible in the yard. Building a "traditional-style" Korean temple compound, including several gates, and multiple buildings with ornate roof architecture, would take much more space, a larger community of monastics and laypeople for ongoing support, and a significant larger and more enduring donor base than most Korean American Buddhist communities have at their disposal. (There are some examples nonetheless, e.g., Muryangsa in Honolulu, Tahlmahsa in Los Angeles, and Taegosa in Tehachapi, California.)

The plain exterior of most temples correlates with the multipurpose use of many interior spaces. Unlike the spatial separation of chanting, sitting in meditation, or studying sutras that one may find in a more spacious Korean temple compound (with, e.g., a sutra hall devoted to study and different halls dedicated to Bodhisattvas and ancestors or, e.g., regional/mountain spirits), almost all Korean Buddhist temples in North America combine all of these activities and their various iconographic representations in the main Dharma hall. This—largest—room of the building also provides space for communal gatherings, memorials, weddings, or baby-naming ceremonies, as well as less formal get-togethers. If there are other rooms available, they may serve as tea-room, residential or guest quarters for monastics or guest teachers, library, functional rooms such as kitchens and dining rooms, and administrative offices.

Translation into English: Convert Lineages Founded by Korean Teachers

While almost all Korean Buddhist teachers who came to North America during the second half of the twentieth century initially ministered to the existing Korean Buddhist communities, some also focused on teaching non-Korean (and mostly non-Buddhist) Americans. Several of these Korean teachers founded centers and organizations that became popular with non-Korean converts, and some of these organizations continue to exist and shape what we today encounter as English-speaking Buddhism based on Korean lineages in North America.

Perhaps the earliest Korean teacher to promote Korean Seon Buddhism in America was Seo Kyung-bo, who visited Columbia University in 1964 and then traveled around giving talks (Yu 1988, 83). Pursuing his PhD at Temple University in Philadelphia, he gave talks in the community and had several students who formed groups and small organizations, most of which no longer exist today.

Another teacher, Kusan Sunim, visited the United States in the early 1970s and inspired several North American students to return to Korea with him and undergo Seon monastic training at Songgwang Sa.[8] One prolific American scholar of Korean Buddhism, Robert E. Buswell, was such a student of Kusan Sunim.[9]

Samu Sunim (1941–2022) was the first Korean monk to stay permanently in North American and teach Korean Buddhism by founding several convert communities based in Korean monastic practice. Samu Sunim arrived in New York City in 1967 and established the "Zen Lotus Society." Moving to Montreal and then Toronto, he established a temple and residential community in Toronto in 1979. Further temples were founded in Ann Arbor, Michigan (1981), Mexico City (1985), Chicago (1992), and New York City (2014). "Zen Lotus Society" was renamed in 1990 as "Buddhist Society for Compassionate Wisdom." It is described as "a non-celibate (celibacy optional) North American Buddhist order" based on the Korean monastic training Samu Sunim received. A three-year training program for non-Korean Dharma teachers exists, and at least two of his students have received teaching authorization from Samu Sunim (Yu 1988, 84).

The arguably most influential Korean teacher in the United States was Zen Master Seung Sahn (1927–2004), who arrived in the United States in 1972. Having received transmission from his teacher Ko Bong, Seung Sahn had previously been active in the revitalization of the Jogye order in Korea. He arrived in America as an official Jogye missionary at the invitation of the existing Korean Buddhist community in Los Angeles in order to tend to their needs. Seung Sahn did minister to the existing Korean Buddhist communities in several cities, founded three new Korean temples, and assisted in the maintenance of several others. However, his main focus was on teaching non-Korean American practitioners and forming convert residential communities (Zen Centers) where men and women as well as monastics and laypeople lived communally and integrated Zen practice into everyday life. Formed in 1983, the "Kwan Um School of Zen" is currently the largest collective of authorized Zen teachers in the Korean lineage in America, and the largest group of practitioners of Korean-lineage Buddhism as practiced by primarily non-Koreans in North America. While some practitioners are monastics (trained by Seung Sahn or now through monastic training in Korea) the vast majority of Kwan Um members and teachers are non-monastic. Currently, thirty-nine

---

[8] One of the oldest and most famous Korean temples in Korea and especially focused on monastic education. Also see Kusan's popular *The Way of Korean Zen* (1985).

[9] See Buswell 1992b.

Zen centers and groups are affiliated with the school in North America (plus sixty centers in other parts of the world). The centers range from small practice groups to large residential centers, but all follow in one way or another Seung Sahn's core teachings and the school's practice schedule (with daily chanting and sitting schedules that accommodate work or school requirements for Zen Center residents or members of the community). Twenty-eight authorized teachers (plus thirty outside North America) within the Kwan Um School lead retreats ranging from one to 100 days.[10] Diamond Hill Zen Monastery, built in traditional Korean temple style in 1984, located in Cumberland, Rhode Island, serves as a retreat center for the annual three-month winter and one-month summer intensive meditation retreats (*kyol che*) open to monastics and laypeople alike. A robust "online sangha" that reaches many more practitioners in places without physical Zen centers pre-dates by several years the need of many Buddhist groups to explore online practice due to the COVID-19 pandemic.

While there are some other well-known Korean monastic teachers who currently have followers in North America, they tend to not have particularly formalized communities. However, "Korean Buddhism in North America" can also point to the visibility of some Korean Buddhist teachers (especially via the internet or through international teaching tours that reach many in North America). One popular teacher, Pomnyun Sunim, teaches about happiness and freedom and the relevance of Buddhism to daily life. His diverse non-monastic audiences, and the members of the "Jungto Society" he founded, participate in classes or Dharma talks and also engage in various humanitarian, environmental, or peace activities.[11] Pomnyun Sunim's practical and eclectic teaching (besides Seon, he also teaches *vipassanā* meditation, for example) has wide appeal to both Korean and non-Korean practitioners in North America and beyond. He may also be a good example for the difficult task of finding meaningful definitions or boundaries of *Korean* Buddhism in *America* (especially when considering the increasingly robust transnational and online presence of various teachers, schools, and lineages).

Academic Study of Korean Buddhism in North America

In comparison to other forms of Buddhism that are practiced in North America, Korean Buddhism has received little attention in the scholarship of religion in America. The vast majority of work among religion scholars interested in the communities and practices of Koreans in North America has been devoted to studies of Christianity in the context

---

[10] The numbers of current authorized teachers are accurate as of September 14, 2022. Any changes and updates can be viewed through the digital archive (http://zmss.cah.ucf.edu/timelines) or the Kwan Um School's website (https://kwanumzen.org/).

[11] See, e.g., https://www.jungtosociety.org/

of immigration and subsequent phases of acculturation (e.g., Kwon, Kim, and Warner 2001). Besides a few studies investigating specific local communities, some sociological comparative work about Koreans in America includes select reference to Korean Buddhists. Reflected in the limited data available, three themes appear important to consider in the developing academic study of Korean Buddhism in North America.

Jinul's Inclusive Legacy

Due to his enduring influence, Jinul (Chinul) (1158–1210) is often considered the founder of Korean Seon Buddhism. Concerned with divisions and tensions among various doctrinal and meditation schools during the twelfth century, he "incorporated doctrinal teachings into Sŏn practice and promoted the basic unity of Sŏn and doctrinal teachings" (Samu 2001, 232). Jinul taught "sudden awakening and gradual cultivation" and was invested in revitalizing monastic education and in formalizing Korean Seon training, as well as providing comprehensive guides for meditation practice and cultivation in everyday life.

As part of his syncretic program which skillfully negotiated sectarian divisions at the time, Jinul promoted the practice of meditative investigation through *hwadu* (gong-an) which would become a unique feature of Korean Buddhism (cf. Buswell 1992a). Muller (1997, n.p.) suggests that "[d]own to the present, modern Seon practice is thought not to be far removed in content from that which was implemented by Jinul—an integrated combination of the practice of [. . .] meditation with the study of selected Buddhist texts." Jinul's inclusive teaching continued earlier influences such as Wonhyo (617–686) and was further developed by others, but the impulse to find connections and unity among different approaches, as well as the affirmation of the oneness of scholarly study and meditation practice, appears an important aspect of much of Korean Buddhist teachings since then (see also Park 2009).

We can see one example of Chinul's influence in Suh's study of a Korean temple in Los Angeles. While few of the temple's members referenced explicit textual sources, their comments about their motivation and assumed goal of Buddhist practice (as "finding and knowing one's mind") reflect a doctrine of Buddha Nature as developed in Jinul's commentaries. Suh writes:

> This potential to become a Buddha takes on a particularly nuanced meaning in Korean Buddhism through the commentaries of Chinul. . . . Chinul believed that individuals must have faith not only in their own potential to become Buddhas but also the fact that they already *are* Buddhas. In other words, the individual awakens to his or her own enlightenment through self-realization wherein one "realize[s] directly the nature of our own True Mind." (2004, 17)

Here Jinul's "sudden awakening followed by gradual cultivation" is translated into an affirmation of self which, as Suh explores in detail throughout her study, with particular attention to gender differences, leads to skillful tactics of "coping with struggles for self-confidence experienced by many immigrant groups" (2004, 6).

Double Minority Status and Comparison with Christianity

Of particular importance in the context of Korean Buddhists in North America is their minority status, not just in terms of ethnic identity within the wider North American context, but within the Korean immigrant community. In Korea today, Christians and Buddhists make up minorities with 28 percent and 15 percent, respectively—the vast majority of Koreans are "not religious."[12] The situation is different in North America, where an overwhelming majority of Koreans identify as or associate with Christianity. "An estimated 70 to 80 percent of all Korean Americans claim affiliation with Korean Christian churches, yet 40 percent of that population is said to have converted to Christianity following immigration" (Hurh quoted by Suh 2004, 3).

Korean Buddhists in North America thus face the challenge of potentially feeling more isolated from others in the immigrant community, including exclusion from social and economic networking possibilities that larger community connections (e.g., facilitated in Christian churches) entail.[13] At the same time, and as a reaction to their double minority status, in some instances Korean Buddhists proclaim more national pride in the Korean-ness of their Buddhist practice. Suh writes about a man who, like others in the community, "equated Buddhism with a strong sense of nationalism and a Korean identity that has been undermined not only by Japanese imperialism but also by Christians attracted to the West" (2004, 141).

Kim suggests, "it is impossible to discuss Korean American religion without discussing Christianity," as Korean practitioners of other religions have come to define themselves in contrast to the more powerful and more steadily growing Christianity within the immigrant Korean community (2008, 177). As observed in fieldwork at a Korean temple in Boston, "[v]irtually every *dharma* talk ('sermon') at the temple includes a comparison of Christians and Buddhists, whereas Christians rarely compare themselves to other religious groups, except when they talk of a need to evangelize non-Christians" (2008, 164). We can observe such definition-by-comparison/contrast even in scholarly accounts, such as Park's *One Korean's Approach to Buddhism* (2009). Frequent comparison or refence to Christian theological constructs or points of refence are here integrated into an otherwise quite disciplined "dharmatological" exploration of key Buddhist concepts and sutras.

---

[12] https://www.state.gov/reports/2019-report-on-international-religious-freedom/south-korea.
[13] As Hickey reminds us, "ethnically focused communities [developed] partly in response to the white racism promoted by law, propaganda, and force" (2015, 44).

The potential tension that Korean Buddhists may experience with Korean Christians within an immigrant context of course differs from relationships that English-speaking convert communities may have with other religious traditions and communities—and with Korean-ness as potential identity. Much work remains to be done, as generational shifts within Korean American communities, together with increasingly transnational teachers and virtually facilitated community formations, introduce new issues and necessary negotiations of what appears as Korean Buddhism in North America.

Relationship to Japanese Colonialism: Resistance and Hybridity

A third topic worthy of scholarly attention is related to the Korean colonial experience. Japanese rule in Korean (1910–1945) brought great suffering for Koreans, and it also created (new) difficulties for Korean monastic institutions. While Korean Buddhist orders were released from the limitations imposed during the previous Joseon (1392–1909) period, they simultaneously were forced to accommodate (or change) traditions and practices to colonial demands. The Japanese convention of married monks is the most often noted enforced change; the Jogye Order's resistance to the mandate partially contributed to its central role in the reinvigoration of Korean Buddhism after 1945.[14]

Many of the post-1965 immigrants arriving in North America (or their parents) had lived through the suppression experienced under Japanese colonial rule. These formative events may help contextualize the frequent mention of significant pride in Korean history—and especially the importance of Korean Buddhist monastics in resisting earlier Japanese rule, maintaining distinct Korean Buddhist traditions, and then reinstating Korean Buddhist institutions. Armed groups of "righteous monks" in the late sixteenth century who helped expel an earlier Japanese invasion are often cited as defenders of Korean Buddhist national pride. The distinct Korean approach to *gong-an* practice is frequently explained (to outsiders) in distinction from Japanese Zen.[15]

While Korean immigrants to North America and their descendants may negotiate their relationship to a history of Japanese suppression by reclaiming a sense of national pride in the reinvigoration of the dominant Jogye Order that continued celibacy in defiance of Japanese mandates for monks to marry, the relationship between Korean and Japanese expressions of Buddhism took on another characteristic in the 1960s/1970s convert communities.

When Korean Seon teachers came to North America, they encountered a public image (and several practice communities) shaped by Zen teachers from Japanese lineages.

---

[14] See Pori Park's thorough exploration of these negotiations in their 2009 study of the reform movements from the early 1900s to 1945 in light of particular forms of "modernity."

[15] Unlike the Japanese style of a developing series of koans that are contemplated one after another, the Korean approach, as developed by Jinul and practiced to the present day, is focused on only one *hwadu* that the practitioner holds during their entire life.

Unlike the initial transmission of Buddhism from Korea into Japan in the sixth century, in twentieth-century North America, Japanese Zen had already set the stage when Korean teachers arrived. Most Korean teachers who founded convert communities developed their brand of Buddhism in North America in direct relationship with this already existing cultural imaginary. For example, while Korean monastic training and lay practice are not solely focused on meditation, the image of Zen in America was preoccupied with sitting meditation, sidelining (as "cultural trappings" or through other white supremacist perspectives) practices of sutra chanting or devotional rituals that may be more central in the Korean Buddhist lived context (cf. Cheah 2011).

While Seung Sahn maintained traditional forms in Korean temples, for his English-speaking communities he created a "hybrid" style of Korean Seon that was grounded in Korean tradition but was also innovative and departed from existing institutional formations (e.g., in the creation of "Bodhisattva monks" as an avenue for non-celibate monastics).[16] Seung Sahn tried to maintain the practice's "Korean-ness" while borrowing liberally from Japanese Zen styles; for example, in his creation of a graduated series of *gong-an*s that is more closely related to Japanese than to Korean *hwadu* style.[17] In many other ways he also embodied the syncretic and inclusive style characteristic of Korean Buddhism and negotiated his public teachings to non-Korean American audiences within the emergence of a nascent American style of Zen that was influenced by both Japanese and Korean contexts (among several other sources of influence). How the "Korean-ness" of the Kwan Um School will develop in North America among increasingly transnational developments of Buddhist communities will be interesting to observe.

Conclusion

Korean Buddhism in North America, especially as practiced in heritage communities, is understudied and deserves more scholarly attention in order to uncover its role in complex negotiations of ethnic identity, religious heritage, and life in an increasingly globalized world. Formal intersections of heritage communities with English-speaking Korean-lineage Buddhist communities appear limited. Yet, any typology akin to the "two streams" will need to become more layered. As some second- or third-generation Koreans in North America (who may or may not have grown up Buddhist), as well as non-Korean Americans who grew up with Buddhist parents (of various lineages), have joined some of the "English-speaking" "convert" groups, the fluidity of organizing identity markers increasingly renders existing typologies inaccurate (also see Han 2021). How some of the inclusive and syncretic impulse of Korean Buddhism will affect

---

[16] Low calls this "clearly a concession" and even "a tacit acknowledgment of the successful immersion of Japanese Zen in America" (2010, 277).

[17] See Jang 2014.

heritage communities and how "Korean Buddhism" will function amidst the transnational and globalizing settings of the twenty-first century remain to be seen and deserve scholarly attention.

References

Buswell, Robert E. 1992a. *Tracing Back the Radiance: Chinul's Korean Way of Zen*. Honolulu: University of Hawai'i Press.

Buswell, Robert E. 1992b. *The Zen Monastic Experience: Buddhist Practice in Contemporary Korea*. Princeton, NJ: Princeton University Press.

Chai, Karen J. 2001. "Intra-Ethnic Religious Diversity: Korean Buddhists and Protestants in Greater Boston." In *Korean Americans and Their Religions: Pilgrims and Missionaries from a Different Shore*, edited by Ho-Youn Kwon, Kwang Chung Kim, and R. Stephen Warner, 273–294. University Park: Pennsylvania State University Press.

Cheah, Joseph. 2011. *Race and Religion in American Buddhism: White Supremacy and Immigrant Adaptation*. New York: Oxford University Press.

Ching, Key Ray. 1997. *Won Buddhism: A History and Theology of Korea's New Religion*. Lewiston, NY: Edwin Mellen Press.

Choi. Joon-sik. 2015. *Won-Buddhism: The Birth of Korean Buddhism*. Seoul, Korea: Jimoondang.

Han, Chenxing. 2021. *Be the Refuge: Raising the Voices of Asian American Buddhists*. Berkeley, CA: North Atlantic Books.

Hickey, Wakoh Shannon. 2015. "Two Buddhisms, Three Buddhisms, and Racism." In *Buddhism beyond Borders: New Perspectives on Buddhism in the United States*, edited by Scott A. Mitchell and Natalie E. F. Quli, 35–56. Albany: State University of New York Press.

Hurh, Won Moo, and Kwang Chung Kim. 1990. "Religious Participation of Korean Immigrants in the U.S." *Journal for the Scientific Study of Religion* 29 (March): 19–34.

Jang, Eun-hwa. 2014. "An Investigation of Seung Sahn's Seon: Don't Know Mind, Ten Gates, and Systems of Hierarchy and Authorization." *Korea Journal* 54, no. 4 (Winter): 29–51.

Kim, Bok In. 2001. "Won Buddhism in the United States." In *Korean Americans and Their Religions: Pilgrims and Missionaries from a Different Shore*, edited by Ho-Youn Kwon, Kwang Chung Kim, and R. Stephen Warner, 259–272. University Park: Pennsylvania State University Press.

Kim, Karen Chai. 2008. "A Religious Minority within an Ethnic Minority: Korean American Buddhists." In *North American Buddhists in Social Context*, edited by Paul David Numrich, 163–184. Leiden and Boston: Brill.

Kim, Kwang Chung, R. Stephen Warner, and Ho-Youn Kwon. 2001. "Korean American Religion in International Perspective." In *Korean Americans and Their Religions: Pilgrims and Missionaries from a Different Shore*, edited by Ho-Youn Kwon, Kwang Chung Kim, and R. Stephen Warner, 3–24. University Park: Pennsylvania State University Press.

Kusan Sunim. 2009. *The Way of Korean Zen*. Translated by Martine Batchelor. Boston and London: Weatherhill.

Kwon Ho-Youn, Kwan Chung Kim, and R. Stephen Warner, eds. 2001. *Korean Americans and Their Religions: Pilgrims and Missionaries from a Different Shore*. University Park: Pennsylvania State University Press.

Low, Sor-Ching. 2010. "Seung Sahn: The Makeover of a Modern Zen Patriarch." In *Zen Masters*, edited by Steven Heine and Dale S. Wright, 265–284. New York: Oxford University Press.

Min, Pyong Gap. 2011. "The Immigration of Koreans to the United States: A Review of 45 Years." *Development and Society* 40, no. 2, December, 195–223.

Muller, Charles. 1997. "Korean Buddhism: A Short Overview," updated 2015. http://www.acmuller.net/kor-bud/koreanbuddhism-overview.html.

Numrich, Paul David. 2006. "Two Buddhisms Further Reconsidered." In *Buddhist Studies from India to America: Essays in Honor of Charles S. Prebish*, edited by Damien Keown, 207–233. New York: Routledge.

Park, Sung Bae. 2009. *One Korean's Approach to Buddhism: The* Mom/Momjit *Paradigm*. Albany: State University of New York Press.

Park, Pori. 2009. *Trial and Error in Modernist Reform: Korean Buddhism under Colonial Rule*. Berkeley: University of California Press.

Samu Sunim (Kim, Sam Woo). 2001. "Turning the Wheel of Dharma in the West: Korean Sŏn Buddhism in North America." In *Korean Americans and Their Religions: Pilgrims and Missionaries from a Different Shore*, edited by Ho-Youn Kwon, Kwang Chung Kim, and R. Stephen Warner, 227–258. University Park: Pennsylvania State University Press.

Suh, Sharon. 2004. *Being Buddhist in a Christian World*. Seattle: University of Washington Press.

Yi, Jong Kweon. 2012. *The Sangha Book of Korean Buddhism*. http://www.koreanbuddhism.us/SanghaBook.html.

Yi, Jong Kweon. 2014. "The Founder of Korean Buddhism in America Is Zen Master Seung Sahn," translated by Jong Kweon Yi and Kathy Park, originally published in *Bulgyo Sinmun/Buddhist Newspaper* No. 2998, March 31. http://www.ibulgyo.com/news/articleView.html?idxno=132745.

Yu, Eui-Young. [1988] 2001. "The Growth of Korean Buddhism in the Unites States, with Special Reference to Southern California." *The Pacific World: Journal of the Institute of Buddhist Studies*, new series 4: 82–93 (slightly revised, reprinted in *Korean Americans and Their Religions: Pilgrims and Missionaries from a Different Shore*, edited by Ho-Youn Kwon, Kwang Chung Kim, and R. Stephen Warner, 211–226. University Park: Pennsylvania State University Press, 2001).

CHAPTER 10

THERAVĀDA BUDDHISM IN AMERICA

ERIK BRAUN

SOME years ago, I went to the Bhāvanā Society in West Virginia to attend a weeklong meditation retreat. Founded by the Sri Lankan monk Henepola Gunaratana, the Bhāvanā Society is a both a meditation center and a monastery for monks in the Theravāda tradition of Buddhism. At the time I went to Bhāvanā, Gunaratana still ran the society, assisted by a vice abbot who was also Sri Lankan, along with four other monks in residence. One morning, a few days after the start of the retreat, a junior monk named Bhikkhu Jayasara warned us of a disruption to the schedule that day. A group of laypeople from the Washington, D.C., area (a couple of hours drive away) would be coming to make a meal offering to the monks. Jayasara told us they might also offer something to us retreatants. He seemed concerned that the occasion might create a distracting environment. And so it did. The visitors that day to Bhāvanā were a merry group of all ages, including young children. They filled the main building and walked around the monastery grounds, talking and laughing. Their lively behavior contrasted sharply with the solemn comportment of those attending the meditation retreat. So it is perhaps not surprising that many of the retreat participants were clearly uncertain what to do when, seated in silent rows for their main meal of the day, one of the day-visitors began to walk among them with a cooler in tow, handing out slightly melted Milky Way ice cream bars.

It struck me that the meditators were the odd ones out in the situation. The day-trippers clearly knew their way around the Bhāvanā Society, knew how to act with the monks, and understood the role of giving *dāna* (offerings) in Theravāda Buddhism. They obviously also knew the role of meditation in the functioning of the society and seemed mildly approving of the rows of meditators. On the other hand, many of the meditators looked nonplussed at the chatting, the laughter, and, above all, the ice cream. I wondered if the retreatants' discomfort stemmed from a sense that all the activity surrounding them, but especially receiving the ice cream treat, had drawn them into a

framework of morality and even karma—we might call it a cosmological framework—
that outstripped their understandings and perhaps their inclinations.[1]

THERAVĀDA AND THE TWO BUDDHISMS MODEL

By the end of that day, the visitors from Washington, D.C., had left and the retreat went on as planned. The rupture in its flow, however, had highlighted a still-present divide within Theravāda Buddhism in America between what many scholars have called the "two Buddhisms."[2] In this model, on one side is a group consisting mostly of people from non-Buddhist backgrounds, usually white, relatively affluent, and well-educated. The other side is made up largely of those born Buddhist, often having recently immigrated, and clustered in groups of Asian heritage. Scholars of American Buddhism have commonly used the labels "convert" and "heritage" to describe the two sides of the split, though many other terms have been suggested.[3]

Yet for some time resistance has been growing not only to common terms describing either side of the model, but to the very model itself. The anthropologist Jiemin Bao captures a fundamental critique of the paradigm when she observes that it often ends up "reducing social complexity to an act of simple contrasts and erasing the vigor and diversity of practices."[4] Wakoh Shannon Hickey makes a related point, noting that the model can cast Buddhists into two camps along racial lines and so erase the existence of people who are neither white nor Asian. Hickey and others have argued that, besides

---

[1] Such culture clashes had happened before at Bhāvanā. See Wendy Cadge, *Heartwood: The First Generation of Theravada Buddhism in America* (Chicago: University of Chicago Press, 2005), 37.

[2] This divide was first described in Charles Prebish's *American Buddhism* (North Scituate, MA: Duxbury Press, 1979), though Emma Layman in her *Buddhism in America* (Chicago: Nelson-Hall, 1976), 262–263, prefigures the model in her analysis. For a critical overview, see Chenxing Han, "Describing the (Nonexistent?) Elephant: Ethnographic Methods in the Study of Asian American Buddhists," in *Methods in Buddhist Studies: Essays in Honor of Richard Payne*, ed. Scott A. Mitchell and Natalie Fisk Quli (New York: Bloomsbury Academic, 2019), 109–125. Jeff Wilson also offers an insightful analysis of the model in "Mapping the American Buddhist Terrain: Paths Taken and Possible Itineraries," *Religion Compass* 3, no. 5 (2009): 839–840.

[3] Jan Nattier has analyzed the makeup of Buddhist groups into a tripartite model, based on whether a form of Buddhism was imported to America by those already here, exported to the country by Buddhists elsewhere interested in missionization, or brought by immigrants coming to America. See Jan Nattier, "Buddhism Comes to Main Street," *The Wilson Quarterly*, Spring 1997, http://archive.wilsonquarterly.com/essays/buddhism-comes-main-street (accessed June 23, 2022). Jeff Wilson argues for approaching Buddhism in America in terms of regionalism in *Dixie Dharma: Inside a Buddhist Temple in the American South* (Chapel Hill: University of North Carolina Press, 2012). This chapter, however, will focus on the still-pertinent split into two groups in terms general enough to forgo discussion of regional variation.

[4] Jiemin Bao, *Creating a Buddhist Community: A Thai Temple in Silicon Valley* (Philadelphia: Temple University Press, 2015), 8.

leaving many people out, such a model has frequently created a binary in which Asian American Buddhists are seen to hold a static, ritualistic, and implicitly moribund "traditional" Buddhism, while white convert Buddhists are taken to practice a Buddhism that is innovative, experiential, and relevant to modern life.[5] These criticisms underscore the fact that any simplistic or essentializing application of the two Buddhisms model is likely to misconstrue profoundly Theravāda in America.[6] If used carefully as a heuristic tool, however, this chapter will argue that the two Buddhisms model can still be put to good use.[7] As the anecdote at the start of this essay suggests, the two Buddhisms model can still capture the development of two broadly distinct Buddhist communities in local circumstances.[8] In other words, the model can shed light on Theravāda in the United States if thought of not as the juxtaposition of two groups of people reified by purportedly essential features, but rather as two cultures which various groups express and contest. In using the word "culture," I mean an anthropologically oriented set of conceptions of the self, right and wrong, how we relate to others, what is good and what is bad, and so on.[9] The two Buddhisms can be understood as divergent, though changing and ever

---

[5] Wakoh Shannon Hickey, "Two Buddhisms, Three Buddhisms, and Racism," *Journal of Global Buddhism* 11 (2015): 1–25. See also Bao, *Creating a Buddhist Community*; Ann Gleig, *American Dharma: Buddhism beyond Modernity* (New Haven, CT: Yale University Press, 2019), esp. 34–36; Joseph Cheah, *Race and Religion in American Buddhism: White Supremacy and Immigrant Adaption* (New York: Oxford University Press, 2011); Todd LeRoy Perreira, "*Sasana Sakon* and the New Asian American: Intermarriage and Identity at a Thai Buddhist Temple in Silicon Valley," in *Asian American Religions: The Making and Remaking of Borders and Boundaries*, ed. Tony Carnes and Fenggang Yang (New York: New York University Press, 2004), 313–337; Natalie Fisk Quli, "On Authenticity: Scholarship, the Insight Movement, and White Authority," in *Methods in Buddhist Studies: Essays in Honor of Richard Payne*, ed. Scott A. Mitchell and Natalie Fisk Quli (New York: Bloomsbury Academic, 2019), 154–172; and Cadge, *Heartwood*.

[6] The critique of the model came to explicit consciousness in reaction to Helen Tworkov's 1991 editorial "Many Is More," *Tricycle: The Buddhist Review* 1, no. 2 (Winter 1991), https://tricycle.org/magazine/many-more/ (accessed July 15, 2022). Many took the editorial to be saying that, unlike white Buddhists in America, Asian American Buddhists did not express a genuinely "American Buddhism." See Scott A. Mitchell, *Buddhism in America: Global Religion, Local Contexts* (New York: Bloomsbury Academic, 2013), 208; Peter N. Gregory, "Describing the Elephant: Buddhism in America," *Religion and Culture: A Journal of Interpretation* 11, no. 12 (2001): 246–247; and Hickey, "Two Buddhisms, Three Buddhisms, and Racism," 8–9. An Orientalist trope of passive Asians opposed to dynamic whites appeared to work hand in hand with racialization to privilege one group over another. See Joseph Cheah, "Buddhism, Race, and Ethnicity," in *The Oxford Handbook of Contemporary Buddhism*, ed. Michael Jerryson (New York, Oxford University Press, 2017), 650–661; Adeana McNicholl, "Buddhism and Race in the United States," *Religion Compass* 15, no. 8 (2021): 4; and Bao, *Creating a Buddhist Community*, 9.

[7] See Richard Payne's related point that "categories or typology should be motivated by the question being asked," in "Religion, Self-Help, Science: Three Economics of Western/ized Buddhism," *Journal of Global Buddhism* 20 (2019): 70.

[8] Kenneth K. Tanaka makes this point in "Epilogue: The Colors and Contours of American Buddhism," in *The Faces of Buddhism in America*, ed. Charles S. Prebish and Kenneth K. Tanaka (New York: Oxford University Pres, 1998), 288.

[9] I am following the general description of culture by Charles Taylor in "Two Theories of Modernity," in *Alternative Modernities*, ed. Dilip Parameshwar Gaonkar (Durham, NC: Duke University Press, 2001), 172.

more entangled, cultures that carry profound and even inarticulable notions of self and world.

I will refer to the culture typically associated with "convert" Buddhists as "meditation-oriented Buddhism." (The term "meditation-oriented Buddhism" sounds similar to Ann Gleig's "meditation-based convert Buddhist lineage," though my concern is sketching deep-seated outlooks rather than Gleig's nuanced exploration of particular expressions in the contemporary period.)[10] As the name indicates, meditation is at the core of what defines this form of Buddhism. But meditative practice should be understood as embedded within an encompassing cultural vision. So it is also with the other form of Buddhism in this approach to the two Buddhisms model, that associated with heritage Buddhists, which I term "cosmology-oriented Buddhism." This form centers on a vision of reality within a karmic framework of good and bad results based on prior actions (committed often in previous lives). Both include much more than specific practices, as important as those may be. Each depends on broader, often unconscious, outlooks. Approaching each as a distinct culture defined in these terms will allow us to gain a better sense of how they take shape in complex environments as the products of distinct histories. Viewing the two Buddhisms as cultural formations also helps us to see how they interrelate and endure in the United States under the rubric of Theravāda.

To be sure, the two Buddhisms defined here as two cultures both must be understood as shaped in their formations by the encompassing power of ideas about race—and even flat-out racism—in the American context. As Joseph Cheah has pointed out, the category of culture has often served as the basis of what he calls a methodological disassociation that neglects the stratifying power of race by dismissing it as merely an "extension of ethnicity."[11] Only a benighted view, however, could overlook the fact that one of the Buddhisms within the two Buddhisms model, the one typified by converts who have been mostly white, has received up to now the lion's share of scholarly attention and social prominence. Its members have wielded far greater resources than the largely Asian American Buddhists on the other side of the divide. Because of this, Buddhists in meditation-oriented Buddhism have usually been the ones to define what counts as Buddhist and to set the terms of engagement with the broader culture. An analysis of the two Buddhisms model cannot skate over this fact. On the contrary, the aim of a focus on these Buddhisms as cultures is to allow, first, for a richer sense of the origins of their respective demographic makeups and differences in power, and this includes consideration of the twinned roles of racism and Orientalism. Following from this analysis is the opportunity to observe how they are changing—not necessarily to meld, let alone assimilate—but nonetheless changing in complex ways that undercut any lasting characterization or single trajectory of development.

While my focus here on cultural formation does not leave room to delve into important, related issues—particularly present-day racism, the treatment of women, and the

---

[10] Gleig, *American Dharma*, 6ff.
[11] Cheah, *Race and Religion in American Buddhism*, 15; see also 75.

effects of class—understanding the two Buddhisms as cultures can frame a useful approach to such matters. For such a propaedeutic can help us gain a more accurate understanding of a significant portion of the American population, and, moreover, can allow us to assess the role that Theravāda Buddhism has played (and continues to play) in shaping American culture as a whole.[12]

THE NOTION OF BUDDHISM AND THE LABEL THERAVĀDA

How the Buddhist with a cooler of ice cream bars and the meditator came together at the Bhāvanā Society depends, first, on the creation of a widespread conception of a single form of Buddhism—namely, Theravāda—that includes them both. And the notion of Theravāda depends on the Western—really, European—creation of the idea of a world religion called Buddhism in which the Pali canon, as the body of texts seen as the earliest, stood as the religion's most authentic expression.[13] In the Orientalist interpretation, such Buddhism was anti-ritualistic, anti-clerical, rational, text-based, and tied to a charismatic reformer. In other words, true Buddhism was remarkably Protestant in character. It is no wonder, then, that such a notion of Buddhism would resonate in an American culture inflected with a Protestant sensibility and would continue to shape attitudes about what counts as authentic Buddhism up to the present day. Recent scholarship has called our attention not just to how this outlook tacitly or even overtly supported colonial subjugation, but also undergirded attitudes of racial superiority by juxtaposing a pure Buddhism to its degraded expressions among Asian

---

[12] In their 2012 survey of the Asian American population, the Pew Research Center estimated that Asian Americans comprised around 67–69 percent of Buddhists in America. Among this group, only 8 percent identified as Theravāda and 2 percent as "Vipassana" (a term for insight meditation derived from Theravāda). See The Pew Forum on Religion and Public Life, *Asian Americans: A Mosaic of Faiths* (Washington, DC: Pew Research Center, 2012). If we restrict ourselves to this 10 percent, the 2020 census yields a population of 278,405 Theravāda Asian Americans. If we include those who report themselves to be both Asian and belonging to one or more other racial groups, we can add 57,609, for a total of 336,014 (see https://www2.census.gov/programs-surveys/decennial/2020/data/redistricting-supplementary-tables/redistricting-supplementary-table-01.pdf, accessed July 22, 2022). Pew has not parsed the Buddhist makeup of the non-Asian population (nor, so far as I'm aware, has any other survey organization). Among whites and Blacks, Pew reports in its 2014 Landscape Survey that less than 1 percent identify as Buddhist. Among Latinos, the percentage is 1 percent. If we take 1 percent, then, as the proportion of Buddhists among whites, Blacks, and Latinos, we get 3,680,722 using 2020 census numbers; with more than one racial group identification, the number rises to 4,235,223. Yet we do not know what percentage would identify as Theravāda.

[13] Tomoko Masuzawa, *The Invention of World Religions: Or, How European Universalism Was Preserved in the Language of Pluralism* (Chicago: University of Chicago Press, 2005), 126. See also Nathan McGovern, "The Contemporary Study of Buddhism," in *The Oxford Handbook of Contemporary Buddhism*, ed. Michael Jerryson (New York: Oxford University Press, 2017), 705.

locals.¹⁴ Such racializing attitudes have cropped up in American contexts—indeed, even in some emic uses of the heritage-convert distinction among Buddhists.¹⁵

Attitudes about a "pure" Buddhism found in the Pali canon often aligned with the outlooks of influential Asian monks and lay scholars. South and Southeast Asian Buddhists' assertions of purity in origins affirmed and even helped to articulate the Orientalist view. The Western notion of historical degradation drew support from the Buddhist conception of cycles of decline and revival that obscured or even rejected any idea of local innovation.¹⁶ These commonalities do not mean that Asian Buddhists shared the same agenda with Western interlocutors. Acknowledging these convergences, however, keeps us attentive to the complex relationships among actors that now shape forms of Buddhism in America. For even today in the United States, assumptions about the nature of Theravāda often depend on a textualist predilection among teachers of all sorts of backgrounds that finds an amplifying affinity with many meditators.¹⁷

Those who came to be called Theravāda Buddhists had always named their practices and teachings, of course, above all through the use of the still-widespread Pali term *sāsana*. Yet it was only recently that Theravāda became the common name for this form of Buddhism.¹⁸ Prior to the colonial era, Buddhists across South and Southeast Asia had known Theravāda as a time-honored term that could indicate a monastic lineage or even could name a broad group of Buddhists.¹⁹ Yet it was not a dominant marker for a religious identity until the early twentieth century.²⁰ Its use in that way depended on the philological conceptions described above. The culmination of this sense of Theravāda as a reified, transnational entity can be seen in the inaugural conference of the World Fellowship of Buddhists, held in May 1950, in Colombo, Sri Lanka. The event marked a high-water moment of Buddhist revivalist spirit. At the World Fellowship, a resolution

---

[14] See Charles Hallisey, "Roads Taken and Not Taken in the Study of Theravada Buddhism," in *Curators of the Buddha: The Study of Buddhism under Colonialism*, ed. Donald S. Lopez (Chicago: University of Chicago Press, 1995), 31–61.

[15] Cheah's *Race and Religion in American Buddhism* is a foundational work concerning such issues; see especially chapter 3. See also Ryan Anningson's *Theories of the Self, Race, and Essentialization in Buddhism: The United States and the Asian "Other," 1899-1957* (New York: Routledge, 2021).

[16] See Anne M. Blackburn, *Buddhist Learning and Textual Practice in Eighteenth-Century Lankan Monastic Culture* (Princeton, NJ: Princeton University Press, 2001), especially 5–9.

[17] See Paul David Numrich, "Two Buddhisms Further Considered," *Contemporary Buddhism* 4, no. 1 (2003): 68. Carolyn Chen's "'True Buddhism Is Not Chinese': Taiwanese Immigrants Defining Buddhist Identity in the United States," in *North American Buddhists in Social Context*, ed. Paul David Numrich (Boston: Brill, 2008), 145–161, gives an example of Buddhism understood explicitly outside of ethic terms.

[18] Todd Perreira has argued that in 1910 the English-born monk Ananda Metteyya was the first to use the term "Theravāda" in English to refer wholesale to the Buddhism of South and Southeast Asia; Todd LeRoy Perreira, "Whence Theravāda? The Modern Genealogy of an Ancient Term," in *How Theravāda is Theravāda? Exploring Buddhist Identities*, ed. Peter Skilling, Jason A. Carbine, Claudio Cicuzza, and Santi Pakdeekham (Chiang Mai, Thailand: Silkworm Books, 2012), 551.

[19] Anālayo, "A Note on the Term *Theravāda*," *Buddhist Studies Review* 30, no. 2 (2013): 215–235.

[20] Peter Skilling, "Theravāda in History," *Pacific World* 3, no. 11 (2009): 62.

was passed to designate the Buddhisms of Sri Lanka and peninsular Southeast Asia as "Theravāda."[21] This move put an official stamp on a title that had gained in prominence over the prior decades of the twentieth century, at least at the elite level that overlapped with scholarly textual approaches.

The adoption of the term "Theravāda" at the conference also signaled another crucial development in self-conception. For, in taking to the world stage as newly independent and, excepting Thailand, self-consciously postcolonial countries, Theravāda became an integral aspect of identity now coupled to the idea of the nation-state. The use of the label "ethnic" reflects the melding of nationalist identities with Buddhism. This sense, in fact, often remains today stronger than identification with the label "Theravāda." As Wendy Cadge noted in her ethnographic work: "Few people I met in the course of this research actually identified themselves as Theravada Buddhists. Most identified just as Buddhists or, for Asians, occasionally as Sri Lankan Buddhists or Thai Buddhists."[22] A sense of nationalist identity has also helped to sustain transnational linkages that remain vital to many people, especially within cosmology-oriented Buddhism.

BUDDHISM IN AMERICA BEFORE 1965

Starting in the mid-nineteenth century, immigrants from China and Japan established Buddhist communities in America, mostly in Hawaii and on the West Coast. But the Chinese Exclusion Act of 1882 began a process of the legal barring of Asian peoples from America. It culminated in the Johnson-Reed Act of 1924, which stopped all Asian immigration. No significant groups of Theravāda Buddhists from Asia, therefore, came to America prior to changes in the law in the mid-1960s. Nor was there any development of Theravāda among those born in the United States. The Sri Lankan reformer Dharmapala (1864–1933), who spoke in 1893 at the World Parliament of Religions in Chicago and toured the country, typically begins the story of Theravāda in America. Yet he did not use the term "Theravāda," nor did his approach match exactly with what emerged from colonialist and Orientalist perspectives.[23] What is more, Dharmapala would see his efforts as having died on the vine by 1921, when he wrote: "At one time there was some kind of activity in certain parts of the U.S. where some people took interest in Buddhism; but I see none of that now."[24] Generally speaking, in the period between the world wars, Buddhisms of all stripes disappeared within the dominant American culture.[25]

---

[21] Perreira. "Whence Theravāda?," 450.

[22] Cadge, *Heartwood*, 222, fn.10.

[23] Steven Kemper, *Rescued from the Nation: Dharmapala and the Buddhist World* (Chicago: University of Chicago Press, 2015), 222; see also Perreira, "Whence Theravāda?," 550.

[24] Thomas Tweed, *The American Encounter with Buddhism, 1844–1912* (Bloomington: Indiana University Press, 1992), 157.

[25] See Tweed, *The American Encounter with Buddhism*, 1992.

The "Zen boom" of the 1950s signaled the first significant interest in Buddhism among white Americans since the Victorian period. This boom matters to the story of Theravāda because it shaped American assumptions about Buddhism that set the parameters for the culture of one of the two Buddhisms, that of meditation-oriented Buddhism, and created the context that the other side, cosmology-oriented Buddhism, would encounter. The 1950s was a period of postwar trauma, mounting Cold War existential anxiety, and, in reaction to such factors, a romantic pull toward the "East." Due to military and political connections, the pull was especially to Japan.[26] It was this turn to Japan that helped to fuse Zen and psychology, thus joining meditation and psychological healing in American consciousness. In the same period, the Beat movement, impelled by the same social factors, gravitated to a vision of Buddhism, and once again particularly to Zen, that served as a foil to an American society seen as mechanistic and soulless. Buddhism could offer a response to a crisis of meaning in modernity, a way to live spontaneously and authentically in the world.[27]

Just as Buddhism *qua* Buddhism first took shape in a European philological mode, the academic study of Buddhism in America would adopt and popularize many of the same assumptions. Formulated within the outlook of the field of Religious Studies, Buddhist Studies grew by leaps and bounds after World War II. This growth at the collegiate level depended on the demographic bulge of the Baby Boomers. Students in large numbers sought spiritual alternatives in the countercultural context of the Civil Rights movement and protests against the Vietnam War. The field of Buddhist Studies was ready to answer this need, thanks to the Supreme Court's imprimatur for the state-sponsored study of religion in the 1963 *Abington School District v. Schempp* (374 U.S. 203) decision. Academic categorizations within Buddhist Studies reaffirmed notions of Buddhism and Theravāda formulated in the colonial era. Such study thus ordered American engagement with South and Southeast Asian Buddhist traditions around the conceptions described above.

The Formation of Two Buddhisms

Meditation-Oriented Buddhism

The moment often used to mark the arrival of Theravāda as a permanent entity in the United States is the founding of the Washington Buddhist Vihara, a Sri Lankan temple,

---

[26] D. T. Suzuki (1870–1966) was perhaps the most influential figure to meld a certain notion of Zen with psychological and avant-garde artistic perspectives. See Jane Iwamura's *Virtual Orientalism: Asian Religions and American Popular Culture* (New York: Oxford University Press, 2010), especially chapter 2.

[27] Asian Americans, particularly Japanese Americans, did not play much of a public role in this engagement with Zen because the larger culture privileged Asian origins and textual resources. See Caroline Chung Simpson, *An Absent Presence: Japanese Americans in Post-War American Culture, 1945–1960* (Durham, NC: Duke University Press, 2002).

in Washington, D.C., in 1966.[28] But it was in the prior year that two events really set in motion the development of Theravāda in America. The first led to what I am calling meditation-oriented Buddhism. This event was the departure of Joseph Goldstein (1944–) for Thailand as a Peace Corps volunteer in 1965. After years spent meditating in Asia, he would become in 1975 one of the founders of the Insight Meditation Society (IMS), the first center in the United States to teach *vipassanā*, a form of meditative practice (often called insight meditation) based upon Theravāda texts and teachings. Two years after Goldstein, Jack Kornfield (1945–), another founder of IMS, would also go to Thailand as a Peace Corps volunteer and then ordain as a Thai forest monk. And, four years after him, Sharon Salzberg (1952–), the third founder, would go to India on a college study-abroad trip to meditate.[29] Although by no means the only progenitors of meditation-oriented Buddhism in the United States, these figures have played a critical role in its formation, for IMS and, subsequently, its sister center Spirit Rock, have been the nodes out of which this form of Buddhism has ramified across the country.

At the moment such seekers arrived in India and Thailand, they met a newly burgeoning mass meditation movement created by Theravāda Buddhists in response to colonial and postcolonial pressures. Here there was a productive affinity between Western meditators and Asian meditation masters, who found a receptive audience for their calls to practice using simplified techniques appropriate to laypeople.[30] Such meditative practices were, to be sure, grounded in Theravāda Buddhist doctrine, and many Western practitioners would come to see themselves as Buddhists. Yet the IMS founders' approach to meditation would also depend on their understandings shaped by the Zen Boom of the 1950s, the ferment of cultural change in the 1960s, and the academic presentation of Buddhism in terms indebted to assumptions created in the colonial context noted above. The resulting outlook put meditation at the heart of a Buddhism seen as experiential, pragmatic, individualistic, and therapeutic.

Goldstein and Salzberg would practice under the guidance of the Burmese-born Indian teacher S. N. Goenka (1924–2013).[31] Salzberg would also study under the Calcutta-based teacher Dipa Ma (1911–1989), while Goldstein would train as well with Munindraji (1915–2003), a Bengali Indian who lived much of his life in Bodh Gaya.

---

[28] Cadge, *Heartwood*, 19.

[29] Cadge, *Heartwood*, 26–31. Jaqueline Schwartz is a key fourth figure in the early history of IMS, though she seems to have become a leading teacher along with the other three shortly after the establishment of IMS.

[30] On the start of mass lay meditation, see Erik Braun, *The Birth of Insight: Meditation, Modern Buddhism, and the Burmese Monk Ledi Sayadaw* (Chicago: University of Chicago Press, 2013). For details on the meditation methods the IMS founders learned, see Braun, *Birth of Insight*, esp. the conclusion; and Lance Cousins, "The Origins of Insight Meditation," *The Buddhist Forum* 4 (1996): 35–58.

[31] The only lengthy biography of Goenka is Daniel Stuart's *S. N. Goenka: Emissary of Insight* (Berkeley, CA: Shambhala, 2020). Though somewhat hagiographical, biographical treatments of Dipa Ma and Munindraji can be found, respectively, in Amy Schmidt, *Dipa Ma: The Life and Legacy of a Buddhist Master* (New York: BlueBridge Books, 2005); and Mirka Knaster, *Living This Life Fully: Stories and Teachings of Munindra* (Berkeley, CA: Shambhala, 2010).

Kornfield ordained as a forest monk under the Thai master Ajaan Chah (1918–1992), but would also practice extensively in Burma at the meditation center of the Burmese monk Mahasi Sayadaw (1904–1982). Dipa Ma and Munindraji also had trained with Mahasi, and it was this Mahasi method that would become the charter technique of insight practice at IMS and, subsequently, within meditation-oriented Theravāda Buddhism in America.

The three founders came together for the first time in 1974 at the inaugural summer study session of the Naropa Institute in Boulder, Colorado.[32] They—along with, it should be noted, many others in the meditation "scene"—joined forces a year later to establish, as it was put in a 1975 fundraising letter, "a continuous retreat environment devoted exclusively to the Vipassana meditation practice of Therevada [sic] Buddhism."[33] At the center, the focus was (and remains) on conducting insight retreats. While monastic teachers sometimes lead retreats at IMS (including Mahasi and Chah), a board of laypeople runs the center. Unlike in a Theravāda context in Southeast Asia, the *sangha* or community at IMS refers primarily to lay meditators, rather than monastics—in fact, to even refer to such people as lay frames the community too much within an explicitly Buddhist view. Focused on insight practice, little other activity takes place, and the culture does not assume a Buddhist identity or outlook. An important feature, then, of meditation-oriented Buddhism is the significant number of participants who have loose connections to it. Many of these folks could be termed sympathizers or, in Thomas Tweed's well-known phrase, "nightstand Buddhists," meaning those who do not hold an exclusively Buddhist identity but are the sort who keep Buddhist books on their nightstands for spiritual sustenance.[34] Such people indicate the relatively porous boundaries of belonging within this culture, as well as the important role of print culture in its formation.

The porousness in affiliation reflects a porousness in sources shaping this worldview. For meditation-oriented Buddhism draws from a tradition of spirituality outside of orthodox Buddhism. Sometimes called a metaphysical strain in American religiosity, it focuses on individual mystical experience, a cosmopolitan and combinative ecumenical outlook, and an abiding concern for healing, particularly a flourishing in the here and now that is both mental and physical.[35] The IMS approach reflects such an outlook. But it is the founding of Spirit Rock some years later in California that shows most clearly the logic of development from such a basis. Jack Kornfield left IMS for the Bay Area of

---

[32] Rick Fields, *How the Swans Came to the Lake: A Narrative History of Buddhism in America* (Berkeley, CA: Shambhala, 1992), 319–320.

[33] Insight Meditation Society letter dated November 12, 1975. Jack Kornfield provides an overview of this history in his article "This Fantastic, Unfolding Experiment," *Buddhadharma* (Summer 2007): 32–39.

[34] Thomas Tweed, "Nightstand Buddhists and Other Creatures: Sympathizers, Adherents, and the Study of Religion," in *American Buddhism: Methods and Findings in Recent Scholarship*, ed. Duncan Ryuken Williams and Christopher S. Queen (New York: Routledge, 1999), 71–90.

[35] See Leigh Schmidt, *Restless Souls: The Making of American Spirituality* (Berkeley: University of California Press, 2012), especially the introduction; Catherine Albanese, *A Republic of Mind and Spirit: A Cultural History of American Metaphysical Religion* (New Haven, CT: Yale University Press, 2008), 10–15.

San Francisco in 1984 and, subsequently, he took the lead role in the founding of Spirit Rock (called at first Insight Meditation West) in Marin County, north of San Francisco.[36] From its start, the center has incorporated into its programs not only Buddhist teachers and teachings from outside the Theravāda tradition, but even non-Buddhist teachers and influences, such as Advaita Vedanta and Sufism. Spirit Rock, to be sure, maintains Theravāda teachings at the core of its identity, but the spectrum of possible spiritual resources it offers aligns it even more closely than IMS with a metaphysical outlook that is eclectic, free-ranging among religious perspectives, and shaped by senses of oneness and wellness. The dominance of psychologists among Spirit Rock faculty is one example of a therapeutic sensibility, which tracks to a larger sense in meditation-oriented Buddhism of meditation as a means to psychological health.[37]

Spirit Rock's inclusivity, in fact, marks a divergence from IMS and suggests that the lines of development within the culture of meditation-oriented Buddhism do not tend in just one direction. IMS has recently defined itself as rooted in a conception of "early Buddhism," while Spirit Rock has expanded the basis of its identity even beyond Buddhism. Neither organization dictates an approach to other insight centers. Yet the numerous centers now dotting the country are often bound by affective ties among teachers trained through IMS or Spirit Rock, by broader senses of shared lineages of insight practice, and by common origins in American metaphysical religion.

Although the scope of this chapter prevents much exploration of it, perhaps the most influential development on American society that comes out of the culture of meditation-oriented Buddhism is secular mindfulness, preeminently in the Mindfulness-Based Stress Reduction (MBSR) program of Jon Kabat-Zinn. A hallmark of the technique is that its practitioners understand it as decoupled from Buddhism or any system of belief. It is a cultural product that sees itself as outside of cultural contingency. Secular mindfulness practice draws techniques and inspiration not just from Theravāda sources. Its combinative nature is captured well in Kabat-Zinn's quip that "MBSR is mostly vipassana practice (in the Theravada sense as taught by people like Joseph [Goldstein] and Jack [Kornfield] etc.) with a Zen attitude."[38] Still, the basic technique comes from Mahasi-style insight practice. Since he underwent a visionary experience at an IMS retreat in 1979 that inspired him to start the MBSR program, Kabat-Zinn's mindfulness movement has spread throughout American culture.[39]

---

[36] Cadge, *Heartwood*, 35.

[37] See Ann Gleig, "Wedding the Personal and Impersonal in West Coast Vipassana: A Dialogical Encounter between Buddhism and Psychotherapy," *Journal of Global Buddhism* 13 (2012): 129–146; see also David McMahan, *The Making of Buddhist Modernism* (New York: Oxford University Press, 2009).

[38] Richard Gilpin, "The Use of Theravāda Buddhist Practices and Perspectives in Mindfulness-Based Cognitive Therapy," *Contemporary Buddhism* 2, no. 8 (2008): 238.

[39] On mindfulness in contemporary America, see Jeff Wilson, *Mindful America: The Mutual Transformation of Buddhist Meditation and American Culture* (New York: Oxford University Press, 2014). On Jon Kabat-Zinn and his religion vision, see Jon Kabat-Zinn, "Some Reflections on the Origins of MBSR, Skillful Means, and the Trouble with Maps," in *Mindfulness: Diverse Perspectives on Its Meaning, Origins and Applications*, ed. J. Mark G. Williams and Jon Kabat-Zinn (New York: Routledge, 2013),

A final development of meditation-oriented Theravāda Buddhism serves as a bridge to the other of the two Buddhisms, namely the one oriented around a cosmological outlook. The worldwide meditation movement of S. N. Goenka—who taught both Salzberg and Goldstein—established permanent practice centers in the United States beginning in the 1980s. Resolutely focused on *vipassanā* practice, its technique draws from a different practice tradition in Burma from that of Mahasi. The movement traces its lineage from the Burmese monk Ledi Sayadaw (1846–1923), through the laymen Saya Thetgyi (1873–1945) and U Ba Khin (1899–1971), and on to Goenka. Although born and raised in Burma, Goenka was from an ethnically Indian and Hindu family with deep connections to South Asia. His approach to the meditation he learned from U Ba Khin stressed its practicality and emphasized its non-sectarian nature. He is well known for describing the Buddha as someone who "never taught Buddhism. Buddha never made a single person Buddhist."[40] Such statements may sound antinomian, but the organization is in many respects highly orthodox in its perspective, maintaining a close adherence to Theravāda teachings and the Pali canon. Behind a focus on technique is a karmic outlook that governs the logic of practice. In fact, the pervasive metaphysical outlook of much meditation-oriented Buddhism—its inclusivity, even syncretism—is absent. Indeed, Goenka warned the IMS founders that any center in which more than one technique of meditation was taught was doing "the work of Mara" (in other words, deluding people).[41] Despite this attitude, Goenka's approach has appealed to many in this culture because, regardless of the karmic aspects of his teaching, he stressed practice as a practical effort outside of any belief system. What is more, early in his teaching career he forbade any charging of fees for retreats, which made them widely accessible, and he standardized the retreat format, setting up a template that many Western teachers, including those at IMS, would use.[42]

COSMOLOGY-ORIENTED BUDDHISM

The travel of the IMS founders to Asia was one of two originating events in the history of Theravāda in America. The other was the passing of the Immigration and Nationality

---

281–306; and Erik Braun, "Mindful but Not Religious: Meditation and Enchantment in the Work of Jon Kabat-Zinn," in *Meditation, Buddhism, and Science*, ed. David L. McMahan and Erik Braun (New York: Oxford University Press, 2017), 173–197.

[40] Helen Tworkov, "Superscience: An Interview with S. N. Goenka on the Techniques of Buddhist Practice," *Tricycle: The Buddhist Review* 10, no. 2 (Winter 2000), https://tricycle.org/magazine/s-n-goenka/ (accessed June 22, 2022).

[41] Kornfield, "This Fantastic, Unfolding Experiment," 35.

[42] Gil Fronsdal, "Insight Meditation in the United States: Life, Liberty, and the Pursuit of Happiness," in *The Faces of Buddhism in America*, ed. Charles S. Prebish and Kenneth Tanaka (Berkeley: University of California Press, 1998), 164–180.

Act of 1965. The Immigration Act opened up the possibility for Theravāda Buddhists in South and Southeast Asia to move to America. Cadge notes that between 1977 and 2000, over five hundred thousand people came to America from traditionally Theravāda countries.[43] Not all of these folks would be Buddhist, yet many would be, as is evinced in the growth from the 1970s to the present day in the number of Theravāda temples in America.[44]

Naturally, South and Southeast Asians who arrived after 1965 did not approach Buddhism with the American outlook described above. The reasons for immigration vary widely, from war and civil strife to marriage and economic opportunity. Even from a single nation-state, the reasons to move often have differed profoundly from one group, one family, or even one individual to another. Some come with few resources, while others are well off. Yet, even accepting profoundly different social locations and reasons for immigrating, Theravāda Buddhists of South and Southeast Asia could draw, broadly speaking, on shared senses of identity rooted in long-standing Buddhist institutions, texts, and practices—in other words, the *sāsana*.[45] Their Buddhist cultures, then, offered a wide range of similar resources for thinking through lived experience and responding to spiritual and social challenges. The result would be the development in America of a Buddhist culture with a cosmological outlook that posited life within a sweep of karmic history, hence the term "cosmology-oriented Buddhism." In this view, the triple gem of the Buddha, the *dhamma* (the teachings), and the *sangha* (the monastic community) serves as a powerful resource for living well. The *sangha*, in particular, serves as a focus, given its embodiment of the Buddha's teachings, a living sign of Buddhism's vitality. Monasteries and temples are, furthermore, key sites for festivals, such as those for the New Year or those tied to the end of the monastic rains retreat in the fall (called the *kaṭhina*), and other activities that bind the community together, reflecting and reinforcing a shared outlook.

People in such a milieu have certainly not shunned meditation; their communities often include rigorous practitioners, such as Gunaratana of the Bhāvanā Society or Ajahn Silaratano of the Forest Dhamma Monastery in Lexington, Virginia. Yet this perspective folds meditation practice more clearly into a karmic framework. *Dāna* or supporting the ordained community (*sangha*) fits as the cornerstone of another, more common aspect of practice, that of meritorious action (*puñña*). Making merit shapes the karmic arc of an individual just as meditation can—though, to be sure, meditation offers at its more advanced levels the chance to step entirely out of the karmic problem of endless rebirth (*samsāra*). The Bhāvanā Society is a rich example, though not unique, as a site in which meditation-oriented and cosmology-oriented cultures

---

[43] Cadge, *Heartwood*, 20.

[44] Cadge, *Heartwood*, 32–33, notes that in 1980 there were five Thai temples in the United States, while by 1990 there were forty.

[45] Cadge, *Heartwood*, 2005, chapter six, has a nuanced discussion of various formations of identity in her two communities of study.

coexist. The anecdote at the beginning of this chapter illustrates how this can result in what Paul Numrich first observed as "parallel congregations."[46] This idea of separate congregations, one white, the other Asian, has received criticism for presenting a simplistic picture.[47] Yet if we view these groups as cultural formations, we can see why they remain distinguishable without assuming a static ethnic or racial stratification. In fact, while the decades of the 1970s, 1980s, and 1990s saw the proliferation of temples organized according to ethnic identities, Cadge, Bao, Perreira, and others have noted that, especially from the 1990s onward, demographic blending has grown, in which peoples of varied backgrounds interact and create various forms of community.[48]

Converts appear in this setting, too. Thanissaro Bhikkhu, for example, serves as a sort of bridge to a figure such as Goenka from the other side of the two Buddhisms model. Thanissaro, born Geoffrey DeGraff in 1949, learned about Buddhism in high school in Virginia and studied it at Oberlin College. He subsequently traveled to Thailand and ordained there. He is now the abbot in Southern California of Wat Metta, in many respects a traditional Thai monastery. Monks there go on alms round each day, scrupulously follow the monastic rules, and serve the usual range of functions of the ordained in a Thai Buddhist context (above all as the recipients of *dāna*). But Thanissaro is also a well-known meditation teacher who draws in practitioners from meditation-oriented backgrounds.[49]

Cosmology-oriented Buddhism emerged as a culture shaped by the immigrant experience and with deep connections to a karmic outlook formed in the context of South and Southeast Asian Buddhism. Yet the example of Thanissaro and the growing voices of Asian Americans who cross the boundaries of this culture and that oriented to meditation remind us again of the methodological point that a focus on culture in the two Buddhisms model is meant to undercut the sense that either Buddhism is pegged to a particular group or fixed in its nature (and it is useful to remember that only 14 percent of Asian Americans identify as Buddhists).[50] This is so, even as we recognize a history in which specific groups—holding a common ethnic identity, often mostly racially homogenous—largely made them in their initial formulations. Peter Gregory and Richard Seager each argued in the early 2000s that the distinction between the two Buddhisms would likely diminish and even disappear.[51] Highlighting the distinction as one of cultural outlook helps to explain, however, its enduring salience some twenty

---

[46] Paul Numrich, *Old Wisdom in the New World: Americanization in Two Immigrant Theravada Buddhist Temples* (Knoxville: The University of Tennessee Press, 1996), see especially chapter four.

[47] See Cadge, *Heartwood*, 22–23.

[48] See the sources in note 5.

[49] A description of Thanissaro can be found in Richard Hughes Seager, *Buddhism in America* (New York: Columbia University Press, 1999), 156–157.

[50] Pew, *Mosaic*, 11.

[51] Gregory, "Describing the Elephant," 242–243; Richard Hughes Seager, "American Buddhism in the Making," in *Westward Dharma: Buddhism Beyond Asia*, ed. Charles S. Prebish and Martin Baumann (Berkeley: University of California Press, 2002), 118; see discussion also in Numrich, "Two Buddhisms Further Considered," 60.

years after their predictions. Such cultural views are dynamic, continuously refined and reinforced through various activities, including meditation, that can sometimes sharpen group differences rather than weaken them. This perhaps counterintuitive outcome has gained strength in the contemporary period. This is because ever more robust transnational communities, what Bao describes as "interlocking local and transnational circuits,"[52] can transmit influences and experiences from more "cosmological" Theravāda contexts back to Americans in powerful ways that reinforce a certain cultural outlook.[53]

As the point about transnational circuits suggests, the approach to one of the two Buddhisms as a cosmology-oriented culture runs the risk of overlooking its role as a component of ethnic identity. As Numrich points out, it was the formulation of the two Buddhisms model in the early 1990s that first drew scholarly attention to what he calls "ethnic-Asian Buddhism," away from an almost exclusive focus on converts.[54] Such ethnic identities are in many respects as much an American product as that of the convert, and this reminds us again of the powerful salience of race. The pluralistic and often racializing environment of the United States can amplify a group's sense of religiosity and potentially strengthen adherence to a cosmology-oriented Buddhism as a marker of group identity.[55] It is critical to remember that both Buddhisms in the two Buddhisms model are heuristics of differentiation. They clarify lines of development and important distinctions but cannot capture the full complexity of the lived experience of Buddhism on the ground.

Conclusion

In exploring the two Buddhisms as cultures that are historical products, we can see why distinctions have endured even as ongoing change undercuts any stable configuration within or between them. Stressing the genealogies of cultural formation offers a way to understand why Theravāda looks the way it does now—and how it might develop. The conception of Theravāda began as a modern product of Orientalist and colonial conceptions, reworking teachings and traditions that had not understood themselves in such a singular and reified way. The American context shaped the interest of those who would adopt Theravāda here, even as others came to America with different understandings and aims for an entity conceived under the same name.

---

[52] Bao, *Creating a Buddhist Community*, 19.
[53] Bao, *Creating a Buddhist Community*, 19–22.
[54] Numrich, "Two Buddhisms Further Considered," 69.
[55] Carl L. Bankston III and Danielle Antoinette Hildago, "Temple and Society in the New World: Theravada Buddhism and Social Order in North America," in *North American Buddhists in Social Context*, ed. Paul David Numrich (Boston: Brill, 2008), 59. See also Gregory, "Describing the Elephant," 251.

Yet these views are not sealed off from one another. They can align and interact, and they have.

That disjunctive moment at the Bhāvanā Society with which I began this chapter offers one more example in this regard, in which cultural views clashed but could also reconcile. After those ice cream bars were passed out, I noticed one of the meditators near me holding hers with a look of consternation. She was there to meditate, and one can imagine her reasons for doing so connected to a larger vision resonant with the meditation-oriented culture sketched above. Yet here she was holding an offering made to serve a different Buddhist end. She turned to me and asked in a low whisper if I thought it was OK to eat it. I said, yes, it was fine to eat the ice cream bar. The stakes were presumably inconsequential for her. Yet, by taking it, she had become, at least in a small and ephemeral way, a part of a sense of Buddhism that went beyond the usual expectations and behaviors of a meditation retreat. When she ate the ice cream—and she did eat it—she took a small part in reconfiguring the differences of culture and history described here.

References

Albanese, Catherine. *A Republic of Mind and Spirit: A Cultural History of American Metaphysical Religion*. New Haven, CT: Yale University Press, 2008.

Anālayo. "A Note on the Term Theravāda." *Buddhist Studies Review* 30, no. 2 (2013): 215–235.

Anningson, Ryan. *Theories of the Self, Race, and Essentialization in Buddhism: The United States and the Asian "Other," 1899–1957*. New York: Routledge, 2021.

Bankston III, Carl L. and Danielle Antoinette Hildago. "Temple and Society in the New World: Theravada Buddhism and Social Order in North America." In *North American Buddhists in Social Contex*t, ed. Paul David Numrich, 51–85. Boston: Brill, 2008.

Bao, Jiemin. *Creating a Buddhist Community: A Thai Temple in Silicon Valley*. Philadelphia: Temple University Press, 2015.

Blackburn, Anne M. *Buddhist Learning and Textual Practice in Eighteenth-Century Lankan Monastic Culture*. Princeton, NJ: Princeton University Press, 2001.

Braun, Erik. *The Birth of Insight: Meditation, Modern Buddhism, and the Burmese Monk Ledi Sayadaw*. Chicago: University of Chicago Press, 2013.

Braun, Erik. "Mindful but Not Religious: Meditation and Enchantment in the Work of Jon Kabat-Zinn." In *Meditation, Buddhism, and Science*, ed. David L. McMahan and Erik Braun, 173–197. New York: Oxford University Press, 2017.

Cadge, Wendy. *Heartwood: The First Generation of Theravada Buddhism in America*. Chicago: University of Chicago Press, 2005.

Cheah, Joseph. "Buddhism, Race, and Ethnicity." In *The Oxford Handbook of Contemporary Buddhism*, ed. Michael Jerryson, 650–661. New York, Oxford University Press, 2017.

Cheah, Joseph. *Race and Religion in American Buddhism: White Supremacy and Immigrant Adaption*. New York: Oxford University Press, 2011.

Chen, Carolyn. "'True Buddhism Is Not Chinese': Taiwanese Immigrants Defining Buddhist Identity in the United States." In *North American Buddhists in Social Context*, ed. Paul David Numrich, 145–161. Boston: Brill, 2008.

Cousins, Lance. "The Origins of Insight Meditation." *The Buddhist Forum* 4 (1996): 35–58.
Fields, Rick. *How the Swans Came to the Lake: A Narrative History of Buddhism in America.* Berkeley, CA: Shambhala, 1992.
Fronsdal, Gil. "Insight Meditation in the United States: Life, Liberty, and the Pursuit of Happiness." In *The Faces of Buddhism in America*, ed. Charles S. Prebish and Kenneth Tanaka, 164–180. Berkeley: University of California Press, 1998.
Gilpin, Richard. "The Use of Theravāda Buddhist Practices and Perspectives in Mindfulness-Based Cognitive Therapy." *Contemporary Buddhism* 2, no. 8 (2008): 227–251.
Gleig, Ann. *American Dharma: Buddhism beyond Modernity.* New Haven, CT: Yale University Press, 2019.
Gleig, Ann. "Wedding the Personal and Impersonal in West Coast Vipassana: A Dialogical Encounter between Buddhism and Psychotherapy." *Journal of Global Buddhism* 13 (2012): 129–146.
Gregory, Peter N. "Describing the Elephant: Buddhism in America." *Religion and Culture: A Journal of Interpretation* 11, no. 12 (2001): 233–263.
Hallisey, Charles. "Roads Taken and Not Taken in the Study of Theravada Buddhism." In *Curators of the Buddha: The Study of Buddhism under Colonialism*, ed. Donald S. Lopez, 31–61. Chicago: University of Chicago Press, 1995.
Han, Chenxing. "Describing the (Nonexistent?) Elephant: Ethnographic Methods in the Study of Asian American Buddhists." In *Methods in Buddhist Studies: Essays in Honor of Richard Payne*, ed. Scott A. Mitchell and Natalie Fisk Quli, 109–125. New York: Bloomsbury Academic, 2019.
Hickey, Wakoh Shannon. "Two Buddhisms, Three Buddhisms, and Racism." *Journal of Global Buddhism* 11 (2015): 1–25.
Insight Meditation Society letter, dated November 12, 1975.
Iwamura, Jane. *Virtual Orientalism: Asian Religions and American Popular Culture.* New York: Oxford University Press, 2010.
Kabat-Zinn, Jon. "Some Reflections on the Origins of MBSR, Skillful Means, and the Trouble with Maps." In *Mindfulness: Diverse Perspectives on Its Meaning, Origins and Applications*, ed. J. Mark G. Williams and Jon Kabat-Zinn, 281–306. New York: Routledge, 2013.
Kemper, Steven. *Rescued from the Nation: Dharmapala and the Buddhist World.* Chicago: University of Chicago Press, 2015.
Knaster, Mirka. *Living This Life Fully: Stories and Teachings of Munindra.* Berkeley, CA: Shambhala, 2010.
Kornfield, Jack. "This Fantastic, Unfolding Experiment." *Buddhadharma* (Summer 2007): 32–39.
Layman, Emma. *Buddhism in America.* Chicago: Nelson-Hall, 1976.
Masuzawa, Tomoko. *The Invention of World Religions: Or, How European Universalism Was Preserved in the Language of Pluralism.* Chicago: University of Chicago Press, 2005.
McGovern, Nathan. "The Contemporary Study of Buddhism." In *The Oxford Handbook of Contemporary Buddhism*, ed. Michael Jerryson, 701–714. New York: Oxford University Press, 2017.
McMahan, David. *The Making of Buddhist Modernism.* New York: Oxford University Press, 2009.
McNicholl, Adeana. "Buddhism and Race in the United States." *Religion Compass* 15, no. 8 (2021): 1–13.

Mitchell, Scott A. *Buddhism in America: Global Religion, Local Contexts*. New York: Bloomsbury Academic, 2013.

Nattier, Jan. "Buddhism Comes to Main Street." *The Wilson Quarterly*, Spring 1997. http://archive.wilsonquarterly.com/essays/buddhism-comes-main-street. Last accessed June 23, 2022.

Numrich, Paul David. "Two Buddhisms Further Considered." *Contemporary Buddhism* 4, no. 1 (2003): 55–78.

Numrich, Paul David. *Old Wisdom in the New World: Americanization in Two Immigrant Theravada Buddhist Temples*. Knoxville: The University of Tennessee Press, 1996.

Payne, Richard. "Religion, Self-Help, Science: Three Economics of Western/ized Buddhism." *Journal of Global Buddhism* 20 (2019): 69–86.

Perreira, Todd LeRoy. "Whence Theravāda? The Modern Genealogy of an Ancient Term." In *How Theravāda is Theravāda? Exploring Buddhist Identities*, ed. Peter Skilling, Jason A. Carbine, Claudio Cicuzza, and Santi Pakdeekham, 443–571. Chiang Mai, Thailand: Silkworm Books, 2012.

Perreira, Todd LeRoy "Sasana Sakon and the New Asian American: Intermarriage and Identity at a Thai Buddhist Temple in Silicon Valley." In *Asian American Religions: The Making and Remaking of Borders and Boundaries*, ed. Tony Carnes and Fenggang Yang, 313–337. New York: New York University Press, 2004.

The Pew Forum on Religion and Public Life. *Asian Americans: A Mosaic of Faiths*. Washington, DC: Pew Research Center, 2012.

Prebish, Charles. *American Buddhism*. North Scituate, MA: Duxbury Press, 1979.

Quli, Natalie Fisk. "On Authenticity: Scholarship, the Insight Movement, and White Authority." In *Methods in Buddhist Studies: Essays in Honor of Richard Payne*, ed. Scott A. Mitchell and Natalie Fisk Quli, 154–172. New York: Bloomsbury Academic, 2019.

Schmidt, Amy. *Dipa Ma: The Life and Legacy of a Buddhist Master*. New York: BlueBridge Books, 2005.

Schmidt, Leigh. *Restless Souls: The Making of American Spirituality*. Berkeley: University of California Press, 2012.

Seager, Richard Hughes. "American Buddhism in the Making." In *Westward Dharma: Buddhism Beyond Asia*, ed. Charles S. Prebish and Martin Baumann, 106–119. Berkeley: University of California Press, 2002.

Seager, Richard Hughes. *Buddhism in America*. New York: Columbia University Press, 1999.

Simpson, Caroline Chung. *An Absent Presence: Japanese Americans in Post-War American Culture, 1945–1960*. Durham, NC: Duke University Press, 2002.

Skilling, Peter. "Theravāda in History." *Pacific World* 3, no. 11 (2009): 61–93.

Stuart, Daniel. *S. N. Goenka: Emissary of Insight*. Berkeley, CA: Shambhala, 2020.

Tanaka, Kenneth K. "Epilogue: The Colors and Contours of American Buddhism." In *The Faces of Buddhism in America*, ed. Charles S. Prebish and Kenneth K. Tanaka, 287–298. New York: Oxford University Pres, 1998.

Taylor, Charles. "Two Theories of Modernity." In *Alternative Modernities*, ed. Dilip Parameshwar Gaonkar, 172–196. Durham, NC: Duke University Press, 2001.

Tweed, Thomas. "Nightstand Buddhists and Other Creatures: Sympathizers, Adherents, and the Study of Religion." In *American Buddhism: Methods and Findings in Recent Scholarship*, ed. Duncan Ryuken Williams and Christopher S. Queen, 71–90. New York: Routledge, 1999.

Tweed, Thomas. *The American Encounter with Buddhism, 1844–1912*. Bloomington: Indiana University Press, 1992.

Tworkov, Helen. "Superscience: An Interview with S. N. Goenka on the Techniques of Buddhist Practice." *Tricycle: The Buddhist Review* 10, no. 2 (Winter 2000). https://tricycle.org/magazine/s-n-goenka/. Last accessed June 22, 2022.

Tworkov, Helen. "Many Is More." *Tricycle: The Buddhist Review* 1, no. 2 (Winter 1991). https://tricycle.org/magazine/many-more/. Last accessed July 15, 2022.

Wilson, Jeff. *Mindful America: The Mutual Transformation of Buddhist Meditation and American Culture.* New York: Oxford University Press, 2014.

Wilson, Jeff. *Dixie Dharma: Inside a Buddhist Temple in the American South.* Chapel Hill: University of North Carolina Press, 2012.

Wilson, Jeff. "Mapping the American Buddhist Terrain: Paths Taken and Possible Itineraries." *Religion Compass* 3, no. 5 (2009): 839–840.

CHAPTER 11

NICHIREN BUDDHISM IN AMERICA

RALPH H. CRAIG III

INTRODUCTION

"After I have passed into extinction," the Buddha exhorts in the Bhaiṣajyarāja ("Medicine King") chapter in the Lotus Sūtra, "in the last five-hundred-year period you must spread it [J. *kōsen-rufu*] abroad widely throughout Jambudvipa and never allow it to be cut off...."[1] Similar exhortations pepper other chapters in the scripture, such that it could be read as an injunction to spread the sūtra itself. Jambudvipa (S. *jambudvīpa*) is generally understood to mean the entire world. Thus, on one reading the Buddha is here urging that the Lotus Sūtra be propagated throughout the world. This is certainly how some of the sūtra's interpreters understood it. The thirteenth-century Buddhist reformer Nichiren (1222–1282) was one such interpreter who took this passage as his mandate, and *kōsen-rufu*, or the propagation of the Lotus Sūtra, became his life's work. Adherents in the various lineages which comprise Nichiren Buddhism have similarly made propagating the Lotus Sūtra, his teachings, and the practices he delineated the core of their respective lineages. In this sense, Nichiren Buddhism is a missionizing religion, and its missionary imperative has carried it to the United States.

This chapter examines Nichiren Buddhism in the United States. After first providing background on Nichiren, his view of the Lotus Sūtra, and the practices that he outlined,

---

[1] Burton Watson, trans., *The Lotus Sutra and Its Opening and Closing Sutras* (Tokyo: Soka Gakkai, 2009), 330. See also Leon Hurvitz, trans., *Scripture of the Lotus Blossom of the Fine Dharma (The Lotus Sūtra)*, revised ed. (New York: Columbia University Press, 2009), 276. For a translation from Sanskrit, see Hendrik Kern, trans., *The Lotus Sūtra: Saddharma Puṇḍarīka Sūtra or The Lotus of the True Law* ([Sacred Books of the East, Volume XXI, 1884]; Surrey: Eremitical Press, 2011). As Donald Lopez Jr. and Jacqueline I. Stone point out, the "it" that is to be spread refers specifically to the chapter itself. See Donald S. Lopez Jr. and Jacqueline I. Stone, *Two Buddhas Seated Side by Side: A Guide to the Lotus Sūtra* (Princeton, NJ: Princeton University Press, 2019), 231.

the chapter briefly discusses Nichiren Buddhism's representation at the 1893 World's Parliament of Religion. After this, I outline the histories of two of the main Nichiren Buddhist sects established in the United States: Nichirenshū and Nipponzan Myōhōji.[2] The latter half of the chapter discusses Soka Gakkai International–United States of America (SGI-USA) and Nichiren Shōshū. Nichiren Shōshū is a traditional Buddhist order comprising monastics and lay members. Sōka Gakkai (the original, Japanese forerunner of Soka Gakkai International) is a lay religious organization founded in 1930. When Sōka Gakkai first came to the United States, it was one of the lay groups affiliated with Nichiren Shōshū. Because of this history, it makes sense to discuss these two traditions together. It is important to note that owing to the dearth of scholarship on Nichiren Buddhist sects in the United States aside from Sōka Gakkai/Nichiren Shōshū, my treatment of Nichirenshū and Nipponzan Myōhōji must be regarded as a starting point for future studies of these traditions. The presentation below is largely chronological, with the exception that Nipponzan Myōhōji, which came to the United States in the 1970s, is discussed before Sōka Gakkai/Nichiren Shōshū. In the final section of the chapter, I offer three suggestions for future avenues of research.

HISTORICAL BACKGROUND: NICHIREN'S BUDDHISM

Nichiren is often considered to be one of the most important religious figures to emerge during Japan's Kamakura period (1185–1333).[3] He was initially ordained in the Tendai Buddhist school and studied the doctrines and practices of other Buddhist traditions. As Nichiren studied, he became convinced that the Buddhist traditions of his day had irreconcilable doctrinal errors, as they had incorrectly grasped which teachings and practices held the most social, economic, political, and soteriological efficacy in the Final Dharma age (J. *mappō*), when the Buddha's teachings were thought to be in decline. "In his estimation," as Jacqueline Stone explains, "the other Buddhist forms current in his day—Pure Land, Zen, and the esoteric teachings—being provisional and incomplete, no longer led to liberation in the *mappō* era; to embrace them and reject the *Lotus Sūtra* . . . could only invite suffering."[4] Rather than focus on the "Pure Land" sūtras

---

[2] The designation "Nichirenshū" is often used both for all Nichiren-related lineages and for the largest sect in particular. In this chapter, "Nichirenshū" is used only in the latter sense.

[3] For an overview of Nichiren's life, see the Introduction in Nichiren, *Selected Writings of Nichiren*, ed. Philip B. Yampolsky, trans. Burton Watson and others (New York: Columbia University Press, 1990), 1–10. See also Jacqueline I. Stone, *Original Enlightenment and the Transformation of Medieval Japanese Buddhism* (Honolulu: University of Hawai'i Press, 1999), 242–263. On the Kamakura period, see Stone, *Original Enlightenment*, 55–62.

[4] Jacqueline I. Stone, "'By Imperial Edict and Shogunal Decree': Politics and the Issue of the Ordination Platform in Modern Lay Nichiren Buddhism," in *Buddhism in the Modern World:*

as Hōnen and his disciple Shinran did, or on the teachings of Chinese Chan masters as Dōgen did, Nichiren held that the *Saddharma-puṇḍarīka-sūtra* or the "Teaching of the Lotus Blossom of the Wonderful Law" (J. *Myōhōrengekyō*; Lotus Sūtra) was the most universally efficacious scripture.

Nichiren also found fault with the Tendai school in which he was ordained. While the Lotus Sūtra, alongside commentaries written by patriarchs of the Chinese Tiantai school, was the central scripture of Tendai, this school also included fire rituals, silent meditation, and other practices.[5] Instead, Nichiren declared that chanting the title (J. *daimoku*) of the Lotus Sūtra in the form of the mantra *Namu-myōhō-renge-kyō* was the most efficacious Buddhist practice. Nichiren gave concrete form to his teachings when he inscribed the *daimoku* in the form of a calligraphic maṇḍala as the central object of devotion (J. *(go)honzon*). The *honzon* that Nichiren inscribed features the *daimoku* written down the center. Surrounding the *daimoku* are the names of various deities, bodhisattvas, buddhas, and other beings that were present when the Lotus Sūtra was preached. He held that the practice of exclusive devotion to the Lotus Sūtra, through chanting the *daimoku* before the *honzon*, and (crucially) propagating the sūtra, would end the sociopolitical upheaval of his day and establish an ideal world.[6] Such an understanding led him to have controversial views on the need for a monastic ordination platform (J. *kaidan*) officially sponsored by imperial authorities.[7] Traditionally, the *kaidan* was a place where monastics received the precepts and formally joined the Buddhist monastic order. For Nichiren, the question of the *kaidan* was intimately tied to an exclusive acceptance of the Lotus Sūtra. These three elements—the *daimoku*, *honzon*, and *kaidan*—are often referred to as the "three great secret dharmas" (J. *sandai hihō*).[8] The three great secret dharmas index the core doctrines of Nichiren's Buddhism.

Nichiren had a relatively small community of followers in his lifetime. Chief among his followers were six disciples around whom communities of believers began to coalesce, and over time the number of adherents in these communities gradually increased. Over the course of the following centuries different sects emerged, embracing a variety of interpretations of his three great secret dharmas. Nearly all lineages of Nichiren Buddhism emphasize propagation of the Buddhist teachings and the Lotus Sūtra, just as Nichiren had done.[9] Among the Nichiren Buddhist lineages in the centuries after

---

Adaptations of an Ancient Tradition, ed. Steven Heine and Charles S. Prebish (Oxford: Oxford University Press, 2003), 194.

[5] The Tendai tradition's incorporation of various practices extends back to the tradition's founder, Saichō (767–822). See Stone, *Original Enlightenment*, 16–21. On the important Tiantai commentaries to the Lotus Sūtra, see Stephen F. Teiser and Jacqueline I. Stone, eds., *Readings of the Lotus Sūtra* (New York: Columbia University Press, 2009), 31–38.

[6] Stone, "'By Imperial Edict and Shogunal Decree,'" 194.

[7] The extent to which Nichiren endorsed this notion has been a subject of much debate among scholars. See Stone, "'By Imperial Edict and Shogunal Decree,'" 195–197, for a summary of the debates.

[8] Ibid., 196. In establishing his teachings, Nichiren drew on Tendai doctrines such as *ichinen sanzen* ("three thousand realms in one moment of thought"), earlier mantric practices, and historical precedents for the creation of devotional objects.

[9] Stone, *Original Enlightenment*, 302–303.

Nichiren's death, two especially would play major roles in bringing Nichiren Buddhism to the United States: Nichirenshū, itself comprised of several different lineages; and the "Fuji School" of Nikkō, one of Nichiren's six chief disciples. New lineages continued to be founded into the twentieth century, one of which, the Nipponzan Myōhōji lineage, would also play an active role in American Buddhist history. In the next section, I discuss Nichiren Buddhism's representation at the 1893 World's Parliament of Religions.

NICHIREN BUDDHISM IN THE NINETEENTH-CENTURY UNITED STATES

Nichiren Buddhism was first brought to the United States in the nineteenth century. Toward the end of the first half of the century, the Lotus Sūtra appeared in the New England–based Transcendentalist magazine *The Dial: A Magazine of Literature, Philosophy, and Religion*. In 1842, *The Dial* began publishing a series of translations of texts from Asia.[10] Two years later, through the pioneering efforts of educator Elizabeth Palmer Peabody, who worked as the paper's business manager, *The Dial* published a translation of an excerpt of the sūtra.[11] Initially, it did not have much of an impact. In fact, due to the effects of orientalist readings of Indian Buddhist literature and the subsequent elevation of Buddhist sources in the Pāli language, the Lotus Sūtra, as Donald Lopez Jr. explains, "all but disappeared from New England" in subsequent decades.[12] Nonetheless, by the 1870s, Nichiren Buddhism started to be mentioned sporadically in newspapers such as *The Independent* and *The Jewish Messenger*. That is, during the latter half of the nineteenth century, Americans encountered the foundational scripture of Nichiren Buddhism and mentions of Nichiren and Nichiren Buddhist priests in American publications.[13]

Americans would also encounter Nichiren Buddhism at the 1893 World's Parliament of Religions. Part of the Chicago World's Fair, the Parliament had a momentous impact on the trajectory of Buddhism in America.[14] Writing on the heels of the event's centennial

---

[10] Thomas A. Tweed and Stephen Prothero, eds., *Asian Religions in America: A Documentary History* (New York: Oxford University Press, 1999), 62.

[11] On the translation of the Lotus Sūtra in *The Dial*, see Donald Lopez Jr., *The Lotus Sutra: A Biography* (Princeton, NJ: Princeton University Press, 2016), 156ff.

[12] Lopez Jr., *The Lotus Sutra: A Biography*, 168.

[13] Thus, for Nichiren Buddhism in the United States, the nineteenth century can be seen, in agreement with Thomas A. Tweed and Stephen Prothero, as a period of meeting or encounter. See Thomas A. Tweed and Stephen Prothero, eds., *Asian Religions in America: A Documentary History* (New York: Oxford University Press, 1999), 6–7.

[14] See, for example, Richard Hughes Seager, *The World's Parliament of Religions: The East/West Encounter, Chicago, 1893* (Bloomington: Indiana University Press, [1995] 2009); Thomas A. Tweed, *The American Encounter with Buddhism, 1844–1912: Victorian Culture and the Limits of Dissent* (Chapel Hill: University of North Carolina Press, [1992] 2000); Scott A. Mitchell, *Buddhism in America: Global*

celebrations in 1993, Richard Seager stated that the "Parliament deserves a central place in American and modern religious history."[15] Characterizing the Parliament as "a liberal, western, and American quest for world religious unity that failed," Seager explains, it nevertheless "failed" due to the "same parochialism, ethnocentrism, imperial pretensions, and hegemonic intentions as the entire Exposition."[16] Despite its significant limitations, the Parliament introduced many Americans to religious ideas and peoples that they previously had neither heard of nor personally encountered.

Among the Parliament's attendees from all over the world was a delegation of Japanese Buddhist monks, representing different Buddhist schools. Among the members of the delegation was Yoshigiro Kawai,[17] a Nichiren Buddhist priest, who presented a paper via an interpreter. The delegation also included Soyen Shaku (a Zen monk of the Rinzai Zen school; teacher of D. T. Suzuki). In his paper, Kawai focused especially on the three great secret dharmas (mentioned above). Due to its complexity, Kawai's piece, as Richard Seager observes, was among the more "densely-coded papers" presented at the conference.[18] Indeed, a Parliament attendee without background knowledge of Nichiren Buddhism may have found it difficult to make sense of Kawai's discussion of the three great secret dharmas, which he referred to as the "three true secret principles of Buddhism." In his explanation of the *daimoku*, Kawai explained that "happiness will spring from the powerful and benevolent mercy of the principles combined and expressed in the words 'Namu-myo-ho-renge-kyo.'" Regarding the *honzon*, he said that the "Mandala is a grand mirror of enlightenment, in which all things and all phenomena are at once reflected together." The third great secret law, the *kaidan*, was the "place where we practice the doctrines of the holy book [i.e., the Lotus Sūtra]." Kawai concluded by summarizing the core of his order: "To set up the good law and to make the State peaceful—this is the fundamental doctrine of the Nichiren sect." Through the rubric of the three great secret dharmas, Kawai was able to give a succinct account of the salient aspects of Nichiren's biography, explain the fundamentals of Nichiren's teachings, and make a case for the sociopolitical value of Nichiren Buddhism. Similar to Seager's take, in her article on Nichiren Shōshū and Sōka Gakkai, Jane Hurst writes that "[Kawai] did not proselytize or seem to have much impact on the delegates, probably because he spoke only Japanese."[19] Yet, showing the missionary impulse inherited from Nichiren, Kawai offered to the audience, "If any of our brethren desire to ask on the doctrine of our sect we shall be delighted to explain the tenets of our faith as far as our poor

---

Religion, Local Contexts (London: Bloomsbury Academic, 2016); and Rick Fields, *How the Swans Came to the Lake: A Narrative History of Buddhism in America*, 3rd ed. (Boston: Shambhala, 1992).

[15] Seager, *The World's Parliament of Religions*, xxv.
[16] Ibid., xxxviii–xxxix. See also Mitchell, *Buddhism in America: Global Religion, Local Contexts*, 44–47.
[17] Some sources spell his name Yoshigirai.
[18] Seager, *The World's Parliament of Religions*, 103.
[19] Jane Hurst, "Nichiren Shōshū and Soka Gakkai in America: The Pioneer Spirit," in *The Faces of Buddhism in America*, ed. Charles S. Prebish and Kenneth K. Tanaka (Berkeley: University of California Press, 1998), 80.

knowledge and feeble power will permit."[20] Kawai's paper at the 1893 World's Parliament of Religions, then, represents a noteworthy example of Nichiren Buddhism's presence in the United States in the nineteenth century. The presence of Nichiren Buddhism in the United States would expand in the following century.

Nichirenshū and Nipponzan Myōhōji

Nichirenshū was one of the first Nichiren Buddhist sects to establish an institutional presence in the United States. In 1899, Reverend Gyoun Takagi arrived in Honolulu to minister to Nichirenshū Buddhists among the Japanese immigrants that had settled in Hawaiʻi. As Scott Mitchell explains, trade "brought migrant workers to the islands from China, Korea, and Japan through the latter half of the nineteenth century, workers who began establishing cultural and religious communities. Whereas Chinese and Korean immigrants would have undoubtedly brought Buddhist practices with them, Japanese immigrants were the first to establish Buddhist communities in the Kingdom of Hawaiʻi before it was annexed as a US territory in 1898."[21] Among the Japanese immigrants were adherents of different Buddhist schools, including some Nichirenshū Buddhists. To serve them, Takagi established the Kapapala Nichiren Mission in May 1902. Ten years later, he established the Nichiren Mission of Hawaiʻi in Honolulu. In 1914, the Nichiren Sect Mission of Hawaii was formally granted the status of a religious corporation. That same year, a Nichirenshū temple was established on the United States mainland in Los Angeles, and the Nichiren Order of North America was founded. Nichirenshū continued to grow in the United States until World War II and the devasting effects of Executive Order 9066, which saw some 120,000 Japanese Americans sent to internment camps. After the internment, the Nichirenshū began re-establishing temples that continued to be active throughout the twentieth and into the twenty-first century.[22]

Another lineage of Nichiren Buddhism that came to the United States in the mid-twentieth century is the Nipponzan Myōhōji order. The order was founded by Venerable Nichidatsu Fujii (1885–1985) and it includes both monastics and lay supporters. Fujii drew his religious inspiration from Nichiren, ascetic tendencies within the Nichiren school, and from the pacifist activism of Gandhi.[23] Monks and nuns of this order engage

---

[20] All quotes from "Buddhists Present Their Cause," *Chicago Daily Tribune (1872–1922)*, September 27, 1893, 11.

[21] Scott Mitchell, "Buddhist Practice in Europe and North America," in *The Oxford Handbook of Buddhist Practice*, ed. Kevin Trainor and Paula Arai (New York: Oxford University Press, 2022), 94.

[22] All information on Nichiren Shu history has been drawn from "History," Nichiren Mission of Hawaii, accessed January 14, 2023, https://www.nichirenmission.org/history. On the incarceration of Japanese Americans during World War II, see Duncan Ryūken Williams, *American Sutra: A Story of Faith and Freedom in the Second World War* (Cambridge, MA: Harvard University Press, 2019).

[23] Jacqueline I. Stone, "Nichiren's Activist Heirs: Sōka Gakkai, Risshō Kōseikai, Nipponzan Myōhōji," in *Action Dharma: New Studies in Engaged Buddhism*, ed. Christopher Queen, Charles Prebish, and Damien Keown (London: RoutledgeCurzon, 2003), 78–79.

in periodic fasting and extended periods of chanting the *daimoku*, using a hand drum to accompany their recitations. They carry out both practices in adherence to the ascetic proclivities of their founder. At the same time, they maintain a firm commitment to nonviolent social activism. Their activism includes participation at marches and rallies, joining in solidarity with other activist groups, carrying out "peace walks," and building peace pagodas.[24] Nipponzan Myōhōji carried their hallmark practices to the United States in the 1970s.

Nichidatsu Fujii himself first came to the United States in 1968 to protest US involvement in Vietnam. Then, in 1974, Nipponzan Myōhōji's first US temple was opened in Washington, D.C.[25] Two years later, the order received an invitation to participate in the War Resister League's "Continental Walk for Disarmament and Social Justice."[26] This was the first of many activist walks that Nipponzan Myōhōji would participate in. In their activism, the order has "shown particular sympathy for peoples who have suffered Western aggression and colonization," leading them to be "active on behalf of Native American rights," to protest US racism, and even to support Latin American liberation movements.[27] Beyond Nipponzan Myōhōji's presence in US activist movements, the order has also built its peace pagodas in Leverett, Massachusetts, Grafton, New York, and Newport, Tennessee. As a result of this activity, Nipponzan Myōhōji has become recognized as an active participant in the tradition of religious activism in the United States. Their activism is all the more impressive given their small size of roughly 1,500 adherents worldwide, only a fraction of whom are in the United States. Even still, Nipponzan Myōhōji represents (alongside SGI-USA, as we will see below) a significant force in the movement that has come to be called Engaged Buddhism or Socially Engaged Buddhism.[28]

Sōka Gakkai/SGI-USA and Nichiren Shōshū

Sōka Gakkai and Nichiren Shōshū came to the United States during the post–World War II period. These two traditions are responsible for the wide spread of Nichiren Buddhism in the United States seen especially since the 1960s.

Nichiren Shōshū traces its lineage back to Nikkō (1246–1333), one of the six chief disciples of Nichiren. The school that emerged from Nikkō, the "Fuji School," developed

---

[24] Stone, "Nichiren's Activist Heirs," 77.
[25] Paula Green, "Walking for Peace: Nipponzan Myohoji," in *Engaged Buddhism in the West*, ed. Christopher S. Queen (Boston: Wisdom Publications, 2000), 144.
[26] Ibid.
[27] Stone, "Nichiren's Activist Heirs," 78; and Green, "Walking for Peace," 150.
[28] For a discussion of Engaged Buddhism and a summary of the relevant scholarship, see Paul Fuller, *An Introduction to Engaged Buddhism* (London: Bloomsbury Academic, 2022).

many unique interpretations of Nichiren's teachings that set this school apart from the Nichirenshū sect tradition above.[29] One of their most distinctive doctrines relates to their view of Nichiren. The uniqueness of the Fuji School's view of Nichiren can be seen by way of comparison with Nichirenshū's view. In their understanding of Nichiren, Nichirenshū holds that he is either the reincarnation or representative of bodhisattva Superior Practice (S. Viśiṣṭacārita; J. Jōgyō), a figure mentioned in the Lotus Sūtra.[30] For example, in his paper at the 1893 World's Parliament of Religion (discussed above), Yoshigiro Kawai is reported to have explained that the "Bodhisattva Vishishtakarita [sic] was born again in Japan . . . adopting the name of Nichiren."[31] This interpretation extends to how Nichirenshū understands other traditional Buddhist doctrines, such as the three jewels (the Buddha, dharma, and sangha). As Jacqueline Stone outlines, the standard interpretation of the three jewels in Nichirenshū is: "the Buddha is defined as the original Śākyamuni of the 'Fathoming the Lifespan" chapter of the *Lotus Sūtra*, the Dharma is Namu-myōhō-renge-kyō, and the Sangha is represented by Nichiren."[32] The Fuji Schools do not hold this view. Instead, for them, as Stone continues, "the Buddha is Nichiren, the Dharma is Namu-myōhō-renge-kyō, and the Sangha is represented by Nikkō."[33] These and other doctrines distinguish Nikkō's lineage, and therefore Nichiren Shōshū, from other Nichiren Buddhist sects. While Nichiren Shōshū remained a small sect before the twentieth century, it would experience phenomenal growth in post–World War II Japan through one of its lay organizations, Sōka Gakkai.

Sōka Gakkai was founded in 1930, by Japanese educators Tsunesaburō Makiguchi (1871–1944) and Jōsei Toda (1900–1958).[34] Two years prior to the organization's founding, Makiguchi had converted to Nichiren Shōshū Buddhism. As a result, though the organization primarily focused on disseminating Makiguchi's educational theories in its early years, by 1941 it gradually began to focus on the proselytization of Nichiren's teachings. Even as the organization was changing its focus, so was the Japanese empire, which was mobilizing for war. That same year, Sōka Kyōiku Gakkai came to the attention of Japan's Special Higher Police. Levi McLaughlin's *Soka Gakkai's Human Revolution* provides one of the most thorough accounts of this period of the organization's history. McLaughlin explains that during this time, "Japan's Special Higher Police were clamping down on religious organizations. They invoked the 1925 Peace Preservation Law,

---

[29] For the most detailed discussion of Nikkō's lineage in English, see Stone, *Original Enlightenment*, 334–343.

[30] On the identification of Nichiren with this bodhisattva, see Lopez Jr. and Stone, *Two Buddhas Seated Side by Side*, 176 and 210–217.

[31] See "Buddhists Present Their Cause," *Chicago Daily Tribune (1872–1922)*, September 27, 1893, 11.

[32] Stone, *Original Enlightenment*, 341–342.

[33] Stone, *Original Enlightenment*, 342.

[34] The organization was originally named the Sōka Kyōiku Gakkai ("Value Creation Education Study Association"). Sōka Kyōiku Gakkai held its first official meeting on January 27, 1937, but dates its founding to the publication of the first volume of Tsunesaburō Makiguchi's *Sōkakyōikugaku taikei* ("System of Value-Creating Educational Study"). See Levi McLaughlin, *Soka Gakkai's Human Revolution: The Rise of a Mimetic Nation in Modern Japan* (Honolulu: University of Hawai'i Press, 2019), 41. Much of the following understanding of Sōka Gakkai's early history in Japan is drawn from McLaughlin's work.

legislation that gave governmental authorities sanction to interfere in the daily operations of all organizations."[35] In 1943, while Sōka Kyōiku Gakkai was under surveillance by these authorities, Nichiren Shōshū faced mounting government pressures to merge with Nichirenshū. Things would come to a head when Makiguchi was arrested that summer on charges of violating the Peace Preservation Law, along with his disciple Jōsei Toda and other Sōka Kyōiku Gakkai leaders. Makiguchi died in prison the following fall.[36] During his time in prison, Toda's religiosity deepened when he experienced two spiritual awakenings as a result of prolonged chanting of the *daimoku*. These visions also confirmed for Toda that his mission was *kōsen-rufu* (discussed above).[37]

Toda was released from prison in July 1945. The following year, he set out to rebuild the Sōka Kyōiku Gakkai, which had essentially folded during his and Makiguchi's imprisonment. Toda began lecturing on the Lotus Sūtra at Nichiren Shōshū's head temple and dropped Kyōiku from the organization's name, rebranding it solely as Sōka Gakkai. In 1951, Toda was named second president of the Sōka Gakkai (Makiguchi had been the first) and by that point he had attracted a number of disciples, one of whom, Daisaku Ikeda (1928–2023), would later become the third Sōka Gakkai president. Faced with the challenge of rebuilding in the upheaval of post–World War II Japan, Toda did as other proponents of Nichiren Buddhism had done before him. He drew on Nichiren's conviction that times of social strife required aggressive propagation of the Lotus Sūtra, known as *shakubuku*.[38] While president, Toda launched a full-scale proselytization campaign known as the "Great March of Shakubuku" (J. *shakubuku daikōshin*).[39] Toda's Great March of Shakubuku proved tremendously successful. By the time of his death in April 1958, the organization had achieved and surpassed Toda's lifetime goal of achieving 750,000 member households and had become a formidable force in Japanese politics. At the same time, throughout his presidency, Toda worked to strengthen the organization's connection to the Nichiren Shōshū lineage by refurbishing buildings at the order's Taisekiji headquarters, building branch temples around Japan, and forming alliances with amenable high priests of the order (though relations were at times rocky). As a result of Sōka Gakkai's initiatives and conversion drives, as the former grew, so did their clerical parent body Nichiren Shōshū.

In the 1950s, members of Sōka Gakkai and adherents of Nichiren Shōshū began arriving in the United States as Japanese immigrants. These immigrants, as Scott Mitchell explains, were "Japanese women who had married US servicemen stationed in Asia during the Allied occupation of Japan and the Korean War [and who] brought the tradition back to the United States with them."[40] These women shared with

---

[35] McLaughlin, *Soka Gakkai's Human Revolution*, 43.
[36] Ibid., 43–44.
[37] On these visions, see ibid., 46.
[38] On this term, see Richard Hughes Seager, *Encountering the Dharma: Daisaku Ikeda, Soka Gakkai, and the Globalization of Buddhist Humanism* (Berkeley: University of California Press, 2006), 55.
[39] McLaughlin, *Soka Gakkai's Human Revolution*, 48.
[40] Mitchell, *Buddhism in America*, 128–129.

their fellow members in Japan the organizational imperative to propagate Nichiren Buddhism. But, with no organizational support, language barriers, and being spread out around the country, they struggled to share Nichiren Buddhism with others in the United States. According to George M. Williams, who came to the United States in 1957 as a student from Japan, at that time there were roughly one hundred Sōka Gakkai members spread out around the country.[41] This would change during the following decade with the inauguration of Daisaku Ikeda, Toda's disciple, as the third Sōka Gakkai president.

Daisaku Ikeda became Sōka Gakkai president in May 1960. Though Ikeda's leadership style differed significantly from Toda's, *shakubuku* remained one of his primary concerns. Beyond Japan, Ikeda set his sights on global *shakubuku*. Under Ikeda's direction, Sōka Gakkai established an "Overseas Branch" two months after his inauguration.[42] In October of that same year, Ikeda himself traveled abroad, making the United States one of his first stops. The visit galvanized the organization's members then living in the United States.[43] During his travels, Ikeda organized small chapters in major urban cities around the United States and established the "America General Chapter." When he returned to the United States in 1963, the organization opened its first community center in the Little Tokyo neighborhood of downtown Los Angeles. During this same year, the organization was formally "recognized as a non-profit religious corporation."[44] Because the organization was still a lay group affiliated with Nichiren Shōshū, they established the name Nichiren Shōshū Sōka Gakkai of America (hereafter, NSA). NSA also began hosting English-language meetings. An English-language newspaper followed in 1964. According to Jane Hurst, "NSA grew slowly through the 1960s, relying on techniques of street *shakubuku* and discussion meetings to recruit new members."[45] Summarizing the format of these meetings, Hurst explains that the meetings were "held complete with songs, chanting *Nam-myōhō-renge-kyō*, and introduction to Nichiren Shōshū Buddhism, and several members' experiences with chanting."[46] NSA augmented these discussion meetings by holding unifying "general chapter meetings" and large-scale "conventions."[47] As NSA grew, it established the first Nichiren Shōshū temples in the United States in Honolulu and Los Angeles.[48] Into the 1970s, the combination of "street *shakubuku*," discussion meetings,

---

[41] George M. Williams, *Freedom and Influence: The Rule of Religion in American Society, an NSA Perspective* (Santa Monica, CA: World Tribune Press, 1985), 155.

[42] James Allen Dator, *Sōka Gakkai, Builders of the Third Civilization: American and Japanese Members* (Seattle: University of Washington Press, 1969), 17.

[43] Hurst, "Nichiren Shōshū and Soka Gakkai in America," 86.

[44] Williams, *Freedom and Influence*, 156–157. See also Ralph H. Craig, III, *Dancing in My Dreams: A Spiritual Biography of Tina Turner* (Grand Rapids: William B. Eerdmans Publishing Company, 2023).

[45] Hurst, "Nichiren Shōshū and Soka Gakkai in America," 87.

[46] Ibid.

[47] See ibid., 87–88.

[48] Williams, *Freedom and Influence*, 158.

conventions, and urban locations proved highly effective in attracting a diverse membership body.[49]

Several prominent African American celebrities, including Tina Turner and Herbie Hancock, joined the organization during this time.[50] While there are many reasons why such figures were attracted to NSA, I suggest that it was due in part to what Hurst characterizes as NSA's "ethos as a religious movement." In Hurst's assessment, NSA developed an organizational "ethos" that indexes "themes of individual power, change, and the mission for world peace." She continues by explaining that this ethos is "confident, positive, and free of anxiety. It is optimistic, hopeful, goal-oriented, extroverted, and energetic. It places the responsibility for each person's life on his or her own shoulders and does not need bad luck or scapegoats to account for the reversals of fortune."[51] Turner, in particular, exemplifies the embodiment of this ethos. Turner frequently discussed her conversion to Nichiren Buddhism in interviews throughout her career. She credited the practice with giving her the necessary confidence to end her abusive marriage to her ex-husband Ike Turner, to overcome racism and sexism in the music business, and to experience career success.[52] Alongside NSA's various meetings and *shakubuku* efforts, celebrities also helped to add profile and prestige to NSA and Nichiren Buddhism in America.

Successful conversion drives led to the rapid growth of NSA throughout the late 1960s and into the 1970s. At the same time, dramatic changes were on the organization's horizon. In 1975, Daisaku Ikeda founded the Soka Gakkai International organization in Guam and became its first president. Four years later, due to ongoing issues with the Nichiren Shōshū priesthood, he resigned as third president of Sōka Gakkai in Japan. This eventually led to the restructuring of Nichiren Shōshū Sōka Gakkai of America throughout the 1980s, as Sōka Gakkai attempted to shield its US members from ongoing disputes in Japan. Nonetheless, in 1991, Nikken Abe, the sixty-seventh High Priest of Nichiren Shōshū, excommunicated Sōka Gakkai's leadership, and eventually their entire membership body.[53] Sōka Gakkai considers November 28, 1991, the day of its excommunication, as its "Spiritual Independence Day." The excommunication rendered Sōka Gakkai a separate, entirely lay religious group in the lineage of Nikkō (discussed

---

[49] David W. Chappell, "Racial Diversity in the Soka Gakkai," in *Engaged Buddhism in the West*, ed. Christopher S. Queen (Boston: Wisdom Publications, 2000), 184. Seager, *Encountering the Dharma*, 146–150, discusses the demographics of SGI-USA during this period.

[50] See Richard Hughes Seager, *Buddhism in America*, revised ed. (New York: Columbia University Press, 2012), 92–93.

[51] Hurst, "Nichiren Shōshū and Soka Gakkai in America," 87. Hurst's analysis should be nuanced with considerations of the unique ways in which African Americans and people of color have embodied this ethos in the context of their own experience. See, for example, Chappell, "Racial Diversity in the Soka Gakkai," 193–198. See also Seager, *Encountering the Dharma*, 147–150.

[52] For an extended discussion of Turner's conversion to Buddhism and its place in career, see Ralph H. Craig III, "Some Will Hear: Tina Turner, African American Buddhist Teacher," *American Religion* 4, no. 1 (Fall 2022): 1–33.

[53] For a detailed discussion of the split, see Hurst, "Nichiren Shōshū and Soka Gakkai in America," 91–96. See also, Seager, *Encountering the Dharma*, 127–139.

above).⁵⁴ Throughout its history, SGI members have seen their organization, with its bureaucratic leadership structure and lay participation model, as fulfilling the role of both clergy and laity.⁵⁵ This model of lay participation emboldens members to take on leadership roles in the organization, which also entails taking on roles as teachers. Thus, each member is trained to be a lay Buddhist teacher, thereby fulfilling the role that Nichiren Shōshū monastics would have filled.

In the 1990s, Sōka Gakkai rebranded its American branch as the Soka Gakkai International-USA. Throughout the 1990s, Daisaku Ikeda returned to the United States on multiple occasions. On these trips, Ikeda laid the groundwork for solidifying the ideals that underpin SGI-USA's focus on social engagement. SGI-USA adheres to the broader vision of Soka Gakkai's engaged Buddhist movement. This includes SGI's role as a nongovernmental organization (NGO) affiliated with the United Nations Economic and Social Council (UNESCO), Daisaku Ikeda's yearly peace proposals, and five "key action areas" comprising "peace and disarmament," "education for sustainable development and climate action," "human rights education," "humanitarian relief and disaster risk reduction," and "gender equality and women's empowerment."⁵⁶ Given the prevalence of racism in the United States, SGI-USA has also worked to address this issue, largely in the form of published statements affirming the values of social justice. In January 1993, Daisaku Ikeda visited Los Angeles in the wake of the 1992 LA Riots. In a speech broadcast to SGI-USA locations around the United States, he presented a poem titled, "The Sun of Jiyu over a New Land." The poem addresses the roots of racial conflict. *Jiyu* in the title of the poem refers to *jiyu no bosatsu*, or the "Bodhisattvas of the Earth," that are described in the Lotus Sūtra as emerging to propagate the scripture in the most difficult times.⁵⁷ In the poem, Ikeda refers to *jiyu* as the "primordial 'roots' of humankind" which he describes as "beyond all differences of gender and race."⁵⁸ This poem has become an important touchstone in SGI-USA, especially for Black members. The organization continues to grow and expand as a social force in the United States into the twenty-first century. At present, the organization reports having some 350,000 members in North America, with the majority of them in the United States and "more than 2,500 monthly neighborhood discussion meetings and 90 Buddhist centers throughout the

---

⁵⁴ Sōka Gakkai maintains a small body of priests in Japan to fulfill ceremonial roles for elderly Japanese members.

⁵⁵ Daisaku Ikeda, *The New Human Revolution*, vol. 24 (Santa Monica, CA: World Tribune Press, 2013), 161. Ikeda has written two novelized histories of the organization, *The Human Revolution* and *The New Human Revolution*. Both serve as canonical scriptures for SGI members around the world. In the novel, Ikeda appears as Shinichi Yamamoto. For an in-depth discussion of both novels and how they function as history and scripture, see chapter four of McLaughlin, *Soka Gakkai's Human Revolution*, 88–111.

⁵⁶ See, "Action on Global Issues," Soka Gakkai Global, accessed January 16, 2023, https://www.sokaglobal.org/in-society/action-on-global-issues.html; and "Engaged Buddhism," SGI-USA, accessed January 16, 2023, https://www.sgi-usa.org/engaged-buddhism/.

⁵⁷ This idea also relates to Toda's awakening in prison.

⁵⁸ See Daisaku Ikeda, *My Dear Friends in America: Collected Addresses to the SGI-USA since 1990*, 3rd ed. (Santa Monica, CA: World Tribune Press, 2012), 208. Forthcoming work by the author will examine this poem in the context of race in American Buddhism.

country."⁵⁹ Today, Sōka Gakkai operates as its own lineage of Sōka Gakkai Nichiren Buddhism/SGI Nichiren Buddhism.

For its part, Nichiren Shōshū has six temples in the United States and its own lay group, called "Hokkeko." They do not have any publicly accessible membership statistics. The order outlines the role of its Hokkeko members by saying, "As members of the Hokkeko, the believers make efforts, day and night, to accumulate good fortune and positively influence society. They visit their local temples, where they deepen their faith through listening to the priest's sermon, sharing encouraging experiences with their fellow members, and carrying out various activities in faith and practice."⁶⁰ Thus, Nichiren Shōshū remains a traditional Buddhist order centered on temples and their resident priests.⁶¹

Avenues for Further Research

The brevity of the above exploration of Nichirenshū, Nipponzan Myōhōji, Sōka Gakkai/SGI-USA, and Nichiren Shōshū should make clear that there are many fruitful areas of research to pursue in the study of Nichiren Buddhism in the United States. To conclude this chapter, I will point to three potential research areas: identity, adherence, and the study of chanting-based Buddhist communities in the United States.

The first area of future research would be to carry out detailed studies of race and gender in the US Nichiren Buddhist lineages. While SGI-USA is often noted for its racial diversity and female leadership,⁶² and Nipponzan Myōhōji is noted for its activist work and standing in solidarity with marginalized communities (as discussed above), there have been few studies that specifically center an analysis of how race and gender operates in these communities. For Nichirenshū and Nichiren Shōshū, there have been no scholarly studies of these issues. Recent works by scholars like Jan Willis, Chenxing Han, Rima Vesely-Flad, and Pamela Ayo Yetunde and Cheryl A. Giles provide expert models for how scholars might begin to investigate race and gender identities in the study of US Nichiren Buddhist communities.⁶³

---

⁵⁹ "About Our Community," SGI-USA, accessed January 16, 2023, https://www.sgi-usa.org/about-our-community/.

⁶⁰ "Practice of True Buddhism," Nichiren Shoshu, accessed January 16, 2023, https://www.nichirenshoshu.or.jp/eng/practice.html.

⁶¹ It should be noted that Hokkeko members also host meetings in their home.

⁶² See, for example, Chappell, "Racial Diversity in the Soka Gakkai," in *Engaged Buddhism in the West*, ed. Christopher S. Queen (Boston: Wisdom Publications, 2000), 184–217; and Seager, *Encountering the Dharma*, especially 146–50.

⁶³ See Jan Willis, *Dharma Matters: Women, Race, and Tantra* (Somerville, MA: Wisdom Publications, 2020); Chenxing Han, *Be the Refuge: Raising the Voices of Asian American Buddhists* (Berkeley, CA: North Atlantic Books, 2021); Rima Vesely-Flad, *Black Buddhists and the Black Radical Tradition: The Practice of Stillness in the Movement for Liberation* (New York: New York University Press, 2022); and Pamela Ayo Yetunde and Cheryl A. Giles, eds., *Black and Buddhist: What Buddhism Can Teach Us about Race, Resilience, Transformation, and Freedom* (Boulder, CO: Shambhala, 2020). See also Adeana

A second area of future research is to study issues related to affiliation/membership and succession in US Nichiren Buddhist communities. Each of the four US Nichiren Buddhist sects that I center in this chapter are transnational religious communities. When adherents of these traditions move from other countries and join Nichiren communities in the United States, they inevitably shape and transform what it means to practice Nichiren Buddhism in the US. How are these Nichiren Buddhist communities in the United States contending with these transformations, especially given the changes in their own aging demographics? Alongside these transformations, how do these communities contend with changing notions of adherence, affiliation, and membership? For example, SGI-USA requires that its members receive their own personal *gohonzon* to officially join the organization. Once inside the organization, they are fitted into a highly structured system of members and leaders that prioritizes regular, communal practice and active participation in the daily activities of the organization. How will such a group deal with increasing numbers of young practitioners that adhere to flexible rubrics of "spirituality" and do not necessarily share the willingness to participate in the same ways as older generations? Finally, how do US Nichiren Buddhist lineages deal with the succession of their aging leaders? Nichirenshū, Nipponzan Myōhōji, and Nichiren Shōshū are composed of both monastic and lay adherents. While there are clear processes for ordination and the choosing of bishops, these communities face dwindling numbers of ordinands, especially in the United States. The issue of succession is even more complicated for SGI/SGI-USA due to the November 15, 2023 passing of Daisaku Ikeda whose charismatic leadership has been the guiding force of the organization since he assumed leadership of Sōka Gakkai in 1960. Ikeda's passing is sure to exert a profound impact upon this community, and it will likely have ripple effects across US Nichiren Buddhist communities. Accessing these shifts will be important for understanding the future of US Nichiren Buddhist communities.[64]

The last area of future scholarly research is studying the Nichiren traditions as instances of chanting-based practice lineages in American Buddhism. Scholarly monographs on American Buddhism tend to focus on so-called meditation-based lineages. David McMahan's *The Making of Buddhist Modernism* (2008)[65] and Ann Gleig's *American Dharma* (2019) are two prominent examples.[66] In their respective studies on Buddhism and modernity, both McMahan and Gleig focus heavily on figures and communities associated with meditation-based lineages such as those with roots in Zen Buddhism. Both studies only briefly mention Sōka Gakkai, while leaving other Nichiren sects unexplored. Future scholarship that integrates chanting-based Buddhist traditions may nuance our understanding of both American Buddhism and Buddhist modernist discourse.

McNicholl, "Buddhism and Race," in *The Oxford Handbook of Religion and Race in American History*, ed. Kathryn Gin Lum and Paul Harvey (New York: Oxford University Press, 2018), 223–240.

[64] I am grateful to Levi McLaughlin for suggesting some of these areas of concern.

[65] David McMahan, *The Making of Buddhist Modernism* (Oxford: Oxford University Press, 2008).

[66] Ann Gleig, *American Dharma: Buddhism beyond Modernity* (New Haven, CT: Yale University Press, 2019).

Attention to each of these three areas will enable scholars to form more complete portraits of Nichiren Buddhism in the United States. In turn, this will offer a valuable contribution to understanding the history of American Buddhism.

FURTHER READING

Craig, Ralph H., III. *Dancing in My Dreams: A Spiritual Biography of Tina Turner*. Grand Rapids: William B. Eerdmans Publishing Company, 2023.

Fields, Rick. *How the Swans Came to the Lake: A Narrative History of Buddhism in America*. 3rd edition. Boston: Shambhala, 1992.

Fuller, Paul. *An Introduction to Engaged Buddhism*. London: Bloomsbury Academic, 2022.

Lopez, Donald S., Jr. *The Lotus Sutra: A Biography*. Princeton, NJ: Princeton University Press, 2016.

Lopez, Donald S., Jr., and Jacqueline I. Stone. *Two Buddhas Seated Side by Side: A Guide to the Lotus Sūtra*. Princeton, NJ: Princeton University Press, 2019.

McLaughlin, Levi. *Soka Gakkai's Human Revolution: The Rise of a Mimetic Nation in Modern Japan*. Honolulu: University of Hawai'i Press, 2019.

Mitchell, A. *Buddhism in America: Global Religion, Local Contexts*. London: Bloomsbury Academic, 2016.

Prebish, Charles S., and Kenneth K. Tanaka, eds. *The Faces of Buddhism in America*. Berkeley: University of California Press, 1998.

Queen, Christopher S., ed. *Engaged Buddhism in the West*. Boston: Wisdom Publications, 2000.

Seager, Richard Hughes. *Buddhism in America*. Revised edition. New York: Columbia University, 2012.

Seager, Richard Hughes. *Encountering the Dharma: Daisaku Ikeda, Soka Gakkai, and the Globalization of Buddhist Humanism*. Berkeley: University of California Press, 2006.

Seager, Richard Hughes. *The World's Parliament of Religions: The East/West Encounter, Chicago, 1893*. Bloomington: Indiana University Press, 2009 [1995].

Stone, Jacqueline I. "'By Imperial Edict and Shogunal Decree': Politics and the Issue of the Ordination Platform in Modern Lay Nichiren Buddhism." In *Buddhism in the Modern World: Adaptations of an Ancient Tradition*, edited by Steven Heine and Charles S. Prebish, 193–219. Oxford: Oxford University Press, 2003.

Stone, Jacqueline I. *Original Enlightenment and the Transformation of Medieval Japanese Buddhism*. Honolulu: University of Hawai'i Press, 1999.

Teiser, Stephen F., and Jacqueline I. Stone, eds. *Readings of the Lotus Sūtra*. New York: Columbia University Press, 2009.

Tweed, Thomas A., and Stephen Prothero, eds. *Asian Religions in America: A Documentary History*. New York: Oxford University Press, 1999.

Watson, Burton, trans. *The Lotus Sutra and Its Opening and Closing Sutras*. Tokyo: Soka Gakkai, 2009.

Williams, Duncan Ryūken. *American Sutra: A Story of Faith and Freedom in the Second World War*. Cambridge, MA: Harvard University Press, 2019.

Yetunde, Pamela Ayo, and Cheryl A. Giles, eds. *Black and Buddhist: What Buddhism Can Teach Us about Race, Resilience, Transformation, and Freedom*. Boulder, CO: Shambhala, 2020.

CHAPTER 12

VIETNAMESE BUDDHISM IN AMERICA

TODD LEROY PERREIRA

Introduction

The study of Buddhism in North America has yet to prioritize what is, arguably, the single most important demographic development in its recent history: the emergence of monastic-centered Southeast Asian Buddhism conveyed by refugees following the communist takeover and "reunification of Vietnam" in 1975 and the subsequent immigrant and transmigrant flows this has engendered to the present day. Among the mass exodus that found its way to North America from the mid-1970s through 2010, nearly 2.9 million people entered the United States as refugees. Fleeing war-torn Cambodia, Laos, and Vietnam, they constitute the single largest resettled refugee population in American history. Religion plays an important role in the lives of many. Some 30 percent of Vietnamese Americans identify as Roman Catholic today, while the majority broadly affiliate as Buddhist or may claim Buddhism as part of their cultural heritage.[1] Together, they have established 650 Buddhist centers, monasteries, and temples throughout the United States, with roughly two out of every three built by Vietnamese Americans, who now operate more than 400 Buddhist centers in 42 of the 50 states.[2] These range from lay associations to converted single-family homes tucked away in suburban neighborhoods, to full-service temples serving large overseas populations living in major metropolitan areas, to meditation centers, monasteries, and nunneries with impressive architectural

---

[1] *Asian and Pacific Presence: Harmony in Faith*, a 2001 study developed by the Committee on Migration of the United States Conference of Catholic Bishops (USCCB), 9.

[2] A definitive enumeration remains a desideratum. Carol A. Mortland's *Cambodian Buddhism in the United States* (Albany: State University of New York Press, 2017) cites a 2011 report identifying 109 Khmer temples (p. 113); the "Lao Temple Directory in USA" maintained online by Wat Lao Buddhavong in Catlett, Virginia, reports 133 Lao temples in 2023; and our own research findings (see note 4) have determined there were 408 Vietnamese Buddhist centers in America as of 2021.

footprints found in sparsely populated rural settings for short- and long-term retreats. In addition, there are three monasteries and 396 "local practice communities" in 48 of the 50 states modeled in the "Plum Village tradition" established in southern France by the late Thích Nhất Hạnh (1926–2022), the most widely recognized Vietnamese monk in America, whose Order of Interbeing (Tiếp Hiện), an international organization embracing an ethnically diverse community of laity, monks, and nuns, is now a flourishing global sangha.[3] Assuming our data are accurate, Vietnamese Americans now constitute the single largest population group in Buddhist America today.[4]

Of the 2.2 million Americans of Vietnamese ancestry, approximately half are from overseas and consist of political refugees, asylees, and family reunification sponsorships. The other half are American-born Vietnamese who are fluent in English, have no direct memories of war and communism, and know of Vietnam only through stories and culture. These children and grandchildren of the inaugural settlers are joined by transmigrants who travel with ease back and forth to live and work in both nations. Following the normalization of relations in 1995, the United States eventually stopped accepting former political detainees still living in Vietnam for admission. Since then, Vietnamese émigrés have gradually transitioned from refugees into immigrants and transmigrants. Given that US state department officials continue to press for progress on religious freedom and human rights as a necessary condition for continued improvement in bilateral relations, the study of Vietnamese Buddhism is of particular importance today since, at present, there is little understanding of how Southeast Asian overseas Buddhist communities in America pass from the diasporic logic of the refugee to a new era of transnational actors engaged in religious diplomacy and trans-Pacific rapprochement.[5]

STUDIES OF VIETNAMESE BUDDHISM IN AMERICA

The study of Vietnamese Buddhism in America is situated at the crossroads of three academic discussions: (1) immigrant religions establishing ethnic congregations

---

[3] See *The Mindfulness Bell* sangha directory, https://www.parallax.org/mindfulnessbell/sangha-directory/.

[4] Our research for this chapter was conducted exclusively in the Vietnamese language over a four-month period (December 2020–March 2021) by my research assistant Duong Preciado via website survey, Facebook Messenger, and voice and video contact. To enumerate the total number of Vietnamese Buddhist centers in the United States, we correlated our findings with two earlier efforts aiming at a comprehensive count: Le Huu Do's *Sounds of the Bamboo Forest* which reports a total of 204 as 2003, and Quang Minh Thich's 2007 dissertation on "Vietnamese Buddhism in America" which provided us with data for the years 2000 and 2005. These two sources were consolidated into a single list and cross-referenced against the temples identified in our survey.

[5] Office of International Religious Freedom, US Department of State, *Vietnam 2021 International Religious Freedom Report*, 22. The report is accessible online via the US State Department at: https://www.state.gov/reports/2021-report-on-international-religious-freedom/vietnam/.

comprising transnational kinship groups; (2) social, cultural, and racial dimensions of Asian American religions; and (3) modernist and globalized formations of Buddhism. Their success and impressive numbers notwithstanding, Vietnamese Buddhists have yet to figure prominently in mainstream accounts of Buddhism or in scholarly discussions of Buddhism in America.[6] This, in spite of the fact that Vietnamese Americans are among the most documented populations in the nation, indicates a shortfall in the scholarship on US religious history and Asian American religions. Some scholars attribute this to a lingering Marxist orientation or "secular bias" in Asian American studies that, until recently, regarded religion as "ephemeral in nature" and easily dismissed as a mere "cultural relic" of immigrant nostalgia.[7] Others have called attention to the "overdocumentation" of Vietnamese refugees through mainstream US narratives focused on the memory of war and how this effectively elides the complexity of Vietnamese American religious life today.[8] Whatever the case may be, Vietnamese Buddhism remains persistently under-documented in our studies of Buddhism in the United States. Though many decades have elapsed since Thích Thiên Ân (1925–1980) arrived in Los Angeles in 1966 to became the first transmitter of Thiền or Vietnamese-styled Zen Buddhism in the US, the publication of a full-length scholarly monograph on the history and development of Vietnamese Buddhism in America remains a desideratum. Journalist Le Huu Do's 2003 self-published directory, entitled *Sounds of the Bamboo Forest: Buddhist Churches of America in the Vietnamese Tradition*, is the only documentary history, thus far, to attempt coverage of the first three decades of this development. The anecdotal and qualitative data Do has painstakingly gathered is historically significant in that it is the first attempt at a state-by-state survey documenting the activities, facilities, and leaders of every then known Vietnamese Buddhist temple in the US; however, a lack of critical analysis and methodological rigor limits its value. Quang Minh Thich's landmark 2007 dissertation on "Vietnamese Buddhism in America" is the first attempt at a formal academic study of the history and development of the South Vietnamese diaspora and, as such, remains an indispensable resource nearly two decades on.[9] Apart from these pioneering efforts, what has emerged over the past half century is a gradual and uneven development of scholarly attention devoted to the study of Vietnamese Buddhism in the United States that has both contributed to and disrupted the metanarrative about Buddhism in America, one that cleaves along a familiar, if problematic, distinction between "traditional," "ethnic," and "immigrant" Buddhist communities and "modern," "white," or "convert" Buddhist practitioners.

---

[6] Truitt 2021, 4.
[7] Discussed in Yoo 1999, 8–9 and Kim 2020, 20–21.
[8] Both Khúc 2020, 123–124 and Espiritu 2006 address this lingering problem.
[9] Quang Minh Thich's Florida State University dissertation builds on and updates the data reported by Do in *Sounds of the Bamboo Forest* through the year 2005, but its methodological approach for collecting, analyzing, and reporting data is similarly vague and unstated.

Early scholarship on the study of Vietnamese Buddhism in America shows a tendency to conflate "ethnicity" with the transmission of "traditional Buddhism" in one of two ways. On the one hand, Vietnamese Buddhists are portrayed as regressive in their attempts to transplant what is characterized as an archaic and obsolete form of Buddhism to America, one that hails from a "vanished time" seemingly untouched by colonialism, war, dislocation, and the acids of modernity and, as such, is irrelevant, not only to successive generations of Vietnamese Americans born in the United States, but to Westerners who, as scholars consistently note, have shown no practical interest in adopting the Vietnamese form of Pure Land Buddhism.[10] The other approach emphasizes the role of immigrant religion as a vehicle for preserving, maintaining, and transmitting the cultural heritage of the homeland to the resettled population in America. In this latter case, examples of acculturation and assimilation are marshalled to show how the traditional Buddhism which the Vietnamese brought to America not only contributes to the stabilization of ethnic identity, but has also proven to be dynamic and resilient in its ability to change and adapt as it responds creatively to the vicissitudes of immigration, displacement, resettlement, and generational succession.[11] The first approach sees the transmission of Vietnamese Buddhism to America as static and in danger of dying out by clinging to an imagined past.[12] The latter approach emphasizes Vietnamese Buddhism's capacity for change, but that change is only accounted for on the American side of the Pacific. In other words, what both of these approaches share is an ahistorical assumption that the Buddhism transmitted to America arrives on our shores prepackaged in an unsullied "traditional" form, obscuring the fact that this trans-Pacific community has been strenuously preoccupied with revitalizing and modernizing Vietnamese Buddhism since at least the 1920s, and doing so under conditions most extraordinary and unpropitious.[13]

The portrayal of Vietnamese Buddhists in America as ethnic sentimentalists or nostalgic custodians of "traditional" Buddhism belies the modernizing forces of institutional reform that were well underway in Vietnam and throughout the broader Buddhist world of South and Southeast Asia during much of the twentieth century.[14] Emphasis in recent scholarship on how contemporary Vietnamese Buddhist identity is constituted is increasingly focused on historically complex processes that are resistant to tidy and totalizing categorizations like ethnicity. Cultural maintenance of

---

[10] See Nguyen and Barber 1998, 141 and 146; and Soucy 2017a, 22.

[11] Studies like Do and Khúc 2009 often invoke a widely used theoretical framework in Asian American Studies for identifying acculturation, assimiliation, and adaptation strategies among Asian immigrant communities.

[12] This cautionary critique of Vietnamese Buddhism in America as nostalgic and fossilized was first advanced by Nguyen and Barbar 1998, 145–146.

[13] Elise Anne DeVito 2007 traces the origins of the institutional and conceptual roots of Vietnam's modern Buddhist revival known as Chấn Hưng Phật Giáo to the influence of the Chinese Buddhist reformer Taixu.

[14] The first to draw attention to the problems which an "ethnic Buddhist" or "traditional Buddhist" analytical frame creates in the study of modern Vietnamese Buddhism is Soucy 2017a, 25.

ethnic identity was not the aim of Vietnam's Buddhist revival movement during the past century; rather, the focus was on reorienting Pure Land Buddhism's traditional soteriological emphasis on a world apart from the human realm of saṃsāric existence toward embracing *Nhân Gian Phật Giáo*, or a "Buddhism for this world."[15] Grappling with a dizzying surfeit of challenges—including Western imperialism, nationalist independence movements, communist insurgency, lay- and monastic-led political activism, the establishment of monastic colleges, the formation of a national Buddhist congress, an emergent pan-Buddhist consciousness through participation in internationalized networks of Buddhist clergy, the Buddhist Youth Family Movement and various social welfare projects, and rural and agricultural development programs—Buddhist revivalists continued to remain engaged in such efforts right up through the period when a new geopolitical territorial status was imposed on the region making it the de facto frontier of the "hot" Cold War following the collapse of French colonialism and the partitioning of Vietnam in 1954.

There is growing acknowledgment among scholars today that the very presence of Vietnamese Buddhists in the United States is inextricably bound up in America's rise to global power as the Cold War defender of democracy in the free world. The fact that US policymakers and counter-intelligence operatives worked to "instrumentalize" the Buddhism of South and Southeast Asia into an anti-communist asset during the 1950s and 1960s[16] means that the advent of Vietnamese Buddhism in America from the 1970s onward "is not an ethnic story that can be told apart from US empire" but is a narrative inseparably linked to US foreign policy and its failure to fully contain the spread of communism in Southeast Asia.[17] By the mid-1960s and early 1970s, with a catastrophic proxy war underway, propping up the Soviet Bloc–backed Việt Cộng in the north against the US-backed premiership of the staunchly pro-Catholic regime of Ngô Đình Diệm (r. 1955–1963) in the south, Western Buddhist scholars began to describe the scene as a *Buddhism in Transition* while journalists reported on "a faith in flames."[18] Prominent Vietnamese Buddhist leaders like Thích Nhất Hạnh took a more optimistic view by situating these developments in the waxing light of a "renaissance of Buddhism in Southeast Asia" that had already been well underway in the years leading up to Vietnam's double occupation as a French colony overtaken by the Japanese during the Second World War.[19] What recent scholarship has made clear is that a Buddhism forged in the unraveling "crucible of colonialism" cannot, in its diasporic context, be meaningfully framed by any stretch of the imagination as "traditional."[20] The array of Vietnamese

---

[15] DeVido 2007, 252 and DeVido 2009, 414.

[16] For the instrumentalization of Buddhism as a Cold War asset see Ford 2017, 41.

[17] Like Soucy 2017a, Allison J. Truitt sees reliance on an ethnic model as problematic and apolitical and insists on utilizing an analytical framework that centers racialization and US imperialism during the Cold War. See Truitt 2021, 11.

[18] This is the title of Swearer's 1970 monograph. Citation is from Schecter 1967, xi.

[19] Discussed in Nhat Hanh 1967, 40–41.

[20] Soucy 2017a, 24.

Buddhist communities and institutions flourishing in America today therefore reflect, to varying degrees, an ongoing engagement with the enduring legacy of these and other global and transnational forces.

Vietnamese Compatriot Buddhists: A New Direction

In her recent monograph *Pure Land in the Making: Vietnamese Buddhism in the US Gulf South* (2021), Allison J. Truitt takes the study of Vietnamese Buddhism in America in a promising new direction by locating religious institutions within a nexus of generational and geographical contexts that emphasize the mediating role they play between ancestors and descendants and between remembrance of the homeland and aspirations in the land of resettlement. Careful analytical attention to this dynamic compels her to see Vietnamese temples not only as religious centers for propagating the Dharma, but also as venues for legitimizing broader political and historical concerns for engaging conceptions of freedom and liberation that are decidedly more this-worldly in orientation:

> Temples are not only formal spaces of worship. They are also sites of sociability and memory where practitioners make sense of their place in history and reclaim their dignity as they reckon with the legacies of the Cold War and racial segregation. They are also sites where practitioners demonstrate fidelity to US ideals, in how they sometimes invoke "freedom" in ways more akin to gratitude for having escaped oppression at the hands of a communist government and for having adapted to US market-based liberalism, than to Buddhist ideals of liberation ... making these temples political sites for representing the unsettled past of what Americans call the Vietnam War.[21]

While the notion that migrant temples are not merely ceremonial places of worship is not new, this recognition of the temple as a valid space for doing the hard work of reckoning with the legacies of US empire, war, and refugee resettlement transforms our understanding of the role that Buddhist centers play in the lives of Vietnamese Americans today. Previous scholarship reliant on the ethnic model approach casts the temple as a site of cultural preservation that strives to meet the spiritual and mundane needs of the community as they arise.[22] While this is certainly true of most immigrant-based religious centers, it fails to adequately foreground and contextualize the political and historical forces that created the need for resettlement in the first place. America's Vietnamese Buddhist temples are not simply cultural repositories for installing, preserving, and

---

[21] Truitt 2021, 5.
[22] Representative of this approach is Huynh 2000, 165. See also Do and Khúc 2009, 133–134.

transmitting the religious tradition that refugees and immigrants brought with them, as the familiar "Baggage Buddhism" ethnic model suggests.[23] Vietnamese temples can also function as collective spaces of worship that foster what Truitt has identified as "compatriot Buddhists" (đồng hương Phật tử), a distinctive discourse of obligation and mutual aid for soliciting participation from people who share a common diasporic identity but may not explicitly self-identify as Buddhist.[24] Compatriot Buddhists build on what Phuong Tran Nguyen calls "refugee nationalism"—the articulation of a sense of belonging while reclaiming fidelity to the memory of a pre-revolutionary ancestral homeland—by sanctifying the symbols and anthems of the old US-backed regime within a Buddhist milieux.[25]

The symbols that mark these transnational entanglements can be easily observed at temples like Chùa Di Lặc, located in the heart of San José's Little Saigon business district. Each spring, Chùa Di Lặc celebrates Phật Đản, the birth of the Buddha, and, like many Vietnamese Buddhist temples across the United States, they have given new meaning and purpose to the annual staging of this festival in its American context. The opening ceremony typically features young adults and children smartly dressed in áo dài or in the familiar ceremonial blue-gray lay temple attire (áo tràng lam), carrying aloft a figure of the newborn baby Buddha (Phật sơ sinh) who stands upright with one hand pointing down to the earth and the other extended up with a finger pointing to the sky. Led in procession by the Venerable Thích Pháp Lưu, the temple's founding abbot, participants strike a hand gong (chiêng) and march in a solemn procession, chanting "Nam Mô Bổn Sư Thích Ca Mâu Ni Phật" ("Praise to Shakyamuni Buddha"), with flag bearers who carry, shoulder-to-shoulder, the US flag, the Vietnamese Freedom and Heritage flag—a bright yellow flag with three red stripes that keeps alive the memory of the old Republic of Vietnam (RVN) or South Vietnam—and the international Buddhist flag. The procession through temple grounds terminates at a raised platform where monks, dressed in saffron-colored robes, some overlayed with a gossamer ceremonial robe of bright red embroidered with gold-threaded panels, gather around a flower-bedecked image of the newborn baby Buddha, while nearby a bouquet of "Happy Birthday" balloons billow in the wind. Before dignitaries speak, the US flag is elevated prominently above the others as a woman sings "The Star-Spangled Banner," flanked by her cohorts dressed resplendently in colorful áo dài who respectfully extend their right hands to cover their hearts. Then the yellow RVN flag is raised above the others and the women on stage proudly sing "Tiếng Gọi Công Dân" ("Call to the Citizens"), the "Free Vietnam" anthem cherished by anti-communist Vietnamese expatriates. Finally, the international Buddhist flag is hoisted above the others, and to it is sung an anthem to Vietnamese Buddhism ("Phật Giáo Việt Nam"). The song celebrates Vietnamese Buddhism as the

---

[23] For a discussion of this typology see Nattier 1998, 189–190.
[24] Truitt 2021, 42.
[25] Although the scope of Phuong Tran Nguyen's 2017 engaging study *Becoming Refugee America* is focused on the political dynamics of Little Saigon, his notion of "refugee nationalism" can also be observed at Vietnamese Buddhist temples across the United States.

great unifier of the three main regions of the nation and calls upon the people to follow the example of Shakyamuni to liberate sentient beings by joining hands together in the form of a lotus and imbue Vietnam with Buddhism in all directions.

Public displays like these, affirming fidelity to the United States with an unwavering commitment to an anti-communist identity in solidarity with fellow Buddhists across the ancestral homeland, signals not so much a refusal to assimilate as it does a resilience-based mode of adaptation that strategically utilizes the Buddhist temple for maintaining allegiance to a South Vietnamese geopolitical identity while championing America as "the arbiter of freedom for Vietnamese people abroad and domestically."[26] Anthropologist Allison J. Truitt, who has been studying and writing about the Vietnamese Buddhist communities in the southern Gulf Coast states since 2013, contends that this complex process of grounding diasporic identity in the legitimizing activities of the Buddhist temple "cannot be explained by the category of ethnicity but should instead be framed in terms of racialization" to reveal how Vietnamese Buddhists in America actually understand their identities in relation to political, social, and institutional structures.[27] If we designate events like *Phật Đản* as "ethnic celebrations," the argument goes, then the ritual behavior of parading the newborn Buddha with national flags and anthems might be cavalierly dismissed as a mere staging of refugee fantasies for a triumphant return to a communist-free Vietnam under American protection. In so doing, we would fail to see how lay disciples (*đệ tử*) and their fellow "compatriot Buddhists" (*đồng hương Phật tử*) utilize the *Phật Đản* festival to manage the transgenerational effects of war, displacement, and marginalization while navigating the vicissitudes of US citizenship, immigration status, and generational succession by invoking the legacies of a dual citizenship within a Buddhist idiom. We would also fail to appreciate the fact that while the Cold War ended for most Americans in 1989, there are many Vietnamese, as well as some American veterans, who are still reeling from the lingering traumas and phantoms of the war's effects half a century later.[28]

One might reasonably presume that annual observances like Vesak or *Phật Đản* to commemorate the birth of the Buddha have long been a part of the traditional Vietnamese Buddhist calendar, as the ethnic model would have us believe. In fact, it is not until 1934 that the celebration of Vesak can first be documented in Vietnam.[29] Indeed, it is not until mid-century that Vesak observance is promoted at the national level as a result of Vietnam's participation in the inaugural World Fellowship of Buddhists (WFB) conference held in 1950 in what was then a newly independent Ceylon (Sri Lanka). Thích Tố Liên (1903–1977), who led a delegation of Vietnamese monks to the WFB meeting in Sri Lanka, returned with the international Buddhist flag and raised it for the first time in Vietnam on May 6, 1951, the full moon of Vesak, in the city of

---

[26] Bui 2018, 22.
[27] Truitt 2021, 14.
[28] For more on the long-term consequences of the war in Vietnam see Kwon 2008 and Nguyen 2016.
[29] The first to date Vesak or *Phật Đản* observance in Vietnam is Soucy 2017b, 191, note 8.

Huế where the first nationwide Buddhist congress had convened at Từ Đàm pagoda to form the General Buddhist Association of Vietnam (Tổng Hội Phật Giáo Việt Nam) with the aim of promoting unity among six Buddhist associations from southern, central, and northern Vietnam. The fifty or so delegates gathered at this meeting voted to reorganize the Buddhist sangha, provide religious instruction to lay and youth groups, codify Buddhist religious rites, and abolish superstitions (phế bỏ mê tín dị đoan). At the same time, they formally ratified membership in the WFB and adopted the use of the international Buddhist flag and anthem as a symbol of Vietnamese Buddhism's common cause with the people's desire for nationalist independence.[30]

The international Buddhist flag was the unifying symbol of this rising global profile of Buddhist resolve. As a 1967 US military pamphlet on "The Religions of Vietnam" reports, this was this same flag that an "American ex-Army officer, a Civil War Veteran" had a direct hand in redesigning and standardizing during his visit in 1886 to Ceylon.[31] That veteran, of course, was Colonel Henry Steel Olcott (1832–1907), the first American convert to Buddhism, whose book, *A Buddhist Catechism*, originally published in 1871, is today widely circulated in Vietnamese Buddhist temples across the United States in the form of a bilingual edition (Phật Giáo Vấn Đáp) to serve as an aide and primer for language learners in both Vietnamese and English. It was Olcott who facilitated the globalization of the Buddhist flag's initial adoption at the end of the nineteenth century by introducing it to various world leaders at international gatherings held in Burma (Myanmar), Siam (Thailand), Japan, and India. Half a century later, it was formally adopted as the official flag of Buddhists throughout the world at the First General Conference of the WFB in Ceylon. Indeed, this was the very same flag that the Diệm government, after failing to abolish Vesak as an official holiday in 1957, infamously forbade Buddhists to raise during Vesak celebrations in 1963, citing a regulation dating back to the French colonial period prohibiting the display of nongovernmental flags. At the same time, that ordinance was not invoked when the public was encouraged to display papal flags to celebrate the twenty-fifth anniversary of the ordination of Phêrô Máctinô Ngô Đình Thục (1897–1984), the Catholic archbishop of Huế who also happened to be Diệm's older brother. Such blatant preferential treatment was seen as nepotistic and discriminatory, and it triggered thousands-strong mass protests outside a radio station in Huế where Buddhists had gathered to hear the Vesak Day broadcast.[32] These events were among the catalyzing forces in the subsequent development of Phật giáo dấn thân, what Thích Nhất Hạnh styled in his 1964 publication as Đạo Phật Đi Vào Cuộc Đời ("Buddhism Entering into Society") and transmitted to the West as

---

[30] See discussion in Nhat Hanh 1967, 44.

[31] The flag was first flown in Ceylon in 1885 as an expression of Buddhist solidarity during the Vesak season, while signaling resistance to colonial efforts aimed at imposing Christianity. The military pamphlet misattributes credit for the design of the flag to Olcott (see "The Religions of Vietnam," April 1967, MACV Command Information Pamphlet, p. 11); however, by Olcott's own admission, he was never involved in the actual design of the flag, only in the standardization of its size (see Deegalle 2018).

[32] Roberts 1965, 240.

"Engaged Buddhism."[33] Suppression of the protestors by government security forces resulted in the deaths of nine unarmed demonstrators, a government ban on further protests, and multiple raids on Buddhist monasteries to quash what came to be called the "Buddhist crisis" in which thousands were jailed and hundreds more would die. In solidarity with these protestors, Thích Quảng Đức (1897–1963), a sixty-seven-year old monastic educator and administrator who taught meditation and spent years in meditative seclusion before his involvement with the reformist monks demonstrating in Huế, famously pleaded with Diệm to lift the ban on the Buddhist flag and implement religious equality, before publicly sacrificing himself in the busy streets of Saigon on June 11, 1963—a day widely regarded as a seminal moment for having shocked the consciousness of the world—by setting his seated body aflame while remaining fixed in a meditative posture. This courageous, if desperate, act of compassion would be replicated by at least fifty-seven others who subsequently committed self-immolation. Thousands of students, along with hundreds of South Vietnamese army veterans and widows, began protesting peacefully in the pagodas. Soldiers and peasants took to wearing patches of saffron to demonstrate their support for the Buddhists.[34] The cumulative effect of these demonstrations proved to be a decisive turning point that would eventually culminate in the arrest and assassination of Diệm. Washed in the flaming blood of martyrs, the flag which an American ex-Army officer and Civil War veteran helped design and popularize as a global emblem of Buddhist unity had now been transformed into a powerful symbol of Buddhist solidarity and the free exercise of religion.

Today, many Vietnamese Buddhist temples across America display the international Buddhist flag as an adjacent symbol of "compatriot Buddhist" festival regalia. The earliest account we have of its first appearance in the United States is by Rick Fields, who observed it being paraded through the streets of Los Angeles in 1986 to commemorate the 2,530th year since the birth of Shakyamuni Buddha by members of the Vietnamese Buddhist Temple also known as Chùa Việt-Nam, the first and historically most important Vietnamese Buddhist center in the United States. The procession was led by the Venerable Thích Mãn Giác (1929–2006), formerly the Supreme Patriarch of Vietnamese Buddhism in America. Alongside the international Buddhist flag were three others, cheek by jowl: the US flag, the South Vietnam RVN flag, and the United Nations flag. These were followed in procession by a Vietnamese brass band and members of the Buddhist youth group *Long Hòa*, an organization modeled after the Boy Scouts and Girl Scouts of America, bearing a palanquin with a large incense burner and an oil painting depicting Thích Quảng Đức, his robes aflame. Multilingual banners undulating in the wind proclaimed:

---

[33] Use of the term "Engaged" to describe a form of Buddhism that is more "this worldly" in orientation was likely an homage to Jean-Paul Sartre's familiar concept of "littérature engage," as French existentialism was *de rigueur* among Vietnamese intellectuals, including Thích Nhất Hạnh, during this period. See DeVido 2009, 436–439.

[34] These firsthand accounts are documented in Hope 1970, 160.

There Is No Religious Freedom in Vietnam.
Long Live the Sacrificial Spirit of the Venerable Thích Quảng Đức.
Long Live World Buddhism.
Unity Is Strength.
950 Million Buddhists All Over the World United with Other Religions to Serve World Peace.[35]

While the Vietnamese Buddhist community of southern California was celebrating *Phật Đản* with a jubilant parade and lively political demonstration in the streets of Los Angeles, some 330 miles north the Venerable Sư Bà Đàm Lựu (1932–1999) was earnestly collecting recyclables in the streets of San José to finance the construction of the first Vietnamese Buddhist nunnery in the United States. Đàm Lựu was among the hundreds of thousands of "boat people" who fled Vietnam in the late 1970s in the hopes that a neighboring country would grant them political asylum. After a harrowing six-day journey overseas, she and 200 others landed in a squalid refugee camp in Kuching, Sarawak (Malaysia), where more than a year passed before she was finally accepted for resettlement in the United States. In the Vesak season of 1980, her sponsor, Thích Thanh Cát, the abbot of Chùa Giác Minh in East Palo Alto, assigned her to the San José area, where she founded a temple in a modest 1,424-square-foot residential rental home and rededicated it as Chùa Đức Viên ("Perfect Virtue Temple")—a name that, in part, pays homage to the memory of Thích Quảng Đức ("Bright Clear Virtue Son of Shakya"). She converted the living room into a Buddha Hall (*Phật Điện*) and transformed the backyard into a convivial gathering space for dining, Dharma talks, and Vietnamese language classes for children. She oversaw the printing and distribution of sūtras and produced copies of her Dharma talks on tapes and CDs, which were freely given to other temples and circulated in Southeast Asian refugee camps. These activities attracted the interest and support of a growing number of lay disciples (*đệ tử*) and "compatriot Buddhists" (*đồng hương Phật tử*) so that the burgeoning community rapidly outgrew its original home and, in 1985, was able to relocate to a much larger 9,000-square-foot site several blocks south of the central retail district that would eventually be designated by the City of San José as "Little Saigon." Over a ten-year period, Đàm Lựu diligently collected discarded recyclables and managed to accumulate a remarkable sum of $120,000 that was put toward the $400,000 down payment for the new site, while some 3,000 donors from throughout the Bay Area contributed the balance.[36]

---

[35] Rick Fields's account of "Los Angeles Vesak Day" appears in an undated and unpaginated pamphlet published by Chùa Việt-Nam entitled *Vietnamese Buddhist Temple in Los Angeles*. It was later reprinted in Tweed and Prothero 1999, 318–319. This same account can also be found in the concluding pages of Field's *Taking Refuge in L.A.: Life in a Buddhist Temple* (1987) with a photo of the parade by Don Farber on p. 37.

[36] Details concerning the purchase and donor information are from Jim Dickey's feature article, "A Special Buddhist Temple: A Spiritual Haven on a Busy S.J. Street," *San Jose Mercury News (CA)*, August 24, 1993, p. 1B.

Construction of the one-million-dollar temple was completed a decade later and features a striking modern tiled roof, incorporating traditional upswept eaves capped with dragons (rồng) in a Sino-Vietnamese style, with a prominent *dharmacakra* (wheel of dharma) motif atop the ridge of the gabled roof. Past the central gate, the main entrance to the temple is flanked by two guardian deities or Dharma Protectors (Vi Đà). A large statue of A Di Đà Phật (Amitābha Buddha) stands in front of the main entrance as if beckoning devotees to his paradise. Placed in front of the Buddha image is an impressive Tiangong censor in the open air of the courtyard with two celestial dragons rising up on either side, grasping pearls (signifying good fortune). It attracts visitors throughout the day who pause to leave incense after paying their respects to A Di Đà Phật, or else snap selfies and post them online.

At ground level nearby is a raised physical map of Vietnam carved into a large slab of black granite, with the names of dozens of cities inscribed in gold lettering. Significantly, the current name of the capital has been completely obliterated, and below the defacement someone has scratched the old capital name "Saigon" onto the stone. An inscription at the top of the map is taken from a poem attributed to General Lý Thường Kiệt (1019–1105), celebrating the well-known story of Thánh Gióng, the legendary giant boy revered for protecting Vietnam from enemy invasion. An image of Thánh Gióng, riding his famous iron horse and wielding his staff like a mighty sword, is etched into the granite along with these words written in Sino-Vietnamese:

Nam quốc sơn hà nam đế cư
Tiệt nhiên định phận tại thiên thư
Như hà nghịch lỗ lai xâm phạm
Nhữ đẳng hành khan thủ bại hư.

Over Mountains and Rivers of the South, reigns the Southern Emperor
who knows the fate of what is written in the Book of Heaven
Do those barbarians dare to invade our land?
Beware intruders! You will, without pity, be annihilated.[37]

One might be forgiven for seeing nothing more in this monument stone than an effort aimed at paying tribute to a popular Vietnamese folk hero who is here being invoked, perhaps, to protect the temple from malevolent forces and thus perform a similar function as the Dharma Protectors guarding the main entry or the aquatic dragons rising from the corners of the temple roof. But it is also possible to see in this a concerted effort to reclaim the homeland by linking the legendary figure most famous for protecting and defending the nation against foreign occupation with a modern map of Vietnam that conspicuously effaces "Ho Chi Minh City" as the name of the capital while simultaneously restoring it to "Saigon," the capital of ancestral memory so firmly fixed at the center of the South Vietnamese diasporic exile imaginary. This is a vivid reminder of

---

[37] Author's translation in consultation with Duong Preciado.

how Buddhist spaces like the temple grounds of a nunnery are leveraged to protect ancestral time and space by legitimizing anti-communist sentiment and opposition to the socialist republic of Vietnam as a capstone legacy of the community's enduring pre-revolutionary identity. It can also be read as an olive branch extended to the more extremist elements in the community who, on several occasions, have staged raucous anti-communist demonstrations on the temple's grounds.

On one such occasion, during the Vesak season of 1998, protestors started gathering outside Chùa Đức Viên to oppose Đàm Lưu's decision to host a respected monk visiting from Vietnam. The ninety-three-year old Venerable Thích Trí Dũng (1906–2001) was in the United States to participate in *Phật Đản* celebrations in southern California, where he was warmly greeted by high-ranking Buddhist leaders and followers. However, when word spread that he was coming to San José to visit Đức Viên for an overnight stay, a local Vietnamese radio station and magazine provoked a political storm by insinuating that the venerable monk, who was originally from northern Vietnam, was a patsy for the communist government, a known operative with ties to the Việt Cộng during the war, and a recipient of the Second-Class Anti-American Resistance Medal by the Communist Party of Vietnam (CPV). Rumors began to spread that the head abbess Đàm Lưu was herself a "wicked communist" cleverly disguised as a Buddhist nun.[38] This provoked confusion and outrage in the community, and some 150 protestors descended upon the temple, yelling at the nuns through bullhorns, harassing temple visitors, displaying banners warning: Đừng nghe những gì cộng sản nói. Hãy nhìn kỹ những gì Cộng Sản làm ("Don't listen to what the communists say. Look at what the communists do"), and waving placards accusing Đức Viên of being a covert spy center for the CPV. When they broke into the nuns' living quarters and started pounding on doors, the nuns became frightened and called the police. Six protestors were arrested. Among those protesting were donors who had helped finance the construction of the temple. They were angry when they learned from media reports that the temple was harboring a "communist sympathizer" who was "disguised as a religious person."[39] Đàm Lưu encouraged the nuns to treat protestors with care and respect: "No matter how bad their deeds may be," she explained, "they still have Buddha nature.... They may be protesting out of ignorance or because they were given biased information. In any case, they should not be blamed for what they are doing. The real troublemakers are greed, anger, and ignorance—not human beings."[40]

After two weeks of sustained protesting, leaders sought a "mutual agreement" with the nuns and finally agreed to call off the protest if three conditions were met: (1) henceforth, the temple shall hang the South Vietnam flag on all major holidays; (2) the head nun Đàm Lưu must state she is anti-communist; and (3) anti-communist community leaders will be informed in advance of all future special visitors to the temple. In response, Đàm

---

[38] For a fuller account of the character assassination targeting Sư Bà Đàm Lưu and her magnanimous response see Duc 2000, 117–119.

[39] Duc 2000, 117.

[40] Duc 2000, 118.

Lưu agreed to hang the flag as requested and publicly declared: "I am not a communist. I am a refugee just like hundreds of thousands of others."[41] Two days later, the entire monastic community of northern California issued a joint statement supporting Đàm Lưu, and the demonstrators called off their protest.[42]

Had Đàm Lưu not been undergoing chemotherapy treatments for cancer at the time, she might have had the strength to tell them about her own days as a demonstrator for freedom and democracy when she and other monastics protested Diệm's unjust treatment of the Buddhist community back in 1963, following Thích Quảng Đức's self-immolation. She was among the thousands of monastics who were rounded up and jailed when the government cracked down on Buddhist monastics.[43] Đàm Lưu's health, however, continued to decline, and she died the following year. Today a spirit altar adjacent to the main worship hall displays a framed photograph of Đàm Lưu, before which is placed a glass display box containing her robes and alms bowl, flanked on either side with offerings of orchids and fresh fruit. Behind her is an incense memory board (*khung thờ hương linh*) of photographs of deceased monastics who were important teachers in her life; among these is an arresting image of Thích Quảng Đức, not as a monk in flames but as a haloed bodhisattva (Bồ Tát) evoking a new Pure Land that mingles and intertwines notions of civil liberty with spiritual liberation.

FUTURE STUDIES: THE INTERSECTION OF BLACK BUDDHISM AND THE VIETNAM WAR

When Đàm Lưu instructed her nuns to adopt a compassionate stance toward the angry protestors storming their temple in 1998, her argument was premised on the same logic Thích Nhất Hạnh used in 1965 when he wrote an open letter to the Rev. Dr. Martin Luther King, Jr., explaining that the self-immolations of Buddhists in Vietnam were not "acts of suicide" or "self-destruction" as characterized by the media, but, in fact, constituted an "act of self-sacrifice for the sake of others." He drew a parallel to the courageous act of the Buddha in a former life celebrated in the well-known Jātaka story of the hungry lioness in which he sacrifices himself for the benefit of others. "The enemies are not man," he explained to Dr. King:

> They are intolerance, fanaticism, dictatorship, cupidity, hatred, and discrimination which lie in the heart of man. I also believe with all my being that the struggle for equality and freedom you lead in Birmingham, Alabama, is not really aimed at the

---

[41] "Monk's Visit Touches Off Temple Siege," *San Jose Mercury News (CA)*, June 7, 1998, p. 5F. See also Stacy Finz's report in the *San Francisco Chronicle*, "New Protest at Buddhist Temple: Vietnamese Monk's Visit to San Jose Provokes Anger," May 20, 1998, A19.

[42] Duc 2000, 119.

[43] Duc 2000, 106.

whites but only at intolerance, hatred, and discrimination. These are the real enemies of man—not man himself.[44]

By linking the Buddhist struggle in Vietnam with the civil rights movement in America and acknowledging that the cause of true justice and liberation may ultimately demand the sacrifice of one's life for the greater good, Thích Nhất Hạnh opened a moral pathway to fostering a powerful sense of solidarity between the Buddhists of Vietnam and African Americans and, more broadly, with oppressed people of color everywhere in the world. This link remains one of the most momentous and underexamined outcomes to mark the transformation of Buddhism in American life, and it points to some promising new directions our future studies might take by examining the advent of Vietnamese Buddhism in the United States through a broader racialized lens.

A common motif threading its way through several memoirs of the first generation of Black Americans to embrace Buddhism is how their memory of the war in Vietnam is inextricably bound up in their decision to formally take refuge in the Three Jewels.[45] In *Meeting Faith*, Faith Adiele describes her experience as a *maechi* (Buddhist nun) in Thailand and recalls an early memory of seeing a black-and-white image of a Buddhist monk setting himself ablaze while seated in meditation. "Am I only a toddler . . . watching Vietnam's Buddhist crisis . . . as it unfolds on American television screens?" she wonders, "Or is this years later, perhaps a war documentary with footage of Thich Quang Duc . . . who performed the first self-immolation the year of my birth?"[46] In *Dreaming Me*, Jan Willis, one of the earliest American scholar-practitioners of Tibetan Buddhism, recalls the moment when her interest in Buddhism, which was awakened during her freshman year at Cornell University, intersected with her experience of marching in Dr. King's 1963 direct-action campaign in Birmingham:

> Every night on the evening news, we watched as Buddhist monks and nuns set fire to themselves, with prayers for peace on their lips. I wondered how those peace-loving people could continue to endure the constant terrors of air and chemical warfare, the relentless bombing assaults, the day-to-day hell—and still hold on to loving-kindness and peace. In Birmingham, we civil rights marchers had been given instructions on how to meet violence without striking back, but I found it hard to hold my anger in check. Because of the war and the way Vietnamese Buddhists were dealing with it, my interests gradually turned to Buddhism. I became determined to learn more about it.[47]

---

[44] Nhat Hanh 1967, 107.

[45] I draw here on Carolyn M. Jones Medine's (2019) fascinating survey of memoirs from African American Buddhist practitioners in "'Beyond Vietnam': Martin Luther King, Jr., Thích Nhất Hạnh, and the Confluence of Black and Engaged Buddhism in the Vietnam War," 119–141.

[46] Adiele 2005, 196.

[47] Willis 2001, 83.

The memory of how such powerful images ignited an interest in Buddhism is also a story of cross-cultural mimesis. Just as America's Black citizens found common cause with Vietnamese Buddhist monks and nuns in their unwavering fidelity to nonviolent methods of peaceful protest while enduring the terrors of violence perpetrated by local police in the streets of Saigon, so too did these same monks and nuns look to emulate African Americans in their struggle for freedom and civil rights as they contended with riot police in the streets of Birmingham. American peace activists doing fieldwork in Vietnam in 1963 interviewed monastic leaders directly involved in the demonstrations and were informed that their peaceful protests were not only fortified by a strict adherence to their monastic vows and training as Buddhists, but that they found inspiration in the examples of Mahatma Gandhi and "the American Negroes' silent protest by sitdown" which they had learned about in news stories and black-and-white images.[48] They were referring to Dr. King, an ardent student of the teachings of Gandhi, and his direct-action campaign in Birmingham, which included a series of marches and sit-ins at lunch counters in April 1963. Two months later, a cadre of several hundred Buddhist monks and nuns marched through the streets of Saigon, and one of them, Thích Quảng Đức, famously staged his own "sit-in." Explaining this convergence in their respective movements, one unnamed monk declared: "Everything in this world has relations—it is the law of interdependent causes."[49]

Scholars are just beginning to reckon with the implications of the mimetic effect of these racialized correspondences that intersect the civil rights movement with the war in Vietnam.[50] Some even see in this convergence an expansion of Dr. King's global vision for "the Beloved Community," drawing Buddhists and Christians into a shared moral realm for bringing about a new "Pure Land" or "Promised Land" overflowing, not with milk and honey, but with Buddhist *karuṇā* (compassion) and Christian *agape* (unconditional love).[51] The aspiration to build on this legacy has already begun to materialize

---

[48] Hope 1970, 165.

[49] Hope 1970, 165.

[50] In addition to Medine (2019), Sharon Luk investigates the encounters between the first generation of engaged Buddhists in Vietnam and their Black liberation theology cohorts in the United States from 1965 to 1968 in "'Sea of Fire': A Buddhist Pedagogy of Dying and Black Encounters Across Two Waves," *Souls: A Critical Journal of Black Politics, Culture, and Society* 20, no. 3 (2018): 267–288. Judy Tzu-Chun Wu's study of Robert S. Browne, an African American economist who served as a development program officer and economic aid advisor in Cambodia and Vietnam and subsequently became a leader in the antiwar movement, provides an important historical narrative for foregrounding the rise of this "internationalist" form of social and political activism that spanned the globe during this period. See Wu's *Radicals on the Road: Internationalism, Orientalism, and Feminism during the Vietnam Era* (Ithaca: Cornell University Press, 2013).

[51] *Agape* is defined in this context as "unconditional love" based on a 1957 address Dr. King delivered at the General Assembly of the National Council of Churches in St. Louis, in which he described *agape* as "an overflowing love which seeks nothing in return." It means, he further explained, "loving the person who does the evil deed while hating the deed that the person does." A transcript of King's speech is available at: https://kinginstitute.stanford.edu/king-papers/documents/christian-way-life-human-relations-address-delivered-general-assembly-national.

at Magnolia Grove Monastery in Batesville, Mississippi. Just sixty-one miles south of the site where Dr. King was assassinated, this Buddhist meditation practice center dedicated the "Beloved Community Garden" on September 27, 2015, which commemorates the first time Thích Nhất Hạnh and Dr. King met in 1966 with a monumental statue honoring "these two bodhisattvas."[52]

As Duncan Ryūken Williams's groundbreaking history *American Sutra* (2019) reveals, the story behind the mass incarceration of Japanese Americans during World War II is the story of how "American Buddhism" was forged in the crucible of war in defense of religious freedom. The advent of Vietnamese Buddhism in America could very well be the second unwritten volume of that story. Just as people of Japanese ancestry were forcibly relocated and interned in camps, so were people of Vietnamese ancestry forced to flee their homes for resettlement camps, some even passing through the very same camps previously inhabited by Japanese American Buddhists. One of those camps was Fort Chaffee in Arkansas where, in the spring of 1975, when the first wave of refugees began arriving, they were met by Dr. Thích Thiên Ân, founder of the International Buddhist Mediation Center in Los Angeles (IBMC), and his assistant Thích Tịnh Từ, who were assigned to work as Buddhist chaplains at the military base. Drawing on an especially pertinent discourse in which the Buddha cautions against taking refuge in anyone or anything other than one's own self after having gone to "the island of Dharma" for refuge, the monks guided men, women, and children into formally taking the Three Refuges and Five Precepts (*Quy y Tam Bảo, Ngũ Giới*). By the time the camp closed at the end of 1975, more than ten thousand people had departed as "official Buddhists" (*Phật tử chính thức*).[53] During this same period, Thích Thiên Ân also assisted in the effort to process refugees arriving at Camp Pendleton in California, where the US Marines Corps had erected a tent city for some 50,000 people. Among those assisting the refugees was an inaugural group of American Buddhist monks and nuns whom Thích Thiên Ân had ordained the previous year, including Venerable Thích Ân Đức (ca. 1940–2013), better known as "Bhante" Suhita Dharma Ācāriya—the first African American ordained as a Buddhist monk. Bhante would later go on to serve as vice abbot of IBMC and pioneer the first Black, Indigenous, and People of Color (BIPOC) meditation retreats at Dharma centers across the United States before his death, introducing a new generation of practitioners to "sit-ins" that point to the next chapter in the unfolding legacy of Vietnamese Buddhism's American frontier and its heirs to the Dharma of liberation.

---

[52] Both Thích Nhất Hạnh and Dr. King are today recognized as "lineage holders" in what Josiah Royce identified as the "Beloved Community" in *The Problem of Christianity* (1913). Marc Andrus (2021) explores how Thích Nhất Hạnh, through his friendship with Dr. King, helped universalize the expansion of King's vision of spiritual unity and racial equality by becoming the first Buddhist proponent of the Beloved Community. For an account of the dedication ceremony see: "When Giants Meet: Dedication of the Beloved Community Garden at Magnolia Grove Monastery" by Peggy Rowe-Ward and Sister Peace, June 2016, https://www.parallax.org/mindfulnessbell/article/when-giants-meet/.

[53] See Truitt 2021, 3–4 and 155.

References

Adiele, Faith. 2005. *Meeting Faith: An Inward Odyssey*. New York and London: W. W. Norton.

Andrus, Marc. 2021. *Brothers in the Beloved Community: The Friendship of Thich Nhat Hanh and Martin Luther King, Jr.* Berkeley, CA: Parallax Press.

Bui, Long T. 2018. *Returns of War: South Vietnam and the Price of Refugee Memory*. New York: New York University Press.

Dang, Thuy Vo. 2005. "The Cultural Work of Anticommunism in the San Diego Vietnamese American Community." *Amerasia Journal* 31, no. 2: 66–86.

Deegalle, Mahinda. 2018. "Internationalization of Vesak." In *Vesak, Peace and Harmony: Thinking of Buddhist Heritage*, edited by Mahinda Deegalle. Kandy, Sri Lanka: Research Center for Buddhist Studies, chap. 1, Kindle edition, n.p.

DeVido, Elise Anne. 2007. "'Buddhist for This World': The Buddhist Revival of Vietnam, 1920 to 1951, and Its Legacy." *Modernity and Re-enchantment: Religion in Post-revolutionary Vietnam*, edited by Philip Taylor, 250–296. Singapore: Institute of Southeast Asian Studies.

DeVido, Elise Anne. 2009. "The Influence of Chinese Master Taixu on Buddhism in Vietnam." *Journal of Global Buddhism* 10: 413–458.

Dickey, Jim. 1993. "Special Buddhist Temple a Spiritual Haven on a Busy S.J. Street." *San Jose Mercury News* (CA), August 24, 1B.

Do, Hien Duc, and Mimi Khúc. 2009. "Immigrant Religious Adaptation: Vietnamese American Buddhists at Chua Viet Name (Vietnamese Buddhist Temple)." In *Religion at the Corner of Bliss and Nirvana: Politics, Identity, and Faith in New Migrant Communities*, edited by Lois Ann Lorentzen, Joaquin Jay Gonzalez III, Kevin M. Chun, and Hien Duc Do, 124–138. Durham, NC, and London: Duke University Press.

Do, Le Huu. 2003. *Sounds of the Bamboo Forest: Buddhist Churches of America in the Vietnamese Tradition*. Pittsburgh, PA: Dorrance.

Duc, Thich Minh. 2000. "Dam Luu: An Eminent Vietnamese Buddhist Nun." In *Innovative Buddhist Women: Swimming against the Stream*, edited by Karma Lekshe Tsomo, 104–120. Richmond, Surrey: Curzon.

Espiritu, Yến Lê. 2006. "Toward a Critical Refugee Study: The Vietnamese Refugee Subject in U.S. Scholarship." *Journal of Vietnamese Studies* 1, no. 1: 410–433.

Ford, Eugene. 2017. *Cold War Monks: Buddhism and America's Secret Strategy in Southeast Asia*. New Haven, CT, and London: Yale University Press.

Hanh, Thich Nhat. 1967. *Vietnam: Lotus in a Sea of Fire*. New York: Hill and Wang.

Hope, Marjorie. 1970. *Youth Against the World*. Boston: Little, Brown.

Huynh, Thuan. 2000. "Center for Vietnamese Buddhism: Recreating Home." In *Religion and the New Immigrants: Continuities and Adaptations in Immigrant Congregations*, edited by Helen Rose Ebaugh and Janet Saltzman Chafetz, 163–179. Walnut Creek, CA: Alta Mira Press.

Khúc, Mimi. 2020. "Where the History Books End: Religion and Vietnamese America in the Afterlife of the Vietnam War." In *Envisioning Religion, Race, and Asian Americans*, edited by David K. Yoo and Khyati Y. Joshi, 123–142. Honolulu: University of Hawai'i Press.

Kim, Helen Jin. 2020. "Reconstructing Asian America's Religious Past: A Historiography." In *Envisioning Religion, Race, and Asian Americans*, edited by David K. Yoo and Khyati Y. Joshi, 13–40. Honolulu: University of Hawai'i Press.

Kwon, Heonik. 2008. *Ghosts of War in Vietnam*. New York: Cambridge University Press.

Medine, Carolyn M. Jones. 2019. "'Beyond Vietnam': Martin Luther King, Jr., Thích Nhất Hạnh, and the Confluence of Black and Engaged Buddhism in the Vietnam War." In *Buddhism and Whiteness: Critical Reflections*, edited by George Yancy and Emily McRae, 119–141. Lanham, MD: Lexington Books.

Mortland, Carol A. 2017. *Cambodian Buddhism in the United States*. Albany: State University of New York Press.

Nattier, Jan. 1998. "Who Is a Buddhist? Charting the Landscape of Buddhist America." In *The Faces of Buddhism in America*, edited by Charles S. Prebish and Kenneth K. Tanaka, 183–195. Berkeley: University of California Press.

Nguyen, Cuong Tu, and A. W. Barber. 1998. "Vietnamese Buddhism in North America: Tradition and Acculturation." In *The Faces of Buddhism in America*, edited by Charles S. Prebish and Kenneth K. Tanaka, 129–146. Berkeley: University of California Press.

Nguyen, Phuong Tran. 2017. *Becoming Refugee America: The Politics of Rescue in Little Saigon*. Urbana, Chicago, and Springfield: University of Illinois Press.

Nguyen, Viet Thanh. 2016. *Nothing Ever Dies: Vietnam and the Memory of War*. Cambridge, MA: Harvard University Press.

Roberts, Adam. 1965. "Buddhism and Politics in South Vietnam." *The World Today* 21, no. 6: 240–250.

Schecter, Jerrold. 1967. *The New Face of Buddha: The Fusion of Religion and Politics in Contemporary Buddhism*. New York: Coward-McCann.

Soucy, Alexander. 2017a. "A Reappraisal of Vietnamese Buddhism's Status as 'Ethnic.'" *Journal of Vietnamese Studies* 12, no. 2: 20–48.

Soucy, Alexander. 2017b. "Contemporary Vietnamese Buddhism." In *The Oxford Handbook of Contemporary Buddhism*, edited by Michael K. Jerryson, 177–195. New York and Oxford: Oxford University Press.

Swearer, Donald K. 1970. *Buddhism in Transition*. Philadelphia: The Westminster Press.

Truitt, Allison J. 2021. *Pure Land in the Making: Vietnamese Buddhism in the US Gulf South*. Seattle: University of Washington Press.

Tweed, Thomas A., and Stephen Prothero. 1999. *Asian Religions in America: A Documentary History*. New York and Oxford: Oxford University Press.

Willis, Jan. 2001. *Dreaming Me: From Baptist to Buddhist, One Woman's Spiritual Journey*. New York: Riverhead Books.

Yoo, David K. 1999. *New Spiritual Homes: Religion and Asian Americans*. Honolulu: University of Hawai'i Press.

CHAPTER 13

TIBETAN BUDDHISM IN AMERICA

HOLLY GAYLEY AND JOSHUA BRALLIER

A painting by Tsherin Sherpa calls to mind the dispersed worlds of Tibetan Buddhism. *Luxation 1* (2016) is a dramatic image in sixteen panels featuring the disjointed details of a wrathful Buddhist deity. Its many hands cross several panels in a swirl, its bulging eyes and crown of laughing skulls leap out from the central panels. A skull cup, trident, and flames are scattered here and there. As the title suggests, this multipanel painting represents displacement, a response to the 2015 earthquake in Nepal and a representation of the artist's own cultural dislocation as a Sherpa and Tibetan Buddhist in California.[1] It is a potent reminder that Tibetan Buddhism came to the Americas amid various disjunctures, including political upheaval, outmigration, and the conditions of exile, and that North America (the purview of this volume) is but one vector in a global trajectory of Tibetan Buddhism—with various cultural and linguistic gaps and fissures en route—as well as significant points of convergence and productive tension.

This history of displacement needs to be kept in mind to counter the romanticized lens through which Tibet and Buddhism have been viewed and represented in the west. The global spread of Tibetan Buddhism was inadvertently propelled by the social and cultural devastation that followed the invasion of Tibet by Chinese Communist troops in the 1950s. After the Lhasa Uprising of 1959, approximately 80,000 Tibetans followed the Fourteenth Dalai Lama Tenzin Gyatso into exile and established Buddhist institutions in various enclaves in India and Nepal. They emerged into a world already suffused with the myth of Tibet as a Shangri-la, an idyllic and isolated preserve of timeless Buddhist wisdom (Lopez 1998), and soon found allies in spiritual seekers and western academics to support and broaden their efforts. The exotic allure of Tibet facilitated the entry and enthusiastic reception of its most portable elements beyond Asia, including Buddhist

---

[1] This is the cover image (acrylic on sixteen canvases, each 18 × 18 inches) for the exhibition catalog of *Awaken: A Tibetan Buddhist Journey toward Enlightenment*, shown at Virginia Museum of Fine Arts in 2019 and Asian Art Museum of San Francisco in 2020.

teachers, teachings, and material culture. Tsoknyi Rinpoche sums up the situation in pragmatic terms: "Everything has two sides. The unfortunate side is we lost our country. The fortunate side: dharma went all over the world."[2]

In recent decades, Tibetans have generated vibrant, far-reaching transnational networks of Buddhist and Bön lineages that remain anchored to the exile community in South Asia and connected to home institutions on the Tibetan plateau. Tibetan Buddhism is constellating in North America through the circulation of religious texts and practices, people and patronage, art and artifacts, and more.[3] This is not a unidirectional transfer from Asia to America, as often imagined in the transmission process.[4] Instead, we are inspired by Manual Vasquez's model of transnational religion as a vascular network, emphasizing the multidirectional circulation of discourses and practices through various nodes, akin to a living tissue (Vasquez 2017). This is helpful in thinking about the dynamically linked and mobile aspects of Buddhism that become localized in dharma centers, cultural associations, retreat facilities, and research institutes in America, while remaining linked to Tibet as an "idealized homeland."

In this chapter, we attend to the dynamic tension between the transnational scope of Tibetan Buddhism and efforts to localize it geographically, institutionally, culturally, and linguistically in North America.[5] We elaborate a series of tensions between mobility and rootedness, continuity and adaptation, the curated public presentation of Tibetan Buddhism and the ritual arena of Vajrayāna, or Buddhist tantra, a domain restricted to initiates. A focus on tensions suggests a method for approaching the study of Tibetan Buddhism in America that is resonant with assemblage theory and its emphasis on the flexible constellations of heterogeneous elements that branch out rhizomatically and create new centers of gravity (Deleuze and Guattari 1987; Bennett 2010). Drawing from assemblage theory has the added benefit of aligning with Buddhist conceptions of selfhood as an interdependent amalgam of elements rather than a substantive whole. This aids in our commitment to centering Tibetan agents, frameworks, and strategies for enacting the translation and transmission of Buddhist teachings to new lands.

We make several interventions in this chapter. First, we eschew a "western adaptation" model that collapses transformation into modernization and/or westernization.[6] Instead we emphasize Tibetan modalities for localizing Buddhism and challenge the usefulness of the "ethnic/convert" distinction, upending its associations with tradition/modernity in the examples we offer. Second, we focus on processes and tensions in the translation and transmission of Tibetan Buddhism in America, rather than on founding figures and their enduring institutions, which tends to privilege origins as authentic and

---

[2] Remark by Tsoknyi Rinpoche in the documentary, *When the Iron Bird Flies: Tibetan Buddhism Arrives in the West* (2012), directed by Victress Hitchcock and Amber Bemak.
[3] See Appadurai 1996 on "global flows" that result from globalization as well as modern political and cultural disjunctures.
[4] For example, the model delineated in Nattier 1997. For a critique, see Hickey 2015, 46–52.
[5] Our approach here is in line with that taken in Mitchell and Quli 2015.
[6] For example, the paradigm advanced in Coleman 2001.

leaves unexplored the ongoing mechanisms of change. As an extension of this, we center groups that usually receive less attention in anthology chapters on Tibetan Buddhism in America: Tibetan exile communities, established women-led sanghas, as well as emerging BIPOC (Black, Indigenous, People of Color) and queer voices.[7] Third, we consider to what extent Tibetan Buddhism in America is "American" in any way, and just what that would mean—more entrepreneurial and individualistic, more democratic and wedded to social justice, more connected to the land and Indigenous peoples, more secular and aestheticized, or something else entirely. Given that Tibetan Buddhism and America are not stable signifiers, but multivalent assemblages, all of this warrants consideration.

TIBETAN/AMERICAN BUDDHISTS

Building on scholars who critique the "ethnic/convert" distinction to characterize diverse Buddhist communities in America (see Hsu, Chapter 20 in this volume),[8] it is worth noting that equating "ethnic" with Tibetan elides significant heterogeneity. The Kalmyk Mongolian population who settled in New Jersey in the 1950s were among the earliest Tibetan Buddhists in America, and since the first decade of the twenty-first century a significant group of Chinese and Chinese American Buddhists are following Tibetan teachers based on outreach programs to mainland China, Taiwan, and Hong Kong. This binary also risks essentializing Tibetan identity and culture as Buddhist, eliding the indigenous Bön tradition and missing the myriad ways that Tibetan lamas, monastics, artists, and intellectuals operate in secular spaces. Moreover, predominantly white "convert" communities are in their second and third generations, while BIPOC-led saṅghas are among the more innovative new horizons for Tibetan Buddhism in America. The "ethnic/convert" distinction, and even the category of Tibetan Buddhism in America itself, risks foreclosing the multifaceted and multidirectional trajectories of Tibetan Buddhism as a global phenomenon into reductive and value-laden categories, not just "ethnic" and "convert," but associated tropes of "traditional" and "modern."[9]

An example of a saṅgha that confounds the "ethnic/convert" binary is Palyul International with its global network.[10] During retreats at Nyingma Palyul Dharma

---

[7] Given the space limitations of this chapter, our case studies, site visits, and interviews relate predominantly to the Nyingma school of Tibetan Buddhism, while still including examples from all four major schools including Sakya, Kagyu, and Geluk, as well as Bön, an indigenous tradition which developed institutionally alongside Buddhism.

[8] For substantive critiques of the ethnic/convert distinction, see Hickey 2015, 42–46; Mitchell 2016, 7–9; and Gleig 2019, 6–8.

[9] See McLaughlin 2020 for a critique regarding the association of traditional and modern praxis with ethnic and convert Buddhist communities in America.

[10] For counter-examples, where there is a notable disjunct between Tibetan and non-Tibetan interests and activities within Buddhist practice communities, see Mullen 2006.

Center in upstate New York, Tibetan and non-Tibetan children regularly run through the throngs of diverse practitioners during daily practice sessions in a way that is uncharacteristic of more white-dominated saṅghas. During the COVID-19 pandemic, Palyul shifted all of their programming online, creating a more expansive circuit of global conduits. Its annual summer month-long retreat was conducted entirely over Zoom in 2020, which subsequently inspired daily live broadcasts of teachings and practice sessions from their New York temple—sometimes even with *khenpo*s logging in from India and Taiwan to offer additional sessions. Hundreds of practitioners join synchronously from around the world, listening to teachings and receiving empowerments in Tibetan that are simultaneously interpreted into eight languages. The addition of online programming enlivened the already diverse Palyul saṅgha, opening up space for community and practice that is more financially, linguistically, and geographically accessible—not to mention more accessible to the disabled, with closed captioning in each language.

Received binaries also fail to account for the syncretic impulses found in practice communities, such as Sunray Meditation Society and Peace Village in the Green Mountains of Vermont, run by Venerable Dhyani Ywahoo, a Tsalagi/Cherokee medicine woman and teacher in the Drikung Kagyu lineage of Tibetan Buddhism. All this suggests the need to better account for the diversity of Tibetan Buddhist actors and communities in North America, as well as the multidirectional vectors of global networks on the one hand and localizing impulses on the other.

Buddhicizing the American Landscape

Firefighters shouted "Save the temple!" as the Cameron Peak Fire crested the hill into Drala (formerly Shambhala) Mountain Center in northern Colorado in October 2020. The value of the Great Stupa of Dharmakaya, a Buddhist monument towering over the valley at 108 feet tall, was immediately apparent to firefighting crews. For centuries Tibetans have marked the landscape as Buddhist in various ways, including building temples, erecting stūpas (reliquaries), hanging prayer flags, and carving mantras into stone. While not all of this has translated into the American landscape, stūpas, large and small, now pepper North America—the tallest being the towering Stupa de la Paz outside Mexico City, a Bön stūpa built under the auspices of Tenzin Wangyal Rinpoche.

Temple building has been less common than building stūpas and founding meditation centers. Nonetheless, Dzigar Kongtrul's retreat center Longchen Jigme Samten Ling in Crestone, Colorado has a stunning example of the iconic Zangdok Palri temple. This is a Tibetan architectural form prevalent in the Buddhist revival on the Tibetan plateau during the post-Mao period, but in this case the exquisite materials and craftsmanship follow a Japanese aesthetic, creating a syncretic architectural form produced through a confluence of Asian artistic influences in America.

Even here the binary between "traditional" Tibetan forms of Buddhicizing the landscape and "modern" American syncretic or secularizing impulses fails to capture the dynamic tensions involved in place-making. When Chagdud Tulku established centers across the Americas in the 1980s and 1990s, nearly the first thing his non-Tibetan students did—before constructing any permanent facilities—was to erect a life-sized statue of a Buddhist master, for example, Padmasambhava at Iron Knot Ranch in New Mexico.[11] This signals a deep religious commitment to sanctifying the landscape for auspicious and successful practice and study in a way that contests the ubiquity of modernist impulses among converts to Buddhism (cf. McMahan 2008).

Novel forms of sacred architecture in North America have also been part of a Buddhicization process, even as such innovations confound an easy conceptual divide between "modern" secularized aesthetics and "traditional" Buddhist construction. Notable in this regard is the Garden of 1000 Buddhas in northern Montana. Since 2010, it has become a destination for the tourists en route to Glacier National Park, for locals who join in the annual Peace Festival, for Tibetan pilgrims from cities in the United States who visit via bus tours, and for Vajrayāna practitioners who study and practice with Ewam International. Tulku Sang-ngag chose the site, formerly a sixty-acre sheep ranch, based on a vision he had as a child in Tibet. Since it is situated on Confederated Salish and Kootenai Tribal lands, tribal elders were asked for permission prior to construction and were included in the consecration ceremonies.

According to Khen Rinpoche, the abbot of the Garden of 1000 Buddhas, the central statue of Yum Chenmo (the great mother, Prajñāpāramitā) and the one-thousand Buddha statues erected along spokes of the grand dharma wheel around her are meant to bless the land, bring good fortune, and protect from adversity.[12] Below each buddha image is a plaque, identifying the buddha, the donor's name, and their aspiration, with names indicating diverse patronage. In this way, the Garden unifies a cosmic vision of copious buddhas and the aspirations of donors from around the world into a singular monument in rural Montana. It embodies a distinctive form of Buddhist place-making in America, even as Tulku Sang-ngag has a transnational reach with centers in India, Nepal, Bhutan, Taiwan, Hong Kong, and Japan.

Place-making efforts in the Buddhicization of the American landscape based on Tibetan architectural forms, new and old, highlight a tension between mobility and rootedness. This can be productively theorized as the de-territorializing and re-territorializing operations endemic to the assemblage: the Chinese Communist invasion and the subsequent socialist reforms and religious persecution in the Maoist period de-territorialized Buddhism from the Tibet plateau, prompting a wave of re-territorializing moves across South Asia and beyond, and later revitalization efforts by Tibetans on the plateau during the post-Mao era. Tibetan Buddhism does not simply uproot and move

---

[11] Personal communication from Pema McLaughlin.
[12] Site visit to Garden of 1000 Buddhas and interview with Khen Rinpoche on August 16, 2021, with the assistance of Justin Kirkwood. Thanks to Maura Ganz for her help arranging this.

to a new place: elements once dispersed are reconfigured within evolving historical, cultural, geographic, and institutional contexts.

Beyond the Monastery

If we take seriously the idea that one cannot simply transplant Tibetan Buddhism *in toto*—as if it were a thing, like a tree, as lineages are often depicted iconographically—then context matters.[13] We need to consider the entire ecosystem from and within which specific elements of Tibetan Buddhism become dis-embedded and re-embedded. What conditions enable select aspects to take root (or not), and how do elements transform and interact in a new assemblage? Take the now ubiquitous "Dharma center" in North America. The buildings may look Tibetan in their architectural design, color palette, and interior shrines, such as Rigdzin Ling in Northern California founded by the late Chagdud Tulku in 1983 as his North American seat—or his centers in Brazil, Odsal Ling in São Paulo and Khadro Ling in Três Coroas, where he settled in 1996 with his wife Chagdud Khadro. Yet their institutional configuration could not be more different. Dharma centers in North America are generally nonprofit organizations that charge fees for programs and rentals, have a rotating staff living and working onsite, and use websites, listservs, and other advertising and revenue-generating mechanisms. Among the monasteries, encampments, temples, and retreat hermitages on the Tibetan plateau, there is no direct correlate.

This illustrates how elements of Tibetan Buddhism (such as architectural or ritual forms) are reassembled and embedded in different institutional frameworks in the Americas. The emphasis in previous treatments of Tibetan Buddhism within anthologies of Buddhism in America has been to focus on founding figures:[14] early Tibetan lamas who established enduring institutions, thereby "planting" the Vajrayāna in the west, to invoke an oft-used metaphor.[15] When we shift the focus to contextual factors, we see radical disjunctures as distilled elements are adapted to (and transformed within) new geographic, cultural, and institutional ecosystems.

Consider the case of monasticism. In contrast to mass monasticism on the Tibetan plateau, monastic institutions play a relatively minor role in North America. It is but one institutional configuration among many that involve the study and practice of Tibetan Buddhism: dharma centers, research institutes, cultural associations, translation

---

[13] On the importance of context for Buddhist meditation in America, see McMahan 2017. David Germano spoke to this issue in a lecture, "The Profundity of Culture and Context: Tibetan Buddhist Meditation and Modernity," at Naropa University on September 8, 2016.

[14] For example, Lavine 1998, 100–115; Seager 1999, 113–135; Coleman 2001, 103–109; and Mitchell 2016, 133–153, building on an early narrative history by Rick Fields, *How the Swans Came to the Lake* (1981).

[15] Vajrayāna, or the "adamantine vehicle" (*rdo rje theg pa*) refers to Buddhist tantra, a diverse set of esoteric practices involving visualization and mantra recitation, which developed in India and was brought to Tibet starting in its imperial period (seventh to ninth centuries).

committees, rural retreat facilities, academic programs at universities, and online saṅghas. This is a case of a dramatic but easily imperceptible shift. Rather than a singular and linear process of adaptation, we find a proliferation of multiple trajectories, as in the rhizomatic extensions of a living assemblage.

Over the centuries, monasticism has served as one dominant form of Buddhist communities in Tibet. Yet monasticism, as rooted in the Mūlasarvāstivāda Vinaya, has yet to take hold in North America in a substantial way. The scholar and nun Karma Lekshe Tsomo sees this as due, in part, to the lack of financial support and training facilities for monastics. Without a comparable monastic presence, she expresses concern about the depth of Buddhist study within the Tibetan system: "There is no ideal place for monastics to train in North America to receive the systematic monastic training needed to build a strong foundation for Buddhism in a new land. Anyone can ordain, but that's different from monasticism as an institution."[16] While monastics in her generation received their training in Nepal and India, the heyday of prolonged budget travel in Asia is long past, and available grants are generally for academic research, translation training and projects, and even three-year retreats—but not for monasticism per se (see Luke Clossey and Karen Ferguson, Chapter 15 in this volume).

For this reason, akin to the heart and lungs of a vascular system, monastic institutions and yogic training in India, Nepal, and Tibet remain vibrant sources of authority and knowledge for the global spread of Tibetan Buddhism, sites where the next generation of Tibetan and Himalayan lamas and cleric-scholars are emerging. There are a handful of monastic communities in North America—like Deer Park outside Madison, Wisconsin, Karma Triyana Dharmachakra in the Catskills of upstate New York, and Drepung Loseling outside Atlanta—which house small communities of Tibetan monks who offer classes and ritual services to the laity and, in the case of the Drepung Loseling monks, regularly perform ritual music and dances in secular venues under the banner of "The Mystical Arts of Tibet." For training as a monastic in North America, two of the more successful facilities are headed by nuns: Sravasti Abbey in Washington State led by Thubten Chödrön, and Gampo Abbey in Nova Scotia, Canada, led by Pema Chödrön, where Thrangu Rinpoche served as the founding abbot. Each has a modest residential monastic population and the opportunity to explore monastic life prior to ordination through long-term residencies and temporary ordination.

In contrast to the limited uptake of monasticism, the yogic tradition has flourished in the Americas. This includes the majority of lay householders who do tantric practices at home and on occasional retreats—as well as those ordained as *ngakpa*s and *ngakma*s, male and female yogic practitioners who wear red and white robes on ritual occasions (distinguished from the burgundy and saffron robes of monastics) and follow a path that culminates in the advanced tantric practices of the three-year retreat. Historically in Tibet, *ngakpa/ma*s practiced in family lineages, encampments, village temples, retreat hermitages, and large-scale gatherings—and more recently in formal institutes. Some

---

[16] Interview with Karma Lekshe Tsomo on August 3, 2021.

Tibetan lamas who came westward early on, like Kalu Rinpoche and Chagdud Tulku, encouraged dedicated students to complete a three-year retreat, but it is also possible to perform these practices in shorter retreat segments, allowing for a certain flexibility more compatible with contemporary American lifestyles and the constraints of financial self-sufficiency among lay practitioners.

In response to the interest in yogic traditions, Pema Khandro has created a "family-friendly path" through Ngakpa International which she founded in California in 1999, along with its educational center, the Buddhist Studies Institute, for householders who seek to balance rigorous training in Buddhist philosophy with in-depth tantric practice. As a Millennial scholar and dharma teacher, who identifies as an Indigenous woman and feminist, Pema Khandro is committed to inclusivity and lateral religious authority: she shares leadership with three women out of a feminist commitment to a consensus model. This is notably distinct from groups run by a single (most often male) lama, with hierarchically structured authority.[17]

In training students, Pema Khandro adheres to a standard Nyingma curriculum of practice and study, while employing an American-style dialogic pedagogy that includes conversations on race and gender, trauma and mental health, communication skills, and healthy boundaries. In these ways, Pema Khandro fosters a progressive community while teaching a widely recognized ritual cycle among the Nyingma, the *Longchen Nyingtik*. "I try to change things as little as possible," Pema Khandro avers, "so that my students can go to Asia or other saṅghas and practice something recognizable."[18] In this way, she balances a commitment to maintaining Tibetan lineages of teachings and practices with a sensitivity and responsiveness to contemporary issues. She shares this with GenX dharma teachers like Lamas Willa Baker and Liz Monson of Natural Dharma Fellowship and Wonderwell Mountain Refuge. In public forums, all three advocate harm prevention in Buddhist saṅghas in parallel with the #MeToo movement.

Secularizing Impulses

The yogic and monastic are parallel streams in Tibetan Buddhism, aligned with the two key types of training: practice and study. These trainings have taken different shapes in America, modeled loosely on the Tibetan *shedra* (*bshad grwa*) or study center, where a curriculum of Buddhist philosophy is mastered, and a *drupdra* (*sgrub grwa*) or retreat center, for esoteric practice in a three-year retreat at a remove from the monastery. Retreat centers like Drala Mountain Center in Colorado and Wonderwell Mountain

---

[17] Tulku (*sprul sku*) refers to a reincarnate lama; *lama* is the Tibetan translation of the Sanskrit *guru*, meaning "teacher," usually someone who has completed a three-year retreat.

[18] Interview with Pema Khandro on January 7, 2022.

Refuge in New Hampshire offer facilities for residential programs and retreats—but of much shorter duration, typically from a weekend to a month—that include meditation retreats open to the public and advanced Vajrayāna teachings and practices.

Permutations of the *shedra* are more varied. The Tibetan impulse to study the progression of tenets and schools in Buddhist philosophy has taken diverse forms in North America, including the founding of Buddhist-inspired institutes, such as Naropa University in Boulder, Colorado, Maitripa College in Portland, Oregon, and the Mangalam Research Center in Berkeley, California. The Nitartha Institute, a summer study program founded by Dzogchen Ponlop Rinpoche, employs materials from a *shedra* curriculum and even teaches long-standing monastic forms like the syllogisms used in debate practice. Though not explicitly modeled on a *shedra* curriculum, academic programs in Tibetan studies are a flourishing site for the study of Tibetan Buddhism, and university towns became early nodes for Buddhist practice and study due to collaborations between lamas and scholars, some of whom were also practitioners. For example, Seattle retains a strong Sakya presence due to Dezhung Rinpoche, who taught Tibetan language and Buddhist philosophy at the University of Washington from 1960 to 1972 and co-founded the Sakya Monastery in Seattle in 1974 with both Jigdal Dagchen Sakya and his wife Dagmo Kusho.

Since the early 2000s, with the rise of the mindfulness movement, new types of collaborations with universities have unfolded that expand the influence of Tibetan Buddhism into secular arenas. The Mind & Life Dialogues held regularly between the Dalai Lama and neuroscientists and psychologists since 1987 have been a significant node in the burgeoning scientific research on the empirical effects of mindfulness and compassion practices derived from Buddhism. Out of that has come Emory University's longstanding collaboration with the Dalai Lama under the direction of Lobsang Tenzin Negi since 1998, including the Emory-Tibet Science Initiative and the Center for Contemplative Science and Compassion-Based Ethics. Cross-fertilization is evident in the newly accredited monastic degree program at Sera Jey Monastery in India, where Geluk monks who trained at Emory returned to oversee the translation of scientific textbooks and implement them in a newly revised monastic curriculum (Rekjong 2023). In addition, Tibetan-designed secular meditation programs have emerged, such as the Compassion Cultivation Training (CCT), developed at Stanford in 2009 by Thupten Jinpa, a scholar, former monk, longtime translator for the Dalai Lama, and chairman of the board for the Mind & Life Institute. The eight-week CCT curriculum is now taught through the Compassion Institute he founded in 2017 as well at Stanford.

The relationship between high-profile Tibetan lamas and American universities also manifests institutionally via nonprofit foundations that fund the practice and study of Tibetan Buddhism in higher education. Dzongsar Khyentse Rinpoche has emphasized the importance of the academic study of Buddhist traditions alongside their teaching and practice. When asked why his Khyentse Foundation has endowed six chairs and professorships in Buddhist studies and three centers in Buddhist Studies across universities internationally, he responded by naming scholars as "the guardians of Buddhism in the west."[19] Similar to the rigors of *shedra* training, Khyentse Rinpoche insisted, academic programs offer systematic training in philology, historical analysis, and philosophical rigor that mitigate against the "watering down" of "all this mindfulness stuff." For him, training in Buddhist languages facilitates deep textual and ethnographic study, thereby helping to faithfully translate the dharma into new cultural contexts. Yet the Khyentse Foundation cannot simply be viewed as a "Buddhist modernist" actant, because it also invests in curricular development for monastic education in Asia and in the translation of the Buddhist canon into English: activities resonant with more than a millennium of history in the Tibetan cultural world.

Religious Politics, Political Religion

These secular innovations and new forms of patronage undermine previous academic portrayals of "ethnic" Buddhist communities in North America as "traditional." Taking this one step further, many annual observations by Tibetans in North America are historically novel and embody the long-standing notion of the "union of religion and politics" (*chos srid zung 'brel*) in striking new ways.[20] Commemorations, protests, and vigils by the exile Tibetan community are grounded in the Buddhist value of compassion, accompanied by religious prayers, and aimed at Tibetan self-determination, "a populist movement that works in tandem with discourses extended by the Dalai Lama" (Avalos 2015, 189). Here we make space for Tibetan political and cultural expressions which are often overlooked in academic surveys of Tibetan Buddhism in America.

In 1991, Norbu Samphell received the life-changing news from the Central Tibetan Administration in Dharamsala, India, that he had won one of 1,000 lottery spots for exile Tibetans living in India and Nepal to immigrate to the United States under the 1990 Immigration Act and Tibetan Resettlement Project. The project was a coordinated effort between the US government, the Central Tibetan Administration, and a vast network of Tibetan and American volunteers joining together to relocate the lottery winners.[21] Norbu was one of 100 Tibetans to be assigned to Chicago, where volunteers poured forth from the Chicago branches of the Jewel Heart saṅgha and Shambhala International, along with others sympathetic to the Tibetans' political plight. The Project of Chicago was one of twenty-one such immigrant projects across the United States, as a thousand Tibetans journeyed to a new life in major cities, growing roots that would become a

---

[19] Dzongsar Khyentse Rinpoche, "Reflections on the Study and Practice of Buddhist Traditions," delivered virtually to the Khyentse Foundation Buddhist Studies Lecture Series at Northwestern University on February 5, 2021.

[20] For example, Tibetan Uprising Day (March 10) and the Dalai Lama's birthday (July 6). Natalie Avalos has argued that "the union of religion and politics" embodied in the rule of Dalai Lamas in central Tibet has been transformed "from the bottom up" through activism by exile Tibetans in America (2015, 185).

[21] For a detailed account of the Tibetan Resettlement Project in the United States, see Hess 2009.

networked confederation of Tibetan cultural centers dedicated to the promotion of the Tibetan heritage through a variety of cultural events and classes for children in Tibetan language, song, and dance.

Visits by the Dalai Lama have been pivotal to establishing Tibet Associations across North America, offering an opportunity for visibility and fundraising. Canada's largest Tibetan community in Toronto, with more than four thousand Tibetans, hosted the Dalai Lama to bestow the Kālacakra Initiation in 2004 and bless its proposed Tibetan Canadian Cultural Center. In 2008, the Tibetan Alliance of Chicago invited the Dalai Lama to offer two public teachings and invested the profits from ticket sales in their first building just north of the city. Like other branches across North America, the Alliance continues to make fiscal contributions to the Central Tibetan Administration, and is in turn supported with cultural resources in a multidirectional reciprocity. "The connection is an emotional one," Norbu tells us.[22] Tibetan Associations are united as a transnational community in their commitment to the cause of a sovereign Tibet and the leadership of the Dalai Lama.

Religious and political themes likewise weave together in the work of Tenzing Rigdol, a Tibetan artist whose family immigrated from Nepal to the United States in 2002. His masterpiece, *My World Is in Your Blind Spot* (2014), calls attention to the ongoing and underreported tragedy of self-immolations on the Tibetan plateau protesting oppression under Chinese colonial rule. Each of its five panels features the outline of a seated Buddha whose body is filled with photographically reproduced flames, symbolizing the devastating reality of self-immolations and containing them within the calming presence of the five Buddhas. This work was first exhibited in the United States in 2019 at the Emmanuel Gallery on the University of Colorado Denver campus, where Tenzing Rigdol received a BA in Art History and a BFA in Painting and Drawing. In such works, Tenzing Rigdol reconfigures Tibetan artistic techniques and Buddhist iconography in order "to challenge the viewer" in a way that is "simultaneously safe and subversive: beautiful to look at, devastating to comprehend."[23]

Looking at vibrant Tibetan cultural production in North America counters the tendency to reduce Tibetan identity as essentially Buddhist. This is particularly evident when considering the types of cultural events created by Tibetan associations over the past thirty years. One notable event was a performance by Tenzin Mariko in September 2019. Mariko is the first out trans woman in Tibetan history, catapulting to fame after disrobing from her monastic order, coming out as trans, and performing in the Miss Tibet pageant in Dharamshala in 2017. She traveled to North America in the autumn of 2019 to perform at twelve Tibetan associations across the United States and Canada as part of a tour put on by Students for a Free Tibet. At the event in Chicago, she drew a primarily Tibetan-speaking audience, but also a small contingent of queer white

---

[22] Interview with Norbu Samphell on September 8, 2021.
[23] See Sarah Magnatta's introduction in the exhibit catalog for *My World Is in Your Blind Spot* (Denver: CU Denver, College of Arts & Media, 2019).

Americans—creating non-Buddhist queer conduits of connection across Tibetan and American cultural flows.

The Latse Library in New York City serves as another example that challenges the conflation of Tibetan culture with Buddhism. From 1999 to 2020, the Latse Library (now the Latse Project) served as a cultural hub connecting the large community of exile Tibetans living in New York to wider networks of Tibetans in diaspora and on the plateau.[24] Latse championed contemporary Tibetan literary and cultural production, providing space for both academic research and cultural events. They hosted popular courses on Tibetan dance and folk singing, Tibetan ghost-story-telling and love-letter-writing contests, and the first major conference celebrating the modernist monk Gendun Chöpel. Seen in this light, Latse has been a highly trafficked node in the globally dynamic assemblage of Tibetan culture—one that cannot be straightforwardly essentialized as Buddhist, any more than "Tibetan Buddhism" can be cleaved of its "Tibetan" adjective.

Translation and Transmission

Turning now to the processes that have shaped Tibetan Buddhism within America, let us consider more closely the tension between continuity and adaptation, considering elective affinities or synergies between resources drawn from the vast repertoire of Tibetan Buddhism and the exigencies of specific eras and arenas in America over the past fifty-some years.[25] Across the decades, different aspects of Tibetan Buddhism have gained traction: the antinomian bent of Buddhist tantra during the counterculture of the 1970s, the centrality of compassion and nonviolence during the heyday of Free Tibet activism in the 1990s, secular adaptations of Buddhist practices such as *tonglen* (*gtong len*) evolving in tandem with the mindfulness movement since the early 2000s, and the social justice imperatives of recent years, creating disruptions in some of the larger Buddhist organizations while simultaneously providing fertile ground for emergent saṅghas. In each era, distinct aspects of Tibetan Buddhism have come into "central visibility" in America, to borrow Ananda Abeysekara's felicitous term (2002, 4), which acknowledges shifting configurations and expressions of Buddhism over time.

Tibetan lamas and American lineage successors have delicately balanced continuity and adaptation to meet the needs of their students. One example is Anam Thubten, who was among a group of eastern Tibetan lamas invited to California in the early 1990s by Tarthang Tulku. He left Tarthang Tulku's resplendent Odiyan Buddhist Retreat Center in Sonoma County to found the Dharmata Foundation in Richmond just north of

---

[24] Interview with Latse Library director Pema Bhum on December 19, 2021. Note that the Latse Library's building closed because of the COVID-19 pandemic, but their mission continues as the Laste Project online: https://www.latse.org.

[25] Scholars use different terms to capture such affinities: David McMahan uses "harmonies" and "resonance" (2008, 61–62) and Thomas Tweed uses the term "confluences" (2008, 55–62).

Oakland. Although recognized as a *tulku* (reincarnate lama), Anam Thubten eschews the typical formality surrounding tantric masters. Preferring informality, he teaches on a simple platform rather than an elevated throne, refers to his students as "Dharma friends," and asks them not to rise when he enters the room.

Anam Thubten's informality serves as an updated model for the teacher-student relationship in America. For him, the outer forms of the Vajrayāna need to be flexible: "As Buddhists if we don't change with the times, I worry that the whole tradition will become an endangered species."[26] This sense of adaptability is reflected in the contemporary aesthetic of Dhumatala Temple (formerly Dhyana Hall): once a church, constructed from Redwoods at the turn of the twentieth century, today its wood paneling is decorated with just a few banners. Adaptability is also apparent in the way Anam Thubten introduces the *Longchen Nyingtik* ritual cycle: he simplifies parts of the liturgy and has students do six months of preliminary practice, counting by time rather than numbers of recitation. Nonetheless, he takes care to train students in the many details of liturgical forms, including the proper use of ritual instruments and melodies for chanting, while also giving pithy instructions. Harkening to the wandering Chöd practitioners of yore, Anam Thubten has collaborated with Elizabeth-Mattis Namgyal to establish the Wilderness Dharma Movement; they held their first retreat in 2016 in Canyon de Chelly, a national park and canyon sacred to the Diné/Navajo in Arizona.

In exploring the transmission of Tibetan Buddhism to America, it is helpful to consider the twin processes of *linguistic translation* and *cultural translation*. Oral and literary translations have been crucial to render the dharma comprehensible to English speakers and to translate practice and study materials for specific saṅghas, usually by translation committees under the direction of a Tibetan lama. As the Tsadra Foundation's "Translation and Transmission" conferences in Colorado in 2014 and 2017 highlighted, the project of translating Buddhist texts from Tibetan into English is interwoven with transmitting their associated practices and doctrine. Hence the importance of long-term translation projects, an impulse deeply rooted in Tibetan history and epitomized today in Tsadra's numerous translation projects, including the voluminous *Treasury of Oral Instruction* (*Gdams ngag mdzod*), and the Khyentse Foundation's *84000: Translating the Words of the Buddha*.[27] The latter has no less ambition than to translate all Buddhist canonical texts preserved in classical Tibetan into English. In addition, there is a parallel process, the cultural translation of ideas and practices into a new idiom through elective affinity, whereby Buddhist ideas and practices achieve legibility and traction in an American context. This means not only Buddhist ideas expressed in English, but their potential correspondence and dynamic interplay with features of life in America: its secular humanist presumptions, prevailing discourses like psychology, current movements for social justice, and shifting values as previously counterculture movements enter the mainstream.

---

[26] Interview with Anam Thubten on October 2, 2021.
[27] On these translation efforts, see tsadra.org/translation and 84000.co, respectively.

Central to the cultural translation process is addressing needs on the ground. Tara Mandala is unique as a Buddhist retreat center in North America dedicated to the sacred feminine, meeting a significant need in a historically male-dominated tradition. Located outside Pagosa Springs in southern Colorado, its main temple is dedicated to the female Buddha Tārā and constructed as her three-dimensional maṇḍala. The circular shrine room is filled with nearly lifesize statues of the twenty-one Tārās along the rim. The central figure on the shrine is Machig Labdrön, the eleventh-century Tibetan yoginī and female founder of Chöd (*gcod*, literally "severance"), a ritual practice to viscerally cut through attachment to ego. "The sacred feminine has always been part of the tradition," states founder Lama Tsultrim Allione.[28] Not only does the temple have a Tibetan corollary in the Nyethang Drolma Temple near Lhasa, dedicated to Tārā in her twenty-one manifestations and established by the eleventh-century Indian master Atiśa, but the ritual of Chöd has long been a mainstay practice in various lineages of Tibetan Buddhism. Taken in this sense, there's nothing "new" about Tara Mandala aside from Lama Tsultrim's decision to center the feminine in its iconography and ritual practices.

Lama Tsultrim founded Tara Mandala in 1994 based on an aspiration from her early twenties, when she ordained as a Buddhist nun, to create a sanctuary for the "depth of retreat and meditation as it occurred in Tibet alongside the study of western psychology." At Tara Mandala, she offers esoteric teachings and rituals received from Tibetan lamas alongside exoteric practices that are her own secular adaptation. "What is innovative is not the emphasis on the feminine," Lama Tsultrim remarks, "but the psychological emotional work that needs to be done in parallel with spiritual work." Chöd is a thread throughout the lineages Lama Tsultrim holds, and it inspired her development of a secular "Feeding Your Demons" program. After her recognition as an emanation of Machig Labdrön by lamas in Tibet and Nepal, she chose to "specialize in that," transmitting Chöd to her students, who can do the practice in solitary retreat at Tara Mandala under her supervision.

In these examples, we can see the care taken to balance continuity and adaptation in creative tension. Quite often, adaptation happens on the exoteric side of things, where outreach to a broad audience is intended, such as bestselling books or introductory programs that translate Buddhist ideas and practices into an American cultural milieu: coining new terms, crafting new pedagogies, and secularizing practices. By contrast, continuity is emphasized with respect to the esoteric practices of Buddhist tantra. As with theories of textual translation, we can identify a tension between domesticating and foreignizing impulses. The domesticating move of outreach meets audiences where they are, by articulating the dharma in terms compatible with liberal secular values or addressing spiritual-but-not-religious audiences. The foreignizing move of Buddhist tantric practices is more restricted, requiring initiation to enter into the Vajrayāna and the decidedly hierarchical framework of the guru-disciple relationship. Moreover, the recitation of tantric liturgies is routinely done in Tibetan, with phonetics

---

[28] Interview with Tsultrim Allione on September 26, 2021.

and translations provided. Such foreignizing elements, alongside Tibetan iconography, implements, and offerings used in ritual, bring the practitioner closer to a Tibetan cultural milieu in their ongoing Buddhist practice.

This strategy allows for broad outreach and a depth of training to be achieved. Yet it is not without a "bait-and-switch" quality for some who enter in the spirit of open inquiry (given meditation's modernist depiction as a "inner science") and then find themselves over their heads in a hierarchical guru-disciple relationship that can run afoul.[29] Given the "uneven topography" of the assemblage (Bennet 2010, 24), not everything in the translation and transmission process gains traction. The patriarchal bent of the guru figure thus finds both expression and resistance on American soil; the role of land deities becomes decoupled from one land and transplanted into another—or they are left behind; secret empowerments migrate from bounded maṇḍalas forged on the ground to virtual spaces across the globe; the sedimentation of centuries of ritual collides with the allergy to ritual in contemporary mindfulness.

New Horizons

Generational change is in the air and on the ground. As the legacy of the counterculture recedes, social justice issues are coming to the fore, with GenX and Millennials leading the way.[30] Since the 1990s, Tibetan communities in North America have laid the ground by combining political activism with Buddhist practice in horizontally constituted, democratic lay associations. Joining them are several movements breaking the mold inside and outside of predominantly white baby-boomer dominated saṅghas through #MeToo revelations, Queer Dharma initiatives, and emergent BIPOC-led groups. Meanwhile, the shift to online programming during the COVID-19 pandemic entailed the closure of numerous brick-and-mortar centers within larger saṅghas, while communities limited to a single center or region have significantly expanded their geographic reach. All this makes for a painful and fertile time for reform and shifts in demographics for Tibetan Buddhism in America.

Alongside the broader #MeToo movement, allegations of sexual abuse by several high-profile Tibetan lamas ignited scandals for some of the largest and most established Tibetan Buddhist communities in North America, including Rigpa, Shambhala, and the Foundation for the Preservation of Mahayana Tradition (FPMT). While there are a number of contextual factors that have contributed to abuse, we highlight just a few here (see also Amy Langenberg, Chapter 4 in this volume). First and foremost, the western idealization and romanticization of all things Tibetan has allowed for the tantric guru to be elevated beyond human fallibility and accountability in systemic ways. Yet the tantric

---

[29] For this reason, classic and contemporary sources on the Vajrayāna alike emphasize the importance of discernment in choosing and following a guru. For example, see Kongtrul 1999 and Hookham 2021.

[30] For recent work on young Buddhists and social justice, see Gleig 2019 and Han 2021.

injunction "to see the guru as a buddha" does not require that communities minimize misconduct and gloss over it with a veneer of sanctity.[31]

Of course, the guru model itself is another factor, providing tremendous authority to the "vajra master" who bestows tantric initiations and provides access to esoteric teachings. This authority is amplified by ritual injunctions to follow the guru's command, the secrecy surrounding tantra, and the structuring properties of proximal desire that shape nascent institutions (Gayley 2018; Lucia 2018). The counterculture milieu of the 1970s, when a number of Tibetan Buddhist saṅghas were first becoming established in North America, adds another factor: the valorization of tantric antinomianism became entangled with the "free love" ethos of the time in ways that led to profound harm.

Can there be a healthy ecosystem around tantric gurus when they are siloed, as they often are in North America, dis-embedded from mechanisms of social accountability stitched into the fabric of Tibetan clan relations, monastic bureaucracy, place-based religion, and dense lineage networks? Generating such an ecosystem will take more than articulating and adhering to codes of ethics, which are nonetheless a crucial starting point. It will take a cultural shift: humanizing the guru and examining social conditioning around male entitlement and its structural sedimentations—factors of power and privilege that extend well beyond the guru model, as the #MeToo movement has amply demonstrated. We are wary of the "cultural clash" explanation, which suggests that abusive behavior by tantric gurus would somehow be acceptable in Tibetan and Himalayan contexts.[32] Quite the contrary, there are contemporary Tibetan critiques of "fake" (*rdzun ma*) lamas and monks who deceive others for the sake of wealth or sexual gratification (Gayley and Bhum 2022). We are equally wary of the derogatory specter of "cult" used to delegitimize saṅghas and by extension Tibetan Buddhism as a whole. This reductive approach bears disconcerting similarities to the rhetoric that the Chinese Communist state uses to legitimate colonial rule by portraying historical Tibet as a "feudal theocracy" in which lamas ruled by autocratic power.

All this signals the need for the maturation of the Vajrayāna in America. Such a maturation is already proceeding along intersectional lines, recognizing the multiplicity of crises that call for a response by American practitioners of Buddhism in the twenty-first century: racism and white supremacy, widespread ecological devastation, and the global rise of authoritarianism all underscore the interconnectedness of struggles against oppression, which figure deeply in the rising generations of Vajrayāna teachers in America. One such teacher is Lama Rod Owens, a queer Black man who completed his three-year retreat at Palpung (formerly Kagyu) Thubten Choling and then earned his M.Div. in Buddhist chaplaincy from Harvard. Lama Rod is at the forefront of an emergent generation of teachers who center social justice as inseparable from Buddhist praxis: political

---

[31] For an explanation of this point, see the Introduction and Interview with Jetsün Khandro Rinpoche in *Longing to Awaken: Buddhist Devotion in Tibetan Poetry and Song,* edited by Holly Gayley and Dominique Townsend (2024).

[32] See Jacoby 2014 and Gayley 2018 for twentieth-century examples of Tibetan consort practice in committed relationships and women resisting untoward sexual advances by religious figures.

liberation is wedded to spiritual liberation in a way that is resonant with the struggle for Tibetan independence. Alongside Tibetan exile communities in North America, BIPOC-led saṅghas view political protest and social justice as part of their Buddhist practice, a compassionate concern for all who suffer from oppression. Emphasizing the intersectionality of oppression, Lama Rod decries sexual abuse by gurus, teaches on the importance of working with anger at injustice, and adapts yogic and meditative techniques to the challenges of contemporary life in the United States.

The concept of intersectionality not only highlights the compounded precarity of individuals who sit at the nexus of multiple axes of oppression, it also provides a rubric for tracing the rhizomatic extensions of Buddhist groups in America. Shared conditions of oppression have spurred the formation of alliances across Buddhist traditions: Lama Rod, a Tibetan Buddhist teacher, and Rev. angel Kyodo williams, a Zen teacher, have together launched the Radical Dharma initiative, publishing a book by the same name alongside Black Buddhist political theorist Jasmine Syedullah.[33] Another example of the rhizomatic extensions of American Vajrayāna is Justin Miles, a Shambhala teacher who created the Black Power Meditation Group in Baltimore, Maryland, and authored the tantric liturgy, *The Sadhana of Awakened Melanin*, which is "designed to center Black people around their inner, outer and secret Black Power" (Miles 2022, n.p.). Along analogous lines, Black studies scholar and New York–based dharma teacher Shanté Paradigm Smalls has authored a quintessentially American tantric liturgy, *The Sadhana of Araminta Ross*, featuring Harriet Tubman as the central figure.[34] These are compelling Buddhist responses to the violent histories of systemic racism in America. Indeed, what could be more American than the struggle for Black liberation?

Another horizon for Tibetan Buddhism is the expansion of online programming. Despite place-making and institution-building efforts, it would be a mistake to imagine Tibetan Buddhism in America in purely geographic terms. Even those Tibetan lamas who settled in the United States and Canada travel widely and have students and centers around the world. In addition, there are a growing number of Buddhist and Bön lamas who have created robust online learning platforms, such as the CyberSangha of Tenzin Wangyal and Vajrayana Online, a subscription-based online program for the Tergar community under the direction of Yongey Mingyur Rinpoche. The global lockdown between 2020 and 2021 during the height of the COVID-19 pandemic brought financial precarity (or closure) to a number of brick-and-mortar dharma centers, but it also gave rise to widespread Tibetan Buddhist programming on Zoom and other online platforms, allowing a greater intensity of global flows of teachings, rituals, and retreats.

Let us end with two contrasting images of Tibetan Buddhism in America, one solemn, the other irreverent. In 2007, the US Congress honored the Dalai Lama with the Congressional Gold Medal for "his many enduring and outstanding contributions to peace, non-violence, human rights and religious understanding" in then House Speaker

---

[33] See williams, Owen, and Syedullah 2016.

[34] An early version of this liturgy was presented at Harvard's 2021 Buddhism and Race Speaker Series on June 17, 2021 and the Mahasangha Gathering at Drala Mountain Center, July 22–25, 2021.

Nancy Pelosi's words.[35] This is but one prominent example of the way that Americans have embraced the Tibetan cause, admired Buddhist values of compassion and non-violence, and lauded spiritual leaders like the Dalai Lama. Yet a brazen Americanness comes through strikingly in a photograph by Tenzing Rigdol, titled *Empire* (2009).[36] It shows the artist's hand, wearing a Buddhist *mālā* (rosary) on his wrist, giving the finger to the Empire State Building in Manhattan, its top tiers prominently lit by red and yellow lights to celebrate the sixtieth anniversary of the People's Republic of China in 2009—an image of protest, an expression of freedom, a Buddhism beyond Shangri-la clichés.

References

Abeysekara, Ananda. 2002. *Colors of the Robe: Religion, Identity, and Difference*. Columbia: University of South Carolina Press.

Appadurai, Arjun. 1996. *Modernity at Large: Cultural Dimensions of Globalization*. Minneapolis: University of Minnesota Press.

Avalos, Natalie. 2015. "Interdependence as a Lifeway: Decolonization and Resistance in Transnational Native American and Tibetan Communities." PhD dissertation, University of California, Santa Barbara.

Bennett, Jane. 2010. *Vibrant Matter: A Political Ecology of Things*. Durham, NC: Duke University Press.

Coleman, James William. 2001. *The New Buddhism: The Western Transformation of an Ancient Tradition*. Oxford: Oxford University Press.

Deleuze, Gilles, and Félix Guattari. 1987. *A Thousand Plateaus: Capitalism and Schizophrenia*. Translated by Brian Massumi. London: Continuum.

Fields, Rick. [1981] 2022. *How the Swans Came to the Lake: A Narrative History of Buddhism in America*. Boulder, CO: Shambhala.

Gayley, Holly. 2018. "Revisiting the Secret Consort (*gsang yum*) in Tibetan Buddhism." *Religions* 9, no. 6 (June): 1–21. doi:10.3390/rel9060179.

Gayley, Holly, and Somtso Bhum. 2022. "Parody and Pathos: Sexual Transgression by 'Fake' Lamas in Tibetan Short Stories." *Revue d'Etudes Tibétaines* 63 (April): 62–94.

Gayley, Holly, and Dominique Townsend. 2024. "Introduction and Interview with Jetsün Khandro Rinpoche." In *Longing to Awaken: Buddhist Devotion in Tibetan Poetry and Song*, edited by Holly Gayley and Dominique Townsend, 1–31. Charlottesville, VA: University of Virginia Press.

Gleig, Ann. 2019. *American Dharma: Buddhism beyond Modernity*. New Haven, CT: Yale University Press.

Han, Chenxing. 2021. *Be the Refuge: Raising the Voices of Asian American Buddhists*. Berkeley: North Atlantic Books.

Hess, Julia Meredith. 2009. *Immigrant Ambassadors: Citizenship and Belonging in the Tibetan Diaspora*. Redwood City, CA: Stanford University Press.

---

[35] https://www.dalailama.com/messages/acceptance-speeches/u-s-congressional-gold-medal/speech-by-speaker-pelosi (accessed November 27, 2021).

[36] rossirossi.com/exhibition/change-is-the-eternal-law (accessed February 11, 2022).

Hickey, Wakoh Shannon. 2015. "Two Buddhisms, Three Buddhisms, and Racism." In *Buddhism Beyond Borders: New Perspectives on Buddhism in the United States*, edited by Scott Mitchell and Natalie Quli, 35–56. Albany: State University of New York Press.

Hookham, Shenpen. 2021. *The Guru Principle: A Guide to the Teacher-Student Relationship in Buddhism*. Boulder, CO: Shambhala.

Jacoby, Sarah. 2014. *Love and Liberation: Autobiographical Writings of the Tibetan Buddhist Visionary Sera Khandro*. New York: Columbia University Press.

Kongtrul, Jamgön. 1999. *The Teacher Student Relationship*. Translated by Ron Garry. Boulder, CO: Snow Lion.

Lavine, Amy. 1998. "Tibetan Buddhism in America: The Development of American Vajrayāna." In *The Faces of Buddhism in America*, edited by Charles Prebish and Kenneth Tanaka, 100–115. Berkeley: University of California Press.

Lopez, Donald. 1998. *Prisoners of Shangri-la: Tibetan Buddhism and the West*. Chicago: University of Chicago Press.

Lucia, Amanda. 2018. "Guru Sex: Charisma, Proxemic Desire, and the Haptic Logics of the Guru Disciple Relationship." *Journal of the American Academy of Religion* 86, no. 4: 953–988.

McLaughlin, Pema. 2020. "Imagining Buddhist Modernism: The Shared Religious Categories of Scholars and American Buddhists." *Religion* 50, no. 4: 529–549.

McMahan, David. 2008. *The Making of Buddhist Modernism*. Oxford: Oxford University Press.

McMahan, David. 2017. "How Meditation Works: Theorizing the Role of Cultural Context in Buddhist Contemplative Practices." In *Meditation, Buddhism, and Science*, edited by David McMahan and Erik Braun, 21–46. Oxford: Oxford University Press.

Miles, Justin. 2022. "The Sadhana of Awakened Melanin." https://milesinstitute.net/black-power-meditation (accessed January 6, 2022).

Mitchell, Scott. 2016. *Buddhism in America: Global Religion, Local Contexts*. London: Bloomsbury Academic.

Mitchell, Scott, and Natalie Quli, eds. 2015. *Buddhism beyond Borders: New Perspectives on Buddhism in the United States*. Albany: State University of New York Press.

Mullen, Eve. 2006. "Tibetan Religious Expression and Identity: Transformations in Exile." In *Materializing Religion: Expression, Performance and Ritual*, edited by Elisabeth Arweck and William Keenan, 175–189. New York: Routledge.

Nattier, Jan. 1997. "Buddhism Comes to Main Street." *The Wilson Quarterly* (Spring). http://archive.wilsonquarterly.com/essays/buddhism-comes-main-street.

Quli, Natalie, and Scott Mitchell. 2015. "Buddhist Modernism as Narrative: A Comparative Study of Jodo Shinshu and Zen." In *Buddhism beyond Borders: New Perspectives on Buddhism in the United States*, edited by Scott Mitchell and Natalie Quli, 197–215. Albany: State University of New York Press.

Rekjong, Dhondup. 2023. "How Buddhism Met Science: A Monastic Scholar's Journey." *Lion's Roar* (December): https://www.lionsroar.com/monastic-scholars-journey/.

Seager, Richard Hughes. 1999. *Buddhism in America*. New York: Columbia University Press.

Tweed, Thomas. 2008. *Crossing and Dwelling: A Theory of Religion*. Cambridge, MA: Harvard University Press.

Vásquez, Manuel. 2017. "Vascularizing the Study of Religion: Multi-Agent Figurations and Cosmopolitics." In *Entangled Worlds: Religion, Science, and New Materialisms*, edited by Catherine Keller and Mary-Jane Rubenstein, 228–250. New York: Fordham University Press.

williams, Rev. angel Kyodo, Lama Rod Owens, and Jasmine Syedullah. 2016. *Radical Dharma: Talking Race, Love, and Liberation*. Berkeley, CA: North Atlantic Books.

CHAPTER 14

AMERICAN BUDDHISM AND JUDAISM

JAY MICHAELSON

The diverse encounters between American Jews and Buddhism date back to 1893, when Charles Strauss, a Jewish businessman, became the first known American convert to Buddhism at the World Parliament of Religions. Since then, American Jews have been disproportionately present in a variety of Buddhist communities, have integrated Buddhist practices and doctrines into Judaism, and have taken leading roles in the creation of secular mindfulness in America.

The diversity of these encounters, with multiple forms of cross-cultural influence and appropriation, belies the extremely shopworn joke about a Jewish mother visiting Tibet (or India, in some versions) and telling the enthroned guru, "Sheldon, come home!"[1] Implicit in that joke is a single mode of encounter: a neurotic, nerdy Ashkenazic Jew donning the "exotic" drag of Buddhism—and failing to pass, at that. This chapter will show that the reality is far more varied and considered in nature. First, the chapter assesses current scholarship on the phenomenon—variously identified colloquially as JuBu, Jew-Bu, and BuJu—especially the recent works of Emily Sigalow and Mira Niculescu Weil. Second, building on this work, the chapter proposes five modes of how the phenomenon has manifested in the last half century: converts, secularizers, integrators, responders, and hybridizers.

While it is difficult to quantify the extent of the BuJu phenomenon, it is often significant: it is estimated that in American insight meditation communities, up to one-third of practitioners are of Jewish background.[2] The spiritual teacher Ram Dass, himself of Jewish background, is said to have called the percentage of Jews in Buddhist communities "outlandish."[3] A more conservative estimate, cited by Niculescu, is that

---

[1] See, e.g., Sigalow 2019, 1; Niculescu 2017b, 149–150; Rosenzweig 2019, 1; Surya Das 1998, 1. Different versions of the stories have different names, but the story is basically the same.
[2] Gez 2011, 49.
[3] Quoted in Kamenetz 1994, 9.

Jews make up 16–30 percent of American Buddhist practitioners.[4] Either way, this is a strikingly disproportionate representation, given that Jews comprise 2.4 percent of the US population. Similar data are not available for secular/medical mindfulness, though anecdotal evidence suggests that American Jews are overrepresented in that much larger field as well, beginning with its foremost exponent, Jon Kabat-Zinn. And while the new field of "Jewish spirituality" is relatively small, Buddhism's impact on it has been significant.

Two methodological notes are in order at the outset. First, while most of the BuJu phenomenon involves meditation-based convert lineages (MBCLs), other forms are present as well. Numerous American Jews have been ordained or otherwise teach in Tibetan, Zen, Theravādan, and other lineages. Outside of the scope of the present study is the relatively small number of Jews who have affiliated with non-liberal Buddhist communities (formerly known as "heritage" or "Asian" Buddhist communities). Second, as will become clear, the present writer is himself active in the BuJu phenomenon, and has written about it as a practitioner several times.[5] While the intention here is to provide a scholarly overview of the phenomenon, it is inevitable that the author's individual perspectives and social position will affect that presentation.

Literature Review and Historical Background

Scholarly Works

American Jews' involvement with Buddhism has been the subject of sporadic investigation over the years, and concentrated attention in the last two decades.

Emily Sigalow's *American JewBu: Jews, Buddhists, and Religious Change* (2019) is the most significant study of the BuJu phenomenon in America. It identifies three periods in the phenomenon's history. The first extends from Strauss's conversion in 1893 through the growing interest in Buddhism among Jewish intellectuals of the 1920s. The second period discussed by Sigalow is essentially that of "the sixties" (understood culturally, not chronologically) and the New Age, roughly from 1966 to 1990. During this period, many Jews became prominent American Buddhist teachers and leaders, which contributied to the partial secularization of Buddhism in America and the "emphasizing [of] meditation and mindfulness and muting the dogmatic, doctrinal, and mythological elements of Buddhism."[6] These, of course, are similar to the changes that, as McMahan observed,

---

[4] Niculescu 2017b, 151.
[5] See Michaelson 2013, 152–160; 2015, 3–25; 2019, 206–213.
[6] Sigalow 2019, 69.

Asian pioneers of Buddhist modernism wrought in the nineteenth and early twentieth centuries.[7]

The third and most recent period discussed by Sigalow runs from 1991 to the present. Here, Sigalow focuses on two developments in which American Jews played a significant role: secular, medical mindfulness on the one hand, and Buddhist-influenced Jewish spirituality or Jewish meditation on the other. The secular phenomenon is much larger, with estimates of one million Americans trying meditation (mostly secular mindfulness meditation) for the first time each year. But each influenced the other. The secularization of Buddhist meditation made it "kosher" for some traditional Jewish practitioners, and these secular phenomena themselves owe a debt to Jewish culture.

Sigalow then turns to forms of Buddhist-Jewish encounter based on interviews conducted with contemporary subjects: the creation of a "Jewish meditation" largely based on Buddhist-derived mindfulness, the syncretic birth of a "Jewish Buddhist spirituality" focused on the cultivation of beneficial qualities of mind and heart, and the construction of a hybrid Jewish-Buddhist identity, especially among cultural and non-practicing Jews. Setting aside Jewish Buddhists' and Buddhist Jews' own explanations for their syncretic activity—such as filling contemplative gaps in Judaism, finding meaning (spiritual or otherwise) as secular Jews, and enhancing Jewish practice—Sigalow argues that the "most central explanation for the appeal of Buddhism to American Jews is that American Jews and convert Buddhists share a remarkably similar sociodemographic location in society, thus facilitating the mixing of the two groups."[8] Additional factors proposed by Sigalow are that "Judaism and Buddhism do not have a fraught history with each other," that loose Buddhist communal organization rules permitted affiliation, the "modernizing efforts of the Jewish Buddhist teachers" of the twentieth century, and the "familiar territory" created by Buddhist teachers of Jewish background.[9]

Mira Niculescu Weil has authored several articles on the BuJu phenomenon. Here we will focus on Niculescu (2017b), which offers a somewhat different periodization of the American Jewish encounter with Buddhism, which in her presentation coincide with different modes of integration and syncretism. Niculescu Weil does not treat the pre-"sixties" periods of Jewish-Buddhist encounter, and instead proposes three phases of development. First is the 1970s–1980s, in which, she says, Jews leaving "the fold" for Buddhism were seen as threats, and were widely condemned both by prominent

---

[7] See McMahan 2009.

[8] Sigalow 2019, 182.

[9] Ibid. 183–184. Sigalow's accounts of her subjects' motives often differ from what they say themselves. For example, meditation teacher James Baraz states that Joseph Goldstein's Jewish background was initially off-putting, but that Baraz was nonetheless persuaded that "he knew something that I wanted to know, and was saying it's possible to not be run by your neurotic thought patterns." But Sigalow states the opposite, namely, "That Baraz and his teacher came from similar Jewish backgrounds rendered Buddhism permissible to explore."

Orthodox figures such as the Lubavitcher Rebbe and by mainstream American Jews who often sent them to "cult clinics" for deprogramming.[10] Broadly speaking, Jewish explorers in this period were regarded as belonging to the "counterculture." The second period is the 1990s, in which mindfulness and Buddhism became mainstreamed, and in which Niculescu Weil observes that more Jews were "claiming being both Jewish and Buddhist," citing books by Sylvia Boorstein, Alan Lew, and Norman Fischer. And the third period is roughly the early 2000s to the present day, when Niculescu Weil says that Jews began integrating Buddhist insights and practices into Judaism, here citing Jewish meditation centers such as Makor Or and the Institute for Jewish Spirituality.[11]

As with any attempt to align ideological trends with chronological periods, the realities are messier than the periodization. For example, most of the Jewish Buddhist pioneers of the 1970s came from non-religious households, so while the Lubavitcher Rebbe may have disapproved of them, they likely didn't know and didn't care. And the modalities of integration, hybridization, and conversion exist in all of the decades that Niculescu Weil surveys. Yet overall, Niculescu Weil's contribution convincingly rejects the "monolithic, reified approach towards the phenomenon of the 'Jewish-Buddhists'"[12] and persuasively shows how the phenomenon has evolved over time.

Niculescu Weil's other contributions to this field of study include a 2015 chapter in *Buddhism beyond Borders* entitled "Mind Full of God: 'Jewish Mindfulness' as an Offspring of Western Buddhism in America." Here Niculescu Weil shows how the secularization of Buddhist-derived mindfulness facilitated its importation into Judaism. Niculescu Weil identifies certain distinctly American elements to what she calls "Jewish mindfulness": a disillusion with Western modernity, its roots in a "seeker" counterculture, and its experiential rather than dogmatic orientation.

Other scholarly assessments of the Buddhist-Jewish phenomenon include Gez (2011) and Vallely (2008) in English, and Persico (2016) in Hebrew. Gez asserts that the Holocaust was a primary motivating force for Jewish engagement with Buddhism, causing a profound rupture in Jewish identity and an undermining of traditional Jewish theology. Buddhism, in turn, provided a distinctive language and method of managing that trauma and suffering that appealed to Jews.[13] Vallely, in contrast, focuses on the postwar period that produced so many "seekers" among the Baby Boom generation in general, and the alienation of postwar late-modern capitalism that engendered it. She writes, "[I]f a 'no-nonsense,' down-to-earth Judaism works well to ensure ethnic identification and continuity, it offers little to those seeking the inspirational, the ineffable, and, perhaps, even a little of the impractical."[14]

---

[10] Niculescu 2017b, 154–156.
[11] Ibid., 157–160.
[12] Ibid., 152.
[13] Gez 2011, 45.
[14] Vallely 2008, 22.

Other Works

Outside the academy, by far the most influential text on Buddhism and Judaism is Rodger Kamenetz's 1994 bestseller, *The Jew in the Lotus*. On one level, *Lotus* is a travelogue, recounting a historic (or quixotic) meeting between an assortment of rabbis and the Dalai Lama. But because Kamenetz perceptively and astutely detailed the participants' varying ways of relating to Buddhism, including his own, it became a kind of BuJu bible. It did not recount history so much as make it. It would not be an exaggeration to divide American Buddhist Jewish life into the time before and after *Lotus*'s publication.

Within Buddhist Jewish literature, the two most popular and influential monographs are by Sylvia Boorstein (*That's Funny, You Don't Look Buddhist*) and Rabbi Alan Lew (*One God Clapping: The Spiritual Path of a Zen Rabbi*). Both combine memoir with teachings on how the traditions enrich and occasionally conflict with one another. The anthology *Beside Still Waters: Jews, Christians, and the Way of the Buddha* is the most significant (non-academic) anthology in part about the BuJu phenomenon, and includes contributions from Boorstein, Lew, and others. Other BuJu monographs include works by Norman Fischer (*Opening to You: A Zen-Inspired Translation of the Psalms*), Brenda Shoshanna (*Jewish Dharma: A Guide to the Practice of Judaism and Zen*), and this writer (*God in Your Body: Kabbalah, Mindfulness, and Embodied Spiritual Practice*). Jewish meditation/mindfulness books clearly influenced by Buddhism also include Jonathan Slater's *Mindful Jewish Living*, and books by Jeff Roth, David Cooper, and others. Earlier entries in the literature of Buddhism and Judaism include a volume edited by Harold Heifetz, *Zen and Hasidism* (1978), which includes some of the first practitioners' comparisons of the two paths, as well as Martin Buber's essay comparing the two, and Judith Linzer's *Torah and Dharma* (1996).

Important works that either integrate Buddhist practices into Judaism or attempt to develop "native" Jewish practices in response to them include Arthur Green's 1995 essay "Restoring the Aleph," and several of the essays in the *Neo-Hasidism: Branches* anthology that Green co-edited with Ariel Mayse (especially those by Nancy Flam, Jonathan Slater, and James Jacobson-Maisels), as well as Aryeh Kaplan's three volumes on Jewish meditation, and the writings of the Chabad-Lubavitch Rabbi DovBer Pinson.

MODES OF INTERACTION

We now turn to five modes of American Buddhist-Jewish interaction as reflected in five populations of Buddhist-Jewish practitioners.

1. Converts: Jews in Buddhist Communities

The first is *converts*: Jews practicing or teaching Buddhism while largely leaving behind Judaism. Examples include, in the Insight Meditation/neo-Theravādan tradition,

Joseph Goldstein, Sharon Salzberg, Jack Kornfield, Jacqueline Mandell, Bhikkhu Bodhi, James Baraz, Ayya Khema, Mark Epstein, Wes Nisker, and Daniel Goleman. In Tibetan traditions, they include Lama Surya Das, Thubthen Chodron, and others; in Zen traditions, they include Bernie Glassman, Koshin Paley Ellison, Dennis Merzel/Genpo Roshi, and others. This list could also include cultural figures including Philip Glass and Allen Ginsberg.

As the Sheldon joke indicates, this is the most familiar form of Buddhist-Jewish interaction: Jews "leaving the fold" and practicing Buddhism or Buddhist meditation, as these have done. Yet contrary to the exotic imagery of the joke, in Theravādan and Zen contexts (though not in Tibetan ones), most of these secular Jews found a Buddhist modernism that had already diminished the role of ritual, deities, magic, dogma, doctrine, and other "religious" elements. As they brought Buddhist modernism to the West, they amplified this modernist tendency, emphasizing the pragmatic, psychologically oriented, and ostensibly "secular" teachings of the Buddha and de-emphasizing past lives, karma, and other non-"scientific" elements. (Of course, many non-Jewish figures such as Stephen Batchelor also carried this process forward still further.) In addition, while Jews in this segment have generally moved away from Jewish religious practice, many of these American Jews bring with them aspects of American Jewish culture, such as a householder-focused humanism, a rejection of quietism, Jewish humor or other cultural influences, and an emphasis on psychology, psychiatry, and psychotherapy. All of these trends are present particularly in MBCL American Buddhism.

As noted above, scholars have proposed an array of explanations for this striking phenomenon: assimilated Jews' rejection of traditional Judaism in the United States (leading them to seek answers to philosophical/religious questions outside of their "native" religious context), the enduring trauma of the Holocaust (and its erasure of traditional God concepts), the economic success of Jewish immigrants and their children's questioning of American capitalist conceptions of success,[15] and the encounter with Zen, Tibetan, and Theravādan forms of Buddhist modernism which were already reformed by Asian Buddhist modernizers to speak to concerns of the modern subject in pragmatic, "scientific" terms.[16] At the very least, the socioeconomic position of American Jews, as disproportionately educated, middle-class, and apart from American Christianity, rendered them open to new ways of understanding fundamental philosophical and religious questions, with Buddhism, among other philosophies and traditions, being one of them.

Yet the model of "conversion" may be misleading. Judaism does not formally recognize conversion, and MBCL Buddhism does not require or even ritualize it. Even Charles Strauss's taking on of Buddhist precepts was not a "conversion," a term with Christian-normative assumptions that do not apply in his case. Moreover, for some practitioners, "conversion" implies an assumption of a particularist identity, which is part of what the "converts" are leaving behind. In Chodron's words:

---

[15] Green 1995, 10–12.
[16] McMahan 2009.

What does being Jewish mean? I remember discussing it in Sunday school, and when the rabbi asked that on a test, I managed to pass. Am I Jewish because my ancestors were? Because I have dark curly hair...? Am I Jewish because I was confirmed?... One day I went to the Wailing Wall to pray. For a while I recited the mantra of Chenresig and visualized purifying light healing the centuries of suffering in the Middle East. To me, Jewish and Buddhist are merely labels. It is not important what we call ourselves. It is important how we live, how we treat others.[17]

If American Jewish social and economic positions made an embrace of Buddhism available, this lack of ethnic/tribal belonging which characterized postwar American Judaism made it all the more attractive.

2. Secularizers

Related to American Jews who leave Judaism and adopt Buddhism are the *secularizers*: those American Jews who have played a disproportionate role in the creation of secular mindfulness. Obviously, Mindfulness-Based Stress Reduction, Mindfulness-Based Cognitive Therapy, and other forms of secular mindfulness in the healthcare context, are not overtly Jewish, and claim to be not overtly Buddhist either. The number of American Jews in the field also seems less disproportionate in the case of secularizers than in the case of converts. To this day, there has been little scholarly attention to whatever Jewish cultural or religious resonances remain in this material. Yet, given the size of secular mindfulness—36 million Americans have tried it at least once—this category's overall impact is likely the largest of any considered here, suggesting an area for further investigation.

Arguably, the secular Jewish cultural milieu that greatly influenced the founders of American *vipassanā* also influenced the Jewish founders of the contemporary mindfulness movement, including Jon Kabat-Zinn, Daniel Goleman, and bestselling author Dan Harris. Socially, these secularizers overlap closely with the converts: Jon Kabat-Zinn often works with teachers from the Insight Meditation Society, for example, and MBSR is primarily an adaptation of neo-Theravādan forms. And these figures all share several characteristics with convert leaders: non-religious Judaism, liberal to centrist American politics, an awareness of and affinity for psychoanalysis and psychology, and a middle-class, educated, white social position. By the 2020s, the field of secular mindfulness had grown well beyond its initial founders, and has been influenced by corporate actors, insurance companies, and capitalist "wellness" culture, on the one hand, and on the other, by teachers, writers, publishers, and leaders from diverse backgrounds.

---

[17] Chodron 2016.

3. Integrators

A second form of Buddhist-Jewish interaction is the integration of Buddhist teachings and techniques into Judaism, or more specifically, Jewish spirituality. While a far smaller phenomena than secular mindfulness or "convert" Buddhism, this "integration" model has transformed Jewish spirituality. Notable figures include the Institute for Jewish Spirituality, James Jacobson-Maisels, Jonathan Slater, Sheila Peltz Weinberg, Nancy Flam, and Jeff Roth, among many others. The Institute for Jewish Spirituality (IJS), initially founded by the Nathan Cummings Foundation (Rachel Cowan, responsible for much of the funding work at Cummings, later became the executive director of IJS), is the leading organization embodying this approach. Its motto, according to its website (accessed in December 2022), is "Cultivate Mindfulness, Deepen Connection, and Enliven Jewish Life." The explicit use of the term "mindfulness" acknowledges this integration. Other organizations integrating Buddhist teachings into Jewish meditation or spiritual practice include Makor Or, Chochmat HaLev, and the Elat Chayyim retreat center, also founded by Rabbi Jeff Roth, which for ten years hosted Jewish meditation retreats that were almost entirely teaching *vipassanā* meditation. As Niculescu put it, "The very fact of the creation of an 'Institute for Jewish Spirituality,' based on the practice of mindfulness and meditation, shows the depth of this re-claiming process: it has turned into an institutionalization of the use of Buddhist tools within a Jewish frame."[18]

Integrators' accounts of the sources and nature of mindfulness vary. In some cases, mindfulness is described as coming from Buddhism but being grafted, consciously, into Jewish practice. In others, mindfulness is described as essentially secular or universal. And in others still, it is described as indigenous to Judaism. For example, Rabbi James Jacobson-Maisels, who directs the Or HaLev organization (which runs some programs with IJS), says that the Hasidic Piaseczner Rebbe "teaches mindfulness as the intentional, nonjudgmental observation of one's own experience."[19] Sometimes the relationship is simply left undiscussed. For example, Rabbi Jeff Roth's The Awakened Heart Project says that it "was created to promote Jewish contemplative techniques that develop a heart of wisdom and compassion through daily practice and a variety of meditation retreat opportunities."[20] Though the website discusses Jewish contemplative techniques, the primary form of meditation taught by The Awakened Heart Project is mindfulness, and Rabbi Roth has extensive retreat experience in Buddhist contexts. In a sense, these models reflect different iterations of what Beth Berkowitz described as the "Neutralization" strategy, which states that a given innovation is basically secular and thus safe to import, and the "Biblicalization" strategy, which insists that an innovation is actually contained within Judaism.[21]

---

[18] Niculescu 2017b, 160.
[19] Jacobson-Maisels 2019, 255.
[20] https://awakenedheartproject.org/, accessed December 16, 2022.
[21] Berkowitz 2012.

Even beyond the practices of mindfulness and mindfulness meditation, these integrations usually carry an affective quality of American forms of Buddhist modernism. Traditional Jewish values, such as arguing righteously, enforcing boundaries (us/them, righteous/wicked, kosher/unkosher, permitted/forbidden, sacred/profane), and scrupulous ritual performance, though central to biblical and rabbinic traditions, tend to be devalued in Buddhist-influenced Jewish spirituality. Meanwhile, values central to Buddhist modernism that are only secondary in traditional rabbinic Judaism—selfless action for the benefit of all beings, interconnection/universalism, being mindful of "the present moment," and so on—are often foregrounded in this "Jewish" spirituality, even when the spiritual teachers do not mention Buddhism at all.

One example of the integration model of Jewish Buddhism is the way some Jewish spiritual teachers have joined Buddhist-derived meditation techniques with Hasidic teachings filtered through the contemporary movement known as Neo-Hasidism.[22] Consider this presentation by Rabbi Jonathan Slater, in his chapter "Neo-Hasidism for Today's Jewish Seeker." Describing the work of the IJS, Slater states that "the foundation of the [Jewish spiritual] practice is mindfulness meditation, which in turn grounds one in mindfulness in whatever one does."[23] Slater observes that when performed with the orientation of mindfulness, "religious practice is no longer solely a Jewish obligation or ethnic identifier, but a means to cultivate spiritual and ethical dispositions, leading to personal (and ultimately global) transformation."[24] But, Slater continues:

> Introducing the study of Hasidic texts helped to ground the mindfulness practice in Jewish language. Here were teachers who were interested—among other things—in inviting the reader to sense his or her direct connection with God, in feeling the ebbs and lows of spiritual awareness, in seeing the whole of life as an arena for spiritual consciousness and engagement. Furthermore, the texts discussing the spiritual experiences of the Hasidic teachers, the shifts in consciousness that led to deeper awareness of the Divine and connection to God, did not directly teach the practices by which readers could attain these shifts themselves. Readers were often left with the sense of "yes, but how?"
>
> Both mindfulness meditation and mindfulness practice can lead to these experiences. Thus the institute took the best of each form of study—mindfulness as well as Hasidic texts and spirituality—and invited each to reflect on the other, to illuminate each other, to make them more powerful together.[25]

The phrase "yes, but how?" is an apt summation of one of the primary motives of Buddhist-Jewish synthesis.[26] Jewish mystical teachings—here, Hasidic texts mediated

---

[22] Flam 2019; Jacobson-Maisels 2019; and Slater 2019.
[23] Slater 2019, 271.
[24] Ibid. at 272.
[25] Ibid. at 272–273.
[26] Flam quotes Alan Morinis, a leading teacher of the Jewish ethical refinement practice known as *mussar*, as considering to title "one of his books on seeking holiness as a Jew '*Yes, but How?*'"; Flam 2019, 233.

by the reformist/modernist adaptations of Martin Buber, Arthur Green, and others—offer tantalizing promises of mystical experiences, but do not say how to attain them. Mindfulness, writes Slater, "can lead to these experiences." This writer, too, had a similar understanding early on in my encounter with mindfulness meditation in a Jewish context, presented on a "Jewish meditation retreat" at the Elat Chayyim Jewish Retreat Center in 2002. Shortly after those retreats, I wrote that meditation was like "getting the answer key" to Jewish practice, continuing, "This is what they were talking about when they said that God is everywhere! The attention brought to mundane objects renders them everyday miracles, and an opened heart makes *davening* [Jewish prayer] a cathartic, healing experience."[27]

This model is sometimes referred to as "Buddhist roots, Jewish fruits." The roots of the practice are Buddhist in nature, but the fruits are not liberation from the wheel of samsara and extinguishing of the taints, but, in Nancy Flam's words, "how to live in conscious relationship with the Divine Presence."[28] Yet on closer inspection, these "fruits" are themselves affected by the Buddhist-Jewish encounter. For example, consider the words of Jacobson-Maisels:

> The goals of my practice are fundamentally the goals of the early (and some later) Hasidic masters in their own spiritual practice. I am to give up the illusion of dualism and see that I, the Divine, other humans, animals, plants, and the inanimate world are not truly separate. . . . I am to touch the divine nothingness and radical openness (*ayin*) that is my true nature. . . . I am to be present in every moment. . . . I am to see myself clearly, to understand the nature of my heart, mind, body, and soul, to achieve insight (*hasagah*) and understanding. I am to free myself of pain (*tsara*) and suffering, anxiety and depression (*atsvut*).[29]

These goals, particularly insight, reducing suffering, and interconnection, owe a great deal to MBCL Buddhism, Buddhist modernism, the New Age, and twentieth-century American spirituality.[30] Arguably, in their use of Hasidic sources, neo-Hasidic integrators are creating a kind of "Hasidic modernism." Just as Buddhist modernists "reformed" Buddhism to be more rational, scientific, worldly, and so on, so neo-Hasidic modernists "reform" Hasidism to be more contemplative, universalist, and focused on interconnection—in other words, more like Buddhist modernism. Hasidism is no longer about theurgy, the role of the *tzaddik*, or pious observance of the law—it is about cultivating lovingkindness, compassion, and even mindfulness.

Some teachers see the two traditions as even closer in orientation, as simply using different language to describe the same reality. Sheila Peltz Weinberg, for example, writes:

---

[27] Michaelson 2019, 28.
[28] Flam 2019, 223.
[29] Jacobson-Maisels 2019, 251–252.
[30] On the theme of interdependence in Buddhist modernism, see McMahan 2009, 149–182.

> As the days unfolded [at Insight Meditation Society], I started to translate the teachings into a Jewish spiritual language. I understood that the Buddhist reference to suffering, craving, and the conditioned "I" that always wants attention and amusement was equivalent to what Judaism refers to as false gods and idolatry.... I begin to teach mindfulness to Jews using the language of Jewish story and symbol.[31]

Such claims, of course, are homiletical rather than scholarly in nature. When biblical texts mention false gods and idolatry, they are referring to deities worshipped by Canaanites, Egyptians, Assyrians, or other nations in the Ancient Near East—and, archaeological evidence has demonstrated, by many Israelites as well—not the "conditioned 'I' that always wants attention and amusement." The pleasant, expansive, equanimous mind states that result from *samadhi* meditation may or may not align with what Kabbalistic writers "were talking about when they said that God is everywhere." And from the perspective of Theravādan Buddhism, it would be an error to reify an experience, however filled with insight and pleasant sensations, into an ontological claim of "awareness of the Divine and connection to God." That does not mean, of course, that Buddhist means cannot be utilized for Jewish ends by the practitioner—only that there is not necessarily an identity between them historically.

At the same time, integrators' relationships to "native" Jewish meditation practices vary. Some, including IJS and Maisels, utilize such practices as Hasidic contemplation, ecstatic prayer, and techniques adapted from the Kabbalist Abraham Abulafia, while still using mindfulness as the primary technique. Others, including Jonathan Omer-Man, one of the founders of IJS who went on to found the Metivta Center for contemplative Judaism, have focused primarily on Jewish practices. Still others, discussed in the "responders" category, claim to teach only "native" Jewish practices, often with a hostility to Buddhism. Yet while these techniques and practices do exist, they are nowhere as systematic as Buddhist texts on meditation. There is no unified system of Jewish meditation, no manuals describing how to overcome common obstacles, no inventory of psychological traits that can support or obstruct meditation, and no long history of practitioners leaving behind records of their experiences and techniques. They are also traditionally embedded in Jewish theologies that may not resonate with contemporary seekers. As Flam puts it, "The Hasidic texts on self-effacement to make room for God's fullness everywhere intrigued me, but it was only when I began practicing mindfulness meditation that I learned a discipline for training the mind in just this way."[32] Thus practitioners have observed that the mind quieted by meditation is more able to experience wonder and the sacred, including in the contexts of Jewish ritual, and that meditation enables more ethical conduct in personal relationships. Further, insights into emptiness and/or non-self can be, in some Jewish panentheistic theological understandings, insights into the Divine as the sole reality.

---

[31] Weinberg 2010, 85–87.
[32] Flam 2019, 232.

Of course, integrators and hybridzers also face significant challenges and discontinuities between the traditions. For example, traditional Judaism's ban on statues and idolatry conflicts with many Buddhist traditions' customs of bowing or making offerings to statues, and even most MBCL centers have a Buddha statue present. Traditional Judaism's theism and emphasis on rites and rituals may conflict either with Theravādan condemnations of ritual actions or with different Mahāyāna or Vajrayāna rituals. One of the leading hybridizers, Alan Lew, said that the extent of this challenge depends on the tradition:

> So when one asks the question of whether or not Buddhism and Judaism are compatible with each other, one has to first ask, which Buddhism? (And I suppose it might be useful to ask which Judaism as well.) If one is talking about the austere, value free mindfulness practice of Zen or Vipasana, it is hard to see a problem. In these settings, Buddhism has principally concerned itself with the cultivation of awareness. If someone wants to say that the cultivation of awareness is somehow incompatible or threatening to Judaism, I think they really need to take a closer look at what they are saying. On the other hand, a Jew might be forgiven, in my view, if he felt uncomfortable visualizing the host of heavenly and demonic beings Tibetan Buddhism asks him to visualize, or reciting its Mantras, or doing prostrations by the thousands, whether in the direction of a statue of the Buddha or not.[33]

Denominationally, the work of integrators and hybridizers has appeared primarily in nearly all Jewish movements, in various forms. Reform, Reconstructionist, and Jewish Renewal movements have been most receptive to explicitly integrating or hybridizing Buddhist techniques and doctrines, with Conservative and Modern Orthodox ones more reticent and tending to prefer toward techniques presented as natively Jewish. However, there is diversity of opinion everywhere. For example, Rabbi Zalman Schachter-Shalomi, the former Chabad Lubavitch emissary who founded the Jewish Renewal movement, often complained of what he called "vipassana in a *tallis* [prayer shawl]" and promoted Hasidic prayer and contemplation, among numerous other techniques. At the same time, Renewal figures such as Jeff Roth pioneered the integrationist approach, and Schachter-Shalomi himself was a radical syncretist, sampling practices from a wide variety of traditions. The cleavage lines among approaches do not align with denominational ones.

4. Hybridizers

Closely related to, and overlapping with, the integrators are those we might term *hybridizers*, who overtly blend Buddhism and/or mindfulness and Judaism, either in adjacent paths that occasionally intersect, or into a hybridity. As we saw, many integrators

---

[33] Lew 2005b.

would agree that they are making use of Buddhist-derived "technologies" for Jewish ends. However, the experience of this writer, who identifies and teaches in this category, suggests that there are significant differences in approach. Leading hybridizers include Boorstein, Kamenetz, Fischer, Lew, Cooper, Michaelson, and Alison Laichter,[34] as well as artistic figures such as Leonard Cohen.[35] Many have written bestselling books on the Buddhist-Jewish intersection, and while all have, at times, taught wholly within one tradition or the other, they have also affirmed both paths as integral to their identity and conception of the spiritual path. The subtitles of Boorstein's book, *On Being a Faithful Jew and a Passionate Buddhist*, Lew's, *The Spiritual Path of a Zen Rabbi*, and Michaelson's *Kabbalah, Mindfulness, and Embodied Spiritual Practice*, perhaps embody this approach.

While there is no clear line separating integrators and hybridizers, the terms do denote differing approaches to the Buddhist-Jewish interchange. First, for a hybridizer, the approach is not "Buddhist roots, Jewish fruits" but the whole Buddhist tree, ends as well as means. Whereas an integrator utilizes mindfulness for purportedly Jewish ends, the hybridizer may practice Buddhist meditation, ethics, and behavioral norms for their own dharmic ends, whether understood in terms of liberation, *nibbana*, the bodhisattva ideal, living in the light of *rigpa*, a Zen form of enlightenment, or in any other number of ways. There is no assumption that these ends align with Jewish goals of practice, or can somehow be found in Jewish text. The converse is also true. Jewish religious valorizations of "holy" mind-states, personal theistic language, myths—even, for some, its legal strictures—may also be goals of practice for hybridizers, even if they do not align with (or are in some cases contradicted by) Buddhist ones.

While in some quarters, this hybridization is denigrated as a form of New Age/hyper-capitalist dilettantism, others have regarded hybridity as a hallmark of postmodern identity, not only in terms of religious and ethno-religious identity, but also in terms of race, gender, sexuality, migration, and national/civic identification.[36] It makes manifest the bricolage of postmodern identities, rejecting claims to authenticity or identity, claims which invariably involve the invention of some unbroken or recovered tradition. Yet just as integrators inquired into the possible "benefits" of Buddhist practice for Judaism, hybridizers face a converse question: the benefits of maintaining a Jewish practice in a Buddhist or hybrid context. These values may include the resonance, meaning, and comfort that emerge from the Jewish context, family, life-cycle events, daily rituals, culture, and community; the emphasis on worldliness and humanism that can complement the more individualistic activity of meditation, particularly in MBCLs derived from Theravādan monastic practice; the devotionalistic elements of Jewish life that can replace Buddhist devotionalistic elements that were removed by Buddhist modernism

---

[34] Sigalow 2019, 101–104.
[35] Bariman 2021.
[36] Badalescu 2014, McMahan 2009, 242–244; Vallely 2008, 32. At the same time, religious hybridity is at least as old as the overlapping biblical Israelite religions, and many scholars believe it to be more common than non-hybridity. See, e.g., McGuire 2008, 185–213.

and MBCLs; and Jewish spiritual practices that allow for a wider variety of personal, psychological, familial, spiritual, and ethical concerns to be explored in meditation than generally appear in traditional Buddhist contexts.

At the same time, taking Buddhist values, as well as practice, seriously can change what is meant by a Jewish experience in a Jewish space. As Boorstein put it:

> These days it's normal for me not only to go to a synagogue and have people say "let's sit quietly for a few moments" but to really talk about what we're doing there in terms of the transformation of consciousness, of developing kindness and compassion. The message of dharma is more than just the practice of sitting—you can sit quietly and nothing can happen. It's about sitting quietly with the intention to notice those characteristics of heart and mind that lead to unhappiness, and those that lead to happiness, and therefore "choose life." This is not just a groovy way to alter your consciousness, or feel a little bit high or a little bit relaxed, but really to see deeply into the nature of your own character and—whatever language you want to use—the glory of God, or the wonder of creation, or the awesomeness of being alive, and to have that vision transform you into the kindest and most courageous person that you can be for the duration of your lifetime.[37]

While Boorstein is speaking here of an integrationist context—meditation in a synagogue—note that her approach is more hybridist in orientation. It blends MBCL/Theravādan Buddhist values—she refers here to the three characteristics of *anicca*, *anatta*, and *dukkha*, the traditional foci of insight meditation—with Jewish ones (the quotation of "choose life," for example). She explicitly rejects the stress reduction aim of secular mindfulness, and emphasizes both Jewish religious/mystical values and psychological/ethical ones.

Again, the boundary between integration and hybridity is soft and porous, as Boorstein's own work shows. It is not always possible to sort teachers into one category or another. However, they are distinct approaches to how the Buddhist and Jewish traditions relate to one another, and the nuances among them offer intriguing possibilities for future research.

5. Responders

Finally, though in a less innovative mode, are the Jewish spiritual leaders influenced by but hostile to Buddhism, whom I am calling *responders*. Unlike the integrators, the responders omit or disavow any direct positive influence, and purport to present "native" Jewish wisdom regarding meditation and spirituality—sometimes in a continuous lineage (as in Chabad Hasidism) and other times in a recovery of Jewish meditation techniques from centuries past. Yet the responders are influenced by Buddhism in at

---

[37] Quoted in Michaelson 2013, 156–157.

least one way: they feel moved to articulate a Jewish meditation partially in response to the popularity among American Jews of Buddhism, yoga, Hinduism, and other Asian-derived traditions and practices. Moreover, from the ways in which the responders edit and present their material, it is obvious that one of their motivations is seeking to persuade American Jews who might be tempted by these other paths to instead find their meditative spiritual paths within Judaism.

The most famous of the responders, and probably still the most influential single source for Jewish meditation among traditional Jews, was Aryeh Kaplan (1934–1983), an Orthodox rabbi active in *kiruv* (outreach to non-religious Jews) and Orthodox youth groups. Kaplan's works have been enormously popular, especially *Jewish Meditation: A Practical Guide* (1982), which presents meditation practices from Kabbalistic, Hasidic, and even biblical sources. Kaplan only occasionally mentions non-Jewish meditative techniques, often with warnings not to undertake them, but it is clear from the historical context and the methods that he puts forward that he is "competing" with mantra meditation, mindfulness meditation, and other popular practices, and significantly interpreting (or distorting) the Jewish sources in order to do so. For example, Rabbi Nachman of Bratzlav recommends the phrase *Ribbono Shel Olam* ("Master of the Universe") not as a mantra, as Kaplan presents it, but as a plaintive emotional cry when one feels unable to speak in the free-associative method known as *hisbodedus*.[38] And Abulafian techniques in the original sources are far more complex, mythic, and embedded in textual allusions, numerology, and prophecy than in Kaplan's presentations of them. More recently, DovBer Pinson has written a series of books compiling and presenting Jewish meditative teachings, again with the intention (communicated to this author) of presenting "native" Jewish teachings as an alternative to Buddhist ones. The title of one such entry, *Breathing and Quieting the Mind*, reflects this orientation. Ironically, these Orthodox responders, in responding to Buddhism, internalize various Buddhist conceptions of the nature and purpose of meditation.[39]

Perhaps the most remarkable example of this trend is the recent campaign by Chabad-Lubavitch Hasidism described as "Meditation from Sinai: Mindful awareness and Divine spirituality to help you think, feel, and live more deeply."[40] The course description states, "many Jews are unaware of another important facet of the Jewish tradition: deeply meaningful teachings about mindful awareness, spirituality, and meditative practices."[41] While the vocabulary and purposes of the course are obviously drawn from

---

[38] Kaplan, 2011, 57–58. Kaplan notes Rabbi Nachman's usage of the phrase but states "it seems obvious that Rabbi Nachman was prescribing the use of this phrase as a mantra to bring a person into a higher state of consciousness."

[39] See also Glazerson 1981. Glazerson states that Hindu and Buddhist philosophy as we know them were in fact originated by the biblical Abraham.

[40] The same course modules are available on numerous local Chabad websites. See, e.g., https://www.chabadqueenanne.com/templates/articlecco_cdo/aid/5345942/jewish/Meditation-From-Sinai.htm; https://www.chabadsa.com/templates/articlecco_cdo/aid/5395850/jewish/Meditation-from-Sinai.htm; and https://www.chabad101.com/templates/articlecco_cdo/aid/5270132/jewish/JLI-Meditation-from-Sinai.htm.

[41] Ibid.

secular mindfulness and Buddhist modernism, the course offers "the uniquely Jewish approaches to these fascinating topics."

In many of these responder texts by Orthodox figures, Kabbalistic meditative forms with aims wholly different from Buddhist ones—such as theosophy, theurgy, maintenance of cosmic order, the receiving of prophecy—are put to work in the service of cultivating spiritual mind-states and ecstatic experiences. Ironically, the "native" forms of Jewish meditation such teachers present are themselves perhaps the most dramatic example of Buddhist influence on Judaism.

Conclusion

As we have seen, American Jews' encounters with Buddhism have taken many forms over the past 125 years, with new ones still being created. The encounter has greatly shaped American Buddhism on the one hand, and Jewish spirituality on the other, arguably influencing secular mindfulness as well. By way of conclusion, having begun with an overused joke that flattens the BuJu experience into a reductive model of Jews wandering off to "exotic" Asia, perhaps the diversity of that experience could be better captured by a few of the dozens of Buddhist-Jewish jokes in David Bader's *Zen Judaism: For You, A Little Enlightenment*. While these are, of course, jokes, they still reflect some of the actual interplay of Buddhist and Jewish sensibilities, as well as practices and doctrines, and perhaps capture some of the affective quality of the BuJu experience. Or just a laugh.

> There is no escaping karma. In a previous life, you never called, you never wrote, you never visited. And whose fault was this?
> Be aware of your body. Be aware of your perceptions. Keep in mind that not every physical sensation is a symptom of a terminal illness.
> Zen is not easy. It takes effort to attain nothingness. And then what do you have? *Bupkis*.[42]

References

Bader, David. 2002. *Zen Judaism: For You, A Little Enlightenment*. New York: Harmony Books.
Bădulescu, Dana. 2014. "The Hybrids of Postmodernism." *Postmodern Openings* 5: 9–20.
Bariman, Alan. 2021 "The Meanings of Zen Buddhism in Leonard Cohen's Poetry." ProQuest Dissertations Publishing.

---

[42] The Yiddish term *bupkis* means "nothing," but with an untranslatable inflection of frustration and disappointment.

Berkowitz, Beth. 2012. *Defining Jewish Difference from Antiquity to the Present*. New York: Cambridge University Press.

Boorstein, Sylvia. 1997. *That's Funny, You Don't Look Buddhist: On Being a Faithful Jew and a Passionate Buddhist*. San Francisco: Harper.

Cadge, Wendy. 2005. *Heartwood: The First Generation of Theravada Buddhism in America*. Chicago: University of Chicago Press.

Chayes, Bill, and Isaac Solotaroff. 1999. *Jews and Buddhism: Belief Amended, Faith Revealed*. New York: Filmmakers Library.

Chodron, Thubten. "Land of Identities: An American Jewish Tibetan Buddhist Nun Visits Israel." *Tricycle: The Buddhist Review*, February 8, 2016, https://tricycle.org/magazine/land-identities/.

Cooper, Rabbi David A. 1998. *God Is a Verb: Kabbalah and the Practice of Jewish Mysticism*. New York: Riverhead Books.

Cooper, Rabbi David A. 2011. *Three Gates to Meditation Practices: A Personal Journey into Sufism, Buddhism and Judaism*. La Vergne, TN: Turner.

Cooper, Rabbi David A. 2012. *The Handbook of Jewish Meditation Practices: A Guide for Enriching the Sabbath and Other Days of Your Life*. La Vergne, TN: Turner.

Davis, Avram, ed. 1999. *Meditation from the Heart of Judaism: Today's Teachers Share Their Practices, Techniques, and Faith*. Woodstock, VT: Jewish Lights.

Fields, Rick, and Benjamin Bogin. 2022. *How the Swans Came to the Lake: A Narrative History of Buddhism in America*. New York: Shambhala.

Fischer, Norman. 2003. *Opening to You: Zen-Inspired Translations of the Psalms*. New York: Viking Compass.

Fischer, Norman. 2005. "Jewish Meditation and Buber." https://everydayzen.org/teachings/jewish-meditation-and-buber/.

Flam, Nancy. 2019. "Training the Heart and Mind toward Expansive Awareness: A Neo-Hasidic Journey." In *A New Hasidism. Branches*, edited by Arthur Green and Ariel Evan Mayse, 251–270. Philadelphia: Jewish Publication Society.

Gellman, Jerome. 2012. "Judaism and Buddhism: A Jewish Approach to a Godless Religion." In *Jewish Theology and World Religions*, edited by Alon Goshen-Gottstein and Eugene Korn, 299–316. Liverpool: Liverpool University Press.

Gez, Yonatan N. 2011. "The Phenomenon of Jewish Buddhists in Light of the History of Jewish Suffering." *Nova Religio: The Journal of Alternative and Emergent Religions* 15, no. 1: 44–68.

Glazerson, Matityahu. 1981. *The Grandeur of Judaism and the East*. Jerusalem, Israel: Himelsein-Glazerson.

Green, Arthur. 1992. *Seek My Face Speak My Name: A Contemporary Jewish Theology*. Northvale, NJ: Jason Aronson.

Green, Arthur, Barry W. Holtz, and Ariel Evan Mayse. 2017. *Your Word Is Fire: The Hasidic Masters on Contemplative Prayer*. Nashville, TN: Jewish Lights.

Green, Arthur, and Ariel Evan Mayse. 1995. "Restoring the Aleph: Judaism for the Contemporary Seeker." Council for Initiatives in Jewish Education.

Green, Arthur, and Ariel Evan Mayse. 2019. *A New Hasidism: Branches*. Philadelphia: Jewish Publication Society.

Heifetz, Harold. 1978. *Zen and Hasidism: The Similarities between Two Spiritual Disciplines*. Wheaton, IL: Theosophical Publishing House.

Huss, Boaz. 2022. "Jewish Mysticism and Zen Buddhism: Comparative Perspectives." https://www.youtube.com/watch?v=Ds_Kxfbnfbg.

Jacobson-Maisels, James. 2019. "Neo-Hasidic Meditation: Mindfulness as a Neo-Hasidic Practice." In *A New Hasidism: Branches*, edited by Arthur Green and Ariel Evan Mayse, 251–270. Philadelphia: Jewish Publication Society.

Kamenetz, Rodger. 1994. *The Jew in the Lotus: A Poet's Rediscovery of Jewish Identity in Buddhist India*. San Francisco: Harper San Francisco.

Kaplan, Aryeh. 1985. *Meditation and Kabbalah*. York Beach, ME: S. Weiser.

Kaplan, Aryeh. 1995. *Meditation and the Bible*. Northvale, NJ: Jason Aronson.

Kaplan, Aryeh. 2011. *Jewish Meditation: A Practical Guide*. New York: Schocken Books.

Kasinow, Harold. 2015. "Reflections on Jewish and Christian Encounters with Buddhism." *Buddhist-Christian Studies* 35: 21–28.

Kasimow, Harold, John P. Keenan, and Linda Klepinger Keenan. 2003. *Beside Still Waters: Jews, Christians, and the Way of the Buddha*. Boston: Wisdom Publications.

Levin, Alan. 2015. *Crossing the Boundary: Stories of Jewish Leaders of Other Spiritual Paths*. Berkeley, CA: Regent Press.

Lew, Alan. 2005a. *Be Still and Get Going: A Jewish Meditation Practice for Real Life*. New York: Little, Brown.

Lew, Alan. 2005b. "Why Did Bodhidharma Come to the West?" https://elijah-interfaith.org/sharing-wisdom/eight-jewish-glimpses-of-buddhism.

Lew, Alan, and Sherril Jaffe. 2001. *One God Clapping: The Spiritual Path of a Zen Rabbi*. Nashville, TN: Jewish Lights Publishing.

Libin, Nicole. 2009. "The Choosing People: Constructing Jewish Buddhist Identity in America." PhD thesis, Faculty of Graduate Studies, University of Calgary.

Linzer, Judith. 1996. *Torah and Dharma: Jewish Seekers in Eastern Religions*. Northvale, NJ: Jason Aronson.

Marks, Richard Gordon. 1999. "Jewish-Buddhist Meetings: Review Essay." *Shofar (West Lafayette, Ind.)* 17, no. 3: 93–98.

McGuire, Meredith B. 2008. *Lived Religion: Faith and Practice in Everyday Life*. Oxford: Oxford University Press.

McMahan, David. 2009. *The Making of Buddhist Modernism*. Oxford: Oxford University Press.

Meir, Ephraim. 2015. "Buddhist Thought and Heschel's Jewish Philosophy: An Encounter." In *Interreligious Theology*, edited by Ephraim Meir, 50–61. Berlin, München, and Boston: De Gruyter.

Michaelson, Jay. 2009. *Everything Is God: The Radical Path of Nondual Judaism*. Boulder, CO: Trumpeter.

Michaelson, Jay. 2011. *God in Your Body: Kabbalah Mindfulness and Embodied Spiritual Practice*. La Vergne, TN: Turner.

Michaelson, Jay. 2013. *Evolving Dharma: Meditation Buddhism and the Next Generation of Enlightenment*. Berkeley, CA: Evolver Editions.

Michaelson, Jay. 2015. *The Gate of Tears: Sadness and the Spiritual Path*. Teaneck, NJ: Ben Yehuda Press.

Michaelson, Jay. 2019. *Enlightenment by Trial and Error: Ten Years on the Slippery Slopes of Jewish Spirituality, Postmodern Buddhism and Other Mystical Heresies*. Teaneck, NJ: Ben Yehuda Press.

Mitchell, Scott A., and Natalie E. F. Quli. 2015. *Buddhism beyond Borders: New Perspectives on Buddhism in the United States*. Albany: State University of New York Press.

Musch, Sebastian. 2019. *Jewish Encounters with Buddhism in German Culture: Between Moses and Buddha, 1890–1940*. Cham: Palgrave Macmillan.

Niculescu, Mira. 2012. "I the Jew, I the Buddhist: Multi-Religious Belonging as Inner Dialogue." *Crosscurrents* 62, no. 3: 350–359.

Niculescu, Mira. 2013. "Find your Inner God and Breathe: Buddhism, Pop Culture and Contemporary Changes." In *Religion in Consumer Society*, edited by F. Gauthier, and T. Martikanen, 91–108. London: Ashgate.

Niculescu, Mira. 2015a. "Mind Full of God: Jewish 'Mindfulness' as an Offspring of Western Buddhism in America." In Scott Mitchell and Natalie E.F. Quli, eds, *Buddhism beyond Borders: New Perspectives on Buddhism in the United States*, 143–160. Albany: State University of New York Press.

Niculescu, Mira. 2015b. "Going Online and Taking the Plane. From San Francisco to Jerusalem. The Physical and Electronic Networks of 'Jewish Mindfulness.'" *The Heidelberg Journal of Religions on the Internet* 8: 98–114.

Niculescu, Mira. 2017a. "Reading in-Betweenness: Jewish Buddhist Autobiographies and the Self-Display of Interstitiality." *Contemporary Jewry* 37: 333–347.

Niculescu, Mira. 2017b. "JewBus Are Not What They Used to Be: A Call for a Diachronic Study of the Phenomenon of the 'Jewish Buddhists.'" *PaRDeS Zeitschrift der Vereinigung für Jüdische Studien* 23: 149–161.

Obadia, Lionel. 2007. "Etre Juif et Bouddhiste." In *Des cultures et des Dieux: Repères pour une transmission du fait religieux*, edited by Jean-Christophe Attias and Esther Benbassa, 412–413. Paris: Fayard.

Persico, Tomer. 2016 *The Jewish Meditative Tradition* (Heb.). Ramat Aviv: Tel Aviv University Press.

Persico, Tomer. 2022. "Studying Jewish Meditative Techniques: A Phenomenological Typology and an Interdisciplinary View." *Religions* 13, no. 7: 648.

Pinson, DovBer. 2004. *Meditation and Judaism: Exploring the Jewish Meditative Paths*. Lanham, MD: Jason Aronson.

Pinson, DovBer. 2014. *Breathing and Quieting the Mind*. Brooklyn, NY: IYYUN.

Rosenzweig, Rosie, and Sylvia Boorstein. 2019. *A Jewish Mother in Shangri-La*. Boulder, CO: Shambhala.

Roth, Jeff. 2011. *Jewish Meditation Practices for Everyday Life: Awakening Your Heart Connecting with God*. La Vergne, TN: Turner.

Roth, Jeff. 2016. *Me Myself and God: A Theology of Mindfulness*. Woodstock, NY: Jewish Lights.

Sautter, Cia. 2002. "Chochmat: Rhymes with Spirit Rock." *Journal of Religion and Popular Culture* 1, no. 1: 5–5.

Shaw, Sarah. 2020. *Mindfulness: Where It Comes from and What It Means*. Boston: Shambhala.

Shoshanna, Brenda. 2004. *Jewish Dharma: A Guide to the Practice of Judaism and Zen*. New York: de Capo.

Sigalow, Emily. 2019. *American Jewbu: Jews Buddhists and Religious Change*. Princeton, NJ: Princeton University Press.

Slater, Jonathan. 2004. *Mindful Jewish Living: Compassionate Practice*. Charlottesville, VA: Aviv Press.

Slater, Jonathan. 2019. "Neo-Hasidism for Today's Jewish Seeker: A Personal Reflection." In *A New Hasidism: Branches*, edited by Arthur Green and Ariel Evan Mayse, 251–270. Philadelphia: Jewish Publication Society.

Strassfield, Michael, ed. 2022. *Neo-Hasidic Teachings and Practices in Honor of Rabbi Jonathan Slater*. Teaneck, NJ: Ben Yehuda Press.

Surya Das. 1998. *Awakening the Buddha Within: Tibetan Wisdom for the Western World*. New York: Broadway Books.

Tatz, Akiva, and David Gottlieb. 2004. *Letters to a Buddhist Jew*. Southfield, MI: Targum Press.

Teshima, Yūrō. 1995. *Zen Buddhism and Hasidism: A Comparative Study*. Lanham, MD: University Press of America.

Vallely, Anne. 2008. "Jewish Redemption by Way of the Buddha." In *New Age Judaism*, edited by Celia Rothenberg and Anne Vallely, 19–33. London: Vallentine Mitchell.

Weinberg, Sheila Peltz. 2010. *Surprisingly Happy: An Atypical Religious Memoir*. Amherst, MA: White River Press.

PART III
PRACTICES

CHAPTER 15

BUDDHIST MONASTICISM IN NORTH AMERICA

LUKE CLOSSEY AND KAREN FERGUSON

BUDDHIST studies scholar Peter Harvey has observed that "Buddhists invented monastic life" and "no other human institution has had such a long-lasting continuous existence, along with such a wide diffusion, as the Buddhist sangha."[1] The Buddha encouraged his male followers to "go forth" from the householder life to become *bhikkhus*, literally, "mendicants." Mahāpajāpatī Gotamī, the Buddha's aunt and step-mother, repeatedly requested ordination; the Buddha's cautious and conditional agreement launched the female order of *bhikkhunīs*. The community of ordained *bhikkhus* and *bhikkhunīs*, called the sangha ("community"), became one of the "three gems" or "refuges," alongside the Buddha himself and his teachings. As anthropologist Michael Carrithers put it, "No Buddhism without the Sangha, and no Sangha without the Discipline."[2]

In response to arising real-life situations, the Buddha engineered a series of regulations known as *vinaya* ("training" or "relinquishment") designed to optimize community harmony and individual practice. The *vinaya* for the *bhikkhus* and *bhikkhunīs* listed some two or three hundred rules, depending on lineage and gender. These included grave prohibitions on killing and sexual intercourse, as well as institutional rules, such as not eating in the afternoon. Other behavioral norms proscribed private interaction with the opposite sex, in order to minimize the temptation and suggestion of sexual activity, or harkened back to ancient etiquette, like not preaching the doctrine to someone holding an umbrella. The sangha was one of the first corporate bodies not based on kinship relations. Still thriving today, it has also proven to be one of the most successful organizations in world history—a success and continuity that at

---

[1] Peter Harvey, *An Introduction to Buddhism: Teachings, History and Practices* (New York: Cambridge University Press, 1990), 73.
[2] Michael Carrithers, "'They Will Be Lords upon the Island': Buddhism in Sri Lanka," in *The World of Buddhism: Buddhist Monks and Nuns in Society and Culture*, ed. Heinz Bechert and Richard Gombrich (New York: Facts on File, 1984), 133.

times encourages a conservative reluctance to accept gender equality and other phenomena viewed as cultural "fads" begun only centuries ago.

This chapter will first define and describe the development of community temples in North America, and the functions of monks and nuns resident in them. Moving beyond this typical pattern, it will survey the variety of North American monasticism. It will conclude by considering the constructive cultural collision between monastic outreach and the broader American society.

Monks in Community Temples

Ending eight decades of Asian exclusion, the 1965 American and 1967 Canadian immigration acts opened the floodgates to Asian immigration, and the current era of monasticism began in North America. The conditions for monasticism in the United States were further enhanced by the Immigration Act of 1990 and its EB-4 visa for religious workers without employer support.[3] Most of these monks were immigrants and temporary visitors, with limited familiarity with American culture and languages.[4]

Pioneering monastic-led temples, including the Washington, D.C., Buddhist Vihara (est. 1965), Wat Thai in Los Angeles (est. 1971), and Hsi Lai Temple (est. 1991) in Hacienda Heights, California, became anchor institutions for their respective traditions, providing a source of inspiration, support, and monastics for sattelites being established continent-wide.[5] In the early decades, such support for rooting monasticism on North American soil was often nonsectarian and multiethnic. For example, Chinese monk Master Hsuan Hua, the founder of the Dharma Realm Buddhist Association (DRBA), donated land from its monastic headquarters in Northern California, the City of Ten Thousand Buddhas (est. 1977), for the building of Abhayagiri (est. 1995), the flagship North American monastery for the global network of "international" (i.e., non-Thai) Theravādan Forest monastics in the lineage of famed teacher and abbot Ajahn Chah.[6] In another example, Bhikkhu Yogacara Rahula, the first non-Asian Theravādan monastic receiving higher ordination from novice to monk in North America, did so in 1979 at

---

[3] Irene Lin, "Journey to the Far West: Chinese Buddhism in America," in *New Spiritual Homes: Religion and Asian Americans*, ed. David K. Yoo (Honolulu: University of Hawai'i Press, 1999), 140.

[4] Paul David Numrich, "Vinaya in Theravāda Temples in the United States," *Journal of Buddhist Ethics* 1 (1994): 30.

[5] Scott A. Mitchell, *Buddhism in America: Global Religion, Local Contexts* (New York: Bloomsbury, 2016), 73, 75, 101; D. Mitra Barua, *Seeding Buddhism with Multiculturalism: The Transmission of Sri Lankan Buddhism in Toronto* (Kingston and Montreal: McGill-Queen's University Press, 2019), 35; Bandu Madanayake, "Sri Lankan and Myanmar Buddhism," in *Asian Religions in British Columbia*, ed. Larry DeVries (Vancouver: UBC Press, 2010), 124–140; Wendy Cadge and Sidhorn Sangdhanoo, "Thai Buddhism in America: A Historical and Contemporary Overview," *Contemporary Buddhism: An Interdisciplinary Journal* 6 (2005): 7–35.

[6] "Origins of Abhayagiri," Abhayagiri: A Buddhist Monastery in the Thai Forest Tradition of Ajahn Chah, 2021, https://www.abhayagiri.org/about/origins-of-abhayagiri.

Los Angeles's Wat Thai in a ceremony conducted by Sri Lankan monastics; at the time, Bhante Rahula was living at the International Buddhist Meditation Center, an ecumenical monastic residential center founded in 1970 by the Vietnamese Mahāyāna monk Venerable Thich Thien-An. A few years later, Bhante Rahula, along with a dedicated multiethnic group of monastics and laypeople, supported Bhante Henepola Gunaratana Mahathera of the Washington, D.C., Buddhist Vihara to establish the Bhavana Society in West Virginia, the first Theravādan Forest monastery in North America, which, like Abhayagiri, has from the beginning both trained homegrown monastics and offered meditation retreats to laypeople.[7]

Many monastic institutions are networked with others in Asia and the Americas. For example, the DRBA's branches in western Canada and the United States stretch from Calgary to Long Beach. Except for its main center, the City of Ten Thousand Buddhas in Ukiah, every branch is in or near a major metropolitan area. Similarly, Fo Guang Shan has branches in fourteen states across the United States, with many concentrated in California. Most are in suburbs, with a notable exception of Deer Park in the Hudson Valley, eighty miles from New York City. Ten more Fo Guang Shan branches in Latin America (Costa Rica, Paraguay, Brazil, Chile, Argentina) and five in Canada are all in or near major cities. An unusual example of a network of intentionally rural monasteries is the Ajahn Chah lineage of the Thai Forest tradition. Half are just over a hundred kilometers from a metropolitan area; the rest are at least twice that distance, but near a smaller city. In 2017 this network grew a new node, Wat Pah Suddhavāri, in São Lourenço, Brazil, three hundred miles from Rio de Janeiro.

The urban temple serving an (or sometimes more than one[8]) Asian migrant community is the most common monastic institution in North America. The general pattern for their establishment is striking in its similarity across time, place, and tradition, with a few, largely minor, variations: laypeople from the same tradition and nationality begin meeting in private homes or rented facilities to practice Buddhist rites; once established, members of these informal "home temples" work together to raise funds and to connect with monastic institutions in Asia, or sometimes a well-established temple in North America, to send them a monastic or monastics; these eventually arrive to serve the community, after which the monastic and lay community work together to formally establish a temple. Some of these new, monastic-led institutions have grown

---

[7] Mathieu Boisvert, Manuel Litalien, and François Thibeault, "Blurred Boundaries: Buddhist Communities in the Greater Montréal Region," in *Buddhism in Canada*, ed. Bruce Matthews (London: Routledge, 2006), 145; Wendy Cadge, *Heartwood: The First Generation of Theravada Buddhism in America* (Chicago: University of Chicago Press, 2005), 36–37; Bhikkhu Yogacara Rahula, *One Night's Shelter (From Home to Homelessness): The Autobiography of an American Buddhist Monk*, 3rd rev. ed. (High View, West Virginia: Bhavana Society, 2004), 362–363, 366–367.

[8] Small and resource-strapped communities whose Buddhist traditions are closely affiliated with another national ethnic group's Buddhist traditions sometimes join forces in temple building and/or affiliation. Mitchell, *Buddhism in America*, 78, 99, 102–103; Madanayake, "Sri Lankan"; Jiemin Bao, *Creating a Buddhist Community: A Thai Temple in Silicon Valley* (Philadelphia: Temple University Press, 2015), 145.

quickly, including into large and impressive edifices that are now among the most prominent temples in the Western Hemisphere, or splinter groups from the original temple community have branched off to create new temples and monasteries representing different lineages and movements within the broader tradition they represent, beginning to approximate in North America the diversity of the religious ecology in Buddhist countries.[9]

Variations occur within this pattern, as some monastic institutions thrive thanks to demography, local interest, or Asian support. North America's population of Asian Buddhists is geographically uneven; for example, there are hundreds of thousands of residents of Vietnamese descent in Southern California alone, but fewer than five thousand in all of Saskatchewan, resulting in different numbers and varieties of monastics and pagodas in both places. In addition, the temple and monastery landscape depend on the interest in and ability of Asian monastic institutions—like the Sri Lankan missionary monks (*dharmadūtas*, or "messengers of dhamma") sent worldwide since the early twentieth century from the Siri Vajirārāmaya Temple in Colombo—and Buddhist nations—most notably, Thailand—to support these global outposts, including those in North America.[10] Refugee groups, like Tibetans, have struggled to establish "ethnic" religious institutions serving their communities, but many Tibetan monks have founded meditation centers through their teaching to and support from non-Tibetan converts.[11] This latter pattern has also been seen in the case of individual, charismatic monks, such as the Vietnamese monk Thich Nhat Hanh (Order of Interbeing) and Korean Samu Sunim (Buddhist Society for Compassionate Wisdom), who have established popular Buddhist movements in North America that have included both Asian and non-Asian adherents; however, both of these movements deviate from the mainstream of their respective "national" Buddhisms, which have not otherwise attracted significant support outside of their "ethnic" communities.[12] Some refugee groups have overcome herculean challenges to establish any temples at all, given their destitution upon arrival in North America, their forced dispersal (in the United States), barriers to the immigration of mendicant monastics (in Canada, where officials have often failed to recognize religious specialists as skilled labor or socially necessary), and the decimation of the Cambodian sangha through genocide.[13]

---

[9] Mitchell, *Buddhism in America*, 78, 128; Bao, *Creating a Buddhist Community* 36–37, 61–74; Barua, *Seeding Buddhism with Multiculturalism* 45–49.

[10] Steven Kemper, "Dharmapala's Dharmaduta and the Buddhist Ethnoscape," in *Buddhist Missionaries in the Era of Globalization*, ed. Linda Learman (Honolulu: University of Hawai'i Press), 22–50; Bao, *Creating a Buddhist Community*, 121–125; Pattana Kitiarsa, "Missionary Intent and Monastic Networks: Thai Buddhism as a Transnational Religion," *Sojourn: Journal of Social Issues in Southeast Asia* 25 (2010): 109–132.

[11] Mitchell, *Buddhism in America*, 146–147.

[12] Alexander Soucy, "The Buddha and the Birch Tree: The Great Pine Forest Monastery and the Localization of Vietnamese Buddhism to Canada," *Contemporary Buddhism* 15 (2014): 376, 381; Mitchell, *Buddhism in America*, 126.

[13] Janet McLellan, *Cambodian Refugees in Ontario: Resettlement, Religion, and Identity* (Toronto: University of Toronto Press, 2009), 89–92, 111; Mitchell, *Buddhism in America*, 77; Penny Van Esterik,

Monastic Functions

Temples and their resident monks play a fundamental spiritual and cultural role for migrant communities, providing them with essential support as a religious minority in decidedly non-Buddhist societies. The Buddha saw a reciprocal relationship between sangha and laypeople: He advised monks to "teach them the Dhamma" and serve as "an unsurpassed field of merit," while householders would offer monks robes, food, shelter, and medicine.[14] Many Mahāyāna monks perform ceremonies for the dead. For some lay Theravādan Buddhists, a monastery's principal purpose is to receive donations, thus allowing for the generation of spiritual merit.[15]

Monks and temples in Canada and the United States also have functions distinct from those in Asia due to their identity as a minority religious institution serving migrant communities. Beyond the spiritual economy, monks can serve as a culturally consonant supplement or alternative to government social-services counseling for immigrant communities. They can "recognize, mediate, and treat the vast array of mental health concerns caused by spirit possession, bereavement, guilt, and atonement needs."[16] Although exorcism and counseling might be of special urgency for refugee communities from Southeast Asia, mental health is also an important motivation for converts to seek out monastic support.[17]

Fundamentally, Asian monks in North America find themselves responsible for the perpetuation of the faith beyond the first generation of migrants, a primary aspiration of most lay communities who established temples in the first place. This existential responsibility is sometimes complicated by the tension between older generations, seeking to preserve an idealized Asian religious tradition that they had left behind, and their children and grandchildren born in a North American cultural context.[18] Monastics in North America have found a number of ways to address this need. For example, Sri Lankan Buddhist monks in Canada followed the lead of diasporic temple monastics in Malaysia—and all other Asian Theravādan traditions—to offer temporary ordination to the younger generation in order to strengthen both their filial piety and religious knowledge. This overseas innovation has recently been adopted in Sri Lanka, where until recently it had been largely unknown—thus demonstrating the complex circuits of

---

Taking Refuge: Lao Buddhists in North America ([n.p.]: Arizona State University, 1992), 55–58; Jeff Wilson, "What Is Canadian about Canadian Buddhism," *Religion Compass* 5 (2011): 541–542.

[14] Itivuttaka, 90 and 107.

[15] Bao, *Creating a Buddhist Community*, 97–99; Luke Clossey and Karen Ferguson, "Birken Buddhist Forest Monastery: Asian Migration, the Creative Class, and Cultural Transformation in the New Pacific British Columbia," *BC Studies* 208 (2021): 41–43.

[16] Janet McLellan, *Many Petals of the Lotus: Five Asian Buddhist Communities in Toronto* (Toronto: University of Toronto Press, 1999), 148–151.

[17] Clossey and Ferguson, "Birken Buddhist Forest Monastery," 32.

[18] Bao, *Creating a Buddhist Community*, 83, 93; Cadge, *Heartwood*, 199–200; Soucy, "The Buddha and the Birch Tree," 37; Barua, *Seeding Buddhism with Multiculturalism*, 44–45.

influence within global Buddhism.[19] Furthermore, in attracting young people born and bred in North America, many of Toronto's Sri Lankan monks have relaxed their high status in order to recast themselves as spiritual friends to the laity.[20] Thai and Sri Lankan communities in North America have also found in the mostly convert monks of the Thai Forest Sangha, many with global followings among Asian and non-Asian supporters alike, a bridge in communicating the faith effectively to the younger generation with whom they share a "Western" cultural context.[21] Many temples also serve more broadly as de facto cultural centers, providing language, dance, and other instruction aimed at cultural retention, especially for the second and third generations.[22]

In these ways, monastic life in North America is focused primarily on the lay community; few Asian monks in North America serve the sangha as scholars or to train other monks, beyond temporary ordination.[23] Monastic ordination, and thus the worldwide supply of monastics, for the most part remains the preserve of the Asian metropoles of formal and informal transnational networks with nodes in American temples. However, there are some notable exceptions. For example, in California, DRBA at first trained and deliberately sought out American-born white students, but now overwhelmingly attracts ethnically Chinese monastic ordinands from diasporic communities worldwide, including the Americas, to the center of its global monastic community, the City of Ten Thousand Buddhas.[24] Nearby, Abhayagiri Monastery is the North American center of a decentralized global network of monasteries training convert monks in the Thai Forest tradition.

In addition, there are multiple accounts of individual convert Buddhists—white, Black, and Latino—seeking and often obtaining monastic training from Asian monks at North American temples.[25] Beyond anecdotal accounts of such outliers, we know

---

[19] D. Mitra Bhikkhu, "Temporary Ordination for Character Transformation: A Diasporic Practice with Transnational Connections," *Journal of Global Buddhism* 12 (2011): 51–68.

[20] Barua, *Seeding Buddhism with Multiculturalism*, 164–165.

[21] Cadge, *Heartwood*, 42; Barua, *Seeding Buddhism with Multiculturalism*, 145–147; Clossey and Ferguson, "Birken Buddhist Forest Monastery," 34.

[22] Bao, *Creating a Buddhist Community*, 120–127.

[23] On temporary ordination, see Paul David Numrich, *Old Wisdom in the New World: Americanization in Two Immigrant Theravada Buddhist Temples* (Knoxville: University of Tennessee Press, 1996), 85–86, 125; McLellan, *Cambodian Refugees*, 99–100; Bhikkhu, "Temporary Ordination"; Cadge and Sangdhanoo, "Thai Buddhism in America," 20.

[24] Lina Verchery, "An Alternative to the 'Westernization' Paradigm and Buddhist Global Imaginaires," in *Buddhism in the Global Eye: Beyond East and West*, edited by John S. Harding, Victor Sogen Hori, and Alexander Soucy (London: Bloomsbury, 2020), 150–162; Lina Verchery, "The Avatamsaka Sagely Monastery (華嚴聖寺) and New Perspectives on Globalized Buddhism in Canada," in *Understanding the Consecrated Life in Canada: Critical Essays on Contemporary Trends*, ed. Jason Zuidema (Waterloo, ON: Wilfrid Laurier University Press, 2015), 363–376.

[25] See, for example, Bao, *Creating a Buddhist Community*, 86–95; Numrich, *Old Wisdom*, 12; James Placzek and Ian G. Baird, "Thai and Lao Buddhism," in *Asian Religions in British Columbia*, ed. Larry DeVries, Don Baker, and Dan Overmyer (Vancouver: UBC Press, 2010), 114–115; "Tributes Honor Passing of Ven. Suhita Dharma, First African-American Buddhist Monk," *Lion's Roar*, January 1, 2014; Caitlin Yoshida Candil, "'Buddhism in Spanish Is Here': The Latino Monks Building a Unique

little about this phenomenon, including how widespread it is and the trajectory of these monks and nuns. Similarly, aside from snippets and suggestions,[26] no published research considers in depth those laypeople from established Asian migrant communities who seek long-term ordination. The scholarship accounts for the dearth of a homegrown Asian–North American sangha in terms of immigrant parents' disinterest in having their children choose a vocation of penurious monasticism.[27] Like many aspects of the historic and evolving experience of Asian–North American Buddhists, even the most basic research remains to be undertaken on this subject, including the conversion and ordination of Asian–North Americans who were not brought up Buddhist or who now follow Buddhist traditions different from those of their families.[28]

A number of Buddhist monasteries, sometimes in concert with Christian counterparts, have been active in ecology and sustainability. At times this "green monasticism" shares goals with the modern environmental movement.[29] No less striking is a more otherworldly approach to the landscape that is often consonant with local Indigenous understandings. Castle Mountain (Blackfoot: Miistukskoowa) in Alberta has been recognized by the Avatamsaka monastery community as a holy site (bodhimaṇḍala) for the wisdom-bodhisattva Mañjuśrī.[30] Local legend remembers a Tibetan monk from California visiting Vidette Lake in the interior of British Columbia in the 1980s to confirm its location as the "center of the universe," a belief consonant with the tradition of the local Indigenous Skeetchestn Nation.[31] Antonio Velasco Piña, a Mexican spiritual writer whose Mexicanism reached back to Indigenous religious traditions, understood the Dali Lama, during a 1989 visit, to have mentally communed with two local volcanoes[32] and to have chanted a mantra at the Metropolitan Cathedral that called "to the most ancestral forces of Mexico": "I didn't doubt that the energies of the Mexican chakra had suddenly risen and were circulating towards the south, searching for the yearned-for connection with the chakra centered on Machu Picchu" in Peru. The following year in Mexico, eight Tibetan monks performed a ritual at, and "reactivated," the ancient Pyramid of the Sun so that its feelings proved clearly perceptible.[33]

Community," *The Guardian*, April 15, 2022, https://www.theguardian.com/us-news/2022/apr/15/buddhism-latinos-temple-los-angeles.

[26] Kitiarsa, "Missionary Intent and Monastic Networks," 123–124; Verchery, "Avatamsaka," 370; Soucy, "The Buddha and the Birch Tree," 381–383; Chenxing Han, *Be the Refuge: Raising the Voices of Asian American Buddhists* (Berkeley, CA: North Atlantic Books, 2021).

[27] Cadge and Sangdhanoo, "Thai Buddhism in America," 26; Numrich, *Old Wisdom*, 45–46; Natalie E. F. Quli, "Laicization in Four Sri Lankan Buddhist Temples in Northern California," PhD dissertation, Graduate Theological Union, 2010, 72–81.

[28] Han, *Be the Refuge*.

[29] Donald W. Mitchell and William Skudlarek, ed., *Green Monasticism: A Buddhist-Catholic Response to an Environmental Calamity* (New York: Lantern, 2010).

[30] Lina Verchery, "Avatamsaka," 371, citing 華嚴盛宴是歸鄉 *Avatamsaka Celebrates Our Ultimate Return Home* (2007), 115.

[31] Kelly Sinoski, "'Centre of the Universe' Near Kamloops—Really," *The Vancouver Sun*, July 21, 2007, A1 and A6.

[32] Antonio Velasco Piña, *Cartas a Elisabeth* (Mexico City: Punto de Lectura, 2009), 163

[33] Ibid., 147, 266.

Divergences and Tensions

Daily life for temple monks in North America starkly contrasts with the ideal of strict *vinaya* adherence, still found in some monasteries in Asia and (see below) in the Americas. North American monks from a wide range of traditions have been reported to drive cars, handle money, use credit cards, and even prepare food, all of which may or may not, depending on the tradition and lineage, deviate from monastic practice in Asia.[34] Even practitioners of a pristine *vinaya* have had to adapt to American circumstances. Adaptations have focused on transportation, clothing (parka-wearing in cold climates), mealtimes, and distancing formalities between monks and laywomen.[35] In the Americas, the vast distances from one temple to another of the same tradition creates difficulties in gathering the quorum necessary for certain ceremonies, which has required improvisation of informal equivalents. Many Asian monastics arriving in North America to serve in temples expect to have to adapt to their new cultural context, and are sometimes more ready to bend the rules than the laypeople who sponsored them or the sangha leadership back home. So, for example, Ajahn Maha Prasert, the Thai abbot of Wat Buddhanusorn in Fremont, California, for several years supported the residency there of Venerable Tathālokā Mahātherī—an American-born *bhikkhunī* ordained first in Korea and then by Sri Lankan monks in California—and then supported her establishment of Dhammadarini, a groundbreaking hermitage for nuns in California, in contravention of the Thai Sangha's opposition to *bhikkhunī* ordination and the disapproval of some in the temple community.[36] In general, among serious *vinaya* practitioners modifications have been minor, practical, consonant with the spirit of the rules, and developed in consultation with the lay community. One of the more thoroughgoing updates came in 2004, when Thich Nhat Hanh published a new *vinaya* harmonized with modern lifestyles and sensibilities, both adding and removing rules: monks can drive modest cars, and earn and save money, but cannot eat meat, use the phone while driving, or honk out of frustration.[37] In some Sri Lankan and Japanese temples, liberalization is not just an adaptation to America, but a continuation of modernization processes begun in Asia.[38]

Monastics' relationship with their temples' lay community is different than in Asia; in North America, generally monks' authority is less secure and laypeople may expect monastics to serve them and the temple in unexpected ways. To take one example,

---

[34] Jens W. Borgland, "Some Reflections of Thich Nhat Hanh's Monastic Code for the Twenty-First Century," in *Buddhist Modernities: Re-Inventing Tradition in the Globalizing Modern World*, ed. Hanna Havnevik et al. (New York: Routledge, 2017), 259–281; Numrich, "Vinaya," 23–31.

[35] McLellan, *Cambodian Refugees*, 96–99; Numrich, *Old Wisdom*, 46–55.

[36] Bao, *Creating a Buddhist Community*, 90–93; Rachel Antell and Elinor Pierce, *Fremont, USA* (Cambridge, MA: The Pluralism Project, Harvard University, 2009).

[37] Thich Nhat Hanh, *Freedom Wherever We Go: A Buddhist Monastic Code for the Twenty-First Century* (Berkeley, CA: Parallax, 2004), 43–45, 58, 72, 99, 101, 137. See Borgland, "Some Reflections."

[38] Quli, "Laicization in Four Sri Lankan Buddhist Temples."

while in Thailand and Sri Lanka laypeople would chauffeur monks where they need to go, in North America those monks might offer or be asked to drive laypeople to their appointments, a world turned upside down in terms of *vinaya* and social hierarchy.[39] Despite these adjustments, there have also been multiple incidents of conflicts between laypeople and monastics about temple mission, management, and development, sometimes even leading to schisms and offshoot temples. A Sinhalese monk working in Los Angeles observed that some lay communities prefer that monks "remain 'old country' in order to preserve a nostalgia for their old home life, while they themselves pursue the new American dream."[40] These conflicts are unsurprising in a North American context in which laypeople have initiated and invested so much in founding temples, including by procuring and supporting monastics who themselves are newcomers to North America, and in which temple governance is legally mandated by laws regulating nonprofits that require a board of directors, and not just monastic control, to govern the temple's affairs.[41] Recently, D. Mitra Barua, writing about Toronto's various and numerous Sri Lankan temples, some of which were established because of such putative "schisms," long since healed, has reinterpreted these episodes as evidence of the growth, maturation, rootedness, and robustness of Sri Lankan Buddhism in the Greater Toronto Area. Ultimately this partitioning has resulted today in a diverse yet cooperative local religious community in which there are enough laypeople to materially support and enough monastics and monastic institutions to serve the different spiritual needs and desires of the lay community—for example, meditation, rituals, dhamma education, and religious and other forms of diversity within "national" Buddhist groups.[42]

Monks have often found themselves as cultural emissaries in their temple work, defending their religion and communities to an often hostile dominant society—especially when it comes to land-use decisions about building temples—as well as finding ways to establish and legitimate their traditions in the pluralistic and multicultural societies of Canada and the United States. This has been a ubiquitous challenge throughout Canada and the United States for monastic institutions large and small. Fo Guang Shan faced difficulties in building the Hsi Lai Temple in Los Angeles County—billed as the largest temple in North America—where potential neighbors worried about both traffic jams and animal sacrifices. Meanwhile in Orange County, the monks of the tiny Vietnamese Chua Lien Hoa Temple engaged in a decade-long battle with the City of Garden Grove for its very existence, ultimately prevailing by asserting their religious

---

[39] Bao, *Creating a Buddhist Community* 76–77, 83–85; Barua, *Seeding Buddhism with Multiculturalism*, 47.

[40] John Dart, "Los Angeles Monk Advocates an Americanized Form of Buddhism," *Los Angeles Times*, July 8, 1989. https://www.latimes.com/archives/la-xpm-1989-07-08-me-2692-story.html.

[41] Numrich, *Old Wisdom*, 19–39; Cadge and Sangdhanoo, "Thai Buddhism in America," 16; Bao, *Creating a Buddhist Community*, 37–38; Soucy, "The Buddha and the Birch Tree," 378–379.

[42] Barua, *Seeding Buddhism with Multiculturalism*, 48–49. Along with Barua, several other scholars have noted this evolution and diversification of Buddhist institutions. See McLellan, *Cambodian Refugees*; Soucy, "The Buddha and the Birch Tree"; Clossey and Ferguson, "Birken Buddhist Forest Monastery."

rights and testing the limits of the municipal code.[43] At the same time, monastics, sometimes mistaken for Muslims or Hare Krishnas, have endured verbal abuse and assaults.[44] In the 1980s a Laotian monastery in Rockford, Illinois, was shot at and bombed.[45]

Despite this pressure to find acceptance in the dominant culture and society, in many metropolitan regions—including those in Southern California and others like Vancouver and Toronto—large, multigenerational, and ever-growing diaspora communities like the Chinese are so demographically dominant and secure that once their temples are established they can focus inwardly on the "integrity and continuity" of their diverse religious traditions, rather than adaptation and integration.[46] By contrast, monks in many other traditions often find themselves spread thin and isolated in their pastoral role; the stresses of this shortage of monastic support for both monks and laity are especially acute in traumatized refugee communities.[47]

MONASTERIES FOR THE CONSECRATED LIFE

At least one form of Buddhist monasticism in North America acts less like a "minority" religion in North America, and more as a central node in its transnational network—that of modern Chinese "humanistic" Buddhism. While most Asian monks in North America serve in temples tending to the pastoral needs of lay immigrant communities, these monastics live in monasteries populated by monks and nuns, ordinands, and laypeople from around the world who belong to these global diasporic movements. These centers of monastic life range from some of the largest monasteries in the Western Hemisphere (DRBA's City of Ten Thousand Buddhas in Northern California; Fo Guang Shan's Hsi Lai Temple in Los Angeles County; and Fu-chih's (Bliss and Wisdom Foundation) Great Enlightenment Buddhist Institute Society monastery for monks and Great Wisdom Buddhist Institute for nuns in Prince Edward Island), to tiny hermitages like the Po Lam monastery, an outpost of Hong Kong's Po Lin monastery, in exurban Vancouver.[48]

---

[43] Philip P. Pan, "Good Neighbor: Hemisphere's Largest Buddhist Temple Wins Over Residents," *Los Angeles Times*, August 8, 1993. https://www.latimes.com/archives/la-xpm-1993-08-08-hl-21660-story.html; Stacy Anne Harwood, "Struggling to Embrace Difference in Land-Use Decision Making in Multicultural Communities," *Planning Practice & Research* 20 (2005): 362–364. See Barua, *Seeding Buddhism with Multiculturalism*, 100–141; Bao, *Creating a Buddhist Community*, 61–62; Antell and Pierce, *Fremont, USA*.

[44] Numrich, "Vinaya," 26.

[45] *Blue Collar and Buddha*, dir. Taggart Siegel (1987).

[46] Paul Crowe, "Dharma on the Move: Vancouver Buddhist Communities and Multiculturalism," in *Flowers on the Rock: Global and Local Buddhisms in Canada*, ed. J. S. Harding et al. (Montreal: McGill-Queen's University Press, 2014), 150–172.

[47] McLellan, *Cambodian Refugees*, 91–92, 105–109; Soucy, "The Buddha and the Birch Tree."

[48] Verchery, "Alternative"; Jason W. M. Ellsworth, "Glocalization in Buddhist Food Ventures on a Small Canadian Island," in *Buddhism in the Global Eye: Beyond East and West*, ed. John S. Harding,

The "humanistic" Buddhist revitalization movements that founded these monasteries originated in twentieth-century Taiwan and Hong Kong. They are rooted in Chinese Chan and Pure Land traditions, while also often deeply influenced by Theravāda and Vajrayāna elements, and frequently promote an austere and disciplined monasticism for men and women, as well as meditation among laypeople. These are dynamic and growing global movements, with large followings of young people.[49] Similarly, a global Theravādan monastic movement emerging out of Mahamevnawa Monastery in Sri Lanka has recently established more than a dozen meditation centers in North America as part of its worldwide outreach.[50]

The founding of these monastic movements in North America correspond to the late-twentieth-century migration of professional Asian migrants to Canada and the United States, as well as the meditation-based Buddhist movements they support. Unlike temple monks, monastics in these traditions are seeking appropriate locations for maintaining inward-looking monastic tradition, discipline, and training ordinands from around the world (e.g., rural, serene, abundant land and appropriate buildings, local diasporic communities of support), rather than needing to adapt to North America's pluralistic, multicultural, and non-Buddhist societies. Nevertheless, they always offer some form of lay outreach, like dhamma and meditation training, or charitable activities to the monasteries' neighboring communities—diasporic or otherwise—as well as meditation retreats to their worldwide network of lay supporters. For example, the more than seven hundred monastics from throughout the global Chinese diaspora who reside at the Taiwanese Fu-chih (Bliss and Wisdom Foundation) movement's monastic complex and headquarters in Prince Edward Island (population: 160,000), as well as this center's pre-COVID 2,500 annual lay visitors from around the world, have had an outsized and controversial impact on the spiritual life, cultural diversity, tourist economy, and food culture and security of Canada's smallest province, which has historically been characterized as being among the most insular, parochial, and culturally homogenous areas of the country.[51]

Outreach and Convert Monastics

Some Buddhist monks in the Americas from Asia seek opportunities to establish the dhamma in the non-Buddhist local communities in which they find themselves and to teach it to those who seek it out, no matter their background. These efforts vary widely

---

Victor Sogen Hori, and Alexander Soucy (London: Bloomsbury, 2020), 163–716; Ven. Yin Kit, "Founding a Landmark of the Dharma in Canada," *Global Buddhist Door* (blog), December 29, 2016, https://www.buddhistdoor.net/features/founding-a-landmark-of-the-dharma-in-canada.

[49] Mitchell, *Buddhism in America*, 123–125; Verchery, "Alternative"; Verchery, "Avatamsaka."
[50] Barua, *Seeding Buddhism with Multiculturalism*, 214–215.
[51] Ellsworth, "Glocalization."

in focus and meanings across traditions, and often take a back seat to perpetuating the faith among migrant communities. One outreach strategy by Asian monks in the Americas is to develop formal or informal programs of meditation and mindfulness practices conducted in English (or French or Spanish or Portuguese, depending on location), and publicized to the wider community for their psychological benefit, reflecting dominant notions of Buddhism in the Americas. Such efforts have allowed monastics to promote Buddhism in the Americas as a religion of peace and happiness, while others in related efforts have highlighted its potential to bring about harmony in the context of sometimes fractious multicultural societies.[52] Other monastic-led groups, like the New Kandampa Tradition, seek support in North America by branding themselves as "modern" Buddhism, despite their often enduring traditionalism.[53] By contrast, other Buddhist groups have never sought out, or struggled with, outreach beyond their "ethnic" community due to language barriers or a lack of missionary tradition.[54]

Missionary monks arriving with the liberalization of immigration in the 1960s and 1970s found themselves in an alien and benighted land. After a visit to New York and California in 1970, Chögyam Trungpa complained about the ego-reinforcing "spiritual materialism" of Americans spoiled by the "supermarket" of diverse religious traditions available to them.[55] His arrival in their "savage" culture reminded him of the missionary work of the Indian monk Padmasambhava to a similarly "savage" eighth-century Tibet.[56] Like his predecessor, Trungpa would have to skillfully adapt the dhamma to this strange people. At a meditation retreat in New Mexico in the 1970s, the pioneering Sri Lankan missionary monk Bhante Gunaratana found in his room a naked participant who thought the best way to show her appreciation for his teachings was to offer herself for sex. After repeatedly shooing her out of his room, the missionary monk reflected on the gap between Buddhist civilization and this wild New World: "It seemed to me that any person who tried to seduce me was disrespecting me as a monk and as a teacher. It was a slap in the face to 2,500 years of tradition. . . ."[57] Lina Verchery has found that the success of the DRBA in Asia has relied significantly on the promotion of the memory of Master Hsuan Hua's early years in the 1960s Californian "Wild West" when he had considerable success, against the odds, in ordaining undisciplined and hedonistic white hippies in his austere monastic discipline.[58]

---

[52] Numrich, *Old Wisdom*, 63–79; Barua, *Seeding Buddhism with Multiculturalism*, 100–141; Ellsworth, "Glocalization," 169; Placzek and Baird, "Thai and Lao Buddhism," 120.

[53] Christopher Emory-Moore, "Branding a New Buddhist Movement: The New Kadampa Tradition's Self-Identification as 'Modern Buddhism,'" *Journal of Global Buddhism* 21 (2020): 22.

[54] Soucy, "The Buddha and the Birch Tree," 380; John H. Negru, "Highlights from the Survey of Canadian Buddhist Organizations," *Journal of Global Buddhism* 14 (2013): 5.

[55] Chögyam Trungpa, *Cutting through Spiritual Materialism* (Boston: Shambhala, 2002), 42–43.

[56] Ryan Jones, "Fresh Bread from an Old Recipe: Chögyam Trungpa's Transmission of Buddhism to North America, 1970–1977," *Canadian Journal of Buddhist Studies* 18 (2013): 53.

[57] Henepola Gunaratana, *Journey to Mindfulness: The Autobiography of Bhante G.* (Boston: Wisdom, 2017), 220–222.

[58] Verchery, "Alternative," 156–157.

Some monks bypassed the cultural divide entirely by using rebirth to come to the Americas. In 1981 the fifteenth-century Tibetan monk Drubtchok Gualwa Samdrup was reborn as the Brazilian Michel Lenz Calmanowitz, identified by the visiting Lama Gangchen with assistance from a local astrologer.[59] Tactical rebirth was not an unusual strategy for pre-modern missionary work: in 1588 the Tibetan lama Sonam Gyatso died with the intention to be reborn as a Mongolian to continue his efforts to spread Buddhism to the north.[60] Although specific memories are lost in the turbulence of transit, some monks born in North America deduce from their own experiences the probability of previous lives in Asia and in monasteries.[61]

Many have noted significant tension between monastic restraint and the Americas' love of individualism and freedom. Alan Watts denounced monasticism as "square zen."[62] The magazine *Tricycle* (1994) described a popular prejudice against "antiquated patriarchal monasticism."[63] Some builders of and visitors to Theravāda monasteries in Canada compared their regimented or demanding routines, unfavorably, with Russian gulags. Even a long-established tradition like Christianity floundered in these waters: the past half century has seen a 74 percent decrease in Catholic monastic vocations in the United States.[64] It is difficult to imagine a landmass less likely to embrace an imported alien, restraining set of communal regulations and patriarchal hierarchy. In 1988 the scholar Charles Prebish predicted that "for the immediate future, Buddhism will remain an almost exclusively lay community in America."[65] This sentiment led to experiments with hybrid lay/ordained institutions in the 1990s.[66]

However, monasticism's asceticism, anti-consumerism, and ethical orientation have proven attractive to certain communities in the Americas.[67] Buddhist monasticism is

---

[59] Frank Usarski, "Religious Adaptation through Reincarnation? The Role of Lama Michel, the 'Little Buddha' of São Paulo, within the Globalized Tibetan Buddhist Movement of Lama Gangchen," https://www.cesnur.org/testi/lama_michel.htm.

[60] Luke Clossey, "Religious Expansion in Islam, Christianity, and Buddhism," in *Global Reformations: Transforming Early Modern Religions, Societies, and Cultures*, ed. Nicholas Terpstra (New York: Routledge: 2019), 15.

[61] More than one monastic has said this to the authors, including Ven. Sona of Birken Forest Monastery (interview by Luke Clossey and Karen Ferguson, August 28, 2017).

[62] Alan W. Watts, *Beat Zen, Square Zen, and Zen* (New York: City Lights, 1959).

[63] Helen Tworkov, "Zen in the Balance: Can It Survive America?" *Tricycle: The Buddhist Review* 3 (Spring 1994), https://tricycle.org/magazine/zen-balance-can-it-survive-america/.

[64] Erick Berrelleza, Mary L. Gautier, and Mark M. Gary, "Population Trends among Religious Institutes of Women," *CARA Special Report* (Fall 2014), 1–8; Santiago Sordo Palacios, Thomas P. Gaunt, and Mary L. Gautier, "Population Trends among Religious Institutes of Men," *CARA Special Report* (Fall 2015), 1–8.

[65] Charles S. Prebish, "Buddhism," in *Encyclopedia of the American Religious Experience: Studies of Traditions and Movements*, ed. Charles H. Lippy and Peter W. Williams (New York: Scribner's, 1988), vol. 2, 677.

[66] Paul David Numrich, "Theravada Buddhism in America: Prospects for the Sangha," in *The Faces of Buddhism in America*, ed. Charles S. Prebish and Kenneth K. Tanaka (Berkeley: University of California Press, 1998), 147–162.

[67] Sandra Bell, "'Crazy Wisdom', Charisma and the Transmission of Buddhism in the United States," *Nova Religio: The Journal of Alternative and Emergent Religions* 2 (1998): 55–76.

more egalitarian than it appears. Carrithers sees a counterintuitive "archaic, egalitarian, anti-hierarchical principle enshrined" in the dhamma and the *vinaya*, as, for example, in the deference to seniority.[68] Similarly, within the American counterculture there was a countercurrent craving structure and stability. Some saw monasticism as extreme freedom and found liberation in strict *vinaya* adherence in Thai Forest-tradition monasteries. Marine Corporal Greg Klein, from New York, was shot in the back of the head in Vietnam (1967), and became ordained as Ajahn Ānando in a Thai monastery in 1974.[69] Californian Scott DuPrez had spent time in an Afghan prison on drug charges before ordination as a novice named Rahula in a Sri Lankan monastery in 1975; in 1979 Bhante Rahula would become the first US-born monk to receive *bhikkhu* ordination in the United States (see above).[70] An Englishman on the same monastic trajectory described himself as a hippie attracted to the "sharp end of an orthodox tradition."[71]

Today, the secure roots of Buddhist monasticism in the Americas can be seen in a Brazilian monastery's recommendation that aspiring monks learn not Pali or Thai, but English.[72] One Jewish American woman from Los Angeles became a Tibetan nun named Thubten Chodron. Despite previous disinterest in lineage, now when her "energy wanes, I remember the lineage of strong, resourceful monastics who have practiced and actualized the Buddha's teachings for 2,500 years."[73]

Conclusion

The arrival of a millennia-old institution onto a vast landmass with a diverse population of a billion people heralded a complex story of cultural negotiation and misunderstanding, of spiritual transformation and transcendence. This chapter has focused on the past sixty years of a history that stretches back centuries, and has highlighted broad patterns and illustrative exceptions in a complex cultural mosaic. The relative youth of the scholarship upon which this chapter rests—half the entries in the reference list were published since 2010—suggests the potential for new research that will confirm, color, and correct the picture we painted here.

---

[68] Michael Carrithers, "The Modern Ascetics of Lanka and the Pattern of Change in Buddhism," *Man*, new series, 14 (1979): 295.

[69] Mali Klein, "Ānando, A War Veteran in the Monastic Life: The Loss of the Sacred Brotherhood," http://www.maliklein.co.uk/greg%20klein.htm.

[70] Rahula, *One Night's Shelter*.

[71] Ajahn Amaro, "Narration and Reflections on Ajahn Sucitto's *The Dawn of the Dhamma*, Chapter 14, Part 2," https://amaravati.org/audio/chapter-14-nibbana-the-universal-potential-part-2/. See David Chadwick, *Crooked Cucumber: The Life and Zen Teaching of Shunryu Suzuki* (London: Thorson, 1999), 293, 307.

[72] Mosteiro Budista Suddhavāri, "Perguntas Frequentes," https://suddhavari.org/perguntas-frequentes/.

[73] Thubten Chodron, "You're Becoming a What? Living as a Western Buddhist Nun," in *Buddhist Women on the Edge*, ed. Marianne Dresser (Berkeley: North Atlantic, 1996), 227–229.

References

Abhayagiri: A Buddhist Monastery in the Thai Forest Tradition of Ajahn Chah. "Origins of Abhayagiri," 2021. https://www.abhayagiri.org/about/origins-of-abhayagiri.

Antell, Rachel, and Elinor Pierce. *Fremont, USA*. Cambridge, MA: The Pluralism Project, Harvard University, 2009.

Bandu Madanayake. "Sri Lankan and Myanmar Buddhism." In *Asian Religions in British Columbia*, edited by Larry DeVries, 124–140. Vancouver: UBC Press, 2010.

Bao, Jiemin. *Creating a Buddhist Community: A Thai Temple in Silicon Valley*. Philadelphia: Temple University Press, 2015.

Barua, D. Mitra. *Seeding Buddhism with Multiculturalism: The Transmission of Sri Lankan Buddhism in Toronto*. Kingston and Montreal: McGill-Queen's University Press, 2019.

Bhikkhu, D. Mitra. "Temporary Ordination for Character Transformation: A Diasporic Practice with Transnational Connections." *Journal of Global Buddhism* 12 (2011): 51–68.

Boisvert, Mathieu, Manuel Litalien, and François Thibeault. "Blurred Boundaries: Buddhist Communities in the Greater Montréal Region." In *Buddhism in Canada*, edited by Bruce Matthews, 142–150. London: Routledge, 2006.

Borgland, Jens W. "Some Reflections of Thich Nhat Hanh's Monastic Code for the Twenty-First Century." In *Buddhist Modernities: Re-Inventing Tradition in the Globalizing Modern World*, edited by Hanna Havnevik, Ute Hüsken, Vladimir Tikhonov, Koen Wellens, and Mark Teeuwen, 259–281. New York: Routledge, 2017.

Braun, Erik. *The Birth of Insight: Meditation, Modern Buddhism, and the Burmese Monk, Ledi Sayadaw*. Chicago: University of Chicago Press, 2013.

Cadge, Wendy. *Heartwood: The First Generation of Theravada Buddhism in America*. Chicago: University of Chicago Press, 2005.

Cadge, Wendy, and Sidhorn Sangdhanoo. "Thai Buddhism in America: A Historical and Contemporary Overview." *Contemporary Buddhism: An Interdisciplinary Journal* 6 (2005): 7–35.

Chadwick, David. *Crooked Cucumber: The Life and Zen Teaching of Shunryu Suzuki*. London: Thorson, 1999.

Chodron, Thubten. "You're Becoming a What? Living as a Western Buddhist Nun." In *Buddhist Women on the Edge*, edited by Marianne Dresser, 223–233. Berkeley: North Atlantic, 1996.

Clossey, Luke, and Karen Ferguson. "Birken Buddhist Forest Monastery: Asian Migration, the Creative Class, and Cultural Transformation in the New Pacific British Columbia." *BC Studies* 208 (2021): 17–44.

Cook, Joanna. *Meditation in Modern Buddhism: Renunciation and Change in Thai Monastic Life*. Cambridge: Cambridge University Press, 2010.

Crowe, Paul. "Dharma on the Move: Vancouver Buddhist Communities and Multiculturalism." In *Flowers on the Rock: Global and Local Buddhisms in Canada*, edited by John S. Harding, Victor Sōgen Hori, and Alexander Soucy, 150–172. Montreal: McGill-Queen's University Press, 2014.

Ellsworth, Jason W. M. "Glocalization in Buddhist Food Ventures on a Small Canadian Island." In *Buddhism in the Global Eye: Beyond East and West*, edited by John S. Harding, Victor Sogen Hori, and Alexander Soucy, 163–176. London: Bloomsbury, 2020.

Emory-Moore, Christopher. "Branding a New Buddhist Movement: The New Kadampa Tradition's Self-Identification as 'Modern Buddhism.'" *Journal of Global Buddhism* 21 (2020): 11–29.

Gunaratana, Henepola. *Journey to Mindfulness: The Autobiography of Bhante G.* Boston: Wisdom, 2017.

Han, Chenxing. *Be the Refuge: Raising the Voices of Asian American Buddhists.* Berkeley, CA: North Atlantic Books, 2021.

Harrington, Laura. "Anti-Catholicism and Protestant Reformism in the History of Western Imagery of the Buddhist Monk." *Buddhist Studies Review* 28 (2011): 203–232.

Harwood, Stacy Anne. "Struggling to Embrace Difference in Land-Use Decision Making in Multicultural Communities." *Planning Practice & Research* 20 (2005): 355–371.

Hori, C. Victor Sogen. "Japanese Zen in America: Americanizing the Face in the Mirror." In *The Faces of Buddhism in America*, edited by Charles S. Prebish and Kenneth K. Tanaka, 50–78. Berkeley: University of California Press, 1988.

Jones, Ryan. "Fresh Bread from an Old Recipe: Chögyam Trungpa's Transmission of Buddhism to North America, 1970–1977." *Canadian Journal of Buddhist Studies* 18 (2013): 30–74.

Kemper, Steven. "Dharmapala's Dharmaduta and the Buddhist Ethnoscape." In *Buddhist Missionaries in the Era of Globalization*, edited by Linda Learman, 22–50. Honolulu: University of Hawai'i Press, 2005.

King, Robert H. *Thomas Merton and Thich Nhat Hanh: Engaged Spirituality in an Age of Globalization.* New York: Continuum, 2001.

Kit, Ven. Yin. "Founding a Landmark of the Dharma in Canada." *Global Buddhist Door*, December 29, 2016. https://www.buddhistdoor.net/features/founding-a-landmark-of-the-dharma-in-canada.

Kitiarsa, Pattana. "Missionary Intent and Monastic Networks: Thai Buddhism as a Transnational Religion." *Sojourn: Journal of Social Issues in Southeast Asia* 25 (2010): 109–132.

Lin, Irene. "Journey to the Far West: Chinese Buddhism in America." In *New Spiritual Homes: Religion and Asian Americans*, edited by David K. Yoo, 134–166. Honolulu: University of Hawai'i Press, 1999.

McLellan, Janet. *Cambodian Refugees in Ontario: Resettlement, Religion, and Identity.* Toronto: University of Toronto Press, 2009.

McLellan, Janet. *Many Petals of the Lotus: Five Asian Buddhist Communities in Toronto.* Toronto: University of Toronto Press, 1999.

Mitchell, Donald W., and William Skudlarek, eds. *Green Monasticism: A Buddhist-Catholic Response to an Environmental Calamity.* New York: Lantern, 2010.

Mitchell, Scott A. *Buddhism in America: Global Religion, Local Contexts.* New York: Bloomsbury, 2016.

Negru, John H. "Highlights from the Survey of Canadian Buddhist Organizations." *Journal of Global Buddhism* 14 (2013): 1–18.

Nhat Hanh, Thich. *Freedom Wherever We Go: A Buddhist Monastic Code for the Twenty-First Century.* Berkeley, CA: Parallax, 2004.

Numrich, Paul David. *Old Wisdom in the New World: Americanization in Two Immigrant Theravada Buddhist Temples.* Knoxville: University of Tennessee Press, 1996.

Numrich, Paul David. "Theravada Buddhism in America: Prospects for the Sangha." In *The Faces of Buddhism in America*, edited by Charles S. Prebish and Kenneth K. Tanaka, 147–162. Berkeley: University of California Press, 1998.

Numrich, Paul David. "Vinaya in Theravāda Temples in the United States." *Journal of Buddhist Ethics* 1 (1994): 23–31.

Placzek, James, and Ian G. Baird. "Thai and Lao Buddhism." In *Asian Religions in British Columbia*, edited by Larry DeVries, Don Baker, and Dan Overmyer, 107–123. Vancouver: UBC Press, 2010.

Quli, Natalie E. F. "Laicization in Four Sri Lankan Buddhist Temples in Northern California." PhD dissertation, Graduate Theological Union, 2010.

Rahula, Bhikkhu Yogacara. *One Night's Shelter (From Home to Homelessness): The Autobiography of an American Buddhist Monk*. 3rd revised edition. High View, West Virginia: Bhavana Society:, 2004. http://www.nalanda.org.my/nalanda_share/One%20Night's%20Shelter%20Version%203E.pdf.

Soucy, Alexander. "The Buddha and the Birch Tree: The Great Pine Forest Monastery and the Localization of Vietnamese Buddhism to Canada." *Contemporary Buddhism* 15 (2014): 373–393.

Trungpa, Chögyam. *Cutting through Spiritual Materialism*. Boston: Shambhala, 2002.

Van Esterik, Penny. *Taking Refuge: Lao Buddhists in North America*. N.p.: Arizona State University, 1992.

Verchery, Lina. "An Alternative to the 'Westernization' Paradigm and Buddhist Global Imaginaires." In *Buddhism in the Global Eye: Beyond East and West*, edited by John S. Harding, Victor Sogen Hori, and Alexander Soucy, 150–162. London: Bloomsbury, 2020.

Verchery, Lina. "The Avatamsaka Sagely Monastery (華嚴聖寺) and New Perspectives on Globalized Buddhism in Canada." In *Understanding the Consecrated Life in Canada: Critical Essays on Contemporary Trends*, edited by Jason Zuidema, 363–376. Waterloo, ON: Wilfrid Laurier University Press, 2015.

Wilson, Jeff. "What Is Canadian about Canadian Buddhism." *Religion Compass* 5 (2011): 536–548.

CHAPTER 16

FOOD IN AMERICAN BUDDHISM

MELISSA ANNE-MARIE CURLEY

IN 1979, American Zen teacher Kōbun Otogawa introduced the rules of Zen monastic eating (*ōryōki*) to Chögyam Trungpa's American Shambhala community. A decade later, Trungpa's students hosted Otogawa at an *ōryōki* meal. Roland Cohen recalls his astonishment at Otogawa's (relative) informality:

> To my surprise, he received all his food (all three dishes) in his one Buddha bowl. This was totally different from how we had been practicing oriyoki, as we always used all three bowls, one for each dish. Our Vajradhatu version was very strict in terms of "rules," as well as our logic about how and why things were done in oriyoki. (Sullivan 2015, n.p.)

From the beginnings of the Buddhist tradition to the present, Buddhists have disagreed about what Buddhists should eat and how they should eat it. Cohen's pride in the strictness of Shambhala *ōryōki* illustrates how dietary orthodoxies function to establish and enforce boundaries. At the same time, Vajradhatu *ōryōki* —a careful mingling of Japanese and Tibetan monastic etiquette, put into practice at shared tables in Colorado and across the world—demonstrates how meals function as a framework in which boundaries are crossed and new capacities acquired. This chapter examines some of the ways in which complex dynamics of boundary crossing and boundary control shape the American Buddhist foodway: the foods Buddhists eat, how these foods are prepared and shared, and the meanings attached to them.

The material here is organized in terms of three broad categories—food offerings, home cooking, and virtuous eating. Across these categories, I hope to demonstrate that food has particular advantages as an entry point for the study of all kinds of American Buddhism, insofar as it draws our attention to everyday practitioners—including many whose labor within Buddhist communities has been understudied. Given the limits of space, the chapter necessarily leaves out important American Buddhist practices and innovations. At the same time, readers may be surprised by some of the food that *is* included here, either because it strikes them as food Buddhists should not eat, or because it is food they associate more strongly with other foodways. Breaking with the rules of *ōryōki*, I hope that readers will take what they like and leave the rest.

Food Offerings: Feeding Monastics

Not all Buddhist monastics are required to sustain themselves through alms rounds; for those who are, the spatial regimes and temporal routines of everyday American life present significant challenges. When Dhammananda Monastery was first established in the California suburb of Daly City in the 1980s, for example, Burmese American lay supporters scattered across San Mateo County took turns delivering the day's meal to the monastery each morning; after some missed deliveries, the monastery's organizing committee stocked the monastery refrigerator with extra meals that the resident monks could, in an emergency, reheat in the microwave, on the understanding that such reheating would not violate *vinaya* rules that prohibit cooking food (Cheah 2011, 109–111). When the monastery moved to Half Moon Bay, too far from the lay community to expect daily deliveries, a lay volunteer moved in to serve as cook and housekeeper, and the organizing committee sponsored a female novice from Burma to come assist, in this way evolving toward "a setup similar to older Catholic rectories" (Cheah 2011, 111). In the early years at Los Angeles's Wat Thai, monastics had to "fend for themselves": driving to the supermarket, and buying and preparing their own food; in the 1980s, the growth of the local Thai American community allowed them to introduce a weekly walking alms round, relying on a resident cook (and take-out from McDonald's) during the rest of the week (Kaplan 1990). Two decades later, the size of the lay community was such that the monks could not reasonably be expected to eat all the donated food, so Wat Thai introduced a system allowing supporters to purchase gift baskets from the monastery and immediately donate them back to the monks, selling and reselling a single basket. This is food offering "organized along the principle of low cost and high return"—as Wat Thai's abbot puts it, "American-ness is working here" (Bao 2015, 129).

Monastics living in places without large local lay communities have likewise innovated. In White Salmon, Washington, the monks at the Pacific Gorge Hermitage rely on an alms coordinator who schedules their walking route in advance so that those interested in donating can be sure to be at home and in earshot when the monks pass through the neighborhood; they also include local restaurants on their rounds, enabling supporters across the country to call in take-out orders for them (Hastings 2019). As a solitary alms mendicant in Kauai, Bhante Subhūti writes that he relied on orders called into a local Subway franchise by a supporter on the mainland: "The meal tickets were taped to the wall by the register. . . . Upon entering, they would take the slip and make a sandwich for me. They would even cut the sandwich with the magic monk words to 'make it allowable'" (Subhūti 2020, n.p.). In rural Minnesota, Bhikkhu Ashin Cintita made a weekly alms round at a summer farmer's market, a strategy he credits to the American nun Amma Thanasanti (Dinsmore 2014). A farmer's market is, he notes, a suitable place for an alms round, with food "close at hand, available for purchase on a whim" (Dinsmore 2014, n.p.); it is also a place where Buddhist monastics—perhaps especially white, English-speaking monastics—are likely to be welcome, their presence affirming the market as a "convivial" public space (even as the absence of panhandlers alerts us to the limited nature of this conviviality) (Francis and Griffith 2011).

Because going for alms makes monastics publicly present, it can become an occasion for monastics to perform a socially valued religious pluralism. The monks at Pacific Gorge, for example, have been invited to stop at a local school, where students offer food and the monks, in return, offer "an opportunity . . . to meet somebody of a different faith tradition than most of the dominant American faith traditions" (Hastings 2019, n.p.). The task of the monastic here is to embody difference as the representative of a minority tradition. On the other hand, public presence also makes possible the pleasure of recognition. Cintita, who describes himself as a monk "of tall lumbering Nordic descent," recalls the experience of stationing himself at the farmer's market alongside some younger monks from the local Karen community, and meeting there an older woman, "an apparent immigrant . . . who presumably had not seen an alms round in many years"; she was, he writes, "thrilled to be able to explain to her lanky grandson how to drop an offering into each of our bowls" (Dinsmore 2014, n.p.). This is an encounter across ethnic and cultural borders: a white monk in Burmese robes, in the company of four Karen monks, recognized as Buddhist by an Asian American grandmother. The story suggests that for the grandmother, the significance of this encounter lay in the opportunity to teach her grandson the skill of merit making—as she makes her gift to the monastics, she is also making a gift to her grandson by increasing what philosopher David Haekwon Kim might call his "cultural capacity," or his ability to move with ease "between ethnic culture and mainstream culture" (Kim 2014, 107). The alms round is thus both a moment of interethnic religious recognition and an opportunity to transmit a set of dispositions central to religious and ethnic identity.

Food Offerings: Nourishing Communities

In America as in Asia, rituals of food offering are entwined with rituals of commensality. One form this takes is the temple food fair or bazaar, an event crucial for merit making, fundraising, and cultivating particular kinds of taste. For Tamara C. Ho's informants at Azusa Buddhist Monastery, the monastery serves as a site where values understood as distinctively Burmese—respect, community, reciprocity, service—are transmitted to the second generation; by connecting younger members of the community with those values, the monastery connects them to Burma and so, as one of Ho's informants puts it, gives Asian American youth "a place, a past" (Ho 2008, 190). Food fairs offer an opportunity to make this connection in an embodied and enjoyable way. On festival days at Dhammananda, Joseph Cheah writes, people came "to eat authentic Burmese food, listen to Burmese music, and socialize with friends they had not seen for a while... to be in an environment that reminded them of the 'old country'" (Cheah 2011, 101–102). Ho and Cheah encourage us to understanding the feeling invoked here not as simple nostalgia, but as a strategic mode of resistance to assimilation (Cheah 2011, 102): an effort to preserve cultural capacity. At the same time, in keeping with the logic of commensality, the promise of delicious, inexpensive food draws visitors from outside the community, allowing events like these to function as sites of encounter across religious, ethnic, and racial lines.

Sometimes, neighbors have objected to such boisterous commensality. In the 1980s and again in the early 2000s, "neighborhood committees" brought complaints about weekend events at Wat Thai to the City of Los Angeles Zoning Commission, claiming that they caused excessive noise, litter, and traffic congestion. In 1987, a zoning complaint was brought against a small Vietnamese Buddhist center in another Los Angeles suburb, with neighbors complaining about the center's resident monastics sharing meals with visitors in the center's front yard. In 2008, neighborhood residents urged an investigation of the zoning permit for Berkeley's Wat Mongkolratnaram and its Sunday food court, complaining about the noise caused by banging pots and pans, litter, traffic congestion, and the smell of fried food. In each case, complaints about matter out of place were supported by appeals to particular ways of understanding religion as properly focused on "individualized prayer and consumption" (Padoongpatt 2017, 144)—the neighbors who brought the complaint against the Vietnamese Buddhist center, for example, insisted that they could tolerate its use as "a retreat for spiritual contemplation" but not as "a community resource" (Puig 1987, n.p.).

In their negotiations with the regulatory state, Buddhist institutions have sometimes been able to make food fairs legible as religious, and so appeal successfully to the principle of freedom of religion. In its application for a broader use permit, for example, Wat Mongkolratnaram described the Sunday food court as an adaptation of the alms round "traditionally practiced every morning" in Thailand but concentrated to Sundays as part of the temple's "Sunday services" (in part because in the United States, "standing outside with a bowl would be panhandling"). Like the alms round, they explained, the food court is about making merit, not money: "Volunteers still prepare and cook the food as they did in the beginning and all donations received from the Sunday services go to funding the Temple, its services and ultimately the community." Wat Mongkolratnaram's legal victory was due, Jonathan H. X. Lee notes, to the organizing efforts of young Thai American activists who acted as "caregivers of their parents' and grandparents' lifeways, and defenders of the American virtue of religious tolerance" (Lee 2014, 137). In other instances, community members have made deft use of another American strategy: lay supporters of the Los Angeles Vietnamese Buddhist center ultimately resolved the dispute by purchasing the property belonging to the complainants.

Despite this policing, Buddhist communities have continued to use festivals and food fairs to enact more inclusive forms of sociality. In 2005, food writer Jonathan Gold included Wat Thai's weekend food court on his list of ninety-nine essential Los Angeles restaurants:

> At the northern end of drab, endless Coldwater Canyon Boulevard lies this massive, gold-encrusted Thai Buddhist temple, grounds crowded with parishioners, saffron-robed monks, and small children who run about as if the temple were a private playground. On weekend afternoons and during festivals, the air around the temple almost throbs with the smells of Thai cooking: meat grilling at satay stands, the wheat pancakes called *roti* sizzling on massive griddles, pungent, briny salt crabs being pounded for the ultraspicy green-papaya salad. This spread may be more or less the equivalent of the smothered chicken and collard greens eaten after services at some African-American churches, and it feels just as homely; the inexpensive Thai feast is open to everyone who cares to come. (Gold 2005)

Gold's lyrical description emphasizes Wat Thai's foreignness, with the temple appearing as a splash of life in the colorless landscape of the San Fernando valley. At the same time, in implying a connection between Thai Buddhist food and American soul food, Gold seems to affirm Wat Thai's quintessentially American character. Tanachai Mark Padoongpatt argues that Wat Thai has indeed been a place in which Thai Americans have been able to practice "a public sociability that crossed ethnic, citizenship, class, and religious lines" (2015, 83). Against the claims of those "who lament non-white populations, particularly immigrants, for fracturing an otherwise unified American culture or sense of togetherness," in insisting on temple space as public space, food fairs and festivals rehearse an American vision of what public space should be: diverse, pluralist, and democratic (Padoongpatt 2015, 104–105).

Home Cooking for the Temple

Preparing the food that sustains the monastic community and organizing fundraising food fairs are practices of generosity (*dāna*). Community cookbooks—created by committee, with recipes volunteered by individual members, and sales supporting the institution—are another kind of *dāna*. This section focuses on two Jōdo Shinshū cookbooks, each first printed in 1977: *Itadakimasu*, produced by the Gardena Buddhist Church Dana Group, and *Heritage of Japan: Favorite Recipes*, produced by the Pasadena Buddhist Women's Association's Cookbook Committee. Making a case for taking material like this seriously, Isaac West suggests that "cookbooks and recipes invite readers into specific subject positions," allowing cooks to communicate "who they are and who they might want to be" (West 2007, 359). What kind of person do these cookbooks invite us to imagine becoming?

In the United States, Jōdo Shinshū institutions have been and remain closely connected to Japanese American communities; one important function of these cookbooks then, is to invite readers into a Japanese American subject position. This includes sharing Japanese recipes—*Heritage of Japan*'s first and longest section is devoted to "Japanese dishes"; *Itadakimasu* too is full of recipes for Japanese dishes, including a thirty-six-page section of "Japanese delicacies." Both books also gesture toward preserving Japanese cultural forms. *Itadakimasu* takes its title from the customary expression said before meals; on the back cover of the book is the matching phrase *gochisōsama*, or "thank you for the meal." *Heritage of Japan* offers a section titled "What, When, Where, Why" that includes all the recipes required for the New Year's and Children's Day holidays as well as an explanation of the symbolism of these foods, and instructions for preparing and serving a formal Japanese dinner. At the same time, however, the recipes reflect the complex cultural flows that shaped Japanese American communities in places like Gardena and Pasadena. Alongside the many recipes for dishes that register (to this reader) as original to the foodway of the United States—Seafoam Salad, Picnic Ham Packages, Cheesy Macaroni and Meat Balls, Crunchy-Jamble Cookies—the books include recipes that invoke other diasporas: Lilikoi Finger Jello, Mexican Won Ton, Matzo Meal Latkes, Nagayama's Special Chicken Tamale, Shanghai Chicken Wings. And even when the connection to Japan is emphasized, the books suggest a capacious understanding of Japanese identity: in *Heritage of Japan*, the section on Japanese dishes includes a recipe for "Maui Manju"; in *Itadakimasu*, the section on Japanese delicacies includes a recipe for "Maui Mochi." This is biculturalism in an additive mode—"acquiring new cultural ways without losing an original cultural capacity" (Kim 2014, 107).

Community cookbooks are also an important site for more specific kinds of community memory. Personal names and sobriquets appear in recipe titles throughout—Auntie Tomi's Hors d'Oeuvres, Dad's Pancakes, Swedish Meatballs à la Sivan, Vi's Tamale Pie, Mr. Sunairi's Favorite Anpan—sometimes reiterating the name of the person who submitted the recipe and sometimes invoking a family member or friend who invented the recipe (or perhaps just loved it). Insofar as these books are made to circulate within the same community that produced the recipes, these names serve as citations, recalling the skill or taste of persons known to the reader. When the books escape that initial context—in the kitchens of people who inherited the book or, in the case of *Itadakimasu*, through a 2007 reprinting—these names no longer work in quite the same way; instead, they invite the reader to imagine themselves as part of a community extending across generations, and as inheriting the skill and taste of that community through cooking. The community cookbook becomes, as Dina Furumoto puts it, a source of "legacy recipes" (Furumoto 2021).

Furumoto's work suggests that in Japanese American homes, Buddhist cookbooks share space with cookbooks produced by Japanese American churches and other community organizations. In what way do these two cookbooks invite readers into a specifically Buddhist subject position? Both include a foreword from the temple's resident minister; *Heritage of Japan* also offers a grace addressing Amida Buddha to be read at the beginning and end of meals. I want to emphasize, however, the religious work that the women responsible for these books are doing. A note included with *Itadakimasu* expressing thanks to those who have purchased the book is signed "Dana Mothers." The dedication page for *Heritage of Japan* likewise tells us that the book "is published in respect for Mothers and Grandmothers before,—to preserve the heritage of the culinary arts and traditions of Japan,—dedicated to the young people, to be treasured and used for generations to come." Jōdo Shinshū has no tradition of alms rounds; doctrinally, it rejects the notion of merit making. Nonetheless, feeding others is as central to the shaping of Buddhist identity here as it is elsewhere. Like the practices considered above, the creation of community cookbooks relies on the practical knowledge and ability of Buddhist lay women, acquired in the domestic sphere through marriage and motherhood: in donating their recipes, lay women lend their skill as mothers to caring for the temple. The cookbooks extend an invitation to readers not only to borrow the skill of the Dana Mothers as home cooks but also to share in the labor of sustaining the temple by buying the book. Readers are invited, in other words, into a network constituted by *dāna*. Those who accept this invitation might understand themselves as acting as good mothers in multiple senses: by feeding their families well, by supporting the life of the temple, and by providing the next generation "a place, a past." It is in this context that Seafoam Salad becomes a quintessentially Buddhist dish.

Monastery Cooking at Home

Commercial cookbooks—published by commercial presses and designed to circulate widely—also invite readers into a Buddhist subject position, although a somewhat different one. Cooks with experience in American Zen monastery kitchens have produced a number of such books. This section will again focus on just two: Edward Espé Brown's *The Complete Tassajara Cookbook: Recipes, Techniques, and Reflections from the Famed Zen Kitchen*, born out of Brown's years at the Tassajara Zen Mountain Center and his famous *Tassajara Bread Book*; and *Three Bowls: Vegetarian Recipes from an American Zen Buddhist Monastery*, from Seppo Ed Farrey, head cook at Dai Bosatsu Zendo.

Like community cookbooks, these books too draw on a range of culinary repertoires. Here, however, all the recipes are vegetarian (in the American sense of excluding meat, fish, and seafood, rather than the sense normative within East Asian monasticism, where Buddhist vegetarian diets also exclude garlic and other alliums, eggs, dairy, and alcohol). This, Farrey writes, is "global vegetarian cooking, which brings together unlikely ingredients from different cultures in harmonious combinations" (2000, xi): Cucumber-Grape Raita with Tofu, Sesame Crepes with Portobello Mushrooms in Port Cream Sauce, Avocado-Wasabi Dressing. The choice of a vegetarian diet is here part of a shift away from foods marked as bad (variously described in *The Complete Tassajara* as processed food, store-bought food, "quick foods," "*dead* food") to foods marked as good (whole foods, "natural food," homemade food, "actual food," "*live* food"). As we see in *The Complete Tassajara*'s omelet recipe, "good" has both ethical and aesthetic dimensions:

> There are several secrets to preparing this light, spongy omelet. It all begins with eggs from free-range chicken with their deep golden yolks, rather than the watery, pale, yellow-yolked eggs from chickens locked in wire boxes, unable to move, stuffed with pellets and antibiotics. (2009, 177)

In keeping with a vision of choosing good foods rather than bad, the recipes here promise to moderate or correct appetite—*Three Bowls* offers a recipe for muffins "so full of lemony flavor that the thought of spreading anything on them will never cross your mind" (2000, 170); *Complete Tassajara* aims at instilling patterns of eating that leave one "fulfilled and not stuffed to lethargy" (2009, 243). Readers are thus imagined as in the process of learning both how to cook and how to eat: they are given instruction in how to use chopsticks, how to crack a hardboiled egg, and how to appreciate what fruits and vegetables "really" taste like.

On one level, this reflects how the authors and the communities to which they belong—predominantly white and middle-class—have, through training in Zen, enhanced their own cultural repertoire. On another level, inasmuch as "good" food is defined here in opposition to an imagined standard American diet, cooking in this style serves as a refusal of those cultural norms. The effect of this refusal is not described in terms of becoming integrated in an ethnic community with its own cultural affordances, but rather in terms of individual self-expression: when you cook, *The Complete Tassajara* tells us, you are "dreaming up what to do with yourself, with your capacity and willingness; what space and time you have available" (2009, 159). To cook is to learn to access your "innate capacity to taste and sense and decide for yourself what you like" (2009, 4–5); it is worth the effort this kind of cooking demands because refusing processed foods and other such efficiencies is a way of registering a critique of a white, middle-class subject position in favor of reclaiming one's "*original* self-worth" (2009, 4).

This notion of "worth" has political significance—one reader of the *Tassajara Bread Book* whose letter to Brown is excerpted in *The Complete Tassajara* writes, "Since I learned to make bread from your book . . . I feel as though I have re-owned my life from corporate America" (2009, 6). But in a Zen Buddhist context, the notion of an original self-worth also has a religious significance, resonating with the Zen image of realizing one's original face, or Buddha nature. Given their authors' personal histories, it is not surprising to find the books suggesting that cooking can be a vital, transformative kind of Buddhist practice. The books include explicitly pedagogical material explaining the role of the monastery cook in Zen tradition and the ritual forms that structure cooking and eating in Japanese and American Zen monasteries; they also describe the routines of the monastery, encouraging readers to enter into such routines, as in this instruction from *Three Bowls*: "bring all your attention to the food. Food lovingly and mindfully prepared tastes better and satisfies longer" (2000, 1). Similarly, they evoke the space of the monastery, inviting the reader to bring that space into their own homes, as in the recipe for sesame soybeans from *The Complete Tassajara*: "this is a recipe that we prepare for ourselves in the winter ... not a guest season recipe ... for all of you mountain yogis and aspiring mountain yogis, here it is" (2009, 371). The implication here is that cooking can be meditation for the home cook, too—a way to learn, as *Three Bowls* puts it, "about the practice of being in each moment" (2000, xii). If one works hard at cooking, *The Complete Tassajara* promises, "cooking will work on you, and refine you, so that you come out of the fire even more large-hearted" (2009, x). For the relatively small set of readers who have spent time in residence at these monasteries, the continuity between the taste of monastic cooking and the taste of home cooking might be understood as a corollary to a hoped-for continuity between the intensive meditation done in residence at the center and a daily meditation practice at home. But the many readers with no direct connection to these monasteries—and perhaps no connection to any Buddhist community at all—are also invited to imagine themselves as monastics, coming to sense "the liberation in learning a basic cooking skill" (Brown 2009, 6).

MINDFUL EATING AND WHAT TASTES GOOD

An interest in correcting the appetite is also present in Buddhist diet manuals—books that draw on Buddhist practice to address ways of eating understood as disordered or disease-producing. Some of these manuals have only a tenuous connection to the Buddhist tradition. Laura C. Holloway's 1886 *Buddhist Diet Book*, for example, prescribes a grain-centered vegetarian diet based on the regime of European Theosophists; George Ohsawa's popular Zen Macrobiotic diet, which emphasizes brown rice and vegetables, prompted scholar Huston Smith to protest in an interview with the *New York Times* that he had "never encountered brown rice in a Zen Buddhist monastery in Japan" (Alexander 1972, 87). This section, however, will focus on diet manuals by authors with deep ties to Buddhist institutions: *Mindful Eating: A Guide to Rediscovering a Healthy and Joyful Relationship with Food* (2009) by Jan Chozen Bays, pediatrician and Zen teacher in the White Plum lineage, and *Savor: Mindful Eating, Mindful Life* (2010) by Thich Nhat Hanh, founder of the Plum Village Tradition, and his student, Harvard-based nutritionist Lilian Cheung.

Both *Mindful Eating* and *Savor* assert that mindful eating is not about weight loss: it is "not about diets or rules" (Bays 2009, 5); it is doing something "different" (Thich Nhat Hanh and Cheung 2010, iv). But the books do diagnose readers with a problem: "You know something is wrong and you feel not in control of your own body" (Fineberg in Thich Nhat Hanh and Cheung 2010, ix). This problem is rooted in disordered eating habits that are "unhelpful" and "unwholesome" (Bays 2009, 16–17), "destructive and unhealthy" (Thich Nhat Hanh and Cheung 2010, 15 and 38), "imprisoning and deadening" (Kabat-Zinn in Bays 2009, xiv). Pulled along by "habit energy" shaped by inner "wounds" (Thich Nhat Hanh and Cheung 2010, 15 and 76), by negative experiences in childhood that have "ruined our natural appetite," and by an "ancient fear of death by starvation" that "seems to have become part of our very cells" (Bays 2009, 16, 82), we "are not free" (Bays 2009, 82).

The cure for this problem with eating is mindfulness, defined as "the practice of being fully present in each moment" (Thich Nhat Hanh and Cheung 2010, 2) and presented as an "antidote to addictive preoccupations" (Kabat-Zinn in Bays 2009, xiii). Bringing mindfulness to the work of eating makes it possible to choose for ourselves what we want to eat and how much, rather than being guided by the impulsive habits of the body and mind; we discover in this process that we need not "obey" the urging of "stomach hunger" nor respond to "what our mind is demanding" (Bays 2009, 35, 42)—one can instead ask oneself "what it is that you *really* want" (Thich Nhat Hanh and Cheung 2010, 182). We thus gain self-control and so begin to "liberate ourselves from patterns of conditioning" (Bays 2009, 82). Mindful eating is a means by which to "reconnect with our true self," concealed up to this point "by our numbed, autopilot way of life" (Thich Nhat Hanh and Cheung 2010, 181); in learning to regulate the impulses of body and mind, always making conscious choices about what to eat, the reader takes "a major step to giving your life back to yourself" (Kabat-Zinn in Bays 2009, xiv) and eating, once a source of suffering, becomes instead "a source of renewal, self-understanding, and delight" (Bays 2009, 5).

As Jeff Wilson observes, mindful eating practices often promise that approaching food in this way will "increase the pleasure of eating" (2014, 112). This reflects the view that paying attention to one's food will increase one's awareness of "the sensory delight of eating" (Thich Nhat Hanh and Cheung 2010, 119); when we "become truly hungry, and then take time to eat slowly and with attention . . . we find the most enjoyment" (Bays 2009, 147). It may also reflect a sense, shared with the commercial cookbooks discussed above, that there is aesthetic pleasure to be found in cultivating a taste for a style of eating different from the imagined standard American diet. Bays, for example, reports that "in Japan people do not eat whole apples or pears" (2009, 24), and describes with satisfaction an American student's "transforming discovery . . . that one slice of apple eaten mindfully could be as satisfying as an entire apple" (2009, 105). But fundamentally, I think, it reflects an understanding that self-governance—choosing freely, for oneself—is intertwined with pleasure: "Eating this way, you feel that strength, freedom, and pleasure are attainable" (Thich Nhat Hanh and Cheung 2010, 119).

This experience of the self "as a project" to be managed is characteristic of neoliberal conceptions of personhood (Gershon 2011, 539; Rimke 2000, 70). As discussed elsewhere in this volume, contemporary mindfulness practices have been sharply criticized for their entanglements with neoliberal practices of self-governance, which shift social responsibility to the domain of the individual (Rimke 2000, 72). Mindful eating is not free of a tendency to center questions of individual choice. Kabat-Zinn introduces *Mindful Eating* with the suggestion that the book describes a social problem—"a condition of endemic mindlessness"—that we can "take personal responsibility for," and Bays concludes it with a call for self-governance:

> Many people only keep their desires in check because of laws and threats of punishment. People who are more aware realize that it is their own duty to control their

desires. Recognizing, controlling, and rechanneling desires are the essential tasks of a person who is consciously working to realize their own potential. (2009, xiii and 149)

In its emphasis on personal responsibility, mindful eating is recognizable as a form of what Robert Crawford dubs "healthism," a discourse within which "personal action to improve health" functions as a substitute for collective action to improve the social conditions that unevenly expose certain groups to disease and death (Crawford 1980, 368). Crawford reads healthism both as an effort to manage political disillusionment and as itself politically demobilizing, insofar as it represents a retreat from the political sphere into self-care (1980, 377 and 385). This may give us cause to wonder about the limits of the individualizing message of "giving your life back to yourself."

At the same time, we also see efforts to bend mindful eating to the task of cultivating political capacity. In *Occupy This Body: A Buddhist Memoir*, Sharon Suh describes discovering in Bays's mindful eating program "a Buddhist practice that spoke to me and the suffering I had been carrying for decades" (2019, 230). Against an understanding of the body as an oppositional force to be managed, Suh approaches mindful eating as a practice of learning to "occupy" her body—to trust and respond to the body's "innate and intuitive hungers" (2019, 60 and 230). As a person of color practicing mindful eating in community with people of color, Suh's use of mindful eating has a political valence in its assertion that racialized bodies deserve care and compassion (2019, 214).

ETHICAL EATING AND DOING GOOD WITH FOOD

Savor too connects the pursuit of individual health with more concrete forms of political participation, suggesting that reducing consumption of red meat and dairy products is good for the individual—"a great way to keep your weight in check, [and] improve your overall health"—but also a meaningful step "toward improving the health of our planet," and so a source of ethical pleasure: "we can be happy knowing that we are supporting a new kind of society in which there is enough food for everyone and no one will have to suffer from hunger" (2010, 51). I'll close this chapter by considering a handful of ways in which American Buddhists have worked with food in pursuing more just relationships with human and nonhuman beings.

Some American Buddhists eat meat, and others do not. In some cases, American Buddhist practitioners who choose vegetarianism are set against what is mainstream within the larger tradition. In Japanese Zen, for example, monastics are expected to refrain from eating meat only in specific circumstances; the American Zen teacher Philip Kapleau, however, maintains that a "strict rejection of flesh eating" is mandated both by the precept against doing harm and by the doctrine of Buddha nature (1981, 67). There has, Kapleau writes, "never been a genuine spiritual master either before, during, or after the Buddha's time who has defended meat eating or denied that it is a bar to realization of the highest states of spirituality" (1981, 53). For Kapleau, choosing a vegetarian diet is a way of accessing an authentic Buddhist tradition, distinct from what he characterizes as "the cultural prejudices and debased practices that have grown up around Buddhism" in certain parts of Asia; vegetarianism can thus, in his view, serve as a point of distinction for American Buddhism, separating legitimate Western teachers from those "Western teachers trained in Asia, or in the West by Asians, [who] often ape the dubious practices of their teachers and teach them to their own students" (1981, 74–75). In this respect, vegetarianism serves as a form of boundary maintenance. At the same time, Kapleau understands the choice of a vegetarian diet as a means of affirming human connection with animals, as "our fellow earthlings, who share a common destiny with us on this imperiled planet" and as living beings who might, like us, someday realize their "innate perfection—that is, become Buddha" (1981, 20 and 39). In this respect, vegetarianism represents a boundary-crossing practice affirming the value of nonhuman life.

In other contexts, choosing vegetarianism is a way for American Buddhist practitioners to connect with a global Buddhist community. Tzu Chi USA, a branch of the Taiwanese Buddhist Tzu Chi Charity Foundation, has made the promotion of vegetarianism a key area of focus through its Very Veggie Movement (VVM) initiatives, including an annual Ethical Eating Day event that invites participants to join together to "be vegetarian and locavore for a day" (Tzu Chi USA, 2022, n.p.). VVM's emphasis on the merits of choosing a vegetarian diet for even a day is rooted in the Chinese Buddhist tradition of the vegetarian fast (*zhaijie*), associated with purification and repentance (Tzu Chi Foundation 2011), and so embeds American practitioners in that larger tradition. At the same time, VVM innovates by adding "locavore" to the Buddhist ethical repertoire. This concern for local food both encourages American practitioners to connect with local food producers in their own regions, and reflects a contemporary understanding of Buddhist vegetarianism as motivated by compassionate concern not only for individual animals but for the environment writ large: thus, the VVM website explains, "ethical eating means a lot of things, but at Tzu Chi, it means choosing a vegetarian diet and locally produced food, because such personal choices prevent global warming and combat climate change" (Tzu Chi USA, 2022, n.p.). In the wake of the COVID-19 pandemic, VVM added a new piece of evidence for the global benefits of vegetarianism to its website, suggesting that shifting to a vegetarian diet could "minimize the outbreak of the next animal-borne disease" (Very Veggie Movement, n.d., n.p.) VVM thus offers American practitioners a way to participate in a transnational community through a diet regime that is simultaneously framed in terms of individual choice and social responsibility.

Other Buddhist communities also seek to connect with what is local and sustainable through working with food. The Green Gulch Farm Zen Center, associated with the San Francisco Zen Center, has been a leader in the development of environmentally sustainable farming practices; the Odiyan Retreat Center, under the leadership of Lama Tarthang Tulku, likewise offers a residential organic garden training program, integrating Buddhist ritual practice into daily routines. In the urban setting of Hamtramck, Michigan, the Detroit Zen Center established an organic grocery store and vegan café, seeking to make local foods more available in the neighborhood—"a small but sincere response to the deeply interwoven personal & global issues around food" (Living Zen Organics, n.d., n.p.). I want to end the chapter, however, by mentioning a product that American readers will likely be able to find on their supermarket shelves no matter where they live.

In 1982, Bernie Glassman, a Zen teacher in the White Plum lineage, founded Greyston Bakery in the New York City suburb of Riverdale. The bakery initially employed students from Glassman's Zen Center of New York, but in its early years of operation, turned its focus to supporting unemployed people living in the nearby working-class neighborhood of Yonkers. Greyston instituted an open-hiring policy, making positions available to people with disabilities, those with a history of incarceration, and others facing hiring discrimination. Recognizing the interrelated ways in which employees hired under this policy continued to be disadvantaged by structural inequalities, Greyston moved to support employees and their families in accessing healthcare, child care, housing, social services, and more. Greyston Bakery thus became Greyston Mandala: a network organized around "five energies" informing an aspect of each person's path to "self-sufficiency" or "wholeness." The growth of the Mandala was enabled by the success of the bakery, which was enabled by Greyston's transformative partnership with Ben and Jerry's—the brownies in Ben and Jerry's Fudge Brownie Ice Cream come from Greyston.

Do Greyston brownies count as Buddhist food? Employees working for the bakery are not asked to become Buddhist practitioners, and Greyston's spiritual repertoire is eclectic, with management practices drawn from Native American traditions and, as of 2020, one key Mandala staff role funded by Westchester Jewish Community Services (Fromartz 2001; Pirson and Livne-Tandarach 2020, 240). But it is impossible to understand Glassman's organizing efforts at Greyston separately from his religious concern for feeding hungry ghosts: inviting in "the people who society has forgotten and [sharing] the best meal we can share" (Glassman 2017, n.p.). Rooted as it is in a specifically American vision of equality and a specifically Buddhist notion of interdependence, Greyston Mandala's use of food as a mechanism for shifting power relations and sustaining community resonates deeply with other instances of commensality we have considered above. To borrow a phrase from the abbot at Wat Thai: American Buddhism is working here.

References

Alexander, George. 1972. "Brown Rice as a Way of Life." *New York Times*, March 12, 87.
Bao, Jiemin. 2005. "Merit-Making Capitalism: Re-Territorializing Thai Buddhism in Silicon Valley, California." *Journal of Asian American Studies* 8, no. 2 (June): 115–142.
Bays, Jan Chozen. 2009. *Mindful Eating: A Guide to Rediscovering a Healthy and Joyful Relationship with Food*. Boston: Shambhala.
Brown, Edward Espe. 2009. *The Complete Tassajara Cookbook: Recipes, Techniques, and Reflections from the Famed Zen Kitchen*. Boulder: Shambhala.

Cheah, Joseph. 2011. *Race and Religion in American Buddhism: White Supremacy and Immigrant Adaptation*. New York: Oxford University Press.

Crawford, Robert. 1980. "Healthism and the Medicalization of Everyday Life." *International Journal of Health Services* 10, no. 3: 365–388.

Dinsmore, Ashin Cintita. 2014. "Alms Round in America?" *Buddha-Sāsana*, January 28. https://bhikkhucintita.wordpress.com/2014/01/28/alms-round-in-america/.

Farrey, Seppo Ed, with Myochi Nancy O'Hara. 2000. *Three Bowls: Vegetarian Recipes from an American Zen Buddhist Monastery*. Boston: Houghton Mifflin Company.

Francis, Mark, and Lucas Griffith. 2011. "The Meaning and Design of Farmers' Markets as Public Space: An Issue-Based Case Study." *Landscape Journal* 30, no. 2 (January): 261–279.

Fromartz, Samuel. 2001. "A Path, Not a Program: Greyston Mandala." *Lion's Roar*, July 1. https://www.lionsroar.com/a-path-not-a-program-greyston-mandala/.

Furumoto, Dina. 2020. "(Almost) Brand New Recipes." *Yo! Magazine*, December 3. https://www.itsyozine.com/posts/legacy-recipes.

Gershon, Ilana. 2011. "Neoliberal Agency." *Current Anthropology* 52, no. 4: 537–555.

Glassman, Bernie. 2017. "Zen Buddhism and Obon: Feeding the Hungry Spirits." *Huffington Post*, December 6. https://www.huffpost.com/entry/zen-buddhism-and-oban-fee_b_644860.

Gold, Jonathan. 2005. "Jonathan Gold's 99 Essential L.A. Restaurants, Part 3." *L.A. Weekly*, June 30. https://www.laweekly.com/jonathan-golds-99-essential-l-a-restaurants-part-3/.

Hastings, Patty. 2019. "The Monks of White Salmon." *The Columbian*, May 5. https://projects.columbian.com/2019/05/05/the-monks-of-white-salmon/.

Ho, Tamara C. 2008. "Women of the Temple: Burmese Immigrants, Gender, and Buddhism in a U.S. Frame." In *Emerging Voices: Experiences of Underrepresented Asian Americans*, edited by Huping Ling, 183–198. New Brunswick, NJ: Rutgers University Press.

Kaplan, Tracey. 1990. "'Bending Like a Bamboo': Monks at Thai Buddhist Temple 'Beg' for Breakfast, Solve Parking Problems and Learn to Adapt." *Los Angeles Times*, February 3. https://www.latimes.com/archives/la-xpm-1990-02-03-me-868-story.html.

Kapleau, Philip. 1981. *To Cherish All Life: A Buddhist View of Animal Slaughter and Meat Eating*. Rochester, NY: The Zen Center.

Kim, David Haekwon. 2014. "Shame and Self-Revision in Asian American Assimilation." In *Living Alterities: Phenomenology, Embodiment, and Race*, edited by Emily S. Lee, 103–132. Albany: State University of New York Press.

Lee, Jonathan H. X. 2015. "Acting Out: Thai American Buddhists Encounters with White Privilege and White Supremacy." In *Southeast Asian Diaspora in the United States: Memories and Visions, Yesterday, Today, and Tomorrow*, edited by Jonathan H. X. Lee, 120–142. Newcastle Upon Tyne: Cambridge Scholars.

Living Zen Organics. n.d. "Living Zen Organics." https://www.detroitzencenter.org/lzo.

Padoongpatt, Tanachai Mark. 2015. "'A Landmark for Sun Valley': Wat Thai of Los Angeles and Thai American Suburban Culture in 1980s San Fernando Valley." *Journal of American Ethnic History* 34, no. 2 (Winter): 83–114.

Pirson, Michael, and Reut Livne-Tandarach. 2020. "Restoring Dignity with Open Hiring: Greyston Bakery and the Recognition of Value." *Rutgers Business Review* 5, no. 2 (Summer): 236–247.

Puig, Claudia. 1987. "Meditative Temple Becomes Center of a Sepulveda Zoning Controversy." *Los Angeles Times*, November 16. https://www.latimes.com/archives/la-xpm-1987-11-16-me-14088-story.html.

Rimke, Heidi Marie. 2000. "Governing Citizens through Self-Help Literature." *Cultural Studies* 14, no. 1: 61–78.

Subhūti. 2020. "As Long as You Stand on the Road." *American Buddhist Monk: Bhante Subhūti*, December. https://americanmonk.org/stand-on-the-road/.

Suh, Sharon A. 2019. *Occupy This Body: A Buddhist Memoir*. Nepean, ON: Sumeru Press.

Sullivan, Judy Sachs. 2015. "Vajradhatu Oriyoki." *Shambhala Times*, July 15. https://shambhalatimes.org/2015/07/15/vajradhatu-oriyoki/.

Thich Nhat Hanh and Lilian Cheung. 2010. *Savor: Mindful Eating, Mindful Life*. New York: HarperOne.

Tzu Chi USA. n.d. "Ethical Eating Day." https://tzuchi.us/ethical-eating-day.

Very Veggie Movement. n.d. "Our Vision." https://veryveggiemovement.org.

West, Isaac. 2007. "Performing Resistance in/from the Kitchen: The Practice of Maternal Pacifist Politics and La WISP's Cookbooks." *Women's Studies in Communication* 30, no. 3 (October): 358–383.

Wilson, Jeff. 2014. *Mindful America: Meditation and the Mutual Transformation of Buddhism and American Culture*. New York: Oxford University Press.

CHAPTER 17

MINDFULNESS AND MEDITATION IN THE UNITED STATES

NALIKA GAJAWEERA

As a Sri Lankan American from a Sinhalese Buddhist family, I was taken aback when I walked up the stairwell into a meditation center in Southern California to see a statue of the Buddha placed at the foot of the front door. "Buddha as door stopper?" I wondered to myself. In most Asian countries where Buddhism is practiced, and in many Asian American Buddhist temples in the United States, placing the Buddha anywhere but above eye level would be considered heretical. But there it was, a statue of a meditating Buddha placed firmly on the ground, welcoming members of the meditation center into their rented space at a local nonprofit organization.

While culturally inappropriate in other contexts, the placement of the Buddha statue also symbolized the pragmatic, psychological approach to Buddhist meditation at the center. The center aimed to "bring the Buddha down to earth" by anchoring Buddhist teachings on meditation in the daily lives of American practitioners. In the first session of a six-week mindfulness class, students shared therapeutic aims such as "I want to deal with the chaos in my mind" and "I need to find some stillness and clarity in my mind." Notably absent were expressions of Buddhist soteriological goals, such as pursuing a moral path toward enlightenment.

This therapeutic approach—untethered from the ethical, communal, and soteriological experience of Buddhism as a culturally embedded religious tradition—is the predominant presentation of mindfulness meditation in North America. Mindfulness is taught in a wide range of non-religious contexts such as university campuses, clinical settings, corporate offices, and even the halls of government. In such spaces, Buddhist signifiers are either completely absent or recontextualized as aesthetic accessories.

This chapter investigates the historical shifts, culturally contingent forces, and power dynamics that have enabled the emergence of mindfulness as a therapeutic modality that countenances the placement of the Buddha as door stopper. It traces the multiple ways that Buddhist meditation has been deployed and presented in the United States, examining the factors that have shaped its expression, both historically and in the contemporary period. Doing so crucially relies on an interdisciplinary approach. While religious studies scholars have traced and contextualized the modernization of Buddhist meditation that began under the conditions of colonialism, given the impact that meditation practice has had in explicitly non-religious settings, other fields such as psychology, business management, sociology, and anthropology have also contributed to a thriving discussion and debate.

Engaging with an interdisciplinary body of scholarship on meditation and mindfulness and its emergence in North America, this chapter is structured into three sections. First, it will trace the multiple historical confluences, sociocultural shifts, and individual innovators that have shaped the emergence of mindfulness meditation in contemporary America today, highlighting the influences and conditions, both Asian and Western, that particularly inform contemporary understandings of meditation. It will draw particularly on scholarship that attends to the historical conditions in Asia, such as colonial-era Burmese reform movements; the Thai forest traditions deriving from Ajahn Chah, which have shaped these developments in meditation; as well as explore the ways in which European modernist thought, late-Victorian values and American liberal spirituality have impacted the emergence of *vipassanā*/insight groups today.

The second section of this chapter examines scholarly frameworks that have applied a comparative and ethnographic lens to understand the contemporary meditation and mindfulness phenomenon. Here I turn to primarily fieldwork-based research that examines mindfulness proponents' own reportage of how they engage with meditation techniques and Buddhist teachings, and that attends to the power-laden and often interconnected meanings about mindfulness, as well as the generational differences and emergent cultural sensibilities and economic demands that shape the contemporary phenomenon.

The final section of the chapter engages with critiques of contemporary mindfulness, ranging from its departure from the classical tradition to its complicity with neoliberalism, whiteness, and patriarchy. It considers a subset of literature in Buddhist studies that delegitimizes contemporary forms of mindfulness meditation in America because of their departure from classical Buddhist doctrines and meditative practices. It discusses how these critiques have also been problematized by parallel scholarship for their reifying notions of the authenticity of "real Buddhism." This section also considers the growing debate and controversies around the neoliberal socioeconomic context in which mindfulness and meditation take place. Yet, as many ethnographers suggest, theorizing mindfulness as always in service of a neoliberal agenda can also flatten out the diversity of experiences, meanings, and efforts of people practicing mindfulness as a form of resilience. The section then concludes with critical interrogation of the intersection of race and whiteness in secular and Buddhist meditation institutions and mindfulness spaces, and recent literature that draws on theories of embodiment to theorize meditation and mindfulness in relation to gender and race in America.

FROM *VIPASSANĀ* TO MINDFULNESS: HISTORICAL TRAJECTORIES

The history of how the word "mindfulness" entered into English parlance in the late nineteenth century, as a translation of the Pali term *sati*, is well documented by scholars, particularly in the efforts of early Indologists, translators, and orientalists who played a key role through early translations of Pali texts in standardizing the English word for *sati*.[1] These were largely based on a canon of such Pali literature as the Establishing of Mindfulness Sutta (Satipaṭṭhāna Sutta), the Mindfulness of Breathing Sutta (Ānāpānasati Sutta), and the Path of Purification (Visuddhimagga).

As Erik Braun notes, in these early framings, *sati* is both subtle and complex, and not reducible to simply meditation, but rather describes "a quality of mind that brings the object of attention to the forefront of awareness, sustains that object in awareness through its recollective function, and, by guarding the mind's focus and engendering a self-awareness about that focus, enables an ethical evaluation aiming at awakening."[2] In this framing, *sati* is a tool for cultivating all forms of meditation, including calming (*samatha*) meditation—a technique for calming the mind by focusing attention on a single object—that precedes insight practice.

The translation of the Pali canon by these early Indologists remains an important point of departure for scholars of Theravāda Buddhism and Western practitioners. Yet, it is also important to situate this now "classical" point of view of *sati* in the colonial biases of nineteenth-century Indology, in order to understand its implications for us today. Pali canon translators like T. W. Rhys-Davis (1842–1922), for example, renowned for establishing the Pali Text Society, was posted in Ceylon as a British civil servant and functioned as a magistrate, part of whose duties was to adjudicate points of Buddhist ecclesiastical law concerning procedure from the Theravāda Vinaya; he learned Pali to handle these cases. Embedded as he was in this colonial project, an important aspect of Rhys-Davis translations of these texts on *sati* were his own claims to power and authority to speak as a Western white author for the "tradition" and the "real Buddhism."[3]

---

[1] For details on the use of mindfulness as the English word for *sati* and other early translations, see Rupert Gethin, "On Some Definitions of Mindfulness," in *Mindfulness: Diverse Perspectives on Its Meaning, Origins and Applications*, ed. J. Mark, G. Williams, and Jon Kabat-Zinn (New York: Routledge, 2013), 263–265; Donald S. Lopez, *The Scientific Buddha: His Short and Happy Life* (New Haven, CT: Yale University Press, 2012), 93; Jeff Wilson, *Mindful America: The Mutual Transformation of Buddhist Meditation and American Culture* (New York: Oxford University Press, 2014), 15–19.

[2] Erik Braun, "Seeing through Mindfulness Practices," in *The Oxford Handbook Buddhist Practice*, ed. Kevin Trainor and Paula Aria (New York: Oxford University Press, 2022), 634.

[3] Natalie Quli, "On Authenticity: Scholarship, The Insight Movement, and White Authority," in *Methods in Buddhist Studies: Essays in Honor of Richard K. Payne*, ed. Scott A. Mitchell and Natalie E. F. Quli (London: Bloomsbury, 2019), 154–172.

Indeed, a popular notion introduced by Anglophone scholarship of the time was that the Pali canon as preserved in Theravāda Ceylon (now Sri Lanka) was the earliest and therefore most authentic account of the Buddhist teachings. Textual translations of Pali became standard-bearers of truth about concepts such as *sati*. This glossed over other coexisting vernacular ideals of *sati* and other concepts idealized in Theravāda and other Buddhist traditions. From the outset, Western authorizing ideals about mindfulness were entangled within broader discourses and institutions of Western imperialism.

Beyond textual interpretations of *sati* by orientalists, an important genealogical root of contemporary formulation of mindfulness practice lies in the influential teachings and efforts of Burmese monk Ledi Sayadaw (1846–1923). Ledi, an influential figure in Myanmar (formerly known as Burma) during colonial modernity at the turn of the twentieth century, innovated existing ideas of *sati* to formulate a new pedagogical form that emphasized that a person could start meditating relying only on "momentary concentration" (*khaṇikasamādhi*), without the need for first developing forms of calming meditation (*samatha*) and rarified states of absorption (*jhāna*)—as had been classically emphasized.[4] A charismatic monastic figure in Burmese Buddhist society, Ledi was instrumental in mobilizing a mass movement of meditation among the Burmese laity. As a result of Ledi's distinctive take on cultivating *sati*, the pursuit of insight became plausible not only for monastics but also for lay Burmese Buddhists who could integrate the practice into to their day-to-day life.

Ledi's particular engagement with *sati* was historically situated in the power dynamics of colonial modernity. His pedagogical efforts were intrinsically linked to broader political goals of the emerging Burmese Buddhist civil society whose efforts centered on the revitalization of the traditional Buddhist polity that was in decline as a result of the disruptive effects of British colonial power.[5] Transforming what had been a long-standing, elite practice of cultivating mastery of Buddhist literature, Ledi sought to make highly valued Buddhist philosophical texts accessible to the non-elite populace. This emphasis on lay meditation emerged out of a rich genealogy of lay authority in Buddhist cultures.

This "Burmese method" of *vipassanā* was the initial spur that framed meditation as accessible to ordinary non-monastic laypeople. It paralleled other lay meditation movements in other Theravāda regions, namely in Thailand[6] and Sri Lanka.[7] In the Thai

---

[4] Erik Braun, *The Birth of Insight: Meditation, Modern Buddhism and the Burmese Monk Ledi Sayadaw* (Chicago: University of Chicago Press, 2013).

[5] Ibid.; Juliane Schober, *Modern Buddhist Conjunctures in Myanmar: Cultural Narratives, Colonial Legacies, and Civil Society* (Honolulu: University of Hawai'i Press, 2011).

[6] Joanna Cook, *Meditation in Modern Buddhism: Renunciation and Change in Thai Monastic Life* (New York and Cambridge: Cambridge University Press, 2010); Kate Crosby, *Theravada Buddhism: Continuity, Diversity, and Identity* (Sussex, UK: John Wiley & Sons, 2013). Stanley J. Tambiah, *The Buddhist Saints of the Forest and the Cult of Amulets: A Study in Charisma, Hagiography, Sectarianism, and Millennial Buddhism* (Cambridge: Cambridge University Press, 1987), 53–78.

[7] George D. Bond, *The Buddhist Revival in Sri Lanka: Religious Tradition, Reinterpretation and Response* (Delhi: Motilal Banarsidass, 1992); for Sri Lankan twenty-first-century reformist text in Sri Lanka, see Soma Thera, *Introduction to the Sati-paṭṭhāna-sutta* (Dodanduwa, Sri Lanka: Island Hermitage, 1941).

context, along with the influence of Ledi's *vipassanā* approach, there also emerged the modern reformation movement shaped by the Thai forest tradition lineage. Here, key monastic teachers of the Thai forest tradition advocated for the everyday world as a site of Buddhist moral perfection accessible to ordinary people in the present life.[8] There were echoes of these trends in revitalization movements in East Asian Mahāyāna and Central Asian Vajrayāna Buddhism too, wherein small movements began to stress the importance of meditation practice that focused on awareness rather than concentration or visualization.[9]

Although differences emerged among these various innovators in the radical simplification of the technique, in each of these contexts, *sati* remained closely connected to its ethical valences in the Pali texts—particularly in relation to the cultivation of wholesome qualities of self-awareness and the ultimate conquering of the "three poisons" in Buddhism, which results in nirvana.[10]

A key shift that eventually made way for the circulation of ideas about *sati* in the West was in the articulation of *sati* as "bare attention" by German-born Theravāda monk Nyanaponika (1901–1994). Nyanaponika, a student of Sri Lankan monk Soma Thera (1898–1960), who in turn was a student of the Burmese monk Mahasi Saysaw (1904–1982), started using the English expression "bare attention" to refer to *sati*, and it came to be circulated in the West through Buddhist literature he authored, such as *The Heart of Buddhist Meditation*. In it, Nyanaponika joined several other Buddhist writers of the time to popularize the novel *vipassanā* meditative method as a "Science of Mind."[11] Through this interpretive lens, meditation was presented as a technique that offered unique access to universal truths about human consciousness, *and* Buddhism itself was framed as an empirical "interior science" for understanding consciousness and "mental culture."

In a time when ideas of science and religion were being constructed in oppositional relation to one another—with science supplanting the latter in its authoritative claims on universal truths—the political stakes were significant for Buddhist reformers like Nyanaponika in presenting Buddhism in general, and meditation in particular, as scientific.[12] Indeed, their attempts in the late nineteenth and early twentieth centuries to align Buddhism with scientific rationalism, to forge what David McMahan has described as a

---

[8] Anne Hansen, *How to Behave: Buddhism and Modernity in Colonial Cambodia, 1860–1930* (Honolulu: University of Hawai'i Press, 2007); Brooke Schedneck, *Thailand's International Buddhist Centers: Tourism and the Global Commodification of Religious Practices* (London: Taylor & Francis, 2015); see also Ann Gleig, *American Dharma: Buddhism beyond Modernity* (New Haven, CT: Yale University Press, 2019): 26–27.

[9] Wilson, *Mindful America*, 22–25.

[10] For a detailed discussion of these various shifts in meaning in the expression of *sati* and mindfulness, see Braun, "Seeing through Mindfulness."

[11] Nyanaponika Thera, *The Heart of Buddhist Meditation (Satipaṭṭhāna): A Handbook of Mental Training Based on the Buddha's Way of Mindfulness* (London: Rider, 1969). See the historical discussion of Nyanaponika in Wilson, *Mindful America*, 23–29.

[12] Thomas Tweed, *The American Encounter with Buddhism:1844–1912: Victorian Culture and the Limits of Dissent* (Chapel Hill: University of North Carolina Press, 2000).

discourse of "scientific Buddhism," powerfully resonated with parallel discourses circulating in Euro-American liberal religion about the power of the mind, the affirmation of ordinary life, and the autonomous pursuit of truth.[13]

Western metaphysical religion, spirituality, and liberal religion were concerned with the primacy of individual experience and consciousness, and ideals about the power of the mind to effect healing.[14] This confluence of Western philosophical, political, religious, and other cultural traditions, stemming from the European Enlightenment tradition, with Asian Buddhist counterparts, has been described by scholars through the analytical concept of Buddhist modernism.[15]

In the name of commitments to science and tolerance, these religious liberals denounced fundamental beliefs and values of the Protestant-Christian framework and the Anglo-American Victorian culture. They also had a cosmopolitan fascination with religious diversity and a perennialist attitude that sought to make the claim for the existence of a mystical universal truth behind all religious traditions.[16] The New Thought movement, theosophists, Transcendentalists, and many others represented various cohorts of liberal religion in America, each spiritually disenchanted with Christianity and interested in metaphysical tradition, making significant overtures to Asian religions, and Buddhism in particular. As argued by Thomas Tweed, "Despite their many differences, esoterics, rationalists and romantics all were drawn to Buddhism by reports of its greater compatibility with science and tolerance."[17]

The 1893 World Parliament of Religions in Chicago, organized and funded in large part by liberal religion advocates, was a watershed moment. Here, Soēn Shaku (1859–1919), a Japanese Zen master, and Anagarika Dharmapala, well-known Buddhist reformer in Ceylon, boldly proclaimed the essential compatibility of Buddhist and scientific concepts to an audience of liberal, upper-middle-class, Protestants prejudiced against Catholicism, ritual, and superstition, and eager for a form of spirituality that appealed to their progressive Victorian sensibilities.[18]

---

[13] David McMahan, *The Making of Buddhist Modernism* (New York: Oxford University Press, 2008), 89–116; Donald Lopez, *Buddhism and Science: A Guide for the Perplexed* (Chicago: University of Chicago Press, 2008).

[14] Wakoh Shannon Hickey, *Mind Cure: How Meditation Became Medicine* (New York: Oxford University Press, 2019); Catherine Albanese, *A Republic of Mind and Spirit: A Cultural History of American Metaphysical Religion* (New Haven, CT: Yale University Press, 2006). Matthew Hedstrom, *The Rise of Liberal Religion: Book Culture and American Spirituality in the Twentieth Century* (New York: Oxford University Press, 2013).

[15] See Christopher Emory Moore, Chapter 1 in this volume, for a thorough examination of Buddhist modernism.

[16] Robert H. Sharf, "Is Mindfulness Buddhist? (And Why It Matters)," *Transcultural Psychiatry* 52, no. 4 (2015): 470–484.

[17] Tweed, *American Encounter*, 110.

[18] Leigh Schmidt, *Restless Souls: The Making of American Spirituality* (San Francisco: HarperCollins, 2005); S. Amunugama, *The Lion's Roar: Anagarika Dharmapala and the Making of Modern Buddhism* (Delhi: Oxford University Press, 2019).

These representations of mindfulness (and Buddhism itself) as science were, however, taking root in the specter of orientalist discourses. For underlying liberal religious claims to the rationalism of Buddhism were deep prejudices and Western imperial logics, such as Western authorizing claims to distinguish an authentic rational "Pure Buddhism" only identifiable in the Pali texts by Westerners (such as Rhys Davids, Paul Carus, and Henry Steel Olcott), to be saved from degradation by Asian mismanagement and practices of superstition and ritualism. As will be discussed later, such tropes continue to be reproduced in contemporary representations of Buddhism in the West.

We may understand the significance of such rationalized representation of meditation by Buddhist figures through their historical situatedness in the colonial project when the rhetoric of science was used by Buddhist intellectuals as authorizing discourses to legitimize and equate Buddhism to Western secularity, while at the same time countering orientalist characterizations.

These exchanges bring to sharp relief how Asian Buddhists subjectified by Western imperialism also informed Western representations of Buddhism and meditation as well. Drawing on the work of Charles Hallisey, we can interpret the meaning of such forceful theorizations of Buddhism and mindfulness itself *as* science as a type of "local production of meaning" wherein the local circumstances and power dynamics of colonial modernity shaped the production of such local meanings about mindfulness.[19]

MEDITATION-BASED CONVERT LINEAGES

Moving into the mid- and late twentieth century, other socioeconomic and political forces come together to bring *sati*-based meditation more centrally into American popular consciousness. These include: (1) the counter-culture movement, in which a generation of Beat writers, such as Jack Kerouac, Gary Snyder, and Alan Ginsberg, turned to Buddhist thinkers and teachers like D. T. Suzuki and his intellectual successors to formulate their counterculture imaginary;[20] (2) repeal of racist anti-Asian immigration policies, which enabled the arrival of missionary-minded Asian Buddhist teachers like Sri Lankan monk Banthe Henepola Gunaratana, introducing meditation to the American public;[21] and (3) the founding of American meditation-based centers by Western laypeople who were attempting to master mindfulness in Southeast Asia under the tutelage of teachers such as U Ba Khin and Mahasi Sayadaw.[22]

[19] Hallisey, Charles, "Roads taken and not taken in the study of Theravada Buddhism," in *Curators of the Buddha, in Curators of the Buddha: The Study of Buddhism Under Colonialism*, ed. Donald Lopez (University of Chicago Press, 1995), 49.
[20] McMahan, *Making of Buddhist Modernism*, chapter 5.
[21] Richard Seager, *Buddhism in America* (New York: Columbia University Press, 2012).
[22] Wendy Cadge, *Heartwood: The First Generation of Theravada Buddhism in America* (Chicago: University of Chicago Press, 2008); Gil Fronsdal, "Insight Meditation in the United States: Life, Liberty, and the Pursuit of Happiness," in *The Faces of Buddhism in America*, ed. Charles Prebish and Kenneth

The latter trend was to have far-reaching consequences in shaping the development of what Jeff Wilson has described as the "mindfulness movement," wherein beginning in the 1970s, the center of the mindfulness movement shifts toward the United States. Jeff Wilson sites three specific sources for mindfulness teachings that are important for this trend. First, American teachers trained in Asia in the *vipassanā* movement returned to the United States to provide retreats and workshops and eventually found meditation centers for lay Americans. Second, the US college–educated Vietnamese monk Thich Nhat Hanh started teaching meditation to Westerners, emphasizing the practice of mindfulness paired with a "socially engaged Buddhist" ethic. Third, doctor and scientist Jon Kabat-Zinn began innovating new modes of teaching and promoting mindfulness, which he learned as a graduate student at the Massachusetts Institute of Technology (MIT) under the guidance of several Zen teachers, including Thich Nhat Hanh.

It is in the context of these twentieth-century cultural shifts in the United States, and the history of liberal religion in North America, that scholars have pointed to the ways in which meditation became detraditionalized, privatized, and unmoored from institutional authority and its traditional soteriological significance.[23] Indeed, it is in such a context that mindfulness became increasingly imagined in middle-class North America as a technique which one can choose in fashioning one's own individual religious practice without having to commit to an institutional structure.[24]

The transfer away from monastic authority over mindfulness occurred through several overlapping phases which, as we have already seen, were of both Asian and Western origin. There were the laicization movements described above, pioneered by monastics in Asia. These monastics, both Asians and Westerners, produced literature in English for the general public, both in Asian Buddhist contexts, but also for Western audiences.

Indeed, it was the appeal of these works to Western students that attracted the first cohort of Anglo-Americans like Jack Kornfield, Joseph Goldstein, Sharon Salzburg, and Ruth Denison to take temporary ordination in monastic settings in Asia. Having received training under Theravāda teachers, like Burmese monk Mahasi Sayadaw, Thai forest monks Ajahn Chah, and lay Indian teacher S. N. Goenka, many returned to the United States to teach an adapted version of Buddhist *vipassanā* meditation to young people. Shorn of Buddhist cosmological notions and devotional practices, many went on to establish *vipassanā* meditation-based centers like Insight Meditation Center and Spirit Rock Meditation Center, as well as *vipassanā* training schools in the tradition of S. N. Goenka.[25] A "lineage of American meditation-based converts" emerged under their tutelage.[26]

Tanaka (Berkeley: University of California Press, 1998),163–182; Rick Fields, *How the Swans Came to the Lake: A Narrative History of Buddhism in America* (Boulder, CO: Shambhala, 1981).

[23] Wilson, *Mindful America*.

[24] McMahan, *Making of Buddhist Modernism*, chapter 7; Wilson, *Mindful America*, 48.

[25] For an ethnography of the Goenka school of *vipassanā*, see Michel Pagis, *Inward: Vipassana Meditation and the Embodiment of the Self* (Chicago: University of Chicago Press, 2019).

[26] Gleig, *American Dharma*, 34–49.

At the same time, Vietnamese monk Thich Nhat Hanh, associated with Mahāyāna Buddhism through the Thien tradition, established Communities of Mindful Living. Herein, he outlined a Zen that looked a lot like mindfulness, which emphasizes a Theravāda-type mindfulness exercise, but with a Mahāyāna, especially Zen, interpretation.[27] In this same context, molecular biologist and MIT graduate Kabat-Zinn developed Mindfulness-Based Stress Reduction (MBSR) at the University of Massachusetts Medical Center, innovating on the meditation practices of several Zen teachers like Thich Nhat Hanh. Kabat-Zinn's eventual establishment of benchmark programs in esteemed public and private entities, such as Google, Brown University, and MIT, eventually established the legitimacy and credibility of mindfulness among the American public.[28] Through a process of what Jeff Wilson describes as mystification, wherein meditation is presented as a non-religious secular technique disassociated from the broader religious system of Buddhist thought, MBSR presented mindfulness as a universal human capacity, one that particularly catered to the empowered individual American self.[29]

The next section turns to a discussion of the contemporary meditation and mindfulness phenomenon in the United States, focusing on fieldwork and ethnographic-based scholarship that unpacks the ways in which mindfulness emerges in the lived reality of teachers, practitioners, and institutional leadership, as well as the evolving cultural sensibilities and generational trends that shape the contemporary phenomenon.

Multiple Mindfulness: Ethnographic Approaches

The contemporary emergence of Buddhist-derived meditation practices in the United States has been characterized by scholars as informed by a particular configuration of cultural norms, attitudes, and practices ushered in with the post-medieval age of modernity. These include processes of rationalization, laicization, and individualism meeting with traditional forms of Buddhism. Indeed, the privileging of meditation by convert-based Buddhist groups in the United States is regarded as an outcome of this process of Buddhist modernism.

Yet, while accounts of Buddhism modernism tend to emphasize a singular linear development of meditation and mindfulness movements in America, the ethnographic record of contemporary trends among meditation-based convert Buddhists

---

[27] See Ben Van Overmeire, Chapter 8 in this volume; see also Seager, *Buddhism in America*.
[28] Jaime Kucinskas, *The Mindful Elite: Mobilizing from the Inside Out* (Oxford: Oxford University Press 2021).
[29] Wilson, *Mindful America*, 43–74.

reveals a much more heterogenous and complicated picture of Buddhist modernities, recognizing the presence of multiple modernist narratives and sub-narratives.[30]

Research on the American Insight networks—a loose affiliation of individuals and communities that prioritize *vipassanā* meditation practice—have brought into sharp relief such differences. As Ann Gleig has illustrated, even in the process of this development of Buddhist modernism in the West, critiques have emerged among American convert Buddhist communities related to its limitations.[31] Such critiques have included the perceived privileging of a model of individualized meditative practice, the neglect and omission of elements discarded in the laicization process such as ritual and sangha, the psychologization of Buddhism, a claim to authority and truth in defining "true Buddhism," as well as critique of meditation institutions' privileging of the needs of an overwhelmingly white, educated, upper-middle-class demographic. Based on her research on "meditation-based convert Buddhist" lineages, namely Theravāda and Zen Buddhism–derived communities, Gleig characterizes such transformation as displaying features more quintessentially postmodern than modern, signaling the development of what Gleig describes as a period marked by enlightenment beyond the (European) Enlightenment. Underlying such a shift is a postmodern resistance to the totalizing grand narratives of modernity such as science, reason, and progress, a postcolonial critique of Eurocentrism, and a turn toward contingency, relativity, difference, and attention to experiences of marginality.

As Gleig's research shows, even within these major currents there is further differentiation between first- and second-generation teachers, preferred styles of practice, conceptions of enlightenment, and modes of legitimatization. Natalie Quli similarly points to how, among groups that turn to the more textual and goal-oriented approaches, there are distinct differences among those who pursue forms of *jhāna* meditation as it is presented in the West. These include those groups that emphasize the authority that "the tradition" (i.e., the commentaries) carries, some who reject anything not located in textual accounts of what the "Buddha himself" said, and still others that locate authority in the de-traditionalized self.[32]

Nuance and heterogeneity are also found in the way psychotherapists in the United States have approached the Buddhist tradition and have engaged with meditation for therapeutic ends. As Ira Helderman argues, a dominant overarching narrative that religious studies scholars rely upon to interpret and classify clinical approaches to Buddhist teachings tends to be based in binary understandings of "religious" and "secular."[33] This

---

[30] Scott Mitchell and Natalie Quli, "Buddhist Modernism as Narrative," in *Buddhism beyond Borders: New Perspectives on Buddhism in the United States*, ed. Mitchell and Quli (Albany: State University of New York Press, 2018), 197–215).

[31] Gleig, *American Dharma*, 209; see also Ann Gleig, "Wedding the Personal and the Impersonal in West Coast Vipassana: A Dialogical Encounter between Buddhism and Psychotherapy," *Journal of Global Buddhism* 13 (February 2012): 129–146.

[32] Natalie Quli, "Multiple Buddhist Modernisms: Jhāna in Convert Theravāda," *Pacific World: Journal of the Institute of Buddhist Studies* 3, no. 10 (2008): 241.

[33] Ira Helderman, *Prescribing the Dharma: Psychotherapists, Buddhist Traditions, and Defining Religion* (Chapel Hill: University of North Carolina Press, 2019).

sweep of totalizing interpretations tends to gloss such developments in terms of either new religious forms (i.e., "new faces of Buddhism") or, in contrast, as a product of secularization. Based on ethnographic observations and interviews with clinicians, however, Helderman shows how "clinicians' treatment of Buddhist doctrine is molded by their own presumptions about what defines the religious and the not-religious and their relative levels of investment in preserving psychotherapy's qualification as a secular biomedical discipline," as well as their own status as secular, scientific, and/or biomedical practitioners.[34] In tracing out six often overlapping approaches in the way clinicians engage with Buddhist teachings—therapized, filtered, translated, personalized, adopted, and integrated—Helderman shows how clinicians maneuver within these imagined religious/secular binaries, and the breakdown that such maneuvers sometimes can entail.

For Buddhist teachings on meditation to become so integrated into standard psychotherapy, meditation had to first be institutionalized.[35] A network of American scholar-practitioners, including Joseph Goldstein, Jack Kornfield, Jon Kabat-Zinn, Roshi Joan Halifax, Ram Dass, Daniel Goldman, Franscisco Valera, and Marabai Bush, came together to collaborate, at first as an informal network of insiders, to establish institutions. These "contemplative leaders," as Kucinskas ethnographically describes them, created organizations using consensus-based mobilization tactics and elite networks to bring Buddhist-inspired practiced into mainstream American public life. As I discuss later, these power dynamics that are foundational to Insight networks and institutions in North America have significant impact on how marginalized communities experience and engage with the practice.

The next section will turn to a subset of literature in the field of Buddhist studies that is critical of the contemporary mindfulness movement, particularly in regard to its alignment with Western psychotherapy's investments in individualism and personal self-development, as well as what is regarded as a departure from the Buddhist soteriological goals underlying *vipassanā* practice. The discussion then centers around critical questions of how both mindfulness proponents and its critics are ensconced in debates over the authenticity of "real Buddhism" or "real meditation," and the ways in which ideas of authenticity reinforce a rhetoric of exclusion.

MINDFULNESS CRITIQUES: DECONTEXTUALIZING AND RECONTEXTUALIZATION

With the popular embrace of mindfulness in mainstream America, there have been prominent critical currents among both scholars and practitioners that are as diverse and distinct as the phenomenon itself.

---

[34] Ibid., 5.
[35] Kucinskas, *Mindful Elite*.

First is a subset of critiques that might be regarded as evaluative in nature in terms of their examination of the fidelity of contemporary mindfulness with canonical or classic mindfulness. Questions are raised by these intellectuals, monastics, and scholars alike, concerning common understandings of mindfulness as nonjudgmental "bare attention" or "bare awareness" and ways in which these frameworks, particularly in secular mindfulness, dismiss Buddhist ethical imperatives that are foundational to Buddhist soteriological goals and are thereby uncoupled from ideals of awakening and liberation.[36]

Relatedly, there is the assessment by Buddhlogists of the Western focus on scientific Buddhism that critically calls into question a reduction of Buddhism to a set of techniques for self-discovery, self-discipline, and self-transformation. For critics like C. W. Huntington, this turn ultimately compromises the Buddhist goal of "relinquishing self-interest," "the linchpin on which the entire apparatus of Buddhist soteriology turns."[37] Indeed, what some of these Buddhologists point to is that the Buddhism that psychotherapeutic communities engage with, as well as forms they help construct, are often highly distinct from those practiced by the majority of Asian Buddhists over the course of history.[38]

Indeed, a cursory search on Google of mindfulness highlights how popular American consciousness about Buddhist meditation is often restricted to the idea of the silent seated practice and its concomitant mental states. As scholars and practitioners of Buddhism have long argued, however, such popular preconceptions that evaluate silent seated meditation as the only valid form of Buddhist practice rely upon an underlying Western dichotomization between meditative practice and ritual.[39] This is one that privileges the former over the latter as the more "authentic" or "true" expression of Buddhist practice. Such a dualism is shaped by a Protestant theological preoccupation, in secular rhetoric, in which the development of the inner self and its experience is valorized over ritual form and practice, where the latter is reducible to mere symbolic expression.[40] The implications of such Eurocentric discourses are orientalist, where Asian and Asian American forms of Buddhist practice that emphasize ethics, doctrine,

---

[36] Bhikkhu Bodhi, "What Does Mindfulness Really Mean? A Canonical Perspective," *Contemporary Buddhism* 12, no. 1 (2011): 19–39.

[37] Huntington, C. W. "The Triumph of Narcissism: Theravāda Buddhist Meditation in the Marketplace," *Journal of the American Academy of Religion* 83, no. 3 (2015): 614. See also Geoffrey Samuel, "The Contemporary Mindfulness Movement and the Question of Nonself," *Transcultural Psychiatry* 52, no. 4 (2014); Georges Dreyfus, "Is Mindfulness Present-Centred and Non-Judgmental? A Discussion of the Cognitive Dimensions of Mindfulness," *Contemporary Buddhism* vol. 12, no. 1 (2011): 41–54; Robert H. Sharf, "Buddhist Modernism and the Rhetoric of Meditative Experience," *Numen* 42 (October 1995): 228–283.

[38] Lopez, *Buddhism and Science*.

[39] Richard Payne, "In Defense of Ritual," *Lion's Roar* (2018). https://www.lionsroar.com/in-defense-of-ritual/.

[40] Talal Asad, *Genealogies of Religion: Discipline and Reasons of Power in Christianity and Islam* (Baltimore, MD: John Hopkins University Press, 1998), 75.

art, and ritual are framed as "folk Buddhist" practices that are less authoritative or authentic, and different from Buddhist meditative experience.[41]

A closely related critical approach of convert-based meditation takes the historical analysis of Buddhist modernism as its point of departure. While scholars such as David McMahan have advanced a generally sympathetic reading of Buddhist modernism as a legitimate form of Buddhism co-produced by Western and Asian Buddhist innovators, others take a more critical stance. Robert Sharf, scholar of Zen/Chan Buddhism, for example, describes Buddhist modernism as a "distortion" and scrutinizes the modern valuing of meditative experience over ritual practice, ethical training, and scripture, as couched within nineteenth-century Protestant theological hermeneutics.[42] For Donald Lopez, as well, the selective modernist revisioning of the Buddha threatens to drain Buddhism of its vibrancy, complexity, and power, while the superficial focus on "mindfulness" turns Buddhism into merely the latest self-help movement.

An overarching concern that frames the above strands of critique are issues of rupture, discontinuity, and an underlying narrative of the decline of Buddhism in relation to the historical record. Yet, as others have argued, caution should also be raised on the implications of such scholarship because such critiques rely upon an authorizing discourse that assesses contemporary Buddhist forms according to what *real* or original Buddhism is or should be. As Natalie Quli (2019) has forcefully argued, while concerns about determining authenticity might be a legitimate concern for Buddhists acting within their various traditions, it is an ill-suited activity for scholars of social science and humanities who produce knowledge about Buddhists, practicing meditation or engaging in other activities.[43]

A different set of critiques of mindfulness from these are those mounted by scholars who situate the phenomenon within the politics of contemporary capitalist culture and neoliberalism. Jeremy Carrette and Richard King for instance, describe the commodification of Buddhist-inspired practice as a form of corporate wellness, branding, and ultimately its adoption for personal profit and corporate gain.[44] As a commodity now available for consumption in the capitalist marketplace, mindfulness, Jeff Wilson shows, dovetails with gendered forms of marketing, wherein mindfulness is envisioned as enhancing a lifestyle to help build or manage an identity as modern women, with mindfulness as an expression of Euro-American femininity.[45]

---

[41] Funie Hsu, "We've Been Here All Along," *Buddhadharma: The Practitioner's Quarterly* (Winter 2016): 24–31, https://www.lionsroar.com/weve-been-here-all-along/; Paul Numrich, "Two Buddhisms Further Considered," *Contemporary Buddhism* 4, no. 1 (2003); Shannon Wakoh Hickey, "Two Buddhisms, Three Buddhisms, and Racism, *Journal of Global Buddhism* 11 (2010): 1–25.

[42] Robert Sharf, "Experience," in *Critical Terms for Religious Studies*, ed. Mark C. Taylor (Chicago: University of Chicago Press, 1998), 94–116; see also Bernard Faure, *The Rhetoric of Immediacy: A Cultural Critique of Chan/Zen Buddhism* (Princeton, NJ: Princeton University Press, 1991); Donald Lopez, *Prisoners of Shangrila* (Chicago: University of Chicago Press, 1998).

[43] Quli, "On Authenticity," 162.

[44] Jeremy Carrette and Richard King, *Selling Spirituality: The Silent Takeover of Religion* (London: Routledge, 2005).

[45] Jeff Wilson, "Mindfully Feminine," in *Buddhist Feminisms and Femininities*, edited by Karma Lekshe Tsomo (Albany: State University of New York Press, 2018): 285–301.

Similarly, Ronald Purser and David Loy draw on Foucauldian-informed analyses of neoliberal governmentality to frame the widespread adoption of mindfulness as representing changing frameworks of state governance. In the context of increased privatization, mindfulness advocates promote the individualized "responsibility" of the subject for their own self-management and welfare.[46] These critiques unpack the links between spiritual self-help techniques and the rhetoric of "emotional self-optimization" and happiness, outlining ways in which mindfulness programs reframe stress, anxiety, and depression as a personal issue, rather than a political one.

Another related site of scrutiny of the neoliberalization of mindfulness has been what Edwin Ng terms the "mindfulness of critique." Here, Ng calls for a form of critique examining how mindfulness might function as a disruptive technology of the self within and against normative operations of power. In this modality of critique, "the objective is to experiment with ways to better articulate and actualize the potential of mindfulness as a critically, ethically and politically enabling practice grounded in the care of self." Taking inspiration from Foucault's emphasis on the resistive or transformative potential immanent in the process of subject formation, Ng is interested in how, through mindful attention and care of the somatic and emotional dimensions of experience, subjects may also foster "critical sensibilities and the political will to address the sociopolitical conditionings behind interpersonal and institutional acts of discrimination, exploitation, and other forms of injustice."[47]

Critical race theory scholarship has been a productive framework for many scholars interrogating the underlying racial discourse in Euro-American authorizing narratives of Buddhist authenticity. It helps to shed light on what Joseph Cheah has described as the "racial rearticulation" in the Western adaption of Buddhism, especially revealing the implicit and invisible racialized discourses that underlie this adaption.[48] Its effects are manifold on Asian American Buddhist heritage communities: from issues of decontextualization and appropriation of Buddhist practice away from cultures of origin, to the centering of convert-Buddhist practice vis-à-vis the scrutinization of authenticity of Asian Buddhist forms as "cultural baggage," as well as the amplification of the racial superiority of whiteness and the legitimacy of white experience in Buddhist practice.[49]

These racial articulations also have implications for the experience of non-white, non-heritage Buddhist practitioners' and converts' engagement with the practice. As I have

---

[46] Nikolas Rose's canonical work on the "psy disciplines" has shown that they have played a pivotal role in normalizing the social mechanisms of subjectification; see Nikolas Rose, *Inventing Our Selves: Psychology, Power, and Personhood*, (Cambridge: Cambridge University Press, 1998).

[47] Edwin Ng, "The Critique of Mindfulness and the Mindfulness of Critique," in *Handbook of Mindfulness: Culture, Context, and Social Engagement*, ed. Adam Burke, David Forbes, and Ronald E. Purser (Cham: Springer International, 2016), 148.

[48] Joseph Cheah, *Race and Religion in American Buddhism: White Supremacy and Immigrant Adaptation* (New York: Oxford University Press, 2011), 59–60.

[49] Nalika Gajaweera, "Reclaiming Our So-Called 'Cultural Baggage,'" *Buddhadharma*. https://www.lionsroar.com/reclaiming-our-so-called-cultural-baggage (October 2021).

argued elsewhere, based on ethnographic research with Insight networks in California, a normative assumption that many non-white practitioners (People of Color, or POCs) encounter in Insight meditation teachings is an underlying view of the human subject as a universal individual unmarked by race.[50] That is, there is a distinct hegemonic discourse that POCs encounter in predominantly white meditation groups which claims that all people as human beings are subject to a universally shared experience of suffering and dissatisfaction. In effect, it disavows the particular racialized experiences of embodiment that POCs carry in the United States.

Resisting normative ideals of resilience that advocate individuals to improve their lives through mindfulness practice by knowing how to adapt as agents of their own well-being, non-white practitioners of Color draw attention to how the social and political contexts of American race relations produce racialized subjectivities that impact their everyday suffering. They do so by creating POC "safe spaces" to meditate and by encouraging practitioners to empathize with the intertwinement of lived embodied experience as racialized Others and the shared sociopolitical nature of their emotions.[51] In line with what Edwin Ng identifies as the "mindfulness of critique," these modes of practice attend to the emergent and contested outcome of mindfulness as a technique of the self.

This engagement with mindfulness as a disruptive technology of dominant assumptions of whiteness is the explicit intent of a recent set of scholarship.[52] The scholar/practitioners in this conversation have interrogated "mindfulness as a site of temporal disruption vis-à-vis the sedimented and habitual practices of whiteness," with many of them exploring ways in which embodied experiences of race and Blackness manifest in Buddhist sanghas. Experiences of isolation, marginalization, and overt discrimination in convert-Buddhist spaces and secular contexts capture just some of the felt impacts of racial rearticulation for non-white practitioners in Western Buddhism. At the same time, they unpack how American ideals of individualism and personhood are upheld and empowered through spiritual practice, while offering alternative visions consisting of anti-racist strategies to remake institutions, curricula, pedagogies, rituals, and methodologies of meditation-based practice spaces.[53]

---

[50] Nalika Gajaweera, "Sitting in the Fire Together: People of Color Cultivating Radical Resilience in North American Insight Meditation," *Journal of Global Buddhism* 22, no. 1 (2021): 121–139.

[51] Sharon A. Suh, "'We Interrupt Your Regularly Scheduled Programming to Bring You This Very Important Public Service Announcement...': aka Buddhism as Usual in the Academy," in *Buddhism and Whiteness: Critical Reflections*, ed. George Yancy and Emily McRae (New York and London: Lexington Books, 2019).

[52] See, for a philosophical engagement with race/whiteness and Buddhist philosophy, George Yancy and Emily McRae, *Buddhism and Whiteness: Critical Reflections* (New York and London: Lexington Books, 2019), xx, and for an analysis of Black Buddhists' interpretation of Buddhism through the Black radical tradition, Rima Vesely-Flad, *Black Buddhists and the Black Radical Tradition: The Practice of Stillness in the Movement for Liberation* (New York: New York University Press, 2022).

[53] Ann Gleig, "Enacting Social Change through Buddhist Meditation," in *The Oxford Handbook of Meditation*, ed. Miguel Farias, David Brazier, and Mansur Lalljee (Oxford: Oxford University Press, 2021), 748–768; Ann Gleig, "Undoing Whiteness in American Buddhist Modernism," in *Buddhism and Whiteness: Critical Reflections* (New York and London: Lexington Books, 2019), 21–42.

Conclusion

As much as current formulations of mindfulness have uncoupled Buddhist meditation practices from the traditional Buddhist authoring power and soteriology, equally significant are the nuanced new meanings, significance, and forms of power relations that have taken hold and are emergent in its ongoing formation. As the preceding discussion has hopefully shown, the historical itinerary taken by the Buddha from his exalted position in an Asian Buddhist household shrine among a pantheon of other divine beings to his quotidian role as door stopper at the entryway of a mindfulness meditation center in Southern California is one propelled by numerous culturally contingent forces and power dynamics, such as colonial modernity, liberal secularism, neoliberalism, and whiteness. An interdisciplinary approach helps trace out how these diverse trajectories of mindfulness meditation are co-constituted by these broader systems of power.

References

Albanese, Catherine. *A Republic of Mind and Spirit: A Cultural History of American Metaphysical Religion*. New Haven, CT: Yale University Press, 2006.
Amunugama, Sarath. *The Lion's Roar: Anagarika Dharmapala and the Making of Modern Buddhism*. Delhi: Oxford University Press, 2019.
Asad, Talal. *Genealogies of Religion: Discipline and Reasons of Power in Christianity and Islam*. Genealogies of Religion. Baltimore, MD: Johns Hopkins University Press, 1993.
Bond, George D. *The Buddhist Revival in Sri Lanka: Religious Tradition, Reinterpretation and Response*. Chapel Hill: University of South Carolina, 1988.
Braun, Erik. *The Birth of Insight: Meditation, Modern Buddhism, and the Burmese Monk Ledi Sayadaw*. Chicago: University of Chicago Press, 2013.
Braun, Eric. "Seeing through Mindfulness Practices." In *The Oxford Handbook Buddhist Practice*, edited by Kevin Trainor and Paula Aria, 632–648. New York: Oxford University Press, 2022.
Cadge, Wendy. *Heartwood: The First Generation of Theravada Buddhism in America*. Chicago: University of Chicago Press, 2008.
Carrette, Jeremy, and Richard King. *Selling Spirituality: The Silent Takeover of Religion*. London: Routledge, 2005.
Cheah, Joseph. *Race and Religion in American Buddhism: White Supremacy and Immigrant Adaptation*. New York: Oxford University Press, 2011.
Cook, Joanna. *Meditation in Modern Buddhism: Renunciation and Change in Thai Monastic Life*. Cambridge: Cambridge University Press, 2010.
Crosby, Kate. *Theravada Buddhism: Continuity, Diversity, and Identity*. Sussex, UK: John Wiley & Sons, 2013.
Dreyfus, Georges. "Is Mindfulness Present-Centred and Non-Judgmental? A Discussion of the Cognitive Dimensions of Mindfulness." *Contemporary Buddhism* 12, no. 1 (2011): 41–54. doi:10.1080/14639947.2011.564815.
Faure, Bernard. *The Rhetoric of Immediacy: A Cultural Critique of Chan/Zen Buddhism*. Princeton, NJ: Princeton University Press, 1991.

Fields, Rick. *How the Swans Came to the Lake: A Narrative History of Buddhism in America*. Boulder, CO: Shambhala, 1981.

Fronsdal, Gil. "Insight Meditation in the United States: Life, Liberty, and the Pursuit of Happiness." In *The Faces of Buddhism in America*, edited by Charles Prebish and Kenneth, 163–182. Berkeley: University of California Press, 1998.

Gajaweera, Nalika. "Reclaiming Our So-Called 'Cultural Baggage.'" *Buddhadharma: Practitioners Quarterly* (Fall, 2021a). https://www.lionsroar.com/reclaiming-our-so-called-cultural-baggage/.

Gajaweera, Nalika. "Sitting in the Fire Together: People of Color Cultivating Radical Resilience in North American Insight Meditation." *Journal of Global Buddhism* 22, no. 1 (2021b): 121–139. doi:10.5281/ zenodo.4727595.

Gethin, Rupert. "On Some Definitions of Mindfulness." In *Mindfulness: Diverse Perspectives on Its Meaning, Origins and Application*, edited by Mark G. Williams and Jon Kabat-Zinn, 263–265. Oxon: Routledge, 2013.

Gleig, Ann. *American Dharma: Buddhism beyond Modernity*. New Haven, CT: Yale University Press, 2019a.

Gleig, Ann. "Enacting Social Change through Buddhist Meditation." In *The Oxford Handbook of Meditation*, edited by Miguel Farias, David Brazier, and Mansur Lalljee, 748–768. London and New York: Oxford University Press, 2021.

Gleig, Ann. "Undoing Whiteness in American Buddhist Modernism." In *Buddhism and Whiteness: Critical Reflections*, edited by George Yancy and Emily McRae, 21–42. New York and London: Lexington Books, 2019b.

Gleig, Ann. "Wedding the Personal and Impersonal in West Coast Vipassana: A Dialogical Encounter between Buddhism and Psychotherapy." *Journal of Global Buddhism* 13 (2012): 129–146.

Hallisey, Charles. "Roads taken and not taken in the study of Theravada Buddhism." In *Curators of the Buddha, in Curators of the Buddha: The Study of Buddhism Under Colonialism*, edited by Donald Lopez, 31–62. Chicago: University of Chicago Press, 1995.

Hansen, Ann R. *How to Behave: Buddhism and Modernity in Colonial Cambodia, 1860–1930. Southeast Asia: Politics, Meaning, and Memory*. Honolulu: University of Hawai'i Press, 2007.

Hedstrom, Matthew. *The Rise of Liberal Religion: Book Culture and American Spirituality in the Twentieth Century*. London and New York: Oxford University Press, 2013.

Helderman, Ira. *Prescribing the Dharma: Psychotherapists, Buddhist Traditions, and Defining Religion*. Chapel Hill: University of North Carolina Press, 2019.

Hickey, Wakoh Shannon. "Two Buddhisms, Three Buddhisms, and Racism." *Journal of Global Buddhism* 11 (February 2010): 1–25.

Hsu, Funie. "We've Been Here All Along," *Buddhadharma: The Practitioner's Quarterly* (Winter, 2016): 24–31.

Huntington, C. W. "The Triumph of Narcissism: Theravāda Buddhist Meditation in the Marketplace." *Journal of the American Academy of Religion* 83, no. 3 (2015): 624–648.

Kucinskas, Jaime. *The Mindful Elite: Mobilizing from the Inside Out*. Oxford: Oxford University Press, 2021.

Lopez, Donald S. *Buddhism and Science: A Guide for the Perplexed*. Chicago: University of Chicago Press, 2009.

Lopez, Donald S. *Prisoners of Shangri-La: Tibetan Buddhism and the West*. Chicago: University of Chicago Press, 1998.

Lopez, Donald S. *The Scientific Buddha*. New Haven, CT: Yale University Press, 2012.

McMahan, David L. *The Making of Buddhist Modernism*. New York: Oxford University Press, 2008.

Mitchell, Scott, and Natalie Quli. "Buddhist Modernism as Narrative." In *Buddhism beyond Borders: New Perspectives on Buddhism in the United States*, edited by Scott Mitchell and Natalie Quli, 197–216. Albany: State University of New York Press, 2018.

Ng, Edwin. "The Critique of Mindfulness and the Mindfulness of Critique." In *Handbook of Mindfulness: Culture, Context, and Social Engagement*, edited by Adam Burke, David Forbes, and Ronald E. Purser, 135–152. Cham: Springer International, 2016.

Numrich, Paul David. "Two Buddhisms Further Considered." *Contemporary Buddhism* 4, no. 1 (2003): 55–78.

Pagis, Michel. *Inward: Vipassana Meditation and the Embodiment of the Self*. Chicago: University of Chicago Press, 2019.

Payne, Richard. "In Defense of Ritual," *Lion's Roar*. 2018. https://www.lionsroar.com/in-defense-of-ritual/.

Quli, Natalie. "Multiple Buddhist Modernisms: Jhāna in Convert Theravāda." *Pacific World: Journal of the Institute of Buddhist Studies* 3, no. 10 (2008): 225–250.

Quli, Natalie Fisk. "Brief Critical Appraisal of the Buddhism Modernism Paradigm." In *Routledge Handbook of Buddhist-Christian Studies*, edited by Carol Anderson and Thomas Cattoi. London: Routledge, 2022.

Quli, Natalie Fisk. "On Authenticity: Scholarship, The Insight Movement, and White Authority." In *Methods in Buddhist Studies: Essays in Honor of Richard K. Payne*, edited by Scott A. Mitchell and Natalie Fisk Quli, 1–16. London: Bloomsbury Publishing, 2020.

Rose, Nikolas. *Inventing Our Selves: Psychology, Power, and Personhood*. Cambridge: Cambridge University Press, 1998.

Samuel, Geoffrey. "The Contemporary Mindfulness Movement and the Question of Nonself." *Transcultural Psychiatry* 52, no. 4 (2014): 485–500.

Schedneck, Brooke. *Thailand's International Meditation Centers: Tourism and the Global Commodification of Religious Practices*. London: Taylor & Francis, 2015.

Schmidt, Leigh. *Restless Souls: The Making of American Spirituality*. San Francisco: HarperCollins, 2005.

Schober, Juliane. *Modern Buddhist Conjunctures in Myanmar: Cultural Narratives, Colonial Legacies, and Civil Society*. Honolulu: University of Hawai'i Press, 2011.

Seager, Richard H. *Buddhism in America*. New York: Columbia University Press, 2012.

Sharf, Robert H. "Buddhist Modernism and the Rhetoric of Meditative Experience." *Numen* 42 (1995): 470–484.

Sharf, Robert H. "Experience." In *Critical Terms for Religious Studies*, edited by Mark C. Taylor, 94–116. Chicago: University of Chicago Press, 1998.

Sharf, Robert H. "Is Mindfulness Buddhist? (And Why It Matters)." *Transcultural Psychiatry* 52, no. 4 (2015): 470–484.

Soma Thera. *Introduction to the Sati-paṭṭhāna-sutta*. Dodanduwa, Sri Lanka: Island Hermitage, 1941.

Suh, Sharon A. "'We Interrupt Your Regularly Scheduled Programming to Bring You This Very Important Public Service Announcement . . .': aka Buddhism as Usual in the Academy." In *Buddhism and Whiteness: Critical Reflections*, edited by George Yancy and Emily McRae, 1–20. New York and London: Lexington Books, 2019.

Tambiah, Stanely J. *The Buddhist Saints of the Forest and the Cult of Amulets*. Cambridge Studies in Social and Cultural Anthropology. Cambridge: Cambridge University Press, 1987.

Tweed, Thomas. *The American Encounter with Buddhism, 1844–1912: Victorian Culture and the Limits of Dissent*. Durham: University of North Carolina Press, 2000.

Vesely-Flad, Rima. "Black Buddhists and the Body: New Approaches to Socially Engaged Buddhism." *Religions* 8, no. 11 (2017): 239.

Wilson, Jeff. *Mindful America: The Mutual Transformation of Buddhist Meditation and American Culture*. Oxford: Oxford University Press, 2014.

Wilson, Jeff. "Mindfully Feminine." In *Buddhist Feminisms and Femininities*, edited by Karma Lekshe Tsomo, 285–301. Albany: State University of New York Press, 2018.

Yancy, George, and Emily McRae. *Buddhism and Whiteness: Critical Reflections*. New York and London: Lexington Books, 2019.

CHAPTER 18

AMERICAN BUDDHISM AND HEALTHCARE

C. PIERCE SALGUERO

MINDFULNESS and other therapeutic meditations have increasingly been researched scientifically, lauded in the mainstream media, and broadly popularized and adopted across US society.[1] All of this attention to meditation has tended to overshadow the wide range of other practices that American Buddhists engage with in pursuit of health and well-being. This chapter begins to address that lacuna by providing an introduction to the complete spectrum of Buddhist healing practices currently being used by American Buddhists. It opens with a section on historical background and a literature review. The remainder of the chapter then introduces data from recent interviews with thirty-six Buddhist healers based in the United States—clerics, lay meditation teachers and sangha leaders, traditional medicine practitioners, and healthcare industry professionals who actively promote Buddhist therapies and practice them with clients or patients. I give both a summary of the data collected as well as an analysis of four distinct "positionalities" that emerge from the interviewees' responses. In the chapter, I quote extensively from the interviews in order to give voice to diverse orientations toward Buddhist healing that currently are found among American Buddhists. In so doing, I hope to move the conversation about Buddhist practices, ideas, and perspectives related to health beyond the current focus on just meditation.

HISTORICAL BACKGROUND

Virtually every Buddhist tradition that has ever existed has had something to say about health.[2] An interest in the mind-body relationship and how to overcome mental and

---

[1] I am grateful to Ryan Rose, Paola Xhuli, Kin Cheung, Somtanuek Chotchoungchatchai, Patrick Kim, Binh Le, Sasha Greendyk, Michael Cadigan, and Ashley Cole for various forms of research assistance.
[2] Some of the text in this section has been adapted from a blog I wrote, Salguero 2016.

physical suffering goes back to the very origins of the religion. A particular set of medical ideas and healing practices was incorporated into the Indian Buddhist tradition during its nascent phase, and these were subsequently spread across Asia along with the transmission of Buddhism in the first millennium CE.³ Influential philosophical or doctrinal aspects included traditional Indian understandings about human anatomy and physiology, an emphasis on the forbearance and equanimity of the patient in the face of illness, and a priority on compassion and appreciation of interdependence on the part of healers and caretakers. Early Buddhist texts also prescribe contemplative exercises, moderation of diet and lifestyle, chanting sutras or the names of deities, and rituals for curing disease and enhancing health. Buddhists have continued to value all of these facets over the centuries, and as we will see below, many American Buddhists continue to engage with them in the current day.

Nevertheless, even as the religion spread throughout Asia in the pre-modern period, and subsequently around the world in the modern period, the specifics of these Buddhist approaches and understandings have never been fixed. In many parts of the world, certain aspects of ancient Indian thought have been replaced, hybridized, or "domesticated" through processes of adaptation and translation.⁴ For example, in East Asia, many Buddhist healers were more interested in working with *qi* and other Chinese medical concepts than with classical Indian medical models. Meanwhile, in Tibet, Buddhist ideas imported from India were combined with medical theories from China and Western Asia in order to produce a unique form of healing known as Sowa Rigpa (literally, the "science of healing"). Likewise, in modern times, the benefits of Buddhist interventions are often interpreted and explained in scientific and biomedical terms.⁵ Modern American Buddhists, like their counterparts all over the world, resituate Buddhist approaches within contemporary American society, culture, and worldviews. Their ideas and practices are no less "Buddhist" for being thus translated.

In addition to Buddhist ideas being reinterpreted through contact and exchange with other medical cultures, healing traditions in many parts of the world have been transformed to varying degrees by exposure to Buddhism. Buddhism was a major catalyst for the development of medical models and approaches in Thailand, Tibet, Burma, Sri Lanka, and Mongolia, for example, where ideas originally derived from Indian contexts became the foundation of local systems of traditional medicine. Many of these medical systems are widely practiced in Asia as well as globally, and institutions specializing in Buddhist or Buddhist-inspired healing exist all over the world today.⁶ These Asian models feature prominently in the survey responses discussed below, as do spin-off forms of alternative healing with more tangential connection to Buddhism, such as Reiki, crystal healing, and other forms of New Age practice.

---

³ For fuller discussion of the history of Buddhist medicine, see Salguero 2022a.
⁴ Salguero 2022a, 124–143.
⁵ Salguero 2022a, 144–158. See relevant translations of texts and ethnographic interviews in Salguero 2020a.
⁶ Salguero 2022a, 159–176.

More than any other Buddhist-inspired practice, therapeutic meditation has in the twentieth and twenty-first centuries become an integral part of modern healthcare around the globe.[7] Americans have associated Buddhist meditation with better health outcomes since at least the late nineteenth century, and scholars have traced its movement from the religious margins to the medical mainstream since that time. Importantly, the popularization of Buddhist meditation in the United States has been a two-way dialogue between Buddhism and science. It has involved not only a process whereby meditation has become increasingly secularized and medicalized, but also a reciprocal process where contemporary neuroscience, psychiatry, and psychology have been influenced by Buddhist models of the mind, attention, and consciousness.[8] There has also been a multidirectional flow of ideas between Asia and the West, and not just a simple transmission from the former to the latter.[9] As the topic of therapeutic meditation is well represented elsewhere in this volume, we will not say much more about it here. It is predictable that therapeutic meditation looms large in our survey of US Buddhists. But, as we will see, meditation is far from the only form of therapy American Buddhist healers are employing with their patients and clients.

Literature Review

Aside from the literature on mindfulness and other therapeutic meditation techniques, only a handful of scholars have described in any detail connections between Buddhism and healthcare in the United States. Among these, Wu Hongyu conducted a survey in 2001–2002 of members of the Greater Boston Buddhist Cultural Center, an organization with links to the Taiwanese organization Foguang Shan.[10] Although a small study ($n = 19$), it found that 100% of respondents believed that Buddhism was beneficial to one's health. Respondents cited Buddhist philosophy and worldviews, increased ability to emotionally self-regulate, enhanced mental health, vegetarianism, traditional herbal medicine, meditation, and moral restraint as positive Buddhist influences on their overall health. While none rejected conventional biomedical care, they advocated prayer, chanting, meditation, repentance, and karmic rectification as complementary therapies.[11]

More detailed treatment of the repertoire of Chinese American Buddhist healing practice is available in the work of Kin Cheung, who has written about the practices of a Cantonese-speaking community healer in Brooklyn, New York, who also happens to be his father. Both Cheung's article and an interview of his father we collaboratively

---

[7] See, inter alia, Wilson 2014; Stuart 2017; Hickey 2019; Purser 2019.
[8] Some of these interactions are discussed in Braun and McMahan 2017; Helderman 2019.
[9] See, e.g., Joo 2011; Salguero 2020b; Salguero, Cheung, and Deane 2024.
[10] Wu 2002. This article, produced in association with Harvard's Pluralism Project, appears to have gone missing from that website but is still available in various online archives at the time of this writing.
[11] Ibid., 42.

produced describe "Master Cheung's" eclectic mix of meditation, Buddhist "life-release" practice, chanting of *sūtra*s and *dhāraṇī*s, *qigong*, *taiji*, Reiki, and a range of Chinese medical arts such as cupping, *guasha*, massage, and herbal preparations.[12] This particular case study is notable for the hybridity of Buddhist, Daoist, medical, and popular religious healing methods, as well as for the importance of diverse sources of healing knowledge, ranging from formal training to YouTube videos.

Beyond the Chinese American experience, Paul D. Numrich (2005) conducted thirty interviews with what he calls "culture" and "convert" Buddhists in the United States, identifying broad differences in orientation between these two categories of practitioner.[13] This study found that Chinese, Japanese, Korean, Thai, Tibetan, and Vietnamese Buddhists reported extensive use of what Numrich calls "folk healing." However, the survey also registered official disapproval of these practices by many monastics and a general privileging of biomedical interventions, particularly among second- and third-generation Asian immigrants. In contrast, the "convert" population—the majority of whom are characterized as "middle-class, educated, European-American baby boomers"—was found to be increasingly interested in alternative approaches to healing such as herbalism, shamanism, Feldenkreis, "Zen therapy" bodywork, and energy work, as well as more traditionally Buddhist forms of visualization and chanting. A more detailed glimpse of the intersection of Buddhist practice and such New Age therapies is provided in an interview I published with a white Californian "spiritual channel," who describes her decades-long practice tapping into the power of the bodhisattva Guanyin to heal clients.[14]

My own publications have also included a comprehensive report on connections between Buddhism and healthcare in the Greater Philadelphia area, based on an ethnographic project completed between 2015 and 2020.[15] The Jivaka Project Philadelphia (www.jivaka.net/philly) involved interviews, photography, audio-video recordings, and mapping of forty-five Buddhist temples, community centers, and other organizations around the metropolitan area. The project is, to the best of my knowledge, one of a very small number of attempts to capture a comprehensive picture of Buddhist institutions within a single Western city, and the only one to focus specifically on healthcare activities.[16] In my published report, as well as on the project website, I describe how Buddhist spaces facilitate involvement in health and healing along six different axes: the therapeutic practice of meditation; a variety of healing rituals; connections between food and health; increased access to traditional Asian medicines; enhancements of the social dimensions of health; and facilitation of intersections with the mainstream healthcare

---

[12] Salguero 2020a, 241–251; Cheung 2024.

[13] Numrich 2005.

[14] Salguero 2020a, 264–272.

[15] Research results are reported in Salguero 2019a; pedagogical methods are described in Salguero 2021.

[16] For other surveys of Buddhist institutions, see McLellan 1999; Starkey and Tomalin 2016. The Pluralism Project (https://pluralism.org) has some information on Buddhism in Philadelphia on their website. However, their list of Buddhist institutions, which was never comprehensive, is now outdated and quite inaccurate.

system. These six dimensions of Buddhist healthcare are also explored in a series of brief documentary films designed for use in the classroom that I co-produced with filmmaker and medical humanities scholar Lan A. Li, which are available on the website.

In an effort to further showcase Philadelphia's religious and medical pluralism, I have also published a series of excerpts of interviews conducted around the city. These transcripts provide brief snapshots of healing among Buddhists of Thai, Cambodian, German, Vietnamese, African American, and Taiwanese descent.[17] Despite their backgrounds, the interviewees all shared a conviction that Buddhist practices and perspectives were a source of truly efficacious healing.[18]

Finally, my most recent article on Buddhist healing in the United States reported on a survey of a broad swath of Buddhists from diverse racial, cultural, socioeconomic, and sectarian backgrounds about their attitudes toward health and healing.[19] The most important overall finding in that study was that Buddhists across the gamut saw their participation in a wide range of Buddhist activities as a source of mental, physical, emotional, and social well-being. In light of this result, the essay argues that Buddhism is playing a larger than appreciated role in shaping American's attitudes about health, and that the entire range of Buddhist approaches needs to be taken into account by scholars. The current chapter can in many ways be seen as building on these conclusions, investigating more closely the range of therapies that Buddhist monastic and lay healers are offering to their communities, beyond simply teachings about meditation.

A Survey of American Buddhist Healers

Between 2015 and 2019, my research assistants and I conducted extensive interviews with thirty-six different American Buddhist healers. Thirteen of these interviewees were practitioners based in the Philadelphia area, whom I discovered while conducting the Jivaka Project described in the previous section. The remainder were identified through internet searches or via my extended social networks. Almost all interviews were conducted in person (two were conducted remotely via phone or Skype), and two were translated into English from Asian languages by research assistants.

Despite the small sample size, an attempt was made to be representative in terms of location, type of practitioner, sectarian affiliation, gender, age, and race. Table 18.1 presents, in the left-hand column, a breakdown of the interviewee's demographic information. The right-hand column presents additional sectarian, cultural, and occupational information.

---

[17] Salguero 2020a, 317–328.
[18] Salguero 2020a, 318.
[19] Salguero 2022b.

Table 18.1 General Information about Interviewees (*n* = 36)

Race
White, 55.5%
Asian, 36%
Black, 3%
Latino, 0%
Other or mixed, 5.5%

Age
Generation X, 58%
Baby Boomer, 42%

Gender
Female, 56%
Male, 44%

Immigrant status
First generation, 33%
Other, 67%

Location
East Coast, 44%
West Coast, 36%
Southwest, 14%
Other, 6%

Buddhist sect
Zen/Seon, 25%
Vajrayāna, 22%
Other Mahāyāna, 19%
Theravāda, 11%
Modern forms of Buddhism, 17%*
Nonsectarian, 6%

Cultural origin of tradition
Japan, 28%
Tibet, 25%
Thailand, 8%
China/Taiwan, 11%
Korea, 11%
Vietnam, 8%
Cambodia, 3%
Nonspecific, 6%

Primary practitioner identity
Professional healer, 31%[†]
Monastic, 19%
Priest, 19%
Lay community leader, 14%
Chaplain, 11%
Meditation teacher, 6%

* Includes Shambhala, Soka Gakkai, and Won Buddhism.

[†] Includes practitioners of acupuncture, massage, yoga therapy, medical qigong, Sowa Rigpa, channeling, etc.

All of the practitioners in our study were long-term practitioners of Buddhism. While only some of the interviewees referred to themselves as "healers," all of the individuals in the study reported being currently involved in healing others or teaching others to heal themselves using techniques, methods, or perspectives drawn from their particular tradition of Buddhism. Lasting from twenty minutes to over two hours, our interviews were open-ended and unstructured, continuing for as long as the practitioners were willing to talk. Across the board, nearly all of the respondents at one point or another mentioned that Buddhist practice was not a replacement for, but rather an adjunct to, modern scientific medical therapies. Conversations centered on the question of how Buddhism and healing are related in the participants' own practice and life. We asked follow-up questions as necessary to elicit specific details about their healing activities with clients or patients.

Because the data collected amounted to almost 300,000 words, we used corpus-level analysis to initially identify some common themes and to direct our attention toward specific areas worthy of further investigation. Some of the most significant key concepts from this corpus-level analysis are reported in Table 18.2. Although these are admittedly crude measures, these data are useful for making some general observations. For example, it is notable that meditation was discussed by every interviewee without exception, as were Asian energetic terms such as *qi, prana*, winds, and chakras. Also universal were discussion of education (including references to studying, learning, teaching, and teachers) as well as specific practices, techniques, or methods. Words related to Buddhist teachings on compassion were mentioned by nearly everyone, and it is evident that almost all interviewees are interested in both mental and physical health.

It is also perhaps interesting to note what is not present among the most common key concepts. We saw far less discussion of karma (total number of mentions = 96), happiness ($n = 78$), belief/faith ($n = 73$), religion ($n = 48$), science ($n = 33$), or vegetarianism ($n = 21$) than anticipated. While doctors, nurses, and caretakers are mentioned frequently, the only therapeutic specialty we see among the most common concepts is psychology. Likewise, while some practitioners mentioned specific ailments such as cancer ($n = 38$),

Table 18.2 Key Concepts in the Corpus

1. Study, learn, teach, teaching, teacher, class, school, student, training (1,740 in 100%)*
2. Buddhist, Buddhism, Buddha, Dharma (1,294 in 100%)
3. Practices, practical, techniques, methods (1,223 in 100%)
4. Mind, mental, thinking, thought (896 in 100%)
5. Body, physical (832 in 97%)
6. Meditation, meditator (756 in 100%)
7. Medicine, medical, medication (534 in 91%)
8. Energy, qi, chi, prana, chakra, wind (478 in 100%)
9. Work, working (477 in 97%)
10. Health, healthy, healthcare (353 in 91%)
11. Monk, nun, priest, sangha (345 in 77%)
12. Compassion, compassionate, love, kindness (321 in 97%)
13. Patient, patients (297 in 63%)
14. Tradition, traditional (294 in 89%)
15. Doctor, physician, nurse (295 in 80%)
16. Temple, monastery (292 in 83%)
17. Chant, chanting (245 in 77%)
18. Zen (244 in 57%)
19. Breathing, breath (234 in 74%)
20. Chaplain, chaplaincy, pastoral, ministry (230 in 34%)
21. Service, volunteer (223 in 51%)
22. Pain, painful (220 in 66%)
23. Yoga (217 in 54%)
24. Tibet, Tibetan (199 in 54%)
25. Community (193 in 63%)
26. Suffering (185 in 74%)
27. Book (181 in 77%)
28. Feelings, emotions (173 in 80%)
29. Mindfulness (171 in 74%)
30. Spirituality, spiritual (167 in 77%)
31. Hospital, hospice (162 in 66%)
32. Ritual, ceremony (160 in 46%)
33. China, Chinese (153 in 74%)
34. Care, caretaker, caregiver (148 in 77%)
35. Calm, peace, quiet (148 in 80%)
36. Sutra, scripture (146 in 57%)
37. Pray, prayer (127 in 66%)
38. Psychological, psychologist, psychotherapy, counseling (126 in 63%)
39. Stress, anxiety (119 in 66%)
40. Death, dying (111 in 51%)

*Total number of mentions in the corpus, appearing in what percent of interviews.

depression ($n = 25$), and chronic pain ($n = 15$), the only diagnosis that made the top forty list is stress/anxiety.

Drilling down further in order to connect these key concepts with demographic and sectarian data, our analysis revealed some interesting patterns. For example, Table 18.2 shows that more interviewees mentioned chanting than mindfulness. However, when we analyzed who mentioned these terms, we saw a preference for mindfulness among white respondents, while Asians were more likely to mention chanting (see Table 18.3). We found that mindfulness was more frequently mentioned by Zen and nonsectarian practitioners, while chanting was more common among Mahāyānists and adherents of modern Buddhist sects. We also noted that mindfulness was mentioned by all the chaplains in our sample, while chanting was favored by community leaders and monastics. (Perhaps counterintuitively, the meditation teachers we interviewed all mentioned both of these terms.) Finally, we detected a preference for mindfulness among women and a preference for chanting among men.

A few other demographic patterns emerged from the data, but these seemed predictable and of relatively minor importance. Much more significant than demography, in my view, was a factor I identified as the interviewees' "positionality"; that is to say, the position that the practitioner occupies within the broad landscape of American Buddhism, and how that practitioner uses their position to engage in certain types of healing practices within their particular communities. In analyzing trends in the data, I found the coherence between the perspectives, ideas, and practices expressed by members of each of these positionalities—and the clear differences across positionalities—to be the

Table 18.3 Respondents Mentioning Mindfulness versus Chanting

Concept	Primary identity	Tradition	Gender	Age	Race
Mindfulness	Meditation teacher, 100%* Chaplain, 100% Healer, 83% Priest, 71% Lay community leader, 25% Monastic, 57%	Zen, 88% Tibetan, 75% Other Mahāyāna, 60% Theravāda, 80% Modern, 60% Nonsectarian, 100%	Female, 86% Male, 57%	Gen X, 69% Boomer, 79%	White, 90% Asian, 46% Black, 100% Mixed, 100%
Chant, chanting	Community leader, 100% Meditation teacher, 100% Monastic, 100% Priest, 86% Healer, 58% Chaplain, 33%	Zen, 63% Tibetan, 50% Other Mahāyāna, 90% Theravāda, 80% Modern, 100% Nonsectarian, 67%	Female, 71% Male, 86%	Gen X, 75% Boomer, 79%	White, 58% Asian, 100% Black, 100% Mixed, 100%

*Percentage of people in this category who mentioned mindfulness.

most striking finding. I argue that this method of breaking out practitioners is more useful than essentializing groups of American Buddhists based on a priori categories such as race, age, immigration status, or sectarian affiliation.[20]

Positionalities of Buddhist Healing

Four distinct positionalities emerge from the data. Each of these categories cuts across demographic lines to include a mix of races, genders, age brackets, locations, sectarian affiliations, and cultural origins. Identifying these four positionalities helped to reveal significant patterns in the respondents' attitudes toward Buddhist healing. Below I describe each positionality in general terms, summarize the viewpoints common to this set of respondents, and provide an excerpt from a representative interview.

Incorporating Buddhism into Mainstream Healthcare ($n = 5$)

Our survey included four chaplains who served in hospitals, hospices, and other settings. These included two white women, a white man, and a first-generation Asian American woman. Although their chaplaincy training had taught them to be cautious about introducing explicitly Buddhist ideas and practices into these professional settings, they all reported practicing Buddhism both for the benefit of their patients and to enhance their own compassion and resilience at work. I also included in this category a first-generation Asian American male leader of a Buddhist charity who is involved in organizing doctors, dentists, surgeons, and other medical personnel to offer free medical clinics for the poor, since this work involves close collaboration with medical professionals. Collectively, this group comprised two practitioners of Mahāyāna and three Zen priests; two East Coasters and three West Coasters; and a mix of four from the Baby Boomer generation and one from Gen X.

This group spoke more than any of the others about the importance of Buddhist values such as equanimity, generosity, and forbearance. These values were themselves attributed with significant healing power for patients, and also with protective power for healthcare workers in order to help them deal with the stress, emotional toll, and burnout associated with encountering illness and death on a daily basis. When they discussed specific Buddhist practices such as meditation, chanting, or prayer, all of the individuals in this group downplayed the need for elaborate preparations, training, or ritual complexity. Rather, they emphasized the simplicity of Buddhist practice and its ability to be easily introduced into everyday healthcare settings without much fanfare. For example, all of

---

[20] See Hickey 2015; Salguero 2019 for further thoughts on the limitations of current scholarly categories. On race in American Buddhism more generally, see also Cheah 2011; Han 2021.

the chaplains we interviewed mentioned how a few moments of simply being aware of the breath could transform the experience of a dying patient. Aside from meditation, these practitioners also talked about chanting a simple mantra or phrase, basic visualizations, compassion, and prayer. Moreover, and in contrast to any other group, most of these individuals emphasized that "just being present" was the core of their healing practice.

One chaplain with many years of experience serving in hospitals, hospices, and military settings shared some details from her practice in a way that is representative of this positionality:[21]

> I'm a bit of a rule bender, but a lot of my chaplaincy work comes out of spontaneity—just really being with what's arising in the moment. I remember being with this woman, and I just started belting out a song and she sang with me. Or, I would go into the room and someone would be eating and I would sit next to them and share a meal together, and it would feel like holy communion. Or, there was another instance when this guy came in and he was so angry, and I said, "I'm going to do a chant for you." And then there was this other guy who had prostate cancer and I sat at the bottom of his bed and put my hands on his feet and did a meditation, visualizing the flow of energy pulling through him.
>
> There would be times where I would go and visit someone and my back would start hurting, or my neck, hip, or foot, like maybe I was picking up their pain. I would just deepen my breathing, like I would when in meditation. I would be tending to these parts of my body that are feeling tense, tight, anxious, fluttering, or whatever, and I would be consciously sending light to the patient.
>
> I'm just really using the ingredients that are there in the moment to make a simple and spontaneous ritual. To bear witness and take action, and to try not to do it from a place of self. As I enter the room I try to put down my badge, my ideas, my expectations, who I think I am, and to instead be that arising of being in the moment.
>
> I think being with someone who is transitioning or close to that place, there's an honoring of life that arises. I don't even know how to describe it—I would use words like magical or otherworldly. The person is so alive even though they are seemingly in so much pain, and all pretenses are dropped. It's really a gift if someone allows me into that space with them. It's hard to explain, but I have grown to trust that stripping away, that whatever happens in the moment was supposed to happen.

Integrating Buddhism with Traditional Asian Medicine ($n = 11$)

Our survey included two practitioners of Chinese acupuncture, two of Korean movement therapies, two of Thai massage, three of Tibetan herbal medicine, and two of

---

[21] All quotes from the interviews have been excerpted and compressed to be more succinct, condensed to remove filler words and repetition, and slightly modified for grammatical consistency and clarity. Some have been cleaned up more than others, but the meaning of the contents has not been affected, and I have in all cases preserved the speaker's own personal style.

yoga therapy. Some of these traditions are historically more explicitly influenced by Buddhism than others; however, all of the Asian medicine practitioners in our survey reported integrating Buddhist practices into their patient care, self-care, and the physical setup of their clinical spaces or other healing environments. Individuals in this category identified as adherents of Seon, Theravāda, Tibetan, Won, and Zen Buddhism. They included six men and five women; eight white people and three Asian Americans (two of whom are first-generation immigrants). Three lived on the East Coast, four on the West Coast, two in the Southwest, and two in other places. There were eight Gen Xers and three Baby Boomers.

Generally speaking, this group was distinctive in its emphasis on traditional methods of training, including studying ancient texts in the original language. This was the only group to consistently prioritize the "authenticity" of Buddhist and traditional medicine teachings, a factor that they explicitly connected with formal lineages and/or institutions. Practitioners in this group described both traditional Asian medicine and Buddhism as complex systems of self-transformation and healing that took proper training to begin and many decades to internalize. The services they offered to patients normally consisted of both physical and spiritual medicine—for example, a massage session that also included blessing the client with loving kindness (*metta*) in order to enhance the pain relief of the treatment, or an herbal tea that was empowered with mantras invoking the healing powers of the Medicine Buddha. Practitioners frequently utilized chanting, visualization, and compassion practice in conjunction with Asian medicine for their own protection and well-being as well. They often mentioned practicing meditation as a core part of their self-care routine, and also occasionally prescribed Buddhist meditations to their patients as well.

One of our interviewees, a practitioner of Tibetan medicine, touched on all of these themes in a concise way:

> The system of medicine I practice is from a Buddhist tradition. It's been kept by a Buddhist lineage and is directly related to Buddhist teachings. So, diagnosing, treating disease, and all of the methodology is rooted in the four noble truths. Traditionally in the Buddhist universities—I'm talking hundreds of years ago—medicine or healing was one of the sciences that you had to learn.
>
> Treatment is really a combination of multiple things. One is lifestyle changes: eating habits, diet, sleeping patterns, exercise, different things like that. Another has to do with incorporating medicines from plants, minerals, or animals. Another is different rituals, like for example making offerings, or making donations, or accumulating merit by practicing generosity, which helps to alleviate certain symptoms. Then, of course, all kinds of meditation and visualization. And chanting.
>
> The pulse is really one of the most important diagnostic methods because you can read the three main *doṣa*s and the elements of wind, fire, and water. With pulse diagnosis you need to do apprenticeship, because you need a personal teacher to show you, otherwise just reading from the text or talking about case studies in class isn't enough. Just like an MD goes through a residency.

We don't separate things out into categories like spiritual practices, magical practices, and mystical practices. Imagine a patient comes in and they have negative influences from black magic, or from a spirit, and they have physical symptoms or conditions—maybe they're feeling sick, maybe they feel dizzy, who knows, it depends on the situation. So the doctor gives them herbal medicine for that, but then at the same time might give them some rituals, like cleansing using a leaf or holy water, or a knife to cut the tie they have with the spirit, or a tool to wipe it out of their body. These things go hand in hand: on the one hand, you're taking herbal medicine to treat your physical ailment, but at the same time if the root cause of that ailment is coming from a spirit or black magic, you have to also cut that out too. Otherwise, the medicine will not have much effect.

People recorded these types of therapies in two kinds of books. One is the ones that have been passed down from generations, which is like a collection of historical formulas and theories, and then we have the texts which are like handbooks from our living teachers or their teachers, with their own experiences and their own notes about what they've done.

Optimizing Dharma Teachings for Health Outcomes ($n = 16$)

A number of our respondents identified primarily as Buddhist clerics, monastics, priests, or sangha leaders, rather than as healers per se. However, these individuals emphasized how, in the course of teaching and guiding their congregations, they routinely focus on the health benefits of the Dharma. They regularly teach their followers how to modify Buddhist practices such as meditation, chanting, and rituals in order to maximize positive health outcomes. (There was no one in the survey who believed that healing was only ever an incidental or unintentional side effect of Buddhist practice.) Individuals in this group included practitioners of Mahāyāna, Seon, Shambhala, Soka Gakkai, Theravāda, Won, and Zen Buddhism. They included nine women and seven men. Ten were located on the East Coast, three on the West Coast, and three in the Southwest. The racial breakdown was seven Asian Americans (six of whom were first-generation immigrants), six white people (one of whom was first-generation), two people of mixed race, and one African American. The age breakdown was six Baby Boomers and ten Gen Xers.

More than any other, this group emphasized the health benefits of serious long-term practice of the Dharma. This group was the only one who discussed advanced meditation attainments in any detail, such as particular states of concentration, absorption, emptiness, or stages of insight. Practitioners in this category spoke about the integration of body and mind that occurs at the advanced stages of practice, bringing one the ability to spontaneously heal even the most serious illnesses or bodily complaints. All individuals in this category were Dharma teachers or clerics who led congregations, and all reported teaching their students certain types of chanting, prayer, and ritual specifically designed for healing or health maintenance. Frequent mention was made of the healing powers of chanting mantras associated with the Medicine Buddha and Avalokiteśvara Bodhisattva, as well as the *Heart Sūtra* and *Lotus Sūtra*. In addition, this group was also more likely than the others to emphasize the importance of Buddhist practice for helping to address well-being at the collective and social level.

One priest who runs a Zen center in a major metropolitan area summarized the range of individual, collective, and social health benefits that emerge through long-term Buddhist practice in the following terms, which are representative of this group:

> I guess the first thing I'd say is that our Zen meditation practice is something that really supports so much of our own health and wellness. There is so much that we know about how the state of our mind has very significant effects on the state of our body and our wellness. There is sort of a ground of calm, or evenness, which actually supports health and wellness.
>
> When we are working with this practice, we begin to recognize the precious nature of our life. It's hard to be mindful about spiritual practices without also becoming more mindful about other things we engage in: How do I eat? Do I exercise? Am I taking care of myself? And so, in fact, as we begin to deepen our own practice, I think very naturally, and spontaneously, and maybe in small increments, there are other changes that might come about in our life. It's harder to engage in things that are self-destructive, if you're also practicing a great wisdom tradition that is about opening yourself up to the truth of who we are. And if that involves recognizing our own Buddha nature, then we begin to respect and honor this body we've been given. Which means that we might be taking care of ourselves better.
>
> We do also have a healing service at the Zen center. There are times where someone in the sangha is ill or is working with a parent who may have a terminal illness. We chant the *Heart Sūtra*, and at the end we pause and the priests will ask that this individual be healed of their ills. There is a tantric side to this liturgy that involves invoking energies. When we are holding someone in that light of healing, we are bringing into our awareness someone who's suffering, who is ill, and directing that energy towards their healing.
>
> Additionally, there's a component of social healing or cultural healing that we also are actively engaged in—what you could consider a sort of social justice concern. We think about how we're struggling as a nation with racism, with all kinds of injustice, with people whose education is failing them, with a prison system where people are not being rehabilitated. In Zen practice, there's a real commitment to that kind of healing. Our work as Zen students also includes outreach to the wider community or the culture to offer healing that's needed in so many places.
>
> This is direct action that is not separate in some way from our own contemplative meditation. When we begin to embody our realization, it translates into action in the world. Then it's just about taking care of this Great Self that includes everybody I meet, wherever they are. It's a very natural offering, not coming from a place of wanting to be seen as doing good for others. It's a healing practice for that Great Oneness that is who we are.

Eclectically Mixing Religion, Spirituality, and Healing (*n* = 4)

Finally, a small number of our respondents were neither clerics, trained practitioners of Asian medicine, nor mainstream healthcare workers, yet drew from some or all of these bodies of knowledge in order to create idiosyncratic blends of healing techniques that they offered to paying clients. The survey included three respondents whose personalized practices could be characterized as blends of Tibetan Buddhism, New Age, and Western Esotericism; and one respondent whose practice is a blend of Buddhism, Chinese popular religion, and traditional Chinese healing arts. This group included three women and one man; three white people and one first-generation Asian American; three West Coasters and one East Coaster; and was split evenly between the two generations represented in the survey.

This final group was the only one in which the spiritual attainments, magical powers, or supernatural gifts of the individual healer emerged as an overarching theme. Practitioners in this category described themselves as individuals with special abilities to diagnose and treat diseases. Since this is the most eclectic group representing the broadest assortment of Buddhist and non-Buddhist healing practices, the specific details tended to vary widely. However, respondents in this group all mentioned being able to perceive invisible energies, karmic influences, or "patterns of information" within their patients' bodies. They also all claimed to be able to affect these invisible forces through the use of certain movements, gestures, sounds, objects, or other tools. All of these practitioners mentioned using mudras, mantras, and/or invoking blessings from Buddhist deities both to empower their therapeutic practice and to protect themselves and their patients. Two of these practitioners communicated directly with Buddhist deities and other spirits through channeling or spirit mediumship, but all practitioners in this category described receiving visions, auditory messages, or "intuitions" that conveyed important information about their patients' illnesses.

Although each practitioner in this category differed in terms of the details of their practice, some of these general patterns can be seen in the response quoted below, from an interview with a practitioner of "Buddhist medicine and crystal healing":

> I trust this healing method as a truth shared by a fully awakened Buddha, and am using that to relieve suffering. I think the outcomes are so astounding and magnificent and revealing that it needs to be spoken about, shared, and made available to all beings.
>
> I can speak to one case that happened just recently. This man was a seventy-five-year-old consultant who travels all over the world and works with many big companies. He's very influential and his opinions and attitudes affect many people around the world, but he had intractable facial pain. I identified precisely what thinking was giving rise to that particular pain, and showed him a method using mantra and mudra to remove that information. Within three days, he had

improvement. Within two weeks, he was significantly better. And several weeks beyond that, it was basically gone.

In the course of the healing, change occurs in the thinking of the individual. They begin to realize that their thinking affects all beings, and that if they change their thinking then those who are connected with them will also be released from suffering. I don't need to teach this: people just realize it and they become a bodhisattva.

I use certain tools that are helpful to remove information from their body [i.e., jades, crystals, mantras, meditations, and various other techniques mentioned in the interview]. Sometimes I've had this experience with patients when we both see something leap from their body—like a black cloud will jump from the patient to the stone that I'm using or something like that. They think of it as almost magic. They see me as a shaman or someone who does miracles, but really it just takes an understanding of the Buddhist teachings.

Our entire universe is created completely by virtue of thinking. You create your universe, I create my universe. And everything that manifests, everything that I perceive, is the result of my previous thinking. Every single thought that we have goes into our body, into every single cell, and it is stored there and it stays there until we change it, delete it, purify it, or till it manifests. That's what the Buddha taught.

I use a jade [or another tool] to help suck—like a vacuum cleaner—information that's negative out of a body. I have a range of different types of healing objects that I can use based on the person's capability, acceptance, interest, or dedication, to help the person to remove some of that negative information energetically.

Conclusion

Created from the bottom up on the basis of detailed ethnographic information, the taxonomy of positionalities introduced in the previous section reveals a much wider range of American Buddhist healing and a broader spectrum of healers than has previously been considered in the scholarly literature. This survey shows that practitioners across demographic and sectarian categories share an interest in many forms of Buddhist healing. But it is evident that these are being thought about and practiced in quite divergent ways by people occupying different positions within the US Buddhist landscape. The positionalities described here represent distinct ways of integrating the Dharma into mainstream medicine, traditional Asian medicine, and eclectic New Age practices. Ranging from medical institutions to Dharma centers to private clinics, there are divergent social, doctrinal, and institutional settings in which these sorts of healing are taking place. These positionalities involve not only multiple types of practitioners with differing education, backgrounds, and goals, but also varying target populations for their interventions.

Showing that the contents and contexts of American Buddhist healing is much more diverse than previously has been described is merely a beginning, but this is an important recognition that opens up new avenues for more nuanced research. Scholarly literature on this subject is sorely wanting, and it is hoped that future research will further illuminate the rich variety of American Buddhist healing, beyond simply focusing on meditation.

References

Cheah, Joseph. 2011. *Race and Religion in American Buddhism: White Supremacy and Immigrant Adaptation*. New York: Oxford University Press.

Cheung, Kin. 2024. "Buddhist Healing in Practice: A Chinese American Community Healer in New York City." In Salguero, Cheung, and Deane 2024.

Cheung, Kin, and C. Pierce Salguero. 2019. "Interview with a Contemporary Chinese American Healer." In *Buddhism and Medicine: An Anthology of Modern and Contemporary Sources*, edited by C. Pierce Salguero, 241–251. New York: Columbia University Press.

Han, Chenxing. 2021. *Be the Refuge: Raising the Voices of Asian American Buddhists*. Berkeley, CA: North Atlantic Books.

Helderman, Ira. 2019. *Prescribing the Dharma: Psychotherapists, Buddhist Traditions, and Defining Religion*. Chapel Hill: University of North Carolina Press.

Hickey, Wakoh Shannon. 2015. "Two Buddhisms, Three Buddhisms, and Racism." In *Buddhism Beyond Borders: New Perspectives on Buddhism in the United States*, edited by Scott A. Mitchell and Natalie E. F. Quli, 35–56. Albany: State University of New York Press.

Hickey, Wakoh Shannon. 2019. *Mind Cure: How Meditation Became Medicine*. Oxford: Oxford University Press.

Joo, Ryan Bongseok. 2011. "Countercurrents from the West: 'Blue-Eyed' Zen Masters, Vipassanā Meditation, and Buddhist Psychotherapy in Contemporary Korea." *Journal of the American Academy of Religion* 79, no. 3: 614–638. doi: 10.1093/jaarel/lfr006.

McLellan, Janet. 1999. *Many Petals of the Lotus: Five Asian Buddhist Communities in Toronto*. Toronto: University of Toronto Press.

McMahan, David, and Erik Braun. 2017. *Meditation, Buddhism, and Science*. Oxford: Oxford University Press.

Numrich, Paul D. 2005. "Complementary and Alternative Medicine in America's 'Two Buddhisms.'" In *Religion and Healing in America*, edited by Linda L. Barnes and Susan S. Sered, 343–357. Oxford and New York: Oxford University Press.

Purser, Ron. 2019. *McMindfulness: How Mindfulness Became the New Capitalist Spirituality*. London: Repeater.

Salguero, C. Pierce. 2016. "What Is Buddhist Medicine?" *Patheos*, https://www.patheos.com/blogs/americanbuddhist/2016/01/what-is-buddhist-medicine.html.

Salguero, C. Pierce. 2019. "Varieties of Buddhist Healing in Multiethnic Philadelphia." *Religions* 10, no. 48. doi: 10.3390/rel10010048.

Salguero, C. Pierce, ed. 2020a. *Buddhism and Medicine: An Anthology of Modern and Contemporary Sources*. New York: Columbia University Press.

Salguero, C. Pierce. 2020b. "Countercurrents and Counterappropriations: The Role of Mindfulness in Traditional Korean Medicine." *Asian Medicine* 15, no. 2: 291–300.

Salguero, C. Pierce. 2021. "Buddhist Healthcare in Philadelphia: An Ethnographic Experiment in Student-Centered, Engaged, and Inclusive Pedagogy." *Religions* 12, no. 6. doi: 10.3390/rel12060420.

Salguero, C. Pierce. 2022a. *A Global History of Buddhism and Medicine*. New York: Columbia University Press.

Salguero, C. Pierce. 2022b. "Beyond Mindfulness: Buddhism and Health in the US." *Pacific World Journal*. Fourth Series 3, https://pwj.shin-ibs.edu/2022/7006.

Salguero, C. Pierce, Kin Cheung, and Susannah Deane. 2024. *Buddhist Medicine in the Modern World*. Honolulu: University of Hawai'i Press.

Starkey, Caroline, and Emma Tomalin. 2016. "Building Buddhism in England: The Flourishing of a Minority Faith Heritage." *Contemporary Buddhism* 17, no. 2: 326–356.

Stuart, Daniel M. 2017. "Insight Transformed: Coming to Terms with Mindfulness in South Asian and Global Frames." *Religions of South Asia* 11, no. 2–3: 158–181.

Wilson, Jeff. 2014. *Mindful America: The Mutual Transformation of Buddhist Meditation and American Culture*. New York: Oxford University Press.

Wu, Hongyu. 2002. "Buddhism, Health, and Healing in a Chinese Community." http://pluralism.org/wp-content/uploads/2015/08/Wu.pdf, last accessed February 10, 2018.

CHAPTER 19

RITUAL, RITUALS, AND RITUALIZING IN AMERICAN BUDDHISM

RICHARD K. PAYNE

Introduction

THE idea that Buddhism is in some significant sense identical with meditation is widespread in American popular religious culture. Scott Mitchell has noted, however, that "the equation of 'Buddhist practice' with 'Buddhist meditation' obscures the wider array of practices in which Buddhists have engaged" (Mitchell 2016, 178). Joseph Cheah and Sharon Suh point out that "this valorization of meditation reproduces the very same devaluation of devotional practice that was rendered backward [to the origin of Buddhism] both in Orientalist scholarship and its modernist inflections in the U.S." (Cheah and Suh 2022). The positive valorization of meditation in popular religious culture is generally paired with a negative valorization of ritual. This includes specific rhetorical claims to the effect that Buddhism rejects ritual, and that instead it promotes a spontaneous state of natural awareness, unsullied by the premeditated actions of ritual—or claims to that effect in different phrasing.

This image of Buddhism in popular religious culture largely derives from the influence of modernist Zen rhetoric from the middle of the twentieth century, which was in turn grounded on representations of Zen in Japan from the late nineteenth and early twentieth centuries that were themselves molded by the adoption of German Idealist thought. Griffith Foulk has explained that the "conceit that Zen is a mode of enlightened spirituality unencumbered by superstitious religious beliefs and practices not only played well in early twentieth-century Japan, it also struck a sympathetic chord among a number of intellectuals in the West and even a few in China, each of whom had their own culturally and historically specific reasons to find it attractive" (Foulk 2008, 25, see also Faure 2010).

The oppositional valorization contributes to the idea that ritual and meditation are two distinctly separate kinds of activities. Located in American religious culture, American Buddhism is also heir to a view of ritual formed by the history of Christian thought, particularly in the agonistic contestations of the Protestant Reformation.

This chapter cannot provide a comprehensive overview of Buddhist ritual practices found in contemporary American Buddhism. Not only is that field far too expansive to cover in a single essay, but as indicated here, the very category of "ritual" is amorphous, such that the boundaries of the category cannot be clearly demarcated. Instead, the goal of this chapter is to suggest a framework that can clarify the different levels of discourse about ritual.

History: Preconceptions and Valorizations

Ideas about ritual in American popular religious culture largely follow from the Reformation (early sixteenth to mid-seventeenth century). Although the Reformers' attitudes were not uniform, questioning the nature, function, number, and justification of the sacraments molds American attitudes toward ritual.[1] American Buddhists exist within this religious culture, and the expectations of what a religion is and how one practices a religion are framed by it. Despite the diversity of individual religious identities, popular religious culture is dominated by America's Protestant heritage. Whether accepted or contested, it provides a conceptual framework, including an implicit theory of ritual. Usually this framework is not formulated explicitly, as claims that might be evaluated critically. It is instead taken as natural, and thereby implicilty constrains how one can think about religion or ritual.

American popular religious culture evidences two ways of thinking about ritual. One is its value, axiological preconceptions, and the other is its existence, ontological preconceptions. Axiological preconceptions pair a positive valorization of prayer with a negative one of ritual. While the former is understood as a way of communing with God, the latter is thought to be empty of meaning or of any authentically experiential basis.[2] Ontologically, ritual is considered to be a distinct and separate category of religious activity, or, more strongly, ritual and prayer are mutually exclusive.

---

[1] The term "mold" does not mean "determined by this one singular source." Instead it points to the ways in which individuals are exposed to ideas about religion, about what activities are understood as religious. These same ideas about religion are embedded in the legal system, which imposes certain strictures on religious organizations and activities.

[2] This of course is not the case for members of the Counter-Reformation. However, American popular religious culture is more dominated by Reformation thought, than by Counter-Reformation thought.

Further, American culture more generally privileges mental (prayer/meditation) over physical (ritual). This privileging is deeply rooted in the intellectual history of the West, a history that Buddhist praxis prior to its engaging with the West did not share. In other words, the most important factor in Western misunderstandings of Buddhism is treating the concepts, categories, and concerns of the religious cultural history of the West as unproblematically ahistorical and universal, when they are not.

Axiological Dichotomy

Half a century ago Evan M. Zuesse pointed out "that there is a very strong anti-ritual prejudice in the West, stemming from certain emphases in the New Testament and intensified by the Protestant Reformation" (Zuesse 1975, 517). While Zuesse was speaking specifically of academic attitudes, this same negative valorization is found throughout popular religious culture. Stereotypes of ritual as performing activities by rote, without conscious reflection, without meaning, and without effect are common. Evidencing this is the enduring debate in American Buddhist communities regarding chanting—whether it is meaningful to chant, especially in a foreign language. If rarely explicit in scholarly writing, negative valorizations of ritual are the axiological background for both popular and academic cultures. In her study of Buddhist practice in two Tibetan centers in Toronto, for example, Patricia Q. Campbell describes the popular conception. "Popular usage of the word [ritual] usually evokes images of empty repetitive performance, fossilized by long-standing tradition, often specifically religious tradition" (Campbell 2011, 10). Ritual has also been interpreted as indicating a more general conservative opposition to change and progress.[3]

This follows from the idea that ritual is static and unchanging. This image of ritual continues in popular religious culture and was largely unquestioned in academic culture into the second half of the twentieth century. Recently, several scholars have explicitly argued against the idea that ritual is fixed and unchanging—though accepting that ritual is socially constructed and therefore mutable remains uneven. Christiane Brosius and Ute Hüsken describe this situation succinctly, noting that:

> until the mid-sixties of the twentieth century, the term [ritual] was imbued with stereotyping connotations referring to the odd, obsolete, primitive, timeless and thus unchanging, opposed to the notions of modern, civilized and progressive. Rituals were tied to religion and, according to a secular worldview, deemed an inappropriate

---

[3] The negative valorization of ritual is also found, for example, in Sigmund Freud's pathologizing equation of religious ritual and obsessive-compulsive disorders. The view that ritual per se is dysfunctional was shared also by the Romantics. While few today explicitly reference Freud as such, this Freudian-rooted suspicion, if not pathologization, of ritual remains in popular religious culture in the United States. This axiological evaluation of ritual as meaningless and obsessive repetition also derives from the Protestant Reformation, mediated through the Enlightenment and nineteenth-century European culture.

form of action in a civilized, "enlightened" society. . . . Once stamped as "ritual," a performative action was normally not investigated any further, and in particular not with respect to its dynamics for this would have also subverted scholarly logics of the time. (Brosius and Hüsken 2010, 2–3)

Contrasting with the negative valorization of ritual is the positive one of meditation. Modern popular perceptions of meditation treat it as analogous to contemplative prayer—which is positively valued in contrast to the historically negative valuation of the sacraments in popular religious culture in America. Also, since the nineteenth century, Buddhism has been located within the conceptual frameworks of Romanticism, resurgent in the second half of the twentieth century as neo-Romanticism. Romantic emphasis on transformative religious experience, often treated as equivalent to aesthetic experience, contributed to representing Buddhist meditation as primarily mental with experiential consequences. This representation is overdetermined—because some aspects of Buddhist praxis are similar to aspects of Western religious culture, those aspects are decontextualized and selectively highlighted.

Ontological Dichotomy

The paired opposition of a negative valorization of ritual with the positive valorization of meditation is itself a dialectic relation, each side of the opposition semiotically bound to the other.[4] This oppositional bond is not limited to their valorizations, but also informs an ontological dichotomy as well. That is, each is treated as if they exist separately from the other. As Catherine Bell points out, most "attempts to define ritual proceed by formulating the universal qualities of an autonomous phenomenon. They maintain, however provisionally, that there is something we can generally call ritual and whenever or wherever it occurs it has certain distinctive features" (Bell 1992, 69). Dualistic systems of this kind are instances of an impoverished ontology in which the complexity of the actual is reduced to two alternatives (Payne 2005).

Neither ritual nor meditation is a natural kind, however (see Bird and Tobin 2022). They do not refer to things in the world in the same way that the categories "tables" and "chairs" do. Both are social categories, meaning that the objects of reference are themselves concepts, not abstracted from any actual instances. Because these are social constructs, they are neither essences nor generalizations over a body of instances. Griffith Foulk explains that "[s]ocial scientists become profoundly confused, however,

---

[4] The dialectic relation meant here is not the teleological kind as found for example in Hegel. Rather, it is intended to simply describe the dynamic of mutual interaction between two concepts as an ongoing process. This also does not assume that the process is a form of rationality working through history, but rather disjoins the rational from the actual. Instead of step-wise progress, Theodore Adorno characterized the systemic relations as "constellations" (Harcourt 2019).

when they conceive of ritual as a single, identifiable mode of human behavior and seek to determine its essential characteristics by looking for a common denominator in all of the various activities that get called ritual in ordinary language" (Foulk 2008, 21). Being socially constructed, the categories are enmeshed in the cultural history of the West. In the history of Buddhist thought, there is a distinctly different set of categories, ones that do not match the usages in American popular religious culture. Two of these emic categories, *pūjā* and *sādhana*, will be introduced below.

Ritualizing, Rituals, and Ritual

The artifice that ritual and meditation are ontologically distinct and axiologically opposed distorts understanding the historical role of ritual in Buddhism, and its present role in American Buddhisms. This section presents an alternative way of conceptualizing ritual that does not prejudice our study of Buddhist praxis by uncritically presuming the axiological and ontological dichotomies between ritual and meditation. At the same time, this alternative resists the dichotomizations between bodily and mental activities, and between religious and secular activities, which also distort our understanding of Buddhist ritual practice.

The approach presented here distinguishes three categories. The first is ritual as activity, that is, "ritualizing"; the second is abstracted forms of rituals, as with specific named kinds; and the third, ritual as a general category, that is, a higher-order abstraction. Looking at activity, rather than abstractions, provides a means for understanding the distinction between ritual and meditation as a matter of perspective.

Ritualizing versus Ritual; Activity versus Abstraction

Many theorists emphasize that ritual is activity, but do not articulate a distinction between that understanding and both "ritual" as a general category and "rituals" as specific entities. "Ritualizing" is used here to explicitly identify lived activity, in contrast to "rituals" and "ritual," both of which are abstract conceptual objects. Discussions of ritual seem to often elide activity and abstraction, talking about ritualized activity, rituals, and ritual, without clearly delineating the three levels.

This section first briefly explains sources for the concept ritualizing; second, usages in which ritualization is treated as a process that produces ritual; third, a distinction between ritualizing and ritualization; and finally a three-part analytic framework.

Ethology, Cognitive Science, and Ritual Studies

In 1914 Julian Huxley introduced the concept of ritualizing for the study of animal behavior, ethology. This is used when instrumental actions lose any practical function, becoming (purely) symbolic acts communicating information (Stephenson

2018, 19). If such acts enhanced species' survival, then they became an evolutionary adaptation. Cognitive theories of religion have also employed the term ritualization when considering instances in which the ordinary, or mundane goal of instrumental behavior is "demoted" in favor of a symbolic significance (Stephenson 2018, 21–22).[5] The point for our study of ritual in American Buddhism is that ritual is not a subset of religion, despite how frequently it is treated as such in the field of religious studies.

Catherine Bell gave an additional nuance to the concept of ritualization, arguing that "ritualization is a strategy for the construction of a limited and limiting power relationship," one that involves contestation and negotiation (Bell 1992, 8). Rather than a Foucaultian perspective, however, we emphasize here that ritualization is something done all the time, and quite normally, rather than constraining it to situations that involve strategies in power relations.

The Process–Product Model

Ethological and cognitive approaches share the idea that ritual is the static product of ritualizing (Stephenson 2018, 19, 21; Humphrey and Laidlaw 1994, 155). This process–product theory is employed by Campbell in her study of Buddhist ritual at two Tibetan centers in Toronto. Campbell explains that "ritualizing, as emergent ritual, may eventually become more formal, repetitive, and stable. With time, it can become ritual" (Campbell 2011, 94). Similarly, Ronald Grimes claims that "[r]itualizing is a process which occurs continually, and it may or may not result in stable structures that a culture deems 'rituals'" (Grimes 1982, 541).

However, lived activities (ritualizing) and abstractions (rituals and ritual) are actually ontological categories, and consequently ritualizing is not a process that stops when a ritual is produced.[6] As Bell notes, there is a "tendency to cast activity, ritual or otherwise, as an object and thus as the completed or 'dead,' execution of a system. When activity is analyzed and categorized as something already finished, the very nature of activity as such is lost" (Bell 1992, 72). In other words, ritualizing as activity and ritual as abstraction are distinct.

The process of ritualizing is ongoing, it develos and changes over time and with use. Consequently, there is no clearly definable moment when a ritual as a static entity is produced. The process–product model of ritualizing and ritual is, therefore, mistaken. Rituals are not a product of a process, but are instead abstracted from the lived practice. This may be done by a practitioner composing a ritual manual, or by a scholar in an academic study such as this one. In addition to employing the process–product model, Grimes and Campbell also distinguish ritualizing from ritualization.

---

[5] We note that the symbolic/instrumental distinction is an analytic artifice, which despite its long history in the study of ritual is itself problematic.

[6] It seems likely that conceiving ritualizing and ritual as process and product results from unconsciously applying an industrial metaphor.

Ritualizing versus Ritualization: A Distinction That Doesn't Make a Difference

Like Grimes, Campbell distinguishes "ritual," "ritualization," and "ritualizing." For her, ritual is a polythetic class characterized as "typically repetitive, formal, embodied, special, set aside from ordinary time and space, elevated, and sometimes spiritual or religious" and also "sometimes described as stylized, communal, deliberate, received, traditional, symbolic, or reflexive (Campbell 2011, 11). "Ritualization" is "the preconscious enactment of our bodily movements" (Campbell 2011, 94), and "ritualizing" is consciously intentional. This distinction between ritualization and ritualizing is, however, based on a false dichotomy. Bell noted that the thought–action dichotomy pervades ritual studies (Bell 1992). Campbell's distinction is based on artificially bifurcating activity and reflective thought, but also marks ritualization as lacking reflective thought.[7]

Distinguishing between ritualization as unreflective or unintentional, and ritualizing as reflective or intentional, simply deploys mind–body dualism, and privileges mind over body (Bell 1992). Consider grocery shopping, just the kind of mundane, instrumental activity that religious studies scholars might automatically exclude from the category ritual. Given that people generally shop the store in more or less the same pattern, though without much explicit reflection, grocery shopping is ritualized—though at a relatively low level. If we have a long list and a short amount of time, however, we might think through how to shop most efficiently. But there is no clear point at which unreflective activity gives way to reflective planning, organizing, and enacting. Making two categories—unreflective activity as the "preconscious enactment of our bodily movements," and reflectively thinking through activity as consciously intentional—is an undemonstrated presumption. In lived experience there is no sharp dividing line between preconscious, unreflectively structured activity and conscious, reflectively structured activity. Despite the appearance of greater clarity, distinguishing ritualizing and ritualization comes at the cost of dichotomizing mind and body, together with the privileging of the mental. Despite the centrality of the distinction between thought and action in theorizing ritual (Bell 1992, 19), the Cartesian dichotomization is neither supported by contemporary cognitive science (see Varela, Thompson, and Rosch 1991), nor is it native to Buddhist praxis. It does, however, appeal to the long-standing prejudice that human reflective consciousness, particularly that exhibited by intellectuals (see Kilminster 1998, 17), is exceptional, and serves to differentiate us from animals. Ungrounded in lived experience, the distinction between ritualization and ritualizing is simply a conceptual one, not an actual difference.

Three Levels: Ritualized Activity, a Ritual, and Ritual

Ritualizing is a strategy applied to important activities. Activities are ritualized when one needs to be careful and precise. The more important the activity, the more ritualized it will

---

[7] Characterizing ritual as unreflective is part of the colonialist legacy of anthropology that has been adopted into religious studies.

be. Ritualizing is normal for human activity, it is not distinct from more regular or ordinary forms of activity. It is a range, running from habitual actions to full ceremonials scripted down to the last detail. Ritualization is an ongoing and open-ended process, an aspect of how we function in the world, specifically, how we organize activities. It is natural, part of daily life, evident in the way we go about our daily activities. Scripts and ritual manuals are abstractions—rituals—that prescribe (or proscribe) activities to be performed.

Rather than employing dichotomies, especially ones that appeal to human exceptionalism, a better approach to the study of ritual delineates three different levels. Most basic is lived activity that is ritualized in various ways and to different extents. The idea of some specific ritual, such as the offerings to hungry ghosts ritual examined below, is the first level of abstraction. The second level is ritual as a general category, which groups together various kinds of organized activities identified as rituals.

A frequent topic in ritual studies is how to distinguish "ordinary activity" from ritual (e.g., Gaenszle 2010, 141; and Humphrey and Laidlaw 1994, 155). From the perspective provided by these three levels, at the level of lived activity no dichotomous distinction—such as that between ritual and meditation—can be made. Such distinctions are made at the third level, meaning that the debates are over socially constructed concepts, and as such can never be brought to closure by anything objectively observable.

Two Perspectives on Activity: Mental and Bodily

The distinction between ritualized activity (lived), a ritual (first order of abstraction), and ritual (second order of abstraction) reveals that the ritual and meditation distinction is made at the second level of abstraction. It is about concepts, and not actual, concrete, lived activity. In other words, the distinction between meditation and ritual (both second-order abstractions), and the accompanying treatment of meditation as more valuable than ritual, is based on dualistic presumptions and cultural history. The difference between ritual and meditation is not found at the concrete level, but instead follows from the way that each is characterized, specifically whether a mental or bodily aspect is being emphasized. Conventionally, practices that are primarily described or conceptualized in mental terms are called meditation, and those primarily described or conceptualized in bodily terms are called rituals. Abandoning an unreflective acceptance of Cartesian dualism allows us to see lived, concrete activity as it is ritualized.[8] Campbell indicates the problematic character of mind–body dualism when she says that "Mindful attention to the mind is . . . the ritualized act or the rite that the mind performs in meditation" (2010, 93).

The proximate source for characterizing meditation as mental is located in nineteenth-century Romantic ideas regarding pure experience, and the religious

---

[8] This is not to be confused with phenomenology, which often in application seems to tend toward a kind of crypto-Platonism.

significance of that experience. Global culture in the nineteenth century circulated these ideas (Ama 2011), particularly in the form of German idealism. This was the basis of a shared understanding of meditation, such that Japanese proponents of Zen adopted the rhetoric of Rudolf Otto and William James (see Foulk 2007, 2013). In other words, the Buddhism circulating in mid-twentieth-century America was already interpreted in a way that it could simultaneously be adopted into and give shape to the neo-Romantic religiosity of the 1960s and 1970s. "As William James's emphasis on 'religious experience' influenced Japanese thought in the first decade of the twentieth century, Zen came to be understood as 'pure experience itself,' and that transhistorical personal experience, the popular interpretation goes, has shaped all aspects of Japanese culture, which is spiritually and aesthetically superior" (Tweed 2013, 202). By the mid-twentieth century it was possible for some "middle- and upper-class Americans" to have "selectively and creatively appropriated" this conception of Buddhist meditation as disembodied experience "because it had been removed from its institutional context (the discipline of the monastery and the authority of the priest) and from its ritual forms (the rigors of seated meditation and the aims of *kōan* practice)" (Tweed 2013, 194). And not just removed from the context of seated meditation and *kōan* practice, but from the full range of monastic ritual (Wright 2007; Buswell 1992, 38–48).

In popular religious culture the distinction between meditation and ritual (second-order abstractions) is naturalized. However, from the concrete level of lived activity, the two are simply selective representations of systematically organized lived activities. Both the first-order abstractions—some specific, named ritual—and the second-order abstractions—ritual and meditation as general categories—are social constructs having their own cultural histories in the West. Those histories are not part of the Buddhist tradition prior to about the mid-nineteenth century. In the next section two Indic Buddhist categories of practice provide contrast to the conceptions of ritual and meditation native to the cultural history of Western religions.

Models of Buddhist Ritual: Adaptations and Origins

Dale Wright has noted the semantic difficulties involved in the study of Buddhist ritual, noting, for example, that "there is no word in Buddhist languages that corresponds precisely to our word 'ritual.' The Japanese *gyōji* [行事], observances, is perhaps closest in connotation" (Wright 2008, 292, n.10). Some instances of ritual in American Buddhism adhere more closely to Western models of ritual than others. Two instances are the program of Sunday services found in the Buddhist Churches of America, and a wedding ceremony created for use in the Sacramento Shingon temple.

Michihiro Ama's study of Shin Buddhism in America highlights the complexity of processes of ritual adaptation. Shin Buddhists in America did not simply adopt or adapt

Christian models in reaction to the new religious environment. Rather than a unidirectional causal process, Ama demonstrates the plurality of factors involved. A program of modernization by church leadership in Kyoto in the nineteenth century initiated many of the changes to earlier Shin practice (Ama 2011, 92, 93). Creating a common book of service for use in Shin temples in America was also complicated. Published in 1939, *Standard Buddhist Gathas and Services: Japanese and English* "involved complex exchanges among the Nishi Honganji Translation Committee in Kyoto, the BMNA [Buddhist Mission of North America], and the HHMH [Honpa Honganji Mission of Hawaii]" (Ama 2011, 93). Already in the nineteenth century, part of modernizing Buddhism was a "cosmopolitan Buddhism" understood as nonsectarian and international, but which drew heavily on Theravāda (Ama 2011, 86). This is evident today in the Buddhist Churches of America, where services quite normally include recitation of the Three Treasures in Pāli. Other innovations came from local and individual sources. For example, Ume Hirano wrote songs for the service book that "used a traditional connotation of *oya-sama* (parent) for Amida Buddha and praised 'her' virtue, creating an image of Amida as a loving mother" (Ama 2011, 95). Hirano also drew upon her own personal experience in portraying "the 'turning of the mind,' or conversion (*eshin* [*āśrayaparāvṛtti*]), and stressed the importance of first being in a state of despondency" (Ama 2011, 95).

Wedding ceremonies have also become a common part of American Buddhism. One instance is a wedding ceremony composed by Taisen Miyata, former bishop of the Los Angeles Koyasan Buddhist Temple, during his earlier appointment to the Sacramento Buddhist Temple. Monastic Buddhism traditionally had no wedding service. In nineteenth-century Japan, as part of a series of modernizing reforms, clerical marriage became more widely accepted and normalized (Jaffe 2001, 95). Despite this history, in the United States new ceremonies for lay sangha members were created on the model of Christian ceremonies.

The wedding ceremony written by Miyata is clearly both structured by and contains elements from Christian weddings in America. Within that basic overall framework, Buddhist elements are found, such as the use of rosaries (*nenju*), deities evoked, and Shingon doctrinal elements. While the exchange of *nenju* had substituted for the exchange of rings earlier, Shin weddings in early twentieth-century Hawai'i began to include both *nenju* and rings (Ama 2011, 90), as in the Shingon ceremony. Reference is made in the ceremony to both Mahāvairocana Buddha and Kōbō Daishi, the main buddha for Shingon, and the tradition's founder in Japan, respectively. In the officiant's declaration, the teaching of "two but not two" is mentioned as well. This is an expression of nondualism, and in various forms is found not only as a central teaching in the Shingon tradition, but also in Zen (Nagatomo 2020, 2) and other Buddhist traditions as well. Thus, the process of adaptation reflected in the Shingon wedding ceremony reflects both Christian structures and contents to which Buddhist ones have been added. While both the Sunday service program and wedding ceremony are convergent with rituals of American popular religious culture, other Buddhist rituals diverge from those models.

In the Indic context within which Buddhist praxis was formed, two classic organizational models have structured ritual practice into the present: *sādhana* and *pūjā*. As with

Wright's comment regarding semantic range, these two also do not correspond precisely to the semantic range of "ritual" in contemporary English. *Sādhana* refers to methods or techniques, or "a means for accomplishing" (as in the Tibetan translation, *sgrub thabs*) (Gyatso 1997, 266). *Sādhana* has a wide semantic range, including formalized practices and meditative aspects such as visualization, as well as devotional and recitative aspects. More fully, sādhana has been described as "[r]itual practice organized into sessions and dedicated to a particular goal, the act of achieving or accomplishing one's purpose in general" (Dharmachakra Translation Committee 2020, g.115). *Pūjā* refers to worship in which an offering is made, or to the offerings themselves.

A classic Indic Buddhist source discussing *pūjā* is Śāntideva's "Introduction to the Practices of Awakening" (*Bodhicaryāvatāra*), particularly chapters two and three. The "supreme worship" (*anuttarapūja*) presented by Śāntideva has seven parts, also known therefore as the "seven limbed" (*saptānga*) practice. The seven parts are: (1) praise, (2) worship, (3) confession of faults, (4) rejoicing in merit, (5) requesting the teaching, (6) supplication for the buddhas to remain, and (7) dedication of merit (Harris 2021). The supreme worship is also found in Śāntideva's "Training Manual" (*Śikṣāsamuccaya*), where in addition to minor differences in the names for the seven, a version drawn from the *Inquiry of Upali* (*Upalipariprcchā*) is given (Goodman 2016, 167–168). In the *Inquiry of Upali* the rite is known as the "Three Sections" and along with the *Inquiry of Ugra* (*Ugrapariprcchā*) is the primary canonic source for this rite (UCSB Buddhist Studies Translation Group 2021, i.5). This version has a primarily confessional purpose, reflecting the malleability of Buddhist ritual forms.

While these seven parts are one model for Buddhist practice, variations in both content and number were not uncommon. Crosby and Skilton note that "the constitution of these seven parts varied, some being more stable than others, and that we can count up to as many as nine elements used variously to make up the Supreme Worship" (Śāntideva 1995, 10). They note that the purpose for practicing the supreme worship ritual is generating and supporting the intent toward awakening (*bodhicitta*). Śāntideva defines the intent toward awakening as having two steps. First, the resolution to awaken, and then guided by that resolve, intention moves the practitioner toward awakening (Śāntideva 1995, 11–12).

These two models, *pūjā* and *sādhana*, are not the only ones that influenced the development of Buddhist ritual. As Koichi Shinohara notes, that history was "complex and many-sided ... and more complex scenarios did not completely displace simpler ones" (Shinohara 2014, xiv). Other types of practices might be included in more extensive systematizations. For example, discussing the practices related to the Medicine Buddha, Barbara Gerke has described a threefold system that developed "over centuries," and was employed in various Tibetan schools: "permission rituals" (Skt. *anujna*, Tib. *rjes snang*), *sādhana*, which she renders as "means for attainment," and "empowerment rites" (Skt. *abhiṣekavidhi*, Tib. *dbang chog*) (Gerke 2017, 580). Considering different categories of Buddhist practice highlights the social construction of the familiar categories of ritual and meditation.

This theoretical discussion first distinguished between the three levels: that of lived activity, the first-order abstraction of some particular named ritual, and the second-order abstraction of ritual as a general category. Although this specificity may seem artificial and unnecessary, failure to distinguish between the three has contributed to the seemingly unending definitional confusions marking the field of ritual studies.

Clarified by this three-part schema is the wholly ordinary character of ritualizing lived activity. Ritualizing is quite natural and is neither distinct from "ordinary activity" nor a subset of "religious activity." As second-order abstractions, ritual and meditation are distinguished by two different perspectives being taken on ritualized lived activity. Looked at as physical activities, then the category ritual is applied. But if looked at instead as mental, then the category meditation is applied. The next section examines some specific examples that reveal the heuristic value of this schema of three levels.

Examples

Orienting on lived activity, some rituals are meditative, and some meditations are ritualized.

Meditation as Ritual

Consider the following instructions:

> At your sitting place, spread out a thick mat and put a cushion on it. Sit either in the full-lotus or half-lotus position. In the full-lotus position, first place your right foot on your left thigh, then your left foot on your right thigh. In the half-lotus, simply place your left foot on your right thigh. Tie your robes loosely and arrange them neatly. Then place your right hand on your left leg and your left hand on your right palm, thumb-tips lightly touching. Straighten your body and sit upright, leaning neither left nor right, neither forward nor backward. Align your ears with your shoulders and your nose with your navel. Rest the tip of your tongue against the front of the roof of your mouth, with teeth and lips together both shut. Always keep your eyes open, and breathe softly through your nose.
>
> Once you have adjusted your posture, take a breath and exhale fully, rock your body right and left, and settle into steady, immovable sitting. (Dōgen 2013)

This is from the "Universally Recommended Instructions for Zazen" (Fukanzazengi) by Dōgen (1200–1253), the section that focuses on bodily posture—exemplifying the ritualized character of Sōtō style Zen meditation (see also Bielefeldt 1988).[9]

---

[9] Perhaps more significantly in terms of the ritualization of Zen Buddhism, the text of the "Universally Recommended Instructions for Zazen" is chanted as part of services in many Sōtō Zen temples, in both the United States and Japan.

While these instructions are highly ritualized, similar if less detailed instructions are commonly found in teachings of many other kinds of meditation, such as insight (*vipassanā*), mindfulness, and Mindfulness Based Stress Reduction and Mindfulness Based Cognitive Therapy (MBSR/MBCT) (Canda and Warren 2013; see also Helderman 2020; and Salguero 2018). A website devoted to mindfulness meditation provides a set of instructions in eleven parts that begins with taking a stable posture, attending to one's legs and feet, sitting up straight. Then one is directed to align their upper arms with their torso, and allow the gaze to drop slightly downward. Closing the eyes is an option. Relax in that posture for a few moments, then begin to follow the breath, mentally focusing attention on some part of the body, and noting in and out breaths. Bring attention back to the breath when the mind wanders, and pause a moment before making any adjustments to the posture. Again, bring attention back to the breath when the mind wanders, and when finished raise the gaze and gradually begin attending to one's surroundings (Mindful Staff 2019). Another mindfulness training program offers a set of practices that employ visualization, converging with the kinds of visualization practices employed in tantric rituals (Pennock and Alberts, 2019).[10] Such instructions give a great deal of attention to the physical body, thus calling into question the portrayal of meditation in exclusively mental terms.

Ritual as Meditation

One of the ways in which lived ritualized activity is categorized is by its scale. Large social events are sometimes referred to as ceremonies or festivals, rather than rituals. Again, because these categories are socially determined, there is no sharp dividing line between them. One instance of a large-scale social event is the Japanese practice of floating lanterns conducted in conjunction with the annual return of the ancestors who visit our world for a few days in the fall. Mental practices of contemplation, remembrance, and visualization are in one way or another a part of all Buddhist rituals—the meditative dimension of ritualized activity—and they comprise an important part of floating lanterns as well. Because of the social nature of such events, there are various modes of engagement, and therefore not every participant is going to engage the meditative character of the event in the same way.

Floating Lanterns and Feeding Ghosts

On Memorial Day, the Hawai'i branch of Shinnyo-en holds a lantern-floating ceremony (Jpn. *toro nagashi*). In recent years this has been at the Ala Moana beach in Honolulu. When the event was first held in 1999, it drew about a thousand participants. More

---

[10] There are also, of course, many directions regarding meditation that do focus on the practitioner's mental states, attitudes, and orientations toward the world. See, for example, Buddhaghosa's *Path of Purification* (Ñāṇamoli 2010), and Kumārajīva's *Sutra on the Concentration of Sitting Meditation* (Yamabe and Sueki 2009).

recently it has become a major public celebration with as many as 40,000 participants from the entire community. Part of the appeal of the ceremony is the opportunity for participants to write the name of a recently deceased person on a paper lantern that is then floated out onto the waters of the Pacific Ocean. This memorial function of the traditional lantern floating practice led to scheduling the event to accord with the American celebration of Memorial Day, and also foregrounding military dead (Montrose 2014, 183).

Despite being relatively conventional by the standards of Japanese religion in the modern era, Shinnyo-en is frequently classed as one of Japan's "new religions" (Jpn. *shin shukyō*). Its roots are in the centuries-old Shingon tradition of tantric Buddhism.[11] Shingon was established both in Hawai'i and on the mainland in the late nineteenth and early twentieth centuries, while Shinnyo-en's presence in the United States is more recent.

In Japan, lantern floating traditionally takes place in conjunction with the annual celebration of O-Bon (Jpn. *bon*, abbrev. for *urabon*, Skt. *ullambana*), held in late summer. For its O-Bon celebration, the Sacramento Shingon temple has also held lantern-floating ceremonies, usually at William Land Park on the American River. The temple community comes together for the service, and socializes with a potluck picnic. The traditions associated with O-Bon derive from Buddhist practices of India and China, and point back to the early sangha's practice of a rainy season retreat, understood to have begun at the time of Śākyamuni (Teiser 1988, 31).

At the heart of the lantern-floating ceremony conducted in the Shingon tradition is the ritual feeding of hungry ghosts (Payne 1999). In this ritual, the hungry ghosts (Skt. *preta*, J. *gaki*) are invited to the ceremony with an aspiration, mudrā, mantra, and visualization. The aspiration is for the benefit of all the hungry ghosts throughout the *dharmadhātu*, and reads in part:

> Fulfilling my vow, abandoning attachment to my body, [I pray that] they may speedily escape the hell-realms, start on the good path, and take refuge in the Three Jewels, thereby generating the aspiration for enlightenment [*bodhicitta*] and in the end realizing the highest awakening and merit without limit. Til the end of time may all sentient beings be equally filled with food. (Payne 1999, 163)

Forming the mudrā that beckons all hungry ghosts, the officiant recites the mantra "*Naubo bo ho rikya tatagyataya*" (Homage to the Tathāgata who resides everywhere on earth, fulfilling his mission for the salvation of all beings) three times (Payne 1999, 163). Visualizing all the hungry ghosts gathering together, the practitioner uses the mudrā that breaks open the earth so that the hungry ghosts imprisoned there are

---

[11] Pamela Winfield has noted the problematic character of including Shinnyo-en in the category of Japan's new religions, as many of the groups included in this category are either "unconventional" or "downright dangerous" (Winfield 2014, 171). The essay helpfully calls into question many of the dichotomies employed in the study of contemporary religious movements.

free; and loosens the constriction of their throats, so they can take in food and drink. Empowering the food and drink offerings with mudrā and mantra, the practitioner visualizes each hungry ghost receiving 49 bushels of food. Finishing this food, they are reborn in a pure land where they perform devotions, their evil karma is eradicated, and their lifetime extended.

Next, the practitioner visualizes food and drink becoming ambrosia, and that all the hungry ghosts receive equal shares. Next, visualizing a flow of water from the water bīja mantra (*vam*), that water becomes milky ambrosia, and there being no scarcity, all the hungry ghosts are equally satisfied. The ritual closes with further mudrā and mantra, recitation of the Heart Sutra, leave-taking, and transfer of merit.

This brief ritual includes many of the acts frequently found in tantric practices, such as the use of mudrā, mantra, and visualization in conjunction. The three correspond to the set of body, speech, and mind, identifying the three dimensions of human existence.[12] The summary given here purposely foregrounds visualization in the performance of the ritual, which is one way in which ritual can have a meditative, mental dimension.

Avalokiteśvara and Medicine Buddha Sādhanas

The Foundation for the Preservation of the Mahayana Tradition (FPMT) is "a transnational federation of local organizations that spans the globe and has a changing cast of characters, visions, and projects" (Falcone 2018, 44). FPMT currently lists twenty-five centers across the United States (FPMT 2022, FPMT Centers, Projects and Services in the United States). Founded by Lama Thubten Yeshe and Lama Zopa Rinpoche, it is in the Gelug lineage deriving from Tsongkhapa (ca. 1357–1419) (FPMT 2022, Mission Statement). Tsongkhapa's teachings combine sutra and tantra, as well as Madhyamaka, epistemology (*pramana*), and yogic practice (Powers 2007, 467). Educational programs emphasize a balance of practice, training, and service.

Available on the FPMT website are several manuals for both *pūjā* and *sādhana* practice. Some of these are intended for any practitioner, while others are restricted to those who have received the appropriate tantric initiations. This distinction is evident in many of the manuals, such as a short sadhana for Ārya Avalokiteśvara Siṃhanāda, the Noble Lord who Looks Down [in Empathy] and Issues a Lion's Roar. While the requirements for practice say that anyone can perform the sādhana, only proper tantric initiation allows the practitioner to visualize themself as the deity (ritual identification) (FPMT 2020a, 2). The *sādhana* begins with taking the triple refuge, followed by prayers to the four immeasurables, a special bodhisattva prayer, and a stages of the path (Tib. *lamrim*)

---

[12] Unlike many tantric rituals, this feeding of hungry ghosts does not include the symbolic construction of an elaborate ritual enclosure into which deities from the maṇḍalas are evoked, and where they are given offerings. The ritual is not structured as five sets of offerings to deities, and there is no chief deity (J. *honzon*, 本尊), with whom the practitioner becomes ritually identical. This visualized identity between the practitioner and the deity evoked is at the center of many tantric rituals, both structurally and symbolically.

prayer.[13] The meditative core of the *sādhana* begins with the practitioner visualizing the syllable HRĪḤ in front of themself. From this syllable, Avalokiteśvara Siṃhanāda arises. His body is white with one face, two arms, three eyes, and at his heart is a moon disc with the syllable HRĪḤ on it. He is seated in the posture of royal ease, that is, with his left leg extended in front, and leaning back on his left hand. His right hand is in the mudrā of granting supreme awakening.

While usually Avalokiteśvara is portrayed with the princely regalia of a bodhisattva, this visualization notes that he is "without ornaments, in the aspect of an ascetic" (FPMT 2020a, 5), and wears the cord of a twice-born brahmin. Also in the style of an ascetic, his hair is in a topknot, he wears a red silk lower robe and the skin of a black deer over his left shoulder. To his right side is a green trident entwined by a white snake, and on his left a lotus, atop which is a flower-filled skull-cup. There is a white lotus blooming on his left, and upright on the lotus beside his head is a sword of wisdom. On his crown is the syllable OṂ in white, at this throat the syllable ĀḤ in red, and at his hear the syllable HŪṂ in blue. The *sādhana* ends with dedication prayers.[14]

The Medicine Buddha Sādhana (FPMT 2004) refers to the seven-limbed *pūjā* in the form of a prayer. While presented above as the seven parts that structure a *pūjā*, here the seven acts are performed by recitation. The Seven-Limb Prayer of this *sādhana* reads:

> I prostrate to Guru Medicine Buddha.
> Each and every offering, including those actually performed and those mentally transformed, I present to you.
> I confess all non-virtuous actions accumulated since beginningless time.
> I rejoice in the virtues of both ordinary and noble beings.
> As our guide I request you, O Buddha, to please abide well and turn the wheel of Dharma until samsara ends.
> All virtues, both my own and those of others, I dedicate to the ripening of the two bodhichittas and the attainment of buddhahood for the sake of all sentient beings.
> (FPMT 2004, 4)

Despite the artifice of clarity created by abstractions, the lived activity of practice is ambiguously both meditative and ritualized. Taigen Leighton characterizes meditation in the Soto Zen tradition as a form of "enactment ritual" (Leighton 2007). Sitting, breathing, bringing the attention back to the breath is exactly the awakened presence of a buddha. While Leighton's essay focuses on Dōgen Zenji's teaching of the identity of zazen practice and awakening, it highlights the integral character of meditative and

---

[13] These are found in other publications (FPMT 2021a, and FPMT 2020b).

[14] As in n. 10, these are again found in another publication (FPMT 2021b). The way that ritual elements from other texts are employed at the beginning and end of the sādhana reflects what is sometimes referred to as the "modularity" of ritual. The metaphor of modules is useful for understanding how some rituals are structured, but more complex metaphors become necessary for longer and more complicated rituals (Payne 2022).

ritualized activity that we here argue is true across the tradition, whatever theory of awakening is held.

Conclusion

Many authors have noted the constructed and conventional nature of the category "ritual." Distinguishing between abstract concepts and lived performance clarifies the study of ritual in American Buddhism. Fuller clarity requires an additional step, which is distinguishing three levels: the concrete level of performance of ritualized activities, the first order of abstraction in which "a ritual" is the conceptualized object, and the second order of abstraction in which the general category "ritual" is the conceptualized object.

At the second level of abstraction, ritual and meditation are often characterized as distinct and mutually exclusive. The two are, however, better understood as two perspectives, either of which can be taken toward the same activities. Meditation is usually described from the perspective of what one is doing mentally, while ritual is usually described from the perspective of physical actions. At the lived, concrete level, the activities that are otherwise categorized as ritual and meditation are not definably distinct. Some sets of activities involve sitting quietly, while others involve performing elaborate actions. But that alone does not resolve the ambiguity of something like the performance of a ritual purely by mentally visualizing the actions. Since it involves perhaps many elaborate actions, is that ritual? Or, since it is performed mentally while sitting quietly, is it meditation? The dichotomy between physical and mental is simply a social construct, but one that obscures the actuality of lived experience.

Depending upon which aspect is emphasized, the same practice may be identified as meditation or as ritual. Rather than distinct categories or kinds of activities, meditation and ritual are simply two separate conceptual frameworks for understanding Buddhist practice. The distinction between activity and the two levels of abstraction allows us to recognize that ritual and meditation are conventional concepts, only distinguished by differing emphases. Both ritual and meditation are activities, and the distinction between them made in American popular religious culture is perspectival.

References

Ama, Michihiro. 2011. *Immigrants to the Pure Land: The Modernization, Acculturation, and Globalization of Shin Buddhism, 1898–1941.* Honolulu: University of Hawai'i Press.

Bell, Catherine. 1992. *Ritual Theory, Ritual Practice.* Oxford and New York: Oxford University Press, 1992.

Bielefeldt, Carl. 1990. *Dōgen's Manuals of Zen Meditation.* Berkeley and Los Angeles: University of California Press.

Bird, Alexander, and Emma Tobin. 2022. "Natural Kinds." In *The Stanford Encyclopedia of Philosophy*, edited by Edward N. Zalta (Spring 2022 edition). https://plato.stanford.edu/archives/spr2022/entries/natural-kinds/.

Brosius, Christiane, and Ute Hüsken. 2010. "Change and Stability of Rituals: An Introduction." In *Ritual Matters: Dynamic Dimensions in Practice*, edited by Christiane Brosius and Ute Hüsken, 1–25. London, New York, and New Delhi: Routledge.

Buswell, Robert E., Jr. 1992. *The Zen Monastic Experience: Buddhist Practice in Contemporary Korea*. Princeton, NJ: Princeton University Press.

Campbell, Patricia Q. 2011. *Knowing Body, Moving Mind: Ritualizing and Learning at Two Buddhist Centers*. Oxford and New York: Oxford University Press.

Canda, Edward R., and Sherry Warren. 2013. "Mindfulness-Based Therapy." In *Encyclopedia of Social Work*. editor in chief Cynthia Franklin, n.p. Oxford and New York: Oxford University Press. doi.org/10.1093/acrefore/9780199975839.013.988.

Cheah, Joseph, and Sharon S. Suh. 2022. "Western Buddhism and Race." In *The Oxford Encyclopedia of Buddhism*, edited by Richard K. Payne and Georgios Halkias, n.p. Oxford and New York: Oxford University Press. https://doi.org/10.1093/acrefore/9780199340378.013.72.

Csikszentmihalyi, Mark. 2020. "Confucius." In *The Stanford Encyclopedia of Philosophy*, edited by Edward N. Zalta (Summer 2020 edition). https://plato.stanford.edu/archives/sum2020/entries/confucius/.

Dharmachakra Translation Committee. 2020. *The Bhūtaḍānara Tantra*. 84000: Translating the Words of the Buddha. https://read.84000.co/translation/toh747.html.

Dōgen. 2018. "Fukanzazengi: Universally Recommended Instructions for Zazen." https://www.ancientdragon.org/fukanzazengi/.

Falcone, Jessica Marie. 2018. *Battling the Buddha of Love: A Cultural Biography of the Greatest Statue Never Built*. New York: Columbia University Press.

Foulk, T. Griffith. 2008. "Ritual in Japanese Zen Buddhism." In *Zen Ritual: Studies of Zen Theory in Practice*, edited by Steven Heine and Dale S. Wright, 21–82. New York and Oxford: Oxford University Press. doi:10.1093/acprof:oso/9780195304671.001.0001.

Foulk, T. Griffith. 2013. "Denial of Ritual in the Zen Buddhist Tradition." *Journal of Ritual Studies* 27, no. 1: 47–58.

FPMT. 2004. *Medicine Buddha Sadhana: A Practice for the Prevention and Healing of Disease*. Taos, NM: Foundation for the Preservation of the Mahayana Tradition.

FPMT. 2020a. *Ārya Avalokiteśvara Siṃhanāda: Exalted Chenrezig Lion's Roar Who Dispels All Diseases*. Portland, OR: Foundation for the Preservation of the Mahayana Tradition.

FPMT. 2020b. *Lamrim Prayers*. Portland, OR: Foundation for the Preservation of the Mahayana Tradition.

FPMT. 2021a. *Daily Prayers*. Portland, OR: Foundation for the Preservation of the Mahayana Tradition.

FPMT. 2021b. *Dedication Prayers*. Portland, OR: Foundation for the Preservation of the Mahayana Tradition.

Gaenszle, Martin. 2010. "Grammar in Ritual Speech: The Use of Binomials in Rai Invocations." In *Grammars and Morphologies of Ritual Practices in Asia*, Section I, edited by Axel Michaels and Anand Mishra, 141–158. Wiesbaden: Harrassowitz Verlag.

Gerke, Barbara. 2017. "Buddhist Healing and Taming in Tibet." In *The Oxford Handbook of Contemporary Buddhism*, edited by Michael Jerryson, 576–590. Oxford and New York: Oxford University Press. doi:10.1093/oxfordhb/9780199362387.013.38.

Goodman, Charles, trans. 2016. *The Training Anthology of Śāntideva: A Translation of the Śikṣā-samuccaya*. New York: Oxford University Press.

Grimes, Ronald L. 1982. "Defining Nascent Ritual." *Journal of the American Academy of Religion*, 50, no. 4: 539–555.

Gyatso, Janet. 1997. "An Avalokiteśvara Sādhana." In *Religions of Tibet in Practice*, edited by Donald S. Lopez, Jr., 266–720. Princeton, NJ: Princeton University Press.

Harcourt, Bernard E. 2019. "Introduction to 7/13 on Negative Dialectics." http://blogs.law.columbia.edu/critique1313/bernard-e-harcourt-introduction-to-7-13-on-negative-dialectics/.

Harris, Stephen E. 2021. "Śāntidevas' Introduction to the Practices of Awakening (Bodhicaryāvatāra)." In *The Oxford Encyclopedia of Buddhism*, edited by Richard K. Payne and Georgios Halkias, . New York and Oxford: Oxford University Press. doi.org/10.1093/acrefore/9780199340378.013.727.

Helderman, Ira. 2020. "Psychological Interpreters of Buddhism." In *The Oxford Encyclopedia of Buddhism*, edited by Richard K. Payne and Georgios Halkias. Oxford and New York: Oxford University Press. doi.org/10.1093/acrefore/9780199340378.013.603.

Humphrey, Caroline, and James Laidlaw. 1994. *The Archetypal Actions of Ritual: A Theory of Ritual Illustrated by the Jain Rite of Worship*. Oxford and New York: Oxford University Press.

Jaffe, Richard M. 2001. *Neither Monk nor Layman: Clerical Marriage in Modern Japanese Buddhism*. Honolulu: University of Hawai'i Press.

Kilminster, Richard. 1998. *The Sociological Revolution: From the Enlightenment to the Global Age*. London and New York: Routledge.

Leighton, Taigen Dan. 2007. "Zazen as an Enactment Ritual." In *Zen Ritual: Studies of Zen Theory in Practice*, edited by Steven Heine and Dale S. Wright, 167–184. New York and Oxford: Oxford University Press.

Mindful Staff. 2019. "Mindfulness: How to Do It." https://www.mindful.org/mindfulness-how-to-do-it/.

Mitchell, Scott. 2016. *Buddhism in America: Global Religion, Local Contexts*. London and New York: Bloomsbury Academic.

Montrose, Victoria Rose. 2014. "Floating Prayer: Localization, Globalization and Tradition in the Shinnyo-en Hawaii Lantern Floating." *Journal of Religion in Japan* 3: 177–197.

Ñāṇamoli, trans. 2010. *The Path of Purification* (Visuddhimagga). 4th edition. Kandy: Buddhist Publication Society.

Nagatomo, Shigenori. 2020. "Japanese Zen Buddhist Philosophy." In *The Stanford Encyclopedia of Philosophy*, edited by Edward N. Zalta (Spring 2020 edition). https://plato.stanford.edu/archives/spr2020/entries/japanese-zen/. Accessed July 6, 2022.

Payne, Richard K. 1999. "Shingon Services for the Dead." In *The Religions of Japan in Practice*, edited by George J. Tanabe, Jr., 159–165. Princeton, NJ: Princeton University Press.

Payne, Richard K. 2005. "Overcoming an Impoverished Ontology: Candrakīrti and the Mind-Body Problem." In *Soul, Psyche and Brain*, edited by Kelly Bulkeley, 197–218. New York: Palgrave Macmillan.

Payne, Richard K. 2022. "Ritual Syntax Revisited." *Numen* 69: 390–420.

Pennock, Seph Fontane, and Hugo Alberts. 2019. *Three Mindfulness Exercises for Helping Professionals*. Maastricht, The Netherlands: PositivePsychology.com. https://positivepsychology.com/.

Powers, John. 2007 [rev. ed., 1995]. *Introduction to Tibetan Buddhism*. Ithaca, NY, and Boulder, CO: Snow Lion.

Salguero, C. Pierce. 2018. "Buddhist Medicine and Its Circulation." In *The Oxford Research Encyclopedia of Asian History*, editor in chief David Ludden. Oxford and New York: Oxford University Press. doi.org/10.1093/acrefore/9780190277727.013.215.

Śāntideva. 1995. *The Bodhicaryāvatāra*, trans. Kate Crosby and Andrew Skilton. Oxford and New York: Oxford University Press.

Shinohara, Koichi. 2014. *Spells, Images, and Maṇḍalas: Tracing the Evolution of Esoteric Buddhist Rituals*. New York: Columbia University Press.

Stephenson, Barry. 2018. "Ritualization and Ritual Invention." In *The Oxford Handbook of Early Christian Ritual*, edited by Risto Uro, Juliette J. Day, Rikard Roitto, and Richard E. DeMaris, 18–36. New York and Oxford: Oxford University Press.

Teiser, Stephen F. 1988. *The Ghost Festival in Medieval China*. Princeton, NJ: Princeton University Press.

Tweed, Thomas. 2013. "Buddhism, Art, and Transcultural Collage: Toward a Cultural History of Buddhism in the United States, 1945–2000." In *Gods in America: Religious Pluralism in the United States*, edited by Charles L. Cohen and Ronald L. Numbers, 193–227. New York and Oxford: Oxford University Press.

Tweed, Thomas. 2000 [1992]. *The American Encounter with Buddhism, 1844–1912: Victorian Culture and the Limits of Dissent*. Chapel Hill and London: University of North Carolina Press.

UCSB Buddhist Studies Translation Group, trans. 2021. *Ascertaining the Vinaya: Upāli's Questions*. 84000: Translating the Words of the Buddha. https://read.84000.co/translation/toh68.html.

Varela, Francisco J., Evan Thompson, and Eleanor Rosch. 1991. *The Embodied Mind: Cognitive Science and Human Experience*. Cambridge, MA, and London: MIT Press.

Wilson, Jeff. 2009. *Mourning the Unborn Dead: A Buddhist Ritual Comes to America*. New York and Oxford: Oxford University Press.

Winfield, Pamela. 2014. "New Wine in Old Bottles? Questioning the Category of New Religious Movments (NRMs)." *CrossCurrents* 64, no. 2: 170–179.

Wright, Dale S. 2007. "Introduction: Rethinking Ritual Practice in Zen Buddhism." In *Zen Ritual: Studies of Zen Theory in Practice*, edited by Steven Heine and Dale S. Wright, 3–20. New York and Oxford: Oxford University Press.

Yamabe, Nobuyoshi, and Fumihiko Sueki, trans. 2009. *The Sutra on the Concentration of Sitting Meditation*. Berkeley, CA: Numata Center for Buddhist Translation and Research.

Zuesse, Evan M. 1975. "Meditation on Ritual." *Journal of the American Academy of Religion* 43, no. 3: 517–530. doi:doi.org/10.1093/jaarel/XLIII.3.

CHAPTER 20

ENGAGED BUDDHISM IN THE UNITED STATES

FUNIE HSU/CHHI

Introduction

With a focus on the postwar period shaped by the influences of Asian figures like Thich Nhat Hanh and his peace movement, scholarship on engaged Buddhism has been characterized as centering nonviolent action (King 2009; Queen 2005), a collective-oriented perspective of interdependence (Queen 2013), a separation from state-sponsored Buddhism (Queen 2003), and addressing issues of environmental (Blum 2009) and social justice (Gleig 2019; Mitchell 2016). Academic debate on the topic includes interrogations of the Buddhist and engaged qualifications of the category (Gleig 2021; Hsu 2022; Yarnell 2000). Recent research has introduced analyses that problematize the tendency toward the postwar temporal focus (Main and Lai 2013), extend the debate on how "engaged" is constituted (Fuller 2021; Main and Lai 2013), and challenge who gets to define and use the category (Temprano 2013; Hsu 2022). These contributions pose important considerations for interpreting the varied academic and community-oriented projects that are categorized as engaged Buddhism in the United States. Of additional consequence, however, is an examination of the US-specific formation of Buddhism that has been employed for engagement.

In the American context, studies on the coterminous relationship of race and religion that has structured the historical conditions of Buddhism in the United States (Cheah 2011, 2016; Masatsugu 2008; Williams 2020; Yoo 2000) are of particular significance to the conversation on engaged Buddhism in America. These works highlight an integral aspect of deliberation that has been generally unaccounted for in formulations and analyses of American engaged Buddhism. Because Buddhism was quickly incorporated into the schemata of what Omi and Winant (1994) refer to as "racial formation" in the United States, American Buddhism was always racialized (Cheah 2011), and was used to racialize, producing the racial-religious trope of the superstitious, "heathen Chinee" foreigner (Lum 2022, 161). This context, then, provides important considerations for rethinking the development of engaged Buddhism in the United States.

This chapter argues that engaged Buddhism in the United States has been relatively disengaged with examining the sociohistorical formulations of the Buddhism it operationalizes as a pathway to enter into social life. Rather than a race-neutral tool for social improvement, mainstream American Buddhism emerged out of a history of Asian and Asian American Buddhist disavowal—a heritage of power still embedded in hegemonic American Buddhism that requires investigation as a crucial aspect of engagement. Inattention to these legacies reflects the conditioning of a white settler Christian nationalism that has structured Buddhism's, and Asian American Buddhists', racialized and segmented (settler) positioning in American society. Thus, the American-ness of engaged Buddhism in the United States has played a defining, yet underexamined, role in molding the contours of its expression and scholarly exploration.

While strains of American engaged Buddhism have critiqued aspects of US nationalism, such as American foreign military interventions in Vietnam, even these projects of engaged Buddhism have left relatively undisturbed the longer historical dynamics of American nationalism and Asian exclusion that have shaped the development of the American Buddhism being offered as a guiding source of intervention. This chapter further argues that contending with the structures of white settler Christian nationalism that have sought to racialize, restrict, and alienate Buddhism is critical for discussions of American engaged Buddhism. It calls for analytical attention to the continued denial and disavowal of Asian American Buddhists enacted through hegemonic American engaged Buddhism, and asks us to consider its purposes and implications. In doing so, it attempts to make visible the historical influences of anti-Asian sentiments that have been woven through American engaged Buddhist projects, and, to borrow from Alexander O. Hsu, clarify the "social location[s] from or against which we might speak" about engaged Buddhism (Hsu 2022, 23).

Situating Engaged Buddhism in the United States

In his recent assessment of the complexities entangled in the Anglophone conceptualization of "engaged Buddhism," Hsu offers an inquiry that speaks directly to the issues highlighted in this chapter: "How, if at all, does a contemporary Engaged Buddhist think about their relationship to the past or other non-Engaged Buddhists, especially given ongoing movements within Western Buddhism to address, in today's language, its own whiteness as a field and its ongoing acts of cultural appropriation?" (2022, 24). Referring to American Buddhist subjects profiled in Ann Gleig's (2021) encyclopedia article on the same topic, Hsu wonders if they identified with the term "engaged Buddhist"; and relatedly, what this identity construct might mean in terms of acknowledging patterns of hierarchical domination embedded in American Buddhism. It is my view that these questions are central to understandings of engaged Buddhism in America. Yet, as a general rule, they have not historically been incorporated into the analytical equation.

Rather than simply an oversight, this absence hints at the anti-Asian structures of denial and disavowal that have bolstered much of American engaged Buddhism. Here, some points of clarification may be helpful in regard to the usage of term "American engaged Buddhism" in this chapter. In this work, the label incorporates both community/activist practices and what Hsu refers to as "Academic Engaged Buddhism" (2022, 21) situated in the United States. Furthermore, just as engaged Buddhism in Asia can be understood as encompassing several forms and functions (King 2018), so too does American engaged Buddhism reflect a plurality of communities, intentions, and actions. While recognizing that there are many engaged Buddhisms in the United States, the term "American engaged Buddhism" is used here to emphasize the hegemonic discourse and frameworks that have dominated the discussion. For example, as Hsu notes with academic engaged Buddhism more broadly, the default Anglophone framing has asserted a naturalized positionality that speaks over other paradigms (2022). This dynamic holds true in the American context, keeping various non-English or multilingual articulations of Buddhist-based society-entering projects at a distance, by choice or by design (Gleig's [2021] incorporation of social engagement actions stemming from heritage sanghas in the United States is a rather uncommon exception to the norm). Thus, the use of American engaged Buddhism in this chapter is also meant to illuminate the existence and social location of the programs that may be disassociated as a matter of volition, and/or denied and disavowed as part of the workings of the dominant discourse.

As the linguistic prioritizing of English in both academic and American engaged Buddhism demonstrates, the omissions that result are not accidental. Rather, they are produced by a logic that asserts, in Kay Anderson's description, "the centred white male subject of western liberal humanism" and the "idealisation of an over-intellectualised, rational 'human' who arrogated to himself the power to speak on behalf of all people" (2007, 10). This rationale is rendered invisible through the cloak of the universal, so that its traces are camouflaged in the hegemonic landscape of liberal humanism. Such reasoning has coursed through academic engaged Buddhism, and consequently, American engaged Buddhism. Detailing the former, Hsu notes that it:

> sowed seeds of discontent by asserting itself as the most evolved and inclusive vision of Buddhism, best able to "see things as they are," when it was actually unable to account for the positionality of the universalism it claimed. It flattered its Western proponents into imagining themselves as vanguard, "countercultural" spiritual progressives, leading Asia, Buddhism, and the rest of the world out from a violent, illiberal past. (2022, 21)

Thomas Freeman Yarnall's identification of modernist engaged Buddhism's tendencies toward "recognition," "appropriation," and "distancing" (2000, 34), and Victor Temprano's critique of David Loy and Sallie King's definitional authority also help to illuminate these issues (2013). Since academic engaged Buddhism bolsters much of American engaged Buddhism, this ideological dynamic is ever-present. Moreover, it is further made manifest through the strange absence of Asian American Buddhists.

While American engaged Buddhism has often located its genesis in relation to postwar Asian engaged Buddhist projects (King 2009; Yarnall 2000), it has normatively omitted discussion of Asian American Buddhists, let alone Asian American expressions of Buddhist engagement. Given their shared American context, this is a rather glaring lacuna—one that cannot be duly explained by oversight alone, especially considering its pervasiveness (in both the literature and practice). The presence, and present-ness, of such an overt absence, despite the historical contributions of Asian Americans to the development of American Buddhism, reveals the discourse of a white Western liberal humanism coupled with settler Christian nationalism. Furthermore, it exposes the manner in which American engaged Buddhism has relied on a particular formation of the Asian exclusionary characteristics of American nationalism.

How can this differential regard for the Asian versus the Asian American Buddhist context be understood? Looking at the major debates within engaged Buddhism helps to uncover this dynamic. The title of Yarnall's 2000 article, "Engaged Buddhism: New and Improved!(?) Made in the U.S.A. of Asian Materials," provides a pithy snapshot of the forces at work. One of the foremost issues in the scholarship on engaged Buddhism has been its relationship to, and location within, Buddhism. The major camps in this debate have been categorized around the "traditionists," who have argued that engagement has historically been present in Buddhism, and the "modernists," who have taken the stance that it represents a new progression of the religion (Yarnall 2000). Yarnall's work takes a critical view of the modernist position (hence the title), but in tracing the arguments on the two sides, reveals how both necessitate an association with Asia to establish their various claims of Buddhist legitimacy. Temprano's analysis of King's invocation of Asia to establish a "traditionist *and* modernist" (2013, 266) case provides just such an example:

> King informs readers that not only is engaged Buddhism something positive in the world, but it is something with a clear Asian pedigree. No one need fear its corruption by the West; she repeatedly points to Buddhist texts, the Buddha, and Asian Buddhists as engaged Buddhism's ultimate source. (2013, 265)

Temprano's notion of a "clear Asian pedigree" points to how engaged Buddhism requires Asia to produce the validity of its very existence. Though this positioning of Asia often echoes orientalist relationalities, especially in the modernist vein (Temprano 2013; Yarnall 2000), Asia maintains an essential centrality. This peculiar reverence for Asia, with its curation of a "canon of saints" (Hsu 2022, 21), was made safe through a geographic, temporal, and developmental sense of the continent's distance from the so-called West; that is to say, in this ideological formation, Asia is, and will forever remain, hopelessly foreign. This foreignness permits the celebration of the Asiatic other insomuch as it affords the trappings of authenticity and legitimacy (Quli 2009). Because "religious authenticity is a discourse of power" (Quli 2019, 155), this same rationale denies the foreign as it is perceived to exist within its own borders, in this case, the United States—a move that enables the preservation of white superiority and authority (Cheah 2011; Quli 2019).

Thus, while academic and American engaged Buddhism has been preoccupied with defining its identity in relation to Asia and constructions of "traditional" Buddhism, it has actively disregarded Asian America. The American Buddhism that is taken up for engagement, then, is one infused with differential power. In this manner, American engaged Buddhism functions to enforce Asian American erasure as a matter of course. This disavowal, however, is not only a product of academic engaged Buddhism's intellectual framing. It is also tied to a longer history of US racial-religious settler nationalism and its particular articulations through Asian exclusion, which hegemonic American engaged Buddhism continues to animate.

Collective Spiritual Bypassing: Engaging with a Hegemonic American Buddhism

John Welwood's term "spiritual bypassing" describes a phenomenon he observed in American Buddhist communities. "Although most of us were sincerely trying to work on ourselves, I noticed a widespread tendency to use spiritual ideas and practices to sidestep or avoid facing unresolved emotional issues, psychological wounds, and unfinished developmental tasks," he has explained. Though as a psychotherapist, Welwood was speaking to the context of individual practice and behavior, his idea of spiritual bypassing is helpful in clarifying similar patterns that exist in American engaged Buddhism. "When we are spiritually bypassing, we often use the goal of awakening or liberation to try to rise above the raw and messy side of our humanness before we have fully faced and made peace with it" (Fosella 2011). This chapter demonstrates that American engaged Buddhism demonstrates a kind of collective spiritual bypassing. Hegemonic American Buddhism's tendency to deny and disavow Asian Americans has not been fully attended to before being applied for engagement. The results, then, have often reproduced the complex Asian exclusionary dynamics of white settler Christian nationalism, even within contemporary American engaged Buddhist projects that aim to address racial inequality.

Academic engaged Buddhist scholarship has, to an extent, examined the presence of nationalism in some manifestations of engaged Buddhism (Fuller 2018; King 2018; Main and Lai 2013; Victoria 2001). These investigations, however, have generally focused on examples in Asia. American engaged Buddhism has in large part excused itself from a duty to investigate the bearings of nationalism in its own practices. Ann Gleig and Brenna Grace Artinger's 2021 work on the "Buddhist culture wars" in the United States is, in this chapter's view, rather helpful in illuminating the varied ways that white American nationalism surfaces in convert Buddhist spaces. Though their article is framed around cultural debates rather than nationalism, their examination of the "longstanding clashes between religious conservatives and progressive[s]" (2021, 21) inadvertently reveals how the legacies of white settler nationalism infuses both sides. In their opening scene, they describe a moment during the racial reckoning of the Trump years, when Tenku Ruff, the president of the Soto Zen Buddhist Association (SZBA), was confronted with an inquiry about racial exclusion in the sangha. "Another teacher asked her how the SZBA, which is 95% demographically white, was welcoming and relevant for African American practitioners" (2021, 20). Thus, while Gleig and Artinger focus on tracing the development of right-wing sentiments—ideologies that are often readily identified as overtly nationalistic—in white convert American spaces, they also help to highlight how the progressive left can be similarly complicit in an exclusionary nationalism.

Yet, as a rule, this nationalism is not properly addressed in American engaged Buddhism. Moreover, in moments when racial exclusion is brought to the fore, it is within the discourse of a dualistic Black-and-white binary paradigm predicated upon the continued disavowal of Asian American Buddhists as structured by white settler Christian nationalism. Even progressive American engaged Buddhism, therefore, can uphold power dynamics that render Asian American Buddhists liminal to American Buddhism and its engaged practices. This point will be further explored later in the section. First, it is important to establish the context of white settler Christian nationalism in the United States.

American nationalism is distinctly situated in the ongoing occupation that is settler colonialism. As Patrick Wolfe has explained, "settler colonization is a structure rather than an event" (2006, 390). Instead of being relegated to a particular moment in time, it is continuously reinstated through the "historical *and* contemporary matrix of relations" that maintain settler presence (Tuck and Gaztambide-Fernández 2013, 73), and a logic of native elimination (Wolfe 2006). Within the context of the United States, Eve Tuck and Wayne Yang argue that settler colonialism established itself through an "entangled triad structure of settler-native-slave" (2012, 1). This structure facilitates what Tuck and Rubén Gaztambide-Fernández term "settler futurity," an intended permanency of settlers on Indigenous lands (2013, 80).

Christianity has been central in this occupation, serving as "covenant for [the] settler nation-state" (Tuck and Yang 2012, 29), perhaps most clearly evidenced through the Protestant premise of Manifest Destiny. Explaining the role of Christianity and racial formations in the United States more broadly, Jacobson and Wadsworth note, "White Christianity in the United States and other imperialist frontier outposts has positioned itself and its whiteness as the universal norm, thereby rendering the racial and religious baggage behind it invisible (though hardly invisible to people of color)" (2012, 5). The result has been the institutionalization of what Rev. Dr. William J. Barber II and Jonathan Wilson-Hartgrove refer to as "Christian nationalism," or "a movement that has promoted white identity politics in the name of God" (Barber and Wilson-Hartgrove 2018), and what Khyati Joshi refers to as a normative white Christian privilege (2020).

These foundations of white settler Christian nationalism have conditioned individuals, institutions, and social movements within the United States, including American engaged Buddhism. Thus, those thinking about and/or practicing engaged Buddhism in the United States must contend with this reality of settler occupation and the white settler Christian nationalism that established this structure.

The majority of American Buddhists, engaged or otherwise, are settlers. As Eve Tuck and Wayne Yang explain, "Settlers are diverse, not just of white European descent, and include people of color, even from other colonial contexts" (2012, 7). To be clear, Asian American Buddhists and their historical exclusion are part of this settler structure, both as Asian settlers and people racial-religiously disciplined to maintain white settler Christian occupation. Here, it is important to state that this chapter's argument for acknowledging anti-Asian disavowal and Asian exclusion in hegemonic American Buddhism and American engaged Buddhism is not intended to assert what would be a false parallel to Indigenous elimination, or a means to deflect complicity in US settler colonialism (even through formal exclusionary periods, Asian Buddhists maintained a settler presence). Nor is its purpose to argue for a more representative inclusion in the white settler logic, or to locate an authentic Buddhist exceptionality within Asian America.

Rather, it is intended to take seriously the way that Buddhism in the United States has been incorporated within the white settler Christian structure as a field for violent, orientalized racialization; that is, developing a critical analysis of the denial and disavowal of Asian American Buddhists sheds light on how the very category of American Buddhism itself is a racial experience. Relatedly, it helps to illuminate how such racial-religious orientializing was employed for advancing the supremacy of white settler Christian occupation. In describing what she terms "settler orientalism," Juliana Hu Pegues notes the manner in which conceptions of the Asiatic other were used to associate Indigenous peoples in Alaska with the geographical and ideological foreignness of Asia—a white settler Christian methodology to sever Indigenous claims to land. The mapping of orientalized Asian religions onto Indigenous practices functioned as one avenue by which such connections were established. As Pegues explains, "[White] [t]ourists described Native religious practice as Asian idolatry" (2021, 35). She provides an elucidating example of one tourist's account to emphasize this point:

> Shamanism is a religion of awful superstition which prevails in Northern Asia, consisting in a belief in evil spirits, and in the necessity of averting their malign influence by magic spells and horrid rites. The prevalence of this religion among the Alaska Indians is one of the many evidences of their Asiatic origins. (2021, 35)

This passage highlights how in the context of US nationalism, Asian religions, including Buddhism, are both rendred heathen and co-opted for race-making, producing the "superstitious" other as exterior to the white settler nation-state. Furthermore, it reveals how this process intends to delegitimize orientalized religious practices to erase ancestral proprietorship and enable white settler ownership. In the case of the example above, it is ownership of Indigenous land. While in the case of hegemonic American Buddhism, it is ownership of an Asian religion.

The project of dealing forthrightly with the denial and disavowal of Asian American Buddhists in American engaged Buddhism, therefore, is urgently needed to facilitate a critical understanding of at least three significant dynamics: (1) the racial-religious construction of the Asian figure; (2) the white settler Christian purposes this formation serves; and (3) the way Buddhism has been appropriated for this process. While the last two points have been addressed above, the first one deserves more dedicated attention. Here, it is helpful to remember that race is a social construction. Asian American Buddhists have not always been Asian. Historically, their racialized taxonomies have ranged from Mongoloid, Oriental, Heathen, and Hindoo, to list just a few. The paradigm of Asian was a term later applied; its popular usage grew in conjunction with the Cold War and the rise of area studies as an extension of the national security state. Through the various classifications, however, the notion of the Asiatic other was intimately tied to orientalized religious practices such as Buddhism to affix certain behaviors as intrinsic to their perceived foreignness. Understanding these intertwined elements as forces of white settler Christian nationalism that have acted upon American Buddhism is crucial for rigorously analyzing American engaged Buddhism. It requires that we interrogate the construction of the hegemonic American Buddhism being operationalized for engagement, and the ramifications of such actions.

Moreover, in the specific context of American Buddhism, and its use for engagement, taking a serious account of Asian American Buddhists' erasure requires us to think about the complexities this disavowal adds to conceptions of race and racial dynamics in the US. How does the continuously erased Asian American Buddhist complicate convenient model minority assimilationist narratives and dismissals? What does it mean when the practitioners who first established Buddhism in the United States are rendered nonexistent, or at best, oriental liabilities to be diminished for the ascendance of "non-oriental" authority? How does this structure become so thoroughly naturalized such that purposeful interventions must be made simply for accountability to historical fact? *What does it mean for this hegemonic American Buddhism to be used as the basis of engagement?*

Acknowledging the Distinctive Racialization of Asian American Buddhists

"Race," Cheah argues, "has been an important factor in naming and defining Buddhism" (2011, 75). Through racial rearticulation, or "the acquisition of the beliefs and practices of another's religious tradition and infusing them with new meanings derived from one's own culture in ways that preserve the prevailing system of racial hegemony," Buddhism continues to be employed as a tool of white settler Christian nationalism to delegitimate Asian American Buddhists as superstitious heathens (nineteenth century) and superstitious baggage Buddhists (twentieth and twenty-first centuries). Racial rearticulation, Cheah further explains, "deals explicitly with power relationship. It is an adoption or adaption of Buddhist practices into forms that help preserve, for example, the system of racial hegemony initiated by Orientalist racial projects of the middle and late Victorian era" (2011, 59–60). Without an explicit awareness of such dynamics and an understanding of the history of Asian immigrants' development of American Buddhism in the context of white settler violence, engaged Buddhist advocates and organizations in the United States may perpetuate the orientalist project of racial rearticulation.

Though Cheah identifies engaged Buddhism as cultural rearticulation (2011, 69), or "a way of representing religious tradition from another's culture into ideas and practices that are familiar and meaningful to people of one's own culture" (2011, 60), rather than racial rearticulation, Yarnall and Temprano's critiques of the orientalist veins in engaged Buddhism demonstrate that the category can, in fact, serve as a vehicle of the latter. Indeed, the fallacy that white Americans visiting Asia brought Buddhism and meditation to the United States in the postwar period, and the idea that the majority of American Buddhists are white, when two-thirds are Asian American ("Asian Americans: A Mosiac of Faiths" 2012), are dominant forms of the racial rearticulation that serves to perpetuate the denial and disavowal of Asian American Buddhists from both hegemonic American Buddhism and, therefore, American engaged Buddhism.

Honestly contending with the anti-Asian dynamics that continue to silently propel much of American engaged Buddhism, therefore, is paramount. Prioritizing discussions of Asian American Buddhists—that is, their roles in establishing Buddhism in America; the particular ways they are racialized through their religion; the active disavowal and negation of these histories; and the growth of their American Buddhist practice as a means of navigating these racial-religious structures—enables an accountable path forward. As Adeana McNicholl has argued, "By centering Asian American religio-racial subjectivities in our histories of American Buddhism, we reveal the racial whiteness underlying normative understandings of American Buddhism" (2021, 9).

Hsiao-Lan Hu's Buddhist feminist ethics of "reconditioning" (Hu 2011) offers a useful approach for the broader American engaged Buddhist community to explicitly address the racial framework of Asian American Buddhist exclusion that dominates the literature and discourse of engaged Buddhism in the United States. Hu explains that the "Buddhist discourse on kamma, is a discourse on the fundamental sociality of human existence and the interconditionality of individual beings." Thus, kamma (karma) is a social phenomenon. "One comes into being in the matrix of material and sociocultural forces and has been conditioned by them, and those material and socio-cultural forces are in place as a result of people's actions up to this moment" (Hu 2011, 108). This context of intentionally remaking oneself highlights the possibility of what Hu terms reconditioning, or learning to engage in behaviors that "sto[p] the cycle of dukkha-production" (2011, 127). The initial step in the direction of reconditioning involves an awakening to the social process of conditioning, "To recondition, actively, the dukkha-inducing socio-cultural sediments that have been conditioning one's 'self,' first of all, one has to be aware of the subtle ways in which socio-cultural conditioning is taking place" (2011, 139).

While many contemporary American engaged Buddhist projects, especially among a younger generation of self-identified engaged Buddhists (Gleig 2021), seek to address issues of racial inequality and suffering (Mitchell 2016), this work is often approached through a framework of racial rearticulation that leaves unchallenged racialized narratives of white authority—and relatedly, Asian superstition and "cultural baggage"—in American Buddhism, thus enacting the continued denial of Asian American Buddhists as part of their engagement for racial justice. Integrating the paradigm of reconditioning can facilitate an urgently needed attentiveness to how these racial justice projects themselves may be predicated on a foundational racialization. Otherwise, such engaged efforts for racial justice can reify the white settler orientalist narrative of white discovery, rescue, and authority in American Buddhism.

Even intended "radical" attempts at expanding the scope of engaged Buddhism can still uphold racial rearticulations and white settler nationalist exclusion. For example, Michael Slott's (2015) theorizing of a "secular, radically engaged Buddhism" maintains an orientalist stance in its alignment with the broader secular Buddhist "rejection of supernatural beings and the cosmology of realms found in Asian Buddhisms, as well as the notion of *karma* linked to literal rebirths" (2015, 280). Though Slott cautions that a "militantly secular Buddhism can entail an intolerance or unwarranted dismissal of others' spiritual beliefs and practices that reflects a lack of compassion and an attachment to a particular viewpoint" (2015, 280), the racialized component of white settler orientalist nationalism remains unexamined. Thus, it also remains embedded in this form of American engaged Buddhism.

Returning to engaged examinations of race, in 2013, the Buddhist Peace Fellowship (BPF), which has been described as "the main socially engaged Buddhist organization in North America" (Rothberg 1998, 270), underwent a "radical rebirth." Among the principles of this framework was an intention to "confront and heal racism," with specific mention of the racialization of Asians and Asia:

> [W]e feel that Buddhism's historical legacies, having spread through many parts of Asia and beyond, should push all of us who feel indebted to the Dharma to give Orientalism particular attention. This means, for instance: pushing back against the romanticizing of "Eastern Wisdom!" It means pushing back against stereotypes of Asian people as inherently calm, submissive, intuitive, or "Ching-Chong" moronic. (Loncke 2013, n.p.)

Here, though Asians were acknowledged in the development of Buddhism across the globe, Asian Americans and their contributions to American Buddhism remained an enigma in this articulation of a radical rebirth of engaged Buddhism. Conversations with Asian American Buddhists directed BPF to "bring attention to and challenge the racism faced by Asian American Buddhists, who have long been marginalized in meditation-based convert Buddhism and patronized and dismissed for practicing 'cultural' rather than 'essential' Buddhism" (Gleig 2019, 256).

Yet having such critically necessary discussions, even within a radically engaged Buddhist organization like BPF, remained difficult. Leaders were hesitant to center the historical contributions of Asian American heritage Buddhists. Expressing a fear that highlighting the position of Asian American Buddhists in American and engaged Buddhism might serve to reproduce hierarchies of white supremacy, co-director Katie Loncke notes that this "is why I balked, at first, at the idea of BPF prioritizing anti-racist projects that re-center Asian American Buddhists in Western dharma. I worried that without greater political clarity, it might somehow lead us to a conservative place" (Loncke 2016, n.p.). Loncke's concerns point to the historical reality of some Asian Americans (including Asian American Buddhists) colluding with white settler power to maintain the racial political order of whiteness (Wu 2015). In some regards, it is understandable that Loncke might have apprehensions, as such Asian American collusions have facilitated the continued production of unequal material effects, especially for Indigenous and Black communities. Furthermore, due to the very structures of white settler Christian nationalism that have historically conditioned US society and American Buddhism, the mainstream discourse on Asian Americans has been limited to racialized tropes of hyper-capitalist model-minority assimilation, and (courtesy of racial-religious orientalism) a conservative, destructive, superstitious otherness (themes resonant with portrayals of Asia and "traditional Buddhism" in academic engaged Buddhism).

However, the immediate assumption of a self-interested, conservative model minority stance on the part of Asian American heritage Buddhists asserting their historical belonging in American Buddhism perpetuates anti-Asian animus, leading to their continued disavowal—only within a discourse of radical engagement. In interrogating the racialized and economized construction of the Asian laborer figure as the vile embodiment of abstract labor, Iyko Day reminds us that the model minority is merely the other side of the "heathen Chinee." "Indeed, the model minority stereotype seems far afield from the historical repertoire of yellow perilism denoting disease, vice, and destruction," Day explains. "But rather than expressions associated with two distinct phases, 'yellow peril' and the 'model minority' stereotype function as complementary aspects of the same form of racialization, in which economic efficiency is the basis for exclusion or assimilation." They are both "part of a continuum of settler colonial capitalism and its racial formations" (Day 2016, 7).

Though the constraints of space prohibit a detailed discussion of how settler colonial capitalism is undeniably interwoven into the racialized exclusion of Asian American Buddhists, Day's appraisal of the complimentary yellow peril and model minority function is important for our analysis here. It highlights how the default model minority/yellow peril ("heathen Chinee") positioning of Asian American Buddhists forecloses the possibility of their existence outside the settler (orientalist) colonial continuum. In doing so, it demonstrates the very ways hegemonic American Buddhism is employed to racialize Asian American Buddhists—even within radical, engaged

Buddhism. Such formulations of engaged Buddhist practice negate the history of Asian American Buddhists like the late Isao Fujimoto, who, inspired by the teachings of his family's Shin Buddhist tradition, cultivated explicit forms of grassroots, worker-led coalition building and community development (Fujimoto 2017). Moreover, they preclude Asian American Buddhist practitioners' definitions of engagement, an orientalist maneuvering that Temprano has cautioned against in his discussion of engaged Buddhist scholarship (2013).

Loncke's reflection, however, also provides a useful path forward. It demonstrates how such reasoning is the product of a broader historical system that has structured the exclusion of Asian American Buddhists from many social arenas, including American Buddhism itself. Quite importantly, it also evidences how engaged Buddhism can operate as a vehicle to not only perpetuate, but enforce, this logic. Moreover, Loncke's willingness to examine their presuppositions, and to do so publicly, demonstrates the commitments that are needed for a reconditioning that takes seriously the systematic erasure of Asian American Buddhists. Indeed, Loncke acknowledged, "Asian diasporic Buddhists have not only seen their spiritual traditions taken up and repackaged by powerful white individuals and institutions, but have been shamed and belittled for 'superstitious' forms of buddhadharma in their own family heritage. Not okay. Let's work together to change this" (Loncke 2016, n.p.). Such reconsideration represents the kinds of practices that need to be replicated in order for American engaged Buddhism to reconcile its foundational exclusionary basis.

The struggle, however, to enact this change within BPF persists. Thanks to the ongoing work of Asian American Buddhists in highlighting the institution's history of denying and disavowing heritage Buddhists, the current BPF Board has made this issue integral in the reformation of the organization. In an update shared in spring 2022, BPF expressed that they had "immensely generative discussions around the present state of American Buddhism(s), especially the gaps in relationship between the majority of Western converts with Heritage Buddhist sanghas, tradition and context" (Buddhist Peace Fellowship 2022a, n.p.). In a later communication, they added, "we continued to surface the ongoing tensions and patterns of erasure of Heritage Buddhist community and culture in relation to Western convert Buddhism, including BPF's own karma in this regard" (Buddhist Peace Fellowship 2022b, n.p.). It is important to note that Asian American Buddhists have been responsible for establishing the validity of these conversations within and beyond BPF—insisting on them in the face of repetitive pushback and disavowal. As the organization noted in their spring update, "Mushim Ikeda pointed out that this gap has been a long fraught area in the history of BPF; a divide that the current BPF stewards are committed to bridging" (Buddhist Peace Fellowship 2022a, n.p.). Thus, for Asian American Buddhists, contending with the hegemony of American engaged Buddhism can become part of their own engaged Buddhism. It can be a vital aspect of their Buddhist practice in the United States—highlighting how Asian American Buddhists have historically turned to their religion to exist beyond their racialization in America.

Conclusion

This chapter demonstrates that popular American engaged Buddhism has been disengaged with the reality of the sociohistorical denial and disavowal of Asian American Buddhists ingrained in its practice. It highlights how the hegemonic construction of American Buddhism that serves as the foundation for engagement stems from white settler Christian nationalist formations of Asian exclusion. Inattention to these realities while proceeding with engaged Buddhist scholarly and community projects evidences a spiritual bypassing that rehearses the racial-religious denial at hand. Moreover, such neglect disregards the impact of this disavowal as a distinct and continual mode of Asian American Buddhist racialization. Even American engaged Buddhist projects attuned to issues of race have generally ignored, or have been hesitant to address, the exclusionary positioning of Asian American Buddhists. This demonstrates an urgent need for a reconditioning. Engaged Buddhist projects in America must have honest conversations about the embedded anti-Asian sentiments, racialization, and exclusion of Asian American Buddhists in their formulations of engagement.

References

Anderson, Kay. 2007. *Race and the Crisis of Humanism*. Abingdon: Routledge.

"Asian Americans: A Mosaic of Faiths." 2012. Pew Research Center. https://www.pewresearch.org/religion/2012/07/19/asian-americans-a-mosaic-of-faiths-overview/#:~:text=The%20survey%20finds%20a%20plurality,agnostic%20or%20nothing%20in%20particular).

Barber, William J., II, and Jonathan Wilson-Hartgrove. 2018. "The Unveiling of Christian Nationalism." *The Herald Sun* (Durham, NC), January 27. https://www.heraldsun.com/opinion/article196961234.html.

Blum, Mark. 2009. "The Transcendentalist Ghost in EcoBuddhism." In *TransBuddhism: Transmission, Translation, Transformation*, edited by Nalini Bhushan, Jay L. Garfield, and Abraham Zablocki, 209–238. Amherst: University of Massachusetts Press.

Buddhist Peace Fellowship. 2022a. "Spring 2022 Update." April 18. https://www.bpf.org/blog/spring-2022-update.

Buddhist Peace Fellowship. 2022b. "Vesak Update." July 12. https://www.bpf.org/blog/vesak-update.

Cheah, J. 2016. "Buddhism, Race, and Ethnicity." In *The Oxford Handbook of Contemporary Buddhism*, edited by Michael Jerryson, 650–661. New York: Oxford University Press.

Cheah, Joseph. 2011. *Race and Religion in American Buddhism: White Supremacy and Immigrant Adaptation*. New York: Oxford University Press.

Day, Iyko. 2016. *Alien Capital: Asian Racialization and the Logic of Settler Colonial Capitalism*. Durham, NC: Duke University Press.

Edwards, Sachi. 2017. "Intergroup Dialogue and Religious Identity: Attempting to Raise Awareness of Christian Privilege and Religious Oppression." *Multicultural Education* 24, no. 2: 18–24.

Fossella, Tina. 2011. "Human Nature Buddha Nature: An Interview with John Welwood." *Tricycle: The Buddhist Review*, Spring. https://tricycle.org/magazine/human-nature-buddha-nature/.

Fujimoto, Isao. 2017. *Bouncing Back: Community Resilience and Curiosity*. Sacramento, CA: I Street Press.

Fuller, Paul. 2018. "The Narratives of Ethnocentric Buddhist Identity," *Journal of the British Association for the Study of Religion* 20: 19–44.

Fuller, Paul. 2021. *An Introduction to Engaged Buddhism*. London: Bloomsbury.

Gleig, Ann. 2019. *American Dharma: Buddhism Beyond Modernity*. New Haven, CT: Yale University Press.

Gleig, Ann. 2021. "Engaged Buddhism." In *Oxford Research Encyclopedia of Religion*.

Gleig, Ann, and Brenna Grace Artinger. 2021. "The #BuddhistCultureWars: BuddhaBros, Alt-Right Dharma, and Snowflake Sanghas." *Journal of Global Buddhism* 22: 19–49.

Hickey, Wakoh Shannon. 2015. "Two Buddhisms, Three Buddhisms, and Racism." In *Buddhism beyond Borders: New Perspectives on Buddhism in the United States*, edited by Scott A. Mitchell and Natalie E. F. Quli, 35–55. Albany: State University of New York Press.

Hsu, Alexander O. 2022. "Coming to Terms with 'Engaged Buddhism': Periodizing, Provincializing, and Politicizing the Concept." *Journal of Global Buddhism* 23, no. 1: 17–31.

Hu, Hsiao-Lan. 2011. *This Worldly-Nibbana: A Buddhist Feminist Social Ethic for Peacemaking in the Global Community*. New York: State University of New York Press.

Hu Pegues, Juliana. 2021. *Space-Time Colonialism: Alaska's Indigenous and Asian Entanglements*. Chapel Hill: University of North Carolina Press.

Jacobson, R. D., and N. D. Wadsworth, eds. 2012. *Faith and Race in American Political Life*. Charlottesville: University of Virginia Press.

Joshi, Khyati Y. 2020. *White Christian Privilege: The Illusion of Religious Equality in America*. New York: New York University Press.

King, Sallie B. 2005. *Being Benevolence: The Social Ethics of Engaged Buddhism*. Honolulu: University of Hawai'i Press.

King, Sallie B. 2009. *Socially Engaged Buddhism*. Honolulu: University of Hawai'i Press.

King, Sallie B. 2018. "The Ethics of Engaged Buddhism in Asia." In *The Oxford Handbook of Buddhist Ethics*, edited by Daniel Cozort and James Mark Shields, 479–500. Oxford: Oxford University Press.

Lee, Catherine. 2010. "'Where the Danger Lies': Race, Gender, and Chinese and Japanese Exclusion in the United States, 1870–1924." *Sociological Forum* 25, no. 2: 248–271.

Loncke, Katie. 2013. "10 Principles of Our Radical Rebirth." Buddhist Peace Fellowship. October 29. https://buddhistpeacefellowship.org/10-principles-of-our-radical-rebirth/.

Loncke, Katie. 2016. "'We've Been Here All Along': Love for Asian American Buddhists." Buddhist Peace Fellowship. December 7. https://buddhistpeacefellowship.org/weve-been-here-love/.

Lum, Kathryn G. 2021. *Heathen: Religion and Race in American History*. Cambridge: Havard University Press.

Main, Jessica L., and Rongdao Lai. 2013. "Introduction: Reformulating 'Socially Engaged Buddhism' as an Analytical Category." *The Eastern Buddhist* 44, no. 2: 1–34.

Masatsugu, Michael K. 2008. "'Beyond This World of Transiency and Impermanence': Japanese Americans, Dharma Bums, and the Making of American Buddhism during the Early Cold War Years." *Pacific Historical Review* 77, no. 3: 423–451.

McNicholl, Adeana. 2021. "Buddhism and Race in the United States." *Religion Compass* 15, no. 8: 1–13.

Mitchell, Scott A. 2016. *Buddhism in America: Global Religion, Local Contexts*. London: Bloomsbury.

Omi, M., and H. Winant. 1994. *Racial Formation in the United States: From the 1960s to the 1990s*. Abingdon, UK: Routledge.

Queen, Christopher. 2003. "Introduction: From Altruism to Activism" In *Action Dharma: New Studies in Engaged Buddhism*, edited by Christopher Queen, Damien Keown, and Charles S. Prebish, 1–37. London: Routledge.

Queen, Christopher. 2005. "Engaged Buddhism." In *Encyclopedia of Religion*, edited by Lindsay Jones, 2785–2791. New York: Macmillan.

Queen, Christopher S. 2013. "Socially Engaged Buddhism: Emerging Patterns of Theory and Practice." In *A Companion to Buddhist Philosophy*, edited by Steven M. Emmanuel, 524–535. Hoboken: John Wiley and Sons, Inc.

Queen, Christopher. 2018. "The Ethics of Engaged Buddhism in the West." In *The Oxford Handbook of Buddhist Ethics*, edited by Daniel Cozort and James Mark Shields, 501–530. Oxford: Oxford University Press.

Quli, Natalie F. 2009. "Western Self, Asian Other: Modernity, Authenticity, and Nostalgia for 'Tradition' in Buddhist Studies." *Journal of Buddhist Ethics* 16: 1–38.

Quli, Natalie F. 2019. "On Authenticity: Scholarship, the Insight Movement, and White Authority." In *Methods in Buddhist Studies: Essays in Honor of Richard K. Payne*, edited by Scott A. Mitchell and Natalie Fisk Quli, 154–172. New York: Bloomsbury Publishing.

Rothberg, Donald. 1998. "Responding to the Cries of the World: Socially Engaged Buddhism in North America." In *The Faces of Buddhism in America*, edited by Charles S. Prebish and Kenneth K. Tanaka, 266–286. Berkeley: University of California Press.

Saranillio, Dean Itsuji. 2013. "Why Asian Settler Colonialism Matters: A Thought Piece on Critiques, Debates, and Indigenous Difference." *Settler Colonial Studies* 3, no. 3–4: 280–294.

Seager, Richard Hughes. 2012. *Buddhism in America*. New York: Columbia University Press.

Slott, Michael. 2015. "Secular, Radically Engaged Buddhism: At the Crossroads of Individual and Social Transformation." *Contemporary Buddhism* 16: 278–298.

Temprano, Victor Gerard. 2013. "Defining Engaged Buddhism: Traditionists, Modernists, and Scholastic Power." *Buddhist Studies Review* 30, no. 2: 261–274.

Tuck, Eve, and Rubén A. Gaztambide-Fernández. 2013. "Curriculum, Replacement, and Settler Futurity." *Journal of Curriculum Theorizing* 29, no. 1: 72–89.

Tuck, Eve, and K. Wayne Yang. 2012. "Decolonization Is Not a Metaphor." *Decolonization: Indigeneity, Education & Society* 1, no. 1: 1–40.

Vesely-Flad, Rima. 2017. "Black Buddhists and the Body: New Approaches to Socially Engaged Buddhism." *Religions* 8, no. 11: 239.

Victoria, Brian Daizen. 2001. "Engaged Buddhism: A Skeleton in the Closet?" *Journal of Global Buddhism* 2: 72–91.

Williams, Duncan Ryūken. 2019. *American Sutra: A Story of Faith and Freedom during the Second World War*. Cambridge, MA: Harvard University Press.

Wolfe, Patrick. 2006. "Settler Colonialism and the Elimination of the Native." *Journal of Genocide Research* 8, no. 4: 387–409.

Wu, Ellen D. 2015. *The Color of Success: Asian Americans and the Origins of the Model Minority*. Princeton, NJ: Princeton University Press.

Yarnall, Thomas Freeman. 2000. "Engaged Buddhism: New and Improved? Made in the USA of Asian Materials." *Journal of Buddhist Ethics* 7: 1–90.

Yoo, David. 2000. *Growing Up Nisei: Race, Generation, and Culture among Japanese Americans of California, 1924–49*. Urbana: University of Illinois Press.

PART IV

FRAMES

CHAPTER 21

AMERICAN BUDDHISM AND SECULARISM

KIN CHEUNG

SCHOLARSHIP on secular Buddhism in North America tends to fall into two main approaches.[1] The first includes more descriptive works that trace and contextualize the emergence of secular Buddhists and Buddhisms in the United States.[2] For example, Mitchell details how Buddhist meditation practices moved into secular settings and the formation of online spaces that connect secular Buddhists in the United States, the United Kingdom, and Australia.[3] The second includes more analytic work focused on issues of whiteness, neoliberalism, and colonialism.[4] For instance, the edited volume *Secularizing Buddhism* emphasizes the dynamic processes involved when groups and individuals claim to be secular Buddhists or are positioned as agents secularizing Buddhism. Payne's Chapter 19 in this volume illuminates how the rhetoric of secularization rests on Protestant foundations, which include "the historical trajectory of religion as an institution, the subjectivity of adherents, why ritual is not a meaningful form of practice, how only some texts are considered authentic, and the authority of a supposedly original teaching."[5] Doing so allows him to explicate how applying the label "secular" is dependent on its opposite (religious or non-secular) and other contrasting pairs.

In this chapter, I further this analysis by using perspectives from the anthropology of religion to explain these *hierarchical* pairings. The most prominent contrast that secular Buddhists use is the pairing of natural versus supernatural—explained in detail below. This hierarchical construction is *political* in that classifiers adjudicate aspects of

---

[1] I presented a draft of this chapter to the Philadelphia-Area Buddhist Studies Work Group and am grateful for their feedback.
[2] Gleig 2019; Mitchell 2016.
[3] Mictchell 2016, 160–165.
[4] Hsu 2021; McNicholl 2021; Cheah 2017.
[5] Payne 2021, 289.

Buddhism deemed superior, denigrating the rest as inferior. My attention to race and whiteness focuses not on skin color, but on racialization—the classification of difference.

In the sections that follow, I: (1) describe secular Buddhist online spaces; (2) overview theories of secular-ity, -ism, -ization along with anthropological warnings against the label "supernatural"; (3) situate secular Buddhists in contrast to other secular religious groups and new Buddhist developments in the United States, secularization of Buddhism via tourism in Asia, and other "Shades of Whiteness in American Buddhism"[6]; (4) provide a close reading of media by the Secular Buddhism Podcast (SBP); (5) critique the two defining principles of the Secular Buddhist Association (SBA); and (6) conclude with reflections on the role of internet transmission of secular Buddhism.

Secular Buddhist Online Spaces

Secular Buddhists groups have been growing through Anglophone online spaces with audiences in the United Kingdom, continental Europe, Australia, New Zealand, Canada, and the United States. Payne and Kemp (2021) provide a literature review on the topic and discuss key figures—Stephen Batchelor (United Kingdom), Winton Higgins (Australia), Rike Bateman (Canada), and groups—the SBA (based in the United States)[7] and the Secular Buddhist Network (SBN, based in Europe). The SBA's and SBN's online presence is eclipsed by the focus of this chapter: the US-based SBP, founded by Noah Rasheta.[8] As of Janurary 2024, the SBP Facebook page has over 93,000 followers.[9] The SBP produced 173 podcast episodes, twenty to forty minutes long, beginning in January 2016. Their first few episodes have been played over 200,000 times each, and a typical episode has approximately 50,000 plays.[10] The SBP has the largest visible online presence of secular Buddhists around the world. Though it is unclear how many or what percentage of their social media (including Instagram, Twitter, and Reddit) followers, podcast listeners, article readers, and forum commenters are based in the United States, Rahesta is US-based and has a local community of practice in Utah.

Who are secular Buddhists? What makes them secular or Buddhist? Rasheta states: "Secular Buddhism is a non-dogmatic way of understanding and practicing Buddhism."[11] The SBA had a motto that is no longer mentioned explicitly on the main pages of their site, but is still referenced in forum discussion posts as late as 2014.[12] The

---

[6] McNicholl 2020.
[7] Payne and Kemp 2021. See Payne 2021 for more on the SBA, especially 298–290 and 309–310.
[8] https://secularbuddhism.com/.
[9] https://www.facebook.com/Secularbuddhism.
[10] https://soundcloud.com/secularbuddhism.
[11] https://secularbuddhism.com/what-is-secular-buddhism/.
[12] It is also cited as appearing on the SBA website in Durazzo 2015, 594 n1.

motto sums up secular Buddhism as "[a] natural, pragmatic approach to early Buddhist teachings and practice." Early denotes an emphasis on Pali *sutta*s. "Natural" is a rejection of literal rebirth and other "supernatural" claims found in various Buddhist traditions. "Practice" denotes following the Eightfold Path and one specific type of sitting meditation, while relegating other types of Buddhist practice—for example, recitation of texts, chanting spells, use of prayer wheels—as ritual or "cultural attachment."

Delineating the "natural" from the "supernatural" is not neutral. Klass convincingly shows that the latter term is ethnocentric and that using it posits a universal distinction between a "natural" and "supernatural" world, when in fact, this division changes over time and varies in local contexts.[13] Secular Buddhists argue their emphasis on the natural is a way of "updating" the ancient wisdom of Buddhist insights to be more palatable for "scientifically minded" or secular audiences. To understand the ways in which this naturalization or secularization of Buddhism is a racialized process, it is helpful to turn to work on religion and race.

In the introduction to the volume *Race and Secularism in America*, the co-editor Lloyd writes:

> We hypothesize that race and secularism are entwined. Put more starkly, whiteness is secular, and the secular is white. The unmarked racial category and the unmarked religious category jointly mark their others. Or, put another way, the desire to stand outside religion and the desire to stand outside race are complementary delusions, for the seemingly outside is in fact the hegemonic.[14]

In the context of theories of religion and the genealogical influence of white supremacy and settler colonialism in America, scholars of religion argue for the interplay between race, religion, and secularism. Hart explains that "[t]o theorize religion is simultaneously to theorize race."[15] Jennings shows that "[a]n ostensibly secular space is in fact a space of whiteness, a space for whites."[16] Focusing on theory and methodology, Driscoll and Miller argue that the study of religion is "particularly suited to address questions of normative white identity and singular logics."[17] These scholars engage with historical and contemporary Black-white relations and Spaniard colonial settlement

---

[13] Klass 1995.

[14] Lloyd 2016, 5. Furthermore, Lloyd continues, "We ask whether it is ever possible to talk about secularism without talking about whiteness. America is a prime site to study secularism in practice and to study the intersection of secularism and racialization. As imagined, or fantasized, America is a place of religious and racial diversity, a place where the freedom to be who you want to be has allowed for varied religious and racial communities to call for and achieve recognition of their distinctiveness. Together with the rhetoric of freedom is the reality of management, the subtle technologies of control that create the horizons of possibility for both religious and racialized lives" (2016, 7). See Thomas 2019 for how American political leaders and scholars of religion wielded the rhetoric of religious freedom to justify US occupation of Japan.

[15] Cited in Stromback 2019, 23.

[16] Cited in Lloyd 2016, 18.

[17] Driscoll and Miller 2018, xxvi.

of the Americas. I apply their theoretical contributions to secular Buddhist groups in America.

I will focus on how the "secular" functions as a frame. What does it hide or reproduce? Is "secular" code for white or whiteness? Whiteness is not merely about skin color or phenotypes. Heng defines race to emphasize how it "is a structural relationship for the articulation and management of human differences, rather than a substantive content."[18] Hart also theorizes race and religion as classification systems, in which whiteness and white religion indicate positions of power and privilege, and includes white-passing people of all skin tones.[19] I only concentrate on a narrow band of how secularity within Buddhism is expressed: the secular Buddhism articulated by Rasheta.[20]

Secular, Secularity, Secularism, and Secularization

There is no consensus on one neat way to define the term "secular" as delineated from the terms "secularity," "secularism," and "secularization." The fact that "this cluster of related terms" plainly has "a common linguistic root should not obscure the fact that they operate in different conceptual frameworks with distinct histories."[21] I follow Casanova in his "distinction between 'the secular' as a central modern epistemic category, 'secularization' as an analytical conceptualization of modern world-historical processes, and 'secularism' as a worldview and ideology."[22] For Casanova, secularity is the state of being secular, in which there are three ways: (1) being secular, like being religious, are both considered to be "normal viable option[s]"; (2) "living without religion" is considered "a normal, quasi-natural, taken-for-granted condition"; and (3) "the phenomenological experience not only of being passively free but also actually of having been liberated from 'religion'" is considered "a condition for human autonomy and human flourishing."[23] As will be shown later, SBP members display tendencies for all three, and their founder displays the third.

Scholars of religion emphasize that the "secular" is always already constructed in relation to the "religious," and at times a third term, such as "superstitious," "magic," or "spiritual."[24] Using Casanova's definition, I will show that secular Buddhists employ the

---

[18] Heng 2018, 27.
[19] Hart 2017.
[20] See the work of McMahan (2012, 2017) on other forms of this-worldly Buddhism or Buddhist modernism by Asian Buddhist teachers in the United States such as Thich Nhat Hanh, Chögyam Trungpa, and Shunryu Suzuki.
[21] Calhoun et al. 2011, 5–6.
[22] Casanova 2011, 55.
[23] Ibid., 60.
[24] See Arnal and McCutcheon 2012; McMahan 2012, 2017; Josephson-Storm 2017; and Payne 2019.

label "secular" in attempts to "construct, codify, grasp, and experience a realm or reality differentiated from 'the religious.'"[25] In other words, I am not addressing the political management of the United States as a nation-state. I am interested in whether and how secular Buddhists present a triumphalist history of the secular (Casanova's third stance of secularity) and how the rhetorical positioning of Buddhism as a religion, as opposed to a "philosophy," a "way of life," or a set of ideas and practices backed by "science" has always been contested, negotiated, and politically motivated.[26]

The use of secular as a frame by white secular Buddhists can be illuminated by how anthropologists of religion explain the problems with the term "supernatural." Sered proposes a continuum, rather than a dualistic binary between the "natural" and "supernatural," by arguing for attention toward "the political value judgments in employing dichotomous labels."[27] When the secular is constructed against the religious, it posits *hierarchical* binaries between the following pairs: science/superstition, rational/irrational, philosophy/blind faith, universal/provincial, universal/cultural "baggage" or attachment or accruement, white/non-white, West/the rest, modern/primitive, pragmatic/"nonsense," practice/dogma, meditation/ritual, and so on. Ultimately, these hierarchies map onto evaluative binaries of true/false and superior/inferior.[28] Furthermore, secular Buddhists equate practice and meditation with a specific type of quiet sitting, while relegating the chanting of sutras or spells, spinning of prayer wheels, or prostrating to deities as ritual and irrational. In other words, they assume sitting is natural—in Casanova's sense of taken-for-granted, as a matter of course, and against the "supernatural"—and rational because it does not unsettle their metaphysical and ontological worldviews. As will be detailed below, secular Buddhists are "uncomfortable" with ritual and rebirth.

North American Secular Buddhists in Context

It is helpful to situate secular Buddhists in the larger North American religious context. Secular Judaism or Jewish secularism emphasizes "Jewishness" as an ethnic

---

[25] Casanova 2011, 54.

[26] See Karlin 2013 for the rhetorical positioning of Buddhism. In writing about how mindfulness has been constructed as secular and backed by science, McMahan (2017) states, "We need hardly note the irony that the initial reframing of Buddhism in scientific language among figures like Taixu, Dharmapāla, and Sōen Shaku was connected to projects to strengthen Buddhism and its institutions, while the distant descendant of this discourse, the mindfulness movement that now returns to Asia from the West, has shucked off most of the Buddhist doctrines, ethics, and institutions in which meditation was embedded for centuries" (122).

[27] Cited in Cheung 2022, 137. See Sered 2003. Elsewhere, I argue for the category of a natural—rather than supernatural—miracle to understand healing in a contemporary Chinese American Buddhist community (Cheung 2022).

[28] Dempsey 2008, 4.

category. Levitt addresses how Jews are presumed white in the United States, yet marked as different.[29] Goldstein details the complicated categorization of Jews in terms of American racial and religious consciousness.[30] Secular Muslims or secular Islam may refer to the Free Muslims Coalition, which claims to have a dozen chapters in the United States, or a number of other online groups wishing to distance themselves from the pejoration of Islam in the post–9/11 United States.[31] The urge to distance is a direct result of the racialization—that is, classification as *other*—of Muslims in the United States. Less commonly referenced in the United States are self-identified secular Hindus, secular Catholics,[32] or secular Daoists (besides being noted in a scatter of individual blogs or article posts that do not indicate any sizable community or coherent group). Asad provides an influential critique of the genealogy of Protestant influence on US and global secularism.[33] The field-changing contribution of Asad is to emphasize how the "secular" *is* a specific culture, *pace* the claims of secular Buddhist spokespersons. Moreover, "scholars like Janet Jakobsen, Ann Pellegrini, and Tracy Fessenden, ... have argued that the dominative formation of secularism in the United States is dependent upon and tangled up in the Protestant Christianity that shapes the country's legal and political traditions."[34] In other words, the terms "secular Protestant" and "secular Protestantism" are redundant, especially in America. I will point out how SBP members assume Protestant notions of religion as interior private belief.[35]

Secular Buddhists settled on this term over other ways to present themselves, such as atheist Buddhist or agnostic Buddhist. All three terms owe their popularity to the work of Stephen Batchelor, who is based in the United Kingdom. His 1997 publication, *Buddhism without Beliefs: A Contemporary Guide to Awakening*, mentions "agnostic Buddhist" and "secular agnosticism."[36] His other notable publications include *Confession of a Buddhist Atheist* (2010), *After Buddhism: Rethinking the Dharma for a Secular Age* (2016), and *Secular Buddhism: Imagining the Dharma in an Uncertain World* (2018). The founder of SBA, Ted Meissner, credits Batchelor for coming up with the term "secular Buddhism" and for registering the secularbuddhism.org domain name before handing it over to Meissner's SBA in 2012.[37] This is in contrast to a group that presents

---

[29] Levitt 2007.

[30] Goldstein 2008.

[31] Rasaba et al. 2007, 129.

[32] See Bruce 2018 for how the term "cultural Catholic" is used in the United States. The history of how Irish and Italian Catholics shifted from immigrant other to presumed white reinforces the need to study religion and race together. Investigating cultural Catholics and cultural Jews along with secular Buddhists would be fruitful in explicating why the first two groups embrace culture while the latter rejects it, and how that relates to whiteness.

[33] Asad 2003.

[34] Hulsether 2016, n.p. See Fessenden 2007; Jakobsen and Pellegrini 2008.

[35] See King 1999, 150–152, and Quli 2009 on colonial agents and the term "Protestant Buddhism."

[36] Batchelor 1997, 18.

[37] Meissner 2020.

themselves as interested in Speculative Non-Buddhism (formerly x-Buddhism), created by others based in the United States.[38]

Besides using the term "secular Buddhism," Americans write about Buddhism in ways that range from embracing its religious aspects to selectively highlighting (mainly by white men) its secular features using the language of science and philosophy.[39] In *The Bodhisattva's Brain: Buddhism Naturalized*, when Flanagan presents a Buddhist philosophy that is compatible with science by subtracting the "hocus pocus" of flying bodhisattvas and lamas who are reborn, he at least admits his version of naturalistic Buddhism is more aptly named "'Buddhaganism'—Flanagan's interpretation of Buddhism."[40] In *Buddhist Biology: Ancient Eastern Wisdom Meets Modern Western Science*, Barash presents a materialist version of a "biological Buddhism" that is in agreement with scientific consensus on ecology and evolution, while dismissing rebirth and healing rituals as "hocus-pocus," "abracadabra," "poppycock," "ludicrous," "mumbo-jumbo," and "arrant nonsense."[41] The self-proclaimed "new atheist" Harris presents mindfulness, meditation, and enlightenment as "spirituality without religion."[42] Wong and Vinsky point out the racist and colonialist overtones of how white or whitewashed practices are more often labeled "spiritual," while practices in non-white communities are labeled "religious."[43] Wright presents the "validity of core Buddhist ideas" as "true," but only the science and philosophy of meditation and enlightenment, not the "supernatural" parts such as rebirth.[44]

The tendency of the above authors to present Buddhist ideas as philosophy and compatible with or backed by science is a mark of a global Buddhist modernism, found not only in the United States and Europe, but also in Asia.[45] Americans secularizing Buddhism is different than secularizing meditation, or mindfulness.[46]

---

[38] Glenn Wallis, one of the co-founders of Speculative Non-Buddhism, is also credited (along with Batchelor) for creating the first version of the SBA's guiding principles; https://secularbuddhism.org/about/guiding-principles/. Wallis criticizes Batchelor's version of secular Buddhism (Mitchell 2016, 168–169). In other words, Wallis may take issue with being credited for the SBA's principles. This raises larger questions of the trustworthiness, politics, and performative nature of online publications. Turning to trending search terms used on Google to shed light on term popularity over time, the first recorded cases of searches for "secular Buddhism" were found in April 2004, with the highest spike in January 2005. These searches were inputted by internet users in the United Kingdom and the United States. The term "secular Buddhist" was used only by Google users in the United States. The term "agnostic Buddhism" also used only in the United States, with the earliest instance in March 2004 and peaking in September 2004, higher than other terms listed here. The term "atheistic Buddhism" first used in May 2004 and peaked then, and only in the United States. Though their search activity has since peaked, the above terms are still regularly searched by Google users, mainly in the United States.

[39] See Mitchell 2016 and Gleig 2019 for overviews of Buddhist communities in America. See Han 2021 on Asian American Buddhist communities from a range of religious backgrounds.

[40] Flanagan 2011, xiii.

[41] Cited in Cheung 2016, 228.

[42] Harris 2015.

[43] Wong and Vinsky 2009.

[44] Wright 2017, xii.

[45] McMahan 2012, 2017.

[46] See Wilson 2014; Helderman 2019; Hickey 2019.

In 1979, Jon Kabat-Zinn founded Mindfulness-Based Stress Reduction (MBSR), which he trademarked. Kabat-Zinn explained his reasoning for presenting MBSR as secular and distanced from Buddhism in order to make it "accessible to mainstream Americans."[47] Hsu argues: "The very need to secularize mindfulness for mass appeal reveals the American cultural baggage of racial-religious hierarchy upon which Asian Buddhist immigrants were constituted as inferior others who required salvation."[48]

Secular Buddhists want more than a secular mindfulness practice, as they are interested in reading Buddhist texts for insight. Elsewhere, I have written on how Meissner explains that students in his mindfulness courses not only learn to reduce stress, but also develop compassion and care toward each other.[49] Mindfulness is one element of the Noble Eightfold Path, with which secular Buddhists are concerned.

Outside the United States, in a difference context, secular Buddhism may take the form of the Dalai Lama's project of creating a humanist ethics or "secular ethics" that is presented as universal.[50] It may look like Japanese Buddhists engaging in secular and commercial activity for financial support in the face of declining temple membership.[51] Bruntz and Schedneck provide examples of contemporary secularization of Buddhism across Asia by government forces, the tourism industry, and commercial interests that "encroach" on Buddhism, along with instances of Buddhists using tourism as a secular front to proselytize, internationalize, or modernize.[52] The tourist-pilgrim distinction is not a strict binary, but rather a continuous spectrum. Likewise, the secular-religious labels are constructed by agents in local contexts.[53] Arnal and McCutcheon argue for the *arbitrariness* of setting apart X for religious and non-X for secular.[54] Thus, in examining American secular Buddhists, I am arguing for the utility of race in explaining what SBP members chose to keep or discard.

Though the SBP are classified as American by the SBN, Mitchell links the conversation in the United States to ones in the United Kingdom and Australia to suggest that "the secular Buddhist discourse is one of concern across the Anglophone West."[55] The SBP is at once founded by an American and also an online transnational group. The SBP online spaces provide not only one directional transmission of ideas—via podcasts and articles, but also comments and exchange—via Twitter tweets, Facebook posts,

---

[47] Kabat-Zinn 2011, 282.
[48] Hsu 2021, 85.
[49] Cheung 2018, 315. Meissner's stance is that mindfulness can change ethical behavior without explicit ethical instruction, which he deems outside the purview of mindfulness courses. Secular Buddhists are interested in Buddhist ethics, epistemology, and metaphysics—categories that blur the philosophy-religion binary, but only a naturalized metaphysics that fits a particular modern materialist worldview.
[50] Bstan-'dzin-rgya-mtsho 1999, 2011.
[51] Reader 2020.
[52] Bruntz and Schedneck 2020, 10-11.
[53] See Kalmanson 2019 for an example of how Buddhist philosophy is racialized in Meiji-era Japan.
[54] Arnal and McCutcheon 2012.
[55] Mitchell 2016, 164.

and forum discussion threads. Williams points out that the internet is a site of dharmic transmission around the world.[56]

That the SBP and other secular Buddhist organizations are led by mainly white men[57] does not mean that American secular Buddhism is the same as American white Buddhism. McNicholl describes two ends of the spectrum of the "Shades of Whiteness in American Buddhism," in which one extreme employs a color-blind universalization of whiteness as a default, in contrast to the other end that asserts an Aryan alt-right superiority.[58] She did not mention secularity. The chapters in *Buddhism and Whiteness: Critical Reflections* predominately address American white Buddhism, but the term "secular Buddhism" is only used twice in the reference section, listing the title of Batchelor's book, and is not discussed in any detail.[59] In other words, non-secular American Buddhist communities also contend with race. The contribution of this chapter is to make explicit the connection between secularizing and racializing. After this overview of various contexts to provide background for the SBP, I now turn to a closer examination of what they mean by "secular."

The Secular Buddhism Podcast

The creator of the SBP, Rasheta, was raised Mormon, with some Catholic influence, but no longer identifies as religious, even though he still engages with the Church of Jesus Christ of Latter-day Saints community.[60] "With a U.S.-born father and a Mexican-born mother," Rasheta is visibly and audibly white.[61] He has read Batchelor and interviewed Batchelor for his podcast. Rasheta teaches Buddhism, meditation, and mindfulness in the Park City area of Utah.[62] Rasheta's definition of secular Buddhism diminishes differences between Buddhist groups to extract "humanistic values." On the page explaining secular Buddhism, he writes:

> I quickly realized that these [Buddhist] teachings were relevant and useful to anyone, *regardless of their beliefs or non-beliefs*. Secular Buddhism allows for this *ancient wisdom to be added* to whatever background/world view you already possess.

---

[56] Williams 2020.

[57] The SBP credits only Rasheta. The SBA's page of organization leaders lists thirteen people, of which twelve appear white and five self-identify with female pronouns; https://secularbuddhism.org/us/. The SBA credits seven white men for articulating the first version of their guiding principles. The SBN team consists of ten members, who all appear white, and three members who self-identify with female pronouns; https://secularbuddhistnetwork.org/about/.

[58] McNicholl 2020.

[59] Yancy and McRae 2019.

[60] Dehlin 2017; Evans 2020.

[61] Dehlin 2017.

[62] https://www.youtube.com/watch?v=d1oXXnCgJvk (2:40).

Whether you're a Christian, Muslim, Atheist, Hindu, Believer, Non-believer, it doesn't really matter; Secular Buddhism is about helping you to become a better whatever you already are. This website, podcast, and the content I share represents [sic] my own individual understanding of the *essential teachings of Buddhism without any of the supernatural or cultural attachments* that have been added in the past 2500 years.[63]

Elsewhere, Rasheta mentions learning Buddhism from a Tibetan Buddhist teacher, Zen and Pure Land–influenced traditions, but does not make explicit what exactly the cultural attachments are that he is setting aside.[64] Rasheta received lay ministry training from the Bright Dawn Center of Oneness Buddhism established by Koyo Kubose in California that exposed Rasheta to Japanese American Buddhist teachings and practices.[65] Rasheta continues, "my goal was to take the deep philosophical concepts taught in Buddhism and make them accessible and easy to understand for secular-minded, 'westerners' like me."[66] When the SBA and other writers mentioned above are presenting Buddhist philosophy or aspects of Buddhism that are compatible with science, they make explicit what they reject (rebirth, flying bodhisattvas), but Rasheta leaves the "supernatural" undefined and assumes that listeners and readers understand him.

In *Secular Buddhism: Eastern Thought for Western Minds*, Rasheta introduces "key teachings found in Buddhism regarding the nature of reality . . . [in order] to present these teachings in a secular language—not as a religion, but as a way of life, not as something to believe in but as something to notice or observe."[67] Referring to "truth, spirituality, faith," he delineates "[t]he Buddhist or Eastern understanding of these words and concepts . . . from what we Westerners typically understand them to mean."[68] In *No-Nonsense Buddhism for Beginners: Clear Answers to Burning Questions about Core Buddhist Teachings*, he organizes the answers into four sections: (1) the Buddha as a historical figure (i.e., "a teacher, not a god": a dismissal of the Buddha's "supernatural" powers or *siddhi*s mentioned in early Buddhist texts);[69] (2) the core concepts; (3) core teachings; and (4) core practices. The last section mentions chanting and how Buddhist chants are "not like a prayer, because in Buddhism, there's no deity to direct a prayer to."[70] He does not mention rebirth, bodhisattvas, or healing rituals; the title of that work would imply that exclusion indicates these are "supernatural" "nonsense."

---

[63] Rasheta n.d., emphasis mine.
[64] Rasheta 2018.
[65] Kubose 2019, 6. Rasheta continues to recommend this lay ministry training program to others as indicated by the Bright Dawn Center newsletters in which inductees explain that they came to the center after listening to SBP or taking workshops with Rasheta.
[66] Rasheta n.d.
[67] Rasheta 2020, 9.
[68] Ibid., 15.
[69] See Guang 2005.
[70] Rasheta 2018.

According to the book's Amazon.com page, *No-Nonsense Buddhism for Beginners* is on the Best Sellers Rank: #2 in Buddhist History (Books) as of January 2024, substantially higher than every single aforementioned book (including Batchelor's). His podcast episodes have over seven million downloads.[71] Clearly, he has built a large audience, despite not expecting this growth when he first started. In an interview for a marketing and business podcast, he says, "I didn't realize there's a very large community of people who were disaffected with religion, in general, but still want something. And to be able to take a system like Buddhism and be able to approach it without feeling like you're investing into a new ideology, there's a big demand for that."[72] Rasheta used to work as a marking director, has extensive experience in entrepreneurship and starting his own businesses, and is executive director of Foundation for Mindful Living. He is profiting from this labor on secular Buddhism.[73]

Rasheta's emphasis on personal growth and choice of belief and practice places him in the third stance of Casanova's secularity: one that liberates the individual from religion as a condition for human autonomy and human flourishing. The type of individual practice advocated is quiet sitting meditation, not chanting Buddhist spells petitioning bodhisattvas for healing.

There is no indication of engagement in anti-racism or examination of race by Rasheta's SBP. Some secular Buddhists, such as the SBA, has recently been trying to change their role in racial discourse. Meissner admits to "strong push back against Secular Buddhism," examples of which will be detailed when I describe Ackerman's work below.[74] As of February 2021, the SBA home page advertises Bhumisparsha.org's "BIPOC Affinity Care Circle" and the SBN gives links to anti-racist resources for secular Buddhists.[75]

The Secular Buddhist Association

Payne and Kemp (2021) (1) explain the positive (creation of a new Buddhism) and negative (critique of the old Buddhism) discourses of secular Buddhism; (2) analyze the institutionalization of secular Buddhism through virtual communities, academic and informal education, and claims of authority; and (3) apply Bruno Latour's four traces of group formation to the emerging groups. Payne and Kemp give significant attention

---

[71] Evans 2020.

[72] Ibid.

[73] His latest podcast, episode 146, published February 3, 2021, uses the language of branding and personal brand to explain how "non-attachment to our brand may allow us to experience greater freedom to be ourselves"; https://secularbuddhism.com/146-the-freedom-to-be-you/. This shows how he uses marketing and business frames to explain Buddhist doctrine.

[74] Meissner 2020. They are aware that self-identity as secular Buddhist could be problematic, and has led to others claiming this label or identity to do harm. However, the type of harm is not made explicit.

[75] https://secularbuddhistnetwork.org/anti-racist-resources-for-secular-buddhists/.

to Batchelor and the SBA, including the latter's definition of secular Buddhism, one of which deals with race.

The SBA has updated their Guiding Principles and Frequently Asked Questions pages to assert that secular Buddhism differs from other forms of Buddhism in two key ways:

1. We [secular Buddhists] allow questioning of a literal interpretation of rebirth.
   . . .
2. We reject the appropriation of Asian/Diasporic culture/s as part of engagement with the Dhamma.[76]

This is starkly different than earlier versions of these pages (most recently archived on November 27, 2020) that present secular Buddhism as "naturalistic and pragmatic" and argues for *necessarily* suspending acceptance of "supernatural" assertions, such as literal rebirth.[77] The new framing to suggest that secular Buddhists *allow* questioning erases the active rejection of rebirth by "many," including Meissner. This also paints other—that is, Asian—Buddhists as blindly accepting rebirth without any deliberation.[78] See Lin and Yen (2015) for a serious consideration of rebirth that concludes with a reinterpretation of rebirth that aids ethical development.

Though Hawkins of the SBA claims no intention of cultural appropriation, Ackerman responds directly to her assertions and explains precisely how secular Buddhists continue cultural appropriation.[79] Addressing the second delineation that secular Buddhists reject appropriation, Ackerman explains that Hawkins fundamentally misunderstands cultural appropriation as people from one culture merely participating in or sharing practices and ideas from another culture.[80] Rather, appropriation happens when the dominant culture takes from, changes the meaning of, and erases the contributions of a non-dominant or marginalized culture (see Brunk and Young 2009 and Borup 2020 for discussions of appropriating indigenous religions and Buddhism, respectively). In other words, Hawkins's example of a Thai person being able to practice Japanese Zen by secularizing Buddhism misses the point that Thai and Japanese people do not have the same power relationship between them as white people have with Thai or Japanese people. Ackerman also shows how the claim that Dhamma can be separated from culture renders "whiteness, and its attendant cultural assumptions invisible, while

---

[76] Hawkins, n.d.; https://secularbuddhism.org/faq/. This update happened between November 28, 2020, and early February 2021 when I first accessed this version of the page.

[77] Cached version of older versions of the Frequently Asked Questions and Guiding Principles pages available here: http://web.archive.org/web/20201127115554/https://secularbuddhism.org/faq/ and http://web.archive.org/web/20201127113708/https://secularbuddhism.org/about/guiding-principles/.

[78] Ackerman 2020.

[79] Ackerman 2020, 2021. He posted his essay on the Buddhism Reddit page on December 23, 2020, and as of February 2021, the post has 198 comments with 73 up votes. His essay is published on Medium.com as a post, which has 69 claps (indicating praise or agreement, similar to a Facebook "like") as of February 2021. I provide this to indicate a sense of engagement with his ideas.

[80] Ackerman 2021.

marking [Asian] Buddhism as constrained, limited and provincial."[81] Ackerman writes: "This Western, colonial gaze continues to frame living Buddhist traditions as simply collections of moribund rituals and superstitions."[82] He ends with a description of secular Buddhists that applies to the SBA and the SPB:

> Secular Buddhists continue to build institutions, invoking the name of a world religion, of which they claim to be—simultaneously—members and secular detractors of.
>
> This astounding position however, makes perfect sense if one factors in cultural appropriation, driven by materialist, scientific, capitalist concerns and reinforced by orientalism, a form of racial essentialism.[83]

The points about materialist and capitalist concerns apply especially to Rasheta, who profits from the secular framing. Though the SBA is a nonprofit, it still gains social capital from its popularity.

Conclusion

Anālayo devotes one of four sections in his *Superiority Conceit in Buddhist Traditions: A Historical Perspective* to secular Buddhism and focuses mainly on how it is presented by Batchelor. Anālayo concludes that secular Buddhists are appealing because of their superiority conceit, "iconoclastic attitude," and "rebelliousness."[84] He states: "It is simply a form of bondage … for Secular Buddhists to look down on traditional Buddhists as stagnant dogmatists caught up in rituals who lack a proper understanding of the teachings of the historical Buddha."[85]

Secular Buddhists wish to differentiate themselves as following a different Buddhism, and in the process have been creating a distinct Buddhist movement because they claim to see a growing need for one in like-minded voices. Yet, this distancing from "other forms" of Buddhism posits a universalizing of truths that they claim are free from cultural contexts. These truths are at once universal and individualistic. By the latter, I mean an assumption of an autonomous self with the free will and ability to extract the "essential teachings of Buddhism" without the accompanying cultural "baggage" or "attachment" of ritual and "superstition" found in Asian Buddhist traditions. Mitchell's description that this group may merely be loosely connected through an online platform fits secular Buddhists in terms of their autonomy and freedom from more traditional

---

[81] Ackerman 2020, n.p.
[82] Ackerman 2021, n.p.
[83] Ibid.
[84] Anālayo 2021, 137–138.
[85] Anālayo 2021, 139.

relationships of dependency and commitment between laity and monastics. Secular Buddhists focus on concerns with personal growth and private practice. Some form local communities where they gather in person for quiet sitting and discussion. Some participate in community virtually. How do internet platforms or online transmission contribute to this universalizing of or broadcasting to a global Anglophone secular Buddhist community? In light of the increasing freedom to choose and consume whatever suits one's tastes from the religious buffet found in the American online-global-spiritual marketplace,[86] is community even the proper word? Perhaps the SBA and SBP are closer to online performance spaces. Though Meissner and Rasheta have their own local communities of practice, the SBP and SBA are subjected to the instability of online groups and media. Even if both groups disappear or change dramatically in a few years, this analysis still serves as an application of turning to race in examining the use and construction of the secular.

In this chapter, I further the work of scholars on religion and race by examining how American secular Buddhists present themselves. My use of race is concerned not with skin-tone or other phenotypes, but rather as classification in relations of power. I argue that the construction of secularity is entangled with a hierarchical judgment elevating white extraction of "core" Buddhist doctrine and practice that disregards Asian cultural "nonsense" and "superstition." I do not claim that there are no white Buddhists who accept rebirth, nor that all non-white Buddhists accept it (see Anālayo 2018). In other words, I make explicit how noticeable white secular Buddhists are classifying aspects of Asian Buddhist practices and beliefs to their benefit. I examine the publicly available media produced by the SBA and the SBP to explicate the hierarchies of their categorization. There is more work that can be done by ethnographers (see examples in Gleig 2019 and Han 2021) and netnographers to provide a more nuanced picture of secular Buddhists other than organizational leaders or website team members. Future efforts in this area can contribute to understanding the construction of race and religious identity and the transmission of global or transnational religion via online platforms.

References

Ackerman, Yaseen. 2020. "Secular Buddhism and the Superior Whiteness of Being." *Medium*. December 23, 2020. https://yaseenkerman.medium.com/secular-buddhism-and-the-superior-whiteness-of-being-9d1514f83ee0.

Ackerman, Yaseen. 2021. "The Secular Buddhist Movement and Cultural Appropriation: Buddhism, but Better(?)." *Medium*. January 22, 2021. https://yaseenkerman.medium.com/the-secular-buddhist-movement-and-cultural-appropriation-buddhism-but-better-e3692b71550c.

Anālayo, Bhikkhu. 2018. *Rebirth in Early Buddhism and Current Research*. Somerville, MA: Wisdom Publications.

---

[86] See Lofton 2017 on American consumption of religion.

Anālayo, Bhikkhu. 2021. *Superiority Conceit in Buddhist Traditions: A Historical Perspective.* Somerville, MA: Wisdom Publications.

Arnal, William, and Russell T. McCutcheon. 2012. *The Sacred Is the Profane: The Political Nature of "Religion."* New York: Oxford University Press.

Asad, Talal. 2003. *Formations of the Secular: Christianity, Islam, Modernity.* Stanford, CA: Stanford University Press.

Barash, David P. 2014. *Buddhist Biology: Ancient Eastern Wisdom Meets Modern Western Science.* Oxford: Oxford University Press.

Batchelor, Stephen. 1997. *Buddhism without Beliefs: A Contemporary Guide to Awakening.* New York: Riverhead Books.

Batchelor, Stephen. 2010. *Confession of a Buddhist Atheist.* New York: Spiegel & Grau.

Batchelor, Stephen. 2016. *After Buddhism: Rethinking the Dharma for a Secular Age.* New Haven, CT: Yale University Press.

Batchelor, Stephen. 2018. *Secular Buddhism: Imagining the Dharma in an Uncertain World.* New Haven, CT: Yale University Press.

Borup, Jørn. 2020. "Who Owns Religion? Intersectionality, Identity Politics, and Cultural Appropriation in Postglobal Buddhism." *Numen* 67 (2–3): 226–255.

Bruce, Tricia C. 2018. "Cultural Catholics in the United States." In *The Changing Faces of Catholicism: National Processes and Central, Local and Institutional Strategies*, edited by Solange Lefebvre and Alfonso Pérez-Agote, 9:83–106. Annual Review of the Sociology of Religion, Volume 9. Leiden: Brill.

Brunk, Conrad G., and James O. Young. 2009. "'The Skin off Our Backs': Appropriation of Religion." In *The Ethics of Cultural Appropriation*, edited by James O. Young and Conrad G. Brunk, 93–114. London: John Wiley & Sons.

Bruntz, Courtney, and Brooke Schedneck, eds. 2020. *Buddhist Tourism in Asia.* Honolulu: University of Hawai'i Press.

Bstan-'dzin-rgya-mtsho, Dalai Lama XIV. 1999. *Ethic for the New Millennium.* New York: Penguin.

Bstan-'dzin-rgya-mtsho, Dalai Lama XIV. 2011. *Beyond Religion: Ethics for a Whole World.* Boston: Houghton Mifflin Harcourt.

Calhoun, Craig J., Mark Juergensmeyer, and Jonathan VanAntwerpen, eds. 2011. *Rethinking Secularism.* Oxford: Oxford University Press.

Casanova, José. 2011. "The Secular, Secularizations, Secularisms." In *Rethinking Secularism*, edited by Craig J Calhoun, Mark Juergensmeyer, and Jonathan VanAntwerpen, 54–74. Oxford: Oxford University Press.

Cheah, Joseph. 2017. "US Buddhist Traditions." In *The Oxford Handbook of Contemporary Buddhism*, edited by Michael Jerryson, 316–331. Oxford: Oxford University Press.

Cheung, Kin. 2016. "Review of Buddhist Biology: Ancient Eastern Wisdom Meets Modern Western *Science* by David P. Barash." *Religious Studies Review* 42, no. 3: 228.

Cheung, Kin. 2018. "Implicit and Explicit Ethics in Mindfulness-Based Programs in a Broader Context." In *Handbook of Ethical Foundations of Mindfulness*, edited by Steven Stanley, Ronald E. Purser, and Nirbhay N. Singh, Mindfulness in Behavior Health Series 9, 305–321. Cham: Springer International, 2018.

Cheung, Kin. 2022. "Miracle as Natural: A Contemporary Chinese American Religious Healer." In *Miracles: An Exercise in Comparative Philosophy of Religion*, edited by Karen Zwier, David Weddle, and Timothy Knepper. The Comparison Project Series 3, 131–154. Cham: Springer International.

Dehlin, Josh. 2017. "691–692: Noah Rasheta, Founder of SecularBuddhism.Com." Mormon Stories (blog). January 30. https://www.mormonstories.org/podcast/noah-rasheta-secular-buddhism/.

Dempsey, Corinne G. 2008. "Introduction: Divine Proof or Tenacious Embarrassment? The Wonders of the Modern Miraculous." In *Miracle as Modern Conundrum in South Asian Religious Traditions*, edited by Corinne Dempsey and Selva J Raj, 1–19. Albany: State University of New York Press.

Driscoll, Christopher M., and Monica R. Miller. 2018. *Method as Identity: Manufacturing Distance in the Academic Study of Religion*. Lanham, MD: Lexington Books.

Durazzo, Leandro Marques. 2015. "Post-Religional Perspective and Secular Buddhism: Stephen Batchelor and the Post-Metaphysical Religion." *Horizonte* 13, no. 37: 592–604.

Evans, Chemain. 2020. "Who Is Noah Rasheta, Host of the 'Secular Buddhism' Podcast?" *Marketing and Business Stories*, Lemonade Stand Blog (blog). September 8. https://blog.lemonadestand.org/noah-rasheta-paramotoring-master-and-host-of-the-secular-buddhism-podcast/.

Fessenden, Tracy. 2007. *Culture and Redemption Religion, the Secular, and American Literature*. Princeton, NJ: Princeton University Press.

Flanagan, Owen. 2011. *The Bodhisattva's Brain: Buddhism Naturalized*. Cambridge, MA: MIT Press.

Gleig, Ann. 2019. *American Dharma: Buddhism beyond Modernity*. New Haven, CT: Yale University Press.

Goldstein, Eric L. 2008. *The Price of Whiteness: Jews, Race, and American Identity*. Princeton, NJ: Princeton University Press.

Guang, Xing. 2005. *The Concept of the Buddha: Its Evolution from Early Buddhism to the Trikāya Theory*. London and New York: RoutledgeCurzon.

Han, Chenxing. 2021. *Be the Refuge: Raising the Voices of Asian American Buddhists*. Berkeley, CA: North Atlantic Books.

Harris, Sam. 2015. *Waking up: A Guide to Spirituality without Religion*. New York: Simon & Schuster.

Hart, William David. 2017. "Theorizing Race and Religion: Du Bois, Cox, and Fanon." In *Religion, Theory, Critique: Classic and Contemporary Approaches and Methodologies*, edited by Richard King, 563–571. New York: Columbia University Press.

Hawkins, Jennifer. n.d. "Frequently Asked Questions about Secular Buddhism." Secular Buddhist Association. Accessed February 2. https://secularbuddhism.org/faq/.

Helderman, Ira. 2019. *Prescribing the Dharma: Psychotherapists, Buddhist Traditions, and Defining Religion*. Chapel Hill: University of North Carolina Press.

Heng, Geraldine. 2018. *The Invention of Race in the European Middle Ages*. Cambridge: Cambridge University Press.

Hickey, Wakoh Shannon. 2019. *Mind Cure: How Meditation Became Medicine*. New York: Oxford University Press.

Hulsether, Lucia. 2016. "Review of *Race and Secularism in America* edited by Jonathon S. Kahn and Vincent W. Lloyd." *Reading Religion*. August 24. https://readingreligion.org/books/race-and-secularism-america.

Hsu, Funie. 2021. "American Cultural Baggage: The Racialized Secularization of Mindfulness in Schools." In *Secularizing Buddhism: New Perspectives on a Dynamic Tradition*, edited by Richard K. Payne, 79–93. Boulder, CO: Shambhala.

Jakobsen, Janet R, and Ann Pellegrini, eds. 2008. *Secularisms*. Durham, NC: Duke University Press.

Josephson-Storm, Jason Ānanda. 2017. "The Superstition, Secularism, and Religion Trinary: Or Re-Theorizing Secularism." *Method & Theory in the Study of Religion* 30: 1–20. https://doi.org/10.1163/15700682-12341409.

Kabat-Zinn, Jon. 2011. "Some Reflections on the Origins of MBSR, Skillful Means, and the Trouble with Maps." *Contemporary Buddhism* 12, no. 1: 281–306. https://doi.org/10.1080/14639947.2011.564844.

Kalmanson, Leah. 2019. "Whiteness and the Construction of Buddhist Philosophy in Meiji Japan." In *Buddhism and Whiteness: Critical Reflections*, edited by George Yancy and Emily McRae, 61–77. Lanham, MD: Lexington Books.

Karlin, Ashley S. 2013. "Rhetorical Motives for Engagement in Dialogues between Buddhism and Science." PhD dissertation, Carnegie Mellon University.

King, Richard. 1999. *Orientalism and Religion: Post-Colonial Theory, India and "The Mystic East."* London: Routledge.

Klass, Morton. 1995. *Ordered Universes: Approaches to the Anthropology of Religion*. Boulder, CO: Westview.

Kubose, Koyo S. 2019. "Book Review of Noah Ma-Yo Rasheta's *The 5-Minute Mindfulness Journal*." *Oneness: Quarterly Newsletter of Bright Dawn Center of Oneness Buddhism* 23, no. 1: 6. https://brightdawn.org/2019-SPRINGNewsletter.pdf.

Levitt, Laura. 2007. "Impossible Assimilations, American Liberalism, and Jewish Difference: Revisiting Jewish Secularism." *American Quarterly* 59, no. 3: 807–832.

Lin, Chien-Te, and Wei-Hung Yen. 2015. "On the Naturalization of Karma and Rebirth." *International Journal of Dharma Studies* 3, no. 1: 1–18. https://doi.org/10.1186/s40613-015-0016-2.

Lloyd, Vincent W. 2016. Introduction to *Race and Secularism in America*, edited by Jonathon S. Kahn and Vincent W. Lloyd, 1–19. New York and Chichester, West Sussex: Columbia University Press.

Lofton, Kathryn. 2017. *Consuming Religion*. Chicago: University of Chicago Press.

McMahan, David L. 2012. "The Enchanted Secular: Buddhism and the Emergence of Transtraditional 'Spirituality.'" *The Eastern Buddhist* 43, no. 1–2: 205–223.

McMahan, David L. 2017. "Buddhism and Global Secularisms." *Journal of Global Buddhism* 18: 112–128. https://doi.org/10.5281/zenodo.1251845.

McNicholl, Adeana. 2020. "Shades of Whiteness in American Buddhism." Virtual Presentation, American Academy of Religion Annual Meeting, December 1.

McNicholl, Adeana. 2021. "Buddhism and Race in the United States." *Religion Compass* 15, no. 8): 1–13.

Meissner, Ted. 2020. "Ted Meissner Reflects on the Past, Present, and Future of Secular Buddhism." Secular Buddhist Network (blog). June 2, 2020. https://secularbuddhistnetwork.org/ted-meissner-reflects-on-the-past-present-and-future-of-secular-buddhism/.

Meissner, Ted. n.d. "Starting Out." Secular Buddhist Association. Accessed February 2, 2021. https://secularbuddhism.org/starting-out/.

Mitchell, Scott A. 2016. *Buddhism in America: Global Religion, Local Contexts*. New York: Bloomsbury.

Payne, Richard K. 2019. "Religion, Self-Help, Science: Three Economies of Western/Ized Buddhism." *Journal of Global Buddhism* 20: 69–86.

Payne, Richard K., ed. 2021. *Secularizing Buddhism: New Perspectives on a Dynamic Tradition.* Boulder, CO: Shambhala.

Payne, Richard K., and Casey Alexander Kemp. 2021. "Secular Buddhism." In *Oxford Research Encyclopedia of Religion*. Retrieved 12 Jan. 2024, from https://oxfordre.com/religion/view/10.1093/acrefore/9780199340378.001.0001/acrefore-9780199340378-e-630.

Quli, Natalie. 2009. "Western Self, Asian Other: Modernity, Authenticity, and Nostalgia for 'Tradition' in Buddhist Studies." *Journal of Buddhist Ethics* 16 (January): 1–38.

Rabasa, Angel, Cheryl Benard, Lowell H. Schwartz, and Peter Sickle. 2007. "Secular Muslims: A Forgotten Dimension in the War of Ideas." In *Building Moderate Muslim Networks*, edited by Rabasa Angel, Cheryl Benard, Lowell H. Schwartz, and Peter Sickle, 121–138. Santa Monica: RAND Corporation.

Rasheta, Noah. 2016. *Secular Buddhism: Eastern Thought for Western Minds.* San Francisco: Blurb.

Rasheta, Noah. 2018. *No-Nonsense Buddhism for Beginners: Clear Answers to Burning Questions about Core Buddhist Teachings.* Emeryville, CA: Althea Press.

Rasheta, Noah. n.d. "What Is Secular Buddhism." Secular Buddhism. Accessed February 4. https://secularbuddhism.com/what-is-secular-buddhism/.

Reader, Ian. 2020. "Turning to Tourism in a Time of Crisis? Buddhist Temples and Pilgrimage Promotion in Secular(ized) Japan." In *Buddhist Tourism in Asia*, edited by Courtney Brunt and Brooke Schedneck, 161–179. Honolulu: University of Hawai'i Press.

Sered, Susan. 2003. "Afterword: Lexicons of the Supernatural." *Anthropological Forum* 13, no. 2: 213–218.

Stromback, Dennis. 2019. "Nishida's Philosophical Resistance to the Secular-Religion Binary." PhD dissertation, Temple University. http://cdm16002.contentdm.oclc.org/cdm/ref/collection/p245801coll10/id/596338.

Thomas, Jolyon Baraka. 2019. *Faking Liberties: Religious Freedom in American-Occupied Japan.* Chicago: University of Chicago Press.

Williams, Duncan. 2020. "Response to Panel on 'Buddhism and Racism across Asia, Europe and North America.'" Virtual Presentation, American Academy of Religion Annual Meeting, December 1.

Wilson, Jeff. 2014. *Mindful America: The Mutual Transformation of Buddhist Meditation and American Culture.* New York: Oxford University Press.

Wong, Yuk-Lin Renita, and Jana Vinsky. 2009. "Speaking from the Margins: A Critical Reflection on the 'Spiritual-but-Not-Religious' Discourse in Social Work." *The British Journal of Social Work* 39, no. 7: 1343–1359. https://doi.org/10.1093/bjsw/bcn032.

Yancy, George, and Emily McRae, eds. 2019. *Buddhism and Whiteness: Critical Reflections.* Lanham, MD: Lexington Books.

CHAPTER 22

AMERICAN BUDDHISM AND PSYCHOTHERAPY

IRA HELDERMAN

For over two centuries, particular Buddhist communities in the United States have taken a keen interest in the disciplines of psychology and psychotherapy. Religious studies scholars like Richard Hughes Seager (2012) have long distinguished so-called convert US Buddhist communities (communities populated predominantly by individuals of European descent who were not born into Buddhist families) from "traditional" or "heritage" Asian Buddhist immigrant communities by, in part, their tendency to interpret Buddhist doctrine in psychological terms and to concentrate their attention on meditation practices they view as excavating the interior mind. Both practitioners and scholars who observe them, like Seager, have advanced different explanations for how these highly specific Buddhist communities in the United States have approached psychology.[1] But the very language that they use to do so and the metaphors they employ to convey how Buddhists have approached psychotherapy and psychology are often as informative as the interpretations themselves.

Buddhism has been described as having a "dialogue" with psychology (e.g., Safran 2003) or a "relationship" with psychotherapy (e.g., Jennings 2010). Some observers name an "interface of Buddhism and western psychology" (e.g., McMahan 2008, 52) that others believe is "developing" or even "maturing" (e.g., Parsons 2009). Of course, neither "Buddhism" nor "psychology" can actually "encounter" each other; they are

---

[1] Both practitioners and scholars like Seager have frequently referred to the role of psychotherapy in "American Buddhism" which defines "American Buddhism" in such a way that focuses on these convert communities and obscures and marginalizes the Asian Buddhist communities in the United States. It was three decades ago that Charles Prebish (1993) published "Two Buddhisms Reconsidered" challenging this tendency, but the "two Buddhisms" schema often seems to remain. Meanwhile, my focus in this chapter is also largely on predominantly white Buddhist communities. And, while I will attempt to explore the issues that arise as a result, this could itself perpetuate the problematic US scholarly practice of continually shining more light on convert Buddhists (even if in their interactions with Asian Buddhists) rather than Asian and Asian American communities.

conceptual categories that cannot interact—only people can. But the metaphors used by both practitioners and scholars have often become *models* for those practitioners and scholars, not only models for describing and explaining how these Buddhist communities in the United States *have* viewed psychology, but for how they think the psychological and psychotherapeutic *should* be approached.

Over the course of this chapter, we will survey a variety of metaphors-as-models and other rhetorical devices used by both practitioners and scholars to talk about an over 200-year history of how these particular Buddhists in the United States have approached psychology and psychotherapy. We will find that *the way* this history is talked about often expresses differing opinions on whether it is positive or negative to mix or blend the Buddhist with the psychotherapeutic, and how diligently boundary lines between the Buddhist and the psychological should be maintained in defining what it means to be Buddhist. Examining these dynamics grants us greater insight into not only how communities of convert Buddhists have approached psychotherapy and psychology, but also the very concept of a "convert Buddhist" and the ways this category intersects with a multiplicity of racialized and gendered identity markers. All of this is fundamental to understanding the ongoing construction of contemporary Buddhism in the United States and beyond—beginning with the very definition of the word "Buddhism."

Metaphors of Philology

One of the more common metaphors that has been employed to describe how predominantly white Buddhist communities in the United States have approached psychology and psychotherapy is "translation," that the psychotherapeutic is a means for "cultural translation" of Buddhist teachings and writings for new populations in the United States (Cho 2012; Parsons 2010). The Buddhist author and psychotherapist Mark Epstein, for example, has written that "in our culture, it is the language of psychoanalysis . . . that the insights of the Buddha must be presented to Westerners" to make them comprehensible to new communities in the United States. Meanwhile, we cannot overstate the role that *actual* translators—philologists like the Pāli Text Society's Thomas and Caroline Rhys Davids—had in constructing the "Buddhism" that we know today as a fundamentally psychological religion. "Buddhism" is, after all, an English word only introduced into the lexicon in the nineteenth-century colonial era to name a newly "discovered" (Almond 1988) "world religion" (Masuzawa 2005), a monolithic category for a wide swath of disparate traditions stretching across an entire continent of peoples.

And one of the defining qualities of this "Buddhism," according to the first individuals to use the word, was that it was a religion founded on a turn inward—a retreat from sociality and withdrawal into psychological examination of the interior mind—a process often referred to at this time as "self-absorption." Caroline Rhys Davids had been an early student of, importantly, the then nascent academic discipline of what was often called "the new psychology." Readers picking up one of her or her husband's translations and commentaries to learn what Buddhism was exactly would read that it was, at its core, "an ethical psychology" that should be "assigned its due place" (Rhys Davids 1900, xviii) in the history of psychological science.

Asian Buddhist popularizers living under colonial rule sought to ward off both Christian and secular critique by playing to common assumptions that Buddhist teachings anticipated the latest scientific truths such as those found in "the new psychology." When the Sri Lankan/Ceylonese Buddhist leader Anagārika Dharmapāla and the Japanese monk Shaku Sōen appeared at the 1893 World Parliament of Religions in Chicago, they both drew upon the language of the psychological in their efforts to legitimate Buddhist teachings and practices. As a result, when the first psychologists of religion took up translations of Buddhist doctrine, they expected to find a religion of the mind, a proto-psychology. It is not surprising that a scholar like James Bisset Pratt (1934) would proclaim that the so-called historical Buddha, Shakyamuni Siddhārtha Gautama, "was probably the greatest psychologist of his age" (21) with the mind of a "scientific physician" (22).

Taking all of this together, the Asian Buddhist popularizers and early scholars who first introduced "Buddhism" to Europe and the United States were not so much describing a mixing or blending between the Buddhist and the psychological. To them, to be Buddhist *was* to be fundamentally concerned with the psychological. The notion that Buddhism is a uniquely psychological religion is often now simply assumed, passed from generation to generation down to this day.

Rhetoric of Essentiality

Carrying forward these inheritances, the theosophist Henry Steel Olcott believed that Buddhism was a fundamentally psychological religion of scientific rationalism. But, living in colonial Ceylon (Sri Lanka), Olcott regularly came into contact with Buddhist communities who were far more interested in economies of karma then employing empirical research methods for cataloguing forms of cognition and consciousness. Resolving this seeming contradiction, Olcott and others asserted that these communities practiced a "popular religion" that had strayed from the earliest, true original teachings of the Buddha.

One of the primary ways that practitioners and scholars alike have spoken about the Buddhist and the psychotherapeutic is using this language of the "pure" and "essential." Numerous new categories have been constructed to distinguish a purportedly core essence of Buddhism from the popular forms named by Olcott, including "original Buddhism" and "classical Buddhism." Many scholars now view figures like Olcott and his contemporary Paul Carus as reproducing the violence of colonialism, as these European men took it upon themselves to educate Asian communities on the essential truths of their own traditions through the publication of texts like, respectively, *Buddhist Catechism* (1881) and *The Gospel of the Buddha* (1917) (Quli 2009).

Turn-of-the-twentieth-century Buddhist Asian leaders also strived to preserve what they believed to be essential elements of their teachings and practices—elements they similarly presented as psychological in nature—but precisely because they feared they would otherwise not withstand imperial pressures. As described by scholars like Erik Braun (2013), in Burma/Myanmar, for example, the monk Ledi Sayādaw aimed to make certain Buddhist philosophical teachings widely accessible, simplifying meditation methods for probing the interior mind that the populace could preserve even in the face of the cultural erasure threatened by Christian hegemony.

Meanwhile, the Japanese Zen Buddhist thinker D. T. Suzuki had been intrigued by the burgeoning academic field of psychology throughout his life and also used it to promote Zen teachings which he portrayed to be the essence of Buddhist doctrine. Suzuki also argued that "Zen" held unparalleled means for accomplishing one of psychoanalysts' primary aims, to uncover the contents of the unconscious. When he published his *Introduction to Zen Buddhism* in German (1927) (later translated into English [1964]), he wrote the prominent psychotherapist C. G. Jung requesting that he pen the foreword and thus stamp it with the imprimatur of psychotherapy's authority over scientific truths of the interior. Jung believed that Buddhist traditions offered superior practices that were evolutionarily designed for Asian peoples to fulfill a universal human drive toward a self-actualization that he called individuation, the ultimate in psychological health.[2]

Jung was convinced that only psychotherapeutic methods could cull psychological truths from the Buddhist metaphysical beliefs that would otherwise be dispelled as illusions by scientific advancement. Contemporaries like Franz Alexander similarly asserted that, for example, the concept of nirvana, what Alexander called "the central core of Buddhism[,] can be understood in its deepest meaning only in the light of psychoanalytical interpretation" (1931, 138). But where Jung saw health, Alexander believed that Buddhism's "central core" confirmed psychological theories of a pathological narcissistic wish to return to a feminized infantile state of union with the mother.

From these perspectives, the psychological reveals the essence of Buddhist traditions, and the essence of Buddhist traditions is fundamentally psychological. The mixing of the Buddhist and psychotherapeutic is de-emphasized by figures like Suzuki or Jung and, instead, a pure ancient Buddhism is legitimated by analyzing it with the latest high-technology psychological sciences. This tradition may be continued today in the neuropsychological fMRI (functional magnetic resonance imaging) studies of meditation practice by cognitive scientists like Richie Davidson.

---

[2] Importantly, however, Jung strongly believed that Buddhist practice should only be taken by communities of Asian descent, a belief that ultimately stems from what Gomez has called a "psychology of race" (1995, 210) that rests upon the German racial theories of Jung's day. For an explication, start with Gomez 1995, followed by Helderman 2019, 71–72, 271 fn 20, 21.

Discourse of Entropy

In some of the most prominent metaphorical language used to describe this topic, "Buddhism" is said to be swallowed up, subsumed, reduced, and/or transmuted by psychology into something radically different (e.g., Payne 2022), part of what Natalie Quli (2009) has observed is a larger scholarly "discourse dominated by tropes of decay and decline" (14). Narratives of a "psychologization of Buddhism" may seem to be describing metaphorical processes, but what is happening on the ground can often seem anything but metaphorical and has long-standing effects.

Many English-language readers were first introduced to Buddhist traditions through a text like W. Y. Evans-Wentz's publication of *The Tibetan Book of the Dead* (1927), which gives over its very first words to Jung for a preface of "psychological commentary." In writings such as this, Jung can seem to be literally psychologizing or therapizing Buddhist teachings. He explains to readers that, for example, the bodhisattvas and divinities that Buddhist communities propitiate should not be considered literal metaphysical realities, but should themselves be considered metaphors of a sort, as representations of psychological realities. Jung's understanding is then passed on to future generations until communities assume without discussion that a basic Buddhist concept like rebirth should not be taken literally, but is instead best understood psychotherapeutically. Adding additional metaphors of the market into the mix, a scholar like Donald Lopez has argued that Jung treats Buddhist concepts as little more than "raw materials in the factory of his analytic psychology, yielding yet further products of the collective unconscious. These products were then marketed to European and American consumers as components of therapy and exported back to Asian colonials as the best explanation of their own cultures" (Lopez 1998, 59).

Critical-historical narratives of psychologization (like those concerning its cousin, "secularization)" portray a historical "Buddhism" that is mutated by social forces like "therapeutic culture." This rhetoric does not so much conjure mixture as a degradation or erosion of the Buddhist by the psychological.

Metaphors of Geography

As is the case in Lopez's above use of metaphors of importation and exportation, scholars and practitioners have also often spoken of Buddhism as an agent traveler that is transformed when arriving in new geographical locations with new cultural norms. At these times, "Buddhism" becomes a reified entity that travels across the globe, seemingly of its own will, where it "meets" and is transformed by additional entities like "psychology." For instance, when explaining that the seemingly radical changes made to contemporary mindfulness practices are not "without precedent" but instead "reflect significant patterns within Buddhism's Asian history" (2014, 105), Jeff Wilson writes that this "is actually how Buddhism moves into new cultures and becomes domesticated" (2014, 3).

If the United States is defined by a so-called therapeutic culture (rather than, for example, the cultural norms of African American communities in the rural South), then the "psychologization of Buddhism" becomes a component of a larger "Americanization of Buddhism." Buddhist teachers like Harvey Aronson (2004) have argued that US cultural norms foundationally shaped convert Buddhist institutions established through the 1960s and 1970s, such as Philip Kapleau's Rochester Zen Center. These norms led attendees of such centers to have the expectation that, for example, a Buddhist teacher would meet their relational therapeutic needs. The Tibetan Buddhist teacher Chögyam Trungpa believed that the psychotherapeutic was necessary for his Shambhala Buddhist teachings to set down roots in a new home when creating his Naropa Institute in Boulder, Colorado (later to become Naropa University). Convert Buddhists seeking what he called the "brilliant sanity" of enlightenment could attend *maitri* retreats which taught Buddhist practices, such as *metta* compassion cultivation, within a psychotherapeutic group-therapy structure.

And recent leading convert Buddhist figures like Jack Kornfield often speak of geography when they cite their travels abroad in Asia as deeply influential for their development of psychotherapeutically informed communities like the Insight Meditation Center in Barre, Massachusetts. They describe returning to the United States carrying with them the meditation practices which they then adapt for the psychotherapeutic needs of their students.

Discourse of Chronology

At other times, Buddhism is described as an aging or developing agent that is changed more by time than place. The phrases "modern Buddhism" and "Buddhist modernism" were coined to name Buddhisms of a recent era that, as Donald Lopez has written about the first term, is an "international Buddhism that transcends cultural and national boundaries" (2002, xxix). This new form is distinguished then from Buddhisms of the past, from "historical Buddhism" or "traditional Buddhism." "Modern Buddhism" could be more easily mistaken for a purely chronological indicator, while a scholar like David McMahan has stressed that "by 'Buddhist modernism' [he] do[es] not mean all Buddhism that happens to exist in the modern era but, rather, forms of Buddhism that have emerged out of an engagement with the dominant cultural and intellectual forces of modernity" (2008, 6). And, in all cases, the influence of the psychological and psychotherapeutic has been centered as a crucial aspect of these new Buddhist forms.

In the language of some, the passage of time overlays popular dross over original Buddhist teachings, but for others Buddhist traditions begin to disintegrate in an encounter with the new. Donald Lopez employs a Buddhist conception of time, "the decline of the dharma, the process whereby Buddhism slowly disappears in the centuries after the Buddha's passage into nirvana" (Lopez 2008, 211), to express concern that the dominance of contemporary ideologies like the psychotherapeutic threatens the "disappearance of the dharma" (Lopez 2008, 212).

Meanwhile, others believe what we actually witness is a Buddhism made up-to-date by incorporating the new insights of the psychological and psychotherapeutic. Buddhist leaders no less prominent than the Dalai Lama himself have suggested that those aspects of Buddhist doctrine that are disproven by new scientific revelations of, for example, neuropsychology should be revised. Many will simultaneously pick back up on the rhetoric of a Caroline Rhys Davids to assert that the latest high technology only confirms the truth of the Buddha's ancient teachings.

The religion and psychology scholar William Parsons has drawn on metaphors of evolutionary development as a model for understanding these activities. In a periodization schema, he traces an advancement away from the reductive approaches of the turn of the twentieth century wherein the Buddhist is subsumed into the psychological (a phase he calls "1880s–1944 Initial Encounters"). In the mid-twentieth century, he sees Buddhist figures like D. T. Suzuki as engaging in fuller exchanges with psychotherapists like the humanistic Erich Fromm (what he calls "1944–1970 The Zen Files"). Until, in what he calls "1970–2007 The Flowering of Dialogue," contemporary communities are equipped with superior scholarship on Buddhist traditions (improved translations, historical analyses, etc.) and can better blend it with the discoveries of psychology in an egalitarian fashion.

Building in part off Parsons's work, Ann Gleig has more fully explicated how contemporary convert Buddhist communities have, over time, grown past exclusively reductive approaches to psychology. She names these communities to have moved "beyond modernity" and observes that convert Buddhists today often mean to resist the trajectories associated with modernism such as psychologization. Increasingly, she explains, these communities take "dialogical approaches" which "put religion and psychology into conversation with each other as two distinct systems and generally employs psychology as a tool to extend, through dialogue, the aims of religion" (2019, 108). The idea is that dialogical approaches are an improvement that have developed within convert Buddhist communities over time as they have entered a new chronological era, a postmodern age.

Rhetoric of Hybridity

The language of other practitioners and scholars explicitly evokes mixture and the idea that communities are blending the Buddhist and modernist or the psychological and the spiritual. As I have written, "scholars now have a surfeit of phrases to describe [such activities]: eclecticism, religious borrowing, hybridity, ritual mixing, syncretism, combinativeness, bricolage, creolization; the list goes on and on" (Helderman 2019, 232). Many of these terms draw on metaphors to convey the nature of such mixing from the biological roots of the concept of "hybridity" to the day-laborers at work in the notion of "bricolage." And both scholars and the communities they study will at times select which of these terms to utilize in order to express relative degrees of comfort with mixing.

The term "syncretism," for instance, has fallen out of favor with scholars, in part because of its imperialist history wherein it was employed in a racialized fashion to out colonized convert communities for being inauthentically Christian and still harboring commitments to "crypto" versions of their own indigenous traditions (Kane 2020; Robbins 2011; Sered 2008). Predominantly white "convert" Buddhist communities have indeed been described in ways that paint them as crypto-Protestants of a sort. A practitioner like psychoanalyst and Buddhist thinker Jeremy Safran draws on the negative valences of the term "syncretism" that imply mixing is frivolous and superficial when he denigrates "the emergence of New Age spirituality, which involves a syncretic blend of various traditional Eastern and Western spiritualties with pop psychology" (2003, 21). The sociologist of religion Emily Sigalow, on the other hand, has argued that it is actually the category of syncretism that "helps to move beyond the various metaphors—bricolage, salad bar religion, and so on" that she sees as the true culprits for the "dismiss[al] of religious mixing as trifling and/or ephemeral" (2019, 179). The same term, then, can connote a negative approach to mixing to some and, for others, offer a superior way to convey the blending at issue here.

The term "hybridity" is another example that both scholars and practitioners have used with a similar awareness of the legacy of colonial imperialism. The concept was initially advanced by cultural theorist Homi Bhabha (1994) as a specific way to name distinct forms of cultural blending in which, as McMahan has noted, "a colonized people imitate[s] cultural and discursive forms of the dominant power, often turning them in subtle ways against it" (2008, 194). Practitioners like the aforementioned Mark Epstein capitalizes on these understandings when appropriating the word "hybrid" to portray psychology as playing an essential role in the contemporary construction of a new Buddhist form that would be "analogous to that of China two thousand years ago" which, he says, saw "the 'Sinification' of Buddhism, producing a new hybrid—Chinese Buddhism, or Zen." Referencing histories of previous instances of transformations of Buddhist traditions is intended to remind us that, as McMahan has also noted, "through incorporating elements of a new culture and leaving behind irreconcilable ones, traditions inevitably become hybrids of what were already hybrid traditions" (2008, 18–19). And, as Thomas Tweed famously wrote earlier in commentary on US Buddhist identities, Buddhist traditions may be far from unique in this regard; across religious traditions, he reminds us, "there is hybridity all the way down" (1999, 19).

For many members of contemporary predominantly white Buddhist communities, mixing has now become desirable and advantageous. Gleig has named an "embrace of hybridity and bricolage" (2019, 9) as one of the qualities that helps define these communities as "postmodern," that they are "marked by a broad-ranging eclecticism, which included a borrowing of teachings across Buddhist and non-Buddhist lineages" (2019, 277), from feminist and deep ecological thought to practices drawn from 1970s encounter groups and modern US versions of yoga techniques. At the same time, members of these communities have increasingly had their consciousness raised about the power dynamics of "cultural appropriation," wary of when such eclecticism can seem "less religious borrowing than theft" (Helderman 2019, 251). They seek methods of blending the Buddhist and psychotherapeutic in ways that take such concerns into account and do not dilute the Dharma (as they understand it). The terms they use to describe their mixing, and the metaphors those terms are often based on, can reflect this search.

Metaphors of Instrumentality

In another common metaphor, psychology is presented as a set of tools or instruments, as a toolkit or pool of resources that can aid convert Buddhist communities. Buddhist teacher and psychoanalyst Paul Cooper, for example, has observed that his Zen students will at times encounter intrapsychic obstacles that block them from progressing in their meditation practice. He believes that psychoanalytic methods can assist practitioners to work through these blockages and help clear their path toward enlightenment. (Helderman, 2019, 186–187). A number of convert Buddhist leaders, such as Zen teacher and psychologist Grace Schireson, have argued that the psychotherapeutic not only can be helpful to contemporary Buddhist communities, but is a necessity to address abuses of power and sexual violence (Gleig 2019, 86–94). As Gleig has observed, "Schireson believes that Western insights on transference, projection, and defense mechanisms" (2019, 94) are essential tools that can, for example, assist in both better understanding and responding to teachers' violation of students' boundaries.

Scholars have long used similar metaphors as models to describe religious traditions in general and Buddhist traditions in particular. The anthropologist Levi-Strauss (1966) referred to religious actors as "tinkerers" and Wendy Cadge (2004) has described predominantly white Buddhist communities as collecting Buddhist ideas, styles, and practices into "ragbags" and "tool kits" (11–14). This language could convey something of an openness to admixture; the metaphor of the toolkit evokes a collection of religiocultural elements treated as resources that can be grouped together. But items in a toolbox remain differentiated from each other—a hammer is clearly distinct from a screwdriver. Framing psychotherapies as helpful tools accessible to Buddhist communities has the effect of centering those communities as active agents standing in front, or perhaps *above*, psychotherapeutic and Buddhist traditions laid out before them. What often seems to determine whether or not they take up a particular item then is a kind of utilitarianism of "what works" (Helderman 2019, 231–234).

Buddhist teachers such as Barry Magid (2002) have critiqued what he calls the "instrumentalism" of, for example, the contemporary widespread use of therapeutic mindfulness practices (2016 with Rosenbaum) in which Buddhist elements are approached as techniques for stress reduction or performance enhancement. Importantly, therapeutic mindfulness practices have had significant influence on convert Buddhist communities who study texts from authors like Jon Kabat-Zinn or Ruth King. But practitioners like Magid can view an instrumental use of mindfulness practices as a threat to the integrity of an authentic Buddhist path which he believes offers liberation from a "means-to-ends" approach to life.

When it is psychology, on the other hand, that is framed as the tool used for Buddhist aims, it may appear to teachers like Schireson to be a manageable resource. Jeff Wilson has suggested that, while religious traditions in general can be understood as metaphorical toolkits or "rag bags," "Buddhism especially is concerned with the confrontation of suffering" and thus "it might be best to think of the particular category of bag that Buddhism represents as a survival kit" (2009, 842). "All types of Buddhists in America," he continues "tot[e] around Buddhism as survival kits from which they draw the particular medicines and so on that they need to deal with the suffering" of life (2009, 842). In the perspective of some practitioners, then, psychotherapeutic "medicines" can simply be added to these "survival kits."

Metaphors of Relationality

One of the single most prevalent metaphors that both scholars and practitioners have used is that of "dialogue" or "conversation," at times naming this entire subject as "the Buddhism and psychology dialogue." Parsons and Gleig, meanwhile, draw the concept of "dialogical approaches" from the larger field of "religion and psychology" to distinguish specific approaches that they believe avoid reducing the Buddhist to the psychological. Relational metaphors of conversation are used to suggest contact, influence, and exchange, but also differentiation. In interpersonal encounters, we can engage in a give-and-take of ideas to our mutual benefit, but we also still walk away as differentiated people(s).

To a certain extent, a phrase like "the dialogue between Buddhism and psychotherapy" transforms these categories into personified actors as if "Buddhism" could have a conversation with "psychotherapy." But literal public dialogues between actual psychologists and Buddhist practitioners have also had significant influence over US predominantly white Buddhist communities and beyond—from Jung's meeting with the professor and Nishida philosopher Shin'ichi Hisamatsu; to D. T. Suzuki's conference with Erich Fromm's analyst students; to, more recently, the much publicized "Mind-Life Dialogues" between the Dalai Lama and neuropsychologists (among other scientists). Further, communities are often described, or describe themselves, as agents who metaphorically place the Buddhist and the psychotherapeutic "into dialogue." This language summons the image of practitioners, standing outside or, again perhaps better, above Buddhist and psychotherapeutic traditions choosing which elements they believe are compatible and can be put into conversation.

Buddhist authors and psychotherapists like Jeffrey Rubin and Pilar Jennings have at times expanded relational metaphors beyond the terminology of "dialogue." Drawing on relational psychoanalysis and first-wave feminist psychology, they emphasize the need for healthy boundaries in order to maintain an "egalitarian relationship" (Rubin 2003a, 41) in "the relationship between Buddhism and psychoanalysis" (Jennings 2010, viii). Interpersonal interactions, after all, can become unhealthy; we can become enmeshed with the other, feel engulfed by the other, or be disempowered by the other. A healthy relationship "between traditions," as Jennings has written (2010, 233), is one in which neither Buddhist nor psychotherapeutic worldviews are unreflectively privileged, and differences between them are respected and maintained. These differences have even been described as incommensurable—the most oft-discussed being the Buddhist aim to achieve awareness of non-self and the therapists' aim to restore a healthy self. However, the dialogue then often seems to pivot toward resolving or, as the above-mentioned Aronson (2004) has put it, "reconciling" these incommensurables. The most famous of these reconciliations is likely Jack Engler's (1983, 1986, 2003) developmental schema which outlines that one first heals psychological wounds to the self before awakening to the illusion of its permanence.

Rhetoric of Unity

Practitioners have also used language that suggests that, despite appearances, disparate Buddhist and psychological traditions actually share a common essence; that they are, at a fundamental level, the same. Predominantly white Buddhist communities in the 1960s through the mid-1980s were especially apt to hear this sort of rhetoric. Texts from Alan Watts (1961), Ken Wilber (2000), and transpersonal psychotherapists like Abraham Maslow (1964) heralding forms of psychological perennialism were frequent points of reference. These thinkers proclaimed that, not only Buddhist and psychotherapeutic, but a vast multiplicity of traditions were actually all bound together by a unified psychological core. These essential psychic forces were often described as a universal evolutionary development throughout humanity as it activated its full potential.

For thinkers like Ken Wilber, an evolutionary realization of human potential is a positive force sweeping through history that produces both contemporary Buddhist forms and modern psychologies. Critics like Jeremy Carrette and Richard King (2005), however, perceive there to be quite different cultural trajectories at the essence of these activities that are actually quite harmful for society. First, it should be noted that practitioners may compare Buddhism and psychology and find there to be a common unifying essence between them. But typically the "Buddhism" in these comparisons can easily be labeled as already psychologized, a Buddhism that simply assumes that the cycle of rebirth and the wonderous powers of bodhisattvas are only psychological metaphors. Richard Payne (2012) has observed that both this psychologized Buddhism and "psychotherapy . . . arise within the same cultural milieu, and the ease with which Buddhism is interpreted as psychotherapeutic is a consequence of that common background" (234). To critics like Carrette and King, the "common background" Payne names here is defined by pernicious societal movements of, variously, "therapeutic culture," individualism, and capitalism. From this perspective, what is at the core of these activities are larger processes of secularization in which Asian religious traditions are transformed into consumable goods for a "neo-liberal market where spirituality is for sale" (Borup 2016, 41).

Discourse that discerns common unifying factors at work in the way communities relate the Buddhist and the psychotherapeutic may not evoke mixture exactly. In positive interpretations, practitioners instead portray a cutting through the seeming diversity of traditions to discover a unity that resides within all things; while, in negative interpretations, both the Buddhist and psychological are not so much blended together as both equally consumed by (and further consume on behalf of) totalizing social trajectories.

Of course, what may truly unify contemporary convert Buddhist communities are simple demographics—demographics that would plainly explain why these communities could be drawing from a common pool of cultural resources. Convert Buddhist communities have historically been strikingly homogenous, made up of peoples predominantly of European descent, living primarily on the coasts, and largely of middle to upper socioeconomic status. Whether theories of therapeutic culture are applicable to all US communities, they may very well be for this population who have the means to access mental healthcare like talk therapy. Interestingly, though sometimes perceived as a perpetuation of a dominant narcissistic consumer culture, these communities also overwhelmingly tend to see themselves as *counter*-cultural, working to bring liberation from these structures. Identifying as socially and politically liberal progressive, members of these communities report being highly opposed to, for example, the worst ills of late global capitalism and have played key roles in innovating "engaged Buddhist" strands in the United States.

Discourse of Intersectionality

An additional demographic factor that may, indeed, be a unifying element in these activities is that the people engaged in, to use one of the above metaphors, the "dialogue between Buddhism and psychology" are often *themselves* both convert Buddhists and psychotherapists. We have met a striking number of figures (Pilar Jennings, Paul Cooper, etc.) who fall into this category over the course of this chapter. The seminal "Buddhism and psychology" scholar Franz Metcalf has observed that since "the maturing of the Baby Boomers, the dialogue has been overwhelmingly propelled by people who personally combine both traditions." Metcalf stresses that "the impact" of the rise of "the psychologist-as-Dharma-teacher across the board in the spectrum of convert American Buddhism . . . cannot be overstated . . . it is changing the face of Buddhism in America" (2002, 354). As post-"Boomer" generations of convert Buddhist communities continue to come of age (Gen X, millennial, etc.), the sociologist of religion Emily Sigalow recently reaffirmed that "there is a notable concentration of practicing psychologists in the Buddhist convert community" (2019, 183).

In the discourse surrounding the psychologist-as-Dharma-teacher (itself a hyphenated hybrid designation), Buddhist practitioners do not stand outside of Buddhist and psychotherapeutic traditions, mixing them together. Instead, the mixture metaphorically occurs *within their very personhood*. For figures like Grace Schireson and Pilar Jennings, this blending entails working through how they relate their multiple identities, not only as Buddhist teachers and therapists, but also as white cisgender women, feminists, liberal progressives, and so on. Gerald Fogel (2018) has declared it his "personal quest to better integrate my two lives in psychoanalysis and Buddhism" (157), which he suggests requires "serious interdisciplinary dialogue that include[s] examples of actual experiences" (138) from one's own personal practice. Some practitioners may seem, at first glance, to bifurcate their identities as psychologists and leaders of Buddhist communities. Barry Magid, for example, would no more teach meditation to analysands than he would attempt analysis with his meditation students. Others, such as Polly Young-Eisendrath, have raised up a process of "the blending of Buddhism with psychoanalysis [as] form[ing] a core aspect of my development as a human being, writer and psychotherapist throughout most of my adult life" (2013, 52). Figures like Paul Cooper and Joe Loizzo have fully named themselves as embodying both roles, using labels such as "Zen psychoanalysts" and "Buddhist psychotherapists."

The contested concept of "multiple religious belonging" could provide a rubric here if one can simultaneously feel a sense of belonging to Buddhist traditions and to psychotherapies as alternative worldviews (even if they are not classified as religious). So-called JuBus or JewBus are frequently mentioned as an example of multiple religious belonging, and it's worth noting that, as observed by Sigalow (2019), there is tremendous overlap in the Venn diagram between US Buddhist teachers who are also both psychotherapists and born into Ashekanzi Jewish families (many of the psychotherapists discussed above fall in this category, e.g., Epstein, Magid, Kornfield, Aronson, Schireson, etc.). Referring to these communities as "converts," however, may be at odds with the notion of "multiple religious belonging." The language of conversion suggests instead a total transformation from one identity to another. Adopting an entirely new name during ceremonies to mark taking refuge in the Dharma may be meant to mark this complete transformation. Though historically they have predominantly been of European descent, convert Buddhist leaders in the United States such as Pema Chödrön may not immediately be recognizable as such by name alone. Analyses of convert Buddhist communities have at times focused less on the process of conversion from a religion-of-origin, then the adoption of Asian religious traditions by white practitioners. But the presence of JewBus (whose racial status has long been fraught) and so-called Black Buddhists—Buddhists of African American descent—have complicated this paradigm for some decades now.

The increased visibility of Black Buddhists is a sign not only of the growing diversification of contemporary convert Buddhist communities, but a concerted effort to build greater awareness around the racial dynamics of power and privilege in these communities and beyond. And, again, some of the most prominent Black Buddhists, such as Cheryl Giles, also happen to be psychotherapists and psychotherapeutic caregivers. Jan Willis—who has named herself "Black, Baptist, and Buddhist"—have long described their multiple identities in ways that align with theories of "intersectionality." And the more recent work of a figure like Pamela Ayo Yetunde explicitly uses the language of "intersecting identities" (e.g., 2018b, 6). Yetunde's writings directly connect the way she embodies multiple identities and her working through how she relates the Buddhist and the psychotherapeutic. She delves deeply into how she practices the specific form of psychotherapeutic caregiving that is pastoral counseling from a Buddhist location.

The growing fields of Buddhist chaplaincy and spiritual or contemplative care have become one of the main arenas in which practitioners intentionally blend elements from both Buddhist and psychotherapeutic traditions. Buddhist chaplains and contemplative caregivers can increasingly be found in hospitals, prisons, and other institutions, and often seem to speak of using psychotherapeutic practices "instrumentally," as additional tools to aid them in their caregiving. A practitioner like Yetunde, meanwhile, frames her approach to Buddhist pastoral care and counseling as inevitably shaped by her intersecting identities. She has written on the topics of multiple religious belonging and "spiritual fluidity" and identifies not only as a Buddhist, but as a Womanist (a blended identity unto itself that includes US Black church traditions, Protestant feminist theologies, and critical race theories) and as influenced by the Africana NTU (also a mixture of contemporary African diasporic religiosities, especially Bantu-Rwandaise philosophies).

Yetunde draws on Buddhist concepts of interdependence and nondualism to explain how she works through the tensions that arise from belonging to multiple locations. She explicitly positions her own embodiment of a "black lesbian Buddhist hermeneutic [as] giv[ing] rise to a particular gestalt or womanist universalist orientation regarding the inclusion and fusion of multiple perspectives . . . [which] cannot fit neatly into dualistic frameworks" of either one orientation or another. "Interdependence," Yetunde suggests, "from a Buddhist perspective, transcends racial, gender, even human constructs in the ultimate or absolute reality; therefore, more perspectives can be included" (2018, 21–22). Yetunde conceives of interdependence as expressing an enmeshment of religio-racial identities and, beyond this, to include not only one's gender and sexual orientation, but the psychotherapeutic as well.

Conclusion

So-called convert Buddhist communities continue to diversify, significantly expanding the cultural repertoires from which they draw. It is an open question how centrally or overtly the psychotherapeutic will figure within future Buddhist communities in the United States and beyond. Nonetheless, psychologist-as-Dharma-teachers currently retain positions of prominence. And, perhaps most importantly, members of today's convert communities will likely continue to find their way to Buddhist centers and meditation groups in a search for healing from suffering they define as psychological, such as trauma and depression.

How to relate the Buddhist and the psychotherapeutic thus remains a topic of regular discussion among Buddhist practitioners and their scholarly observers. This chapter has demonstrated that *the ways* people talk about this topic, the metaphors or other rhetorical devices they use, convey differing opinions about whether mixing the psychotherapeutic into Buddhist teachings is a positive phenomenon or whether it endangers the integrity of an authentic Buddhist path. Some commentators may tell totalizing tales in which contemporary Buddhist practice has been all but completely "psychologized." But we have heard from practitioners who view themselves as protecting Buddhist doctrine from being reduced within the psychotherapeutic (even if the doctrine they are committed to can itself be perceived as psychologized or therapized).

Practitioners and scholars have also long observed the impossibility of conserving a pure Buddhist doctrine that goes untouched by "outside" influences. No matter how hard they might try, Buddhist communities simply cannot totally sequester themselves from an external world deeply impacted by contemporary psychologies and psychotherapies. Neither can it silence the experience of community members who have felt the injustices of heterosexism, racism, ecological disaster, or, for that matter, disparities in access to mental healthcare. In a practitioner like Yetunde's understanding of personhood, we are all unavoidably a blending of influences from outside of what we conceive as our self. In the future, perhaps the best metaphors, if not models, for representing how communities work through relating the Buddhist to the psychotherapeutic could be found by the many psychologists, anthropologists, and philosophers—not to mention a Buddhist thinker or two—who have all deeply contemplated the relationship between the self and the other. Both Buddhist and postmodern psychoanalytic thinkers have considered how we can be "strangers to ourselves," and how we can awaken to realize that our seemingly bounded embodied selves actually mutually co-arise out of our interactions with the other.

References

Alexander, Franz. 1931. "Buddhistic Training as an Artificial Catatonia (The Biological Meaning of Psychic Occurrences)." *Psychoanalytic Review* 18: 129–145.

Almond, Philip. 1988. *The British Discovery of Buddhism*. Cambridge: Cambridge University Press.

Aronson, Harvey. 2004. *Buddhist Practice on Western Ground: Reconciling Eastern Ideals and Western Psychology*. Boston, MA: Shambala.

Bhabha, Homi. 1994. *The Location of Culture*. London: Routledge.

Borup, Jørn. 2016. "Branding Buddha: Mediatized and Commodified Buddhism as Cultural Narrative." *Journal of Global Buddhism* 17: 41–55.

Cadge, Wendy. 2004. *Heartwood: The First Generation of Theravada Buddhism in America*. Chicago: University of Chicago Press.

Carrette, Jeremy, and Richard King. 2005. *Selling Spirituality: The Silent Takeover of Religion*. New York: Routledge.

Carus, Paul. 1917. *The Gospel of the Buddha Compiled from Ancient Records*. Chicago: Open Court.

Cho, Francisca. 2012. "Buddhism and Science: Translating and Re-Translating Culture." In *Buddhism in the Modern World*, edited by David McMahan, 273–289. Oxon: Routledge.

Cooper, Paul. 2010. *The Zen Impulse and the Psychoanalytic Encounter*. New York: Routledge.

Engler, Jack. 1983. "Vicissitudes of the Self According to Psychoanalysis and Buddhism: A Spectrum Model of Object Relations Development." *Psychoanalysis and Contemporary Thought* 6: 29–72.

Engler, Jack. 1986. "Therapeutic Aims in Psychotherapy and Meditation: Developmental Stages in the Representation of Self." In *Transformations of Consciousness: Conventional and Contemplative Perspectives on Development*, edited by Ken Wilber, Jack Engler, and Dan Brown, 17–51. Boston, MA: Shambhala.

Engler, Jack. 2003. "Being Somebody and Being Nobody: A Reexamination of the Understanding of Self in Psychoanalysis and Buddhism." In *Psychoanalysis and Buddhism: An Unfolding Dialogue*, edited by Jeremy Safran, 35–79. Somerville, MA: Wisdom Publications.

Epstein, Mark. 1995. *Thoughts without a Thinker: Psychotherapy from a Buddhist Perspective*. New York: Basic Books.

Evans-Wentz, W. Y. [1927] 1960. *The Tibetan Book of the Dead or the After-Death Exprinces on the* Bardo *Plane, according to Lama Kazi Dawa-Samdup's English Rendering*. Oxford: Oxford University Press.

Fogel, Gerald I. 2018. "My Lives in Psychoanalysis and Buddhism." In *Freud and the Buddha: The Couch and the Cushion*, edited by Alex Hoffer, 135–169. New York: Routledge.

Giles, Cheryl A., and Willa B. Miller, eds. 2012. *The Arts of Contemplative Care: Pioneering Voices in Buddhist Chaplaincy and Pastoral Work*. Boston, MA: Wisdom Publications.

Gleig, Ann. 2019a. *American Dharma: Buddhism beyond Modernity*. New Haven, CT: Yale University Press.

Gleig, Ann. 2019b. "Undoing Whiteness in American Buddhist Modernism: Critical, Collective, and Contextual Turns." In *Buddhism and Whiteness: Critical Reflections*, edited by George Yancy and Emily McRae, 21–43. Lanham, MD: Lexington Press.

Gomez, Luis. 1995. "Oriental Wisdom and the Cure of Souls: Jung and the Indian East." In *Curators of the Buddha: The Study of Buddhism under Colonialism*, edited by Donald Lopez, 197–251. Chicago: University of Chicago Press.

Helderman, Ira. 2015. "'The Conversion of the Barbarians': Comparison and Psychotherapists' Approaches to Buddhist Traditions in the United States." *Buddhist Studies Review* 32, no. 1: 63–97.

Helderman, Ira. 2016. "Drawing the Boundaries between 'Religion' and 'Secular' in Psychotherapists' Approaches to Buddhist Traditions in the United States." *Journal of the American Academy of Religion* 84, no. 4: 937–972.

Helderman, Ira. 2019. *Prescribing the Dharma: Psychotherapists, Buddhist Traditions, and Defining Religion*. Chapel Hill: University of North Carolina Press.

Jennings, Pilar. 2010. *Mixing Minds: The Power of Relationship in Psychoanalysis and Buddhism*. Boston, MA: Wisdom Publications.

Jung, C. G. [1939] 1969. "Foreword to Suzuki's *Introduction to Zen Buddhism.*" In *Psychology and Religion: West and East.* Volume 11 of *Collected Works of C. G. Jung.* Translated by R. F. C. Hull. Bollingen Series, no. 20. 2nd edition, 538–558. Princeton, NJ: Princeton University Press.

Jung, C. G . [1953] 1969. "Psychological Commentary on *The Tibetan Book of the Dead.*" In *Psychology and Religion: West and East.* Volume 11 of *Collected Works of C. G. Jung.* Translated by R. F. C. Hull. Bollingen Series, no. 20. 2nd edition, 509–529. Princeton, NJ: Princeton University Press.

Kane, Ross. 2020. *Syncretism and Christian Tradition: Race and Revelation in the Study of Religious Mixture.* New York: Oxford University Press.

King, Ruth. 2018. *Mindful of Race: Transforming Racism from the Inside Out.* Boulder, CO: Sounds True.

Kornfield, Jack. 2008. *The Wise Heart: A Guide to the Universal Teachings of Buddhist Psychology.* New York: Bantam Books.

Lévi-Strauss, Claude. 1966. *The Savage Mind.* Chicago: University of Chicago Press.

Loizzo, Joseph. 2012. *Sustainable Happiness: The Mind Science of Well-Being, Altruism, and Inspiration.* New York: Routledge.

Lopez, Donald, ed. 1995. *Curators of the Buddha: The Study of Buddhism under Colonialism.* Chicago: University of Chicago Press.

Lopez, Donald. 1998. *Prisoners of Shangri-La: Tibetan Buddhism and the West.* Chicago: University of Chicago Press.

Lopez, Donald, ed. 2002. *A Modern Buddhist Bible: Essential Readings from East and West.* Boston, MA: Beacon Press.

Lopez, Donald. 2008. *Buddhism and Science: A Guide for the Perplexed.* Chicago: University of Chicago Press.

Lopez, Donald. 2012. *The Scientific Buddha: His Short and Happy Life.* New Haven, CT: Yale University Press.

Magid, Barry. 2002. *Ordinary Mind: Exploring the Common Ground of Zen and Psychoanalysis.* Somerville, MA: Wisdom Publications.

Maslow, Abraham H. 1964. *Religions, Values, and Peak-Experiences.* Columbus: Ohio State University Press.

Masuzawa, Tomoko. 2005. *The Invention of World Religions, or, How European Universalism Was Preserved in the Language of Pluralism.* Chicago: University of Chicago Press.

Mathers, Dale, Melvin Miller, and Osamu Ando. 2009. *Self and No-Self: Continuing the Dialogue between Buddhism and Psychotherapy.* Oxford: Routledge.

McMahan, David. 2008. *The Making of Buddhist Modernism.* Oxford: Oxford University Press.

Metcalf, Franz Aubrey. 2001. "Buddhism and Psychology: A Perspective at the Millennium." *Religious Studies Review* 27, no. 4: 349–354.

Metcalf, Franz Aubrey . 2002. "The Encounter of Buddhism and Psychology." In *Westward Dharma Buddhism beyond Asia,* edited by Charles Prebish and Martin Baumann, 348–365. Berkeley: University of California Press.

Muramoto, Shoji, Polly Young-Eisendrath, and Jan Middledorf, trans. 2002. "The Jung-Hisamatsu Conversation. Translated from Aniela Ja e's Original German Protocol." In *Awakening and Insight: Zen Buddhism and Psychotherapy,* edited by Polly Young-Eisendrath and Shoji Muramoto, 105–119. East Sussex, UK: Brunner-Routledge.

Olcott, Henry Steel. [1881] 1915. *The Buddhist Catechism.* 44th edition. Madras, India: Theosophical Publishing House.

Parsons, William. 2009. "Psychoanalysis Meets Buddhism: The Development of a Dialogue." In *Changing the Scientific Study of Religion: Beyond Freud?*, edited by Jacob Belzen, 179–209. New York: Springer.

Parsons, William. 2010. "Of Chariots, Navels, and Winged Steeds: The Dialogue between Psychoanalysis and Buddhism." In *Disciplining Freud on Religion: Perspectives from the Humanities and Social Sciences*, edited by Gregory Kaplan and William Parsons, 107–146. Lanham, MD: Lexington Books.

Payne, Richard K. 2006. "Individuation and Awakening: Romantic Narrative and the Psychological Interpretation of Buddhism." In *Buddhism and Psychotherapy across Cultures*, edited by Mark Unno, 31–53. Somerville, MA: Wisdom Publications.

Payne, Richard K. 2012. "Buddhism and the Powers of the Mind." In *Buddhism in the Modern World*, edited by David McMahan, 233–257. Oxon: Routledge.

Payne, Richard K. 2022. "The Buddhism and Psychology Discourse: A Hermeneutic." *Journal of Global Buddhism* 22, no. 2: 399–420.

Pratt, James Bissett. 1934. "Buddhism and Scientific Thinking." *The Journal of Religion* 14, no. 1: 13–24.

Charles S. Prebish. 1993. "Two Buddhisms Reconsidered." *Buddhist Studies Review* 10: 187–206.

Quli, Natalie E. 2009. "Western Self, Asian Other: Modernity, Authenticity, and Nostalgia for 'Tradition' in Buddhist Studies." *Journal of Buddhist Ethics* 16: 1–38.

Rhys Davids, Caroline, trans. 1900. *Dhammasaṅgaṇi: A Buddhist Manual of Psychological Ethics of the Fourth Century B.C.* London: Royal Asiatic Society.

Robbins, Joel. 2011. "Crypto-Religion and the Study of Cultural Mixtures: Anthropology, Value, and the Nature of Syncretism." *Journal of the American Academy of Religion* 79, no. 2: 408–424.

Rosenbaum, Robert Meikyo, and Barry Magid, eds. 2016. *What's Wrong with Mindfulness (and What Isn't): Zen Perspectives*. New York: Simon and Schuster.

Rubin, Jeffrey. 1996. *Psychotherapy and Buddhism: Toward an Integration*. New York: Plenum Press.

Rubin, Jeffrey. 2003a. "Close Encounters of a New Kind: Toward an Integration of Psychoanalysis and Buddhism." In *Encountering Buddhism: Western Psychology and Buddhist Teachings*, edited by Seth Robert Segall, 31–61. Albany: State University of New York Press.

Safran, Jeremy, ed. 2003b. *Psychoanalysis and Buddhism: An Unfolding Dialogue*. Somerville, MA: Wisdom Publications.

Safran, Jeremy. 2003b. "Psychoanalysis and Buddhism as Cultural Institutions." In Safran, *Psychoanalysis and Buddhism: An Unfolding Dialogue*, 1–35. Somerville, MA: Wisdom Publications.

Seager, Richard Hughes. 2012. *Buddhism in America*. New York: Columbia University Press, 2012.

Sered, Susan. 2008. "Taxonomies of Ritual Mixing." *History of Religions* 47, no. 2/3: 221–238.

Sigalow, Emily. 2016. "Towards a Sociological Framework of Religious Syncretism in the United States." *Journal of the American Academy of Religion* 84, no. 4: 1029–1055.

Sigalow, Emily. 2019. *American JewBu: Jews, Buddhists, and Religious Change*. Princeton, NJ: Princeton University Press.

Snodgrass, Judith. 2007. "Defining Modern Buddhism: Mr. and Mrs. Rhys Davids and the Pali Text Society." *Comparative Studies of South Asia Africa and the Middle East* 27, no, 1: 186–202.

Suzuki, D. T. [1927] 1964. *Introduction to Zen Buddhism*. New York: Grove Press.

Trungpa, Chögyam. 2005. *The Sanity We Are Born With: A Buddhist Approach to Psychology*. Compiled and edited by Carolyn Rose Gilman. Boston, MA: Shambhala.

Tweed, Thomas. 1999. "Night-Stand Buddhists and Other Creatures: Sympathizers, Adherents, and the Study of Religion." In *American Buddhism: Methods and Findings in Recent Scholarship*, edited by Duncan Ryūken Williams and Christopher S. Queen, 71–90. Surrey, UK: Curzon Press.

Watts, Alan. [1936] 1958. *The Spirit of Zen: A Way of Life, Work, and Art in the Far East*. New York: Grove Press.

Watts, Alan. 1961. *Psychotherapy: East and West*. New York: Pantheon Books.

Wilber, Ken. 2000. *Integral Psychology: Consciousness, Spirit, Psychology, Therapy*. Boston: Shambhala.

Willis, Jan. 2001. *Dreaming Me: From Baptist to Buddhist, One Woman's Spiritual Journey*. New York: Riverhead Books.

Willis, Jan. 2008. *Dreaming Me: Black, Baptist, and Buddhist: One Woman's Spiritual Journey*. Somerville, MA: Wisdom Publications.

Wilson, Jeff. 2009. "Mapping the American Buddhist Terrain: Paths Taken and Possible Itineraries," *Religion Compass* 3, no. 5: 836–846.

Wilson, Jeff. 2014. *Mindful America: The Mutual Transformation of Buddhist Meditation and American Culture*. New York: Oxford University Press.

Yetunde, Pamela Ayo. 2018a. *Object Relations, Buddhism, and Relationality in Womanist Practical Theology*. London: Palgrave McMillan.

Yetunde, Pamela Ayo. 2018b. "Buddhist Non-self as Relational Interdependence: An NTU-Inspired African American Lesbian Interpretation?" *Buddhist-Christian Studies* 38: 343–362.

Yetunde, Pamela Ayo. 2019. "*When One Religion Isn't Enough: The Lives of Spiritually Fluid People* Book Review." *Journal of Pastoral Theology* 29, no. 1: 56–59.

Yetunde, Pamela Ayo, and Cheryl A. Giles, eds. 2020. *Black and Buddhist: What Buddhism Can Teach Us about Race, Resilience, Transformation, and Freedom*. Boston, MA: Shambala.

Young-Eisendrath, Polly. 2013. "The Role of No-Self in Creativity: Expanding Our Sense of Interdependent Engagement." In *Crossroads in Psychoanalysis, Buddhism, and Mindfulness: The Word and the Breath*, edited by Anthony Molino, with Roberto Carnevali and Alessandro Giannandrea, 51–63. Lanham, MD: Rowman & Littlefield.

Young-Eisendrath, Polly, and Shoji Muramoto, eds. 2002. *Awakening and Insight: Zen Buddhism and Psychotherapy*. East Sussex, UK: Brunner-Routledge.

CHAPTER 23

AMERICAN BUDDHISM AND TECHNOLOGY

GREGORY PRICE GRIEVE AND DANIEL VEIDLINGER

INTRODUCTION

WRITING about American Buddhism and technology is a bit like recording the behavior of clouds (Peters 1999). You cannot miss them when you look up, the sky is filled with a dizzying array—cirrus, cumulus, nimbus, lenticular. You can even feel their rain on your face. In a similar vein, look around America today, and you see an entire spectrum of technologies that have nourished the blossoming of Buddhisms. But, like flowing clouds, the shape of both the technologies and of Buddhism itself has been changing so quickly that it is difficult to pinpoint exactly the nature of each at any given moment, and their complicated interaction has been mutually transformative over the flowing course of time.

Take, for instance, the video installation *TV Buddha* (1974) by Nam June Paik (1932–2006), the Korean American artist, who was a lifelong Buddhist and is considered to be the founder of video art (Smith 2006). The piece consists of a Buddha statue placed in front of a video camera that projects the image on a TV screen and is considered by many "to unite Eastern religion and Western technology" (Decker-Phillips 1998, 74). What does *TV Buddha* reveal about America, about Buddhism, and about media technologies? Television has proven to be a profoundly American medium (Margolies 1969), but to see the Buddha shining forth from the screen is a jarring mix of Eastern and American imagery. The Buddha himself appears to be staring at the screen in serene contentment, indicating his acceptance of this new mélange. Perhaps his smile belies the enjoyment born from seeing himself on screen, the aura of egolessness be damned. Surely, many of the Hollywood elite who have embraced what often seems the latest faddish Buddhist ideas feel this same satisfaction pulling at the very egos they hope to relinquish through meditation. Paik saw himself operating like a Zen master who tries to shock viewers into a new understanding, and in a way this work acts as a *kōan*, a riddle-like statement used in Zen Buddhism to produce a "great doubt," that directs us to think about the sometimes surprising ways in which technology has contributed to the presence of the Buddha and his Dharma. The Buddhist idea of *pratītya samutpāda,* often translated as mutual causality or interdependent co-arising, stands as a good device to illustrate the kind of complex network of relationships involved here. Rather than a strict one-to-one causal relationship, there is a dynamic many-to-many relationship in which the various aspects of technology become deeply interwoven with the development of the religion itself along several dimensions.

This chapter, then, will consider Buddhism and technology from a variety of perspectives, including the influence of technology on the spread of the religion, the influence of technology on the ideas of the religion itself, and the influence of the religion on local technologies. We will look at the earliest connections between Buddhism and technology in America, for there is a sense in which Buddhism owes the ultimate debt to technology, because the Dharma could never have arrived on these shores if it had not been brought by boats utilizing the latest technologies of their day to cross the great oceans of the world. We will then examine the roles played by telegraphy and radio in setting the stage for the burgeoning of Buddhism in America. Film and television likewise helped to promote and popularize some Buddhist ideas, but were also guilty of contributing to the stereotype of the wise man of the East, which has shaped the perception of Buddhism for many in America. Psychedelic drugs played a pivotal role in opening the minds of many in the 1960s to the new ideas rolling in from Asia, but the nascent computing industry, along with new understandings of systems theory and cybernetics, perhaps helped most of all to usher in a tidal wave of interest in Buddhism that continues to grow.

Buddhism has taken full advantage of the affordances of digital technologies, with cyber-sanghas cropping up every day, hundreds of phone apps with some connection to Buddhism or meditation being developed, and discussions on social media of Buddhist-related topics growing exponentially. Of course, through it all, there has also been a strong countervailing force coming from those who saw Buddhism as being negatively impacted by technological developments. These people have sometimes tried to hold Buddhism up as a way of living that eschews modern technology, as an escape from the fast-paced yet ultimately empty and meaningless flow of "liquid" modern life, and yet others, as exemplified by Peter Hershock (1999) and David Loy (2002, 2007), have tried to protect the Buddha's legacy from being tainted by entanglement with technology. As the technologies have become more advanced and pervasive, some of the critiques have become ever shriller, deriding, for example, computer-mediated forms of what can be called "digital Buddhism" as inauthentic, trivial, faddish, and even toxic (Grieve 2016). However, toward the last part of the twentieth century, many American Buddhists saw their practice as a strategic way to counter the menace of technology.

Early Technology and Buddhism in America

The first glimmerings of the Dharma came to America through the new, streamlined clipper ships that were plying their trade on the oceans of the world, traveling to India and other parts of Asia in the early nineteenth century, often in search of opium. Starting in 1833, Yankee clipper ships began to bring ice to India, and even Henry David Thoreau talks about ice being taken from Walden pond and mixing with the water of the Ganges (Thoreau 1899, 312–313). These oceangoing vessels made it possible for goods and ideas to be traded between Asia and America and helped to bring books about Hinduism and Buddhism to libraries along the East Coast.

Shortly thereafter, in 1852, in San Francisco, the first Chinese began to arrive in California by steamer ships, with the first Chinese temple being built in San Francisco by the Sze Yap Company in 1853, dedicated to Amitābha. In 1867 Chinese workers began to lay the track for the Central Pacific Railroad. Railway technology thus became an unwitting catalyst for the development of heritage Buddhist communities on American shores and drew many thousands of Chinese over the years (Miller 1969). Steam technology also facilitated contact with Japan, another crucial source of Buddhism that was to have a long and fraught relationship with the United States over the ensuing century. In 1854 Commodore Perry arrived in Japan with fully armed paddle-wheeled steamships, and in 1868, year one of the Meiji era, 149 Japanese went to work on Hawaiian sugar plantations, thus laying the foundations of another Buddhist community from Asia (Tanabe and Tanabe 2012). The very earliest developments in the history of Buddhism in America, therefore, moved in lockstep with developments in technology that made them all possible.

Telegraphy, Radio, Spiritualists, and Rationalists

The first formal convert to Buddhism in America took the three refuges in 1893 during the World's Parliament of Religions in Chicago (Tweed 2000, 39), an event held in conjunction with the World Columbian Exposition (Barrows 1893) that was organized to celebrate modern technological wonders such as electricity and railways. Many of the early Buddhist adherents and sympathizers around this period were introduced to Buddhism and other alternative ideas through Spiritualism, which Jeremy Stolow (2009) has shown to be associated with the birth of telegraphy and later radio technology. Stolow argues that the idea that the spirits of the dead can be contacted in seances arose out of growing familiarity with the telegraph and the possibility of communicating messages over great distances without seemingly anything visible connecting the message sender with the recipient. Spiritualists were among the pioneering communities that used the telegraph in their communication with each other around the globe, and they "developed a rich vocabulary for making sense of these ascendant technologies and a repertoire of ritual activities designed specifically to accommodate the performative demands they elicited in various contexts of private and public life" (Stolow 2009, 82). Regular familiarity with the telegraph, according to Stolow, made people more receptive to the ideas of Spiritualism, and this flowed over into an interest in Eastern spiritual traditions, in particular Buddhism. Many of the early Americans who were interested in Buddhism were part of this community and may very well have been influenced by the ideas cited by Stolow.[1] As radio replaced telegraphy, the idea of disembodied spirits became even more popular, marking the height of Spiritualism in America.

Many Americans around the turn of the twentieth century whom Thomas Tweed classifies as "rationalists" were also interested in Buddhism, and particularly Theravāda, because they saw in it a strong ethical system in conformity with the democratic and tolerant ethos of the modern West as well as with evolutionary perspectives of science, and they felt that it did not demand that one abandon the guidance of reason. It could exist in harmony with science and called for individuals to take responsibility for their actions (Tweed 2000, 80). Interest in Buddhism during this period emerged in the context of major changes in many spheres of life, most of which were spurred on by technological advances, especially in transportation with the advent of the railroad, and communication with the development of the telegraph and the explosion of newspapers, magazines, and journals.

In all, there can be no question as to the deep and abiding influence of technological developments on many Americans who had an early interest in Buddhism. Not only did these developments allow Americans to come into contact with Buddhist ideas at all, but the rapidly changing world around them caused them to look beyond the now faltering truths of Western religions to ones that they felt accorded more naturally with the new scientific understandings of the world and the shrinking place of an omnipotent God controlling the fate of humanity (Lopez 2008). Much later, mid-century counterculture figure Gary Snyder would see radio technology as a means of poetic liberation. In his "Look Out's Journal," from his ecological *Earth House Hold: Technical Notes & Queries to Fellow Dharma Revolutionaries*, Snyder collects reports of radio

---

[1] Various "Spiritualist" ways of thinking permeated the early Buddhist pioneers in America. The Theosophical Society, established in 1875, was a veritable clearinghouse of ideas connected with Hindusim, Buddhism, and Spiritualism, all mashed together into an eclectic mix of esoteric ideas. Likewise, the 1888 prospectus for the first American Buddhist magazine published in English, *The Buddhist Ray*, shows that editor Herman Vetterling, also known as Philangi Dasa, had a somewhat eclectic view of Buddhism: "*The Buddhist Ray* will be devoted to the divulgation of the philosophy and life of Buddhism: of Karma, of Transmigration, and of Mystic Communion with the Divine in Humanity. . . . It will set forth the teaching imparted by the Mongolian Buddhists to Emanuel Swedenborg, and published by him in his mystic writings" (quoted in Tweed 2000, 60) (https://tricycle.org/magazine/original-ray/). List of all of the issues: http://iapsop.com/archive/materials/buddhist_ray/index.html.

transmissions between fellow Zen devotees Jack Kerouac and Philip Whalen during two summers (Snyder 1957; Malaby 2009; Williams 2011). While using the airwaves to communicate with interlocutors who were very much embodied, these seminal figures in the explosion of Buddhism in America were able to maintain a robust discussion of the Dharma through this technology.

BUDDHISM IN FILM AND TELEVISION

The very first film about Buddhism to be screened in the United States was the joint German-Indian production *Light of Asia* (*Die Leuchte Asiens*) (Franz Osten and Himansu Rai 1925), based on the popular poem from 1879 of that same name by Sir Edwin Arnold (1879). John Whalen-Bridge, in his collection on Buddhism and cinema, points out that although explicitly Buddhist mainstream films were not made in America for some time, the "Asian wise man with no attachment" has appeared as a character on the screen over the years (2014, 1). For instance, the Buddhist ideal of a self-possessed yet powerful master provided inspiration for the Jedi Knights in the *StarWars* series (Lucas 1977). Themes such as rebirth, karma, the mind-made nature of reality, and the quest for self-mastery have appeared in American films such as *Groundhog Day* and *The Matrix*. Furthermore, since 1989, when the Dalai Lama was awarded the Nobel Peace Prize, big-budget films such as *Kundun* (De fina et al. 1998), *Seven Years in Tibet* (Annaud 2013), and *The Little Buddha* (Bertolucci 1993) have explicitly dealt with Buddhist themes. Whalen-Bridge avers that "Buddhist film is important because it is a marker of the impact of Asian philosophy and religion on American culture" (2014, 3). Film might not have been the first way that Americans came into contact with Buddhism, but it has certainly helped to normalize it as a part of mainstream American culture, and with megastars such as Keanu Reeves playing the Buddha, it solidified this religion in the American consciousness.

While Buddhism has influenced film in many ways, it has not featured prominently in American television, although it has made an appearance in select contexts. One of the earlier and more popular shows with a Buddhist as the main character was *Kung Fu* (Spielman, Thorpe, and Miller) that ran from 1972 to 1975 and featured a Shaolin monk who was travelling through the Old West in search of his half-brother. In *The Simpsons* (Groening et al. 2007), Season 13, Episode 6, Lisa becomes disillusioned with the materialism of her local Christian church and actually converts to Buddhism after meeting actor Richard Gere at the Springfield Buddhist Temple. Gere gives her a pamphlet on the Four Noble Truths and inspires her by explaining that Buddhism holds all things to be impermanent (https://www.youtube.com/watch?v=8QlR626sQ7A, accessed August 13, 2020). There are also some casual references to Buddhism in *King of the Hill*, often in connection to the neighbors who are from Laos. Perhaps the most sustained engagement with Buddhism is the long-running animated series *Avatar: The Last Airbender* that began airing on Nickelodeon in 2005 and quickly gained a cult following. The show focuses on four nations that have control over the various elements, and engages with topics such as reincarnation and the power of nonviolence, and contains many references to Asian culture generally and Tibet in particular (https://tricycle.org/trikedaily/avatar-the-last-airbender/). All of this is not presented without injecting American values and perspectives, some of which are potentially damaging. Jane Iwamura has commented on "virtual orientalism," which she defines as a sort of cultural stereotyping through visual media that makes the figure of the oriental monk not only consumable but also immediate and pervasive. Iwamura traces the origins of the oriental monk figure in American popular culture and media, highlighting its complexity, inconsistencies, and modern manifestations.

BUDDHISM, PSYCHEDELICS, AND TECHNOLOGIES OF THE MIND

Besides the transportation and communication technologies already discussed, pharmaceutic technologies of the mind have also played an outsized role in the story of convert Buddhism in America. Some scholars argue that American Buddhism and experimenting with psychedelics share a common goal: the liberation of the mind (Badiner and Grey 2015). This is particularly true of the 1950s and 1960s countercultural practitioners, the Beats and the hippies. For instance, LSD, according to American Buddhist teacher Jack Kornfield, "prepares the mind for Buddhism." Psychologist Ray Jordan wrote that "LSD might be a useful aid both to the realization of *prajna* and to the development of meditational practice" (Fields 1992, 250). Although he did feel that unaided meditation was a better way to seek the highest states of Buddhist experience, he also acknowledged that psychedelic experiences may have revealed to persons the everyday presentness of the Pure Buddha Land. Other scholars, drawing on scriptural sources, botany, pharmacology, and religious iconography, have explored the use of psychedelic plants within the Buddhist tradition (Crowley and Shulgin 2019). Alan Watts also noted that LSD could help foster "what, in Buddhist terms, would be called an experience of the world as *dharmadhatu*, seeing all things and events, however splendid or deplorable from relative points of view, as aspects of symphonic harmony, which, in its totality, is gorgeous beyond belief" (1971, 136). In the mid-1960s, Robert Aitken noticed that many people who were coming through his Dojo in Maui were heavily involved in the consumption of psychedelic drugs such as LSD, mescaline, or psilocybin, and that they sought to achieve heightened spiritual experiences through the use of these substances. After World War II, once Japan was no longer seen as a threat, the notion that Eastern mysticism defied "the System" became a foundation stone for the many in the 1960s counterculture who perceived Zen as a politics of consciousness—as a means, like psychedelics, to expand one's mind and thereby reach one's authentic human potential.

Cybernetics

Closely tied to psychedelics is cybernetics (Grieve 2016, 103–129). The internet and other cybernetic technologies differ from telecommunications that have a sender and a receiver, because cyberspace occurs in an imagined virtual social environment, in that space between screens, and as such is often thought of as a fantastic place of the imagination that transcends reality (Nelson 1974). As technological fantasy, cyberspace emerged in the late twentieth century from the Cold War marriage of computers and the internet. American mathematician Norbert Wiener (1894–1964) was working on missile-tracking technology when he developed the idea of cybernetics in the late 1940s as a method for improving the accuracy of antiaircraft guns.[2] The problem was that airplanes were much too fast and unproductively wiggly. Only by taking into account the voluntary activity of the pilot as a feedback loop could equations predict an airplane's flight. Wiener argued that cybernetics differed from hard empirical sciences because the focus was not material form, but rather networks made up of users and machines. Eventually, cybernetics became more than just a way to describe systems, but an ontological model of reality itself. By countering the disruptive forces of noise and entropy, Wiener saw communication as the organizing force that created the life of individuals and societies. Wiener himself began, through his studies of cybernetics, to take on a remarkably Buddhist perspective. He famously wrote in *The Human Use of Human Beings*, "We are but whirlpools in a river of ever-flowing water. We are not stuff that abides, but patterns that perpetuate themselves" (1950, 96). The echo of these early Buddhist musings from one of the founders of what became computing technology can be heard down the ages as Buddhism and digital technologies of all kinds have established a close relationship.

Stewart Brand, the founder of the *Whole Earth Catalog* that defined the back-to-the-land movement of the 1960s and 1970s, was among a cadre of idealistic youths influenced by the emerging field of cybernetics who believed that an authentic form of living could be fostered if communications and computer technologies could be harnessed to create collaborative networks. These ideas were highly influential for Brand, as well as many of the most inventive mid-century American artists such as John Cage and Robert

---

[2] As a field, cybernetics falls into three stages. The first, from 1945 to 1960, was stimulated by a series of conferences sponsored by the Josiah Macy Foundation, which laid the foundation for the field by solidifying the concept that both humans and machines could be understood as information-processing systems (see Steve Heims, *The Cybernetics Group* [Cambridge, MA: MIT Press, 1991]). The second stage began in 1960 with the publication of Heinz von Foerster's *Observing Systems* (Seaside, CA: Intersystems Publications, 1981), which understood cybernetics systems not only as self-organizing, but as autopoitic, or reflexively self-making. The third stage began in 1972, when Myron Krueger coined the term "artificial reality" to describe the third Videoplace, which used projectors, video cameras, and other hardware to place users in an interactive computer environment (Krueger, *Artificial Reality 2* [Addison-Wesley Professional, 1991]; *Myron Krueger—Videoplace, Responsive Environment, 1972–1990s*, YouTube video, 7:35, posted by "MediaArtTube," https://www.youtube.com/watch?v=dmmxVA5xhuo [accessed November 6, 2015]).

Rauschenberg who incorporated them into their works (Bernstein 1986; Larson 2013). Cage in particular embraced Buddhism in many of his writings, asserting that nature was "an interrelated field or continuum, no part of which can be separated from or valued above the rest" (quoted in Turner 2006, 46). In the early 1960s, Brand became involved with an avant-garde performance art troupe in New York known as USCO. Their work was "a psychedelic celebration of technology and mystical community . . . intended to transform the audience's consciousness" (Turner 2006, 49). The troupe lived together in communal style and was very influenced by Buddhism and other forms of Eastern mysticism, as well as the newly emerging systems theories. They also were deeply engaged with the latest scientific developments, and in their performance pieces they often included novel technological devices such as tape players, slides, and strobe lights. As a 1968 brochure described them, USCO "unites the cults of mysticism and technology as a basis for introspection and communication" (quoted in Turner 2006, 50). Other seminal American thinkers such as Buckminster Fuller and Gregory Bateson, who were rapidly gaining popularity during the mid-1960s as oracles of the power of technology to catalyze social transformation, also took a Buddhist turn in their thinking. Social life, according to these thinkers, is a complex network of communicative pathways in which the individual should better be considered a "dividual" because each person is nothing but a complex system themselves. This is similar to the Buddhist notion that the person is nothing but an aggregate of a number of different physical and psychological elements that all come together and react with each other to create the illusion of an individual self. These earliest glimmerings of cybernetic culture evolved into the full-blown digital environment in which the world is currently immersed.

Digital Buddhism

Analyzing Buddhism in the age of digital reproduction is significant for two reasons. First, it affords the tools to understand how digital Buddhism is actually being practiced today. Early scholarship on the internet and religion often dichotomized on- and offline as completely separate social realms (Helland 2000; Rheingold 1993). Digital Buddhism, however, rather than providing an alternative social space for a few, has instead altered Buddhist practice for many (Campbell 2013; Grieve 2016, 194–214). In other words, "digital Buddhism" not only refers to online practices, but also indicates how digital media reconfigure Buddhism in the actual world and allow us to articulate the current state of Buddhist practice in relation to its digital reproduction. The spread of this spiritual "mash-up" should come as no surprise. American popular religion often breeds such strange couplings of religion, media technology, and consumerism. Ann Gleig avers that:

> The adoption of technological language to interpret and frame classical Buddhism can be seen as serving two main functions. On one level, it explicitly functions as a

pragmatic pedagogy or "skillful means" way to teach traditional Buddhism in a language that will resonate more with a twenty-first century audience. On another level, it implicitly serves a legitimating function in implying that technological innovations are structurally compatible or even inherent to Buddhism. (2015, 192)

Buddhist Geeks, which started in 2007, is an illustrative example of an online Buddhist organization that embodies many of the features of digital media that we wish to highlight here. It began mainly as a weekly audio podcast and also hosts a digital magazine and conferences that happen every few years. It was started by Vincent Horn and Ryan Oelke as a way to leverage the affordances of digital media to bring Buddhism into the computer age and make it relevant to contemporary life. In particular, they wanted to exploit the social features of digital media to enable discussion of meditation and other features of Buddhism and explore how the practice of Buddhism is evolving in ways salient to contemporary culture. They state that they seek "an ongoing conversation with the individuals and communities who are experimenting with new ways of practicing Buddhism, as well as new ways of bringing Buddhist and contemplative insights into other disciplines" (quoted in Gleig 2014, 16). As such, podcasts discuss not just different forms of Buddhism but also how science, technology, sociology, and the arts can be used to further the practice and understanding of Buddhism. The podcasts became very successful, with hundreds of thousands of downloads, and this prompted them to develop the *Life Retreat*, which was envisioned as a new way to deliver the Dharma, including live instruction online as well as virtual meetings and meditation sessions. Ann Gleig, who has studied the Buddhist Geeks at length, explains that:

> it presents itself as signifying not just the continuation but also the updating of the scientific lineage through the participation of "a new generation of contemplative hybrids" who are equally trained in the "inner and outer technologies," of classical Buddhism and neuroscience and unlike their closeted predecessors are willing to talk openly about the "enlightenment game." (2015, 191)

Buddhist Geeks also recognizes that our modern technological world provides metaphors for speaking about Buddhist ideas that may resonate more deeply with the wired crowd that makes up much of their audience. For example, Horn has talked about what he terms "windowsME" and explains that like a computer that comes loaded with an operating system such as *Windows* that forces it to behave in specific ways, so human beings are programmed to have a mistaken idea of an eternal self that forms the core of their being. Extending the metaphor, he sees meditation as a kind of "mind-hack" that can get past the security firewall guarding the "windowsME" settings and allow us to see our true fluid nature.

Another innovative idea being propounded by Buddhist Geeks is "Open Source Dharma," which according to their website is:

a newly proposed open standard & network, whose aim is to encourage the flourishing of a transparent, collaborative, creative, & evolutionary ecosystem of dharma. The Open Source Dharma protocol serves as a radical alternative to Proprietary Dharma by making it easier for new forms of dharma to emerge. We do this by creating and maintaining an open standard that incentivizes permission-less innovation, cross-lineage collaboration, and transparent organization. Think of it as An Internet of Dharma. (https://www.opensourcedharma.info/)

Buddhism, along with pretty much everything else in society today, has also moved onto social media. There are numerous Facebook groups associated with Buddhism, as well as Instagram and Twitter accounts that post information about events, ideas, practices, debates, and other things connected to Buddhism. Of course, one of the challenges arising out of the use of social media is that they are designed to actually magnify a sense of self, suggesting for example that an experience is not fully had unless one posts many pictures of oneself having the experience. Selfie culture clashes with selflessness on this score. On the other hand, the fact that most people have many different identities online, and present themselves in totally different ways to their friends on Facebook, their colleagues on LinkedIn, their sexual partners on Tinder, and their gaming buddies on Discord may highlight the malleable nature of the self that is a key insight of Buddhism.

Buddhist Apps

There are several hundred mobile apps associated with Buddhism available for both Android and Apple phones. The meditation app *Calm* was awarded the "Best of 2018 Award Winner" by Apple and is estimated to have more than 40 million downloads worldwide and over 1 million paying subscribers, and it is the top grossing health and fitness app and twentieth overall on Apple phones. *Headspace*, its competitor in the meditation app market, is the seventh-highest grossing health and fitness app, valued at $320 million and generating more than $100 million in revenue every year (https://www.cnbc.com/2019/02/05/calm-raises-88-million-valuing-the-meditation-app-at-1-billion.html). These apps utilize all the trappings of successful apps to help the user track their meditative accomplishments and to set up an environment in which they can presumably meditate during their busy daily schedule. However, like all apps, their main aim is ultimately not self-realization, but rather the creation of a sense of dependency that causes the user to return again and again to the app. Rather than drawing them into themselves, the apps draw the users to the screen and attempt to colonize their attention. This has been criticized by some (Grieve and McGuire 2019) as a potentially damaging practice that betrays the true purpose of meditation. Here we see the complicated nexus of capitalism and technology, where the technology almost inevitably operates in the service of capitalist goals to the detriment of the spiritual. Coining a playful term for this phenomenon, David Forbes writes, "McMindfulness promotes self-aggrandizement; its therapeutic function is to comfort, numb, adjust, and accommodate the self within a neoliberal, corporatized, militarized, individualistic society based on private gain" (2019, 25). On the other hand, there are also less commercially oriented apps that serve their audience with more focus on self-development and less on pleasing investors, such as the *Liberate* app aimed at nourishing the meditation practice of those from Black, Indigenous, and People of Color backgrounds (https://www.buddhistdoor.net/news/liberate-a-buddhist-meditation-app-for-people-of-color-flourishes/). While some apps might not be aimed at ameliorating the social conditions that plague our world today, an argument can be made that Buddhist meditation is not intended to change external conditions, but rather to adjust how one reacts to them internally. This debate is not new to Buddhism in the digital age, but stems back to the classical period of Buddhism, where Mahāyāna texts also criticize Theravāda for an excessive turn inward and an insufficient concern for the well-being of others, which Mahāyāna attempts to rectify through its emphasis on compassion.

Medical Science

Beyond digital media, cutting-edge technologies are being used to strengthen Buddhism in interesting ways in the world of medicine. Numerous studies have been performed using functional magnetic resonance imaging (fMRI), electroencephalography (EEG), and other kinds of measuring devices to assess scientifically the efficacy of Buddhist practices such as meditation. Former Buddhist monk Shinzen Young, for example, has worked with university researchers to examine how meditation affects neurophysiology, in what he has termed a "Science of Enlightenment" (Gleig 2015, 191). In 2007 scientists at the University of Toronto noticed from brain scans of meditators that their neural pathways were actually being changed through meditation in ways that afforded a more immediate experience of reality (Gleig 2015, 191). Erik Braun and David McMahan have chronicled a wealth of such studies and have examined how they are propelling a more general interest in Buddhism in their recent collection *Meditation, Buddhism and Science* (2017).

Conclusion: Resistance and Integration

We have shown that while it is difficult to pinpoint exactly the nature of American Buddhism and technology, they have had a complicated interaction that has been mutually transformative over the past 175 years. To give one last example, a lesser-known work by Paik is *Zen for Film* (1965), a twenty-minute-long movie composed of blank silent film leader. As the film ages and wears in the projector, the viewer is confronted with a constantly evolving work caused by the media technologies and events in the environment. Like American Buddhism and media technologies, Paik's work makes the accumulation of traces on film unpredictable, subject to the vagaries of chance, constantly mutating, perpetually evolving, yet possessing a kind of directionality.

Like *Zen for Film* (1965), we have seen that Buddhism and technology in America are stuck between countervailing trends and assumptions. Buddhism in the new world is necessarily a child of globalization, yet also is opposed to those very forces; Buddhists have adopted and even developed many important technologies over time, yet Buddhism is now seen as a potential victim of the long-term effects of those very technologies. Some people inspired by Buddhism, such as Apple founder Steve Jobs, have been key figures in shaping the way that technology has developed in America, while others have been tireless warriors against its steady encroachment on traditional ways of living in the world. Many Buddhist groups have websites, social media accounts, Second Life sims, and phone apps, whereas others eschew what they see as the commercialization and diluting of the tradition. Furthermore, we see medical technologies being used to study and legitimize Buddhism in new and influential ways that have had the effect of bringing many of the key teachings, especially in the realm of meditation, into mainstream American society. Ultimately, like it or not, it is clear that Buddhist practice has been thriving in digital environments, and the transformations to Buddhist spirituality engendered by technology have strengthened the Dharma's impact in America. As Thich Nhat Hanh writes in *Zen Keys*, "Western Civilization has brought us to the edge of the abyss. It has transformed us into machines. With the 'awaking' of a few Westerners, their awareness of the real situation has . . . engaged them in the search for new values" ([1974] 2005, 160).

References

Annaud, Jean-Jacques. 2013. *Seven Years in Tibet*. Film. Sydney: Movies Drama.
Arnold, Edwin. [1879] 2012. *The Light of Asia: The Great Renunciation*. Garfield Heights, OH: Duke Classics.
Badiner, Allan Hunt, and Alex Grey. 2015. *Zig Zag Zen: Buddhism and Psychedelics*. Santa Fe, NM: Synergetic Press.
Barrows, John Henry. 1893. *The World's Parliament of Religions: An Illustrated and Popular Story of the World's First Parliament of Religions, Held in Chicago in Connection with the Columbian Exposition of 1893*. Toronto: Hunter, Rose.
Bernstein, Roberta. 1986. *Introduction to Rauschenberg: The White and Black Paintings 1949–1953*. New York: Larry Gagosian Gallery.
Bertolucci, Bernardo. 1993. *Little Buddha*. Film. Los Angeles: Miramax Family Films.
Braun, Erik, and David McMahan. 2017. *Meditation, Buddhism and Science*. New York: Oxford University Press.

Campbell, Heidi, ed. 2013. *Digital Religion*. New York: Routledge.
Crowley, Mike, and Ann Shulgin. 2019. *Secret Drugs of Buddhism: Psychedelic Sacraments and the Origins of the Vajrayana*. Santa Fe, NM: Synergetic Press.
Decker-Phillips, Edith. 1998. *Paik Video*. Barrytown, NY: Station Hill Press.
Deegalle, Mahinda. 2007. *Popularizing Buddhism: Preaching as Performance in Sri Lanka*. Albany: State University of New York Press.
De Fina, Barbara, Martin Scorsese, Melissa Mathison, Tenzin Thuthob Tsarong, Gyurme Tethong, Roger A. Deakins, Thelma Schoonmaker, and Philip Glass. 1998. *Kundun*. Burbank, CA: Touchstone Home Video.
Fields, Rick. [1992] 2021. *How the Swans Came to the Lake: A Narrative History of Buddhism in America*. Boulder, CO: Shambhala.
Fields, R. 1996. "A High History of Buddhism." *Tricycle: The Buddhist Review* 6, no. 1. https://tricycle.org/magazine/high-history-buddhism/.
Forbes, David. 2019. *Mindfulness and Its Discontents: Education, Self, and Social Transformation*. Halifax: Fernwood.
Gleig, Ann. 2014. "From Buddhist Hippies to Buddhist Geeks: The Emergence of Buddhist Postmodernism." *Journal of Global Buddhism* 15: 15–33.
Gleig, Ann. 2015. "#Hashtag Meditation, Cyborg Buddhas, and Enlightenment as an Epic Win." In *Asian Religions, Technology and Science*, edited by I. Keul, 186–203. London: Routledge.
Grieve, Gregory. 2016. *Cyber Zen: Imagining Authentic Buddhist Identity, Community, and Practices in the Virtual World of* Second Life. New York: Routledge.
Grieve, Gregory, and Beverley McGuire. 2019. "Meditation Apps Might Calm You—but Miss the Point of Buddhist Mindfulness." *The Conversation*, October 30. https://theconversation.com/meditation-apps-might-calm-you-but-miss-the-point-of-buddhist-mindfulness-124859.
Groening, Matt, James L. Brooks, Sam Simon, Alf Clausen, Dan Castellaneta, Julie Kavner, Nancy Cartwright, Yeardley Smith, Hank Azaria, and Harry Shearer. 2007. *The Simpsons*. Los Angeles: Gracie Films.
Helland, Christopher. 2000. "Religion Online/Online Religion and Virtual Communitas." In *Religion on the Internet: Research Prospects and Promises*, edited by Jeffrey Hadden and Douglas Cowen, 205–224. London: JAI Press.
Hershock, Peter. 1999. *Reinventing the Wheel: A Buddhist Response to the Information Age*. Albany: State University of New York Press.
Iwamura, Jane. 2011. *Virtual Orientalism*. New York: Oxford University Press.
Larson, Kay. 2013. *Where the Heart Beats: John Cage, Zen Buddhism, and the Inner Life of Artists*. New York: Penguin.
Lopez, Donald. 2008. *Buddhism and Science: A Guide for the Perplexed*. Chicago: University of Chicago Press.
Loy, David. 2002. "The Lack of Technological Progress." *Revision* 24, no. 4: 27–33.
Loy, David. 2007. "Cyberbabel." *Ethics and Information Technology* 9: 251–258.
Lucas, George. 1977. Film. *Star Wars Episode IV: A New Hope*. Twentieth Century Fox.
Malaby, Thomas. 2009. *Making Virtual Worlds: Linden Lab and Second Life*. Ithaca, NY: Cornell University Press.
Margolies, John. 1969. "TV—The Next Medium." *Art in America* 57, no. 5: 48–55.
Miller, Stuart C. 1969. *The Unwelcome Immigrant: The American Image of the Chinese, 1785–1882*. Berkeley: University of California Press.
Nelson, Theodor. 1974. *Computer Lib: You Can and Must Understand Computers Now/Dream Machines: New Freedoms through Computer Screens—A Minority Report*. Chicago: Hugo Book Service.

Nhat Hanh, Thich. [1974] 2005. *Zen Keys: A Guide to Practice*. New York: Doubleday.
Nye, David. 1994. *American Technological Sublime*. Boston: MIT Press.
Osten, Franz, and Himansu Rai. 1925. *Light of Asia* (*Die Leuchte Asiens*). Münchner Lichtspiel Kunst AG: Great Eastern Film Corporation.
Paik, Nam June. 1965. *Zen for Film*. Film. New York: Museum of Modern Art.
Paik, Nam June. 1974. *TV Buddha*. Sculpture. New York: Museum of Modern Art.
Peters, John Durham. 1999. *Speaking into the Air*. Chicago: University of Chicago Press.
Pirsig, Robert. [1974] 2014. *Zen and the Art of Motorcycle Maintenance*. London: Vintage Books.
Prebish, Charles. 2004. "The Cybersangha: Buddhism on the Internet." In *Religion Online*, edited by Douglas Cowan and Lorne Dawson, 135–147. New York: Routledge.
Rheingold, H. 1993. *The Virtual Community: Homesteading on the Electronic Frontier*. Reading, MA: Addison-Wesley.
Schumacher, Ernest Friedrich. 1973. *Small Is Beautiful: A Study of Economics as if People Mattered*. London: Blond & Briggs.
Smith, Roberta. 2006. "Nam June Paik, 73, Dies; Pioneer of Video Art Whose Work Broke Cultural Barriers." *New York Times*, January 31. https://www.nytimes.com/2006/01/31/arts/design/nam-june-paik-73-dies-pioneer-of-video-art-whose-work-broke.html.
Snyder, Gary. 1957. *Earth House Hold: Technical Notes and Queries to Fellow Dharma Revolutionaries*. San Francisco: New Directions.
Spielman, Ed, Jerry Thorpe, and Herman Miller. 1972–1975. *Kung Fu*. Television. Los Angeles: Warner Bros. Television Distribution.
Stolow, Jeremy. 2009. "Wired Religion: Spiritualism and Telegraphic Globalization in the Nineteenth Century." In *Empires and Autonomy: Moments in the History of Globalization*, edited by Stephen Streeter, John Weaver, and William Coleman, 79–92. Vancouver: University of British Columbia Press.
Tanabe, George, and Jane Tanabe. 2012. *Japanese Buddhist Temples in Hawai'i: An Illustrated Guide*. Honolulu: University of Hawai'i Press.
Thoreau, Henry David. 1899. *Walden or Life in the Wood*. New York: T. Y. Crowell.
Turner, Fred. 2006. *From Counterculture to Cyberculture: Stewart Brand, the Whole Earth Network and the Rise of Digital Utopianism*. Chicago: University of Chicago Press.
Tweed, Thomas. 2000. *The American Encounter with Buddhism 1844–1912*. Chapel Hill: University of North Carolina Press.
Veidlinger, Daniel. 2018. *From Indra's Net to Internet: Communication, Technology and the Evolution of Buddhist Ideas*. Honolulu: University of Hawai'i Press.
Watts, Alan. 1958. *The Way of Zen*. New York: Pantheon.
Watts, Alan. 1965. *The Essential Alan Watts*. Indianapolis: Bobbs-Merrill.
Watts, Alan. 1971. "Ordinary Mind Is the Way." *The Eastern Buddhist New Series* 4, no. 2: 134–137.
Whalen Bridge, John. 2014. "Introduction: Some Hollywood Versions of Enlightenment." In *Buddhism and American Cinema*, edited by Gary Storhoff and John Whalen-Bridge, 1–14. Albany: State University of New York Press.
Wiener, Norbert. 1950. *The Human Use of Human Beings*. New York: Houghton Mifflin.
Williams, John. 2011. "Techne-Zen and the Spiritual Quality of Global Capitalism." *Critical Inquiry* 37: 29.
Wilson, Jeff. 2012. *Dixie Dharma*. Chapel Hill. University of North Carolina Press.
Wilson, Jeff. 2014. *Mindful America*. New York: Oxford University Press.

CHAPTER 24

AMERICAN BUDDHIST EDUCATION AND PEDAGOGY

JUDITH SIMMER-BROWN

AMERICAN Buddhism's diverse educational programs include children's Sunday schools, teacher training programs, textual study institutes, and entire universities, as well as mainstream Buddhist studies degree programs, elementary schools, and adaptations of Buddhist teachings in the civic square in the form of secular mindfulness and compassion programs. This chapter traces American Buddhism's shift from more congregational or monastic focus to broader educational visions serving a larger society of laypeople and non-Buddhists in the United States. It discusses five currents in American Buddhist education—acculturation, authentification, transmission, professionalization, and social transformation—demonstrating the innovative and constantly changing ways in which Buddhism is influencing and being influenced by American society.

In these currents of American Buddhist education, the sheer range and diversity of programs, from a variety of cultural streams of American Buddhism, suggest what Gleig calls "beyond modernity."[1] These programs reveal contemporary educational landscape as pluralistic, hybrid, and global, suspicious of metanarratives, and ready to blur the lines between sacred and secular. How to survey these streams? Asian American scholar-practitioner Chenxing Han was moved by the 2009 TED talk by Nigerian writer Chimamanda Adichie entitled "The Danger of a Single Story": "The single story creates stereotypes, and the problem with stereotypes is not that they are untrue but that they are incomplete. They make one story the only story."[2] This is true about

---

[1] Ann Gleig, *American Dharma: Buddhism beyond Modernity* (New Haven, CT: Yale University Press, 2019), Conclusion.

[2] https://www.google.com/search?q=chimamanda+adichie+ted+talk&oq=Chimamanda+Adichie+TED&aqs=chrome.0.0j69i57j0l2j46j0j0i22i30l2.3728j0j15&sourceid=chrome&ie=UTF-8; Chenxing Han, *Be the Refuge: Raising the Voices of Asian American Buddhists* (Berkeley, CA: North Atlantic Books, 2021), 9, 209.

educational initiatives in Buddhist America. For example, it is difficult to adequately generalize about American Buddhist universities that arise from radically different visions, constituencies, and sociocultural locations.

Additionally, previous tropes of "modernism" versus "traditional," and "convert" versus "ethnic" or even "natal" Buddhism to describe the complex and diverse phenomena of American Buddhism have been shown to be imprecise at best, and racist at worst.[3] Thomas Tweed's body of work suggests that speaking of religious phenomena in the static language of territories and landscapes misses the dynamic, flowing, living quality that Buddhism has in real human lives and communities.[4] He would find it more germane to look at the streams and rivers, currents and eddies in American Buddhism, identifying the many sources and visions that have created these Buddhist educational programs. This chapter offers a series of case studies tracing currents and rivulets in American Buddhist educational initiatives. Like the flow of any river, the specific initiatives are carried by more than one of these currents, sometimes seemingly conflicting or complementary, and along the river of their American history the predominant currents have certainly changed, shifted, and joined larger flows, fed by many streams.

Acculturation Two Ways

For some communities, educational programs express the community's strategy to more fully acculturate into American life, especially for children. In the early 1980s Rev. Harald Oda from the Denver Buddhist Temple (1975–1986), then a member of the US Ministerial Association Dharma School Committee, gifted me the Ministerial Association's loose-leaf notebook of curriculum for a Buddhist Sunday School that he thought might be helpful to my own convert Tibetan Buddhist community.[5] The Denver Temple, also called Tri-State Buddhist Church, is one of the sixty churches associated with the Buddhist Churches of America (BCA), originally the Nishi Honganji subsect of Jōdō Shinshū, a Japanese sect of Pure Land Buddhism founded by Shinran.[6] BCA is the oldest American Buddhist community, originating when

---

[3] Natalie E. F. Quli, Scott A. Mitchell and Wakoh Shannon Hickey, essays in *Buddhism beyond Borders: New Perspectives on Buddhism in the United States*, ed. Mitchell and Quli (Albany: State University of New York Press, 2015), chapters 3 and 12, and Afterword.

[4] Thomas Tweed, *Crossing and Dwelling: A Theory of Religion* (Cambridge, MA: Harvard University Press, 2006); Tweed, "Theory and Method in the Study of Buddhism," in *Buddhism beyond Borders: New Perspectives on Buddhism in the United States*, ed. Scott A. Mitchell and Natalie E. F. Quli (Albany: State University of New York Press, 2015), chapter 1.

[5] *Dharma School Teachers' Guide*, Buddhist Churches of America, 1981 (loose-leaf notebook, no publisher listed, 433 pages).

[6] Judith Simmer-Brown, "Denver Buddhist Temple," in *Encyclopedia of the Great Plains*, ed. David J. Wishart (Lincoln: University of Nebraska, 2011).

two Shin priests came to San Francisco to serve Japanese immigrants there.[7] Decades of racial and ethnic discrimination culminating in the internment of Japanese Americans during World War II led church leaders to initiate a series of postwar "Protestant reforms," such as changing the name of the organization.[8] Other changes were replacing *tatami* with pews and chanting with hymn singing accompanied by organ music to emulate more mainstream Christian services in America. Kenneth Tanaka describes the subsequent developments as juggling "ethnic preservation and ethnic rejection."[9]

The Buddhist Sunday School or Dharma School for children and youth was created in the internment camps during the war, "designed to teach the basics of Buddhist life, organize social and athletics events, coordinate ritual activities, and offer community services."[10] They became even more important after the war. Nothing makes the juggling act of these two clearer than the survey of three Bay Area BCA temple communities conducted by two of Tanaka's students in 1993, asking "Why do you take or send your child/children to Dharma School?" Their answers reflected three priorities—their desire for their children to learn Buddhism and Buddha Dharma, to connect with other Japanese American families and friends, especially children, and to learn Japanese culture.[11]

The 1981 Dharma School curriculum articulates a clear and sophisticated Buddhist teaching, contextualized within an American cultural idiom reminiscent of a white Protestant Sunday school. It enumerates principles of a Buddhist education that detail qualities of "Faith-Mind," framed with expressions of familiar American themes—individual responsibility and democratic values. The detailed curriculum traces a liturgical calendar of "Buddhist Observances"—*gyoji*—that include the Buddha's birthday (*Hanamatsuri*) and nirvāṇa day (*Nehan*) as well Japanese festivals like *Obon* and *Eitaikho* ("perpetually chanting the sūtras day"). They also include adaptations of American cultural holidays like Halloween, Thanksgiving, and Independence Day. Often with brief historical notes about the American origin of these holidays, each of these observances are accompanied by Shin explanations of the holiday, along with children's activities for celebration—American-style craft suggestions, games, songs, and activities. For example, Halloween includes adaptations of trick-or-treating, reminding children to ask softly, remembering to thank their benefactors, and perhaps returning to them a flower. In the case of July 4, Shin Buddhists are asked to celebrate Independence Day as the time when "freedom of religious belief transcending sectarianism was incorporated into the Constitution of the United States ... expressing

---

[7] https://www.buddhistchurchesofamerica.org/about-bca.

[8] Kenneth Tanaka, "Issues of Ethnicity in the Buddhist Churches of America," *American Buddhism: Methods and Findings in Recent Scholarship*, ed. Duncan Ryūken Williams and Christopher S. Queen (London: Curzon Press, 1999), 8.

[9] Tanaka, "Issues of Ethnicity," 8.

[10] Duncan Ryūken Williams, *American Sutra: A Story of Faith and Freedom in the Second World War* (Cambridge, MA: The Belknap Press of Harvard University, 2019), 124; Han, *Be the Refuge*, 37–42.

[11] Tanaka, "Issues of Ethnicity," 8–9.

thankfulness and gratitude with the spirit of Gassho for that freedom of conscience we Buddhists enjoy" as citizens of the United States. As Shin layperson Kanya Okamoto said, "I'm not American like apple pie. But I'm not Japanese like Japan."[12]

For some Chinese Buddhism communities, special emphasis on Chinese culture appears essential to becoming an American Buddhist. Buddha's Light Hsi Lai School was founded in 1989 by Taiwanese Mahāyāna Ven. Master Hsing Yun (b. 1927) as an educational program for children associated with his famous Hacienda Heights, California, temple and University of the West and the Fo Guang Shan movement in Taiwan. His "Humanistic Buddhism" school places an emphasis on integrating Buddhist practices into everyday life and shifting the focus of ritual from the dead to the living. Buddha's Light School purports to "provide quality education, to promote Chinese Cultural and traditional values, to expose our community to a multicultural environment, as well as to bridge cultural differences through learning and appreciating Chinese Culture."[13] Among activities of the school are listed "Halloween costume and pumpkin carving contests: by celebrating Halloween festivity, students express their creativity."[14]

An attempt at reverse acculturation into Buddhist values has influenced some convert communities, as they have welcomed children and grandchildren and wished to raise them with Buddhist identity. These communities have created Sunday schools, summer camps, and especially elementary schools relying on an adaptation of Buddhist values, sometimes in generic form.[15] Reviewing these initiatives, we can ask, what makes them Buddhist? What assumptions underly them, and to what extent are they continuations of Buddhist cultures of Asia and to what extent are they filtered through the lens of white Protestant American values? Whether these values are inculcated through overt storytelling from the Jātaka, ritual holidays adapted from Asian traditions, or through *ikebana* flower arranging, bowing, debate, or martial arts, to what extent are these pedagogies reflecting some version of Buddhist values? The Middle Way School was founded in the Hudson Valley in 2017, declaring its mission "to empower students to take their places in the modern world," drawing on "foundational Buddhist teachings and traditions as well as the latest research in child development, neuroscience, and technology."[16] Founded with a grant from the Khyentse Foundation, Tibetan Nyingma master Dzongsar Khyentse Rinpoche guided the founding, expressing the desire to not discriminate between Buddhist traditions. Director Noa Jones articulates the approach: "But it's not just that we're teaching Buddhism; it's really about the methodology

---

[12] Thomas A. Tweed and Stephen Prothero, *Asian Religions in America: A Documentary History* (New York & London: Oxford Univeristy Press, 1998), 325.

[13] https://www.blhls.org/home. Accessed April 13, 2021.

[14] International Buddhist Progress Society, *Education* (Hacienda Heights, CA.: Hsi Lai Temple, 1997). Quoted in Tweed and Prothero, 1998, 334.

[15] *The Buddhist Door*, June 26, 2015, https://www.buddhistdoor.net/features/educating-buddhist-children-in-america. Accessed April 23, 2021.

[16] https://middlewayschool.org/. Accessed April 23, 2021.

around the education. We will be working from the perspective of recognizing inherent buddhanature in a child rather than just trying to fill them up with knowledge."[17] While declaring they are not tied to a single Dharma lineage or tradition, The Middle Way School promises to cover Buddhist history and philosophy and the fundamentals of the four noble truths, karma, cause and effect, stages of the bodhisattva path, and awareness practices that "grab the present moment."[18] Yet this is not perceived as parochial training. Noa Jones explains: "It's not that you're supposed to simply accept the Buddha's teachings. You're supposed to test them, make them personal, and question the teacher. This concept of debate is really going to run through this educational method, in which we develop curiosity rather than squash it down."[19] Located in Woodstock, New York, the school draws on the communities of Zen Mountain Monastery and Tibetan monastery Karma Triyana Dharmacakra and other Buddhist-identified families in the Hudson Valley.

AUTHENTIFICATION: STUDY AND PRACTICE

In another stream in the river of Buddhist education, some American Buddhist communities have endeavored to ensure a traditional monastic-style education for adults in a Western idiom, especially for those unfamiliar with Buddhist history, texts, and culture. Tibetan Buddhism places special emphasis on scholastic learning as part of traditional training, as reflected in the monastic college (*shedra*) that has played such a pivotal role in Asia. When Nyingma lama Dzogchen Pönlop Rinpoche began teaching in America, he recognized the importance of providing a *shedra* education to his English-speaking American lay students. Initially he founded Nitārtha Institute for Higher Buddhist Studies in 1996 as a study program primarily for Western monastics at Gampo Abbey in Cape Breton, Nova Scotia, based on the curriculum at the famed Karma Kagyü Rumtek Monastery in Sikkim, but offered entirely in English. Eventually Nitārtha Institute became an independent ecumenical educational program serving Buddhists and non-Buddhists from a variety of communities with Western-trained lay practitioner faculty adapting pedagogies from the Tibetan monastery into more experiential, accessible format for lay students. For example, there is much less emphasis on memorization and formal line-by-line discourse, and more emphasis on guided contemplations and interactive learning, entirely in English.[20] Programs are offered primarily in three formats: a month-long Summer Institute, hosted at rented university

---

[17] "Buddhist Elementary School Forging a New Path: Interview with Noa Jones." *Tricycle: The Buddhist Review* 27: 3. April 27, 2018, https://tricycle.org/trikedaily/buddhist-elementary-school./ Accessed April 23, 2021.

[18] https://middlewayschool.org/academics/fundamentals/. Accessed April 23, 2021.

[19] "Interview with Noa Jones," *Tricycle* (27) 3, April 27, 2018.

[20] https://nitarthainstitute.org/. Accessed April 13, 2021.

venues; semester-long classes, offered live online in the United States, Canada, Europe, and Mexico; and asynchronous self-paced online courses. Curriculum topics come from the eight central subjects of a *shedra* curriculum that include foundational texts of the Tibetan Buddhist canon, Abhidharma and Mahāyāna philosophy, logic, debate, and analytical meditation. The Institute is founded on the conviction that meditation practice alone is insufficient without strong grounding in study that bring "certainty from within".[21]

When American *vipassanā* practitioners Joseph Goldstein, Jack Kornfeld, and Sharon Salzberg met at Naropa Institute's 1974 summer session, they had each just returned from intensive retreats in Asia with their respective teachers—Asabha Sayadaw, Anagarika Munindra, Goenka, Achan Chah, and Dipa Ma.[22] When they went on to develop the Insight Meditation Society (IMS) in Barre, Massachusetts, on Valentine's Day of 1976, they emphasized *vipassanā* meditation practice taught in an experiential, ecumenical way, emphasizing popular stories from Sufi, Pāli, and Jewish traditions, far from the style of their Asian teachers.[23] Eventually they developed a nearby center for the study of Buddhist traditions, the Barre Center for Buddhist Studies (BCBS), initially emphasizing textual study of classical Pāli sources. "Their idea was to unify study and practice by creating a center where people could not only study the teachings of the Buddha in more depth and breadth, but also explore various ways of applying the teachings to practice."[24] Very quickly, like Nitartha Institute, BCBS became independent of IMS, with its own board of directors. It is now more ecumenically Buddhist, welcoming faculty from broad *vipassanā*, Zen, and a few Tibetan Buddhist practice communities, some of whom are academics. Among BCBS's guiding values are stated these two: "We value scholarship, inquiry, discernment and experiential embodied wisdom. We are committed to integrating study and practice, scientific understanding, meditative insight, and individual and relational experiences."[25] In other words, unlike Nitārtha that emphasizes contemplative study, BCBS endeavors to balance meditation with study of Buddhist topics in a more ad hoc curriculum adapted to contemporary Western concerns. Academic programs are offered onsite and online, and curriculum offerings are strongly slanted toward social justice issues addressing racism, sexism, homophobia, and environmental justice.

---

[21] https://nitarthainstitute.org/about/the-essence-of-wisdom/. Accessed April 13, 2021.

[22] Jeff Wilson, *Mindful America: The Mutual Transformation of Buddhist Meditation and American Culture* (New York: Oxford University Press, 2014), 32–33.

[23] Gil Fronsdal, "Insight Meditation in the United States: Life, Liberty, and the Pursuit of Happiness," in *The Faces of American Buddhism*, ed. Charles S. Prebish and Kenneth K. Tanaka (Berkeley: University of California Press, 1998), 171.

[24] https://www.buddhistinquiry.org/ims/. Accessed April 13, 2021. Also see Charles S. Prebish, *Luminous Passage: The Practice and Study of Buddhism in America* (Berkeley: University of California Press, 1999), 155.

[25] https://www.buddhistinquiry.org/about-us/. Accessed April 13, 2021.

Transmission: Teacher and Clergy Training

A central torrent in the river of American Buddhism has been teacher and clergy training programs. As the membership and number of local and regional communities have increased, there are growing challenges in preparing the next generations of clergy and teachers to serve their communities, especially because most American Buddhist teachers are not monastic, even though they may hold lay ordination. Educational programs to train American teachers may or may not replicate traditional training from Asian Buddhist lineages, and the needs of American Buddhist communities differ from Buddhist cultures in Asia. Within these diverse Buddhist communities, many leaders reflect about what kind of training is necessary in a contemporary American context, and what adaptations from Asian monastic or clergy training may or may not be relevant.

The first Buddhist clergy training program in the United States is the Institute of Buddhist Studies (IBS), founded in 1966 by Bishop Shinsho Hanayama and Rev. Kanmo Imamura as part of the Berkeley Shin temple of BCA. Originally an informal study center, IBS quickly became a full theological seminary training ministers for Jōdō Shinshū churches in America.[26] Under the academic leadership of Dean Alfred Bloom, in 1985 IBS joined Berkeley's Graduate Theological Union (GTU) to ensure its accreditation as a graduate-level academic institution. This shift has enriched academic offerings for ministerial students, exposing them to other religious traditions and cultures and equipping them to serve the multicultural communities beyond their parishes in interreligious dialogue and Dharma outreach.[27]

Association with GTU also allowed the non-ministerial graduate programs to grow, bringing diverse students with a strong interest in Buddhism. The Institute received candidate accreditation by the Western Association of Schools and Colleges (WASC) in 2020. Now IBS states that its mission is to provide graduate-level education in the entirety of the Buddhist tradition, with specialization in Jōdō Shinshū ministry and Buddhist chaplaincy.[28] Dean Scott Mitchell remarks, "What I think is unique about IBS is our position between the worlds of academic Buddhist studies and Buddhist practice. . . . We take seriously the values of academic freedom and critical inquiry while recognizing the practical applications of our studies, the value of our work for sentient beings and world at large."[29]

---

[26] Kimi Hisatsune, "Introduction to the 100-Year Legacy," *Buddhist Churches of America: A Legacy of the First 100 Years* (San Francisco: Buddhist Churches of America, 1998), vii; Prebish, *Luminous Passage*, 131.

[27] Hisatsune, "Introduction to the 100-Year Legacy," x.

[28] "GTU Welcomes Institute of Buddhist Studies as New Member School," August 5, 2021 https://www.gtu.edu/news/gtu-welcomes-institute-buddhist-studies-new-member-school. Accessed August 12, 2022.

[29] https://www.shin-ibs.edu/meet-dean-scott-mitchell/. Accessed August 12, 2022.

IBS has developed a number of new in-person and online academic programs, including a Master of Divinity (MDiv) chaplaincy program for those who wish to serve outside of BCA parishes, and certificates are offered in six related fields. IBS faculty have been deeply engaged in academic research, publishing in book projects and the Institute's journals such as *Pacific World*.[30] While enrollment remains small, IBS benefits strongly from its many GTU graduate students who participate in programming, and WASC accreditation will continue to provide opportunities for IBS to grow and expand its influence.

Many Zen communities have provided pathways to becoming lay priests or celibate monastics, with training programs as prerequisite. This is a recent endeavor, for the first generation of American Zen teachers were often prepared informally or personally, often given Dharma transmission through the intuition of their Japanese *roshi*s without necessarily undergoing the rigors of training in Japanese monasteries that has been considered foundational. Many American Zen communities have been ambivalent about "education," holding that the completeness of Buddha nature needs no alteration, but only training can fully reveal it. In the wake of sexual abuse scandals, however, there is increasing emphasis on Zen training, a clear code of ethics, and accountability for all teachers.[31]

San Francisco Zen Center (SFZC) has followed the tradition of Dōgen-zenji, who considered "practice-realization" as the best training.[32] This is in contrast with the Japanese Sōtōshū that requires ordination with prerequisites of formal academic as well as monastic trainings, followed by separate training to teach (*kyoshi*).[33] SFZC practitioners are offered levels of ordination from lay (*zaike tokudo*) to priest (*shukke tokudo*) to concentrated monastic training as head student (*shuso*) and eventually Dharma transmission (*shihō*). While in Japan the three aspects of training include academic study of Buddhist teachings, at SFZC this aspect is less emphasized, with primary emphasis placed on *zazen*, ritual training, and monastic service; as always, working with a teacher is also important for ongoing training.[34]

Hozan Alan Senauke, abbot of Berkeley Zen Center, acknowledges that for Zen Center, "spiritual leadership is itself fluid, taking shape according to local needs and circumstances," blurring the distinctions between clergy and laity.[35] Lay teachers receive less ritual training, and are empowered as teachers in a ceremony of lay recognition or

---

[30] https://www.shin-ibs.edu/research/. Accessed August 12, 2022.

[31] Wakoh Shannon Hickey, "Regarding Elephants in the Room: What Buddhists Could Learn from Christians about Preventing Teacher Misconduct," *Buddhist-Christian Studies* 41 (2021): 105–108; Alan Senauke and Teresa Lesko, eds., *Safe Harbour: Guidelines, Process, and Resources for Ethics and Right Conduct in Buddhist Communities* (Berkeley, CA: Buddhist Peace Fellowship, 1998), 4–8.

[32] Alan Senauke, "A Long and Winding Road: Soto Zen Training in America," *Teaching Theology and Religion* 9, no. 2 (2006): 127–132.

[33] For helpful detail that contrasts Japanese training with American Sōtō, see Hickey, "Regarding Elephants in the Room," 105–108.

[34] Senauke, "A Long and Winding Road," 129.

[35] Ibid., 128.

entrustment, considered an "affirmation of a student's strong practice and good understanding, allowing him or her to lead lay practice groups or teach at the home center, though without priestly prerogative to transmit the precepts or ordain others."[36] As for the ethics of teachers, Senauke's 1998 edited resource guide, *Safe Harbour*, follows Suzuki Roshi's advice for centering precepts in a balanced way for Sōtō communities and shows how to prevent and address abuses of power. He argues, "From hard experience I can't emphasize enough how important it is to have guidelines and procedures in place before things go wrong."[37]

Senauke observes that not all priests become teachers, and priests may also seek training outside of Zen Center in areas such as pastoral counseling, social service and social change work, deep listening, and reconciliation, which are not available as part of Zen training.[38] Wakoh Shannon Hickey argues that these additional trainings could prevent clergy sexual abuse in Sōtō communities like SFZC's family of centers.[39]

At Spirit Rock, the monastic training and ordination that have been traditional in Asian Theravāda have been put aside in favor of lay teacher training. From the beginning, American *vipassanā* teachers opted less for a community model with local and regional meditation centers, and instead focused on a more individualistic "retreat" model in which practitioners sustained an "at-home" practice as best they could, refreshing and progressing by attending retreats at a major center like Insight Meditation Society or Spirit Rock. More recently, Spirit Rock has been responding to pleas for more regional practice opportunities, especially for marginalized communities and BIPOC (Black, Indigenous, and People of Color). After some turbulence in the predominantly white community, Spirit Rock eventually prioritized training BIPOC teachers to provide spiritual leadership across diverse communities.[40] Spirit Rock now advertises a succession of centralized lay trainings for "living Dharma," "dedicated," and "advanced" practitioners, and "community Dharma leaders" (CDLs), culminating in "teacher training," probably responding to these requests.[41] Each of these programs, ranging from five months to six years' duration, structure practice around foundational teachings such as the eightfold path, five precepts, three jewels, and four divine abidings (*brahmavihāras*), integrated with a succession of *vipassanā* retreats. The "dedicated" practitioner begins studying Pāli suttas in translation, integrated with intensive practice retreats; CDLs develop leadership skills with a variety of Western modalities, combined with some traditional Theravāda teachings. Some who complete the CDL program are authorized to teach, having demonstrated the following: competency in scriptural knowledge and the ability to apply this to contemporary life; teaching skills in leading practice, guiding classes; training in trauma-informed practice and communication; skill in working with diverse

---

[36] Ibid., 129–130.
[37] Senauke and Lesko, *Safe Harbour*, 4–8.
[38] Senauke, "A Long and Winding Road," 130.
[39] Hickey, "Regarding Elephants in the Room," 112–113.
[40] Gleig, *American Dharma*, 166–173.
[41] https://www.spiritrock.org/deepening-practice. Accessed April 1, 2021.

populations; relational and collaborative savvy; and the ability to create sacred spaces and conduct rituals.[42]

For decades, the extensive Shambhala International mandala of teachers spanned Shambhala Centers throughout North America and Europe due to the popularity of Shambhala Training, a ten-weekend program of meditation teaching, artistic practice, and study of key lineage texts regarding the pervasiveness of basic goodness and the vision of creating an enlightened society. While Shambhala's founder was a Tibetan Buddhist incarnate lama, the Shambhala Training program's emphasis does not include scholastic topics typical of the Tibetan monastic colleges (*shedra*s), such as the classic texts of the Indian *āchārya*s with their detailed commentaries. Instead, Shambhala has trained over 500 teachers in Dzogchen-style meditation, and has discovered treasure texts (*terma*) and commentaries of Chögyam Trungpa and his Dharma heir, teaching skills, "Dharma art" practice, decorum, and teacher ethics, supported with detailed teachers' manuals covering every detail of the Shambhala curriculum. Literally thousands of Buddhists and non-Buddhists have taken this program over the decades.

Beginning in 2010, Shambhala International dismantled teacher training from a centralized system with a few trainers overseen in Halifax into a more localized model, led by a network of Shastris, resident senior teachers, who could identify more personally those most promising for regional needs, representing communication skills, multiple language capabilities, representation by marginalized groups, and attunement to the cultures in which they live. These trainings became monthly local Teachers' Circles encouraging ongoing study, honing of teaching skills, pedagogy workshops, and practice discussions, encouraging emergent teachers while supporting the continuing education of those teaching the Shambhala curriculum.[43] Recently, these trainings have incorporated mitigation of racism, sexism, and homophobia, addressed in the context of basic goodness and firm ethical boundaries for teachers. By the mid-2010s, the distinction between teachers and other leaders became more and more apparent, with multiple opportunities for leadership in governance and community service.

Are these teacher training programs sufficient to provide spiritual leadership and mentorship of practitioners in their communities for the decades to come? Programs like Zen Center emphasize lengthy Zen practice training that extends many more years than parallel training in Japan,[44] likely producing great practitioners who may or may not have knowledge of Buddhist literature, teaching abilities, or the pastoral skills of counseling, conflict resolution, diversity training, and leadership skills. Spirit Rock is ensuring a strong practice and study regimen, with additional leadership skills, but

---

[42] https://www.spiritrock.org/community-dharma-leaders. Accessed April 1, 2021.

[43] It must be acknowledged that as of this printing the Shambhala organization is in disarray following the 2018 disclosures of sexual misconduct on the lineage teacher, Sakyong Mipham Rinpoche. Undergoing major reorganization separating Shambhala from the Sakyong, the organization now has a strong Care & Conduct policy, diversified curriculum, and decentralized structure with an emphasis on the arts, meditation, and Shambhala Training programs. https://shambhala.org/. Accessed April 29, 2021.

[44] Senauke "A Long and Winding Road," 130.

who measures the wisdom and emotional maturity of the graduate who can powerfully lead *vipassanā* practitioners into the future? Shambhala teachers may be able to teach a particular curriculum that they know well, but are they prepared to provide spiritual counsel and leadership where there is no detailed manual instructing them for life's circumstances?

PROFESSIONALIZATION: BUDDHIST CHAPLAINCY

An important current of teacher training in American Buddhist education responds to the quests of some practitioners for careers in Buddhist ministry. The Buddhist teachers described above often serve as volunteers who rely on other livelihoods, and who may receive stipends or donations for Dharma teaching. For the most part, most American Buddhist communities do not presently have the institutional or economic structure to support full-time professional teachers, especially first- or second-generation Western teachers. The consumerist model of American Buddhism has unwittingly forced Dharma teachers to market themselves for financial support. One wonders whether it would be possible to be a professional American Dharma teacher without recourse to advertisements in the Buddhist media with a personal marketing profile complete with product, a published book or two, and a unique trademarked meditation method.

Nevertheless, in the past two decades there has been an increasing demand for professional training programs for Buddhist ministers, chaplains, and social workers who wish to apply their Buddhist training to spiritual care both within and outside of their Buddhist communities. The primary examples of educational programs that address these needs are Buddhist-based chaplaincy programs based at Buddhist-affiliated institutions, secular universities, or nonsectarian divinity schools that offer MDiv degrees. These programs have formed a loose network of Buddhist ministry educators, called the Buddhist Ministry Working Group (BMWG), endeavoring initially to establish standards in Buddhist chaplaincy training.[45] The BMWG has identified the development of resources for Buddhist chaplaincy education as one of its priorities, along with development of professional standards, support for board certification for Buddhist chaplains, and professional networking.[46] Founding members of the BMWG include representatives of Harvard Divinity School, Maitripa College, University of the West,

---

[45] For more information about BMWG, see a description at the Harvard Divinity School site, https://hds.harvard.edu/news/2017/03/23/faculty-explore-possibilities-buddhist-chaplaincy-west#. Accessed April 29, 2021.

[46] The Chaplaincy Innovation Lab at Brandeis University, a clearinghouse for chaplaincy across traditions, serves as a source for information for Buddhist chaplains until a professional society is established. https://chaplaincyinnovation.org/resources/faith-tradition/buddhist-chaplaincy. Accessed April 29, 2021.

Institute for Buddhist Studies, and Naropa University. Founders also included non-academic training programs like Upaya Zen Center and Rigpa International. In recent years, additional institutions have joined the network.[47]

Given the institutional, transmissional, and economic structures of American Buddhism, there is a gap between the professional training of Buddhist ministers and chaplains and the needs of American Buddhist communities. Currently, students who enter professional ministry-training programs may or may not have lineage-based Dharma education and training, with their previous Dharma education coming from popular books, podcasts, and secular mindfulness programs. The Buddhist MDiv programs generally provide curriculum that prepares graduates for Association of Professional Chaplain (APC) board certification. These curricular areas include competencies in integration of theory and practice, professional identity and conduct, professional practice skills, and organizational leadership.[48] For many MDiv students, these studies may be their first introduction to Buddhist history, original texts, ethics, or advanced meditation training.

Wakoh Shannon Hickey argues that Buddhist clergy and teachers need "critical, historical, cross-cultural, and interreligious training—both academic and practical" in order to step outside the insularity of a single Dharma community. She also suggests that they "study the professional standards, credentialing mechanisms, ethical codes, disciplinary procedures, and best practices applying to other religious professionals in American culture."[49] This broader professional education can contribute to safeguarding clergy and teacher ethics, ensuring greater effectiveness, fostering good relationships with other religious communities, and building trustworthy and healthy communities.

Since APC board certification also requires faith endorsement by a recognized Buddhist lineage and organization, MDiv students who plan to seek board certification find themselves shopping around for some kind of affiliation with a Buddhist teacher. This endorsement requirement highlights the chasm between teacher training in Buddhist communities and chaplaincy certification through MDiv and professional training programs. Hemera Foundation's projects have considered how to strengthen the professional development of Dharma teachers for the future of American Buddhism. Jeremy Lowry, a project manager, reported to the Foundation considerations regarding "succession" in Buddhist communities, where "selecting dharma heirs is a closely guarded sole prerogative and primary responsibility on the teacher. In such lineages, the idea of surrendering this responsibility to an external organization is unthinkable."[50] At the same time, he continues, "a young aspiring teacher in many lineages cannot just go

---

[47] https://chaplaincyinnovation.org/resources/faith-tradition/buddhist-chaplaincy.
[48] https://033012b.membershipsoftware.org/files/application_materials/competencies_writing_guide.pdf. Accessed April 29, 2021.
[49] Hickey, "Regarding Elephants in the Room," 118.
[50] Jeremy Lowry, "Rivers & Seas Buddhist Clergy Education Research Summary," Hemera Report, February 12, 2018. Unpublished internal report, used with permission.

to divinity school and then go out in search of a congregation or even have a reasonable certainty of recognition as a teacher.... Indeed, in some lineages, merely identifying oneself as an 'aspiring teacher' is seen with suspicion as a possible manifestation of ego and ambition."[51]

Social Transformation

Another major current in the stream of Buddhist education in American introduces visions of reforms of Western institutions and global communities through Buddhist-inspired education. When Chögyam Trungpa, Rinpoche, founded Naropa Institute in 1974, he declared that he wished to "re-ignite the pilot light" of wisdom in American higher education.[52] He had been a Spalding Fellow at Oxford University from 1963 to 1965, studying comparative religion, philosophy, and fine arts, and came to respect the intellectual traditions of the West. Inspired by the Indian university Nālanda, he wished to transform American higher education through emphasis on contemplative learning, knowing the words as well as the inner meaning, like the namesake Nāropa, the eleventh-century Indian saint and Nālanda abbot.[53] Naropa developed into a year-round Institute offering a few MA degrees, and eventually in 1986 became a fully accredited university with graduate and undergraduate programs. Through its history, Naropa has gone through three phases of development, from a "Buddhist-inspired" university to a university featuring "contemplative education," shedding light on whether it has fulfilled its mission of reigniting the pilot light.

Phase One (1974–1985) focused on psychology, performing arts, interreligious dialogue, and Buddhist studies, building on the slogan, "Let East meet West, and the sparks will fly!"[54] Faculty experimented through co-teaching, workshops, and informal think-tanks, developing what was eventually called contemplative pedagogy.[55] Buddhist meditation was required in every degree program, and large practice events dotted the calendar. With receiving full accreditation in 1986, Naropa began to speak of itself as a "contemplative college of the liberal arts." Rinpoche died in 1987, but not before turning

---

[51] Ibid.

[52] Reed Bye, "The Founding Vision of Naropa University: 'Let East Meet West and the Sparks Will Fly,'" in *Recalling Chogyam Trungpa*, ed. Fabrice Midal (Boston: Shambhala, 2005), 144–145; Ann Hunter, *The Legacy of Chogyam Trungpa at Naropa University: An Overview and Resource Guide* (Boulder, CO: Naropa University, 2008), 6–8.

[53] Herbert Guenther, trans., *The Life and Teachings of Naropa* (New York: Oxford University Press, 1971), 24–27.

[54] Bye, "The Founding Vision of Naropa University," 143–161; Tanya Storch, *Buddhist-Based Universities in the United States: Searching for a New Model in Higher Education* (Lanham, MD: Lexington Books, 2015), chapter 3.

[55] Judith Simmer-Brown, "Contemplative Teaching and Learning: Opportunities for Asian Studies," *ASIANetwork Exchange* 26, no. 1 (2019): 5–25. doi:https://doi.org/10.16995/ane.291.

Naropa over to its own independent Board of Trustees, permanently separating Naropa from his Buddhist organizations.

During the rapid growth of Phase Two (1986–2006), Naropa articulated itself as a nonsectarian, ecumenical university with an increasingly diverse faculty. Robert Goss wrote of this phase, "nonsectarian does not translate to nonspiritual but to an engaged spiritual pluralism and practice; . . . it does not eschew cultural pluralism but embraces religious and cultural pluralism within a contemplative education model."[56] Through this decade, Naropa's heritage was described with the image of a tree with Buddhist roots and wide, religiously inclusive branches.[57]

In Phase Three (2006–present), Naropa joined broader academia with a more diverse, engaged faculty that had both academic and contemplative depth.[58] The Center for the Advancement of Contemplative Education (CACE) was founded in 2006, and Naropa's first non-Buddhist president, Thomas Coburn, led a university-wide articulation of Naropa's contemplative education vision.[59] Naropa's focus on contemplative education is now infused with JEDI, "justice, equity, diversity, and inclusivity," in response to greater emphasis on social justice issues.

Throughout Naropa's history, contemplative practice in the form of Buddhist meditation has evolved into a Buddhist-inspired mindfulness emphasis practiced in every degree program and most classrooms. Yoga has also become important, as well as compassion practice and research.[60] While Naropa's Buddhist roots continue to be honored, with the retirement of the founding faculty a smaller percentage of Naropa's faculty have classical Buddhist training, and an increasing number would consider themselves to be "spiritual but not religious." Has Naropa reignited the pilot light of American higher education, the pilot light of wisdom? That is an ongoing consideration among faculty, alumni, and the Board of Trustees.

Soka University of America (SUA) was founded in 2001 in Aliso Viejo, California, by Daisaku Ikeda (1928–2023), the charismatic Japanese president of the Soka Gakkai International (SGI) movement that emphasizes pacifism, human rights, and global coexistence. The American university is a sister of Soka University in Tokyo, Japan, a private university founded in 1971. While both have been subject to concerns about aggressive proselytization, political entanglements especially in Japan, and vociferous devotion to social activism, their educational institutions are highly regarded. Both universities share a modernist commitment to "value creation"—the meaning of the word *Soka*—emphasizing threefold education, peace-building, and intercultural

---

[56] Robert E. Goss, "Buddhist Studies at Naropa: Sectarian or Academic?," in *American Buddhism: Methods and Findings in Recent Scholarship*, ed. Duncan Ryuken Williams and Christopher Queen (Richmond, Surrey: Curzon, 1999), 232.

[57] https://www.naropa.edu/about-naropa/history/roots.php.

[58] Judith Simmer-Brown, "Contemplative Teaching and Learning: Opportunities for Asian Studies," *ASIANetwork Exchange* 26, no. 1 (2019): 5–25. https://doi.org/10.16995/ane.291.

[59] https://www.naropa.edu/academics/cace/index.php.

[60] https://www.naropa.edu/academics/cace/research-and-initiatives.php. Accessed April 14, 2021.

understanding as the way to mitigate conflict throughout the world. Richard Seager writes that since its inception:

> the movement—like many if not most religions—has set out to transform the world, and it has not been afraid to take concrete action toward that end. In other words, ... social awareness, money, and political will to transform the world. That this has repeatedly meant that the Soka Gakkai has been embroiled in controversy seems simply to go with the territory.[61]

The independent American branch of Soka Gakkai is the fastest-growing, most multiethnic, diverse community of American Buddhism.[62] On the other end of the spectrum financially from Naropa University, in 2021 SUA has an endowment of $2.8 billion, the second-highest endowment per student of any university in the United States, funded by SGI members from all over the world.[63] Their lavish campus was also funded by SGI, and generous scholarships are available to students whose families make less than $60,000.[64]

Soka's liberal arts undergraduate curriculum spans environmental studies, humanities, international studies, life sciences, and social and psychological sciences, with an emphasis on multicultural understanding and global social justice and peace issues.[65] Soka's student body is diverse, with students from all religious traditions and 40 percent from abroad. The Soka curriculum has no courses on Buddhist history, philosophy, or meditation; only Political Buddhism is offered.[66] Nevertheless, founder Daisatsu Ikeda's vision for Soka's education was anticipated in his 1996 address at Teachers' College at Columbia University, reflecting Buddhist principles, when he articulated three qualities of global citizens:

> the wisdom to perceive the interconnectedness of all life ..., the courage not to fear or deny difference, but to respect and strive to understand people of different cultures and to grow from encounters with them, and the compassion to maintain an imaginative empathy that reaches beyond one's immediate surroundings and extends to those suffering in distant places.[67]

---

[61] Richard Hughes Seager, *Encountering the Dharma: Daisaku Ikeda, Soka Gakkai, and the Globalization of Buddhist Humanism* (Berkeley: University of California Press, 2006), xv.

[62] Ibid., chapter 8.

[63] https://www.collegeraptor.com/college-rankings/details/EndowmentPerStudent. Accessed April 15, 2021.

[64] https://www.pri.org/stories/2015-04-17/buddhist-founded-university-now-firmly-mainstream. Accessed, April 15, 2021.

[65] https://www.soka.edu/academics/undergraduate-studies/concentrations. Accessed April 15, 2021.

[66] *Soka University 2020–2021 Academic Catalog*, 126. Also see Storch, *Buddhist-Based Universities in the United States*, 76.

[67] https://www.soka.edu/about/our-stories/founders-message-second-graduate-commencement-ceremony. Accessed April 23, 2021.

These two universities have taken different approaches to social transformation, from the perspectives of divergent Tibetan and Japanese traditions, but both are moving beyond an inward-facing Buddhist educational vision to serving a larger cultural vision of Buddhism contributing to humanistic values beyond Buddhism. In time, perhaps more will be known about the influence of Buddhist educational visions on the larger American culture.

Conclusion: "You Can't Stop the River"

Following the dynamic model of Thomas Tweed, we stand at the delta of the river of American Buddhist education joining the larger cultural flows of Buddhism's contributions as it enters the ocean of American society and culture, recognizing the multiple factors that have shaped its flow, course, and currents. While it is difficult to generalize about any particular project or school, it is clear that, taken as a whole, education in Buddhist America has a few identifying characteristics in common.

The first characteristic is the innovative nature of Buddhist education, not merely replicating the educational approaches in Asian Buddhism but responding to immediate contemporary needs, whether it be for reconciling Buddhist and American identities, providing enough qualified teachers to serve their communities, ensuring unbroken transmissions, or providing livelihood paths for its members. Each of these initiatives have responded to different concerns of their communities, and while the strategies may reflect short-term thinking and even the flaunting of tradition, they have successfully adapted to the particulars of American Buddhism.

The second characteristic is the diversity in what is considered essential in a Buddhist or Buddhist-inspired education. The American Zen communities have emphasized practice training as well as ritual and work practice. The *vipassanā* communities have brought in contemporary psychology in combination with some foundational text training. Shin communities creatively interpret how Buddhism fits in American culture. Soka University doesn't teach Buddhist history, texts, or tenets at all, while Tibetan Buddhist communities have emphasized classical topics from India's monastic universities.

A third theme in American Buddhist education is the constant change in the initiatives as communities respond to larger issues in American society. For example, given the rise in importance of social engagement in American culture, along with other features of postmodernism, curricula have emerged across the American Buddhist landscape featuring responses to patriarchy, white supremacy, heteronormativity, and power dynamics. Even those communities that do not have overt trainings in these topics have demonstrated their inclusion of these topics as part of their Buddhist training, reflecting their responsiveness to the more progressive streams of contemporary culture. On the horizon is Buddhism's response to the climate crisis, likely to be more prominent in Buddhist education in the next decade.

Altogether, these currents in American Buddhist education reveal Buddhism to be a dynamic, living force in contemporary culture, responding to a range of influences from within as well as without. The focus, pedagogy, and content of these educational initiatives assure us that contemporary Buddhism in America is truly "beyond modernity" in Gleig's sense. That is, American Buddhist education is diverse and pluralistic, drawing from a hybrid mixture of traditional and innovative study, culture, and practice, and ready to blur the lines between sacred and secular. Within a few years, there may be nothing overtly "Buddhist" about some of these initiatives as they are absorbed into some version of popular culture. Others may retrench into some kind of seminostalgic reconstruction of what is thought to be a classical form of a specific Buddhist lineage. Still others may be part of a "cross-Buddhism" ecumenical formation, loosely spiritual mixed with streams from psychology, science, and the arts.[68] It is always hard to create an accurate snapshot of an entire moving, flowing, rushing river, but it is impossible to deny its vitality and power.

References

Abrahams, Matthew. "Buddhist Elementary School Forging a New Path: Interview with Noa Jones." *Tricycle: The Buddhist Review* 27: 3, April 27, 2018.

Bye, Reed. "The Founding Vision of Naropa University: 'Let East Meet West and the Sparks Will Fly.'" In *Recalling Chogyam Trungpa*, edited by Fabrice Midal, 143–161. Boston: Shambhala, 2005.

Dharma School Teachers' Guide. Buddhist Churches of America, 1981.

Fronsdal, Gil. "Insight Meditation in the United States: Life, Liberty, and the Pursuit of Happiness." In *The Faces of American Buddhism*, edited by Charles S. Prebish and Kenneth K. Tanaka, 163–182. Berkeley: University of California Press, 1998.

Gleig, Ann. *American Dharma: Buddhism beyond Modernity*. New Haven, CT: Yale University Press, 2019.

Goss, Robert E. "Buddhist Studies at Naropa: Sectarian or Academic?" In *American Buddhism: Methods and Findings in Recent Scholarship*, edited by Duncan Ryuken Williams and Christopher Queen, 215–237. Richmond, Surrey: Curzon, 1999.

Guenther, Herbert, trans. *The Life and Teachings of Naropa*. New York: Oxford University Press, 1971.

Han, Chenxing. *Be the Refuge: Raising the Voices of Asian American Buddhists*. Berkeley, CA: North Atlantic Books, 2021.

Hickey, Wakoh Shannon. "Regarding Elephants in the Room: What Buddhists Could Learn from Christians about Preventing Teacher Misconduct." *Buddhist-Christian Studies* 41 (2021): 95–125.

Hisatsune, Kimi. "Introduction to the 100-Year Legacy." In *Buddhist Churches of America: A Legacy of the First 100 Years*, (anon), 1–32. San Francisco: Buddhist Churches of America, 1998.

---

[68] Gleig, *American Dharma*, 299–304.

Hunter, Ann. *The Legacy of Chogyam Trungpa at Naropa University: An Overview and Resource Guide*. Boulder, CO: Naropa University, 2008.

Lowry, Jeremy. "Rivers & Seas Buddhist Clergy Education Research Summary." Hemera Report, February 12, 2018. Unpublished manuscript.

Mitchell, Scott A., and Natalie E. F. Quli, eds. *Buddhism beyond Borders: New Perspectives on Buddhism in the United States*. Albany: State University of New York Press, 2015.

Prebish, Charles S. *Luminous Passage: The Practice and Study of Buddhism in America*. Berkeley: University of California Press, 1999.

Seager, Richard Hughes. *Encountering the Dharma: Daisaku Ikeda, Soka Gakkai, and the Globalization of Buddhist Humanism*. Berkeley: University of California Press, 2006.

Senauke, Alan. "A Long and Winding Road: Soto Zen Training in America." *Teaching Theology and Religion* 9, no. 2 (2006): 127–132.

Senauke, Alan, and Teresa Lesko, eds. *Safe Harbour: Guidelines, Process, and Resources for Ethics and Right Conduct in Buddhist Communities*. Berkeley, CA: Buddhist Peace Fellowship, 1998.

Simmer-Brown, Judith. "Contemplative Teaching and Learning: Opportunities for Asian Studies," *ASIANetwork Exchange* 26, no. 1 (2019): 5–25. doi:https://doi.org/10.16995/ane.291.

Simmer-Brown, Judith. "Denver Buddhist Temple." In *Encyclopedia of the Great Plains*, edited by David J. Wishart. Lincoln: University of Nebraska, 2011. http://plainshumanities.unl.edu/encyclopedia/doc/egp.asam.009.

Storch, Tanya. *Buddhist-Based Universities in the United States: Searching for a New Model in Higher Education*. Lanham, MD: Lexington Books, 2015.

Tanaka, Kenneth. "Issues of Ethnicity in the Buddhist Churches of America." In *American Buddhism: Methods and Findings in Recent Scholarship*, edited by Duncan Ryūken Williams and Christopher S. Queen, 3–19. London: Curzon Press, 1999.

Tweed, Thomas A. *Crossing and Dwelling: A Theory of Religion*. Cambridge, MA: Harvard University Press, 2006.

Tweed, Thomas A. and Stephen Prothero. *Asian Religions in America: A Documentary History*. New York & London: Oxford Univeristy Press, 1998.

Williams, Duncan Ryūken. *American Sutra: A Story of Faith and Freedom in the Second World War*. Cambridge, MA: The Belknap Press of Harvard University, 2019.

Wilson, Jeff. *Mindful America: The Mutual Transformation of Buddhist Meditation and American Culture*. New York: Oxford University Press, 2014.

CHAPTER 25

AMERICAN BUDDHIST CHAPLAINCY SUPERVISION

JITSUJO T. GAUTHIER

Introduction

CHAPLAINS hold space for care-seekers to express and explore their religious and spiritual views. A person who is sick, incarcerated, dying, or who is in emotional, psychological, or spiritual distress, is in a vulnerable position. Therefore, chaplains are educated and trained to stay grounded in their own worldview or theology without proselytizing. A traditional chaplain is employed by a secular institution (e.g., in the military, government, law enforcement, colleges/universities, hospitals, healthcare systems, prisons/jails, etc.) to serve clients, employees, and families of these institutions. *The Work of the Chaplain* (2006) states: "from a Christian perspective, their role is pastoral, prophetic, and priestly, even while being nonreligious to those who profess no religion. They enter the ministry situation with no personal agenda and the attitude of a servant."[1]

Buddhist chaplaincy in North America emerges within the historical context of Protestant theism. Many Buddhist chaplains are being educated in Buddhist universities, while others attend Interfaith MA/MDiv programs at Christian founded universities, or non-degree Buddhist chaplaincy programs. Educators in Buddhist chaplaincy programs prepare Buddhist chaplains to enter the non-Buddhist context of clinical pastoral education (CPE) to complete their clinical training. University programs combine standards of religious studies, psychology, organizational management, and chaplaincy.[2] The legacy of supervision, spiritual formation, pastoral authority, and spiritual leadership is taught within its theistic context. Programs then

---

[1] Naomi K. Paget and Janet R. McCormack, *The Work of the Chaplain* (Valley Forge, PA: Judson Press, 2006), 6.

[2] Jitsujo Gauthier, "Buddhist Chaplaincy," in *The Oxford Handbook of Buddhist Practice*, ed. Kevin Trainor and Paula Arai (New York: Oxford University Press, 2022), 564–580.

weave Buddhist sources, methods, and praxis into the curricula.[3] It is challenging to teach and learn applied Buddhism using pedagogy based on Western academic and/or interfaith frameworks.[4] This results in Buddhists spending time and energy learning Western academic frameworks, how to build bridges, and how to explain their worldview to non-Buddhist faith systems, rather than developing Buddhist frameworks for applying Buddhist scriptures to real-life issues.

Buddhist chaplains train in CPE chaplain internship/residency programs to minister without proselytizing their own beliefs onto care-seekers. Their supervisors are certified CPE educators, who are most often Christian, know very little about Buddhism, its main traditions, tenets, teachings, and values.[5] At the same time, CPE educators train to approach supervision as pluralistic, meeting in mutuality, shared experience, and partnership. CPE educators make time to create a safe environment for learning in the form of contracts of care with their chaplaincy students.[6] There is transparency around educational models, stages of development within the role of chaplain, and encouragement to experiment with ways to connect intimately with care-seekers.

From a Christian perspective, supervision can be defined as a relationship between educator and student that is developed over time to meet in partnership, reflect upon the practice of spiritual care, and focus all available resources on each supervisee's personal growth within their role as chaplain.[7] Pastoral authority guides a chaplain's actions and decisions. A chaplain's inner authority comes from faith in and relationship to God, and their outer authority is provided through endorsement from a religious tradition and community.

Buddhist hermeneutics and worldviews, in general, are different from theistic chaplains. They most likely do not begin with or share the same perspectives on power dynamics, faith development, authority, and responsibility, even among themselves. Supervision has not been written about in Buddhist chaplaincy. Articulating supervision within Buddhist chaplaincy education can support the work of Buddhist chaplains. A definition of Buddhist supervision may be an engaged relationship with the refuges of Buddha, Dharma, and sangha; where both educator and student together embark on the path to awakening, caring for self and others with an open flexible heart-mind to understand suffering, compassionate action, and spiritual caregiving. A Buddhist chaplain's inner authority comes from confidence in *Dhamma* and practice of the Threefold

---

[3] Guan Zhen, "Buddhist Chaplaincy in the United States: Theory-Praxis Relationship in Formation and Profession," *Journal of International Buddhist Studies* 13, no. 1 (2022): 44–59.

[4] Jitsujo T. Gauthier, Daijaku Judith Kinst, Leigh Miller, and Elaine Yuen, White Paper, "The Path to Buddhist Chaplaincy: Academic Education, Religious Endorsement, Professional Board Certification," 2020.

[5] There are a handful of certified Buddhist CPE educators in the United States and another handful of Buddhist certified educators in training. Chaplaincy Innovation Lab, "Buddhist Chaplaincy." https://chaplaincyinnovation.org/resources/faith-tradition/buddhist-chaplaincy.

[6] Carrie Doehring, *The Practice of Pastoral Care: A Postmodern Approach* (Louisville, KY: Westminster John Knox Press, 2015) 37–52.

[7] David A. Steere, *The Supervision of Pastoral Care* (Eugene, OR: Wipf and Stock, 2002), 66.

Training: (1) ethical virtue (*sila*), (2) mental concentration (*samadhi*), and (3) wisdom/insight (*prajna*). This confidence and practice guide a chaplain's actions and decisions.

This chapter will use the Buddha's final advice to Ānanda as a framework to address and understand supervision in Buddhist chaplaincy education to support the work of Buddhist chaplains. The first section will locate Buddhist chaplains in North America by describing how and when Buddhist chaplains gain entry into the field embedded within Christian contexts. The second section will explain where Buddhist chaplains are educated, some directions they are headed, and challenges they face. The last section will provide a model for supervision, power, and authority from a Buddhist perspective based on a section of the Buddhist scripture *Mahāparinirvāna*.

LOCATING BUDDHIST CHAPLAINS IN NORTH AMERICAN

The word "chaplain" has Christian roots, and the role symbolizes the one who guards the sacred and shares the cloak of compassion. In defining Buddhist chaplaincy in North America, Jennifer Block notes that for over 2,500 years Buddhists have been contemplating old age, sickness, and death to realize suffering and freedom from suffering.[8] The Buddha left the comforts of his palace home in search of refuge within. After many years of practicing with various teachers, he entered a period of retreat, and attained enlightenment. Out of compassion, he went back into the world to share his enlightenment experience and help others attain this realization for themselves.[9] Buddhist chaplaincy connects with the wider tradition of Buddhism as a form of applied, engaged, or humanistic Buddhism.[10] The "way of the chaplain" is a way of serving and attending to suffering outside traditional temple gates, which may take forms of social, political, environmental, charitable, peacemaking, and compassionate action.

When were the seeds of Buddhist chaplaincy first planted? Asian Buddhist leaders and movements inspired many pathways for Buddhist chaplaincy to sprout in North America. Service work outside temple gates is rooted in Asian Buddhisms. Sri Lankan monastics have historically served and supported local communities in times of hardship.[11] A trend in Song dynasty China occurred when Buddhist monastics came down

---

[8] Jennifer Block, "Toward a Definition of Buddhist Chaplaincy," in *The Arts of Contemplative Care: Pioneering Voices in Buddhist Chaplaincy and Pastoral Work*, ed. Cheryl A. Giles and Willa Miller (Boston: Wisdom Publications, 2012), 3–8.

[9] Sanghamitra Sharma, *Legacy of the Buddha: The Universal Power of Buddhism* (Mumbai, India: Eeshwar, 2001), 29–37.

[10] Mikel Monnett, "Developing a Buddhist Approach to Pastoral Care: A Peacemaker's View," *Journal of Pastoral Care & Counseling* 59, no. 1–2 (2005): 57–61.

[11] Joanna Macy, *Dharma and Development: Religion as Resource in the Sarvodaya Self-Help Movement* (West Hartford, CT: Kumarian Press, 1991).

from the mountain monasteries and "out of the cloister" to engage with Confucian diplomats, scholars, and society.[12] In the twentieth century, Indian Buddhists organized along with B. R. Ambedkar to provide literacy to women, medical services, jobs, and housing, and to give Buddhist precepts to hundreds of thousands in the untouchable castes. Similarly, Sulak Sivaraksa advocates for Buddhist principles (i.e., right livelihood) and for Buddhist sanghas to have a voice in contemporary social, economic, and environmental issues in Thailand. Dr. A. T. Ariyaratne's Sarvodaya Shramadana movement empowers and reconnects villages in Sri Lanka. The self-immolation of Vietnamese monk Thich Quang Duc in 1963 caused the world to contemplate true love and engaged compassion. More recently, Zen monastics have come to the aid of many in the most recent Japanese earthquake and tsunami.[13] His Holiness the Dalai Lama continues working for sustainable and nonviolent structural changes globally and within Tibet.

In the mid-nineteenth century, Asian Buddhists immigrated to the United States to live and work in community. Some ministers built temples, published books, and transmitted the Buddha-Dharma to many, while others transmitted Buddhist teachings in subtler ways by beginning families, serving small temples, and supporting one another in community. Through much discrimination and strict immigration laws, Asian Americans remained steadfast in major US metropolitan areas, and by the late nineteenth century an intellectual interest in Buddhist cultures found its way to universities like Harvard, the University of Wisconsin, and Columbia. After World War II, many Buddhist-curious non-Asian Americans traveled to Asian countries to study, train, and take refuge in Buddhist monasteries. Around the same time, immigration laws in the United States became more open, which allowed a variety of Asian Buddhist traditions to become established (e.g., Sri Lankan Buddhist Vihara Society, Taiwanese Dharma Drum, Tzu Chi, Foguanshan, Tibetan Gelug, Nyingma, Sakya, Chinese Humanistic, Taintai, Pure Land, Chan traditions, Korean Son and Jogye Orders, Theravada Thai, Vietnamese Mahayana, Japanese Nichiren, Shingon, Zen).

Military service also has provided a means of cross-pollination between Asia and North America. Doors for Buddhist chaplains began to open as Asian American Buddhists began serving in the US military and non-Buddhist American soldiers were introduced to Buddhism while serving abroad. The first Buddhist chaplain within the

---

[12] Mark Halperin, *Out of the Cloister: Literati Perspectives on Buddhism in Sung China, 960–1279* (Cambridge, MA: Harvard University Asia Center, 2006); Ding-hwa Evelyn Hsieh, "Yuan-wu K'o-ch'in's (1063–1135) Teaching of Ch'an Kung-an Practice," *Journal of the International Association of Buddhist Studies* 17, no. 1 (1994): 75; Ding-hwa Evelyn Hsieh, "A Study of the Evolution of K'an-hua Ch'an in Sung China: Yüan-wu K'o-ch'in (1063–1135) and the Function of Kung-an in Ch'an Pedagogy and Praxis," PhD thesis, University of California, Los Angeles, 1993; Morten Schlutter, *How Zen Became Zen: The Dispute over Enlightenment and the Formation of Chan Buddhism in Song Dynasty China* (Honolulu: University of Hawai'i Press, 2008), 77. The lifestyle of a Chan monastic and Song literati in regard to social engagement, as Schlutter writes, is "largely coextensive."

[13] C. Saito, T. Ohmura, H. Higuchi, and S. Sato, "Psychological Practices and Religiosity (Shukyosei) of People in Communities Affected by the Great East Japan Earthquake and Tsunami," *Pastoral Psychology* 65, no. 2 (2016): 239–253.

Department of Defense was Lieutenant Junior Grade Jeanette Gracie Shin, who was commissioned in 2004.[14] Buddhists have accompanied soldiers into battle, attended to the sick and dying, and served as minsters to kings and government officials for thousands of years in Asian Buddhist countries, although recent discussions raise ethical questions regarding devoted Buddhist monastics disrobing to enlist as US military personnel in order to serve as Buddhist chaplains.[15] Sybil Thornton writes that Buddhists have served the military since 1331 in the Japanese civil war by performing prayer rituals, caring for the wounded, and attending to the dead.[16] Christopher Ives notes that Buddhist priests enlisted as military chaplains during the Japanese Meiji period (late 1800s).[17] Shinsho Hanayama writes about his experience as a Buddhist chaplain in Sugamo Prison in the mid-1940s,[18] and a Vietnamese pamphlet shows Buddhist chaplains serving Vietnamese communities during the Vietnamese War.[19]

Other influences for chaplaincy have arisen out of global peace movements inspired by the social, political, and environmental work of well-known Buddhists such as the Dalai Lama, Sulak Sivaraksa, and Thich Nhat Hanh, who coined the term "Engaged Buddhism." North American organizations like the Buddhist Peace Fellowship, East Bay Meditation Center, Against the Stream, Zen Peacemakers, Prison Mindfulness Institute, Mindfulness-Based Stress Reduction, and Mindful Schools formed to express Buddhist responses to systemic inequality and institutional racism. The first "Buddhism in America" conference (1997) intended to bring Buddhist practitioners together to reflect varied and experiential ways that Buddhism is transmitted in daily life.[20] However, Charles Prebish notes that few Black, Indigenous, Latino, Asian, or People of Color were in attendance. Prebish writes about being "extremely disappointed to learn not only that scholar-practitioners had been almost completely excluded from this conference, but also that the various and important ethnic Buddhist communities in America had not been included, nor had practitioners of the Soka Gakkai tradition."[21] The history where

---

[14] Danny Fisher, *Benefit Beings!: the Buddhist Guide to Professional Chaplaincy* (San Bernardino, CA: Off the Cushion Books, 2013).

[15] Peter Gilbert and Sunil Kariyakarawana, "Military Careers and Buddhist Ethics," *International Journal of Leadership in Public Services* 7, no. 2 (2011): 99–108; Torkel Brekke and Vladimir M. Tichonov, *Military Chaplaincy in an Era of Religious Pluralism: Military-Religious Nexus in Asia, Europe, and USA* (New Delhi: Oxford University Press, 2017).

[16] Sybil Thornton, "Buddhist Chaplains in the Field of Battle," in *Buddhism in Practice*, ed. Donald S. Lopez (Princeton, NJ: Princeton University Press, 2007), 441–446; Daizen Victoria, *Zen War Stories* (London: RoutledgeCurzon, 2012).

[17] Christopher Ives, *Imperial-Way Zen: Ichikawa Hakugen's Critique and Lingering Questions for Buddhist Ethics* (Honolulu: University of Hawai'i Press, 2009).

[18] Shinsho Hanayama, *The Way of Deliverance: Three Years with the Condemned Japanese War Criminals* (Maryland: Pickle Partners Publishing, 2016).

[19] Giác Tâm, *Oriental Culture* (Saigon, Vietnam: Buddhist Chaplain Directorate, 1969).Quân-đội, *The Buddhist Chaplain Branch of the Republic of Vietnam Armed Forces* (Saigon, Vietnam: Buddhist Chaplain Directorate, 1968).

[20] Al Rapaport, *Buddhism in America* (Boston, MA: Charles E. Tuttle, 1998).

[21] Charles S. Prebish, *Luminous Passage: The Practice and Study of Buddhism in America* (Berkeley: University of California Press, 1999), 234.

many European Americans gather, share, and discuss Buddhist practices without including Asian American Theravāda, Mahāyāna, or Vajrayāna needs to be enlightened.

Buddhist Education for Chaplains

Buddhist education sprouted from spiritual movements within the 1960s, and Buddhist chaplaincy developed in this context. There are a few Buddhist universities that employ Buddhist pedagogy in education and offer state-accredited degrees in fields like Buddhist chaplaincy. The Institute of Buddhist Studies (IBS) in Berkeley is the pioneer of Buddhist-based education in North America. IBS was founded by Japanese Master Shinran Shonin in 1949. Its mission is to provide graduate-level education in the entirety of the Buddhist tradition, with specialization in Jōdo Shinshū ministry and Buddhist chaplains. After twenty years of developing ministerial training and educational programs, Revs. Haruyosi Kusada and Hozan Hardiman stewarded IBS to incorporate as a seminary graduate school in the state of California. In 1985, IBS affiliated with the Graduate Theological Union in Berkeley under the leadership of Bishop Seigen Yamaoka and Dr. Richard Payne. The Buddhist chaplain program began in 2008 and was granted Western Association of Schools and Colleges (WASC) accreditation in 2020. IBS currently partners with the Buddhist Churches of America, Ryukoku University in Kyoto, Dharma Drum Institute in Taiwan, Graduate Theological Union, and Sati Institute for Theravada Studies.

Naropa University launched the first Buddhist-based MDiv degree in North America, integrating textual/historical study, meditation practice, pastoral training, ritual, and homiletics. Founded in June 1974 by Tibetan Master Chogyam Trungpa, Rinpoche, its mission is to cultivate compassionate, creative, and critical engagement with an ever-changing world through the discipline of contemplative education. Naropa began as a summer institute that developed into a master's degree in Buddhist studies with twelve students, full-time faculty Reginald Ray and Judith Simmer-Brown, and an array of adjunct faculty. The curriculum was redesigned to incorporate contemplative education and received accreditation by the North Central Association of Colleges and Schools in 1988. Students began to push for a more practical, socially engaged education, which led to the master's degree in Engaged Buddhism in 1995. Coursework consisted of mediation, conflict resolution, contemporary Buddhist theology, sociopolitical issues, organizing skills, and a 100-hour chaplaincy internship CPE. The Engaged Buddhism program brought new students who wanted a recognizable professional degree for future employment. In 2001 the Master of Divinity (MDiv) program opened, and eventually replaced the Engaged Buddhism MA in 2005.

University of the West was born within Hsi Lai Temple of Hacienda Heights, California, in 1988. Hsi Lai Temple, founded by Tawainese Master Hsing Yun, consists of the Foguanshan Taiwanese Mahāyāna monastic order and Buddha's Light International Association lay order. Foguanshan is one of the largest Humanistic Buddhist organizations in the world. Hsi Lai University (西來大學), translated as "Coming to the West," first emerged to offer courses in Humanistic Buddhism in 1991. After years of development, the university moved outside the temple gates to Rosemead, California, and was renamed University of the West (UWest) in 2008. The MDiv degree in Buddhist chaplaincy was WASC accredited in 2010 through the efforts of Naropa MDiv graduate Rev. Danny Fisher and the late UWest Religious Studies Chair Dr. Kenneth Locke. UWest offers several accredited degrees for domestic and international students. Its mission provides a whole-person education in a context informed by Buddhist wisdom and values, and facilitates cultural understanding and appreciation between East and West.

Maitripa College came next to the scene of Buddhist-based education in North America. It was founded in Portland, Oregon, upon three pillars of scholarship, meditation, and service by Yangsi Rinpoche. Maitripa College curriculum combines Western academic and Tibetan Buddhist disciplines rooted within the Gelug School of Tibetan Buddhism and the Foundation for the Preservation of the Mahāyāna Tradition (FPMT). FPMT began in 1975 to teach Buddhism to Western students living in Nepal and has since grown into an international network of Dharma training centers, projects, and educational programs. In 2006 Yangsi Rinpoche began a four-year Advanced Buddhist Studies Program, and in July 2008 Maitripa received accreditation and legal authority to offer graduate degrees by the state of Oregon.

Directions of Buddhist Chaplaincy

There are several pathways to enter Buddhist chaplaincy. One pathway is to enter an MDiv/MA degree program at an accredited Buddhist-based university such as Naropa, Institute of Buddhist Studies, University of the West, and Maitrepa College. Another pathway is to enter an interfaith and/or theistic MDiv/MA program that welcomes Buddhists, such as Harvard School of Divinity, New York Theological Seminary, University of Chicago, Claremont School of Theology, Boston University, and Emmanuel College in Toronto, among others. A non-degree pathway is a chaplaincy program with a Dharma center that may offer a partial MDiv degree, certificate in Buddhist chaplaincy, Buddhist-based clinical training, or that partners with a theistic seminary, (e.g., Sati Center, Upaya Zen Center, New York Center for Contemplative Care, and Rigpa International). New pathways that are developing include non-accredited Buddhist seminaries like Jewel Heart Chaplaincy Program and Shogaku Zen Institute.

Curricula for accredited Buddhist-based MDiv/MA chaplaincy programs need to align with academic, clinical, and professional standards of the field. University programs draw from three North American organizations to create curricula: (1) the Association of Theological Schools (ATS), which holds the highest standard for seminary education; (2) the Association for Clinical Pastoral Education (ACPE), which holds the highest standard for clinical interfaith chaplaincy formation and supervision within internship/residency programs; and (3) the Association for Professional Chaplaincy (APC), which holds the highest standard for board certification.

An accredited MDiv/MA is a requirement for APC Board of Chaplaincy Certification Inc. (BCCI). For those who complete certificates or partial MDiv training programs, it is possible to apply for an equivalency, though this is becoming more of an exception. Three areas of education and training ensure a chaplain's spiritual maturity, professional competency, and healthy boundaries. The first is academic education. Courses are required in Buddhist texts, scriptures, tenets, history, and ethical frameworks within one or more Buddhist traditions, as well as courses in spiritual care, leadership, authority, ritual, homiletics, and so on. The second is clinical training. CPE chaplain internship/ residency (1–4 units) is required, working within a hospital, university setting, nonprofit, or interfaith chaplaincy peer group, and under the supervision of the certified CPE educator. The third is Dharma training and connection to Buddhist sangha to receive guidance from a teacher(s), ethical development, refuge, and endorsement.

Not everyone interested in Buddhist chaplaincy education wants to become a full-time board-certified professional chaplain. Those coming from Asian countries may stay to serve in the US military, healthcare, and university system, while others may return to serve communities and individuals in their home country. Some chaplains only want to work part-time, integrating chaplaincy skills within their temple community or current profession, or serving as a volunteer. Some are spiritual teachers, leaders, ministers, or mentors within Dharma centers. Others aspire to start a humanistic/engaged Buddhist nonprofit, or to work in human resources, administration, or some other helping/caregiving profession. In other words, Buddhist chaplaincy is not a cookie-cutter path.

Ongoing complexity and social suffering are calling a diversity of monastics and lay practitioners to enter Buddhist chaplaincy education today. Buddhist practitioners of different ages, cultures, and walks of life enter chaplaincy education to serve in interfaith settings within hospitals, hospices, police departments, prisons, universities, nonprofit organizations, and the military. Many have had a spiritual opening or awakening experience, a brush with sickness or death within themselves, a close friend, or a loved one. Some identify as Buddhist (i.e., monastic, lay practitioner, ordained priest/minister, scholar-practitioner), while others identify with another religion in addition to Buddhism. All feel drawn to be in right livelihood to benefit all beings. Scott Mitchell notes, "chaplaincy work can be seen as a type of engagement that takes seriously the call to end suffering without necessarily engaging in large scale public protest of activism."[22]

There as many challenges for Buddhist chaplains given their location within the predominately Christian contexts of North America. While many are educated in Buddhist universities or programs, most of their care-seekers and co-workers will be non-Buddhists. They will need to build bridges to theism and may find few bridges being

---

[22] Scott A. Mitchell, *Buddhism in America: Global Religion, Local Contexts* (London: Bloomsbury Academic, 2016), 224.

built back. The suffering and trauma they encounter will affect their body-mind and challenge their practice. They will most likely experience an identity crisis, feel alone in the field, face fears of rejection, have difficulty finding sangha, and burn out. All will most likely struggle to (1) take refuge in this very moment, (2) navigate a Middle Path through suffering (trauma, anxiety, stress, etc.) and transmit this practice, however imperfect, and (3) reconcile a relationship to an inner/outer supervisor—all of which will hopefully deepen their understanding of *Dhamma*. The next section will present a depiction of chaplains as "islands unto yourselves" as a model of Buddhist supervision.

FIND THE REFUGE WITHIN: BUDDHIST SUPERVISION

Supervision has not been written about in terms of Buddhist chaplaincy. Educators have written about methods of spiritual caregiving in the university and clinical settings. Cheryl Giles and Willa Miller compiled a book of pioneering Buddhist voices who use Buddhist frameworks, rituals, and texts to address serving, contemplative care, being with living and dying, prison ministry, and the pastoral role.[23] Ayo Yetunde, Judith Simmer-Brown, Victor Gabriel, Monica Sanford, Guan Zhen, and Duane Bidwell offer ways to bridge gaps in interfaith chaplaincy, and to cultivate right use of power, pastoral authority, and transformation through meeting in mutuality and spiritual friendship.[24] Several Buddhist educators offer methods for being with dying from various perspectives,[25] and some articulate ways that spiritual formation may facilitate

---

[23] Jennifer Block, "Toward a Definition of Buddhist Chaplaincy," in *The Arts of Contemplative Care: Pioneering Voices in Buddhist Chaplaincy and Pastoral Work*, ed. Cheryl A. Giles (Somerville, MA: Wisdom Publications, 2012), 3–8; https://www.sati.org/wp-content/uploads/2013/05/Buddhist-Chaplaincy-definition-Jennifer-Block.pdf.

[24] Victor Gabriel, "Implications for Interfaith Chaplaincy from a Tibetan Buddhist Understanding of Religious Location and the Two Truths" in Snodgrass, Jill Lynnae, and Kathleen J. Greider, *Navigating Religious Difference in Spiritual Care and Counseling: Essays in Honor of Kathleen J. Greider* (Claremont, CA: Claremont Press, 2019), 87–98; Pamela Ayo Yetunde, "I Know I've Been Changed: Black Womanist Buddhist and Christian Spiritual Formation and Spiritual Care for a Homicidal White Male Buddhist," in Snodgrass, Jill Lynnae, and Kathleen J. Greider, *Navigating Religious Difference in Spiritual Care and Counseling: Essays in Honor of Kathleen J. Greider* (Claremont, CA: Claremont Press, 2019), 235–250.; Monica Sanford, *Kalyāṇamitra: A model for Buddhist Spiritual Care* (Manotick, ON: The Sumeru Press, 2020); Duane R. Bidwell, "Deep Listening and Virtuous Friendship: Spiritual Care in the Context of Religious Multiplicity," *Buddhist-Christian Studies* 35 (2015): 3–13; Judith Simmer-Brown, "'Listening Dangerously': Dialogue Training as Contemplative Pedagogy," *Buddhist-Christian Studies* 33 (2013): 33–40; Guan Zhen, "Buddhist Chaplaincy in the United States: Theory-Praxis Relationship in Formation and Profession," *Journal of International Buddhist Studies* 13, no. 1 (2022): 44–59.

[25] Jonathan Watts and Yoshiharu Tomatsu, *Buddhist Care for the Dying and Bereaved: Global Perspectives* (Somerville, MA: Wisdom Publications, 2012); Kirsten DeLeo, *Present through the End: A Caring Companion's Guide for Accompanying the Dying* (Boulder, CO: Shambhala, 2019); Koshin Paley

and challenge Buddhist identity and chaplaincy functioning.[26] There are myriads of recitations, rituals, invocations, prostrations, koans, visualizations, and so on, in the Buddhist canons that provide frameworks for formation and supervision yet to be expounded and applied to Buddhist chaplaincy. The next section will provide one such framework.

Be Islands unto Yourselves

As the Buddha was in his final days, his discipline Venerable Ānanda felt despondent, and his mind unclear as the Buddha was dying. He told the Buddha that he found great comfort in the thought of the *Tathāgata* giving final instructions to the sangha before passing away. The Buddha questioned Venerable Ānanda's motive, and said that anyone who harbors the thought, "I should lead the sangha," or "this sangha is dependent upon me," needs to set down all matters concerning the sangha. The Buddha, or *Tathāgata*, is the embodiment of thusness, founder of Buddhism, leader of the Buddha Way, the one who understands supervision, going beyond this body and mind, and thus rejected Ānanda's request.

> O Ānanda, what more does the Sangha expect of me? I have taught the Dhamma without making distinction between esoteric and exoteric doctrine.[27] In respect of the truths, there is nothing the Tathāgata has held back with a closed fist. Whoever thinks: "it is I who will lead the Sangha," or "the Sangha is dependent upon me," is the person to give final instructions. The Tathāgata, has no such idea, so what instructions should be given concerning matters of the Sangha?
>
> Ānanda, I am now old, decrepit, advanced in years, and coming to the end of my life. I am in my eightieth year. Just as a worn-out cart is rigged to move by being bond with straps, so is the Tathāgata's body, being held together with difficulty. It is only when the Tathāgata dwells in a signless mental concentration, ceasing to attend to outward things, certain feelings, and unmindful of all objects, that the body of the Tathāgata at ease.[28]

Ellison and Matt Weingast, *Awake at the Bedside: Contemplative Teachings on Palliative and End-of-Life Care* (Somerville, MA: Wisdom Publications, 2016); Joan Halifax, *Being with Dying* (Boulder, CO: Shambhala, 2014), 113–123.

[26] Tom Kilts, "A Vajrayana Buddhist Perspective on Ministry Training," *Journal of Pastoral Care and Counseling* 62, no. 3 (2008): 273–282; Tina Jitsujo Gauthier, "Formation and Supervision in Buddhist Chaplaincy," *Reflective Practice: Formation and Supervision in Ministry* 37 (2017); Elaine Yuen, "Humility and Humanity: Contemporary Perspectives on Healthcare Chaplaincy," in *Shadows & Light: Theory, Research, and Practice in Transpersonal Psychology*, ed. Francis J. Kaklauskas, Carla J. Clements, Dan Hocoy, and Louis Hoffman (Colorado Springs: University Professors Press, 2016).

[27] These two terms are sometime translated as inner/outer (*Anantaram abāhiram karitvā*), both individuals and teachings, not limiting the *Dhamma* to an inner circle, or barring the *Dhamma* to others, not discriminating, or making distinctions regarding teachings or disciples.

[28] This refers to the bliss of *Arahantship-phalasamāpatti*.

Therefore, Ānanda, be islands unto yourselves. Be your own refuge. Seek no external refuge. Live with the Dhamma as an island, the Dhamma as your refuge, and with no other as your refuge. How, Ānanda, do you be an island unto yourself, dwell with yourself as a refuge, seeking no external other as your refuge, making the Dhamma your island, dwelling with the Dhamma as your refuge, seeking no other as your refuge? Herein, Ānanda, you live strenuous, reflective, watchful, abandoning covetousness in this world, contemplating body as body, constantly developing mindfulness with respect to feelings, consciousness (mind), and Dhamma (mind-objects).[29] Whoever lives in this way, either now or after my death, will become the foremost amongst those intent on discipline and learning.[30]

On his deathbed, the Buddha did not think he should lead, or want the sangha to be dependent upon him; rather, the Buddha exhorted Ānanda, the sangha, and all practitioners to live yourselves as your island. "Island" can also be translated as "haven" or "lamp," which may represent this body-mind as a vessel, container, or refuge. Understanding the *Dhamma*, developing confidence and maturing in one's spiritual practice, takes time. Ripening to one's full potential relies on inner and outer processes. How can one supervise this process? What type of environment is conducive? What are the responsibilities of supervisor and supervisee? How does one develop a supervisor within? This conversation between Buddha and Ānanda provides a model for Buddhist supervision; the metaphor of being an island unto yourselves provides a framework for developing confidence, authority, and the supervisor from within.

Like the historical Buddha, a Buddhist chaplain needs to master techniques, practices, and skills to develop this refuge of body and mind when encountering suffering. They need to be grounded in the Threefold Training of *sila*, *samadhi*, and *prajna*, which is a framework for the Eightfold Noble Path to the liberation of suffering. The historical Buddha spent many years studying with various teachers, and after at a certain point had to reconcile their inner/outer teacher(s), take refuge in this very moment of suffering, and utilize *satipatthāna* to navigate the Middle Path through the suffering. To follow the Buddhist Path is to undertake this same process of looking within. To develop inner authority, or supervision, is to invoke awakened nature, no-self, and Buddha within. This takes an ardent commitment to signless mental concentration, devout meditation, and patience.

---

[29] These are the four kinds of *satipatthāna*s (Foundations of Mindfulness) stated in the "Mahāsatipaṭṭhāna Sutta: The Greater Discourse on the Foundations of Mindfulness," in Maurice O'C. Walshe, *The Long Discourses of the Buddha: A Translation of the Dīgha Nikāya* (Boston: Wisdom Publications, 2012), 335–350; also: http://www.buddhanet.net/pdf_file/mahasati.pdf.

[30] Nyanaponika Thera, Hellmuth Hecker, and Bhikkhu Bodhi, *Great Disciples of the Buddha: Their Lives, Their Works, Their Legacy* (Boston: Wisdom Publications, 2003), 168–169; Maurice O'C. Walshe, *The Long Discourses of the Buddha: A Translation of the Dīgha Nikāya* (Boston: Wisdom Publications, 2012), 244–245. Nārada, *The Buddha and His Teachings* (Dehiwala: Buddhist Cultural Centre, 2012), 150–152.

Refuge in *Satipatthānas*

The Buddha's instructions for how to live with yourselves as your island and to be your own refuge are to develop mindfulness with respect to the body, feelings, consciousness, and *Dhamma*. These are four kinds of *satipatthānas* found in Greater Discourse on the Foundations of Mindfulness, Mahāsatipaṭṭhāna Sutta.[31] Buddhist scholar-practitioners Jotika and Dhamminda explain *sati* as having mindfulness or awareness of *patthānas*, or that which plunges continuously. *Satipatthāna* is a method for developing concentration, devotion, embodied ethics, and confidence by attending with mindful awareness to body, feelings, consciousness, and *Dhamma* to see reality as it is occurring. Cultivating *satipatthāna* is slowly cultivating *prajna* over time, which eventually leads to discerning right intention, view, and actions. This contrasts with a scattered mind that skips over such phenomena.[32]

In the Buddha's conversation with Ānanda, he says that his body is at ease and his mind is free only when he ceases to attend to outward things, enters signless concentration, and devout meditation. This is *satipatthāna*, which is no other than contemplating body, feelings, consciousness, and *Dhamma*. Contemplating body includes concentration on breathing, awareness of sensations, death, and impermanence. Contemplating feelings is noticing and building awareness of the mind's discernment of sensations as hot, cool, sharp, tingling, pulsating, dull, and so on, and feelings as pleasant, unpleasant, and neutral. Contemplating consciousness is building awareness of when the mind is attached, averse, constricted, enlarged, scattered, concentrated, released, and so on. A practitioner contemplates internal and external phenomena arising and ceasing within the mind, seeing such phenomena as mind-objects or *Dhamma*. Wisdom is knowing that sensations are happening in the body, feelings, mind, and mental qualities of the mind, which are all in and of themselves.

Buddhist chaplains will most likely struggle to reconcile their inner/outer supervisor(s) amidst the most difficult circumstances. There may be difficulty feeling confident and empowered to lead from within. This is part of their spiritual formation. Cultivating this island, lamp, or refuge involves turning inward, being reflexive, exploring the nature of one's suffering, propensities, and conditioning. Each Buddhist chaplain needs to discern how actions of the ego, little self, realized Self, and multi-faceted selves affect interbeing or collective wisdom; thus wisdom is discerning when spiritual leadership is controlling, over-directing, promoting self-interest, unhealthy dependence, and when spiritual leadership is fostering connection, inclusivity, community, or realization of interdependence. Leadership can stimulate experiences to share, as well as skills and insights on how to supervise self and others.

---

[31] "Mahāsatipaṭṭhāna Sutta," 335–350; also: http://www.buddhanet.net/pdf_file/mahasati.pdf.

[32] S. U. Jotika and U. Dhamminda, *Mahāsatipatthāna Sutta: The Greater Discourse on Steadfast Mindfulness* (Ye Chan Oh Village, Maymyo, Burma: Migadavun Monastery, 1986), 49; Anālayo, *Satipatthāna: The Direct Path to Realization* (Birmingham, AL: Windhorse, 2003), 29–30.

Embracing Identity

Buddhist chaplains may struggle taking refuge in this very moment of suffering and transmitting their practice, however imperfect, inadequate, or incompetent it may seem in that moment. Many non-Buddhists automatically assume that all chaplains are Christian; even monastics in Buddhist robes sometimes get called "Father." This leaves Buddhist chaplains in a predicament to either deny, disclose, or safeguard their identity upon saying "hello." Over time this comes at a cost. No matter what direction Buddhist chaplains go, they will each inevitably run up against the many orphaned aspects of themselves. They will face struggles common to all chaplains (e.g., impermanence, sickness, suffering, and death) daily, but they will also meet challenges particular to working at the margins of Christianity. They may experience an identity crisis. Some will easily return to taking refuge in *satipatthāna*, ritual, invocation, recitation, and other devotional practices. Others will find themselves feeling alone with no one close by, yearning for the support of like-minded Buddhist peers, a feeling of sangha to help enlighten their path.

There is a pain in disconnection, feeling invisible, unseen, or lost. Many Buddhist chaplains end up spending much of their time explaining themselves, educating their CPE supervisors and peers about the basics of being Buddhist (i.e., giving lessons in Buddhism 101). Repeatedly quashing, justifying, or explaining their basic Buddhist identity, teachings, tenets, and praxis to others becomes exhausting. Perhaps on some level, some hope the people surrounding them could understand Buddhism and their culture, so then they might not feel alone, separate, and might be seen for who they are. Embracing one's Buddhist identity is living with yourselves as a refuge, with the *Dhamma* as your island, and no other as your refuge.

Functioning as an Island

Buddhist chaplains may struggle to navigate the Middle Path through the suffering (trauma, anxiety, stress, etc.) that arises within spiritual caregiving and receiving. The teaching of "being islands unto yourselves" offers a wonderful framework for supervision. Supervision in this way is learning how to supervise and inhabit this body and mind. An island is not a thing, rather it is an evolution of many things, or aspects of space and time all functioning together. An island is deeply connected to the earth, water, sky, reliant on a multitude of sentient beings that keep it alive and evolving. Buddhism teaches that what we call self or "I" is actually composed of five *skandas*: form/matter (Skt: *rupa*), feeling/sensation (*vedana*), perception (*samjna*), mental formation/volition (*samskara*), and consciousness (*vijnana*).[33] Each Buddhist chaplain will see the interplay of these *skandas* with a different hermeneutic.

---

[33] Walpola Rahula, *What the Buddha Taught* (Bedford, UK: Diemer and Reynolds, 1959).

The functioning of Buddhist supervisor can model a parallel process where supervisees can learn how to accompany and supervise care-seekers in a similar manner that they were accompanied and supervised, or as the Buddha was for Ānanda and the sangha. In the *Handbook of Chaplaincy Studies* (2015), healthcare chaplain, psychotherapist, theological educator, and pastoral supervisor Michael Paterson writes: "Supervision moves beyond a tick box exercise to courageous conversations when it confronts chaplains with their own defenses against feeling useless and inadequate and empowers them to befriend their own vulnerability as a place of deep levelling and commonality with those they encounter."[34] How do supervisors know what to do and how to act? Through the Buddha's own practice of *satipatthāna,* understanding and manifestation of *Dhamma,* he knew how to respond to Ānanda, supervise him, and model a way for Ānanda to find his own answers.

Supervisors and supervisees are on the path, learning, maturing, and accompanying one another through suffering together. Their role is to accompany change. Their function is to be grounded in Buddhist *Dhamma,* refrain from proselytizing and advising, practice the Middle Path, and share the human experience. In time they will learn how to wear their many hats (e.g., spiritual leader, spiritual counselor, spiritual friend, steward, mentor, bodhisattva, teacher, student), explore many aspects of themselves, ask good questions, be curious, and become more flexible. They will find spiritual friendship (*kalyana-mitra*), mentors, stewards, to help them see the *Dhamma* more clearly, take refuge, and cultivate themselves as islands. In this way, Buddhist supervision is not a straight path, but in reality is rather tricky; methods for how to supervise one person may not work for another.

Supervising the spiritual formation of yourselves is a true ministry of presence. Taking refuge in the very moment when everything is chaotic is an inner plunge into the devout heart of meditation and thusness. *Dhamma* is continuously being transmitted, however imperfect things may appear. Chenxing Han's book *Be the Refuge* gathers Asian American Buddhist voices to demonstrate a multitude of subtle and overt ways in which chaplaincy, spiritual care, and engaged Buddhism are manifesting in North America.[35] In a book presentation, Han spoke about the simple and profound experience of being here, "for this moment only" (一期一会), quiet, present, and intimate, as a pretty radical thing to do in this global network of technology, capitalism, and business. It is courageous to leave one's comfort zone, embrace this Buddhist identity, and focus on a path that confronts suffering as it is today.

More important than having a good Buddhist teacher or guide is sangha. Surrounding oneself with spiritual friendships will help uncover the many facets of this island unto yourselves and cultivate the ease of *satipatthāna*. Developing outer-authority is taking

---

[34] Michael Paterson, "Supervision, Support and Safe Practice," in *A Handbook of Chaplaincy Studies: Understanding Spiritual Care in Public Places,* ed. Christopher Swift, Mark Cobb, and Andrew Todd (London: Routledge, 2016), 149.

[35] Chenxing Han, *Be the Refuge: Raising the Voices of Asian American Buddhists* (Berkeley, CA: North Atlantic Books, 2021).

refuge by receiving the Buddhist precepts, and becoming a Buddhist and a part of sangha. Ordination is an empowerment ritual that harmoniously blends inner/outer. Unduly suffering can occur with ideas of self, island, sangha, or "I" as a thing—a one-size-fits-all notion of refuge, identity, place, or sangha that is outside somewhere to seek. Cultivating a relationship with inner/outer sangha can provide a sense of true belonging. To be the refuge is to point directly within to the place where multiple identities converge and many islands coexist, with countless sanghas appearing and disappearing.

Conclusion

Buddhist chaplains get to work in the intersections and gaps of this very being. The growing field of Buddhist chaplaincy is playing a unique role in North America. Buddhist chaplains are in the pursuit of right livelihood. They take Buddhist practices off the cushion to serve suffering outside temple gates and outside their comfort zone. They are widening the idea of sangha. A recent "Mapping Buddhist Chaplaincy in North America" project has begun to research the scope of their identity, education, and functioning with the contemporary landscape.[36] Many islands are creating something together here; a variety of pathways headed in many directions for future chaplains to follow. How can Buddhist chaplains be educated and trained to not only survive in the field, but thrive in the field?

Articulating Buddhist-centered pedagogies may prepare Buddhist chaplains to serve multicultural communities and larger diversities of suffering more effectively. Given Buddhism's long history of compiled systematic methods of critical and pragmatic reflexive praxis,[37] there is a unique opportunity to articulate specific methodologies for "ministry of presence"[38] or spiritual caregiving from a Buddhist view. Real learning happens when students are brought into relationship with the teacher, each other, and the subject.[39] Curricula can include contracts of care, assessment rubrics, and components of research to develop the field of Buddhist spiritual caregiving. Professors may practice teaching as a form of ministry, and consider educational models that include less lecture, and more contemplative, reflexive, and group learning exercises. Future research directions may include developing Buddhist-centered pedagogies

---

[36] "Mapping Buddhist Chaplaincy in North America," Chaplaincy Innovation Lab, December 2022, https://chaplaincyinnovation.org/projects/mapping-buddhist-chaplaincy-n.a.

[37] B. L. Trinlae. "Prospects for a Buddhist Practical Theology," *International Journal of Practical Theology* 18, no. 1 (2014): 7–22.

[38] Wendy Cadge. *Paging God: Religion in the Halls of Medicine* (Chicago: University of Chicago Press, 2013), 77–127; Donald Capps, "The Wise Fool Reframed," in *Images of Pastoral Care*, ed. Robert C. Dykstra (St. Louis, MO: Chalice Press, 2005), 113.

[39] Parker J. Palmer, *The Courage to Teach: Exploring the Inner Landscape of a Teacher's Life* (Newark, NJ: Jossey-Bass, 2017); Paulo Freire, *Pedagogy of the Oppressed* (New York: Bloomsbury Academic, 2018).

where educators and students sit in circles, incorporate self-care, effectively navigate conflict, and go beyond the classroom walls to address suffering.

References

Giles, Cheryl A., and Willa Miller. *The Arts of Contemplative Care: Pioneering Voices in Buddhist Chaplaincy and Pastoral Work*. Boston: Wisdom Publications, 2012.

Guruge, *Humanistic Buddhism for Social Well-Being: An Overview of Grand Master Hsing Yun's Interpretation in Theory and Practice*. Los Angeles: Buddha's Light, 2002.

Mitchell, Scott A. *Buddhism in America: Global Religion, Local Contexts*. London: Bloomsbury Academic, 2016.

Palmer, Parker J. *The Courage to Teach: Exploring the Inner Landscape of a Teacher's Life*. San Francisco: Jossey-Bass, 2007.

Prebish, Charles S. *Luminous Passage: The Practice and Study of Buddhism in America*. Berkeley, CA: University Press, 1999.

Queen, Christopher S. *Engaged Buddhism: Buddhist Liberation Movements in Asia*. Albany: State University of New York Press, 1996.

Walpola, Sri Rahula, *What the Buddha Taught*. Bedford, UK: Diemer and Reynolds, 1959.

Walshe, Maurice O'C. *The Long Discourses of the Buddha: A Translation of the Dīgha Nikāya*. Boston: Wisdom Publications, 2012.

CHAPTER 26

BUDDHIST MATERIAL CULTURE IN THE UNITED STATES

PETER ROMASKIEWICZ

Introduction

The material culture of Buddhism encompasses a stunning array of artifacts. These objects include icons, altars, ritual implements, relics, robes, talismans, scriptural works, musical instruments, monastic complexes, temple souvenirs, and meditation cushions, among many other items produced, replicated, or modified by people in accordance with their ideas and beliefs about Buddhism. In many cases these artifacts are the material manifestations of religious practice, but in a more general sense they are also the means in which Buddhists have come to define their own identity.[1] Over time, many of these artifacts, as well as many people who made or used them, came to the United States to help further shape a Buddhist identity on American soil.

The study of material culture recognizes that artifacts are inherently multivocal with layers of meaning accruing over time. More specifically, meanings are inscribed through the varied uses of objects as they move through the hands of different historical actors and into different physical and social spaces. In short, to study material culture is to examine the rich and varied social lives of artifacts, inclusive of the ideas about them and the behaviors associated with them.[2]

This chapter examines the origins and development of Buddhist material culture in the United States from the late colonial period up through the late twentieth century and explores the meanings these objects evoked. By necessity, this will not be an attempt

---

[1] For studies on Buddhism informed by a material culture approach, see Kieschnick 2003; Rambelli 2007; and Winfield and Heine 2017.
[2] Meyer et al. 2010 and Colwell 2022.

at comprehensiveness, as the types of artifacts are too numerous, their accumulated meanings too complex, and the kinds of Buddhists (and non-Buddhists) who used them too diverse. As a result, a focus will be placed, albeit not exclusively, on a particular kind of artifact, the Buddhist figural icon. This is the type of object for which we have a greater depth of historical documentation and complimentary breadth of interdisciplinary scholarship. In addition, more than simply reiterating the value of icons as part of Buddhist worship and ritual practice, this chapter will explore the varying social, political, and economic conditions that led to the artifactual diaspora of Asian Buddhist objects and examine not only how such objects were used, but also how they were received, resisted, or reconfigured throughout American history. This will push us toward a material culture approach that reads objects as texts that have many stories to tell us, inclusive of the various traditions of Buddhism that supported them and diversity of people who used them.

BUDDHIST MATERIAL CULTURE IN THE COLONIAL AND EARLY REPUBLIC PERIODS

Evidence suggests that the earliest circulation of Buddhist artifacts in the Americas was the result of seventeenth-century global maritime trade. Arguably the first Buddhist objects to arrive in North America were made by Chinese craftsmen during the late Ming (1368–1644) or early to mid-Qing (1636–1912) dynasties. More specifically, around the turn of the seventeenth century, kiln complexes in the Dehua district of coastal Fujian province started to produce fine white porcelain statues of Buddhist figures.[3] These Dehua images would influence artistic traditions both in China and in Europe and form the basis of early American interactions with Buddhist material culture for the next century. Ultimately, such interactions remained superficial in regard to religious understanding, as even the most basic Buddhist beliefs and practices were unfamiliar to most American audiences.

Due to their relatively modest size, it is believed that Dehua porcelain images were not originally intended for use in Chinese monasteries, but for use by regional lay Buddhist associations, temple-guild societies, and local families for display on domestic altars around the region of Minnan in southern Fujian.[4] Notably, images of Śākyamuni Buddha were uncommon in this medium and the majority of surviving statues depict other Buddhist figures who developed ties to local Fujianese communities during the late Ming. These preferences likely reflect, on one hand, broader patterns of decline in Chinese Buddhist monastic landholdings and weakening institutional prestige and, on the other hand, a parallel growth in popular regional cults along the southeastern coast.[5]

---

[3] Donnelly 1969, 130–149.
[4] Yuan 2002, 41–42.
[5] T'ien 1990.

Among the most frequently reproduced Dehua icons are the bodhisattva of compassion Guanyin (Skt. Avalokiteśvara) and the future buddha Budai (Skt. Maitreya), both traditional Buddhist figures who gained widespread appeal for their promises of blessing and protection. Additionally, many icons were made of the legendary Chan monk Bodhidharma who was most commonly grouped among the arhats, the acclaimed disciples of the Buddha, in the popular Chinese imagination of the time.[6]

Through the intermediaries of Dutch and British trading firms, some of these icons originally intended for domestic Chinese use were brought to Europe. Stripped of their religious meaning, these artifacts, soon to be classified as *blanc de Chine* in European markets, were sold as oriental exotica for decorative display atop mantles and shelves. By the late seventeenth century, images of big-bellied Budai and bare-chested arhats were appropriated into the artistic repertoire of European craftsmen. These figures, generically called *pagodes* or *magots*, were sometimes molded as individual statues with nodding heads and appendages or were incorporated into the designs of others objects, such as that of candelabras and clock stands.[7]

It was through the eventual maritime commercial monopoly of the British East India Company that colonial America also became awash with Chinese luxury goods *de rigueur*. Surviving wills, probated estate inventories, and period advertisements from the late seventeenth and early eighteenth centuries attest to the proud collection of Chinese porcelain throughout the coastal colonies. The potential Buddhist origin of some objects escaped the notice of early American consumers, as documents will often record items as "alabaster images," "alabaster toys," and "Indian Babyes," among other obscure names.[8] Unfortunately, in spite of such textual records, surviving colonial estate collections rarely contain Buddhist statuary. Equally, modern archaeological excavations of colonial sites seldom recover images, even in cases where large quantities of other types of Chinese ceramics are unearthed.[9] We can only speculate the loss of early Buddhist artifacts (including their obscuration in contemporary documents) was a legacy of Protestant injunctions against the worshipping of idols. Among the rare surviving Buddhist images of the colonial period is a white porcelain statue of a standing Guanyin, dated to the mid-eighteenth century, which can be found in the Miles Brewton House collection in Charleston.[10]

Direct American trade with China began in 1784, when the merchant vessel *Empress of China* departed New York and returned the following year brimming with Chinese merchandise. According to the ship's cargo manifest, the crew met with Chinese "image makers" at the port of Canton, and one of the financial backers of the voyage, Robert Morris, later had a crate delivered to Philadelphia containing four "Chinese images" and a "marble stone pagoda."[11] East Asian pagodas, based in part on Indian *stūpa*s,

---

[6] Ayers 2002, 26–30.
[7] Kisluk-Grosheide 2002.
[8] Frank 2011, 153–156.
[9] Mudge 1986, 239–243.
[10] Leath 1999.
[11] Mudge 1962, 95.

were traditional repositories for Buddhist relics, but the scaled architectural form was appropriated as a decorative element for Western gardens.[12] The record of "Chinese images" is ambiguous, as "images" could refer to animals or other anthropomorphic figures, such as musicians or dancers. Moreover, Chinese craftsmen had long started to produce modified versions of their old molds, with one of the most famous examples being statues of Madonna and Child, resembling a traditional Guanyin model, and often documented in cargo manifests as "Sancta Maria."[13] Ultimately, the profitable yield of the *Empress*'s landmark voyage convinced numerous other investors to engage in trade with China. Between 1790 and 1812 more than 400 voyages to Canton were undertaken, flooding the Atlantic ports from Boston down to Charleston with Chinese goods and other objects procured en route in India and Southeast Asia.[14]

By the late eighteenth and early nineteenth centuries, a handful of wealthy Americans started to turn their valued collections of Chinese curios and foreign exotica into exhibitions for the general public, some of which included Buddhist objects of various kinds. One of the earliest and largest of such collections was assembled by East India Marine Society, founded in 1799 by a group of mariners in the port of Salem.[15] In 1821, the society's holdings of "natural and artificial curiosities" were catalogued and published as a booklet to assist museum visitors in identification. The entire collection was arranged typologically for the edification of the patrons, grouping items together of similar function or significance from diverse regions of the world.[16] Motivated by an ethnographic classificatory schema, "idols" of the Buddha from China, India, and Burma (Myanmar) were displayed alongside painted clay models of Chinese laborers, porters, and Mandarins in robes.[17] This arrangement effectively informed visitors of the "customs and habits" of foreign peoples while also reducing complex cultural identities into a basic stereotype—the uncultured heathen. Such layered responses to Buddhist icons as both objects of desire and objects of danger directly reflect the dualistic logic of orientalism that endeavors to make sense of an otherwise inscrutable East.

Among the more unique antebellum American exhibitions of Buddhist material culture was commissioned and operated by a British sea captain, Charles Alfred Kellet (1818–1869). He purchased and sailed the Chinese junk *Keying*, manned with thirty Chinese crewmen, from Canton to New York in 1847.[18] While Kellet filled the cargo hold with Chinese goods, the Chinese sailors ensured that the necessary ritual instruments were aboard for safe maritime passage, including a shrine on the lower decks to the "deity of the sea," the popular goddess known as the Empress of Heaven or Mazu, under which the whole vessel received protection. Moreover, an additional shrine was

---

[12] Goldstein 1991.
[13] Zhang 2011, 183, 185.
[14] Mudge 1962, 17.
[15] Schwartz 2020.
[16] Hadad 2008, 105–113.
[17] East-India Marine Society of Salem 1821, 36.
[18] Hadad 2008, 132–151; Zhang 2019.

constructed on the main deck that housed a gilded camphorwood image with eighteen arms and identified as "Chin Tee."[19] This refers to Zhunti (Skt. Cundī), a figure with a complex history in China not only as an esoteric manifestation of Guanyin, but also as a Daoist astral deity (known as Doumu) and a figure of great valor in the famed Ming novel, *Canonization of the Gods*.[20]

Upon arrival in New York harbor, Kellet promoted these icons as points of attraction for visitors during the Chinese crew's celebration of a festival. Kellet's motivations were more sensationalist than education, but unlike the displays in the museum of the East India Marine Society, the icon of Zhunti was spatially contextualized within an authentic ritual setting. Notably, however, Kellet prohibited the crew from practicing their religious devotions while at sea, but he nevertheless found such exercises appealing once a paying audience could be found, and lingering public interest led to additional demonstrations of Chinese worship.[21] While the recurring performances were staged, we might wonder if private devotions were also performed, thus making Zhunti the earliest documented icon of Buddhist heritage to be venerated in the United States.

Buddhist Materiality of First-Wave Asian Immigration

Chinese immigrants in the 1840s and 1850s comprised the first significant wave of Asian immigration to the United States, with most arriving from the Pearl River Delta region of Guangdong province in the south. Not long after landing on the shores of the West Coast, these early pioneers started to rebuild aspects of their religious lives, most visibly through the construction of temples and shrines. These structures were indiscriminately called "joss houses" by the general American public. By the end of the nineteenth century there were approximately 400 Chinese temples scattered across the Western United States, largely mapping to the patterns of employment in the mining, fishing, logging, and railroad industries. More than half of these Chinese temples, about 230, were in California alone.[22] These temples, as well as those established by Japanese immigrants in the coming decades, would be the first to provide traditional spatial and socioreligious environs for Buddhist objects on American soil.

Chinese temples and shrines were not formally Buddhist in their affiliation, but reflected broad patterns of religious practice during the late Qing which can be characterized as syncretic, diffused, and decentralized. These locally diverse forms of worship, however, shared in the same material culture of ritual practice found in

---

[19] *A Description of the Chinese Junk, "Keying"* 1848, 14–18.
[20] Stevens 1998–1999.
[21] Moon 2005, 58–66.
[22] Ho and Bronson 2022, 2.

institutional forms of Chinese Buddhism (as well as Daoism), including the use of icons, altars, incense burners, musical instruments, and other ritual implements. Some of the simplest religious structures included brick or wood open-air shrines equipped with incense burners, such as the one erected by Chinese saltwater fishermen in Pacific Grove on Monterey Bay, perhaps as early as the 1850s.[23] There were also larger freestanding temples housing elaborately decorated altars, such as those still found today in the old Gold Rush towns of Oroville (surviving structure dedicated in 1874), Weaverville (1874), and Marysville (1880).[24]

Many temples in urban areas such as San Francisco were constructed as shrine halls on the top floor of Chinese district association buildings. District associations originated in China as a means for sojourning merchants and travelers to gather with others who hailed from the same geographical region. Thus, members would not only all share the same dialect and customs, but would also worship the same local deities and celebrate the same regional festivals. Well-funded Chinese temples in America were lavishly decorated with gilded shrine enclosures, lacquered altar tables, large bells and gongs, tripod censers, and plaques inscribed with Chinese mottos. While many of the more modest items were made by migrant craftsmen, surviving inscriptions reveal that the more complex cast metal objects and intricate wood carvings were produced in Guangdong and shipped across the Pacific Ocean.[25] These material investments signaled the wealth and strength of the district association, yet for some American observers, the rich material culture of the "joss house" proved too sensuous and garish, and thus eventually became the target of xenophobia-driven condemnation.[26]

Enshrined temple icons depicted an array of heroic tutelary gods, clan ancestors, and powerful trans-local deities. Guanyin was indisputably the most commonly represented figure of traditional Buddhist heritage. Her popularity was a direct reflection of her nationwide cult in China, still flourishing today, and the beneficent protection she offered to her devoted faithful through her material form as an animated living icon.[27] In most cases, Guanyin was worshipped amidst a constellation of different deities, such as was seen at the Temple of Five Saints in San Jose, dedicated in 1889.[28] Surviving examples of nineteenth-century Chinese Buddhist icons are few, but statues of Guanyin from the Weaverville temple, Los Angeles Kong Chow Temple, and old San Bernadino temple are all believed to date previous to 1900.[29]

In rare cases, the bodhisattva of compassion was the main icon of veneration, such as at the Guanyin Temple on Spofford Street in San Francisco and the Guanyin Temple in Honolulu, both of which were operating by the 1880s.[30] Additionally, the

[23] Armentrout-Ma 1981.
[24] Ho and Bronson 2016.
[25] Ho and Bronson 2022, 99–107.
[26] Maffly-Kipp 2005.
[27] Palmer, Tse, and Colwell 2019.
[28] Yu 1991.
[29] Ho and Bronson 2022, 43–44.
[30] Hunter 1971: 42; Ho and Bronson 2022, 191–192.

old San Bernadino temple was dedicated to Guanyin and drew pious Chinese from all over Southern California during annual festivals. This private temple was built and maintained by Wong Nim (1852–1941), a Chinese-American merchant and labor contractor who returned from traveling to China in 1876 with a gold-painted wooden statue of Guanyin.[31] Many of the Chinese immigrants around San Bernadino came from the village of Ganbian, in Guangdong, where a temple dedicated to Guanyin was attached to the regional ancestral hall. Consequently, Wong Nim's temple and icon were not only the site of communal religious activities, but also a means for local migrants to maintain lineage ties in a new home country.[32] As a point of comparison to Guanyin's popularity, icons of buddhas remained exceedingly rare in Chinese temples in America before the twentieth century.

The first Japanese immigrants did not arrive in the United States or Hawaii until after the Meiji Restoration in 1868, with the first wave chiefly arriving from the southern coastal prefectures of Hiroshima, Yamaguchi, Kumamoto, and Fukuoka as contract laborers between 1885 and 1894 and then under terms of unrestricted immigration until 1907. In contrast to contemporary Buddhist institutions across China, Japanese Buddhist temples typically received greater lay support and funding, as was especially the case in the fervently Pure Land Buddhist prefectures of Japan's southwestern coast. Consequently, Japanese Buddhist temples in these regions more readily provided spiritual guidance for their overseas communities.[33]

Buddhist material culture played a significant role in the outreach activities of these Japanese temples. For example, after the Jōdoshū Buddhist lineage sent a reconnaissance mission to Hawaii in 1894, the priest Okabe Gakuō (1866–1922) returned to the Big Island to secure donations to build a temple. It is reported that he carried a statue of Amida Buddha (Skt. Amitābha), the central devotional figure of all Pure Land traditions, on his back to various plantations on the Hāmākua coast to preach the Dharma and solicit funds from Japanese sugarcane harvesters.[34] The icon was likely carried on a wooden frame that also functioned as a portable shrine, similar to what was used by contemporary Japanese pilgrims.

In addition to stirring sentiments of home, the actions of Okabe Gakuō were highly symbolic. There is a long history in East Asia of treating the circulation of Buddhist images as representative of the continued dispensation of Buddhist teachings and as powerful embodiments of the worldly and spiritual protection the Dharma affords to the faithful.[35] Thus, the image was not only a tool for inspired sermonizing, but an affirmation of the missionizing interests of many Japanese Buddhists of the period.[36] After collecting 3,000 dollars, Okabe Gakuō successfully built the first institutionally

---

[31] Costello, Hallaran, and Warren 2004, Vol. 2, 32–37.
[32] Ng 2020.
[33] Williams and Moriya 2010, xi.
[34] Hunter 1971, 59–60.
[35] Lachman 2005.
[36] Tanabe 2005.

sanctioned Buddhist temple on the Hawaiian Islands in 1896 and performed a ceremony for the installation of the Amida icon. The same statue is still enshrined today at Hāmākua Jōdō Mission, placed on an altar carved in 1918 of native Hawaiian koa wood.

Another figure that played an important role in the Japanese Buddhist diaspora was the bodhisattva Jizō (Skt. Kṣitigarbha). Popularly viewed as a protector of women, children, and travelers, images of Jizō carved from local Hawaiian stone were used as grave markers in Japanese cemeteries beginning in the 1890s, following older mortuary practices in Japan. A majority of these figural grave markers were made for children under the age of ten and continued to be carved through the 1930s.[37] It was also during the first decades of the twentieth century that additional figures of Jizō were erected along the Hawaiian coast to protect Japanese fishermen. The oldest images include a pair of statues sponsored by the Sōtō Zen Ryūsen-ji, a site established on the Kawailoa camp in 1904. Following the death of several fishermen and divers due to the turbulent surf of the North Shore, the first Jizō statue, carved by an immigrant Japanese stonemason, was installed along the sandy dunes of the Kawaihāpai camp in 1913. The reported success in preventing drownings led to the installment of a second Jizō statue in 1922, at the Kawailoa camp, which also protected travelers from a new threat: automobile accidents.[38]

On the American mainland, the Jōdo Shinshū lineage established the first Buddhist temple in the United States in 1899. Originally occupying a two-story San Francisco Victorian house and established as a branch office of the Nishi Hongan-ji in Kyoto, the American arm was soon renamed the Buddhist Church of San Francisco in 1905. New Jōdo Shinshū temples, today operating under the banner of the Buddhist Churches of America, quickly opened along the West Coast to serve the Japanese immigrant population and by the end of the 1930s had expanded across the United States to New York City. In almost all cases, an icon of Amida Buddha or a scroll bearing homage to his name was enshrined on the main altar. In one notable campaign, a statue of Amida was flown by two Japanese American pilots from California to the East Coast for a highly celebrated dedication and enshrinement. It was hoped the event would impress the Japanese residents of New York who were increasingly drawn to Japanese Christian congregations.[39]

At first, many buildings purchased by the Jōdo Shinshū organization on the mainland were not remodeled, thus the external design of these early American temples was nearly indistinguishable from their architectural surroundings; some even retained their appearance as a Christian church.[40] In spite of such deviations from traditional temple architecture, the altar arrangement remained largely unchanged. As recorded in *The Light of Dharma*, an English journal started by the San Francisco temple in 1901, multiple sets of elaborate altar furnishings were sent from Kyoto, including flower vases, candleholders, incense burners, and hanging scrolls.[41] Institutionally, in addition

---

[37] Goto 2021.
[38] Clark 2007, 57–89.
[39] Ama 2011, 82.
[40] Ibid., 100.
[41] Buddhist Missions of America 1904.

to performing basic religious services as in Japan, many Japanese temples in America functioned as community centers and as a conservative force to preserve cultural heritage, including the display and use of traditional religious artifacts.[42]

The continuing growth and dissemination of Buddhist material culture in America was significantly disrupted in the late nineteenth and early twentieth centuries by widespread xenophobia and the passage of several exclusionary immigration laws between 1882 and 1924. In regard to the Chinese community, a diminishing population combined with increasingly progressive views toward religion held by many late-Qing overseas Chinese led to the closure of most Chinese temples by the 1910s.[43] Many of the once proudly displayed icons and religious artifacts have long since disappeared (or were lost in fires), while others continued their lives in different spatial contexts. For example, after the San Bernadino Guanyin Temple was demolished in 1944, the icon of Guanyin was displayed in a local Chinese restaurant until the 1980s. Afterward, it was donated to the San Bernadino Historical and Pioneer Society, where it resides currently.[44]

Japanese Buddhist temples came to face unique challenges during World War II. The unlawful wartime internment of Japanese and Japanese Americans in 1942 forced the closure of many Buddhist congregations, and the hysteria of the period also resulted in a rash of vandalism directed at temples and their icons. Moreover, internees tried to re-establish a material Buddhist presence in camps that were often bereft of the most basic ritual implements. According to the memoir of Fujimura Bun'yū (1910–1997), a priest from the Salinas Buddhist Temple, in order to celebrate the Buddha's birthday not long after arriving at the Bismark camp, a Japanese man took a carrot from the kitchen and carved a "splendid image" of the Buddha. This image then became the center of an impromptu and moving devotional service.[45] Elsewhere, resident priests and devotees managed to bring icons of Amida Buddha, such as at Gila River and Heart Mountain. Receiving no assistance from camp authorities, the construction of Buddhist altars required ingenuity, and the altars were often made of salvaged scrap wood.[46] These barrack temples not only provided a place for religious practice, but also a material affirmation of Japanese heritage that was under threat.

Buddhist Artifacts and Early American Consumer Culture

In the postbellum era of the nineteenth century there was a notable upswing in the elite American consumption of Asian antiquities and exotic *objets d'art* that occurred

---

[42] Payne 2005.
[43] Ho and Bronson 2022, 6–16.
[44] Costello, Hallaran, and Warren 2004, Vol. 2, 51–55.
[45] Williams 2003, 266–267.
[46] Williams 2019, 119–120.

in parallel to the devotional and ritual use of Buddhist objects among Chinese and Japanese immigrant communities. In contrast to colonial and early republic eras, this interest of wealthy urbanites included a more conscious attempt to collect artifacts of a specifically Buddhist heritage. This fascination eventually galvanized into a more mainstream appeal for objects related to Buddhist material culture early in the twentieth century.

There were many contributing factors to these shifting consumption patterns, including a growing "vogue" for Buddhism that has been characterized as a response to a Victorian-era spiritual crisis and growing cultural dissent against Western modernity.[47] Barriers to the acquisition of Asian Buddhist artifacts were also lowered through increased ease of trans-Pacific steamship travel and the emergence of international Buddhist art dealers who helped build early American museum collections. The general public was also increasingly exposed to Buddhist visual imagery, especially through the ascendence of illustrated publications and the popular press. It remains unclear, however, if these factors led to a substantive reframing of Buddhist icons as authentic objects of veneration, as the early American discourse on Buddhism veered away from embracing traditional material practices.[48] Within this milieu of early mass consumer culture, the personal possession of a Buddhist statue could publicly signal refined taste and sophistication, or act as the physical embodiment of lofty ancient ideals that, at least for some, also stood in symbolic opposition to a burgeoning urban-industrial world.

The glowing public reception of Japanese goods and antiquities on display at the 1876 Philadelphia Centennial Exposition is often credited for provoking what would come to be known as American Japonisme. This phenomenon refers to the rising popular interest in a Japanese aesthetic idiom that influenced the realms of fine art, architecture, and decorative arts while also fostering interest in the mass consumption of everyday objects. The orientalist caricature of Japan as a land of exotic curios was often bolstered by voyeuristic reports in newspapers and magazines as well as published travelogues by leisure-class globetrotters. These pieces were often lavishly illustrated with etchings and photomechanically reproduced photographs highlighting the object richness of the island nation and various elements of its Buddhist culture.[49]

Just prior to this piquing of American curiosity in Japan, Japanese nativists on the other side of the Pacific Ocean stirred anti-Buddhist sentiment that would have significant ramifications for Japanese Buddhist material culture. These nascent movements soon developed into open Buddhist persecution in 1868, forcing temple closures and the confiscation of monastic assets. Many Buddhist statues were beheaded, burned, or melted down for raw materials (a similar attempt at erasure would occur later in Tibet).[50] While the worst of the looting and vandalism lasted only a few years, surviving temples sometimes remained bereft of their previous economic base, and many strategically

---

[47] Tweed 2000.
[48] Newsome 2010.
[49] Guth 2004, 3–22.
[50] Ketelaar 1990, 3–42.

sold off their icons and artifacts to survive.⁵¹ Due to the sociopolitical and economic conditions on both sides of the Pacific, Buddhist objects continued to flow out of Japan in the coming years, either in the hands of wealthy foreign tourists or through professional intermediaries, such as art dealers, trading firms, and auction houses, who established a base of Western clientele.

Isabella Stewart Gardner (1840–1924) was one among a New England circle of friends who was drawn to Japanese culture and the aesthetics of Buddhist statuary. After touring Japan in 1883, Gardner returned to commission a self-portrait in the veiled guise of a standing Kannon (Avalokiteśvara), reminiscent of a printed talisman she acquired while visiting the famed Kannon icon at Hasedera. Through the assistance of family friend William Sturgis Bigelow (1850–1926), a Bostonian intellectual who had moved to Japan a year prior, Gardner was also able to purchase a small sculpture of a seated buddha which proved to be the seed of a private collection that would grow in the coming decades. Just after the turn of the century, Gardner built a new museum to house her antiquities from around the world, now surviving as the Isabella Stewart Gardner Museum. The original building included a subterranean gallery that Gardner dubbed the Chinese Room. The space was anchored by a triad of large Chinese bronze buddha statues, purchased on recommendation of Bigelow in 1902, and arranged in a row at the end of the room as one might find at a temple.⁵² The incorporation of several other Buddhist statues around the perimeter, from both China and Japan, as well as the addition of hanging banners, altar tables, and other ritual implements, all gave the museum space an aura of the sacred comparable to the interior of a Roman Catholic church or a Buddhist temple hall.⁵³

While Gardner might be considered a Buddhist sympathizer, Bigelow and their mutual friend Ernest Fenollosa (1853–1908) were formal Buddhist adherents, having taken the precepts in the esoteric Japanese Tendai tradition in 1885.⁵⁴ All were connected through their appreciation of Asian art and antiquities. Fenollosa would later become the curator for Boston Museum's new Department of Japanese Art, the first of its kind in the United States. This would emerge as one of the country's finest repositories of Japanese artifacts, built in part upon the large personal collections of Fenollosa and that of his friend Bigelow.⁵⁵ Both dabbled in collecting Buddhist images, especially of Kannon.⁵⁶ In 1909, the museum opened the Buddhist Room, later to be known as the Temple Room, which was reserved for the larger Japanese Buddhist figures of the permanent collection. The new gallery was designed in the fashion of a Japanese temple hall, constructed with walls of plain plaster, pillars of cypress, and Japanese-style bracket arms supporting the ceiling. Museum officials believed this atmosphere was the most appropriate for the religious objects on display.⁵⁷

---

⁵¹ Kiss 2018, 50–52.
⁵² Chong 2009.
⁵³ Tweed 2014.
⁵⁴ Tweed 2000, 40.
⁵⁵ Reed 2017, 125.
⁵⁶ Guth 1995.
⁵⁷ Whitehill 1970, 132–133, 241–243.

Both the Chinese Room and Buddhist Room stood in contrast to earlier nineteenth-century public displays where Buddhist icons were often contextualized as ethnographic enigmas of the Orient, both attractive and menacing. The new spaces were the result of ongoing debates about the ontological status of Asian religious images. In Japan, during Fenollosa's first stint as a university professor in the early 1880s, he helped Japan's intellectual and cultural elite reconceive religious icons as having a modern aesthetic value as fine art.[58] A similar shift in discourse about Buddhist imagery was also occurring among cosmopolitan Americans during this time. For example, the round-the-world travel journal published in 1870 by Harvard geology professor Raphael Pumpelly (1837–1923) describes his apprehension in going to see the colossal Daibutsu in Kamakura, fearing it would be a "grotesque idol." To his astonishment, he found the Kamakura Daibutsu to be a "work of high art" and included a photograph of the thirteenth century bronze as the frontispiece to his travelogue.[59]

Ultimately, the rhetorical distinction between Buddhist images as religious icons and as fine art remained ambiguous, for even the pseudo-temple spaces of the Chinese Room and Buddhist Room were never intended to host authentic Buddhist rituals. A more complex example of this ambiguity can be found in the so-called Buddhist Temple of the eccentric professor Maxwell Sommerville (1929–1904). When the new University of Pennsylvania Museum was constructed in 1899, Sommerville filled a wing of the building with six tons of objects, including numerous Buddhist statues he had acquired during his travels through Japan, China, Thailand, and elsewhere. His intention was not to merely display the icons as a museum exhibit, but to establish an ecumenical space for Buddhist ritual practice that was not tied to specific ethnic or sectarian expressions. Sommerville was considered eccentric by his contemporaries and often dressed in Chinese attire while inside the gallery hall, encouraging visitors to chant and make offerings.[60] It is notable, however, that Japanese residents of Philadelphia appear to have also used the temple for simple devotions, especially during the Russo-Japanese War, and *The Light of Dharma* published a glowing review of the space and its collection of artifacts.[61] The professor's experiment did not last and his temple was closed after his passing in 1904.

Most turn-of-the-century high-end Japanese and Asian art collectors acquired their objects through trusted international brokers. The most influential in this regard were Matsuki Bunkyō (1867–1940), a former Nichiren priest-in-training with a family background in antiquities collecting, and Yamanaka Sadajirō (1866–1936), an art dealer with a family business in Osaka. With Matsuki arriving in America in 1888 and Yamanaka in 1894, both men quickly built a patron base of wealthy connoisseurs and museum curators while also opening stores in Boston and New York.[62] Similar to Gardner,

---

[58] Faure 1998; Storm 2021.
[59] Pumpelly 1870, 80; Suzuki 2011.
[60] Conn 2010, 118–124; McDaniel 2016, 131–135.
[61] Buddhist Missions of America 1904.
[62] Chen 2010; Kuchiki 2013.

Bigelow, and Fenollosa, the sizable collection of industrialist Charles Lang Freer (1854–1919) was also shaped by the acquisitions of Matsuki and Yamanaka, as well as other reputable art dealers, such as Paris-based C. T. Loo (1880–1957).[63] Loo was especially influential in the Westward spread of Chinese Buddhist art in the tumultuous aftermath of the 1911 Revolution that brought about the fall of the Qing dynasty.[64]

The urban middle-class American consumer, unconnected to the elite networks of fine art, could purchase less expensive Buddhist statuary at novelty stores, specialty emporiums, and department stores in larger cities throughout the United States, such as Marsh & Co. in San Francisco and A. A. Vantine & Co. in New York.[65] As mass production and mass marketing continued to ramp up in the early twentieth century, Vantine's was extraordinarily successful in reaching rural markets by focusing on mail order catalogues and national advertising campaigns often targeting women as clientele.[66] By the early 1920s, the company was reorganized as a wholesaler, rebranding itself as "Vantine's, the Buddha of Perfumes" and providing its national retailers, including local pharmacies and gift shops, figural incense burners in the shape of a buddha.[67]

Buddhist Material Culture in Post-1945 America

The periods after the Second World War and the passing of the 1965 Hart-Celler Act saw an acceleration of Asian immigration to the United States and a surge in Buddhist practice communities. As a consequence, Buddhist material culture in America grew increasingly diffuse and diverse over the course of the second half of the twentieth century. Equally, the circulation of Buddhist visual imagery was greatly amplified through modern mass media, appearing in photographic spreads of national magazines, storylines of feature films, and narrative arcs of television programs. These highly stimulating forms of visual media helped create a virtual environment through which Americans could imaginatively interact with aspects of Buddhist materiality in generally positive, albeit still stereotypical, frameworks.[68] It was also during this period in which a critical mass of non-Asian Americans and American institutions started viewing Buddhist icons in closer alignment with traditional Asian Buddhist perspectives, namely as powerful objects worthy of veneration and as animated living icons.[69]

[63] St. Clair 2016; Wang 2016.
[64] Wang 2007.
[65] Brandimarte 1991.
[66] Yoshihara 2003; Yamamori 2008.
[67] Henle 1922.
[68] Tweed 2008; Iwamura 2011.
[69] Seager 2015.

The conditions that caused various groups of practicing Asian Buddhists to come to the United States after 1945 is too complex to outline here, but one example regarding Tibetan forms of Buddhist materiality will help demonstrate the growing diversity of Buddhist material culture in America and the varied meanings it continued to accrue. Beginning in 1951, groups of displaced Kalmyk-Mongols fleeing persecution in Soviet Russia started resettling in New Jersey and quickly established the first Tibetan temple in a converted garage. Furthermore, the year 1955 saw the arrival of Geshe Wangyal (1901–1983), a highly educated Gelugpa lama of Kalmyk-Mongol ancestry, who built his own temple three years later as a nondescript ranch-style house, naming it the Lamaist Buddhist Monastery of America. As seen in a photograph of the building interior in 1959, the back portion of a mid-century living room is devoted to a Buddhist shrine, with walls covered in Tibetan scroll paintings (*thangkas*) and ceiling trimmed with banners and flags. Offering bowls and other ritual instruments are arranged in front of a large bronze icon of a buddha, draped in fabric, sitting on the altar.[70] The procurement and arrangement of such objects were critical for re-establishing the religious lives of the Kalmyk refugee community and creating the proper training environment for students, which included not only young Kalmyks, but also a group of devoted non-Asian Americans.[71]

Tibetan Buddhist icons and ritual implements were known for over a century in the United States but were generally not viewed with the same popular enthusiasm as Buddhist objects from China or Japan, nor was there a similar level of interest among museum institutions. This did not preclude the appearance of select connoisseurs, such as the New York art dealer Jacques Marchais (1887–1948), who built a formidable collection of Himalayan and Tibetan Buddhist artifacts. We might consider Marchais a Buddhist sympathizer in the vein of Gardner and Sommerville, who came several decades before her. Likewise, in order to create a suitable temple-like atmosphere for her collection, Marchais installed a large three-tier stone altar at her Staten Island estate, dubbing her gallery annex the Chanting Hall. Opened to the public in 1947, a photograph shows more than two dozen Buddhist icons of various sizes neatly arrayed along the long altar shelving and a symmetrical balance of Tibetan scroll paintings hanging on the castle-like masonry walls. Marchais envisioned the hall as a space for meditative contemplation and as a venue to learn about Tibetan culture, religion, and art.[72]

Such an enterprise was rather unique at the time. By the 1940s the interest for exhibiting Buddhist artifacts in pseudo-temple settings had waned. This can be seen through a 1938 show at the Metropolitan Museum of Art where medieval Chinese Buddhist bronze statues were displayed with ancient bronze vessels in well-lit glass-paneled vitrines. This arrangement underscored the technical aspects of bronze casting and the value of the objects as fine art antiquities.[73] Comparatively, Tibetan Buddhist

[70] Urubshurow 2013.
[71] Nashold 1981.
[72] Clark 2016.
[73] Leidy 2016.

artifacts in the West remained more likely to be viewed instrumentally as arcane liturgical objects, partly the product of a recurring discourse that envisioned Tibet as a last bastion of mystical knowledge and occult power—the land of Shangri-la.[74] Such a powerful zeitgeist undoubtedly shaped Marchais's temple-inspired display, but her altar was also distinctive from the ritual space created by Geshe Wangyal a decade later. The overall effect was less utilitarian in feel and more reflecting a carefully planned, if not overburdened, museum display, with each of the many images attesting to the refined eye of an art collector.

The decade of the 1950s would ultimately prove significant for the dispersal of Tibetan material culture. Like the political events that hastened the removal of Buddhist objects from Japan and China, the Chinese occupation of Tibet in 1950 and the emergence of a Tibetan exile community in 1959 has had a profound impact on the circulation of Buddhist artifacts. The ensuing decades would lead to not only the systematic destruction of many religious icons, but also concerted efforts at preserving artifacts as part of a threatened Tibetan culture, eventually leading to the establishment of special museum collections.[75] The Tibet House, for example, founded in 1987 in New York, views its collection of Tibetan artifacts as items preserved for repatriation when Tibet is again a free nation. Consequently, these broader sociopolitical contexts tend to paint Tibetan Buddhist objects with greater emotional weight and grant a certain nobility to those who salvage them rather than simply collect them.[76]

The sweeping immigration reforms of 1965 allowed for a larger diversity of Asian Buddhist immigrants, further changing the landscape of Buddhist materiality in the United States as more temples, Dharma centers, and retreat hermitages were constructed in a broader assortment of states, cities, and towns. In some cases, the territorial spread was directly related to governmental resettlement policies for refuges impacted by war and civil unrest in Southeast Asia during the 1960s and 1970s. This growing demographic diversity occurred in parallel with a deepening American embrace of Buddhism, informed not only by increasingly sophisticated presentations in books, but by embedded study abroad in Asia or training within new Buddhist communities in America (such as with Geshe Wangyal, among many others).

Such exposure has led to an emerging American consciousness about the sacrality of Buddhist icons. On one level, since the 1990s, some museums increasingly weigh the ethical considerations of opening consecrated icons, objects treated as living entities by weight of Buddhist tradition, and oftentimes filled with ex-votos and relics such as scriptural passages, written spells, or sacred illustrations.[77] Of similar importance is attention to the inappropriate placement of icons in museum spaces (too near the floor or lavatory) or the public exhibition of esoteric images only previously available for viewing to

---

[74] Lopez 1998, 135–155.
[75] Harris 2012.
[76] Singh 2010.
[77] Reedy 1991.

initiated adepts.[78] Moreover, some museum curators have attempted to establish more immersive multisensory environments with appropriate music, incense, and dramatic lighting, while others have invited Tibetan monks or Japanese Shingon priests to reconsecrate old icons or altar displays.

More generally, there has also been growing vocal resistance to the appropriation of Buddhist imagery into non-Buddhist contexts. This is most conspicuous in advertising, where the ethos of consumerism is founded on a belief that ownership of an object confers some aspect of its identity to the owner. This often forces a framing of Buddhist material culture as stereotypically cool, chic, or exotic, without engendering a deeper commitment to understanding Buddhist doctrine or practice.[79] While such economic entanglements are not new—indeed they form the earliest stages of American encounters with Buddhist materiality—they now come under increased scrutiny as a greater depth of understanding for traditional Buddhist views on sacred materiality is increasingly coming to the forefront of awareness.

Conclusion

This chapter demonstrates that the history of an emerging Buddhist material culture in the United States in inextricably bound to localized sociopolitical and economic factors both in America and abroad. This should not be surprising, as the very nature of Buddhism in America is complex and shaped, in part, by many different Asian Buddhist communities and traditions who arrived on American soil at different times for different reasons. Consequently, Buddhist figural icons, one of the more universal aspects of the global Buddhist diaspora, took on many overlapping roles as critical instruments of religious life (devotional, liturgical, apotropaic), markers of identity (religious, sectarian, ethnic), and remembrances of homeland (aesthetic, didactic, mythic).

In addition, a focus on socio-political and economic factors that helped push Buddhist immigrants to the United States can also be used as a model to understand early periods of Buddhist materiality in the United States. For example, periods of economic growth or political instability in Asian Buddhist countries often led to the selling or mass removal of Buddhist artifacts. As we have seen, such periods include the late seventeenth-century production of *blanc de Chine*, Japanese anti-Buddhist sentiment in 1868, the Chinese Revolution in 1911, and the occupation of Tibet in 1950. These events were counterbalanced by the various pulling forces of wealthy collectors, museums, and other institutions that brought Buddhist artifacts to the United States. Moreover, the American reception of Buddhist materiality has equally been shaped by complex socioreligious and historical factors. This has sometimes led to a suspicion of icons as

[78] Tythacott and Bellini 2020.
[79] Mitchell 2014; Prohl 2020.

dangerous idols, while at other times led to their proud display, if not as exotic curios or refined art, then as objects of devoted reverence and spiritual illumination.

REFERENCES

A Description of the Chinese Junk, "Keying." 1848. 4th edition. London: J. Such.

Ama, Michihiro. 2011. *Immigrants to the Pure Land: The Modernization, Acculturation, and Globalization of Shin Buddhism, 1898–1941*. Honolulu: University of Hawai'i Press.

Ayers, John. 2002. *Blanc de Chine: Divine Images in Porcelain*. New York: China Institute.

Armentrout-Ma, L. Eve. 1981. "Chinese in California's Fishing Industry, 1850–1941." *California History* 60, no. 2: 142–157. https://doi.org/10.2307/25158037.

Brandimarte, Cynthia A. 1991. "Japanese Novelty Stores." *Winterthur Portfolio* 26, no. 1: 1–25. https://doi.org/10.1086/496514.

Buddhist Missions of America. 1904a. "Donation of Our Headquarters." *The Light of Dharma* 3, no. 4: 134.

Buddhist Missions of America. 1904b. "Philadelphia to Have a Complete Buddhist Temple." *The Light of Dharma* 3, no. 4: 108–114.

Chen, Constance J. S. 2010. "Merchants of Asianness: Japanese Art Dealers in the United States in the Early Twentieth Century." *Journal of American Studies* 44, no. 1: 19–46.

Chong, Alan. 2009. "Introduction: Journeys East." In *Inventing Asia: American Perspectives around 1900*, edited by Alan Chong and Noriko Murai, 14–51. Boston: Isabella Stewart Gardner Museum.

Clark, Imogen. 2016. "Exhibiting the Exotic, Simulating the Sacred: Tibetan Shrines at British and American Museums." *Ateliers d'anthropologie* 43. https://doi.org/10.4000/ateliers.10300. Available online: https://journals.openedition. org/ateliers/10300?lang=en.

Clark, John R. K. 2007. *Guardian of the Sea: Jizo in Hawai'i*. Honolulu: University of Hawai'i Press.

Clarke, John. 2015. "Planning the Robert H. N. Ho Family Foundation Gallery of Buddhist Sculpture, 2009–2014." In *Sacred Objects in Secular Spaces: Exhibiting Asian Religions in Museums*, edited by Bruce M. Sullivan, 65–79. New York: Bloomsbury.

Colwell, Chip. 2022. "A Palimpsest Theory of Objects." *Current Anthropology* 63, no. 2: 129–157. https://doi.org/10.1086/719851.

Costello, Julia G., Kevin Hallaran, and Keith Warren. 2004. "The Luck of Third Street Historical Archaeology Data Recovery Report for the Caltrans District 8 San Bernardino Headquarters Demolition Project." California Department of Transportation District 8.

Conn, Steven. 2010. *Do Museums Still Need Objects?* Philadelphia: University of Pennsylvania Press.

Donnelly, P. J. 1969. *Blanc de Chine: The Porcelain of Têhua in Fukien*. New York: Frederick A. Praeger.

East-India Marine Society of Salem. 1821. *The East-India Marine Society of Salem*. Salem: W. Palfray, Jr.

Faure, Bernard. 1998. "The Buddhist Icon and the Modern Gaze." *Critical Inquiry* 24, no. 3: 768–813. https://doi.org/10.1086/448893.

Frank, Caroline. 2011. *Objectifying China, Imagining America: Chinese Commodities in Early America*. Chicago: University of Chicago Press.

Goldstein, Jonathan. 1991. "Cantonese Artifacts, Chinoiserie, and Early American Idealization of China." In *America Views China: American Images of China Then and Now*, edited by Jonathan Goldstein, Jerry Israel, and Hilary Conroy, 43–55. Cranbury: Associated University Presses.

Goto, Akira. 2021. "Jizo (Ksitigarbha) Statues under Palm Trees: The Materialization of Early Japanese Immigrant Culture in Hawai'i." *International Journal of Historical Archaeology* 25, no. 3: 648–662. https://doi.org/10.1007/s10761-020-00570-8.

Guth, Christine M. E. 1995. "The Cult of Kannon among Nineteenth Century American Japanophiles." *Orientations* 26, no. 11: 28–34.

Guth, Christine M. E. 2004. *Longfellow's Tattoos: Tourism, Collecting, and Japan*. Seattle: University of Washington Press.

Henle, James. 1922. "Selling the Exotic to Main Street: A. A. Vantine & Co. Succeed Where Carol Kennicott Failed." *Printer's Ink*, September 14: 77–80.

Haddad, John R. 2008. *The Romance of China: Excursions to China in U.S. Culture: 1776–1876*. New York: Columbia University Press.

Harris, Clare E. 2012. *The Museum on the Roof of the World: Art, Politics and the Representation of Tibet*. Chicago: University of Chicago Press.

Ho, Chuimei, and Bennet Bronson. 2016. *Three Chinese Temples in California*. Seattle: Chinese in Northwest America Research Committee.

Ho, Chuimei, and Bennet Bronson. 2022. *Chinese Traditional Religion and Temples in North America, 1849-1920: California*. Seattle: Chinese in Northwest America Research Committee.

Hunter, Louise H. 1971. *Buddhism in Hawaii: Its Impact on a Yankee Community*. Honolulu: University of Hawai'i Press.

Iwamura, Jane Naomi. 2011. *Virtual Orientalism: Asian Religions and American Popular Culture*. New York: Oxford University Press.

Ketelaar, James. 1990. *Of Heretics and Martyrs in Meiji Japan-Buddhism and Its Persecution*. Princeton, NJ: Princeton University Press.

Kieschnick, John. 2003. *The Impact of Buddhism on Chinese Material Culture*. Princeton, NJ: Princeton University Press.

Kisluk-Grosheide, Daniëlle. 2002. "The Reign of Magots and Pagods." *Metropolitan Museum Journal* 37: 177–198. https://doi.org/10.2307/1513083.

Kiss, Mónica. 2018. "Esoteric Iconography as Curiosum: An Overview of Japanese Buddhist Art Displays with a Specific Example." *Annals of the Faculty of Foreign Languages and Literature* 19, no. 1: 39–58.

Kuchiki, Yuriko. 2013. "The Enemy Trader: The United States and the End of Yamanaka." *Impressions* 34: 32–53.

Lachman, Charles. 2005. "Art." In *Critical Terms for the Study of Buddhism*, edited by Donald S. Lopez, 37–55. Buddhism and Modernity. Chicago: University of Chicago Press.

Leath, Robert A. 1999. "'After the Chinese Taste': Chinese Export Porcelain and Chinoiserie Design in Eighteenth-Century Charleston." *Historical Archaeology* 33, no. 3: 48–61. https://doi.org/10.1007/BF03373622.

Leidy, Denise P. 2015. "Discovery and Display: Case Studies from the Metropolitan Museum of Art." In *Sacred Objects in Secular Spaces: Exhibiting Asian Religions in Museums*, edited by Bruce M. Sullivan, 94–106. New York: Bloomsbury.

Lopez, Donald S. 1998. *Prisoners of Shangri-La: Tibetan Buddhism and the West*. Chicago: University of Chicago Press.

Maffly-Kipp, Laurie. 2005. "Engaging Habits and Besotted Idolatry: Viewing Chinese Religions in the American West." *Material Religion* 1, no. 1: 72–96. https://doi.org/10.2752/174322005778054410.

McDaniel, Justin. 2016. *Architects of Buddhist Leisure: Socially Disengaged Buddhism in Asia's Museums, Monuments, and Amusement Parks*. Honolulu: University of Hawai'i Press.

Meyer, Brigit, Morgan David, Crispin Paine, and S. Brent Plate. 2010. "The Origin and Mission of Material Religion." *Religion* 40, no. 3: 207–211.

Mitchell, Scott A. 2014. "The Tranquil Meditator: Representing Buddhism and Buddhists in US Popular Media." *Religion Compass* 8, no. 3: 81–89. https://doi.org/10.1111/rec3.12104.

Moon, Krystyn R. 2005. *Yellowface: Creating the Chinese in American Popular Music and Performance, 1850s–1920s*. New Brunswick, NJ: Rutgers University Press.

Mudge, Jean McClure. 1962. *Chinese Export Porcelain for the American Trade, 1785–1835*. Newark, NJ: University of Delaware Press.

Mudge, Jean McClure. 1986. *Chinese Export Porcelain in North America*. New York: Clarkson N. Potter.

Nashold, James. 1981. "The dGe-Lugs-Pa Tradition of Tibetan Buddhism in the United States: A Portrait of Geshe Wangyal." *The Tibet Journal* 6, no. 1: 31–38.

Newsome, Jocelyn C. 2010. "Materiality and the Reception of Buddhists and Buddhism in Nineteenth-Century America." PhD dissertation, Claremont Graduate University.

Ng, Laura W. 2020. "Between South China and Southern California: The Formation of Transnational Chinese Communities." In *Chinese Diaspora Archaeology in North America*, edited by Chelsea Rose and J. Ryan Kennedy, 234–249. Gainesville: University Press of Florida.

Palmer, David A., Martin M. H. Tse, and Chip Colwell. 2019. "Guanyin's Limbo: Icons as Demi-Persons and Dividuating Objects." *American Anthropologist* 121, no. 4: 897–910. https://doi.org/10.1111/aman.13317.

Payne, Richard K. 2005. "Hiding in Plain Sight: The Invisibility of the Shingon Mission to the United States." In *Buddhist Missionaries in the Era of Globalization*, edited by Linda Learman, 101–122. Honolulu: University of Hawai'i Press.

Prohl, Inken. 2020. "Branding and/as Religion: The Case of Buddhist-Related Images, Semantics, and Designs." In *Buddhism and Business: Merit, Material Wealth, and Morality in the Global Market Economy*, edited by Trine Brox and Elizabeth Williams-Oerberg, 111–127. Honolulu: University of Hawai'i Press.

Pumpelly, Raphael. 1870. *Across America and Asia: Notes of a Five Years' Journey around the World and of a Residence in Arizona, Japan and China*. New York: Leypoldt & Holt.

Rambelli, Fabio. 2007. *Buddhist Materiality: A Cultural History of Objects in Japanese Buddhism*. Stanford, CA: Stanford University Press.

Reed, Christopher. 2017. *Bachelor Japanists: Japanese Aesthetics and Western Masculinities*. New York: Columbia University Press.

Reedy, Chandra L. 1991. "The Opening of Consecrated Tibetan Bronzes with Interior Contents: Scholarly, Conservation, and Ethical Considerations." *Journal of the American Institute for Conservation* 30, no. 1: 13–34.

Schwartz, George H. 2020. *Collecting the Globe: The Salem East India Marine Society Museum*. Boston: University of Massachusetts Press.

Seager, Richard Hughes. 2016. "Dharma Images and Identity in American Buddhism." In *Buddhism beyond Borders: New Perspectives on Buddhism in the United States*, edited by Scott A. Mitchell and Natalie E. F. Quli, 113–124. Albany: State University of New York Press.

Singh, Kavita. 2010. "Repatriation without Patria: Repatriating for Tibet." *Journal of Material Culture* 15, no. 2: 131–155. https://doi.org/10.1177/1359183510364079.

St. Clair, Michael. 2016. *The Great Chinese Art Transfer: How So Much of China's Art Came to America*. Madison, NJ: Fairleigh Dickinson University Press.

Stevens, Keith. 1998. "Images of Sinicized Vedic Deities on Chinese Altars." *Journal of the Hong Kong Branch of the Royal Asiatic Society* 38: 51–106.

Storm, Jason Ānanda Josephson. 2022. "Excavating the Hall of Dreams: The Inventions of 'Fine Art' and 'Religion' in Japan." *Religions* 13, no. 4: 313. https://doi.org/10.3390/rel13040313.

Suzuki, Hiroyuki. 2011. "The Buddha of Kamakura and the 'Modernization' of Buddhist Statuary in the Meiji Period." *Transcultural Studies* 2, no. 1: 140–158. https://doi.org/10.11588/ts.2011.1.7332.

Tanabe, George J. 2005. "Grafting Identity: The Hawaiian Branches of the Bodhi Tree." In *Buddhist Missionaries in the Era of Globalization*, edited by Linda Learman, 77–100. Honolulu: University of Hawai'i Press.

T'ien, Ju-Kang. 1990. "Decadence of Buddhist Temples in Fu-Chien in Late Ming and Early Ch'ing." In *Development and Decline of Fukien Province in the 17th and 18th Centuries*, edited by Eduard B. Vermeer, 83–100. Leiden: E. J. Brill.

Tweed, Thomas A. 2000. *The American Encounter with Buddhism, 1844–1912: Victorian Culture and the Limits of Dissent*. Chapel Hill: University of North Carolina Press.

Tweed, Thomas A. 2008. "Why Are Buddhists So Nice? Media Representations of Buddhism and Islam in the United States since 1945." *Material Religion* 4, no. 1: 91–93. https://doi.org/10.2752/175183408X288168.

Tweed, Thomas A. 2014. "Smells and Bells: Buddhism, Catholicism, and the Therapeutic Aestheticism of William Sturgis Bigelow and Isabella Stewart Gardner." In *Inventing Asia: American Perspectives around 1900*, edited by Alan Chong and Noriko Murai, 51–61. Honolulu: University of Hawai'i Press.

Tythacott, Louise, and Chiara Bellini. 2020. "Deity and Display: Meanings, Transformations, and Exhibitions of Tibetan Buddhist Objects." *Religions* 11, no. 3: 106. https://doi.org/10.3390/rel11030106.

Urubshurow, David. 2013. "From Russia with Love: The Untold Story of How Tibetan Buddhism First Came to America." *Tricycle: The Buddhist Review* 23, no. 2: 46–53, 103–105.

Wang, Daisy Yiyou. 2007. "The Loouvre from China: A Critical Study of C. T. Loo and the Framing of Chinese Art in the United States, 1915–1950." PhD dissertation, Ohio University.

Wang, Daisy Yiyou. 2016. "Charles Lang Freer and the Collecting of Chinese Buddhist Art in Early-Twentieth-Century America." *Journal of the History of Collections* 28, no. 3: 401–416. https://doi.org/10.1093/jhc/fhv023.

Whitehill, Walter M. 1970. *Museum of Fine Arts, Boston: A Centennial History*. 2 vols. Cambridge, MA: Belknap Press.

Williams, Duncan Ryūken. 2003. "Complex Loyalties: Issei Buddhist Ministers during the Wartime Incarceration." *Pacific World (Third Series)* 5: 255–274.

Williams, Duncan Ryūken. 2019. *American Sutra: A Story of Faith and Freedom in the Second World War*. Cambridge, MA: Harvard University Press.

Williams, Duncan Ryūken, and Tomoe Moriya, eds. 2010. *Issei Buddhism in the Americas*. Champaign: University of Illinois Press.

Winfield, Pamela D., and Steven Heine, eds. 2017. *Zen and Material Culture*. New York: Oxford University Press.

Yamamori, Yumiko. 2008. "Japanese Arts in America, 1895–1920, and the A. A. Vantine and Yamanaka Companies." *Studies in the Decorative Arts* 15, no. 2: 96–126. https://doi.org/10.1086/652831.

Yoshihara, Mari. 2003. *Embracing the East: White Women and American Orientalism*. Oxford: Oxford University Press.

Yu, Connie Young. 1991. *Chinatown, San Jose, USA*. San Jose, CA: San Jose Historical Museum.

Yuan, Bingling. 2002. "Dehua White Ceramics and Their Cultural Significance." In *Blanc de Chine: Divine Images in Porcelain*, edited by John Ayers, 37–48. New York: China Institute.

Zhang, Eva. 2011. "Kannon–Guanyin–Virgin Mary: Early Modern Discourses on Alterity, Religion and Images." In *Transcultural Turbulences: Towards a Multi-Sited Reading of Image Flows*, edited by Christiane Brosius and Roland Wenzlhuemer, 171–189. New York: Springer.

Zhang, Tao. 2019. "The Chinese Junk *Keying* and American Racialization of Chinese." *American Studies in Scandinavia* 51, no. 1: 85–108. https://doi.org/10.22439/asca.v51i1.5792.

CHAPTER 27

AMERICAN BUDDHISM AND VISUAL CULTURE

WINSTON C. KYAN

The diversity of American Buddhism is effectively explored through the multifaceted lens of visual culture, which includes mass media and devotional images used in community, along with more rarefied art forms collected in museums and curated in exhibitions.[1] A visual culture approach, which takes all images as social facts, also facilitates awareness of the transnational currents and localized eddies that contextualize these images.[2] Perhaps most importantly, an inclusive approach to visual production has the potential to challenge historically dominant narratives, such as elite orientalist views of American Buddhism, with the understudied perspectives of those minoritized through race, class, and gender. Accordingly, this chapter situates a broad understanding of American Buddhist visual culture in a chronology of key moments in the practice and reception of American Buddhism. The result is a restitutive overview that brings the Buddhist temples and altars of Chinese and Japanese immigrants into the spotlight given to European American Buddhist converts, juxtaposes the Buddhism-inspired contemporary art practices of women and Blacks with the compositions of the New York avant-garde, and positions mass media representations of Buddhist monks on TV and in cartoons alongside conceptual film and video installations.

---

[1] See Richard Hughes Seager, "Dharma Images and Identity in American Buddhism," in *Buddhism beyond Borders: New Perspectives on Buddhism in the United States*, ed. Scott A. Mitchell and Natalie E. F. Quli (Albany: State University of New York Press, 2015), 113–124. See also Jacquelynn Baas and Mary Jane Jacob, *Buddha Mind in Contemporary Art* (Berkeley: University of California Press, 2004).

[2] See Scott A. Mitchell and Natalie E. F. Quli, *Buddhism beyond Borders: New Perspectives on Buddhism in the United States* (Albany: State University of New York Press, 2015).

The Nineteenth Century

Chinese and Japanese immigrants first brought Buddhism to the United States in the mid- to late nineteenth century. Chinese goldminers and Japanese agricultural workers in California produced a rich visual culture of icons and temples, which are partly illuminated by records of the Tin How Temple and Guanyin Temple in San Francisco's Chinatown before the Great Earthquake of 1906, and by temple-inspired architecture in post-earthquake reconstructions.[3] However, many scholars tend to focus on the European American reception of Buddhism and mark its arrival with the World's Parliament of Religion and the Columbian Exhibition, both held in Chicago in 1893.

In the case of the World's Parliament of Religion, the Buddhist delegates included Soyen Shaku (1860–1919) from Japan and Anagarika Dharmapala (1864–1933) from Sri Lanka. The main point of the Parliament was to show the underlying unity beneath the world's religions, and Protestant Christianity's unique ability to manifest this unity. However, the Buddhist delegates were also eager to incorporate their religion into the narrative of modernity, and strove to present Buddhism as rational, non-theistic, and universal in its own right.[4] These themes of universality also played out on a visual level, when, several months before the official opening on September 11, 1893, the *Chicago Tribune* published a preview of the Parliament on March 5.[5] Among images that constitute the earliest American representations of Buddhist monks, the one depicting the Sri Lankan monk Anagarika Dharmapala stands out. He appears in full-length profile, surrounded by the exotic folds of his robes, and is shown as a distinct individual rather than lumped together with other Asian monastics who attended the Parliament. In a unifying gesture appropriate to the mission of the Parliament, the engraving technique used in the image dualistically divided Dharmapala's body into either black outline or white filler, rendering the skin tone of the Sri Lankan monk as pale as the Caucasian religious figures also shown in the newspaper article.

Further to the south of the city, the World's Columbian Exhibition opened to the public on May 1, 1893, commemorating the four-hundredth-year anniversary of the landing of Christopher Columbus on American shores. As with the World's Parliament of Religions, the World's Columbian Exhibition invited various nations to take part in a hierarchical view of progress that placed America at the top. Japan, with its own

---

[3] See Winston Kyan, "Electric Pagodas and Hyphenate Gates: Folklore, Folklife, and the Architecture of Chinatown," *Amerasia Journal* 39, no. 2 (July 2013): 25–47. See also "Through a Chinese American Lens," accessed February 21, 2023, https://demospectator.tumblr.com/post/650038487091970048/tin-how-temple-of-old-san-francisco-chinatown, and "Map of Temples in San Francisco's Chinatown 1850s–1906," accessed February 21, 2023, https://peterromaskiewicz.com/2020/06/02/map-of-temples-in-san-franciscos-chinatown-1850s-1906/.

[4] See David L. McMahan, *The Making of Buddhist Modernism* (New York: Oxford University Press, 2008), 91–97.

[5] See Jane Naomi Iwamura, *Virtual Orientalism: Asian Religions and American Popular Culture* (New York: Oxford University Press, 2011), 11.

imperialist vision of Asia, expressed early interest in participating and provided three freestanding structures to the exhibition. Most notable of these was the Japanese Pavilion. Modeled on a Buddhist temple located in Uji, this building is arguably the first aesthetic representation of Buddhist architecture in America. The building was completely constructed in Japan, then dismantled and reassembled in Chicago by a team of twenty-four Japanese carpenters. The model for the Japanese Pavilion was the Hōōdō of the Byōdōin, known colloquially as the Phoenix Hall, because its two side corridors and rear corridor resemble a bird spreading its wings and stretching out its tail. The original building dates from the Heian period (794–1185), but the Japanese Pavilion was designed to reflect the architectural idioms of two other periods from Japan's artistic and technological progress. The Muromachi period (1336–1573) was represented in the south wing, and the Edo period (1600–1868) occupied the central wing, while the Heian period, the actual source of the original building, stood in the north wing.

This interest in Asian religions had a prehistory, not only in the founding of the New York Theosophical Society in 1875, with its debts to Hinduism and Buddhism, but also in Ralph Waldo Emerson's *Nature* (1836) and Henry David Thoreau's *Walden* (1854), with their portrayal of religion and spirituality as a form of direct experience and common essence. Nevertheless, the interest in Asian religions in nineteenth-century America existed alongside darker streams of xenophobia, with anti-Chinese sentiment culminating in the Chinese Exclusion Act of 1882. However, at the same time as the Chinese were blamed for taking work away from the European American working class, privileged artists such as John La Farge and James Abbot McNeill Whistler avidly embraced Japonisme, or the craze for Japanese artistic forms.

Consider John La Farge (1835–1910), a New Yorker born to wealthy French parents, who went to Japan for a three-month tour in 1886.[6] La Farge's wife was a grandniece of Matthew Perry, who opened up Japan to trade in 1853. La Farge's traveling companion was the wealthy Henry Adams, who paid for the trip. Through these connections, La Farge met two influential afficionados of Japanese art, Ernest Fenellosa and William Sturgis Bigelow, who had both converted to Tendai Buddhism. Fenellosa was instrumental in introducing Japanese aesthetics to the West, while Bigelow was a prominent collector of Japanese art who would eventually donate 75,000 objects of Japanese art to the Museum of Fine Arts, Boston, many of which were objects of Buddhist art.

The appreciation of Japanese Buddhist art by Fenellosa and Bigelow most likely rubbed off on La Farge, whose watercolors of the Kamakura Buddha completed in 1887 are among the earliest American representations of a Buddha. Based on sketches and photographs done in Japan, La Farge completed this painting as a series of watercolors upon his return to America to commemorate his visit to important Japanese sites. The Kamakura Buddha, thought to date from the thirteenth century, is a massive 44-foot-high bronze Amida Buddha associated with rebirth in the Western Pure Land. At some

---

[6] See Vivien Greene, "Aestheticism and Japan: The Cult of the Orient," in *The Third Mind: American Artists Contemplate Asia, 1860–1989*, ed. Alexandra Munroe (New York: Solomon R. Guggenheim Foundation, 2009), 62–63.

point in its history, the wooden structure enclosing the Buddha, repeatedly damaged from earthquakes and tsunamis, was never rebuilt. For hundreds of years, the sculpture has endured the elements in the open air and stands as one of the most recognizable images of Japan.

La Farge captures the aged grandeur of the sculpture's surface through sharp contrasts of gray and yellow. In one painting he presents the Kamakura Buddha from below, and in another depicts the statue as viewed from the surrounding hills. These two images show La Farge's interest in the high horizon lines, tonal shifts, and color harmonies inspired by Japanese art. His paintings are also done in delicate washes that reference the misty compositions of Japanese Zen painters, such as Sesshū (1420–1506). The resulting fusion between Western linear perspective, in which parallel lines create an illusion of depth, and atmospheric perspective, in which modulating tonalities create recession, captures the monumental yet introspective demeanor of the Kamakura Buddha in a striking cross-cultural manner.

World War II

In 1924, the Johnson Reed Act was passed, which effectively ended all immigration from Asia. State-sponsored surveillance of Asian American Buddhism was likewise carried out in the 1920s and 1930s, when the government kept a close eye on Buddhist organizations in the continental United States and Hawaii, especially those connected with the Japanese diaspora, such as the Buddhist Churches of America.[7] Following the bombing of Pearl Harbor in 1941, this scrutiny culminated in 1942 with the forced relocation of Japanese Americans on the West Coast into concentration camps in the interior of the country. As a consequence, the war years from 1930 to 1945 give us two divergent views onto American Buddhism and visual culture. There are paintings by European American artists for whom Buddhism provided potent visual symbols of resistance to war and violence, and there are Buddhist devotional images created by and for Japanese American internees in the form of elaborate altars.

The Japanese names of these altars reflect multiple religious functions that cannot be captured by the single English word "altar." For example, there were *obutsudan*, large altars enclosed within their own wooden boxes and used communally, *shumidan*, large stand-alone altars without boxes that were also used communally, and *butsudan*, smaller altars for private use.[8] Camp newspapers would proudly report on the installation and commemoration of these altars, noting the specifics of their construction and materials.

---

[7] See Duncan Ryūken Williams, *American Sutra: A Story of Faith and Freedom in the Second World War* (Cambridge, MA: The Belknap Press of Harvard University Press, 2019), 27–34.

[8] See "Buddhist Altars and Poetry Created during the 1942–1945 Relocation of Japanese Americans: Meeting Religious Needs of Internees," http://www.discovernikkei.org/en/journal/2015/1/29/buddhist-altars-and-poetry-1/, accessed May 22, 2021.

For example, reports would mention the lack of nails used in the joinery and the quality of the wood. Distinctions would be made between altars made from scrap lumber and then painted over with opaque colors, and altars made from fine wood imported into the camps and covered with a clear finish to reveal the wood grain. Eventually, networks of craftsmanship were established in which altars built at the busy Heart Mountain Center Cabinet Shop in Wyoming would be shipped to other camps, such as Topaz in Utah.

In the Pacific Northwest, artists not of Japanese descent were able to continue their artistic practice relatively undisturbed. The primary figure in the region to reference an East Asian aesthetic was Mark Tobey (1890–1976). Through his use of "white writing," or the careful application of layers of white paint over the surface of a work, his work acquired the hazy appearance of East Asian paintings, especially those of the Japanese Zen tradition. Among the Seattle painters that formed around Tobey, the one most influenced by Tobey's approach was Morris Graves (1910–2001) and his visually hazy paintings. Graves began his lifelong study of Zen Buddhism in the 1930s and was known to have attended a Buddhist temple in Seattle before the war. A recluse, he built a secluded cabin on Fidalgo Island, sixty miles north of Seattle, where he read books on Japanese culture and lived what he imagined to be a monastic existence. As Graves put it, "Zen stresses the meditative, stilling the surface of the mind and letting the inner surface bloom."[9] As a pacifist, the war would also disrupt his life. Although Graves filed for conscientious-objector status, his file did not go through smoothly, and he was drafted. Refusing military training, he ended up spending a year in detention.

Two of Morris Graves's paintings from the war years stand out as Buddhism-inspired. In 1944, Graves completed *Black Buddha Mandala*, a tempera on paper painting that came to him as a vision. Using the dimensions of a piece of paper as the outer square, he painted a series of circles that abstracted the dizzyingly intricate geometries of a traditional mandala, or Buddhist ritual diagram. He drew one large circle in white at the edges of the paper. Within this, he drew a smaller circle filled with Tobey-esque "white writing." Between these two rings, Graves then drew four smaller circles in white at the cardinal directions, which contained plant forms rather than the tantric deities usually found in traditional mandalas. The background consisted of small interlocking brushstrokes of brown and gray, a neutral palette that constituted the "black" in the title. A year later, in 1945, Graves completed *Lotus*. Also tempera on paper, this painting plays with abstraction but holds a powerful pacifist message. The lotus is the ultimate Buddhist symbol of transcendence, representing a blossom that emerges from the mud but is not contaminated by it. Here, the flower is executed in hazy layers and explodes as a brilliant burst of light, making an overt reference to the horror of the atomic bombs dropped on Japan that year. The painting swallows the horror of the bombing through the mesmerizing play of light and color.

---

[9] See Kathleen Pyne and D. Scott Atkinson, "Landscapes of the Mind: New Conceptions of Nature," in *The Third Mind: American Artists Contemplate Asia, 1860–1989*, ed. Alexandra Munroe (New York: Solomon R. Guggenheim Foundation, 2009), 95.

The 1950s

While Buddhism was viewed as the religion of the enemy during World War II, the postwar years of the 1950s witnessed the revival of Japanese Buddhism as a source for orientalizing by European American artists and audiences. Seemingly counterintuitive ideas in Zen, such as the spontaneous understanding of profound concepts, were embraced by New York artists who found resonances between Zen and avant-garde practices. A crucial translator in this process was Daisetz Teitaro Suzuki (1870–1966), who arrived in the United States in 1950 for his third and most consequential extended stay. Suzuki produced a brand of Japanese Zen Buddhism that wove the exotic insights of Zen into the more familiar threads of New England Transcendentalism. By emphasizing how both found awakening in the direct experiences, Suzuki systematically pushed back the ritual and metaphysical aspects of Buddhism, while establishing a selective model of Zen that underscored concepts of emptiness and intuition. Not surprisingly, Suzuki's popularizations of Zen touched the practices of experimental composers in New York, as well as Beat writers on the West Coast.

Scholars have proposed that the appeal of Suzuki's Americanized Zen was also rooted in his image as the wise and extraordinary "oriental monk."[10] With his wizened face and overhanging eyebrows, he epitomized the stereotypical image of Eastern wisdom. One widely circulated photograph sums up his appeal. We see Suzuki from behind in three-quarters view. His face is barely visible, but his shaved scalp shines in the light, and his eyebrows jut out with their own dynamic energy. He wears a rosary around his neck, and he points to an empty teacup held by the person across from him. This person, the avant-garde composer John Cage (1912–1992), sits obediently—almost childishly—on the floor with his knees pulled up to his chest. His expression is one of beatific comprehension, smiling with eager, knowing eyes. The reference is clear: we are witnessing the *kōan*, or Zen riddle, of the empty cup. In this riddle, the master fills up the teacup of a student to overflowing and continues to pour. Unable to contain himself, the student protests, "stop pouring, the cup is full." The master then teaches, "you are just like this cup, full of your own presumptions, how can I teach you anything until you empty your own cup?"

Suzuki taught at Columbia University from 1952 to 1957, where his lectures became legendary. At these occasions, he came into contact with thinkers and artists, most notably Cage.[11] Shortly after meeting Suzuki, Cage began to incorporate Buddhist ideas into his art, eventually composing *4'33"* in 1952. It was first performed by David Tudor, who opened the keyboard lid and sat silently for thirty seconds. He then closed the lid and reopened it, sitting silently again for a full two minutes and twenty-three seconds.

---

[10] Iwamura, *Virtual Orientalism*, 25–32.

[11] See Jacquelynne Baas, *Smile of the Buddha: Eastern Philosophy and Western Art from Monet to Today* (Berkeley: University of California Press, 2005), 164–177.

He then closed and reopened the lid one more time, sitting silently for one minute and forty seconds. He then closed the lid and walked off stage. As such, the composition was a manifesto on silence and its power to redirect our senses to typically unnoticed phenomena. By presenting silence as substantive rather than empty, Cage attempted to express the Zen principle of the pregnant void. He also conveyed how the absence of the familiar heightens our perception of the unfamiliar. The audience confronted with silent piano keys was forced to focus on the ambient sounds of the auditorium and to scrutinize the visual movements of the performer. The opening and shutting of the piano, rather than marking beginnings and endings, now embodied the visual choreography of the performance.

One of the inspirations for *4'33"* lay in the *White Paintings* of Robert Rauschenberg (1924–2008), who produced a series of paintings executed in white housepaint in 1951. Upon closer inspection, these seemingly blank canvases constantly reflected the fluctuating perceptions of the viewer, which would vary according to the light and shadow in the room. In this sense, the paintings represented a paradigm shift that moved the definition of art from a fixed object *in* time and space to an intuitive experience *of* time and space. Indeed, John Cage has written that "the white paintings came first, my silent piece came later."[12] This shift from object to subject is also at the heart of *Automobile Tire Print*, a collaboration between Rauschenberg and Cage that dates to 1953. In this work, Cage drove his Model A Ford, with black house paint applied to a back tire, over a long strip of twenty sheets of paper that Rauschenberg placed on the street. The car tire's abstract linear imprint created a "quotidian icon."[13] The chance aspects of the work questioned the authority of the artist and alluded to the iconoclastic themes in Zen. Nevertheless, any attributions to Zen in this work are in and of themselves somewhat random. Arguably, *Automobile Tire Print* displays more an appropriation of Zen tropes rather than any deep engagement.

Indeed, the appropriation of Zen in works such as *Automobile Tire Print* would lead the Buddhist writer and speaker Alan Watts (1915–1973) to state, "today there are Western artists avowedly Zen that justify the indiscriminate framing of simply anything—blank canvases, totally silent music, torn up bits of paper dropped on a board and stuck where they fall, or dense masses of mangled wire."[14] Not one to ignore a slight, John Cage responded:

> what I do, I do not wish to be blamed on Zen, though without my engagement with Zen, I doubt I would have done what I have done. I am told that Alan Watts has questioned the relationship between my work and Zen. I mention this in order

---

[12] See John Cage, *Silence: Lectures and Writings* (Middletown, CT: Wesleyan University Press, 1961).

[13] See Alexandra Munroe, "Buddhism and the Neo-Avant Garde: Cage Zen, Beat Zen, and Zen," in *The Third Mind: American Artists Contemplate Asia, 1860–1989*, ed. Alexandra Munroe (New York: Solomon R. Guggenheim Foundation, 2009), 205.

[14] See Gregory P. A. Levine, *Long Strange Journey: On Modern Zen, Zen Art, and Other Predicaments* (Honolulu: University of Hawai'i Press, 2017), 132.

to free Zen from any responsibility for my actions. I shall continue making them, however.[15]

1960S AND 1970S

If in the 1950s, American Buddhist visual culture tended toward Japanese Zen and its appropriation by European American artists, the American Buddhist visual culture of the 1960s and 1970s reflected a heightened consciousness regarding race and ethnicity. More specifically, engagement between America and Asia would intensify in this period through a combination of direct travel to Asia by Americans and increased Asian immigration to the United States following the Hart-Cellar Act of 1965. Moreover, US military engagement in Southeast Asia and the Civil Rights movements of the 1960s and 1970s brought ideas of social justice to the fore. Within this environment, even artists who were not overtly political were politicized because of their race.

Consider the Korean American artist Nam June Paik (1932–2006), taken as the founder of video art, who created a series of Buddhism-inspired works that not only questioned the power of mass media, but also the power of those who could define identity.[16] In Paik's *Zen for Film* (1965), a film projector reels a roll of empty film. The work lacks intentional images, but the film projects the dust and other ephemera that it has gathered from its surroundings each time it is reeled. Likewise, the sound does not come from dialogue or a film score, but rather from the clattering mechanical process of reeling a film. The insertion of shadows and voices from the audience into the screening also becomes part of the experience. The resulting work is ever evolving and unpredictable, thereby playing with ideas of interdependence and propinquity. While these elements would correlate with concepts of chance and trace in the art world of the time, a Buddhist viewer of *Zen for Film* would also think of fundamental Buddhist principles such as co-arising, or *pratītyasamutpāda*, in which all phenomena are caught in a shifting state of mutual causation.

Nine years later, in 1974, Paik created *TV Buddha*, in which a Buddha sculpture watches itself on a TV screen. The screen's image is produced by a live video camera fixed on the Buddha statue, conveying a feeling of being forever caught in the closed-circuit loop of subject and object. The work expresses anxieties between tradition and modernity, art and technology. First purchased for a museum collection in 1977 by the Stedelijk Museum in Amsterdam, successive versions of the work were produced through 2004. Undoubtedly, the work's longevity rests in its particular relevance for the late twentieth and early twenty-first centuries, with its omnipresent surveillance and obsessions with screen culture and self-display. To a Buddhist viewer, *TV Buddha* also

---

[15] Ibid., 130.
[16] Baas, *Smile of the Buddha*, 178–187.

captures the doctrine of non-self, or *anātman*, which denies the existence of any permanent essence in phenomena. Despite the Buddhist titles and iconography of these works, Nam June Paik refuted any deep engagement with Buddhism and resisted any attempts to typecast his interests because of race. When asked if he were a Buddhist, Paik replied, "I am an artist. . . . Because I am a friend of John Cage, people tend to see me as a Zen monk. . . . I am not a follower of Zen but I react to Zen in the same way as I react to Johann Sebastian Bach."[17] In effect, Paik questions whether an artist of Asian descent can ever hold the European American privilege of appropriating Zen without being pigeon-holed as Buddhist.

Around the same time that Paik first created *TV Buddha*, Buddhism was first represented on popular American TV with the series *Kung Fu*. The show follows the wanderings of a mixed-race Chinese Buddhist monk in the Wild West. Because of its themes of vigilante justice and violence, couched within the overarching frame of pacifism, it has been called a "flower children's western."[18] The original ninety-minute movie pilot, *Kung Fu: The Way of the Tiger; The Sign of the Dragon*, first aired on February 22, 1972. By 1973, *Kung Fu* officially became part of ABC's regular lineup until its final episode on June 28, 1975. The promotional photograph that graced the cover of *Esquire Magazine*'s August 1973 issue captures the revolutionary nature of the show. In this image, David Carradine, the actor playing the Buddhist monk, kicks the Lone Ranger out of the picture frame. The caption states in bold font: "Ah, so! A new American hero at last!" The image of a badass Buddhist monk concisely captures the values of a new generation, one with complex attitudes toward war and violence, race and representation.[19]

The show follows the peregrinations of Kwai Chang Caine in the Western frontier. A half-Chinese and half-Caucasian hero, Caine has fled to the United States to escape punishment in China for killing the emperor's nephew. Whether this murder can be warranted or not sets the tone for his future actions in the United States, which also involve the killing of others. Caine thus becomes a fugitive in this country as well. However, his crimes are always presented to the viewer as vigilante justice, and scholars have read the popularity of *Kung Fu* against the fierce debates surrounding the ending years of the Vietnam War.[20] Another debate provoked by the show centered on the playing of a mixed-race character by an actor in yellowface. David Carradine, the actor playing Caine, was in real life fully Caucasian. Scholars have argued that the obvious distortion of Carradine's features into an Asian cast created a character who was artificially foreign, but who was ultimately Caucasian enough for the majority demographic of viewers.[21]

The Buddhist visual culture of the show focused mainly on the flashbacks to Caine's childhood and youth in the Shaolin Monastery in China. This is where the young monk

---

[17] See Hanna B. Holling, *Revisions—Zen for Film* (New York: Bard Graduate Center, 2015), 33.
[18] Iwamura, *Virtual Orientalism*, 121.
[19] Ibid., 119.
[20] Ibid., 113.
[21] Ibid., 138.

learns the wisdom of his instructors, who teach him martial prowess along with the responsibilities that comes with this power. For example, in one encounter between master and student, Master Kan advises his pupil on Buddhist ethics:

> perceive the way of nature and no force of man can harm you. Do not meet a wave head on. Avoid it. You do not have to stop force. It is easier to redirect it. Learn more ways to preserve rather than destroy. Avoid rather than check. Check rather than hurt. Hurt rather than maim. Maim rather than kill. For all life is precious nor can any be replaced.[22]

1980S TO EARLY 2010

The 1980s were a fertile period for Buddhism in America. Not only were the seeds of the meditation and mindfulness movements planted in the 1970s coming to fruition, but post-1965 Asian immigration was having its effects on homegrown Buddhist establishments such as the Dhammananda Monastery in Northern California and the Hsi Lai Temple in Southern California.[23] In terms of scholarship, this led to the "Two Buddhisms" model, with white convert Buddhists focused on meditation and mindfulness, juxtaposed with Asian immigrant Buddhists focused on ritual and merit making. From its inception, the model was problematic.[24] For example, the growing presence of Tibetan meditation and retreat centers in the 1980s were populated with Tibetan immigrants and refugees fleeing increased political oppression in China; however, these institutions catered mainly to white converts. This mainstreaming of Tibetan Buddhism would culminate in 1989 with the 14th Dalai Lama receiving the Nobel Peace Prize.[25]

Artists would react in interesting ways to this evolving context of American Buddhism, rich in meditative practices and references to Tibetan Buddhism. Consider Marina Abromovic (b. 1946), the Serbian American artist, and her work *Nightsea Crossing* (1981–1987). This video work captured twenty-two performances by Abromovic and her collaborator Ulay, which took place in nineteen different locations on several continents over the course of ninety days between 1981 and 1987. The place and the

---

[22] Ibid., 113–114.

[23] See Winston Kyan, "Folklore and the Visual Culture of Burmese America: Domestic Buddhist Practices and the Dhammananda Monastery," in *Asian American Identities and Practices: Folkloric Expressions in Everyday Life*, ed. Jonathan H. X. Lee and Kathleen Nadeau (Lanham, MD: Lexington Books/Rowman and Littlefield, 2014), 15–25. See also Jeff Wilson, *Mindful America: The Mutual Transformation of Buddhist Meditation and American Culture* (New York: Oxford University Press, 2014), 31–36.

[24] See Wakoh Shannon Hickey, "Two Buddhisms, Three Buddhisms, and Racism," *Journal of Global Buddhism* 11 (2010): 1–25.

[25] See Randy Jayne Rosenberg, "Curator's Notes," in *The Missing Peace: Artists and the Dalai Lama*, ed. Committee of 100 for Tibet and the Dalai Lama Foundation (San Rafael: Earth Aware, 2006): viii–ix.

duration of the performances would change, but in each performance, Abromovic and Ulay always sat across from each other, at the same table, with the same chairs. Their faces were also always turned toward each other so that the audience ended up looking at their profiles. One of the twenty-two performances is *Nightsea Crossing/Conjunction* (1981–1987/1983), which involves a Tibetan lama and a high-level Aborigine medicine man. Despite the artist's long and respectful engagement with Tibetan Buddhist communities, the work raises the issue of othering Buddhism and other non-Western religions. For seven hours a day for four days, Abromovic and Ulay sat in chairs in upright, "Western" style, while the lama and the medicine man sat on the floor in a crossed-leg position.[26]

In terms of meditation, Marina Abromovic has stated that *Nightsea Crossing* revealed to her the power of shifting consciousness from the physical to the mental; that is, while sitting motionless, her mind accessed an energy that allowed her to perceive her surroundings in 360 degrees. She later made a connection between the high states of awareness achieved in her performances and similar states arrived at through Buddhist meditation. As she puts it, "most people read the books and then they get interested in Buddhism, my entire relation to Buddhism came out of doing performances, through pure experience ... first experience then the knowledge."[27]

Buddhism in America in the 1990s and early 2000s parallels the development of identity politics in the United States at large, with retreat and teaching centers forced to confront long neglected issues of diversity. Not only have teacher training programs become more inclusive, but sanghas based on affinities of race and/or sexual orientation have also become more common.[28] However, the social justice turn in contemporary American Buddhism is not without its critics, since the Buddhist doctrine of non-self would negate any fixations on individual identity. Consequently, discussions of the suffering associated with race, class, gender, and sexual orientation are seen by some as a hindrance to liberation. What such critics fail to see is that the discourse around non-self has always been shaped by specific historical and cultural conditions, and that in twenty-first-century America, identity is the reality that practitioners need to address—not to bury. Two contemporary artists who take up issues of identity in their Buddhism-inspired work are Mariko Mori and Sanford Biggers.

Mariko Mori (b. 1967) is an artist who lives and works in New York and Tokyo, and in that sense operates as an Asian diasporic artist in America. Reflecting the transnational conditions of Buddhism in an age of globalization, her monumental installation

---

[26] Baas and Jacob, *Buddha Mind in Contemporary Art*, 188.
[27] Ibid.
[28] See Ann Gleig, *American Dharma: Buddhism beyond Modernity* (New Haven, CT: Yale University Press, 2019); Chenxing Han, *Be the Refuge: Raising the Voices of Asian American Buddhists* (Berkeley, CA: North Atlantic Books, 2021); Zenju Earthlyn Manuel, *The Way of Tenderness: Awakening through Race, Sexuality, and Gender* (Somerville, MA: Wisdom Publications, 2015); Jan Willis, *Dreaming Me: Black, Baptist, and Buddhist* (Somerville, MA: Wisdom Publications, 2008); Larry Yang, *Awakening Together: The Spiritual Practice of Inclusivity and Community* (Somerville, MA: Wisdom Publications, 2017).

in three parts, *Nirvana* (1996–1998), was conceived in Tokyo but exhibited in Chicago, Los Angeles, Pittsburgh, and London.[29] It is also a work of Buddhism-inspired contemporary art that foregrounds problems of gender. Throughout the installation, Mori takes on the role of producer, director, costume designer, and star to present herself as a shape-shifting young woman who is the gendered medium for various social and cultural ideas.

Nirvana comprises four billboard-sized, digitally composed photographs encased in glass, a 3-D video also titled *Nirvana*, and a lotus-shaped acrylic *Enlightenment Capsule*. The first of the large photographs is *Entropy of Love* (1996), representing wind. This photograph, along with the three others in the installation, uses images of various locations and objects that are then combined and manipulated on the computer. The images are then blown up to billboard size and encased in glass plates to increase their sense of monumentality. For instance, *Entropy of Love* incorporates images of Arizona's Painted Desert with images of a wind power station in California and a Biosphere dome near Tucson. In the foreground hovers an acrylic bubble that Mori calls the "love shelter," which seems to float as a UFO, enclosing Mori and her sister. Representing fire, *Burning Desire* (1996–1998) uses photographs of a location in the Gobi Desert called Flaming Cleft, considered to be particularly hot and arid, with the terrain looking like flames under certain lighting conditions. Four images of Mori surrounded by flames and wearing a Tibetan monk's hat float above the desert sands. As with a traditional mandala, the figures in flames represent devotees who wish to make contact with the central divinity, which in this image is Mori as a multi-armed deity encircled by a rainbow nimbus. The figure exhibits numerous *mudrā*s, or symbolic Buddhist hand gestures, and holds a lotus flower, one of the attributes of Avalokiteśvara, or the Bodhisattva of Compassion.

Representing water, *Mirror of Water* (1996–1998) is a photograph taken in a French cave that has been sculpted by erosion over millions of years. By integrating futuristic images of herself into a prehistoric cave, she collapses ideas of past, present, and future. Through the use of multiple self-images, sometimes appearing as twins or as triplets, the artist situates identity into a continuous chain of life, death, and rebirth. Completing the cycle is the fourth photograph, *Pure Land* (1996–1998), representing earth. The title refers to a realm of rebirth achieved through the worship of Amitābha Buddha, a paradise marked by its purity from unpleasantness, and consequently, an easier environment in which to focus on the rigors of meditation and enlightenment. Mori places herself at the center, surrounded by anime-influenced Buddhist celestial beings, or *apsara*, who play ancient instruments used in Buddhist ceremonies.

Nirvana (1996–1997), the 3-D video portion of the installation, stars Mori in an elaborate outfit that recalls clothing worn by Buddhist goddesses in traditional Japanese art, such as Kichijōten. The video integrates the same musician figures seen in the

---

[29] Carol S. Eliel, "Interpreting Tradition: Mariko Mori's *Nirvana*," in *Mariko Mori*, ed. Museum of Contemporary Art, Chicago (Chicago: Museum of Contemporary Art, 1999), 27–31.

photograph *Pure Land*. In the video, Mori holds a crystal in the shape of a lotus bud and performs a dance with various *mudrās*. The video has a soundtrack of Buddhist chanting, and sandalwood temple incense is blown into the gallery to give the viewer a multi-sensory experience. *Enlightenment Capsule* (1996–1998) is a lotus-shaped acrylic bubble that is lit by fiber-optic technology. The acrylic lotus is built to be large enough to hold a human being and is a direct reference to the belief that worship in Amitābha Buddha will result in the guaranteed rebirth of the devotee in the Pure Land. Technology in this work is elaborate, with a fiber-optic cable and a solar transmitting device used to bathe the viewer inside the gallery with light from the outside. In short, through the various multimedia and cultural elements of *Nirvana*, Mariko Mori not only demonstrates her mastery of male-gendered technology, but also her reinvention of Buddhist imagery in which female style and panache are celebrated.

In 2004, Sanford Biggers created *Joanin Bell Choir / Hip Hop Ni Sasagu*, or an "offering to hip hop." It is a work of Buddhism-inspired contemporary art that consciously integrates the artist's African American identity with his Buddhist practice. When Biggers went to Japan in 2003, he was connected with the Joanin Soto Zen temple, which had a large collection of large and very old bells. However, the artist decided to create a bell choir of his own design. Upon arriving in Japan, the artist found local artisans who helped him press, cut, and form melted down silver jewelry used by hip hop artists into Buddhist ceremonial bells. As the artist puts it, "melting down these objects was a way of distilling the bling bling materialism out of contemporary hip hop and youth culture. The ceremony is actually a eulogy of sorts."[30]

The ceremony itself consisted of sixteen people in four concentric circles that formed a mandala. Each person was assigned a bell of a different tone and was charged with sounding the bell in a free manner that evoked the improvisations of hip hop performance. The performers were instructed to strike the bell whenever and however they deemed fit, but to keep in mind the cue of the previous bell. The bells would sound from the inner circle to the outer circle. The remarkable aspect of this performance was that there was enough structure for people who were not tonally inclined to play music. However, there was enough freedom so that people who believe themselves to be strict and methodical, such as the Japanese, could express themselves in an open and improvisatory manner. Biggers thus centers this work on the tension between rules and transcendence shared by both Buddhist meditation and Black music-making. Biggers recounts, "because we were performing this bell chorus in the temple, we started with 15 minutes of mediation led by the Temple Master. When you look at the video footage you can barely tell from the facial expressions which part is meditation and which part is the performance."[31]

---

[30] Baas and Jacob, *Buddha Mind in Contemporary Art*, 209.
[31] Baas and Jacob, *Buddha Mind in Contemporary Art*, 210.

Coda: Cartoons as Buddhist Visual Culture

A hallmark of American Buddhism in the twenty-first century is its self-reflexive quality, manifest in numerous studies on how Buddhism is in fact not a religion but a set of secular values.[32] At the level of visual culture, this self-reflexive quality takes the form of Buddhist cartoons, which not only capture the capacity of American Buddhism to poke fun at itself, but also form a bridge between Eastern and Western cultures.[33] Consider the cartoons of Dave Coverly, which situate references to Japanese Buddhist paradoxes into the unexpected context of American domestic situations. For example, in *Zen and the Art of Child Discipline* from October 1, 1994, a bald European American male with downcast eyes sits on the floor in monastic robes, while a small child stands in front of him. In the background, candles and incense burn on a low altar to suggest a sacred space. A speech bubble rising from the mouth of the adult figure reads: "When you feel the urge to act badly, my son, ask yourself this: what is the sound of one hand spanking." The cartoon thus assumes that the reader knows the popular *kōan*, or Zen riddle used to test Buddhist progress, "What is the sound of one hand clapping," attributed to the influential Japanese Rinzai monk Hakuin Eikaku (1686–1769). The humor hinges upon specific educational and class-based presumptions about general Buddhist knowledge, which is part of the self-congratulatory fun of getting the joke. In *Zen GPS* from September 21, 2009, a slouching androgynous figure in monastic robes drives with one hand on the steering wheel. A GPS monitor in front of the figure shouts out: "Follow your bliss"; "The obstacle is the path"; "If you aim for it, you are turning away from it." Again, the cartoon assumes that the viewer understands the use of paradox in Buddhist practice as a way of creating insight. In these two cases, Buddhist cartoons also become a vehicle for social commentary on contemporary parenting obsessions and technological dependence.

The cartoons of Dan Piraro similarly play on a reader's assumed skepticism of religious piety. In one cartoon from February 11, 2016, two figures sit on clouds. One figure clad in monastic robes sits in the lotus posture with a cranial protuberance, or *ushnisha*, on top of his head. These visual cues clearly reference the historical Buddha Shakyamuni. To his left, a Middle Eastern presenting man with dark hair, mustache, and beard sits with a gold halo above his head. This figure clearly represents Jesus. The speech bubble above Shakyamuni reads, "I should've made one of those nobody-can-depict-me rules. They always make me fat." The speech bubble above Jesus reads, "Tell

---

[32] See Stephen Batchelor, *Buddhism without Beliefs* (New York: Riverhead Books, 1997); Evan Thompson, *Why I Am Not a Buddhist* (New Haven, CT: Yale University Press, 2020); Robert Wright, *Why Buddhism Is True: The Science and Philosophy of Meditation and Enlightenment* (New York: Simon and Schuster, 2017).

[33] Levine, *Long Strange Journey*, 158–194.

me about it, I've been a blond, white dude for, like, 2000 years." In a single stroke, the cartoon brilliantly links together certain Islamic restrictions on figural representations, the popular misunderstanding that takes the plump bodhisattva Budai for the Buddha, and the tendency to represent deities in the likeness of the congregation, with a blond and blue-eyed Jesus the norm for Northern European countries and those regions settled by them. By pointing out the seemingly arbitrary nature of religious representation, this cartoon takes a universally offensive approach to religion and humor. In *The Zen Awards* from July 5, 2017, seven monks kneel on what appears to be a flat expanse of gravel. They all face a senior monk who sits on higher ground in the lotus position. He looks out at the other monks and says, "Thanks for nothing." Again, humor hinges on the assumption that the reader will understand that nothingness and emptiness, or *śūnyatā*, is a desired state of wisdom in Buddhist practice.

This overview has explored American Buddhism through the wide lens of visual culture to show that popular images have as much power as high art in reflecting the impact of Buddhism on American culture. By taking visual culture as a social mirror onto the transnational reality of American Buddhism, this chapter has also challenged white convert narratives of Buddhism's reception by highlighting issues of race, class, and gender. Nevertheless, much still needs to be done to write a truly inclusive history of American Buddhist visual culture. For example, some aspects of Asian American Buddhist visual culture have been touched upon, such as Buddhist temples in nineteenth-century Chinatowns and Buddhist altars built in internment camps for Japanese Americans. However, these and other topics related to the American Buddhist visual culture of minoritized individuals require deeper investigations and remain rich mines of potential for further research.

References

Baas, Jacquelynne. *Smile of the Buddha: Eastern Philosophy and Western Art from Monet to Today*. Berkeley: University of California Press, 2005.

Baas, Jacquelynn, and Mary Jane Jacob. *Buddha Mind in Contemporary Art*. Berkeley: University of California Press, 2004.

Batchelor, Stephen. *Buddhism without Beliefs*. New York: Riverhead Books, 1997.

Cage, John. *Silence: Lectures and Writings*. Middletown, CT: Wesleyan University Press, 1961.

Eliel, Carol S. "Interpreting Tradition: Mariko Mori's *Nirvana*." In *Mariko Mori*, edited by the Museum of Contemporary Art, Chicago, 27–31. Chicago: Museum of Contemporary Art, 1999.

Gleig, Ann. *American Dharma: Buddhism beyond Modernity*. New Haven, CT: Yale University Press, 2019.

Greene, Vivien. "Aestheticism and Japan: The Cult of the Orient." In *The Third Mind: American Artists Contemplate Asia, 1860–1989*, edited by Alexandra Munroe, 59–71. New York: Solomon R. Guggenheim Foundation, 2009.

Han, Chenxing. *Be the Refuge: Raising the Voices of Asian American Buddhists*. Berkeley, CA: North Atlantic Books, 2021.

Holling, Hanna B. *Revisions—Zen for Film*. New York: Bard Graduate Center, 2015.

Hickey, Wakoh Shannon. "Two Buddhisms, Three Buddhisms, and Racism." *Journal of Global Buddhism* 11 (2010): 1–25.

Iwamura, Jane Naomi. *Virtual Orientalism: Asian Religions and American Popular Culture*. New York: Oxford University Press, 2011.

Kyan, Winston. "Electric Pagodas and Hyphenate Gates: Folklore, Folklife, and the Architecture of Chinatown." *Amerasia Journal* 39, no. 2 (July 2013): 25–47.

Kyan, Winston. "Folklore and the Visual Culture of Burmese America: Domestic Buddhist Practices and the Dhammananda Monastery." In *Asian American Identities and Practices: Folkloric Expressions in Everyday Life*, edited by Jonathan H. X. Lee and Kathleen Nadeau, 15–25. Lanham, MD: Lexington Books/Rowman and Littlefield, 2014.

Levine, Gregory P. A. *Long Strange Journey: On Modern Zen, Zen Art, and Other Predicaments*. Honolulu: University of Hawai'i Press, 2017.

McMahan, David L. *The Making of Buddhist Modernism*. New York: Oxford University Press, 2008.

Mitchell, Scott A., and Natalie E. F. Quli. *Buddhism beyond Borders: New Perspectives on Buddhism in the United States*. Albany: State University of New York Press, 2015.

Manuel, Zenju Earthlyn. *The Way of Tenderness: Awakening through Race, Sexuality, and Gender*. Somerville, MA: Wisdom Publications, 2015.

Munroe, Alexandra. "Buddhism and the Neo-Avant Garde: Cage Zen, Beat Zen, and Zen." In *The Third Mind: American Artists Contemplate Asia, 1860–1989*, edited by Alexandra Munroe, 199–215. New York: Solomon R. Guggenheim Foundation, 2009.

Pyne, Kathleen, and D. Scott Atkinson. "Landscapes of the Mind: New Conceptions of Nature." In *The Third Mind: American Artists Contemplate Asia, 1860–1989*, edited by Alexandra Munroe, 89–99. New York: Solomon R. Guggenheim Foundation, 2009.

Rosenberg, Randy Jayne. "Curator's Notes." In *The Missing Peace: Artists and the Dalai Lama*, edited by Committee of 100 for Tibet and the Dalai Lama Foundation, viii–ix. San Rafael: Earth Aware, 2006.

Seager, Richard Hughes. "Dharma Images and Identity in American Buddhism." In *Buddhism beyond Borders: New Perspectives on Buddhism in the United States*, edited by Scott A. Mitchell and Natalie E. F. Quli, 113–124. Albany: State University of New York Press, 2015.

Thompson, Evan. *Why I Am Not a Buddhist*. New Haven, CT: Yale University Press, 2020.

Williams, Duncan Ryūken. *American Sutra: A Story of Faith and Freedom in the Second World War*. Cambridge, MA: The Belknap Press of Harvard University Press, 2019.

Willis, Jan. *Dreaming Me: Black, Baptist, and Buddhist*. Somerville, MA: Wisdom Publications, 2008.

Wilson, Jeff. *Mindful America: The Mutual Transformation of Buddhist Meditation and American Culture*. New York: Oxford University Press, 2014.

Wright, Robert. *Why Buddhism Is True: The Science and Philosophy of Meditation and Enlightenment*. New York: Simon and Schuster, 2017.

Yang, Larry. *Awakening Together: The Spiritual Practice of Inclusivity and Community*. Somerville, MA: Wisdom Publications, 2017.

CHAPTER 28

BUDDHISM AND AMERICAN LITERATURE

KIMBERLY BEEK

BUDDHISM has long been a source of inspiration for American writers, and its teachings and principles have played a meaningful role in shaping the landscape of American fiction and poetry. From the Transcendentalists of the nineteenth century to the Beat poets of the mid-twentieth century and the postmodernists of the twenty-first century, many American writers have been drawn to Buddhism for its emphasis on mindfulness, compassion, and the search for meaning and enlightenment. In their works, these writers often explore Buddhist themes such as suffering, the impermanence of all things, and the power of the present moment to transform and heal. Whether they are practicing Buddhists themselves or simply are drawn to its wisdom and insights, writers have used the framework of Buddhism to create works that are both deeply personal and universally resonant. As a result, Buddhism has become an integral part of the American literary tradition and continues to influence and inspire writers to this day. This chapter explores the rich diversity of cultures and imaginative narratives where Buddhism intersects with American fiction and poetry.

American literature and American Buddhism are two interconnected aspects of American culture and society. American literature refers to the body of written works produced in the English language in the United States, covering a wide range of genres and styles and exploring themes such as American history, culture, identity, and concepts of freedom. American literature can be divided into several different periods, including the colonial and revolutionary period, the romantic period, the realism and naturalism period, and the modern and contemporary period. American Buddhism refers to the various forms of Buddhism that have been adapted and practiced in the United States. It is a diverse and multifaceted tradition that encompasses a wide range of schools, styles, and practices, and includes many different ethnic and cultural influences. American Buddhism is unique and evolving, and often incorporates elements from different traditions and teachings, such as Theravāda, Pure Land, Tibetan, and Zen, as well as influences from American culture and society. In general, the development of American

Buddhism reflects democratic values and emphasizes social engagement through activities such as environmentalism. Together, American Buddhism and literature provide a unique and fascinating window into the complexity and diversity of American culture and society. As an interdependent cultural product, Buddhist American literature creates space in the American social imaginary to complicate, develop, and negotiate identities, ideologies, and cultural landscapes.

This brief survey highlights key examples of the intersection of Buddhism and American literature that illustrate the literary trends of their respective time periods. The first section of the chapter focuses on transnational storytelling and covers the Romantic literature of the nineteenth century and early twentieth century. The second section looks at how Buddhist narratives in literature began to trend toward representations of lived Buddhism in the twentieth century. The third section examines contemporary fiction and poetry that inscribes Buddhism into the American social imaginary, thereby embedding Buddhism into American culture and history. Overall, the chapter aims to provide a concise overview of Buddhism in American literature and the ways in which it has evolved over time.

Transnational Storytelling

During the nineteenth century, American understanding and writing about Buddhism flowed through transnational connections influenced by a global context of colonialism. These connections were not directly with Asian peoples, despite the mid-nineteenth-century arrival of Chinese Buddhists to work in American gold mines. For Westerners, Buddhism was primarily understood through texts translated by Anglo-Americans and Europeans in lieu of the practices of Buddhists from Asia. As a result, American knowledge of Buddhism was filtered through Western discourses of imperial dominance, such as orientalism.

One unique group of American writers who were influenced by transnational connections were the Transcendentalists. The philosophical movement known as Transcendentalism originated in the United States in the early nineteenth century. It was largely a reaction to the rationalism and materialism prevalent at the time, and it emphasized the inherent goodness of nature and humanity alongside the importance of individual experience. Many of the Transcendentalists, including Henry David Thoreau, Ralph Waldo Emerson, and Walt Whitman, were influenced by philosophical and religious ideas from the East, including Buddhism. In particular, the Transcendentalists were attracted to the Buddhist emphasis on inner experience and the search for spiritual enlightenment, which resonated with their own beliefs about the power of the individual to transcend the limitations of the material world. They also admired Buddhist teachings of the interconnectedness of all things that foregrounded the importance of compassion in all relationships.

The Transcendentalist poets were known for their use of free verse, a form of poetry that does not adhere to traditional rules of meter and rhyme like the Romantic poetry of the nineteenth century. Ralph Waldo Emerson and Walt Whitman were particularly notable for their use of free verse, which relied on natural rhythms and the use of line breaks to create structure. Emerson also used free verse in his essays and lectures, helping to create a new literary form known as "prose poetry." However, not all Transcendentalist writers used free verse, and some, such as Henry David Thoreau, wrote in more traditional forms of poetry and prose.

The authors of the Transcendentalist movement influenced the American reception of Buddhism in at least two important ways. First, their publishing work helped to introduce Buddhism to American audiences. For example, in 1844 a fragment of the *Lotus Sutra* was translated from French by Elizabeth Peabody and published in *The Dial*, a Transcendentalist journal edited by Ralph Waldo Emerson.[1] Second, the poetry of the Transcendentalists reflects Indian dharmic and Buddhist influences. The famous, seminal poem "Leaves of Grass" by Walt Whitman, the "Bard of Democracy," has often been read as having prominent Buddhist and Hindu themes.[2]

In the years following the publication of Whitman's "Leaves of Grass," the first Chinese Buddhist temple was established in San Francisco and the first Japanese immigrants arrived in the United States. Despite this influx of Buddhists from Asia, Americans continued to be influenced by Western interpretations of Buddhism. One notable example of this is Edwin Arnold's transnational poem "The Light of Asia," first published in 1879 in London.[3] Based on the life of the Buddha as told in sacred Buddhist texts, the poem, written in rhyming verse, gained widespread popularity among Anglophone readers on both sides of the Atlantic.

Arnold's poem has been both praised and criticized as a highly romanticized retelling; for example, Arnold's highly idealized descriptions of the Buddha as a youth in the following lines:

> Like some fair dewdrop on a lotus leaf,
> He shone in all the splendour of his youth. (Book 1, lines 3–4)

The dew drop and lotus leaf are symbols of the Buddha's purity and enlightenment, used to convey the idea that the Buddha was a special and extraordinary person, even from a young age. Arnold attempted to bridge both Indian and Western cultures in order to render the founder of a religion unknown to Anglophone audiences. As a result, there are lines from the poem that characterize the Buddha in somewhat Christian tones, as follows:

---

[1] *The Dial: A Magazine for Literature, Philosophy, and Religion* 4 (1840–1844) (Boston: Russell & Russell, 1961), 391–410.
[2] Allen 1959; Leonard 2008; Schaffer 2016.
[3] Arnold 2005.

> The Lord of Life, the Lord of Love,
> The Lord of all things known above,
> The Lord of all that lies below,
> The Lord of all that can or may be so,
> The Lord of Life, the Lord of Love. (Book 8, lines 1–4)

The use of the term "Lord" and the moniker of "Love" is reminiscent of a statement in the New Testament that "God is love" (1 John 4:16 NIV). This language was, perhaps, required for Arnold's audience. Later in the poem, however, Arnold distinguished the Buddha from Western religion when he wrote:

> He spake of karma and of rebirth,
> Of sorrow and of joy, of love and hate,
> Of all the mysteries that lie beneath
> The veil of Time, and all the secrets hid
> In Life and Death. (Book 5, lines 1–4)

By citing Buddhist cosmology as part of the Buddha's teachings, Arnold firmly situated the Buddha in his Indian culture and belief systems. By retelling his life story in an epic poem in English, Arnold shaped how Western readers imagined the Buddha and his teachings.

"The Light of Asia" was translated into over thirty languages and sparked more interest in Buddhism among the middle classes in Arnold's England and in America than Max Müller's *Sacred Books of the East* series, published in the 1880s. Notwithstanding the circulation of stories about the Buddha in American society, Buddhist immigrants endured the injustices of harsh living conditions and discrimination under laws such as the Chinese Exclusion Act of 1882, which prevented Chinese laborers from competing for mining jobs.

Ezra Pound's poetry and Pearl Buck's fiction from the early twentieth century can be read as correctives to nineteenth-century perceptions of Asian American immigrants. Ezra Pound's poem "Cathay" is a collection of translations of Chinese poems by the poet Li Po (also known as Li Bai), whom he considered to be one of the greatest poets in world literature.[4] The poems in "Cathay" were translated by Pound from the Chinese into English and are notable for their modernist, experimental style. In translating these poems, Pound also included references to Buddhist themes and ideas, as many of Li Po's poems contain Buddhist influences. His translations introduced many readers to Buddhist concepts and themes and contributed to the growing interest in Buddhism in the United States and Europe in the early twentieth century.

In the literary realm, Pound's translations of Li Po's poems have been some of the most influential and important translations of Chinese literature into English, conferring a lasting impact on modernist and experimental poetry in the English language. While

---

[4] Pound 2018.

Pound often employed free verse and other experimental forms in his modernist poetry, his translations in "Cathay" adhere to the traditional forms of Chinese poetry. This was in part because Pound saw these forms as an integral aspect of the poetry, and he believed that preserving them was essential to accurately conveying the spirit of the original poems. Still, the translations helped to establish a new direction in modernist poetry, as Pound sought to blend Western and Eastern literary traditions. In recent scholarship, issues of appropriation in Pound's work have come to the forefront of critical cultural studies.[5]

Pearl S. Buck's 1931 novel *The Good Earth* tells the story of a poor farmer in China named Wang Lung and his rise to prosperity.[6] Set in the early twentieth century, the novel follows Wang Lung as he navigates the challenges and changes of Chinese society, including the overthrow of the Qing dynasty and the rise of the Nationalist government. Through his hard work and determination, Wang Lung overcomes these obstacles and builds a successful life for himself and his family. The novel explores themes of family, tradition, and the relationship between humans and the natural world, and it offers a poignant and nuanced portrayal of Chinese life and culture, including depictions of Buddhist practices. For example, Wang Lung visits a Buddhist temple and is told by the monks there that he should make a donation in order to bring good luck to his family. Further, Wang Lung's wife, O-lan, has a small statue of the Buddha in her room and prays to it for protection and guidance. Overall, Buddhism is depicted in *The Good Earth* as a religion that is deeply rooted in Chinese culture and that provides guidance and comfort to the characters in times of difficulty.

Buck was the daughter of missionaries and she grew up in China. She was fluent in Mandarin and had a deep appreciation for Chinese culture. Her transnational experiences transmuted into nuanced and empathetic portrayals of Chinese people and society at a time when such representations were rare in Western literature. In addition to her writing, Buck was also actively involved in efforts to help Chinese immigrants in the United States. She used her platform to advocate for their rights and to promote understanding and acceptance of Chinese culture. *The Good Earth* won the Pulitzer Prize in 1932 and the 1933 William Dean Howells Medal. Like Pound, Buck's work has also come under contemporary scrutiny for inauthentic romanticizing of Chinese culture.[7] Yet at the time of publication, and for decades after, Buck's writing was significant in the development of Buddhist narratives in American literature because it made Chinese people real for American readers and portrayed Buddhism as a lived religion.

The earliest instances of Buddhism intersecting with American fiction and poetry were often the result of transnational storytelling, as writers and translators sought to bring the cultures, teachings, and themes of Buddhism to an English-speaking audience. During the nineteenth and early twentieth centuries, Buddhism was just beginning to

---

[5] Xie 2021; Yip 2015.
[6] Buck 2020.
[7] See Hayford, http://www.asianstudies.org/wp-content/uploads/whats-so-bad-about-the-good-earth.pdf; Spencer 2002; Zhang 2022.

gain recognition in America. As a result, much of the American fiction and poetry that featured Buddhism was written by transnational voices, such as authors who had lived abroad or translated retellings of Buddhist texts. These voices played a crucial role in introducing Buddhism to American audiences and contributed to the growing interest in the religion. Transnational storytelling around Buddhism also influenced the development of American literature, from the use of free verse to distinguish American poetry from nineteenth-century Romantic verse to the deployment of fiction as a platform for cultural awareness.

From Page to Path

This section explores Buddhism in American literature of the mid-twentieth century up to the turn of the millennium. In the postwar mid-twentieth century, contact between Buddhism and Western cultures increased through immigration and publications. *Siddhartha* by Hermann Hesse was originally published in German in 1922 and was translated into English in 1951.[8] Hesse's novel about a man named Siddhartha who lived at the same time as the Buddha combines teachings on Buddhism with the desire for religious pluralism. The influence of the novel on modern readers should not be underestimated, particularly as it coincided with the growing popularity of Zen Buddhism in America, as well as societal changes like the Civil Rights movement. *Siddhartha*'s popularity marked the beginning of Buddhist narratives around practice, taking Buddhist fiction and poetry from page to path, from a literary concept to a lived reality for millions of Americans.

In the 1950s, Japanese American Buddhist monk D. T. Suzuki introduced Zen Buddhism to Western audiences through his lectures and writing on the subject. This sparked a rise in interest in Buddhism, particularly among American Beat writers who embraced Zen as a countercultural response to postwar society. The Beat poets and writers, including William S. Burroughs, Diane Di Prima, Allen Ginsberg, Jack Kerouac, and Gary Snyder, were known for their spontaneous, free-form writing style and their interest in alternative spiritual practices, including Buddhism. The Beat writers sought inspiration from Asian religions as a way of rejecting the perceived repressive culture of the time. While some have dismissed their movement as a short-lived, disaffected reaction to the values of mid-twentieth-century America, the Beat generation had a lasting influence on the development of Buddhism in the United States. Despite criticisms of misrepresentation of Buddhist teachings, latent racism, and sexism, the Beats played a significant role in the growth of Buddhism in the country.

One writer highly influenced by Suzuki was Gary Snyder, a poet and environmental activist who incorporated Buddhist philosophy and practices into his work. Snyder's

---

[8] Hesse 2002.

poem "Smokey the Bear Sutra" is an example of the transformation of Buddhist concepts into practical action, particularly in support of environmental causes.[9] The poem combines the American icon of Smokey Bear with Buddhist philosophy and teachings. Smokey Bear is a symbol of the United States Forest Service created in 1944. His iconic phrase, "Only you can prevent forest fires," is a reminder of the important role that individuals can play in protecting and preserving the natural world. Through Smokey, this American sutra explores themes of environmentalism, mindfulness, and the interconnectedness of all beings. The poem is structured around the idea that Smokey Bear is the Great Sun Buddha (Vairocana), who teaches the reader about the importance of preserving the natural world and living in harmony with nature.

The poem includes references to various Buddhist teachings and ideas, such as the concept of interdependence, the importance of mindfulness, and the idea of "right action," or ethical conduct. Further, Snyder instantiates these Buddhist concepts into the American landscape, with lines such as: "Now those who recite this Sutra and then try to put it in practice will accumulate merit as countless as the sands of Arizona and Nevada." The instructions from Smokey are grounded in two ideas that Snyder wove together in his poetry. The first idea is an engagement with Far Eastern philosophies and traditions deployed to reconnect with a sense of America that was innate and primordial. The second idea is an appeal for engaged Buddhism, which involves actively working to create positive change in the world and to alleviate suffering, and often involves taking a stand on issues such as social justice, environmentalism, and peace.

Snyder was so influential in spreading the Buddhadharma that he was characterized in the fiction novels of Jack Kerouac, a French-Canadian Catholic American who became interested in Buddhism, particularly Zen, through his association with the Beats. His novels, such as *On the Road* and *Dharma Bums*, combined Buddhist themes with the rhythms of American jazz and blues.[10] Kerouac's conflation of different types of Buddhism and other religious traditions such as Catholicism and Confucianism has been criticized, but his influence on the Beat movement earned him the nickname the "grandfather of the Beats."[11] After his death, the Jack Kerouac School of Disembodied Poetics was opened in his honor at Naropa University, the first Buddhist university in North America.

Another Buddhist poet of note from the mid-twentieth century is Thich Nhat Hanh, a Vietnamese Zen Buddhist monk, teacher, and peace activist. Like D. T. Suzuki, Nhat Hanh purposefully brought Buddhist teachings to the West. During the Civil Rights movement of the 1960s, he met Martin Luther King Jr., and the two became close friends and colleagues, working together for peace and reconciliation during the Vietnam War. Nhat Hanh was deeply impressed by King's commitment to nonviolence and social justice, and King was so inspired by the quiet monk's teachings on love and compassion

---

[9] Snyder 1969.
[10] Kerouac 1957, 1958.
[11] Hakutani 2022; Haynes 2010.

that he nominated Nhat Hanh for the Nobel Peace Prize in 1967.[12] Thich Nhat Hanh published several collections of poetry in English, as well as books and articles on Buddhism and engaged Buddhism.[13]

Some of Thich Nhat Hanh's poetry was published by Shambhala Publications, a publishing house with roots in Tibetan Buddhism. Chögyam Trungpa Rinpoche, a Tibetan Buddhist meditation master and teacher, founded the Shambhala organization in the 1970s after fleeing Tibet during the Chinese invasion in the 1950s. The organization is based on the principles of Shambhala Buddhism, which combines the teachings of the Tibetan Buddhist tradition with the spiritual and cultural heritage of the Shambhala warriors of ancient Tibet. Two members of the Shambhala movement founded Shambhala Publications in 1969. The company is known for publishing works by influential Buddhist teachers, including Thich Nhat Hanh. Likewise, Wisdom Publications, founded in 1975, grew to become the largest Buddhist publishing house in America and publishes books and other materials on Buddhism, mindfulness, and other contemplative traditions. The establishment of Buddhist publishing houses in America raises questions of commodifying the teachings of the Buddha as a means of disseminating Buddhist narratives.

As Buddhist publication companies gained a foothold in American culture, Asian American literature also emerged as a distinct and influential literary tradition within the broader context of American literature. Asian American literature refers to literature written by Asian Americans, or those of Asian descent, who reside in the United States. In the decades following World War II, many Asian Americans experienced significant social and political changes, including the end of exclusionary immigration laws, the Civil Rights movement, and the Vietnam War. These events and the accompanying social and political upheaval had a significant impact on the development of Asian American literature.

Asian American writers began to explore and express their experiences as immigrants and as racial and ethnic minorities in the United States through fiction and poetry. They narrated the struggles and triumphs of their communities, as well as the complexities of their identity construction as Asian Americans. Even though many mid-twentieth-century Asian American writers were Buddhist, Buddhism is not always obvious in their creative narratives; it is sometimes an undercurrent that quietly moves the plot along.

Novels about Japanese internment offer excellent examples of the quiet Buddhist undercurrent present in mid-century Asian American literature. Experiences of forced relocation and internment of Japanese Americans during World War II had a significant impact on Asian American literature, as seen in John Okada's *No-No Boy* (1957).[14]

---

[12] In this same year, Roger Zelazny's Indian Buddhist influenced science fantasy novel *Lord of Light* (1967) was also published by Doubleday in New York. It was nominated for a Nebula Award in 1967 and won the Hugo Award for Best Novel in 1968. While Zelazny's sci-fi story retells the story of Siddhartha Gautama in a futuristic galaxy, it is often read through a lens of modern concepts of Hinduism that conflates Indian ideas of dharma.

[13] Thich Nhat Hanh 2001.

[14] Okada 2019.

Okada's novel is considered the first work of Asian American fiction to deal with the experience of Japanese internment. Over two decades later, *Obasan* (1981), a novel by Japanese Canadian Joy Kogawa, was quickly adopted by Asian Americanists into the canon of Japanese internment literature because of its distinctive and powerful narrative.[15] *Obasan* (Japanese for "aunt") is a compelling novel about the experiences of Japanese Canadians who were forced into internment camps in Canada during World War II. Kogawa blends genres—from adapted folklore, documentary reportage, letters, lyric poetry, and newspaper clippings—to affect a fictional situated testimony of Japanese internment in Canada. Buddhism is most prevalent in the novel in the characterization of Obasan herself, who embodies a silence that is at once attentive, protective, and yet stoic.[16] Obasan's silence functions as a form of mindfulness that allows her to remain calm in difficult situations and withstand trauma in the moment. Her quiet nature also lends Buddhist compassion to her family and community when she uses it to listen deeply to the needs and experiences of others, offering them support and understanding through her attentive silence. *Obasan* won the Before Columbus Foundation American Book Award (1982) and the American Library Association's Notable Book Award (1982) and was widely incorporated into American university syllabi.

Asian American author Maxine Hong Kingston's first novel, *The Woman Warrior: Memoirs of a Girlhood among Ghosts* (1976), also grapples with silence, but not Buddhism per se.[17] Her later novels reveal more of her Buddhist background. In particular, Hong Kingston's third novel, *Tripmaster Monkey: His Fake Book* (1989), relies on the Chinese Buddhist classic novel *Journey to the West* for the characterization of the protagonist.[18] In *Tripmaster*, Hong Kingston developed a *Journey to the West* monkey protagonist named Wittman Ah Sing, after Walt Whitman's name and famous poem "I Sing the Body Electric." The naming of this character alerts readers to Wittman's ongoing identity construction, combining his Asian heritage with his American home. Wittman is a Chinese American beatnik in 1960s San Francisco, struggling to find his own voice while dealing with the influence of Kerouac. Kingston's novel cheekily harnesses the restless and liberatory spirit of the Beat movement to critique its weaknesses in addressing ethnicity, gender, and race. Not surprisingly, *Tripmaster Monkey* won the 1990 PEN-USA West Award.

Asian American literature is not the only American sub-genre to use Buddhist narratives. Charles Johnson is a renowned African American author and professor who has received recognition for his literature, including the Academy Award in Literature from the American Academy of Arts and Letters in 2002. He also identifies as a Buddhist whose work falls into the category of African American literature. Two of his notable slave narrative novels, *Oxherding Tale* (1982) and *Middle Passage* (1990), are set in nineteenth-century America and are structured around Buddhist themes,

---

[15] Kogawa 1981.
[16] Abrams 1997.
[17] Hong Kingston 1976.
[18] Hong Kingston 2011.

although the novels are not explicitly about Buddhism.[19] *Oxherding Tale* follows Andrew Hawkins, a slave born to a slave owner and his African American butler's wife in mid-nineteenth century America, as he grapples with issues of identity and seeks self-fulfillment. Inspired by Kakuan's Zen painting-poems *Ten Bulls*, the novel narrates Hawkins's lifelong search for meaning in a complex world. In the novel *Middle Passage*, Rutherford Calhoun is a former slave who has purchased his own freedom. The plot follows Calhoun as he embarks on a journey that illustrates the Buddhist concept of interdependence. These themes may not be immediately apparent to readers unfamiliar with these Buddhist concepts. Even so, by combining Buddhist and slave narratives, Johnson's work could be considered Afro-Orientalism, a liberatory discourse of solidarity between African and Asian peoples that works toward an international anticolonialism.[20] In liberatory fashion, Johnson's work cuts across cultural and genre labels to blur boundaries.

Only a year after the publication of Johnson's *Middle Passage*, Helen Tworkov created the popular Buddhist periodical *Tricycle: The Buddhist Review* in 1991.[21] In its second issue she claimed that Asian American Buddhists were not prominent in American Buddhism. Jōdo Shinshū priest and professor Ryo Imamura countered that Asian Buddhists had welcomed white Americans into their temples and had introduced them to Buddhism.[22] This controversy highlights the existence of polarized Buddhisms in America and the study of Buddhism in the West. While Tworkov's assumption does not align with the reality of Asian American literature, which had already become a significant and influential voice for Asian Americans and their Buddhist practices, the raucous buzz around Buddhism created by the Beats tended to drown out the voices of the invisible majority of American Buddhists of Asian descent.

Inscribing and Embedding

This section explores the expansion of Buddhist narratives into American literature of the twenty-first century. By this time, authors of Buddhist fiction and poetry are wittingly inscribing Buddhist history, identities, lifeways, and practices into contemporary American literature, thereby continuing the trend started in mid-century American literatures and embedding Buddhism into the ongoing American experiment around freedom. Proof of the expansion of Buddhist narratives into all genres of American literature is marked by scholarly engagement with Buddhism in American fiction and

---

[19] Johnson 1990.
[20] McNicholl 2018.
[21] Tworkov 1991.
[22] Since Tworkov neither responded to nor published Imamura's counter, Charles Prebish published Imamura's letter response in his article "Two Buddhisms Reconsidered," *Buddhist Studies Review* 10, no. 2 (1993): 190–191.

poetry, and by more literary prizes awarded to authors and poets who write Buddhist American literature that propels these works into the public eye.

Wisdom Publications published one poetry and two fiction anthologies between 2004 and 2006 that neatly gathered and packaged Buddhism and literature for belletristic consumption. *Nixon under the Bodhi Tree and Other Works of Buddhist Fiction* (2004), edited by Kate Wheeler, was the first anthology to use the term "Buddhist fiction."[23] The volume contained novel chapter excerpts and short stories by a preponderance of American authors, with a foreword by Charles Johnson. Wisdom's next anthology was Andrew Schelling's edited volume *The Wisdom Anthology of North American Buddhist Poetry* (2005), which included American and Canadian poets from diverse Buddhist sects and schools.[24] The following year, Wisdom published a second volume of Buddhist fiction titled *You Are Not Here and Other Works of Buddhist Fiction* (2006).[25] These anthologies inaugurated a growing body of scholarship around Buddhism in American fiction and poetry.[26] Through the influence of literary and scholarly publications, the literary categories of Buddhist American poetry and Buddhist fiction (mostly American) were realized, which helped avid readers to identify a growing list of poetry, short stories, and novels with Buddhist narrative threads that worked to inscribe Buddhism into the American social imaginary.

Recontextualizing Buddhist sutras and teachings into a contemporary novel genre is another means of inscribing Buddhism into American literature. For example, T. Biringer's novel *The Flatbed Sutra of Louie Wing: The Second Ancestor of Zen in the West* (2009) is set in the American Pacific Northwest, but the story framework imitates the form of *The Platform Sutra of the Sixth Patriarch* (eighth–thirteenth century China) to reference Japanese Buddhist Zen master Dōgen Zenji, *The Lotus Sutra*, and other Mahāyāna texts.[27] Likewise, the novel *Taneesha Never Disparaging* (2008) by M. LaVora Perry replicates the protagonist Bodhisattva Never Disparaging (Sadāparibhūta) from chapter 20 of *The Lotus Sutra* in the characterization of fifth-grade protagonist Taneesha.[28] Her family practices Nichiren Buddhist chanting with Soka Gakkai International (SGI), and Taneesha tries to chant and practice compassion while grappling with bullies, social awkwardness, and her own petulance. Perry even writes SGI President Daisaku Ikeda into the storyline, connecting Taneesha's fictional world to reality.

The recontextualization of Buddhist narrative threads into American literature is not always as obvious. American Canadian film-maker, author, and Zen priest Ruth Ozeki wrote a fictional version of herself into her novel *A Tale for the Time Being* (2013) in

---

[23] Wheeler, ed. 2004.
[24] Schelling, ed. 2005.
[25] Kachtick, ed. 2006.
[26] Listed chronologically, see Loy, Goodhew, and Hirshfield 2000; McMahan 2008, 21–235; Whalen-Bridge and Storhoff 2009; Whalen-Bridge and Storhoff 2011; Normand and Winch 2013; Beek 2015, 2016; Mitchell 2016, 182–185. This list is not exhaustive.
[27] Biringer 2009.
[28] Perry 2008.

order to experiment with subjectivity and "time being."[29] The novel was informed by the writings of Dōgen, whose instructions on awareness of the present moment became a framework for the plot. Ozeki stated that the novel took its final form at a time when she had been reading Dōgen's essays. In particular, she was struck by the essay *Uji*, which could be translated as "time being," "being time," or "for the time being." Dōgen's idea of the time being as one who experiences the present moment as well as (a) being in time would germinate into the novel's other fictional protagonist, a Japanese American teenager named Nao Yasutani. The book opened with an epigraph from *Uji* on the time being, and then the novel began with: "Hi! My name is Nao and I am a time being. Do you know what a time being is? . . . A time being is someone who lives in time, and that means you, and me, and every one of us who is, or was, or ever will be."[30] In the first sentences of the novel, Ozeki presented her reader with a character who defined what it meant to be human, as an interconnected *being* in time. Ozeki's novel was shortlisted for the prestigious Man Booker Prize in 2013 and has been translated into twenty-eight languages.

Poetry is also a powerful medium for expressing being in time. Tsering Wangmo Dhompa is a twenty-first-century poet who writes about the Tibetan diaspora from experience. She is the first Tibetan woman to publish poetry in English, even though she is also fluent in Tibetan, Hindi, and Nepali. Born and raised in Dharamsala, India, and Kathmandu, Nepal, as a Tibetan in exile, Dhompa traveled to the United States for graduate school, where she still resides. Her free verse functions as a form of cultural preservation for Tibetans in diaspora. Dhompa's poetry is dreamlike yet disjointed, a reflection of memories of a home that was never inhabited. She represents spatial displacement through word (dis)placements to affect a sense of a people (beings in time) who are stuck for the time being. Dhompa's unique artistry is evident in her 2005 poem "Autonomy of the Mind" in lines like: "In my family, decisions are made by the lama / who dreams into fate" and "After all, we're living through a conjecture."[31] The phrase "dreams into fate" evokes the orphic power of a lama who juxtaposes a state of consciousness that can influence the future with a karmic destiny not fully under human control. Whatever decision is made by the lama is because "we're living through a conjecture," an opinion, and more specifically, China's opinion of Tibet. Even in diaspora, there is no autonomy of the mind because Tibetan bodies have been displaced from their homeland. Put another way, when history is stolen from a people, their future is uncertain. Dhompa writes about this sentiment in "The History of Sadness."[32] In this poem she talks about everyday activities like visiting a doctor and being asked about her medical history. Not knowing her family's medical history, she fills in the medical intake form with the words "heart disease" because this seems closest to the truth. Clearly Dhompa's

---

[29] Ozeki 2013.
[30] Ozeki 2013, 1.
[31] Dhompa 2005.
[32] Dhompa discusses this poem with Emily DemaoNewton in a 2021 *Tricycle* interview: "Home Defined by Those Who Have Lost Home."

Buddhist identity influences her poetry, yet she prefers to center conversations around "the parts of Tibetan history that were erased through genocide and the inability of Tibetans in exile to return to their homeland."[33] Dhompa's poetry keeps the Tibetan history of exile and diaspora firmly fixed in the present.

Intertwining histories is another means by which Buddhist narratives have expanded into American literature. There are two main ways that fiction authors accomplish this. Some authors retell Buddhist legends using a contemporary cultural lens indicative of American ideologies of freedom, like feminism. Other authors insert Buddhism into the lives of historical Americans to tell a story from a Buddhist perspective. Both methods embed Buddhist narratives into American culture and storytelling.

Jeff Wilson's short story "Buddherotica" (2004) retells the popular tale of the Buddha's conception using the feminist genre of erotica.[34] The story of the Buddha's conception, in which the bodhisattva descends from heaven into the womb of his mother Māyā, is a well-known tale that has been depicted in various art forms and texts across Asia. In Wilson's retelling, Māyā's dream is narrated in the second person, present tense, drawing the reader into the story as the main character. Readers familiar with Buddhism and the story of Māyā's dream will know what role they are playing in this creative reading process, conceiving the Buddhanature always already within them. Wilson's retelling through a feminist lens adds a new layer to the traditional tale.

Feminism plays a prominent role in contemporary re-imaginings of Yasodharā, the wife of Siddhartha Gautama. There is little written about Yasodharā in canonical Buddhist texts, so authors like Gabriel Constans (*Buddha's Wife*, 2009) and Barbara McHugh (*Bride of the Buddha*, 2021) have written novels of her life story using a feminist lens framed with compassion and ingenuity.[35] While Constans's novel tends toward the romantic, McHugh offers an alternative history that follows the broad strokes of what is known and taught of Yasodharā, but places her in the role of Ananda in the Buddha's sangha. Such feminist re-imaginings open spaces for important conversations about the role of women in Buddhism and reflect American Buddhism's democratic ideals and goal of equality in Buddhist sanghas.

In Julie Otsuka's novel *The Buddha in the Attic* (2009), Buddhism is woven into the story of Japanese "picture brides" who come to San Francisco in the early twentieth century for arranged marriages.[36] Narrated in the first-person plural—we—the story follows the shared experiences of these women as they struggle to achieve the American dream and maintain their cultural lifeways. Near the end of the novel, one of the characters creates a hidden altar in the attic, leaving a small brass Buddha to watch over the house before being sent to a Japanese internment camp. The Buddha in the attic

---

[33] DemaoNewton 2021.
[34] Wilson 2004. "Buddherotica" was originally published on the website "Killing the Buddha" in 2002 and later included in the anthology *Nixon under the Bodhi Tree and Other Works of Buddhist Fiction* in 2004.
[35] Constans 2009; McHugh 2021.
[36] Otsuka 2011.

serves as a symbol of the characters' reverence for their religion, even as they are forced to suppress it in their efforts to survive and assimilate in America.

Two stories that incorporate Buddhism into the lives of historical Americans are Charles Johnson's short story "Dr. King's Refrigerator" (2005) and George Saunders's first novel, *Lincoln in the Bardo* (2017).[37] In "Dr. King's Refrigerator," a young Martin Luther King Jr. has a moment of enlightenment while searching for a midnight snack. In *Lincoln in the Bardo*, which won the 2017 Mann Booker Prize, Saunders imagines President Lincoln grieving for his son Willie, who is stuck in a Tibetan Buddhist intermediate state between death and rebirth. While Saunders's conception of the bardo incorporates elements of a Catholic purgatory and the Egyptian afterlife, the novel successfully weaves Buddhist narrative threads into the American social imaginary through its focus on an iconic American president.

In an interview about his novel, Saunders related that for him, writing is a meditative practice.[38] Both Charles Johnson and Ruth Ozeki have also echoed this sentiment, as has prominent American Zen Buddhist poet Jane Hirshfield.[39] If writing Buddhist fiction or poetry can be considered a form of Buddhist practice, then reading is open to this praxis as well. Unsurprisingly, scholars are beginning to read non-Buddhist American literature through a Buddhist lens. Dean Sluyter, Pamela Winfield, and Sang-Keun Yoo have all published works that read classic English literature, Hemingway, and American new wave science fiction, respectively, through a Buddhist lens.[40]

Authors and poets of the twenty-first century have become adept at intertwining Buddhist themes and practices into contemporary American literature, inscribing the ongoing American experiment around freedom with Buddhist concepts and teachings, embedding Buddhism into American culture and history by creating space for Buddhist narratives in the social imaginary of contemporary readers. The impact on the development of American literature is evident in the suggestion that writing is a Buddhist practice, and that the act of reading anything can be done through a Buddhist lens.

Conclusion

This chapter provides an overview of Buddhism in American fiction and poetry since Buddhism came West. In the nineteenth century, Buddhist narratives in American literature took the form of transnational storytelling, transmitted through global activities such as colonialism, missionary work, and translation. However, these works also often incorporated colonial discourse and orientalism, leading to an exoticization of

---

[37] Johnson 2005; Saunders 2017.
[38] Schwartz 2017.
[39] Hirshfield 1997; Johnson 2003; Ozeki in Dwyer interview, 2017.
[40] Sluyter 2022; Winfield 2022; Yoo 2022.

Buddhism. In the twentieth century, Buddhist literature reflected the growth and development of Buddhism in the United States, with convert Buddhists deploying it as a means of social engagement and Asian American Buddhists employing it to address experiences of discrimination and negotiate identities in an unwelcoming environment. Buddhism in twentieth-century American literature was depicted as a lived religion characterized by suffering and the search for freedom.

In the twenty-first century, there has been a shift in Buddhist American fiction and poetry toward narratives inscribing Buddhism more deeply into American culture and life, with a focus on embedding Buddhism into the fabric of American history and reinterpreting Buddhist narratives through an American lens. In all, this chapter has presented a trajectory of Buddhism intertwining with American literature, from transnational storytelling about Asian Buddhism to an American audience, through mid-century narratives that portray Buddhism as a lived religion and describe how to live as a Buddhist in a diversity of ways, to contemporary Buddhist American literature that has embedded Buddhism into the American social imaginary so well, writers consider their craft a Buddhist practice, and readers approach fiction and poetry through a Buddhist lens. The trajectory of this exploration of Buddhism and American literature has moved to Buddhist American literature.

REFERENCES

Abrams, Carlotta Lady Izumi. 1997. "Speaking through the Silence: Uncovering the Buddhist Tradition in Joy Kogawa's 'Obasan.'" Kim Herzinger, Advisor. PhD dissertation, University of Southern Mississippi.
Allen, Gay Wilson. 1959. "Walt Whitman: Passage to India." *Indian Literature* 2, no. 2: 38–44.
Arnold, Edwin. 2005. *The Light of Asia*. Project Gutenberg. EBook-No. 8920. Most Recently Updated, May 31, 2014. https://www.gutenberg.org/ebooks/8920.
Beek, Kimberly. 2015. "Telling Tales Out of School: Buddhist Fiction." In *Buddhism beyond Borders: New Perspectives on Buddhism in the United States*, edited by Scott Mitchell and Natalie Quli, 125–142. Albany: State University of New York Press.
Beek, Kimberly. 2016. "Buddhism and Modern Literature." In *Oxford Bibliographies in Buddhism*, edited by Richard Payne. New York: Oxford University Press. https://www.oxfordbibliographies.com/view/document/obo-9780195393521/obo-9780195393521-0230.xml
Biringer, Ted. 2009. *The Flatbed Sutra of Louie Wing: The Second Ancestor of Zen in the West*. Salt Lake City: American Book Publishing.
Buck, Pearl S. 2020. *The Good Earth*. New York: Simon and Schuster.
Cheng'en, Wu. 2011. *Journey to the West*. Singapore: Asiapac Books.
Constans, Gabriel. 2009. *Buddha's Wife*. First edition. Bandon, OR: Robert Reed.
DeMaioNewton, Emily. 2021. Interview with Tsering Wangmo Dhompa: "Home Defined by Those Who Have Lost Home." *Tricycle: The Buddhist Review* 31, no. 1. https://tricycle.org/magazine/tsering-wangmo-dhompa/.
Dhompa, Tsering Wangmo. 2005. "Autonomy of the Mind." In *The Wisdom Anthology of North American Poetry*, edited by Andrew Schelling, 46–49. Somerville, MA: Wisdom Publications.

Dwyer, Caitlin. 2017. "The Fiction of the Self: Ruth Ozeki." *Buddhistdoor Global*, February 24. https://www.buddhistdoor.net/features/the-fiction-of-the-self-ruth-ozeki/.

Hakutani, Yoshinobu. 2022. "Bashō, Kerouac, and Confucianism." In *Haiku, Other Arts, and Literary Disciplines*, edited by Toru Kiuchi and Yoshinobu Hakutani, 159–172. New York: Lexington Books.

Hayford, Charles W. 1998. "What's so Bad about THE GOOD EARTH?" *Education About Asia* 3, no. 3. http://www.asianstudies.org/wp-content/uploads/whats-so-bad-about-the-good-earth.pdf.

Haynes, Sarah. 2005. "An Exploration of Jack Kerouac's Buddhism: Text and Life." *Contemporary Buddhism* 6, no. 2 (November 1): 153–171.

Hesse, Hermann. 2002. *Siddhartha: An Indian Tale*. New York: Penguin Books.

Hirshfield, Jane. 1997. *Nine Gates: Entering the Mind of Poetry*. New York: HarperCollins.

Johnson, Charles. 1982. *Oxherding Tale*. Bloomington: Indiana University Press.

Johnson, Charles. 1990. *Middle Passage*. New York: Atheneum.

Johnson, Charles. 2003. *Turning the Wheel: Essays on Buddhism and Writing*. New York: Simon and Schuster.

Johnson, Charles. 2005. *Dr. King's Refrigerator: And Other Bedtime Stories*. New York: Scribner.

Kachtick, Keith, ed. 2006. *You Are Not Here and Other Works of Buddhist Fiction*. Somerville: Wisdom Publications.

Kerouac, Jack. 1957. *On the Road*. New York: Viking Press.

Kerouac, Jack. 1958. *Dharma Bums*. New York: Viking Press.

Kingston, Maxine Hong. 1976. *The Woman Warrior: Memoirs of a Girlhood among Ghosts*. New York: Knopf Doubleday.

Kingston, Maxine Hong. 1990. *Tripmaster Monkey: His Fake Book*. London: Vintage.

Kogawa, Joy. 1981. *Obasan*. Toronto, Canada: Lester and Orpen Dennys.

Leonard, Martin. 2008. "Walt Whitman's 'Leaves of Grass' from the Perspective of Modern Mahayana Buddhism." M.A. Thesis. California State University, Fresno.

Loy, David R., Linda Goodhew, and Jane Hirshfield. 2000. *The Dharma of Dragons and Daemons: Buddhist Themes in Modern Fantasy*. First edition. Somerville: Wisdom Publications.

Marpet, Blaze. 2012 "The Beatnik Buddhist: The Monk of American Pop-Culture." In *Teaching Dhamma in New Lands: The 2nd International Association of Buddhist Universities (IABU) Conference*, 69-76. Mahachulalongkornrajavidyalaya University. Ayutthaya, Thailand, International Association of Buddhist Universities.

McHugh, Barbara. 2021. *Bride of the Buddha: A Novel*. Rhinebeck, NY: Monkfish.

McMahan, David L. 2008. *The Making of Buddhist Modernism*. Oxford: Oxford University Press.

McNicholl, Adeana. 2018. "Being Buddha, Staying Woke: Racial Formation in Black Buddhist Writing." *Journal of the American Academy of Religion* 86, no. 4 (November 29): 883–911.

Mitchell, Scott A. 2016. *Buddhism in America: Global Religion, Local Contexts*. London: Bloomsbury.

Normand, Lawrence, and Alison Winch. 2013. *Encountering Buddhism in Twentieth-Century British and American Literature*. London: A&C Black.

Okada, John. 2019. *No-No Boy*. New York: Penguin.

Otsuka, Julie. 2011. *The Buddha in the Attic*. New York: Knopf Doubleday.

Ozeki, Ruth. 2013. *A Tale for the Time Being: A Novel*. New York: Penguin.

Perry, Lavora M. 2008. *Taneesha Never Disparaging*. Somerville: Wisdom Publications.

Pound, Ezra, Christopher Bush, and Haun Saussy. *Cathay: A Critical Edition*. Edited by Timothy Billings. 1st ed. New York: Fordham University Press, 2018.

Prebish, C. S. 1993. "Two Buddhisms Reconsidered." *Buddhist Studies Review* 10, no. 2: 187–206.

Saunders, George. 2017. *Lincoln in the Bardo: A Novel*. New York: Random House.

Schaffer, David. 2016. "Opinion: Walt Whitman, American Buddha." *Los Angeles Times*, December 27. https://www.latimes.com/opinion/readersreact/la-ol-le-walt-whitman-religion-20161227-story.html.

Schelling, Andrew. 2005. *The Wisdom Anthology of North American Buddhist Poetry*. New York: Simon and Schuster.

Schwartz, Dana. 2017. Interview with George Saunders. "How Buddhism Made George Saunders a Better Writer," *Observer*, February 15. https://observer.com/2017/02/how-buddhism-made-george-saunders-a-better-writer/.

Sluyter, Dean. 2022. *The Dharma Bum's Guide to Western Literature: Finding Nirvana in the Classics*. San Francisco, CA: New World.

Snyder, Gary. 1969. "Smokey the Bear Sutra." Self-published, San Francisco, CA.

Spencer, Stephen. 2002. "The Discourse of Whiteness: Chinese-American History, Pearl S. Buck, and *the Good Earth*." *Americana: The Journal of American Popular Culture, 1900 to Present* 1, no. 1. https://americanpopularculture.com/journal/articles/spring_2002/spencer.htm.

"The Preaching of the Buddha: 'White Lotus of the Good Law.'" 1844. In *The Dial: A Magazine for Literature, Philosophy, and Religion (1840–1844); Boston* IV (III), edited by George Ripley, 391–402. Boston: James Munroe and Co.

Tworkov, Helen. 1991. "Many Is More." *Tricycle: The Buddhist Review* 1, no. 2: 4.

Thich Nhat Hanh. 2001. *Call Me by My True Name: The Collected Poems of Thich Nhat Hanh*. Berkeley, CA: Parallax Press.

Whalen-Bridge, John, and Gary Storhoff. 2009. *The Emergence of Buddhist American Literature*. Albany: State University of New York Press.

Whalen-Bridge, John, and Gary Storhoff. 2011. *Writing as Enlightenment: Buddhist American Literature into the Twenty-First Century*. Albany: State University of New York Press.

Wheeler, Kate, ed. 2004. *Nixon under the Bodhi Tree and Other Works of Buddhist Fiction*. Somerville: Wisdom Publications.

Wilson, Jeff. 2004. "Buddherotica." In *Nixon under the Bodhi Tree and Other Works of Buddhist Fiction*, edited by Kate Wheeler, 59–63. Somerville: Wisdom Publications.

Winfield, Pamela. 2022. "To Tame an Ox or to Catch a Fish: A Zen Reading of the Old Man and the Sea." In *The Theory and Practice of Zen Buddhism*, edited by Charles Prebish and On-Cho Ng, 275–298. New York: Springer.

Xie, Ming. 2021. *Ezra Pound and the Appropriation of Chinese Poetry: Cathay, Translation, and Imagism*. London: Routledge.

Yip, Wai-Lim. 2015. *Ezra Pound's Cathay*. Princeton, NJ: Princeton University Press.

Yoo, Sang-Keun. 2022. "Speculative Orientalism: Zen and Tao in American New Wave Science Fiction." PhD dissertation, University of California-Riverside.

Zhang, Chunjie. 2022. "Chinese Rural Realism. Rereading Pearl S. Buck's *The Good Earth* (1931)." *Zeithistorische Forschungen—Studies in Contemporary History* 18, no. 2 (December 13): 363–370.

Index

For the benefit of digital users, indexed terms that span two pages (e.g., 52–53) may, on occasion, appear on only one of those pages.

Tables are indicated by *t* following the page number

A. A. Vantine & Co., 474
Abbey, Gampo, 236
Abe, Stanley, 94–95
Abhayagiri, 272–73, 276
Abington School District v. Schempp, 184
Abromovic, Marina, 492–93
absorption *(jhāna)*, 306
abstraction *versus* ritual. *See* ritualizing, ritual *versus*
academic engaged Buddhism, 361–64
academic study, Korean Buddhism, 170–71
   colonial experiences, 173–74
   inclusive legacy, 171–72
   minority status, 172–73
acculturation, 429–32
activity
   perspectives on, 346–47
   versus abstraction. *See* ritualizing, ritual *versus*
Adams, Henry, 485
Adichie, Chimamanda, 428–29
Adiele, Faith, 225
Ae, Yue Yong, 77–78
African American Dharma Retreat and Conference, 65–66
African Americans, 5–6, 225, 226
After Buddhism: Rethinking the Dharma for a Secular Age (Batchelor), 382–83
aggiornamento, 19
Ahmed, Sara, 75
Akamatsu Renjō, 132–33
Aktor, Mikael, 100–2
Alexander, Franz, 398

Alien Land Laws, 44
Alliance for Bhikkhunis, 80–81
Alphabet Sangha, 86
Ama, Michihiro, 347–48
Ambedkar, B. R., 448–49
American Academy of Asian Studies, 92
American Buddhism, 1–5
   American literature and, 499–513
   chaplaincy supervision, 446–61
   defining, 56–57
   disrupting equation of, 59–60
   education and pedagogy, 428
   exclusion from, 5–8
   food in, 288–300
   foundations. *See* foundations
   frames. *See* frames
   gender and sexuality, 74–89
   internet in recent history of, 50
   Judaism and, 249–64
   mapping terrain of, 8–12
   medicine and, 322–37
   modernity and globalization of, 17–32
   practices. *See* practices
   psychotherapy and, 395–409
   race and whiteness in, 54–72
   rituals in, 339–55
   secularism and, 377–90
   studies and scholar-practitioners of, 92
   survey of healers, 326–30, 327t, 329t
   technology and, 414–25
   traditions of. *See* traditions
   visual culture, 483–97
   Zen Buddhism and, 144–55

American Buddhism: Methods and Findings in Recent Scholarship (Williams), 98, 99–100
American Buddhist, 45
American Dharma (Gleig), 209
American engaged Buddhism, 361–65
American Insight, 312
Americanization, 29, 135, 400
American JewBu: Jews, Buddhists, and Religious Change (Sigalow), 250–51
American literature, 512–13
   expansion of Buddhist narratives in, 508–12
   exploring Buddhism in, 504–8
   overview of, 499–500
   transnational storytelling, 500–4
Amitābha Buddha, 129, 131, 140–41, 222, 494–95
Anālayo, Bhikkhu, 389
Ānanda, 455–56
Ānando, Ajahn, 283–84
anātman, 490–91
Anderson, Kay, 361
Anguttara Nikaya, 21
apps, 423–24
Ariyaratne, A. T., 448–49
Arnold, Edwin, 501–2
artifacts, circulation of, 463–66. See also material culture
Artinger, Brenna Grace, 50, 67–68, 71, 363–64
Aryan, fashioning Buddha as, 55–56
Asia
   origins of Zen in, 145–46
Asian American Buddhism, 3–4, 59–60, 69, 486
Asian Americans
   lay women, 76–77
   ordaining women, 77–80
   recovering voices of, 59–60
Asian Exclusion Act of 1924, 6, 58
Asiatic Barred Zone Act of 1919, 58
Association for Clinical Pastoral Education (ACPE), 452–53
Association for Professional Chaplaincy (APC), 439–40, 452–53
Association of Theological Schools (ATS), 452–53
Austin, Victorian, 82

Automobile Tire Print (Rauschenberg), 489–90
Avalokiteśvara Bodhisattva, 333–34
Avalokiteśvara Siṃhanāda, 353–55
Avatar: The Last Airbender, 418–19
Awakened Heart Project, 256
axial age, 20
axiological dichotomy, ritual, 341–42
Azusa Buddhist Monastery, 290–91

Baker, Lamas Willa, 237
Baker, Richard, 151–52
Baker, Willa Blyth, 87–89
Baldoquín, Hilda Gutíerrez, 63
Baldwin, James, 6
Barre Center for Buddhist Studies (BCBS), 433
Barret, Myoki Caine, 66–67
Barua, D. Mitra, 278–79
Batchelor, Stephen, 378
Bateman, Rike, 378
Bateson, Gregory, 420–21
Baumann, Martin, 28
Baun, Eric, 305
Bays, Jan Chozen, 87–88, 296
BCA. *See* Buddhist Churches of America
BDK. *See* Bukkyō Dendō Kyōkai
"be islands unto yourselves," translating, 455–56
Be the Refuge: Raising the Voices of Asian American Buddhists (Han), 7, 74–75, 81–82, 459
Beat Generation, 144–45
Beats, 45–46, 419, 504, 508
Being Buddhist in a Christian World (Suh), 163
Bell, Catherine, 342, 344
Berkeley Bussei, Tri-Ratna: Buddha, 45
Berkowitz, Beth, 256
Berry, Devin, 65–66
Beyer, Peter, 28
beyond modernity, 428–29
Bhāvanā Society, 177, 189–90
Bhikkhu, Thanissaro, 190
*bhikkhunī*s, 271–72, 278
Biblicalization, strategy, 256
Bidwell, Duane, 454–55
Bigelow, Strugis, 485–86
Bigelow, William Sturgis, 472

Biggers, Sanford, 495
BIPOC. *See* Black, Indigenous, and People of Color
Biringer, T., 509
bla-ma lha (guru-deity), 17–18
Black Buddha Mandala (Graves), 487
Black Buddhism, 65–67
 teachers, 81–85
 Vietnamese Buddhism intersection, 224–27
Black, Indigenous, and People of Color (BIPOC), 68–70, 227, 231–32, 436–37
Black Lives Matter, 1, 65–67
Black Power Meditation Group, 246
blanc de Chine, 477–78
Blavatsky, Helena Petrovna, 23, 42
Bloom, Alfred, 434
Blythe, Willa, 87–88
BMNA. *See* Buddhist Mission of North America
board certification (BCCI), 453
Bodhisattva's Brain, The (Flanagan), 383
Bond, George, 97
Book of Form and Emptiness, The (Ozeki), 4–5
Boorstein, Sylvia, 251–52, 260–61, 262
Borup, Jørn, 102
Boston Museum, Department of Japanese Art in, 472–73
BPF. *See* Buddhist Peace Fellowship
Brach, Tara, 68
brahmavihāras, 436–37
Brand, Stewart, 420–21
Braun, Erik, 24–25, 424
Breathing and Quieting the Mind, 263
bricolage, 401–3
Brief Account of Shin-Shiu, A, 132–33
Brosius, Christiane, 341
Brown, Edward Espé, 294–96
Bruntz, Courtney, 384
Buck, Pearl S., 503
Buddha in the Attic, The (Otsuka), 511–12
buddha-name recitation *(nembutsu/nianfo)*, 129
Buddha-vandana, 17–18
Buddhadharma, 59–60
Buddhaganism, 383
"Buddherotica" (Wilson), 511
Buddhicization, American landscape, 233–35

Buddhification, 39
 first wave of, 40–43
 second wave of, 44–47
 third wave of, 47–50
Buddhish, 4–5
Buddhism in America, conference, 450–51
Buddhism Without Beliefs (Bachelor), 21, 382–83
Buddhism. *See* American Buddhism; foundations; frames; practices; traditions; United States
 protestant reformation, 19–20
 sexual abuse survivors, 87–89
 twin arrival of, 37–39
Buddhist backlash, 49–50
Buddhist modernism, 19–20
 colonialism, 55–57
 demythologization, 21
 detraditionalization, 20
 meditation, 22–23
 psychologization, 21
 whiteness, 55–57
Buddhist Catechism, A (Olcott), 219–20
Buddhist Church of San Francisco, 469
Buddhist Churches of America (BCA), 2, 28, 58–59, 77, 129–30, 429–30, 486
 and Japanese Pure Land in internment, 137–40
Buddhist crisis, 219–20
Buddhist Critical-Constructive Reflection Unit, 100–1
Buddhist Diet Book (Holloway), 296
Buddhist fiction, expansion of, 508–12
Buddhist medicine and crystal healing, 335–36
Buddhist Ministry Working Group (BMWG), 438–39
Buddhist Mission of North America (BMNA), 41–42, 134–35
Buddhist Observances, 430–31
Buddhist Peace Fellowship (BPF), 63–64, 69–70, 368–69, 370
Buddhist roots, Jewish fruits. *See* integrators, American Buddhist-Jewish interaction
Buddhist studies
 introduction of, 48–49
 invention of, 93–99
Buddhist Sunday School, 430

Buddhist Vihara, 272–73
Buddhist Women's Association, 77, 134
Buddhist Youth Family Movement, 214–15
Buddhists of Color, 9, 54–55, 63, 67, 68–69, 70, 89, 105–6
Budge, Stephanie, 62
Bukkyō Dendō Kyōkai (BDK), 103–4
Bukkyō Kakushū Kyōkai (Buddhist Transdenominational Committee), 136
Burning Desire (Mori), 494
Burnouf, Eugène, 37–38, 55–56, 95
Bush, Marabai, 313
butsudan, 486–87

Cabezón, Jose, 97–98
CACE. See Center for the Advancement of Contemplative Education
Cadge, Wendy, 29–30, 48, 188–89, 403
Cage, John, 45–46, 420–21, 488, 489
California Alien Land Laws, 134–35
Calmanowitz, Michel Lenz, 283
calming meditation *(samatha)*, 306
Campbell, Patricia Q., 341, 345
Carrette, Jeremy, 315, 405–6
cartoons, visual culture, 496–97
Carus, Paul, 21, 25, 42–43, 132, 397
Casanova, Jose, 20, 380–81
celibacy, 80–81
Center for the Advancement of Contemplative Education (CACE), 441
Central Asia, Vajrayana Buddhism, 26–27
Central Tibetan Administration, 239–40
Ceylonese Buddhism, 42–43
Chabad-Lubavitch Hasidism, 263–64
Chah, Ajaan, 185–86
chaplaincy education, 438–40
chaplaincy supervision
    Buddhist chaplaincy, 454–60
    Buddhist education, 451–52
    direction of, 452–54
    global peace movements, 450–51
    introduction to, 446–48
    locating chaplains in United States, 448–51
    military service, 449–50
Cheah, Joseph, 28, 55, 56–57, 71, 290–91, 316, 339, 366–67
Chen, Kevin, 7

Cheung, Kin, 324–25
Cheung, Lilian, 296
Chicago Tribune, 484
Chicago World Parliament of Religions, 144–45
China, artifact circulation and, 463–66
Chinese Americans
    Buddhism twin arrival and, 39
    communities, 39, 131–32
    discrimination of, 39
    immigrants, 131–32
    meeting needs of, 47
    religious experiences of, 131
Chinese Buddhism, 126
    Man Chu extraordinary life, 118–20
    mobility and identity, 124–26
    modern student-monk identity, 121–24
    overview, 115–18
Chinese Exclusion Act of 1882, 6, 39, 44, 115–16, 140, 183, 502
Chödrön, Pema, 236
Chödrön, Thubten, 236
Chöpel, Gendun, 241
Christian Examiner, 37–38
Christianity, 364–65
    Christian nationalism, 364–65
    Korean Buddhism and, 172–73
chronology, discourse of, 400–1
Chua Lien Hoa Temple, 279–80
Chung, Park Soon, 77–78
Cintita, Ashin, 290
City of Los Angeles Zoning Commission, 291
City of Ten Thousand Buddhas, 140–41, 272–73, 276, 280
Civil Rights movement, 490, 504, 506
    Vietnam and, 227
clinical pastoral education (CPE), 446–47
Cohen, Roland, 288
Collective Karma, 1
colonial experiences, Korean Buddhism, 173–74
colonialism, 55–57
"Coming Out Whole" (Reed), 85–86
Communist Party of Vietnam (CPV), 223
communities, nourishing, 290–92
community cookbooks, 293–95

community Dharma leaders (CDLs), 436–37
community temples, monks in, 272–74
compatriot Buddhism
　Buddhist flag and, 219–20
　identifying, 216–17
　Perfect Virtue Temple and, 221–22
　protests and, 223–24
　public displays, 217–19
　raised physical map of Vietnam, 222–23
Complete Tassajara Cookbook (Brown), 294–96
Confession of a Buddhist Atheist (Batchelor), 382–83
Constans, Gabriel, 511
consumer culture, American, 470–74
contextual turn, 3–4
"Continental Walk for Disarmament and Social Justice," 202
conversion, monasticism, 281–84
conversion. *See* converts, American Buddhist-Jewish interaction
convert lineages, meditation and, 309–11
converts, American Buddhist-Jewish interaction, 253–55
Conze, Edward, 99–100
Cooper, Paul, 403
cosmology-oriented Buddhism, 180–81
　immigrant experience and, 190–91
　and Immigration and Nationality Act of 1965, 188–89
　meditation practice and, 189–90
　origins of term, 189
Coverly, Dave, 496
COVID-19, 58–59, 74
Cox, Colleen, 97
CPE. *See* clinical pastoral education
CPV. *See* Communist Party of Vietnam
Crawford, Robert, 298
critical race theory, 316
Crosby, Kate, 349
cultural baggage, 62, 76, 78, 316, 368, 383–84
cultural capacity, 290
Cultural Revolution, 120
Curators of the Buddha, 94
Curley, Melissa Anne-Marie, 109
Currents of Change (Usuki), 79

cybernetics, 420–21
CyberSangha, 246

Daihonzan Chozen-ji Rinzai Zen Temple, 77–78
daimoku, 198, 200–2, 203–4
Daisaku Ikeda, 204–8
Daisetsu Teitarō Suzuki, 40, 147–49
Dalai Lama, 17, 26, 27, 141–42, 238, 240, 246–47, 253, 384, 404, 418, 448–49
dāna (offerings), 177–78
"Danger of a Single Story, The," 428–29
Daode jing, 148
Dass, Ram, 249–50, 313
Davids, Caroline Rhys, 396–97, 401
Davids, Thomas Rhys, 42, 55–56, 95–96, 106–8
Davidson, Richie, 398
Day, Iyko, 369–70
decontextualization, mindfulness critiques, 313–18
Deep Time Liberation, 65–66
DeGraff, Geoffrey, 190
DEI. *See* diversity, equity, and inclusion
demythologization, 21
Denison, Ruth, 310
Denver Buddhist Temple, 429–30
detraditionalization, 20
Detroit Zen Center, 299–300
Dhamarapala, Anagarika, 95
dhamma, 189–90
Dhammadarini, 80–81
Dhammadharini Support Foundation, v
Dhammananda Monastery, 289, 492
Dharma age (*mofa* 末法), 122
Dharma Bums, The (Kerouac), 149, 152–53, 505
Dharma Drum, 117
Dharma Realm Buddhist Association, 125–26, 140–41
Dharma Realm Buddhist Association (DRBA), 272–73, 276
Dharma Sangha of Buddha, 136
Dharma teachings, optimizing, 333–34
Dharma, Color, and Culture: New Voices in Western Buddhism, 63
Dharmacakra, Karma Triyana, 431–32
dharmadhātu, 274, 352–53, 419
Dharmapala, Anagarika, 23, 24, 29, 43, 397, 484

Dhompa, Tsering Wangmo, 510–11
Dhrma Drum Mountain, 47
Dial, The, 38, 39, 199
Diệm, Ngô Đình, 215–16
digital Buddhism, 421–23
"Disciplines of Buddhist Studies, The" (Freiberger), 106–7
divergences, monasticism, 278–80
diversity, equity, and inclusion (DEI), 67
diversity, equity, inclusion, and accessibility (DEIA), 83–84
Do, Le Huu, 212–13
Dōgen Zenji, 509
Dorje Shugden, 26
double minority status, Korean Buddhism, 172–73
Doyle, J. D., 85
"Dr. King's Refrigerator" (Johnson), 512
Dreaming Me (Willis), 65, 225
Drepung Loseling, 236
Driscoll, Christopher M., 379–80
Droplets in the Sea of Awakening (*Juehai diandi* 覺海點滴), 121–24
drupdra (*sgrub grwa*), 237–38
Đức, Thích Quảng, 219–20, 221, 448–49

East Asia, Mahayana Buddhism in, 25–26
East Bay Meditation Center (EBMC), 85
East India Marine Society, 465
eating (*ōryōki*), 288. *See also* food American Buddhism
eclectic mixing, 335–36
Ecodharma, 1
education, 428, 443–44
    acculturation and, 429–32
    chaplaincy, 438–40
    social transformation, 440–43
    study and practice, 432–33
    teacher and clergy training, 434–38
Eidō Shimano, 46
Eightfold Noble Path, 17, 378–79, 384, 456
eighties, visual culture in, 492–95
Eihen Dogen (Soto), 146
electroencephalography (EEG), 424
Emerson, Ralph Waldo, 37–38, 485, 500–1
empowerment rites, 349
Empress of China, vessel, 464–65

Emyō Imamura, 136
engaged Buddhism, 48, 202, 219–20, 371, 450–51
    Academic Engaged Buddhism, 361–63
    acknowledging distinctive racialization, 366–70
    American engaged Buddhism, 361–63
    introduction to, 359–60
    situating in United States, 360–63
    spiritual bypassing and, 363–66
"Engaged Buddhism: New and Improved!(?) Made in the U.S.A. of Asian Materials," 362
Enlightenment Capsule (Mori), 494–95
Entropy of Love (Mori), 494
entropy, discourse of, 399
Epstein, Mark, 402
essentiality, rhetoric of, 397–98
Establishing of Mindfulness Sutta (Satipaṭṭhāna Sutta), 305
ethical eating, 298–300
ethnic-Asian Buddhism, 191
ethnic/convert, binary, 232–33
ethnographic approaches, mindfulness/meditation, 311–13
Evans-Wentz, W. Y., 399
exclusion, American Buddhism, 5–8
exclusions, Asian American Buddhists and, 58–59
Executive Order 9066, 44, 58–59, 201
expansion, Buddhist narratives, 508–12
"Extraordinary Memoir, An" (*Bu pingfan de huiyi* 不平凡的回憶), 118

Facebook, 1–2
Fall of Saigon, 119–20
Farge, John La, 485–86
Farrey, Ed, 294–95
feminism, 511
Fenellosa, Ernest, 485–86
Feng Daoyou, 77–78
Fenollosa, Ernest, 472
fiction, Buddhism in. *See* transnational storytelling
field, Buddhist studies as, 93–99
Fields, Rick, 39, 62
fifties, visual culture in, 488–90

film, Buddhism and, 418–19
first wave, Buddhification, 40–43
first-wave Asian immigration, 466–70
Fischer, Norman, 251–52
flag, design of, 219–20
Flatbed Sutra of Louie Wing, The (Biringer), 509
Floyd, George, 1, 54
fMRI. *See* functional magnetic resonance imaging
Fo Guang Shan, 47, 117
folk Buddhism, 314–15
Fonguang Shan, 324
food, American Buddhism
    ethical eating, 298–300
    home cooking, 292–94
    mindful eating, 296–98
    monastery cooking, 294–96
    offerings, 289–92
    overview, 288–89
Forbes, David, 423–24
Forest Dhamma Monastery, 189–90
Foulk, Griffith, 339
Foundation for the Preservation of the Mahāyāna Tradition (FPMT), 244–45, 353–55, 452
foundations
    gender and sexuality, 74–89
    history of Buddhism in United States, 36–51
    modernity and globalization, 17–32
    race and whiteness, 54–72
    studies and scholar-practitioners, 92–109
FPMT. *See* Foundation for the Preservation of the Mahāyāna Tradition
frames
    American literature, 499–513
    chaplaincy supervision, 446–61
    education and pedagogy, 428
    material culture, 462–78
    psychotherapy, 395–409
    secularism, 377–90
    technology, 414–25
    visual culture, 483–97
fraternal organizations (*tang* 堂), 116–17
Free Muslims Coalition, 381–82
Freeman, Thomas, 361–62
Freer, Charles Lang, 474

Freiberger, Oliver, 106–7
Fromm, Erich, 401
Fu-Chih (Bliss and Wisdom Foundation), 281
Fuji School, 202–3
Fujimoto Isao, 369–70
Fujimura Bun'yū, 470
Fuller, Buckminster, 420–21
Fuller, Margaret, 37–38
functional magnetic resonance imaging (fMRI), 398, 424
Fushoushan Temple (Fushoushan si 福壽山寺), 118–19

Gabriel, Victor, 454–55
Gardena Buddhist Church Dana Group, 292
Gardner, Isabella Stewart, 472, 473–74, 475
Gautama, Siddhartha, 17, 93–94
gender and sexuality
    attempting to describe, 89
    Black Buddhist teachers, 81–85
    celibacy, 80–81
    lay women, 76–77
    LGBTQI+ Buddhist teachers and practitioners, 85–86
    ordainment, 77–80
    overview, 74–75
    sexual abuse survivors, 87–89
gender radical, celibacy as, 80–81
gender, Zen sexual misconduct and, 152–54
General Buddhist Association of Vietnam, 218–19
generational patterns, 60–61
generosity (*dāna*), 292
GenX, 237, 244
geography, metaphors of, 399–400
Gerke, Barbara, 349
ghosts, feeding, 351–53
Giác, Thích Mãn, 220
Giles, Cheryl A., 208, 407–8, 454–55
Ginsberg, Alan, 45, 309
Glassman, Bernie, 300
Gleig, Ann, 3–4, 30–31, 50, 67–68, 71, 209, 312, 360–61, 363–64, 401, 404
global Buddhism, 27–29
Goenka, Satya Narayana, 47, 185–86, 310
gohonzon, 209
Gold, Jonathan, 292

Goldberg, Natalie, 149
Goldman, Daniel, 313
Goldstein, Joseph, 47, 184–85, 310, 313, 381–82, 433
Goldwater, Julius, 41, 138–39
Goleman, Daniel, 255
Good Earth, The (Buck), 503
Gospel of Buddha, The (Carus), 21, 132
Graduate Theological Union (GTU), 434
Grant, Hyun Jung, 77–78
Graves, Tobey, 487
Greater Boston Buddhist Cultural Center, 324
Great March of Shakubuku, 204
Great Stupa of Dharmakaya, 233
Green Gulch Farm Zen Center, 299–300
Greyston Bakery, 300
Grimes, Ronald, 344
Grosjean, Glen, 104–5
Grubin, David, 17–18, 29
Guanyin Temple, 467–68, 470, 484
Gunananda, Mohottivatte, 24
Gunaratana, Banthe Henepola, 282, 309
Gyatso, Kelsang, 26
Gyatso, Sonam, 283
Gyatso, Tenzin, 230–31

Hacienda Heights, 272–73
Hahn, Thich Nhat, 141–42
Hairen 海仁, 118–19
Hakuin Ekaku (Rinzai), 146, 496
Halifax, Roshi Joan, 313
Hallisey, Charles, 309
Hāmākua Jōdō Mission, 468–69
Han, Chenxing, 3–4, 7, 60–61, 74–75, 144–45, 428–29, 459
Hancock, Herbie, 206
Handbook of Chaplaincy Studies (Paterson), 459
Hạnh, Thích Nhất, 48, 211–12, 215–16, 224, 274, 296, 310, 311, 359, 450–51, 505–6
Harding, John S., 28, 32
Harris, Dan, 255
Hart-Cellar Act of 1965, 140, 474, 490. See also Immigration and Nationality Act of 1965
Hart, William David, 379–80
Hartman, Blanche, 82
Haruyosi Kusada, 451
Harvey, Peter, 271

Hase, Craig, 62
Hasidic modernism, 258
Hawaii, USA
 first-wave immigration to, 468–69
 immigration to, 40–42
 mainland immigration, 469–70
Hawkins, Jennifer, 388–89
healers, survey of, 326–30
 general information about interviewees, 327t
 key concepts in corpus, 328t
 respondents mentioning mindfulness *versus* chanting, 329t
healing, positionalities of, 330. See also medicine
 eclectic mixing, 335–36
 integration with traditional Asian medicine, 331–33
 mainstream healthcare, 330–31
 optimizing Dharma teachings, 333–34
healthism, 298
Heart Sūtra, 333–34
Hedge, Frederic Henry, 37–38
Hedge's Club, 37–38
Helderman, Ira, 312–13
Hemera Foundation, 439–40
Heritage of Japan: Favorite Recipes, 292–94
Herrigel, Eugen, 45–46
Hesse, Hermann, 504
Hickey, Wakoh Shannon, 28, 57, 76, 436, 439
Higashi Honganji Temple, 133–34
Higgins, Winton, 378
Hirshfield, Jane, 17, 149–51, 512
Hisamatsu Shin'ichi, 404
historical Buddhism, 400
history, Buddhism in United States, 36
 first wave of Buddhification, 40–43
 future history, 50–51
 second wave of Buddhification, 44–47
 third wave of Buddhification, 47–50
 twin arrival, 37–39
Ho, Tamara C., 76, 290–91
Hodgson, Brian Houghton, 37, 55–56
Holloway, Laura C., 296
holy site *(bodhimaṇḍala)*, 277
home cooking
 monastery, 294–96
 for temple, 292–94

home temples, 273–74
Hompa Hongwanji Temple, 58
Hongyu, Wu, 324
Honpa Honganji Mission of Hawaii, 136
honzon, 198, 200–1, 209
Hori, Victor, 28, 32
horizons, Tibetan Buddhism, 244–47
Hozan Hardiman, 451
Hsi Lai Temple, 272–73, 451–52, 492
Hsi Lai University (西來大學), 451–52
Hsu, Alexander O., 360–61
Hsu, Funie, 3–4, 54, 69–70, 74–75
Hsuan Hua, 272–73
Hu, Hsiao-Lan, 367–68
Hua, Hsuan, 140–41, 282
Hudgson, Brian Houghton, 95
Humanistic Buddhism, 431
Humanity (*Rensheng* 人生), 121
Human Use of Human Beings, The (Wiener), 420
hungry ghosts, 352–53
Huntington, C. W., 314
Hurst, Jane, 206
Hüsken, Ute, 341
Huxley, Julian, 343–44
hwadu (gong-an), 171
hybridity
   Korean Seon, 173–74
   rhetoric of, 401–3
hybridizers, American Buddhist-Jewish interaction, 260–62

IBMC. *See* International Buddhist Mediation Center
IBS. *See* Institute of Buddhist Studies
identity
   Chinese Buddhism, 124–26
   embracing, 458
IJS. *See* Institute for Jewish Spirituality
Immigration Act of 1965, 166
Immigration Act of 1990, 272
Immigration and Nationality Act of 1965, 46, 117, 188–89
impulses, secularizing, 237–39
Indigenous Skeetchestn Nation, 277
Inquiring Mind, 85–86
Inquiry of Upali (*Upalipariprccha*), 349

Insight Meditation Center, 310
Insight Meditation Society (IMS), 47–48, 184–85, 255, 433
Instagram, 1–2
Institute for Jewish Spirituality (IJS), 256–57, 259
Institute of Buddhist Studies (IBS), 98, 434–35, 451
instrumentality, metaphors of, 403–4
integrators, American Buddhist-Jewish interaction, 256–60
interconnection, term, 109
International Association of Buddhist Studies, 97
International Buddhist Meditation Center (IBMC), 227, 272–73
internment
   Japanese Americans, 44–47, 58–59
   novels about, 506–7
   Pure Land Buddhism, 137–40
intersectional Buddhism, 60–61
intersectionality, 60–61
   discourse of, 406–9
   Tibetan Buddhism, 246
Introduction to the History of Indian Buddhism (Burnouf), 37
Introduction to Zen Buddhism (Suzuki), 398
Isabella Stewart Gardner Museum, 472
Isenberg, Sarina, 38
island, functioning as, 458–61
Itadakimasu, 292–94
Ives, Christopher, 449–50
Iwamura, Jane, 3

Jackson, Phil, 4–5
Jacobson-Maisels, James, 256
Jambudvipa (S. *jambudvīpa*), 196
James, William, 148, 346–47
Japan
   arrival of the black ships (*kurofune raikō*), 40
   early American consumer culture and, 470–74
   lantern floating, 351–53
   Nichiren Buddhism, 196–210
   O-Bon, 352
   Pure Land Buddhism, 129–42
   rule in Korea, 173–74
   Zen Buddhism and, 144–55

Japanese Americans, 43
    exclusion of, 41–42
    internment of, 44–47, 58–59
    during interwar years, 44–47
Japanese and Korean Exclusion League, 134–35
Japanese Buddhism, 10, 25, 42–43, 130
Japanese Pure Land Buddhism
    early forms of, 133–34
    further development of, 134–37
    in internment, 137–40
Jayasara, Bhikkhu, 177
Jennings, Pilar, 379–80, 404–5, 407
Jew in the Lotus, The (Kamenetz), 253
Jewish meditation retreat, 257–58
Jewish Meditation: A Practical Guide (Kaplan), 263
Jewish meditation, 251
Jim Crow laws, 5–6
Jinul, inclusive legacy of, 171–72
Jivaka Project Philadelphia, 325–26
Joanin Bell Choir / Hip Hop Ni Sasagu, 495
Jōdo Shinshū
    Buddhists, 1, 2, 60–61, 100, 104–5, 129–30, 135
    communities, 59–60, 79
    cookbooks, 292
    ministry, 434, 451
    temples, 79–80, 469
Jogye Order of Korean Buddhism, 161–62
Johnson-Reed Act of 1924, 183, 486
Johnson, Charles, 149–51, 507–8, 512
Johnson, Kate, 83–85
Jones, Noa, 431–32
Jordan, Ray, 419
Joshi, Khyati, 364–65
Jōshū Sasaki, 46
joss houses, 39, 116–17, 131, 466, 467
Journal of Global Buddhism, 107–8
Judaism, 381–82
Judaism-Buddhism, phenomenon (JuBu), 249–50, 264
    historical background of, 250–53
    literature review of, 250–53
    modes of interaction, 253–64
    other works, 253
    overview of, 249–50
    scholarly works, 250–52
Judge, William Quan, 42

Jung, C. G., 398
Jungto Society, 170

Kabat-Zinn, Jon, 24–25, 48–49, 249–50, 255, 297, 310, 311, 313, 383–84, 403–4
Kabbalist Abraham Abulafia, 259
Kagyu Thubten Choling (KTC), 87–88
Kakuryo Nishijima, 135–36
Kālacakra Initiation, 240
Kalama Sutta, 21
Kamakura Buddha, 485–86
Kamakura period, Japan, 197–98
Kamenetz, Rodger, 253
Kanmo Imamura, 45
Kapapala Nichiren, 201
Kaplan, Aryeh, 263
Kapleau, Philip, 46, 148–49, 151–52, 298–99
karma, 4–5
Karma Kagyü Rumtek Monastery, 432–33
Karma Triyana Dharmachakra, 236
karmic benefits, 104
Katagiri, Dainin, 149
Kawamura, Leslie, 97
Kellet, Charles Alfred, 465–66
Kemp, Alexander, 387–88
Kemper, Steven, 24
kensho, 151
Kerouac, Jack, 2, 45, 309, 505
Khandro, Pema, 237
Khin, U Ba, 188
Khyentse Foundation, 238–39
Kim (Kipling), 94–95
Kim, David Haekwon, 290
Kim, Louije, 68–69
King of the Hill, 418–19
King, Martin Luther, Jr., 224, 505–6
King, Richard, 315, 405–6
King, Ruth, 403–4
King, Sallie, 361–62
Kingston, Maxine Hong, 507
kinship organizations (*huiguan* 會館), 116–17
Kipling, Rudyard, 94
kiruv, 263
Kiyozawa Manshi, 132–33
Klein, Greg, 283–84
Kogawa, Joe, 506–7
Koichi Shinohara, 349
Kolvig, Eric, 85

Kong Chow Temple, 116–17
Korean Buddhism, 174–75
    academic study of, 170–74
    arrival in America, 166–67
    groups of, 164–66
    overview of, 161–64
    teachers of, 168–70
    temples, 167–68
Korean Buddhist News USA, 165–66
Korean Jogye Order of Buddhism, 164
Kornfield, Jack, 47, 184–85, 310, 313, 400, 419, 433
kōsen-rufu, 196
Koyozawa Manshi, 132–33
Koyu Uchida, 134–35
KTC. *See* Kagyu Thubten Choling
Kundun (film), 418
Kung Fu (show), 418–19, 491–92
Kwan Um School of Zen, 163, 164, 169–70
Kyung-bo, Seo, 169

labels, Theravāda Buddhism, 181–83
Lamaist Buddhist Monastery of America, 475
lantern floating, 351–53
Latse Library, 241
lay women, 76–77
Lee, Jonathan H. X., 291
Leighton, Taigen, 354–55
LeRoy, Todd, 77
Levi-Strauss, 403
Lew, Alan, 251–52, 260
Li, Lan A., 325–26
Life of the Buddha, 148
Light Hsi Lai School, 431
Light of Asia (Die Leuchte Asiens) (film), 42, 418
"Light of Asia, The" (Arnold), 501–2
Light of Dharma, The, 45, 135–36, 469–70
Lincoln in the Bardo (Saunders), 512
Lion's Roar, 88
literary aesthetic, Zen Buddhism, 149–51
Little Buddha, The (film), 418
Little Saigon, 221
Lloyd, Vincent, 379
Loncke, Katie, 369–70
Longchen Nyingtik, 237
Long Hoa, 220
Loo, C. T., 473–74

Look Out's Journal" (Snyder), 417–18
Lopez, David, 22
Lopez, Donald, 27, 315, 399, 400–1
Lopez, Donald S., Jr., 37
Los Angeles Kong Chow Temple, 467
Lotus (Graves), 487
Lotus Sūtra, 38, 202–3, 333–34
Lourde, Audre, 6
Lowry, Jeremy, 439–40
Loy, David, 316, 361–62
Lum, Kathryn Gin, 131
Lưu, Sư Bà Đàm, 221–24

Ma, Dipa, 185–86
Magid, Barry, 403–4
Magnuson Act of 1943, 140
magots, 464
Mahamevnawa Monastery, 281
Mahathera, Bhante Henepola Gunaratana, 272–73
Mahātherī, Tathālokā, 278
Mahayana Buddhism, 25–26, 333
Mahmood, Saba, 75
mainstream healthcare, incorporating Buddhism into, 330–31
Making of Buddhist Modernism, The (McMahan), 209
Making the Invisible Visible: Healing Racism in Our Buddhist Communities, 63
Makransky, John, 107–8
Man Chu, 117–18
    extraordinary life of, 118–20
    modern student-monk identity of, 121–24
Mandell, Jaqueline, 47–48
Manders, Kevin, 86
Mañjuśrī, 277
Manuel, Zenju Earthlyn, 64–65, 82–83
Marchais, Jacques, 475
Mariko, Tenzin, 240–41
Marsh & Co., 474
Marston, Elizabeth, 86
Masatoshi Nagatomi, 100, 108
Maslow, Abraham, 405
Mason, Konda, 65–66
Master Man Chu of America (*Meiguo de Wenzhu fashi* 美國的文珠法師). *See* Man Chu
Master of Divinity (MDiv), 435, 451

material culture
    in colonial/early republic periods, 463–66
    early American consumer culture, 470–74
    first-wave Asian immigration and, 466–70
    introduction, 462–63
    post-1945 America, 474–78
Matsuki Bunkyō, 473–74
Matsuomoto, Devon, 61
"May We Gather," ceremony, 3–4, 74–75
    Asian American women and, 77–78
    characteristics of, 54–55
    organization of, 54
    recognizing women, 60
    taking cue from, 75
MBCLs. *See* meditation-based convert lineages
MBSR. *See* Mindfulness-Based Stress Reduction
McCarran-Walter Act of 1952, 140
McHugh, Barbara, 511
McLaughlin, Levi, 203–4
McLaughlin, Pema, 105–6
McMahan, David, 19–20, 22, 26–27, 50–51, 250–51, 307–8, 315, 424
McMindfulness, 423–24
McNicholl, Adeana, 57, 67–68, 75, 367
Meadows, James, 62
means for attainment, 349
medical science, 424
medicine, 336–37
    healer survey, 326–30, 327t, 328t, 329t
    historical background of, 322–24
    literature review of, 324–26
    overview of, 322
    positionalities, 330–36
Medicine Buddha, 131–32, 333–34
Medicine Buddha Sādhana, 354
meditation, 22–23
    convert lineages, 309–11
    critiques of, 313–18
    as essence of Zen, 151–52
    ethnographic approaches, 311–13
    overview, 303–4
    as ritual, 350–51
    ritual as, 351–55
meditation retreats *(kyol che)*, 169–70
meditation-based convert lineages (MBCLs), 250, 254

meditation-oriented Buddhism, 180–81
    drawing from spirituality, 186–87
    founders of, 185–86
    marking arrival of Theravāda, 184–85
    secular mindfulness, 187
    worldwide meditation movement, 188
Meditation, Buddhism and Science (Braun), 424
Meeting Faith (Adiele), 225
Meiji era, 40
Meiji Restoration, 468
Meissner, Ted, 382–83, 389–90
Merchasin, Carol, 87–88
metaphors, psychotherapy, 396–97
Metcalf, Franz, 406–7
#MeToo movement, 237, 244–45
Metropolitan Museum of Art, 475–76
mettā, 85
Middle Passage (Johnson), 507–8
Miles, Justin, 246
Millennials, 244
Miller, Willa, 379–80, 454–55
Mills, Martin, 26–27
Mind & Life Dialogues, 238
"Mind Full of God: 'Jewish Mindfulness' as an Offspring of Western Buddhism in America," 252
mind, technology of, 419
mindful pruning, 88
mindful eating, 296–98
Mindful Eating (Bays), 296–98
mindfulness
    bare attention, 307–8
    Burmese method, 306–7
    colonial modernity and, 306
    critiques of, 313–18
    early framings of, 305
    ethnographic approaches, 311–13
    genealogical roots, 306
    historical trajections of, 305–9
    overview, 303–4
    primacy of individual experience and consciousness, 308
    representations of, 309
mindfulness movement, 310
Mindfulness of Breathing Sutta (Ānāpānasati Sutta), 305
mindfulness of critique, 316

Mindfulness-Based Stress Reduction (MBSR), 22, 49, 311, 383–84
mindfulness, term, 256
Mingchang 明常, 119
Minzhi 敏智, 118, 119
Miracle of Mindfulness, The (Hanh), 48
Mirror of Water (Mori), 494
Mitchell, Scott, 2, 30, 31–32, 41, 45–46, 47, 50, 60, 201, 204–5, 339, 384, 434
mobility, Chinese Buddhism, 124–26
modern Buddhism, 18, 23, 24, 123–24, 400
modernism, Buddhist, 19–20
    colonialism, 55–57
    demythologization, 21
    detraditionalization, 20
    meditation, 22–23
    psychologization, 21
    whiteness, 55–57
modernity, term, 19
modernization
    Buddhist modernism, 19–23
    claims of, 18
    global Buddhism, 27–29
    in global, historical perspective, 23–27
    overview of, 17–18
    postcolonial Buddhist postmodernity, 29–31
    three key components, 30–31
modern technology, utilization, 4–5
modes, American Buddhist-Jewish interaction
    converts, 253–55
    hybridizers, 260–62
    integrators, 256–60
    responders, 262–64
    secularizers, 255
Mohanty, Chandra Talpade, 75
momentary concentration *(khaṇikasamādhi)*, 306
monastery cooking, 294–96
monasticism, 235–37, 284
    acting as central node, 280–81
    converts, 281–84
    divergences and tensions, 278–80
    functions, 275–77
    monks in community temples, 272–74
    outreach, 281–84
    overview of, 271–72

monastics, feeding, 289–90
Monson, Liz, 88, 237
Moon, Cristina, 77–78, 80
Mori, Mariko, 493–95
Mrozik, Susanne, 80
Mu Sahn, 162
*mudrā*s, 494
Mūlasarvāstivāda Vinaya, 236
Müller, F. Max, 23, 42, 132, 502
multiple religious belonging, concept, 407
Munindraji, 185–86
My World Is in Your Blind Spot, 240

Naropa Institute, 47–48, 440, 441
    Phase One, 440–41
    Phase Three, 441
    Phase Two, 441
Naropa University, 451
Native Americans, 5
Natural Dharma Fellowship (NDF), 88
natural-supernatural binary, 380–81
Naturalization Act, 5–6
NDF. *See* Natural Dharma Fellowship
neighborhood committees, 291
neutralization, strategy, 256
new Buddhism *(shin bukkyo)*, 25
New Kandampa Tradition, 31–32, 281–82
new religious movement (NRM), 107–8
New York Theosophical Society, 485
New York Times, 296
Ng, Edwin, 316
Ngakpa International, 237
*ngakpa/ma*s, 236–37
Nguyen, Phuong, 216–17
Nhân Gian Phật Giáo, 214–15
Nichidatsu Fujii, 202
Nichiren Buddhism
    further research of, 208–10
    historicla background of, 197–99
    Nichiren Shōshū, 202–8
    Nichirenshū, 201–2
    in nineteenth-century United States, 199–201
    Nipponzan Myōhōji, 201–2
    overview of, 196–97
    Sōka Gakkai, 202–8
Nichiren Mission of Hawai'i, 201

Nichiren Order of North America, 201
Nichiren Shōshū, 196–97, 202–8
Nichiren Shōshū Sōka Gakkai of America (NSA), 205–6
Nichiren, interpreter. *See* Nichiren Buddhism
Nichirenshū, 201–2
Nichtern, Ethan, 83–84
Nightsea Crossing (performance), 492–93
nightstand Buddhists, 4–5
Nikkō, 202–3
nineteenth century
  Nichiren Buddhism in, 199–201
  visual culture in, 484–86
1965, Buddhism and American before, 183–84
Nipponzan Myōhōji, 196–97, 201–2
Nirvana (Mori), 493–95
Nisaburō Hirano, 134
Nishi Hongan-ji, 135–36, 469
Nishi Honganji Jōdo Shinshū, 132–33
Nishi Hongwan-ji, 41, 44
Nitārtha Institute for Higher Buddhist Studies, 238, 432–33
Nixon under the Bodhi Tree and Other Works of Buddhist Fiction (Wheeler), 509
No-No Boy (Okada), 506–7
No-Nonsense Buddhism for Beginners (Rasheta), 386–87
Noble Eightfold Path, 17, 384
nongovernmental organization (NGO), 207–8
North American Buddhists in Social Context, 98–99
North American Review, 37–38
Northern Buddhism, 106–7
NRM. *See* new religious movement
Numrich, Paul D., 98–99, 325
Nyanaponika, 307–8
Nyogen Senzaki, 40, 147

Obasan (Kogawa), 506–7
objective scholarship, 106–9
obutsudan, 486–87
Occupy This Body (Suh), 298
Oda, Harald, 429–30
Odiyan Retreat Center, 299–300
offerings, food
  communities, 290–92
  feeding monastics, 289–90

Ohsawa, George, 296
Okabe Gakuō, 468–69
Okada, John, 506–7
Olcott, Henry Steel, 23, 24, 42, 55–56, 219–20, 397
Oldenberg, Hermann, 42
Omer-Man, Jonathan, 259
Omi, M., 56–57, 359–60
"On the Establishment of the Pure Land in the Human Realm," 25
On the Road (Kerouac), 505
One Korean's Approach to Buddhism, 172
online sangha, 169–70
online spaces, secular Buddhists, 378–80
ontological dichotomy, ritual, 342–43
Opium Wars, 25
ordainment, Asian American women, 77–80
Orient, 93–94, 96–97, 473
Oriental Exclusion Act of 1924, 134–35, 166
Oroville Chinese Temple, 131–32
other-power *(tariki)*, 129
Otogawa, Kōbun, 288
Otsuka, Julie, 511–12
Otto, Rudolf, 346–47
outreach, monasticism, 281–84
Owens, Rod, 245–46
Ownes, Lama Rod, 65
Oxherding Tale (Johnson), 507–8
Ozeki, Ruth, 4–5, 509–10

Pacific Gorge Hermitage, 289–90
Padmasambhava, 282
Padoongpatt, Tanachai Mark, 292
pagodes, 464
Paik, Nam June, 45–46, 414–15, 490–91
Pali canon, translating, 305
Pali Text Society, 23, 95–96, 305, 396
Palyul International, 232–33
Parliament of World Religions, 43, 147–49
Parsons, William, 401, 404
Pasadena Buddhist Women's Association's Cookbook Committee, 292
Paterson, Michael, 459
Path of Purification (Visuddhimagga), 305
Payne, Richard, 387–88, 405–6
Peabody, Elizabeth Palmer, 37–38, 199, 501
Peace Preservation Law, 203–4

Pegues, Juliana Hu, 365
Pelosi, Nancy, 246–47
Pemaratana, Soorakkulame, 30
People of Color (POC), 62, 68–70, 316–17
Perfect Enlightenment Temple, 117–18, 119–20, 125–26
Perfect Virtue Temple, 221
permission rituals, 349
Perry, M. LaVora, 509
Perry, Matthew, 416, 485
Philadelphia Centennial Exposition, 471
philology, metaphors of, 396–97
Piña, Antonio Velasco, 277
Piraro, Dan, 496–97
place-making, 233–35
Plum Village Tradition, 296
podcast, secular Buddhists, 385–87
poetry, Buddhism in. *See* transnational storytelling
political religion, 239–41
post-1945 America, material culture in, 474–78
postcolonial Buddhist postmodernity, 29–31
postcolonialism, 29–31
postmodernity, 29–31
Pound, Ezra, 502–3
practice-realization, 435
practices
    engaged Buddhism, 359, 371
    food, 288–300
    medicine, 322–37
    mindfulness and meditation, 303–18
    monasticism, 271–84
    rituals, 339–55
prajñāpāramitā, 99–100, 234
pratītya samutpāda, 414–15
Pratt, Gladys Sunya, 41
Pratts, Richard H., 5
Prebish, Charles, 28, 97, 98, 99–100, 450–51
prose poetry, 501
Protestant Buddhism, 11–12, 20, 24, 55–56
Protestant Christianity, 19, 20, 25, 139, 381–82
Protestant Reformation, 18, 340, 341
psychedelics, 419
psychologization, 21
psychologization of Buddhism, 399
psychotherapy
    discourse of chronology, 400–1

    discourse of entropy, 399
    discourse of intersectionality, 406–9
    metaphors, 396–97
    metaphors of geography, 399–400
    metaphors of instrumentality, 403–4
    metaphors of relationality, 404–5
    overview of, 395–96
    rhetoric of essentiality, 397–98
    rhetoric of hybridity, 401–3
    rhetoric of unity, 405–6
pūjā, 348–49
Pumpelly, Raphael, 473
puñña, 189–90
Pure Land (Mori), 494
Pure Land Buddhism, 142, 214, 429–30
    early American intellectual encounters, 132–33
    early forms of, 133–34
    first introductions, 131–32
    further developments, 134–37
    in internment, 137–40
    new Pure Lands in America, 140–42
    overview of, 129–30
Pure Land in the Making (Truitt), 216
Purser, Ronald, 316

Queen, Christopher, 29
Quli, Natalie, 31–32, 71, 108–9, 315, 399

Race and Secularism in America (Lloyd), 379
race. *See* whiteness
    Black Buddhism, 65–67
    differences between "people of color," 68–70
    disrupting white Buddhism, 63–65
    intersectionality and, 60–61
    recovering Asian America voices, 59–60
    resistance and receptivity, 67–68
    shaping Buddha, 55–57
    violence and exclusions, 58–59
    white Buddhism, 61–62
    Zen sexual misconduct and, 152–54
racial rearticulation, 316
racialization, acknowledging, 366–70
radical empiricism, 25
Radical Friendship, 84
radio, 416–18
Rahula, Bikkhu Yogacara, 272–73

Rasheta, Noah, 378–79, 385–87
rationalists, technolgy and, 416–18
Rauschenberg, Robert, 45–46, 420–21, 489
Ray, Reginald, 451
Reader, Ian, 107–8
receptivity, white Buddhism, 67–68
reconditioning, 367–68
recontextualization, mindfulness critiques, 313–18
Reed, Caitriona, 85–86
Reform and Opening Up, 117
refugee nationalism, 216–17
relationality. metaphors of, 404–5
Religions of Vietnam, The" (pamphlet), 219–20
religious politics, 239–41
reorienting practices, 78
Republic of Vietnam (RVN), 217–18
resistance, white Buddhism, 67–68
responders, American Buddhist-Jewish interaction, 262–64
Rhys-Davids, Thomas, 23, 305
Rigdol, Tenzing, 240
rigpa, 261
Rinpoche, Chagdud, 234
Rinpoche, Dzogchen Pönlop, 238, 432–33
Rinpoche, Dzongsar Khyentse, 431–32, 440, 451
Rinpoche, Khen, 234
Rinpoche, Lama Zopa, 141–42
Rinpoche, Penor, 26–27
Ripley, George, 38
ritual
  examples of, 350–55
  as meditation, 351–55
  meditation as, 350–51
  models of, 347–50
  overview of, 339–40
  perspectives on activity, 346–47
  preconceptions of, 340–43
  ritualizing *versus*, 343–46
  valorization of, 340–43
ritualization, 345
ritualizing, ritual *versus*, 343–46
  cognitive science, 343–44
  ethology, 343–44
  levels, 345–46

process-product model, 344
ritual studies, 343–44
ritualization, 345
Robertson, Roland, 28
Rochester Zen Center, 400
Romanticism, 20, 22, 25, 132, 342
Roosevelt, Franklin D., 137
Roosevelt, Frankling Delano, 44, 58–59
rosaries *(nenju)*, 348
Ross, Nancy Wilson, 45–46
Rubin, Jeffrey, 404–5
Russo-Japanese War, 134–35
RVN. *See* Republic of Vietnam

sādhana, 348–49
Sadhana of Araminta Ross, The, 246
Safe Harbour, 435–36
Sahn, Seung, 169–70, 174
Sakya Monastery, 238
Salinas Buddhist Temple, 470
Salzberg, Sharon, 47, 184–85, 310, 433
Samdrup, Drubtchok Gualwa, 283
Samphell, Norbu, 239–40
San Fernando Valley Hongwanji Buddhist Temple, 79–80
San Francisco Chronicler, 135–36
San Francisco Zen Center (SFZC), 82, 435–36
Sanford, Monica, 454–55
sangha, 186, 189–90
sāsana, term, 182–83
Sassar, Jade, 66–67
sati, term, 305–9. *See* mindfulness
satipatthāna, refuge in, 457
Saunders, George, 512
Savor (Hanh), 296–98
Sayadaw, Ledi, 24–25, 188, 306
Sayādaw, Mahāsī, 47
SBA. *See* Secular Buddhist Association
SBN. *See* Secular Buddhist Network
SBP. *See* Secular Buddhist Podcast
Schedneck, Brooke, 384
Schelling, Andrew, 509
Schireson, Grace, 87–88, 153–54, 407
scholar-practitioners, 99–102
scholarly objective, 106–9
scholarly works, JuBu, 250–52
scholars, role of, 71–72

Science of Enlightenment, 424
Seager, Richard, 190–91, 441–42
Seager, Richard Hughes, 395
second wave, Buddhification, 44–47
Second World War, 118–19
sectional analysis (*kepan* 科判), 121–22
Secular Buddhism: Eastern Thought for Western Minds (Rasheta), 386
Secular Buddhist Association (SBA), 387–90
Secular Buddhist Network (SBN), 378, 384–85, 387
Secular Buddhist Podcast (SBP), 378, 381–82, 384–87
secular Buddhists, 377–78
   in context, 381–85
   online spaces, 378–80
   overview theories, 380–81
   podcast, 385–87
   Secular Buddhist Association, 387–90
secular mindfulness, 187
secular, term, 380–81
secularism, term, 380–81
secularity, term, 380–81
secularization, term, 380–81
secularizers, American Buddhist-Jewish interaction, 255
Secularizing Buddhism, 377
self-governance, as project, 297–98
Senart, Émile, 42
Senauke, Hozan Alan, 435–36
Seon Buddhism, 333
Sermons of a Buddhist Abbot, 25
settler futurity, 364
Seven Years in Tibet (film), 418
Seven-Limb Prayer, 354
seventies, visual culture in, 490–92
sexual abuse
   survivors of, 87–89
   Zen and, 152–54
SGI-USA. *See* Soka Gakkai International-United States of America
SGI. *See* Soka Gakkai International
Shaku Sōen, 40, 397
shakubuku, 204, 205–6
Shamanic Bones of Zen, The (Manuel), 82
Shambhala Buddhism, 333, 506
Shambhala International, 437

Shambhala Training, 437
Shannon, Wakoh, 56–57
Sharf, Robert, 315
Sharpe, Gina, 83–84
shedra (bshad grwa), 237–38
Sherpa, Tsherin, 230
Shin Buddhism, 36, 347–48
Shingon, 132–33
Shinnyo-en, 351–52
Shinran Shonin, 451
Shinsho Hanayama, 449–50
shumidan, 486–87
Shunryu Suzuki, 46, 151–52
Shuye Sonoda, 135–36
Siddhartha (Hesse), 504
Sigalow, Emily, 249, 250–51, 406–7
Silent Sangha, 99–102
Simmer-Brown, Judith, 451, 454–55
Simpsons, The, 418–19
Siri Vajirārāmaya Temple, 274
sixties, visual culture in, 490–92
Skeleton of a Philosophy of Religion, 132–33
Skilton, Andrew, 349
Slater, Jonathan, 257–58
Slott, Michael, 368
Smalls, Shante Paradigm, 246
"Smokey the Bear Sutra" (Snyder), 504–5
Snyder, Gary, 45, 104–5, 149–51, 309, 417–18, 504–5
social transformation, education and, 440–43
socially engaged Buddhism (*renjian fojiao*), 26, 202
Société Asiatique, 37
Soēn Shaku, 308
Sōka Gakkai ("Value Creation Society"), 26, 82, 196–97, 202–8
Soka Gakkai Buddhism, 333
Soka Gakkai International (SGI), 66–67, 441–43, 509
Soka Gakkai International-USA (SGI-USA), 196–97, 207–8
Soka University of America (SUA), 441–42
Sommerville, Maxwell, 473
Sōryū Kagahi, 41, 58, 133–34
Soto Zen Buddhist Association (SZBA), 66, 363–64

Sōtō Zen Ryūsen-ji, 469
Soucy, Alexander, 28, 29, 32
Sounds of the Bamboo Forest (Do), 212–13
South Asia, Theravāda Buddhism in, 23–25
Soyen Shaku, 200–1, 484
specialization, defining, 98–99
Speculative Non-Buddhism, 50
Spiegelberg, Frederic, 104–5
Spirit Rock Meditation Center, 83–84, 186–87, 310, 436–37
spiritual bypassing, 363–66
Spirutalists, technology and, 416–18
Śrīmālādevī Siṃhanāda Sūtra, 92, 104–5
Standard Buddhist Gathas and Services (Ama), 347–48
Star Wars (series), 418
Still Breathing Zen Sangha, 82
Stolow, Jeremy, 416–17
Strauss, Charles, 249, 250–51, 254
studies, American Buddhism, 92–93
   objective scholarship, 106–9
   scholar-practitioners, 99–102
   scholarly objectives, 106–9
   structures and institutions, 103–6
   studies as field, 93–99
study and practice, 432–33
*stūpa*s, 464–65
SUA. *See* Soka University of America
Subhūti, Bhante, 289–90
subjective turn, 20
Suh, Sharon, 76–77, 298, 339
Sumangala, Hikkaduve, 23–26, 95
Suncha, Kim, 77–78
Sunim, Kusan, 169
Sunim, Myeong Seong, 80
Sunim, Pomnyun, 170
Sunim, Samu, 169, 274
Super Conduct, 202–3
Superiority Conceit in Buddhist Traditions (Anālayo), 389
supervision. *See* chaplaincy supervision
supreme worship *(anuttarapūja)*, 349
Śūraṃgama Sūtra, Lotus Sūtra, 118–19, 121–22
survival kits, 404
Suzuki, D. T., 2, 25, 144–45, 309, 398, 488–89, 504, 505–6

Syedullah, Jasmine, 65
syncretism, 402
SZBA. *See* Soto Zen Buddhist Association
Sze Yap Company, 58, 416

Tada, Tokan, 104–5
Taixu, 140–41
Taizan Maezumi, 46
Takagi, Gyoun, 201
Takakusu Junjirō, 132
Takao Ozawa, 6
Tale for the Time Being, A (Ozeki), 509–10
Tan Xiaojie, 77–78
Tan-Luan, 131
Tanaka, Kenneth, 28
Taneesha Never Disparaging (Perry), 509
Tassajara Bread Book (Brown), 294–96
Taylor, Charles, 19–20
teachers
   Black Buddhism, 81–85
   and clergy training, 434–38
   Korean Buddhism, 168–70
"Teaching of the Lotus Blossom of the Wonderful Law" *(Saddharma-puṇḍarīka-sūtra)*, 197–98
Teachings of the Buddha, 103–4
technology, 424–25
   apps, 423–24
   cybernetics, 420–21
   digital Buddhism, 421–23
   early technology, 416
   film and television, 418–19
   introduction to, 414–15
   medical science, 424
   of the mind, 419
   radio, 416–18
   rationalists and, 416–18
   Spiritualists and, 416–18
   telegraphy, 416–18
telegraphy, 416–18
television, technology and, 418–19
Temple of Five Saints in San Jose, 467
temples
   home cooking for, 292–94
   Korean Buddhism, 167–68
   temple building, 233
Temprano, Victor Gerard, 362–63, 367

Ten Bulls (Kakuan), 507–8
Tendai, 132–33
Tendai Buddhism, 485
tensions, monasticism, 278–80
Thanasanti, Amma, 289–90
Theosophical Society, 23, 42
therapeutic culture, 400
Theravāda Buddhism, 23–25, 69, 191–92, 275, 333
  in America before 1965, 183–84
  cosmology-oriented Buddhism, 188–91
  labels, 181–83
  overview of, 177–78
  "two Buddhisms" model and, 178–81
Therī, Tathālokā, 80–81
Thetgyi, Saya, 188
Thich, Quang Minh, 212–13
Thiên-Ân, Thích, 212–13, 272–73
third wave, Buddhification, 47–50
Thoreau, Henry David, 37–38, 485, 500, 501
Three Bowls (Brown), 294–96
three great secret dharmas, 198
Three Pillars of Zen (Kapleau), 46, 151
Thục, Phêrô Máctinô Ngô Đình, 219–20
Tibetan Alliance of Chicago, 240
Tibetan Book of the Dead (Evans-Wentz), 399
Tibetan Buddhism, 92
  American Buddhists and, 232
  beyond monasticism, 235–37
  Buddhicizing American landscape, 233–35
  new horizons of, 244–47
  overview of, 230–32
  religion and politics, 239–41
  secularizing impulses, 237–39
  translation and transmission, 241–44
TIME, 2–3
Tin How Temple, 116–17, 484
Tobey, Mark, 487
Toko Umehara, 77
traditional Asian medicine, integrating Buddhism with, 331–33
traditional Buddhism, 178–80, 214–15, 363, 369, 400
traditional/modern, binary, 234
traditions
  Chinese Buddhism in America, 115–26
  Judaism, 249–64

  Korean Buddhism, 161–75
  Nichiren Buddhism, 196–210
  Pure Land Buddhism, 129–42
  Theravāda Buddhism, 177–92
  Tibetan Buddhism, 230–47
  Vietnamese Buddhism, 211–27
  Zen Buddhism, 144–55
Training Manual (Śikṣā-samuccaya), 349
trans-sectarian Buddhism, 41
Transcendentalism, 500–1
"Transgender Buddhist Trailblazer 20+ Years Later, A," 86
translation, Tibetan Buddhism, 241–44
transmission, Tibetan Buddhism, 241–44
transnational storyteling, 500–4
Tricycle: The Buddhist Review, 2–3, 59, 78, 86, 283, 508
Tripmaster Monkey (Kingston), 507
Truitt, Allison J., 216
Trungpa, Chögyam, 47–48, 282, 288, 437
Tsomo, Karma Lekshe, 76
Tsunesaburō Makiguchi, 203–4
Tuck, Eve, 364, 365
Tudor, David, 488
Tulku, Chagdud, 235
Turner, Tina, 206
TV Buddha, 414–15, 490–91
Tweed, Thomas, 36, 42–43, 51, 417
twin arrival, Buddhism, 37–39
Twitter, 1–2
two Buddhisms, 28, 76, 102
  and Buddhist studies, 98–99
  criticism of, 165
  formation of, 184–88
  gander/race hierarchies, 81–82
  reinforcement, 105–6
  Theravāda Buddhisms and, 178–81
  visual culture and, 492
two-thousands, visual culture in, 492–95
Tworkov, Helen, 2–3, 59
tzaddik, 258
Tzu Chi, 117
Tzu Chi Charity Foundation, 299

Unitarianism, 37–38
United Nations Economic and Social Council (UNESCO), 207–8

United States
  Buddhist material culture in, 462–78
  Chinese Buddhism in, 115–26
  early Japanese Pure Land Buddhism in, 133–34
  engaged Buddhism, 359, 371
  film and television in, 418–19
  history of Buddhism in, 36–51
  Korean Buddhism in, 161–75
  mindfulness and meditation in, 303–18
  monasticism in, 271–84
  new Pure Lands in, 140–42
  Nichiren Buddhism in, 196–210
  in nineteenth century, 199–201
  Pure Land Buddhism in, 129–42
  Theravāda Buddhism in, 177–92
  Tibetan Buddhism, 230–47
  Vietnamese Buddhism, 211–27
  Zen Buddhism in, 144–55
unity, rhetoric of, 405–6
universities, secularization and, 237–39
University of the West (UWest), 451–52
US Ministerial Association Dharma School Committee, 429–31
USCO, 420–21
ushnisha, 496–97
Usuki, Patricia Kanaya, 76–77, 79–80

vajra master, 244–45
Vajradhatu, 47–48
Vajrayana Buddhism, 26–27
Vajrayana Online, 246
Valera, Franscisco, 313
Varieties of Mystical Experience, 148
Vasquez, Manual, 231
vegetarian fast *(zhaijie)*, 299
Verchery, Lina, 282
Verhoeven, Martin, 21
Versluis, Arthur, 38
Very Veggie Movement (VVM), 299
Vesely-Flad, Rima, 6, 67, 68–69, 82, 208
Vietnam War, 506
Vietnamese Buddhism
  Black Buddhism intersection, 224–27
  compatriot Buddhism, 216–24
  overview of, 211–12

  studies of, 212–16
Vietnamese Buddhist Temple, 220
Vimalakīrti Nirdeśa Sūtra, 92, 104–5
vinaya, 271–72, 278–79
violence, Asian American Buddhists and, 58–59
vipassanā, 29–31, 36, 47–49, 170, 184–85, 188, 255, 256, 260, 304, 306–7, 310, 312, 433, 436–37
virtual orientalism, 418–19
visual aesthetic, Zen Buddhism, 149–51
visual culture, 483
  cartoons as, 496–97
  in eighties, 492–95
  in fifties, 488–90
  in nineteenth century, 484–86
  in seventies, 490–92
  in sixties, 490–92
  in two-thousands, 492–95
  in World War II, 486–87
voices, recovering, 59–60
VVM. *See* Very Veggie Movement

Wangyal, Geshe, 475–76
Washam, Spring, 83–84
Wat Mongkolratnaram, 291
Wat Thai, 272–73
Watts, Alan, 2, 45–46, 283, 405, 489
Way of Tenderness, The (Manuel), 83
"Way of the Bodhisattva" *(Bodhicaryāvatāra)*, 349
Way of Zen, The (Watts), 148–49
Way, Noliwe Alexander, 65–66
Wayman, Alex, 92, 104–5
We've Been Here All Along," 59–61
wedding ceremonies, 348
Weil, Mira Niculescu, 249, 251–52
Weisman, Arinna, 85
Welwood, John, 363
West, Isaac, 292
Western American Buddhist Association, 119–20
Western Association of Schools and Colleges (WASC), 434, 451
Western Buddhism, 7
Western Romanticism, 22
Western scholars, term, 101–2

WFB. 218–19, *See* World Fellowship of
    Buddhists
Whalen-Bridge, John, 418
Whalen, Philip, 45, 149–51
Wheeler, Kate, 509
white awareness practices, 68
white Buddhism, 61–62
    adopting diversity, inclusion, and equity
        plans, 64
    Buddhist teachings and practices, 64–65
    community development, 63–64
    disrupting, 63–65
    Insight leadership, 64
    literature, 63
    POC retreats, 63
    promoting racial justice initiatives, 63–64
    resistance to, 67–68
whiteness
    disrupting, 63–65
    shaping Buddhism, 55–57
    white Buddhism, 61–62
Whitman, Walt, 500–1
Whole Earth Catalog (Brand), 420–21
Wiener, Norbert, 420
Wilber, Ken, 405–6
Willi, Jan, 225
Williams, DaRa, 83–84
Williams, Duncan Ryûken, 3–4, 44, 54, 68–69,
    99–100, 108, 137, 227
Williams, George M., 204–5
williams, Kyodo, 58–59, 65, 246
Willis, Jan, 65, 208
Wilson, Jeff, 49, 98, 297, 310, 399–400, 511
Winant, Howard, 56–57
*Wisdom Anthology of North American
    Buddhist Poetry, The*, 509
Wisdom Publications, 509
Wolfe, Patrick, 364, 365
Woman Warrior, The (Kingston), 507
women
    lay women, 77–80
    ordainment of, 77–80
Won Buddhism, 333
Wong Nim, 467–68
Wonhyo, 171
World Fellowship of Buddhists (WFB), 218–19

World Parliament of Religions, 132–34, 249,
    308
World War II, 41, 96–97, 419, 470, 486–87, 506
World's Parliament of Religions, 199–201,
    202–3, 416–17, 484
World's Columbian Exhibition, 484–85
worth, notion of, 295–96
Wright, Dale, 347
*Writing down the Bones: Unleashing the Writer
    Within* (Goldberg), 149

Xie Bingying 謝冰瑩, 121

Yamanaka Sadajirō, 473–74
Yang, Larry, 64–65
Yarnall, Thomas Freeman, 362, 367
YBE. *See* Young Buddhist Editorial
Yemyo Imamura, 41
Yetunde, Pamela Ayo, 208, 408, 454–55
Yi, Jong Kweon, 165–62, 167
Yinshun 印順, 118
YMBA. *See* Young Men's Buddhist
    Association
yongmaeng jeongjin, 161–62
Yoshigiro Kawai, 200–1, 202–3
*You Are Not Here and Other Works of Buddhist
    Fiction*, 509
Young Buddhist Editorial (YBE), 1–3, 4, 61
Young Men's Buddhist Association (YMBA),
    41, 134
Young, Shinzen, 424
YouTube, 1–2
Yuanshen 遠慎, 118–19
Yue, Yong Ae, 54
Yun, Hsing, 431
Ywahoo, Dhyani, 233

Zen, 132–33
    boom of, 36, 184
    meditation as essence of, 151–52
    modernism of, 147–49
    origins of, 145–46
    square zen, 283
    as visual/literary aesthetic, 149–51
Zen and the Art of Child Discipline (Coverly),
    496

Zen Buddhism, 4–5, 154–55,
   333, 504
   Asian origins of, 145–46
   meditation and, 151–52
   modernism and, 147–49
   overview of, 144–45
   sexual misconduct, 152–54
   visual/literary aesthetic, 149–51

Zen Buddhism and Psychoanalysis, 152–53
Zen for Film (film), 424–25, 490
Zen GPS, 496
Zen Lotus Society, 169
Zen Macrobiotic, 296
Zhen, Guan, 454–55
Zhengxin Buddhist Academy, 119
Zuesse, Evan M., 341